DEAR ADULT FRIENDS,

It is my hope that this book will help your child get to know God better. In *one year* your child can have an in-depth overview of God's story, from Creation through John's Revelation.

    The stories are written in chronological order—in the order in which they occurred. For example, David's psalms are placed with the stories about his life. The Gospels are combined to tell the story of Jesus' life as a whole.

    Every Scripture was considered, word by word, as this book was written. The text has been simplified, but not fictionalized or robbed of it's power, because it is straight from God's Word.

    May your child be blessed by reading through this *Day by Day Kid's Bible* in the next 365 days, starting today!

Karyn Henley

PRESENTED TO

_____

BY

_____

ON

_____

DAY BY DAY
Kid's Bible

by Karyn Henley

TYNDALE HOUSE PUBLISHERS, INC.
CAROL STREAM, ILLINOIS

Visit Tyndale's website for kids at www.tyndale.com/kids.

TYNDALE is a registered trademark of Tyndale House Publishers, Inc. The Tyndale Kids logo is a trademark of Tyndale House Publishers, Inc.

Day by Day Kid's Bible

Edited by Betty Free

Day by Day Kid's Bible published August 2002 by Tyndale House Publishers, Inc. Copyright © 1998 by Karyn Henley. All rights reserved. Exclusively administered by Child Sensitive Communication, LLC. For permission to copy excerpts from this book, send requests by e-mail to: permission@tyndale.com or call 630-668-8300, ext. 5023.

First published by Tyndale House Publishers, Inc., as *God's Story* © 1998 by Karyn Henley. All rights reserved. Exclusively administered by Child Sensitive Communication, LLC.

Cover design by Beth Sparkman

Interior design by Catherine Bergstrom and Beth Sparkman

Interior illustrations by Marlene Ekman. Interior illustrations © 1998 by Karyn Henley. All rights reserved. Exclusively administered by Child Sensitive Communication, LLC.

For manufacturing information regarding this product, please call 1-800-323-9400.

For information about special discounts for bulk purchases, please contact Tyndale House Publishers at csresponse@tyndale.com, or call 1-800-323-9400.

Library of Congress Cataloging-in-Publication Data

Henley, Karyn.
   Day by day kid's Bible : the Bible for young readers / by Karyn Henley.
      p. cm.
Rev. ed. of: God's story. c1998.
Summary: A simplified version of the Bible, from Creation to Revelation, with a pictorial time line showing biblical and world events.
Includes index.
   ISBN 978-0-8423-5536-0
      1. Bible stories, English.   [1. Bible—Paraphrases.   2. Bible stories.]
I. Henley, Karyn. God's story.   II. Title.
BS551.3 .H47 2002
220.9'505—dc21

2002006404

Printed in China

26   25   24   23   22   21
17   16   15   14   13   12

CONTENTS

(See complete lists of stories at the back.)

New Testament

DEAR YOUNG FRIENDS,

Did you ever get really thirsty? You could hardly wait to get a drink. It's kind of like that when you want to know God better. Water can make your body feel fresh again. And God can make your spirit feel fresh again.

This *Day by Day Kid's Bible* can help you get to know God better. These are real, true stories of people who lived long ago. But just think about it. They had the same kinds of feelings and thoughts you have. Their stories are here to show how much God loves his people.

God loves you, too. He wants you to be one of his people. And he wants to be your loving Father forever. So read all about it. It will take you only about seven minutes a day to read two or three pages. If you do that, you'll be able to read through this whole Bible in one year. You'll be glad you did!

Love,

Karyn Henley

DEAR ADULT FRIENDS,

It is my hope that this book will help your child get to know God better. In *one year* your child can have an in-depth overview of God's story, from Creation through John's Revelation. This can be accomplished in about *seven minutes a day* by following the daily readings of two to three pages each.

The stories are written in the order in which they occurred. For example, David's psalms are placed with stories about his life. The Gospels are combined to tell the story of Jesus' life as a whole. Paul's letters are placed between chapters in Acts during the time period in which he wrote them.

To keep the text interesting and meaningful, some passages have been excluded. These include genealogies, repetitive passages, parts of long speeches, detailed laws and rituals, extremely abstract and symbolic passages, sexual scenes, and graphic violence.

This Bible is written at approximately a second-grade reading level. Some words may be readable by the child but are not easily understood, such as "glory" and "grace." In such cases, words with a clearer meaning were chosen, like "greatness" and "kind love." Other words are very hard for young readers, so they have been replaced with words or phrases that represent the meaning. For example, the tabernacle is called the "worship tent." Still other words can be understood when read in context, so one sentence may say that John dipped people in water, while the next sentence says that John baptized the people.

The words "Jews" and "Jewish people" are used for "God's people" throughout the Old Testament instead of different words, such as "Israelite" and "Hebrew," which might confuse children. In this way, children will understand that God's people in the Old Testament are the same group of people referred to in the New Testament. And they are the same group of people referred to today as "Jews."

Every Scripture was considered, word by word, as this book was written. The text has been simplified, but not fictionalized or robbed of its power, because it is straight from God's Word.

May your child be blessed by reading through this *Day by Day Kid's Bible* in the next 365 days, starting today! (Even if today is not January 1, your child can start reading at the beginning. Ignoring the dates, show your child how to check one box each day after reading the stories below it.)

May you also be blessed. You *will* be as you watch your child fall deeper in love with God.

By God's grace, to his glory,

Karyn Henley

OLD TESTAMENT

When the World Was New

When Time Began

GENESIS 1–2

To begin with, God made the earth and space. The earth had no shape. There was nothing on it. It was dark. But God's Spirit floated above the water.

"Let's have some light," said God.

The light glowed. God saw that the light was good. He named it "day." He named the dark "night." So evening came. Then morning came. That was the first day.

Then the second day came. "Let's have some wide, open air around the earth," said God. "It will keep the water below away from the water above." So God made this space. He named it "sky."

The third day came. God said, "Let the water below come together. Let dry ground show."

So the water came together. God named it "sea." The dry ground showed. God named it "earth."

Then God said, "Let the earth grow different kinds of plants and trees. Let plants and trees make fruit with seeds. And let the seeds make more plants and trees. These will be like the ones they came from."

So plants grew. God saw that this was good.

The fourth day came. God said, "Let lights shine in the sky. They will show day and night. They will show seasons, days, and years. They will bring light to earth."

Two bright lights shone. The sun for the day and the moon for the night. God put stars in the sky, too.

Then the fifth day came. God said, "Let animals fill the water. Let birds fly across the sky."

Then God made every kind of sea animal. He made every kind of bird. And he saw that this was good. He said, "Let the fish make more fish like themselves. Let the birds make more birds like themselves."

The sixth day came. God said, "Let all kinds of animals come to life."

So God made all kinds of wild animals. He made all the animals that move on land. Each animal was able to make more animals like itself. And God saw that this was good.

Then God said, "Let's make people to be like us. They can be in charge of the fish and birds and cows. They can take care of the earth and all the animals."

So God made people like himself. First he made a man from dust. Then God breathed life into Adam, and he came alive.

God told Adam, "I'm giving you all plants that have seeds. I'm giving you all trees that have fruit with seeds. This is your food. And I'm giving all green plants to the animals for food."

Then God looked at everything he had made. He saw that it was very good.

So the earth and space were made. God finished making everything by the seventh day. Then he rested from his work. God said the seventh day is good and special. It is holy. That's when he rested from making everything.

Adam's Helper

GENESIS 2

Now God had planted a garden in Eden. It was in the East. God had put beautiful fruit trees in the Garden. Two different trees grew in the middle of the Garden. There was a tree of life. And there was a tree of knowing good and bad.

A river flowed out of the Garden of Eden. It parted to make other rivers. One was the Pishon River. It winds through a land that has gold. Another was the Gihon River. Two more were the Tigris River and the Euphrates River.

God put Adam in the Garden of Eden. Adam could work there and take care of the Garden. God said, "You may eat fruit from the trees. But you may not eat from the tree of knowing good and bad. You will die if you eat from that tree."

Then God said, "It's not good for Adam to be alone. I'll make a helper for him."

Now God had made all the animals. So he showed them to Adam. He wanted to see what Adam would call them. An animal's name became whatever Adam called it. Adam named all the animals.

But God didn't find any animal that was able to help Adam. So God made Adam go to sleep. Adam slept very deeply. Then God took one rib from Adam. He made a woman from it.

God showed the woman to Adam. Adam said, "I will call her 'woman' because she came from a man."

Adam and his wife did not wear clothes. But they did not feel bad about it.

The Snake's Trick
GENESIS 3

Now the snake was tricky. He talked to the woman. "Did God say not to eat fruit from the trees?"

"No," she said. "We may eat fruit. Just not from the tree in the middle of the Garden. God said we can't even touch that tree. We'll die if we do."

"You won't die," said the snake. "God knows that the fruit will make you wise. Just like God. You will know good and bad."

The woman looked at the fruit. It was very pretty. It looked like it would taste good. Since she thought it would make her wise, she ate some. Adam was with her. So she gave some to Adam, too. And he ate it.

Right away they saw they had no clothes on. All of a sudden, they felt bad. So they made clothes out of fig leaves.

Then they heard a sound they knew. It was God walking in the Garden. He came at the cool time of day. The man and woman hid among the trees.

"Where are you, Adam?" called God.

"I heard you," said Adam. "But I hid because I was scared. I didn't have any clothes on."

"Why do you feel bad about that?" asked God. "Did you eat the fruit I said not to eat?"

"My helper gave me fruit from that tree," said Adam. "So I ate it."

Then God asked Adam's helper, "What did you do?"

"The snake lied to me," said the woman. "I ate the fruit."

Then God spoke to the snake. "Now you will be the lowest animal in the world. You'll crawl on your belly. You'll taste dust all your life. The woman will hate you. Her child will hate yours. You'll bite at his heel. But he will pound on your head."

God told the woman, "You will have children. But there will be pain when you have a baby. And your husband will be in charge of you."

God told Adam, "You listened to your wife. You did not obey me.

"You'll eat the plants that grow in the field. But you'll have to work hard to get anything to grow. There will be lots of weeds."

Adam named his wife Eve. Then God made clothes out of animal skin. He gave them to Adam and Eve. "Adam knows good and bad now," said God. "We can't let him eat from the tree of life, too. If he does, he will live forever."

So God sent Adam and Eve out of the Garden. Then he put angels at the east side of the Garden. He also put a sword of fire there. It flashed back and forth. Now no one could get to the tree of life.

The First Children

GENESIS 4

Sometime later, Eve had a baby. She and Adam named him Cain. Then she had another baby. She named him Abel.

Cain and Abel grew to be young men. Cain worked as a farmer. He grew fruit. Abel took care of sheep. He was a shepherd.

One day Cain took some of his fruit. He gave it as a gift to God. Abel took some of his best sheep. He gave them as gifts to God.

God said that what Abel gave him was right. But what Cain gave him was not. Cain got mad, and he frowned.

"Why are you mad?" asked God. "Why are you frowning? Do the right thing. Then I'll like what you bring me. But what if you don't do the right thing? Then sin will wait at your door. Sin wants to catch you. But you must not let it get to you."

Now Cain asked Abel to go out to the field with him. While they were there, Cain killed Abel.

God said to Cain, "Where is Abel, your brother?"

"I don't know," said Cain. "Do I have to keep track of my brother?"

"What did you do?" asked God. "I know what happened. You're in trouble from now on. You will try to farm the land. But it won't grow food. You will have to move around from place to place."

"This is too much!" said Cain. "I can't farm the land anymore! I will be hidden from you. I will have to move around from place to place. Anybody who finds me will kill me."

"If they do, they'll be in trouble," said God. So he put a mark on Cain. Then no one who saw him would kill him.

Cain left. He went east to live in the land of Nod.

Now Adam and Eve had another son. They named him Seth. "This child will take Abel's place," said Eve.

JANUARY 3

A World under Water

GENESIS 6–9

More children were born. They grew up and had children. And

6

their children grew up and had children.

But God saw that people had turned bad. Everything they thought of was bad. It made God's heart hurt. "I will get rid of people," he said. "I'll get rid of people and animals. I'm sorry I ever made them."

But God was happy with Noah. That's because Noah did what was right. He trusted God.

Noah had three sons. Their names were Shem, Ham, and Japheth.

God told Noah, "I'm going to get rid of people. They are mean and hateful. So make a big boat, an ark.

"Make it out of wood. Cover it with tar inside and out. Make it 450 feet long. Make it 75 feet wide and 45 feet high. Make a window in it. Put a door in the side. Build a bottom deck, a middle deck, and a top deck.

"I will bring flood water to cover the earth. I will get rid of everything. So bring two of every animal into the ark. Bring all kinds of food in. You can feed yourselves and the animals."

Noah did everything God told him to do.

Then God said, "Take your whole family into the ark. Take seven of every animal I tell you to take. Take two of the other animals. Next week I will send rain."

So Noah and his wife went into the ark. His sons and their wives went into the ark. The animals also went into the ark, two by two.

A week passed. Then the flood water came. But God had shut the door behind Noah. Rain kept falling for 40 days and 40 nights. The water got higher and higher. The ark began to float.

Soon the water covered all the mountains. Everything living on the earth died. But God didn't forget Noah and his family. He didn't forget all the animals on the ark.

Rain stopped falling. God sent wind to blow across the earth. The water began to go down.

After 150 days, the water had gone down a lot. The ark landed on the Ararat Mountains. Soon the water was down even more. Other mountain tops showed.

Noah opened the window in the ark. He let a raven fly out. It kept flying back and forth. Then he let a dove fly out. Noah wanted to see if the water was off the ground. But the dove couldn't find a place to land. There was too much water on the ground. So she flew back to the ark.

Noah held out his hand. The dove landed on it. And Noah took her back into the ark.

A week passed. Then Noah let the dove fly out again. The dove came back that evening. She had a fresh leaf from an olive tree in her beak! So Noah knew the water had gone down. Trees were showing.

A week later Noah let the dove fly out again. This time she didn't come back.

Then Noah opened the door of the ark. He looked out. He saw that the flood water was going down. Two months later, the ground was dry.

God said, "You may all go out of the ark."

So Noah and his family went out. All the animals went out. Then Noah made a big pile of rocks. It was an altar for worshiping God. Noah put some fresh meat on it as a gift to God.

God said, "I'll never get rid of all living things again. There will always be a time to plant. There will always be a time to pick the crops. There will always be cold and heat. There will always be summer and winter. There will always be day and night. These will be around as long as the earth lasts."

God said, "Have children and fill the earth. You are in charge of the animals now. I'm making a promise to you and all the animals. It's a promise that will last forever. I'll never get rid of everything by flood water again.

"Here is the sign that shows my promise is true," said God. "I am putting a rainbow in the clouds. I will remember my promise when I see the rainbow."

The Tower

GENESIS 11

After some time, there were many people in the world. Everyone spoke the same language. Some of the people moved to a flat land.

"Let's make some bricks," said the people. "Let's stick them together with tar. Let's build a city and a tower. We will build the tower as high as the sky. Then everyone will know who we are. That will help us stay together as a group."

But God saw the city and the tower. He said, "These people speak the same language. So they can plan together to do many things like this. Let's mix up their language. Then they won't understand each other."

So God gave them different languages. Then the people stopped building. They did not stay together. They went here and there around the earth.

Everyone called the city Babel. That's because God mixed up their language there.

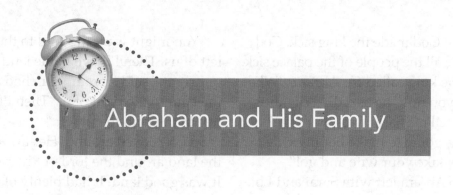

Abraham and His Family

Abram's Travels Begin

GENESIS 12–13

God talked to a man named Abram. God said, "Leave this land. Leave these people. Leave your father's family. I will show you a new land to live in. I am going to give you a family. Your family will become a great nation. Your name will become great.

"I'll do good things for anyone who speaks well of you. I'll send trouble to anyone who says bad things about you. Good will come to everyone on earth because of your family."

Abram was 75 years old. But he did what God told him. He left for another land. His wife, Sarai, and his brother's son, Lot, went with him. They took everything they had. Then they traveled to the land of Canaan.

One day Abram came to a big oak tree. It was at a place called Moreh. "I will give this land to your family," God said.

So Abram piled up stones. He built an altar near the big tree. It was a place to worship God. He built it because God had talked to him there.

Then Abram went south toward the hills. He set up his tent. He built another altar and worshiped God there.

But a time came when there was not enough food. Food would not grow. So Abram traveled again. He went to the land of Egypt.

Before they got to Egypt, Abram had a talk with Sarai. "You are very beautiful," he said. "The men of Egypt will see you. They may want you to be one of their wives. Then they will kill me. So tell them you are my sister. Then I will be safe."

The men of Egypt did see Sarai. Some of them told the king how beautiful she was. So the king took Sarai to his palace. He was very nice to Abram. That's because Sarai was at his palace. Abram got sheep and cows, donkeys and camels, and servants.

But God made the king sick. God made all the people of the palace sick.

The king called for Abram. "What did you do?" he asked. "Why didn't you tell me Sarai was your wife? I was going to make her my wife. Now take your wife and go!"

So Abram left with Sarai and Lot. He took all the things he had gotten in Egypt. He was rich with animals and silver and gold. He traveled back to Bethel. That's where he had set up his tent before. Then Abram worshiped God there.

Lot Chooses His Land

GENESIS 13

Lot was the son of Abram's brother. He had been traveling with Abram. He had been living where Abram lived.

Lot also had many sheep and cows and tents. There wasn't enough land for both Abram's animals and Lot's animals.

Lot's servants took care of Lot's sheep and cows. Abram's servants took care of Abram's sheep and cows. But Lot's servants began to fuss and fight with Abram's servants.

Abram told Lot, "Let's not fuss and fight. Let's not allow our servants to fuss and fight. Don't we have all this land around us? Let's live in different places.

"You might want the land to the left of us. Then I'll live in the land to our right," said Abram. "Or choose the land to the right of us. Then I'll live in the land to our left."

So Lot looked around. He saw all the land around the Jordan River. It was good land. It had plenty of water. It was like a garden. So that's where Lot chose to live. He set up his tents near the city of Sodom. But people in that city were sinful. They did many sinful things.

Abram went to live in Canaan. God told Abram, "Look around you. Look north and south. Look east and west. I'll give all this land to you and your family. It will be yours forever. Your family will be so big that it will be like dust. No one can count the dust. No one will be able to count the people in your family. Walk through the land. I give it to you."

So Abram moved near the big oak trees at Hebron. He set up his tents there. And he built an altar to God.

JANUARY 5

War!

GENESIS 14–15

Now four kings got their armies together. They went to war against five other kings. One of the five kings was the king of Sodom. They all marched out to the Dead Sea Valley. It was four kings against five.

The four kings were winning. The men in the army of Sodom began to run away. But the valley was full of tar pits. Some men fell into the tar pits. Some men ran to the hills.

Then the four kings went into the city of Sodom. They took away everything they could find. They even took the food and some of the people. They took Lot and his family, too.

But one person got away. He ran to Abram and told him what had happened.

Abram got 318 men together. They were all good fighters. They chased the armies of the four kings.

Night came. Abram put his men in different groups. They fought the armies of the four kings. They saved Lot and his family and many other people. They even saved the things that the army had taken. Then they started home.

The king of Sodom met Abram in the King's Valley. Another king met Abram, too. He was the king of Salem. He was a king who worshiped God. He set out bread and wine for Abram.

Then the king of Salem prayed for Abram. He said, "God Most High is the Maker of heaven and earth. He gives his riches to Abram. So worship God Most High. He saved you from your enemy."

Abram took one of every 10 things he got from the war. He gave that to the king of Salem.

The king of Sodom told Abram, "Just give me back my people. You can keep everything else."

"No," said Abram. "I promised God I wouldn't take anything that was yours. I won't even take a string. Not even a tie from your shoe. I'll only take what my men ate."

Sometime later, God told Abram, "Don't be afraid. I am your guard. Good things will come to you."

"Why give me anything?" asked Abram. "I don't have any children. When I die, my servant will get everything I own."

"No," said God. "That is not how it will be. You will have a son."

Then God took Abram outside. "Look up at the sky," God said. "Count the stars if you can. That's how many people will be in your family someday."

Abram believed God. That made everything right between Abram and God.

Then Abram gave some animals to God as a gift. God was happy.

Sarai Tries to Get a Son
GENESIS 16

Abram and Sarai did not have any children. But Sarai had a servant named Hagar. So Sarai told Abram, "Take my servant to be another wife for you. When she has a baby, it can be my baby."

Abram did what Sarai asked. He let Hagar be his wife, too. One day Hagar found out she was going to have a baby. Then Hagar began to hate Sarai.

Sarai told Abram, "You are the one to blame. I let Hagar be your other wife. Now she hates me."

"She is your servant," said Abram. "You can do whatever you want with her."

From then on, Sarai was mean to Hagar. So Hagar ran away.

But God's angel found Hagar. She was out in the desert by a road. The road was near a place where water came out of the ground. "Where did you come from, Hagar?" asked the angel. "Where are you going?"

"I'm running away from Sarai," said Hagar.

The angel said, "Go back to her. Keep being her servant. You will have children. They will grow up and have children. Someday, there will be many people in your family. No one will be able to count them."

The angel also said, "Your baby will be a boy. Name him Ishmael, because God has heard how sad you are. Ishmael will be like a wild donkey. He will fight with everyone."

Then Hagar thought of a name for God. She said, "You are 'The God Who Sees Me.' Now I have seen 'The God Who Sees Me.'"

Hagar went back to Sarai. She had a baby boy. Abram named him Ishmael. That was when Abram was 86 years old.

A New Name
GENESIS 17

God came to Abram again when Abram was 99 years old. God said, "I am God Almighty. Do what is right."

Abram bowed. He put his face toward the ground. God said, "You will not be called Abram anymore. Now your name will be Abraham, father of many nations. Nations will come from your family. Kings will come from your family. I promise to be your God forever. I promise to be the God of your family. And I give you the land of Canaan."

Then God said, "Sarai's name will now be Sarah. She will have a son. She will be the mother of nations."

Abraham laughed. "Will I have a son after I'm 100 years old? Will Sarah have a baby after she is 90? Maybe you can do these good things for Ishmael instead."

"Sarah will have a son," said God. "Name him Isaac. My promise is for him and his family forever. But I hear what you say about Ishmael. I will do good things for him. He will have a big family, too. But my promise is for Isaac."

JANUARY 6

Abraham's Visitors

GENESIS 18

Abraham sat at the front of his tent near the trees. It was the hot part of the day. Abraham looked up and saw three men. So he got up and went to meet them. One of them was really God.

Abraham bowed down. "Stay here for a while," he said. "Rest in the shade of the tree. My servants will get water so you can wash your feet. I'll get some food so you can eat. You can go on after you rest."

"All right," the men said.

Abraham rushed into the tent. "Hurry, Sarah," he said. "Bake some bread."

In a little while, the food was ready. Abraham brought out milk and meat and bread. He gave it to the men. Then he let them eat while he stood under a tree.

"Where is Sarah?" asked the men.

"She is in the tent," said Abraham.

Then God said, "Sarah will have a baby boy. It will happen next year about this time."

Sarah was in the tent, near the door. She was listening. She laughed to herself when she heard what God said. That's because she and Abraham were very old.

"Why is Sarah laughing?" asked God. "Is anything too hard for God?"

Sarah was scared. She said, "I didn't laugh."

"Yes, you did," said God.

Sodom

GENESIS 18

Abraham walked a little way with the men when they left. They could see the city of Sodom far away. They stood and looked at the city.

God said, "There is very bad sin in Sodom. I'm going there to see just how bad the people are."

Then the two men walked toward Sodom. But God stayed there with Abraham.

Abraham could tell that God was going to get rid of the bad people. "You wouldn't get rid of good people, would you? Won't you save the city if 50 good people live there?"

"I'll look for 50 good people there," said God. "If I find 50, I'll save the city."

"I've been brave to talk to you

about this," said Abraham. "But what if you find only 45 good people?"

"I'll look for 45 good people," said God. "If I find 45, I'll save the city."

"But what if you find only 40 good people?" asked Abraham.

"For 40 good people, I'll save the city," said God.

"Don't be angry," said Abraham. "But what if you find only 30?"

"I'll save the city for 30 good people," said God.

"Since I've been so brave, I'll ask again," said Abraham. "What if you find only 20?"

"If I find 20, I'll save the city," said God.

"Please don't get mad," said Abraham. "But what if you find only 10?"

"If I find 10, I'll save the city," said God.

Then God left, and Abraham went back home.

Angels in Sodom

GENESIS 19

It was evening when the two men got to Sodom. They were really angels. Lot was sitting at the city gate. He saw them coming. So he stood up and bowed. "Please come to my house," he said. "You may wash up and stay there tonight. In the morning, you can go on your way."

The angels said, "No. We will stay in the city street tonight."

But Lot kept asking them to stay with him. So at last they went to Lot's house. He baked bread and made dinner. And they ate with him.

Before they went to bed, they heard voices. "Bring out the men who came to see you. We want to take them with us." But the men of the city were mean men.

Lot went outside. He closed the door to his house. He saw all the men of the city around his house. They were asking for Lot's visitors.

But Lot said, "No. This is not right. You must not be mean to my visitors."

The men said, "Get out of the way. Or we'll be meaner to you than we are to them." They kept pushing Lot. They pushed toward the door so they could break it down.

But the angels were inside. They quickly opened the door. They took hold of Lot. And they pulled him inside with them. Then the angels made the men outside lose their sight. They could not find the door.

The angels turned to Lot. "Does anyone else in your family live in this city? If they do, tell them to leave," they said. "God has sent us here to get rid of the city."

Lot went to the men who were going to marry his daughters. "God is going to get rid of this city!" he told them. "So hurry and leave."

But the young men thought it was just a joke.

When morning came, the angels told Lot, "Hurry and leave. Or you'll be in the city when God wipes it away! Take your wife and daughters with you. Now go!"

But Lot did not go. So the angels took him by the hand. They took his wife's hand and his daughters' hands. The angels led them out of the city. God was being good to them.

They got out of the city. Then one of the angels said, "Run for your lives! Don't look behind you. Don't stop until you get to the mountains!"

But Lot said, "No, please. You are very kind to save our lives. But I can't run all the way to the mountains. See the town of Zoar over there? It's a very small town. Let me run to that town."

So the angel said, "All right. But hurry! I can't get rid of Sodom until you get there."

The sun was up when Lot got to Zoar. Then God sent fire from heaven. Fire fell like rain on Sodom. So he got rid of the city and everyone in it.

But Lot's wife looked back. She turned into a post made of salt.

The next morning Abraham got up early. He went back to where he had talked with God. He looked toward Sodom. He saw thick smoke going up from the land.

Lot was too scared to stay in Zoar. So he took his two daughters and moved to the mountains. They lived there.

JANUARY 7

Abraham Lies Again
GENESIS 20

Abraham moved to Gerar for a while. He told people there that his wife, Sarah, was his sister. So the king brought Sarah to his palace. He planned to make her his wife.

But God came to the king one night in a dream. God said to the king, "You are in big trouble. Sarah is already married."

"Abraham told me she was his sister," said the king. "I didn't mean to do anything wrong."

"I know," said God. "Now give Sarah back to Abraham. If you don't, you and your family will die."

The king called his leaders together early the next morning. He told them about his dream. They were very scared.

Then the king called for Abraham. "Why did you do this to me?" asked the king.

"I thought you would kill me," said Abraham. "That way, you could have Sarah to be your wife."

Then the king gave Abraham sheep and cows and servants. He gave Sarah back to Abraham, too. The king said, "Live wherever you want to live in my land."

Then the king spoke to Sarah. "I was wrong to bring you to my palace," he said. "So I will give 1,000 pieces of silver to Abraham. This will make up for the wrong I did."

Two Sons
GENESIS 21

God kept his promise to Sarah. She and Abraham had a son, even though they were old. The baby came just when God said it would. Abraham named the baby Isaac.

Abraham was 100 years old when Isaac was born.

"God has let me laugh," said Sarah. "Anyone who hears about this will laugh and be happy, too. Who would have thought Abraham and I would have a child? But I had a baby boy for old Abraham!"

One day Abraham had a party for Isaac. But Ishmael, Hagar's son, made fun of Isaac.

So Sarah told Abraham, "Get rid of Hagar and Ishmael. I don't want Ishmael to get anything that belongs to Isaac."

Abraham was upset, because Ishmael was his son, too.

But God said, "Don't be upset. Listen to Sarah. Isaac is the son that a whole nation of people will come from. But I'll make Ishmael's family into a nation, too."

So early the next day, Abraham gave Hagar some food. He gave her some water in a bag made from animal skins. Then he sent Hagar and Ishmael away. Hagar carried the food and water on her shoulders. She and Ishmael went off into the desert.

One day Hagar and Ishmael drank the last of the water. Hagar set Ishmael under a bush. Then she sat nearby. "I can't stand to see him die," she thought. She started crying.

Ishmael was crying, too. God heard him. God's angel called out,

"What's wrong, Hagar? Don't be scared. God hears Ishmael crying. Go hold his hand. Tell him to get up. I'm going to make his family into a big nation."

Then God let Hagar see a well of water. She filled her bag with water. She gave Ishmael a drink.

So God watched over Ishmael. Ishmael grew up in the desert. He was good at using a bow and arrow. He married a woman from Egypt.

Now the king of Gerar spoke to Abraham. "I know God takes care of you," he said. "I have been kind to you. So promise that you will be kind to me."

"I promise," said Abraham. "But your servants took one of my wells."

"I didn't know that," said the king. "I don't know who did it."

So Abraham and the king made a deal. Abraham took seven lambs to the king. "I'm giving you these lambs," said Abraham. "This shows I'm telling the truth. I dug this well."

Then the king went home. Abraham planted a tree there, and worshiped God. He lived in that land for a long time.

Abraham's Test

GENESIS 22

One day God gave Abraham a test. God called, "Abraham!"

"I'm here," said Abraham.

"Isaac is your only son," God said. "He is the son you love. Take him to the land of Moriah. I will show you a mountain. Put Isaac on an altar. He'll be the gift you give me on the altar."

So the next morning, Abraham got up early. He put a saddle on his donkey. He cut wood to put on the altar. Then he took Isaac and two servants, and they left.

They traveled for two days. The next day Abraham looked out over the land. He saw the place where God wanted him to go. So Abraham told his servants, "Keep the donkey here. Isaac and I will go worship. Then we'll come back."

Isaac carried the wood. Abraham carried the fire and the knife for the gift. They would give a gift to God on the altar.

Abraham and Isaac walked on together. "Father," said Isaac.

"Yes," said Abraham.

"We have wood," said Isaac. "We can make a fire. But where is the lamb for the altar?"

"God will give it to us," said Abraham. And they walked on.

At last they came to the place God told Abraham about. Abraham piled up stones to make an altar. He put the wood on it. Then he put Isaac on the wood on the altar. Isaac would be the gift on the altar.

But God's angel called out, "Abraham!"

"I'm here," said Abraham.

"Take Isaac off the altar," he said. "Now I know God is the most important one to you. You were going to obey God. You were going to give him your only son."

Then Abraham looked up. He saw a ram. Its horns were stuck in a bush. So Abraham took Isaac off the altar. He got the ram. He put it on the altar as the gift for God.

God's angel called to Abraham again. "Here's what God says. You were going to give me your only son. So I promise I'll give my riches to you. Isaac's children will become a very big family. There will be as many people as stars in the sky. There will be as many as sand on the beach. Good will come to all nations on earth. It's all because you obeyed me."

Abraham and Isaac went down the mountain. The servants were waiting for them. Then they all went home.

JANUARY 8

The Cave

GENESIS 23

Abraham and Sarah went to Hebron in the land of Canaan. While they were there, Sarah died. Abraham cried.

Then he went to the people of that land. "I'm a stranger here," he said. "Sell me some land. I need a place to lay my wife's body."

The people said, "You can put her body in any of our caves. Choose the best one."

Abraham bowed. He said that he wanted the cave in one of the fields. He said he'd buy it.

The man who owned it said, "I'll give you the field and the cave."

Abraham bowed down again. "I'll pay whatever it costs. Take the money. I'll put my wife's body there."

"The land costs 400 pieces of silver," said the man.

So Abraham counted out the money. He bought the field and the cave. He bought all the trees in the field. Then he put Sarah's body in the cave.

Looking for a Wife

GENESIS 24–25

Abraham was old. God had given him all kinds of good things.

One day Abraham called his best servant to him. Abraham said, "Make me a promise. Promise you'll find a wife for Isaac. But she should not be from this land. Go back to the land I came from. Get a wife for Isaac from that land."

"What if she doesn't want to

come?" asked the servant. "Should I take Isaac to the other land to live?"

"No," said Abraham. "God will send his angel ahead of you. He will help you get a wife for Isaac. But if she doesn't want to come, don't make her. Just don't take Isaac to that land."

So the servant promised. Then he took 10 camels. He took all kinds of good gifts. And he left on his trip.

After many days, the servant stopped at a well. It was almost evening. He made his camels sit down. It was almost time for women to come get water.

The servant prayed. "God," he said. "Be kind to Abraham. I am standing by the well. The women are coming to get water here. I'll speak to one of the girls. I'll ask her to get me some water with her jar. Show me the one you choose, God. Have her give me a drink. Have her say that she will give my camels water, too. Then I'll know you want her to be Isaac's wife. And I'll know you are being kind to Isaac's father, Abraham."

Before the servant stopped praying, Rebekah came to the well. She was beautiful. She held her jar on her shoulder. She filled her jar with water.

The servant quickly went over to her. "Please get me a drink of water from your jar."

"Have a drink," said Rebekah. She took her jar down from her shoulder. She gave him a drink.

Then she said, "I'll give your camels some water, too." She gave the rest of her water to the camels. Then she ran to the well again for more water. She got enough water for all the servant's camels.

The servant watched Rebekah carefully. He wanted to make sure God had chosen her.

The camels drank their water. Then the servant gave Rebekah a gold ring. He gave her two gold arm bands. "Who is your father?" he asked.

"Nahor's son," said Rebekah.

Now the servant knew that Nahor was Abraham's brother. "Is there room at your house for us?" he asked. "Could we spend the night?"

"Yes," said Rebekah. "There is plenty of food for your camels. And there is room for you to stay with us."

The servant bowed down. He worshiped God. "Praise God," he said. "He has led me to Abraham's family."

Rebekah ran home. She told what had happened.

Rebekah had a brother named Laban. He heard Rebekah's story. He saw the ring and the arm bands. So he went to find the servant.

Laban found him standing by his camels near the well.

"Come with me," said Laban. "I made a place for you at our house. I made a place for the camels, too."

So the servant went home with Laban. He took the packs off the camels. He fed them and gave them water. He and his men washed up. Then it was time for dinner. Food was ready for them.

But the servant said, "I can't eat yet. I have to tell you something first."

"Tell us," said Laban.

"I'm Abraham's servant," he said. "God made Abraham rich with sheep and cows. He is rich with silver and gold. He has servants and camels and donkeys. Abraham also has a son. He has given his son everything he has."

The servant told Rebekah's family about his promise to Abraham. He told them how he prayed by the well. He told them how Rebekah came to the well. He told how she gave him and his camels a drink.

"Now tell me," said the servant. "May Rebekah come home with me?"

"God made this happen," said Rebekah's father. "So take Rebekah with you."

The servant bowed to God. Then he gave gold and silver dishes to Rebekah. He gave clothes to her. He gave gifts to Rebekah's brother and her mother, too. Then the servant and his men ate dinner. And they stayed there for the night.

The next morning the servant said, "We must go. We have to get back to Abraham now."

But Rebekah's brother and mother didn't want them to go. "Let Rebekah stay here 10 days," they said. "Then she can go with you."

"Don't make us stay here," said the servant. "I have done what I promised Abraham. Now I need to go back to him."

"Let's ask Rebekah what she wants to do," her family said. So they asked her.

"I'll go now," said Rebekah.

So they let Rebekah go with the servant. Rebekah and her maids got on their camels. They rode off with the servant.

One evening Isaac was out in a field. He was thinking. He looked up and saw camels coming his way. So he went to meet them.

Rebekah looked up, too. She saw Isaac. She got off her camel. "Who is that man?" she asked the servant.

"That's Isaac," said the servant.

Rebekah covered her face with a thin cloth.

The servant told Isaac what had happened. Isaac married Rebekah. He loved her.

After Sarah died, Abraham married a woman named Keturah.

They had lots of children. Abraham gave gifts to his children as they grew up. Then he sent them away to live in the East. He wanted them to live away from Isaac. Abraham saved everything else he owned to give to Isaac.

Abraham lived to be 175 years old. When he died, Isaac and Ishmael put his body in a cave. It was the same cave where Sarah's body was.

JANUARY 9

Twins

GENESIS 25

Rebekah could not have any children. So Isaac prayed for her. God answered Isaac's prayer. Rebekah was going to have babies. Two of them. Rebekah could feel them inside her. They were pushing each other around.

Rebekah asked God, "What's happening here?"

God said, "These two babies will start two nations. One will be stronger than the other. The older one will serve the younger one."

Sometime later, Rebekah had her babies. They were twin boys. The first one looked red. His body was hairy. They called him Esau.

The next baby was holding on to Esau's heel. They named him Jacob.

Esau became a very good hunter when he grew up. He liked to go out into the fields. But Jacob was quiet. He liked to stay home around the tents. Isaac loved Esau best. That's because Isaac liked to eat the meat that Esau cooked after hunting. But Rebekah loved Jacob best.

One day Jacob cooked some soup. Esau came in from his time in the fields. And he was hungry. "I'm so hungry, I'm about to die!" said Esau. "Hurry and give me some of that red soup!"

"First you must promise me something," said Jacob. "When our father dies, he will leave most of what he owns to you. Promise me that you'll let me have it all."

"All right," said Esau. "After all, I'm about to die of hunger!"

"Promise!" said Jacob.

So Esau promised. Then Jacob gave him some of the soup and some bread. Esau ate the food and left.

Isaac in the Land of Gerar

GENESIS 26

A time came when there was not enough food. Crops would not grow in the fields. So Isaac moved to the land of Gerar.

God told Isaac, "Stay here for a while. I will do good things for you here. One day you and your family will own this land. It will be part of the promise I gave Abraham. Your children and their children will become a big family. There will be many of them. As many as the stars in the sky. Good will come to all nations because Abraham obeyed me."

So Isaac stayed in the land of Gerar.

Now Rebekah was beautiful. The men of Gerar asked Isaac about her.

Isaac said, "She is my sister." He was too scared to tell them she was his wife. He was afraid they might kill him. One of them might want Rebekah to be his wife.

One day the king looked out his window. He saw Isaac hugging Rebekah. So he called for Isaac. "Rebekah is really your wife!" he said. "Why didn't you tell me?"

"I was afraid someone might kill me," said Isaac.

The king was upset. He said, "No one may bother Isaac or Rebekah!"

Isaac planted seeds in the land of Gerar. Lots of crops grew for him. He had 100 times more than when he started. God was being good to him. He got very rich. He had many sheep and cows and servants.

Now the people of Gerar wished they had what Isaac had. So they

filled up all his wells with dirt. "Leave us," said the king. "You have too much power."

So Isaac moved to the valley. Isaac's servants dug new wells there. They found fresh water.

Now some of the men of Gerar took care of cows. They said, "This is our water!" So Isaac called it "The Well of Making a Fuss."

Then Isaac's servants dug a new well. But the men began to fight over that one, too. Isaac called that well "The Well of Fighting."

So they moved and dug another new well. This time no one came to fight over it. Isaac called the well "Wide Places." He said, "Now God has made room for us."

One night God said to Isaac, "Don't be afraid. I am with you."

So Isaac made an altar at that place. He worshiped God there.

Then the king of Gerar came to see Isaac.

"Why did you come here?" asked Isaac. "You asked me to leave."

The king said, "We can see that God is with you. We want to promise that we won't fight each other. We want to have peace."

So Isaac had a big dinner for the king. The next morning they promised each other to have peace. Then the king and his people left.

On the same day, Isaac's servants came to him. They told him about another well they had dug. "We found water!" they said. So he called that well "Promise."

Jacob Tricks Isaac

GENESIS 27–28

Isaac grew old. He could not see anymore. One day he called Esau to come to him.

"I'm old now," said Isaac. "I don't know when I might die. So take your bow and arrow. Go to the field and get some meat for me. Cook the meat the way I like it. Let me eat it. Then I will pray for God's best to come to you."

Rebekah heard what Isaac told Esau. She waited until Esau had gone hunting. Then she talked to Jacob.

"I heard your father talking to Esau," said Rebekah. "He told Esau to bring him some meat to eat. Then he is going to pray for God's best for Esau. So listen to me. Do what I say. Bring me some goat meat. I will cook it the way your father likes it. Then you can take it to him. He can eat it and pray for God's best for you."

"But Esau is hairy," said Jacob. "I have smooth skin. What if my father feels my smooth skin? Then he will think I'm playing a trick on him. He will pray for bad things for me. He won't pray for good things."

"The bad words can be for me," said Rebekah. "Just do what I tell you."

So Jacob got goat meat for Rebekah, his mother. She cooked it the way Isaac liked it. Then she put Esau's best clothes on Jacob. She put goat skins on Jacob's hands and neck. She also gave the goat meat and bread to Jacob.

Jacob went to Isaac. "Father," he said.

"Who is it?" asked Isaac.

"I'm Esau," said Jacob. "I did what you asked me to do. Eat some of this meat. Then you can pray for God's best for me."

"How could you get the meat so fast?" asked Isaac.

"God helped me," said Jacob.

Then Isaac said, "Let me touch you. I want to make sure you really are Esau."

Jacob moved closer to Isaac. Isaac felt his skin. "Your voice sounds like Jacob. But your hands feel like Esau. Are you really Esau?" he asked.

"Yes," said Jacob.

"Bring me the meat to eat," said Isaac. "Then I will pray for God's best to come to you."

So Jacob took the meat to Isaac. Isaac ate it. Then Jacob gave Isaac some wine. Isaac drank it. "Come and kiss me, Son," said Isaac.

Jacob kissed Isaac. Isaac smelled Esau's clothes on Jacob. So Isaac prayed for God's riches to come to Jacob.

Isaac said, "My son smells like a field. Like a field that God has been good to. I pray that God will give you rain from heaven. I pray that he will give you rich earth. I pray that he will give you lots of grain and wine. I pray that other nations will be your servants. I pray that your brothers and other people will bow to you. May bad come to people who speak bad words about you. May good come to people who say good things about you."

Jacob left Isaac after this prayer.

It was not long until Esau came back from hunting. He brought back the good meat his father loved. He cooked it and took it to Isaac.

"Sit up and eat," said Esau. "Then you can pray for God's best to come to me."

"Who is this?" asked Isaac.

"I'm your son Esau," said Esau.

Isaac began to shake. "Who was in here before? Who cooked food for me? I prayed for God's best to come to him!"

"Pray for me, too, Father!" Esau cried.

"Jacob tricked me," said Isaac. "He took the prayer I was going to pray for you."

"He has tricked me two times!"

said Esau. "He sold me soup. So he gets everything you should give me when you die. And now he took my prayer! Isn't there any prayer you can say for me?"

"All the family will bow to Jacob," said Isaac. "They'll be his servants. He will have lots of grain and wine. What can I do for you?"

"Is there just one prayer for good things, Father? Oh, pray for me, too!" said Esau. Esau cried.

Then Isaac said, "You will not live with rich earth. You will not live with heaven's rain. You will fight. And you will be a servant to Jacob. But a day will come when you won't serve him anymore."

From then on, Esau was angry with Jacob. He said, "It will not be long until my father dies. Then I will kill Jacob."

Someone told Rebekah what Esau said. So she called for Jacob. "Esau plans to kill you," she said. "Run away to my brother, Laban. You can stay there until Esau stops being so angry. I will let you know when you can come back."

Now Esau had married two women. They were from families who did not know or love God. Rebekah talked to Isaac about it. "It's hard for me to live with these women around. What if Jacob marries the same kind of woman?

Then I wouldn't want to live anymore."

So Isaac called Jacob. "Don't marry someone from this land," he said. "Go to Laban's house. Find a wife from his family. May God give you the same promise he gave my father, Abraham. May your family become a big nation."

JANUARY 11

A Ladder up to Heaven

GENESIS 28

Jacob left his home and began his trip to Laban's. The sun went down before he got there. So Jacob stopped to rest. He took a stone and used it as a pillow. He lay down for the night.

That night Jacob had a dream. He saw a ladder that went all the way up to heaven. God's angels were going up and down the ladder.

God stood at the top of the ladder. God said, "I am the Lord. I am the God of Abraham and Isaac. I will give your family the land you are sleeping on. Your family will become big. There will be so many people, they'll be like dust. They will live in the west and the east. They will live in the north and the south. Good will come to all nations because of your family."

God also said, "I'll be with you.

I will watch over you everywhere you go. I won't leave you. I will keep all my promises to you."

Jacob woke up thinking. He said, "God is here, and I didn't even know it!" It made him afraid. "This place is wonderful!" he said. "This is God's house! This is heaven's door!"

Early in the morning, Jacob got up. He set up the stone he had slept on. It made a post. Jacob put oil on the post. He named it "The House of God."

Then Jacob made a promise. "If God watches over me, he will bring me back here safely. He will give me food and clothes. This stone will be God's place. I'll give to God part of every thing he gives me."

Jacob in the Land of the East

GENESIS 29

Jacob kept going on his trip. At last he came to the land of the East. There was a well in a field there. Three groups of sheep sat near the well. That's where they came to get water. But a huge stone covered the top of the well.

The shepherds would wait until

25

all the sheep were there. Then they would take off the stone and give their sheep water. After that, they would put the stone back.

"Where are you from?" Jacob asked the shepherds.

"From Haran," said the shepherds.

"Do you know Laban?" asked Jacob.

"Yes," they said.

"How is he?" asked Jacob.

"He is doing well," they answered. "In fact, here comes his daughter Rachel now. She is bringing their sheep."

"It's too early to gather all of the sheep," said Jacob. "Go ahead and give your sheep some water. Then you can lead them back to the fields."

"We can't do that," said the shepherds. "We have to wait until all the sheep are here. Then we will take the stone off the well. That's when we will water our sheep."

Just then Rachel walked up. She was leading her father's sheep. She was a shepherdess.

Jacob saw Rachel. He took the stone off the well. He gave water to her sheep. Then he kissed her. He began to cry. He told Rachel that he was Rebekah's son. Rachel's father, Laban, was his uncle. Rachel ran back and told her father.

Laban came out quickly to meet Jacob. Laban hugged him and took him home.

Working for a Wife
GENESIS 29

Jacob stayed with Laban for a month. Jacob worked for him. One day Laban said, "You are part of my family. But I should pay you for the work you do. What do you want me to pay you?"

Now Laban had two daughters. Rachel had a big sister named Leah. But Rachel was prettier than Leah. Jacob loved Rachel. So he said, "Will you let Rachel marry me? If you will, I'll work seven years for you."

"That's fine," said Laban. "You may stay here and work for me."

Jacob worked for seven years so he could marry Rachel. But it didn't seem like a long time to Jacob. That's because he loved Rachel so much.

At last the seven years were over. Jacob said, "It is time for me to marry Rachel."

So Laban had a wedding party. He gave the bride to Jacob. But when Jacob saw his bride, he saw she was Leah!

"What did you do to me?" Jacob asked Laban. "I worked to marry Rachel. You fooled me!"

"That's how we do it in this

land," said Laban. "The older girl must get married before her younger sister. You can marry Rachel next week. But you must work seven more years for me."

So the next week Jacob married Rachel. He loved Rachel more than Leah. Then Jacob worked seven more years for Laban.

Lots of Babies

GENESIS 29–30

God saw that Jacob did not love Leah. So God let Leah have children. She had a baby boy. "God saw how sad I was," said Leah. So she called the baby Reuben.

Sometime later, Leah had another baby boy. "God gave me another baby," she said. "It's because he saw that Jacob does not love me." So she called this baby Simeon.

After that, Leah had another baby boy. "Now Jacob will stay with me," she said. So she called the baby Levi.

Later, she had another baby boy. "Praise God!" said Leah. And she called the baby Judah.

But Rachel did not have any children. She wanted to be like Leah. So she told Jacob, "Take my servant. She can be a wife to you. Then I'll have children that I can call mine."

So Rachel's servant had a baby boy. "God heard me!" said Rachel. So Rachel named the baby Dan.

Then Rachel's servant had another baby boy. "I have won the fight with my sister!" said Rachel. So Rachel called him Naphtali.

Now Leah saw that she wasn't having any more babies. So she gave her servant to Jacob. Her servant became another wife for him. That way Leah could have more children in her family.

It was not long before Leah's servant had a baby boy. "This is a good thing that happened!" said Leah. So she named the baby Gad.

Then Leah's servant had another baby boy. "I am so happy!" said Leah. So she called the baby Asher.

Then Leah herself had another baby boy. "This is a gift from God," she said. So she named this baby boy Issachar.

Sometime later, Leah had another baby boy. "This is a wonderful gift!" said Leah. "I have had six sons for Jacob!" So she named the baby Zebulun. Later, she had a baby girl. She named her baby girl Dinah.

Then God answered Rachel's prayers. She had her own baby, a baby boy. "I can feel good now," said Rachel. She named the baby Joseph and said, "May God give me another son."

Jacob Goes Home

GENESIS 30–31

Jacob went to Laban. He said, "I've done a lot of work for you. I want to take my wives and children. I want to go home."

"Please stay here," said Laban. "I know that God has been good to you. Just tell me what you want me to pay you."

"I have worked very hard for you," said Jacob. "Think about when I began working for you. You had only a few animals. Now you have a lot. God has been good to you, because I worked for you. But I should do something for my own family now."

"What do you want?" asked Laban.

Jacob said, "Just do one thing. Give me all the dark or spotted sheep and goats. They will be my pay. Then I will go on working for you."

"All right," said Laban. But that day Laban took all the dark or spotted goats. He gave them to his sons to take care of. They took the goats. They traveled away from Jacob for three days.

Jacob still took care of the sheep. They began having babies that were dark or spotted. So Jacob gathered those sheep for himself. He didn't let them get mixed in with Laban's sheep.

The dark and spotted sheep were very strong. So Jacob got the strong sheep. Laban got the weak sheep. Jacob got lots of sheep. He also got camels and donkeys and servants.

Now Laban's sons said, "Jacob took sheep from our father. He has made himself rich that way."

Jacob heard what they said. He also saw that Laban wasn't as friendly as before.

Then God told Jacob, "Go home. Go where you lived before. I'll be with you."

Jacob called for Rachel and Leah. They went out to the field to meet him. Jacob said, "Your father isn't as friendly to me now. You know how hard I have worked for him. But he tricked me. He changed my pay many times. But God has been good to me. God has taken care of me. Now God wants me to move back to my own land."

Rachel and Leah said, "Do whatever God tells you."

So Jacob got some camels. His wives and children rode on them. Jacob sent his cows ahead with other things he owned. Then Jacob started the trip back to Canaan.

Now Laban had gone to cut wool off his sheep. While he was gone, Rachel stole the handmade gods.

They were idols that Laban kept in his house.

Jacob did not tell Laban that he was leaving. Jacob just left. He crossed the river and set out toward hill country.

Three days went by. Then someone told Laban that Jacob had gone. So Laban got the men of his family together. They chased after Jacob. They found Jacob camped in the hill country. Laban set up his tents there, too.

But that night Laban had a dream. God spoke to Laban in the dream. "Be careful about what you say to Jacob."

The next day Laban spoke to Jacob. "Why did you run away in secret?" he said. "Why did you fool me? Why didn't you tell me you were going? I could have sent you away with joy. We could have had music and harps and singing. You didn't even give me a chance to say good-bye. I didn't get to kiss my daughters and grandchildren.

"You were very foolish," said Laban. "I could have hurt you. But last night God spoke to me. He told me not to say anything good or bad. But why did you steal my idols?"

"I was scared," said Jacob. "That's why I left without telling you. I thought you would make my wives stay here. But we did not take your idols. You can kill anybody you find who took your idols. If you find anything that is yours, take it." Jacob didn't know that Rachel had taken the idols.

Laban looked for his idols in Jacob's tent. He looked in Leah's tent. He looked in her servant's tent. He looked in the tent of Rachel's servant. Then he went into Rachel's tent.

Rachel had hidden the idols in her camel's saddle. The saddle was on the ground. She was sitting on it when her father walked in. Laban looked and looked.

"Don't be mad at me," said Rachel. "But I can't stand up right now. I'm not feeling well." So Laban left Rachel's tent without finding the idols.

Then Jacob was mad. "What did I do wrong? You looked everywhere. You didn't find anything that is yours. I worked for you for 20 years. I took good care of your sheep and goats. I got hot in the day and cold at night. There were many times when I could not sleep. And you changed my pay 10 times. You made it less each time. But God took care of me. If he hadn't, I'd be leaving without anything of my own."

"But these are my daughters and my grandchildren," said Laban. "Let's make peace."

So Jacob set up a stone post. Laban helped make a pile of stones, too.

"These stones are the sign of our promise," said Laban. "God will see if we keep our promise. So we will not hurt each other."

Jacob gave an animal as a gift to God. Then he asked Laban and his men to come to dinner. They ate next to the pile of stones. After they ate, they spent the night. In the morning, Laban kissed his daughters. He kissed his grandchildren. Then he and his men left and went back home.

JANUARY 13

Meeting Esau

GENESIS 32–33

Jacob and his family left for Canaan. God's angels met Jacob on the way. Jacob saw the angels. He said, "This is God's camp!"

Jacob sent some servants ahead. They took this message to Jacob's brother, Esau. "I have been at Laban's. Now I have cows and donkeys. I have sheep and goats and servants. I hope you will be kind to me."

The servants took the message to Esau. Then they came back to Jacob. "Esau is coming here," they said. "He has 400 men with him."

Jacob was scared. He put his family and servants and animals in two groups. Half of the people and animals were in one group. Half of them were in another group. "Esau might fight one group," he thought. "But the other group can get away."

Then Jacob prayed. "God, you have been kind to me. I am not good enough for your kindness. I came across the Jordan River a long time ago. I only had my walking stick with me. But now I am going back across with two groups. I pray that you will save me from Esau. You promised to make my family into a big nation. You said there would be more people than the sand."

Then Jacob chose a gift for Esau. He chose 220 goats and 220 sheep. He got 30 camels with their baby camels. He took 40 cows, 10 bulls, and 30 donkeys. He gave them to his servants.

"You go first," Jacob told them. "Stay in different groups. Esau will meet the first group. When he asks whose animals these are, tell him that these are Jacob's. Say that they are a gift. Say that Jacob is on his way."

Jacob told the other groups to say the same thing. He hoped that the gifts would keep Esau from being angry.

Jacob sent the gifts on. Later that night, he sent his wives and children across the river. But Jacob spent the night by himself.

That night a man came to Jacob. The man had a fight with Jacob. They kept fighting all night long. But the man could not win, because Jacob was strong. So the man touched Jacob's hip. Right away, Jacob's hip was hurt.

"Let me go now," said the man. "Day is coming."

"Only if you pray for God's best for me," said Jacob.

"What is your name?" asked the man.

"Jacob," he said.

"Now your name will be Israel," said the man. "Why? Because you have been fighting with God and with people. And you have won."

"Who are you?" asked Jacob.

"Why are you asking me?" said the man. Then he prayed for God's best for Jacob.

The sun was high in the sky when Jacob left. He could not walk well, because his hip was hurt. "I saw God!" said Jacob. "But I did not die!"

Jacob went on with his family. Then he saw Esau and his 400 men coming! So Jacob put his family into groups. He sent the two servants and their children out first. Next he sent Leah with her children. He sent Rachel and Joseph last. But Jacob went ahead of them all. He bowed down to Esau.

Esau ran up to Jacob. He hugged and kissed him. Then he saw Jacob's big family. "Who are they?" he asked.

"These are my wives and children," said Jacob.

They passed by Esau in their groups. They bowed down to Esau.

"Why did you send all the goats ahead of you? Why did you send sheep and cows?" asked Esau.

"They are a gift for you," said Jacob. "So you will be kind to me."

"I have enough goats and sheep and cows," said Esau. "You may keep them."

"No," said Jacob. "I am so happy to see your kind face. Please keep the animals as my gift to you. For God has been very good to me."

So Esau kept them. "I'll go along with you on your trip and help you," he said.

But Jacob said, "The children can't go very fast. They are too little. So you go on. We will come more slowly."

So Esau went back home. Jacob took his family to a different place in Canaan. He set up his tents. He built an altar to God there, too.

One More Baby

GENESIS 35

God told Jacob, "Go to Bethel. Build an altar to me there."

So Jacob told his family and

servants, "Get rid of all your idols. Then clean yourselves up. Put on clean clothes. We're going to go to Bethel. We'll build an altar to God there."

They all gave their idols to Jacob. Jacob dug a hole under an oak tree. He put the idols in the hole. He covered them up and left them there. Then they set out for Bethel.

At Bethel, Jacob built an altar to God. Bethel was the same place where Jacob had his dream. It was the dream about the angels on the ladder. It was where God talked to Jacob for the first time. That was when he was running away from Esau.

God came to Jacob again there. God said, "Your name will be Israel now. I give this land to you and your children. Kings will come from your people. And this will be their land."

Jacob set up a stone post there. He put oil on the post. He called that place Bethel.

Then Jacob traveled on. Rachel was going to have a baby. While they were on the trip, the baby was born. But Rachel had a hard time having the baby.

"Don't be afraid," said the woman who was helping Rachel. "You have a baby boy."

But Rachel was dying. Before she died, she named the baby Ben-Oni.

Jacob called him Benjamin. Then Rachel died. Jacob made a grave for Rachel. He set up a post to mark where her grave was.

Jacob stayed in the land of Canaan.

Sometime later, Jacob went home to see his father, Isaac. Then Isaac died. Esau and Jacob put his body in a grave.

JANUARY 14

The Dreamer

GENESIS 37

Jacob and Rachel's older son, Joseph, was growing up. He was 17 years old. He took care of sheep with his brothers. His brothers were not acting right. So he told his father, Jacob.

Jacob was also called Israel. He loved Joseph more than his other sons. He made a beautiful, long coat for Joseph.

Now Joseph's brothers saw that Jacob loved Joseph best. They hated Joseph for that. In fact, they could hardly say anything kind to him.

One time Joseph had a dream. He told his brothers about it. "We were making piles of wheat in the field. My pile of wheat stood up. Your piles of wheat came all around mine. They bowed to mine."

Joseph's brothers hated him even more because of his dream. "Do you think you'll be our boss?" they asked.

Joseph had another dream. He told his brothers about this dream, too. "The sun and moon bowed down to me," he said. "And 11 stars bowed down to me."

Joseph told his father, Jacob, about this dream. Jacob spoke. "Now, Joseph, do you really think our whole family will bow to you?"

Joseph's brothers were angry. They wanted to be special, too. His father just kept thinking about what Joseph had said.

One day Jacob called for his son Joseph. "Your brothers are taking care of the sheep. I want you to go to them. See if everything is going well for them. Then come back and tell me."

So off Joseph went. He came to where his brothers were supposed to be. But they were not there.

A man saw Joseph in the field. He asked, "Who are you looking for?"

"My brothers," said Joseph. "Do you know where they took their sheep?"

"I heard them say they were going to Dothan," said the man.

So Joseph went to Dothan. That's where he found his brothers. But they saw him coming before he got there. They made plans to kill him.

"Here's the dreamer!" they said. "Let's kill him and throw him into a well. We'll tell our father a wild animal ate him up. Then we'll find out what happens to his dreams!"

But Reuben tried to save Joseph. He said, "Let's not kill him. Throw him into this dry well. But don't kill him." Reuben was planning to save Joseph. He planned to take Joseph home later.

Joseph walked up to his brothers. They pulled his beautiful, long coat off. They threw him into the dry well.

Then they sat down and ate their lunch. Now along came a line of men with camels. The camels had packs of spices on their backs. They were on their way to Egypt.

Judah said, "It won't do us any good to kill Joseph. Let's sell him to these men."

The others thought that was a good idea. The line of camels came close. The brothers took Joseph out of the well. They sold him to the

men. They got 20 pieces of silver for him. Then the men and camels went on to Egypt.

Now Reuben did not know his brothers had sold Joseph. He went back to the well to save him. But Joseph wasn't there. Reuben ran to his brothers. "Joseph is not there!" he said. "Now what can I do?"

They took Joseph's coat. They killed a goat. They dipped the coat in the goat's blood. Then they took the coat to their father.

"Look at what we found," they said. "Does this belong to Joseph?"

Jacob saw at once that it was Joseph's coat. "It is Joseph's coat!" he said. "A wild animal has eaten him!"

Jacob was so upset that he tore his clothes. Then he put on clothes made of old sack cloth. He cried for days and days. His family tried to make him feel better. But he would not cheer up. "I'll be sad until the day I die," he said.

While this was happening, the men and camels got to Egypt. There they sold Joseph. The captain of the king's guard bought him.

At the Captain's House
GENESIS 39

God took care of Joseph. He lived in the captain's house. The captain saw that God helped Joseph. Good

things happened when Joseph was around. So the captain put Joseph in charge of everything in his house. With Joseph in charge, the captain didn't worry about anything. God took care of his house.

Now the captain's wife saw that Joseph was very handsome. So she said to Joseph, "Come and be like a husband to me!"

But Joseph wouldn't. He said, "The captain trusts me. How could I do such a thing? It would not be right. It would be a great sin against God."

Every day the captain's wife said the same thing. Every day Joseph answered the same. In fact, he tried not to be around the captain's wife.

One day Joseph went into the house. He was going to take care of some work. No one else was around.

But the captain's wife was there. She took hold of Joseph's coat. "Come and be like a husband to me!" she said.

Joseph ran out of the house. He left his coat in her hands.

Then the captain's wife called her servants. "See this?" she said. "Joseph came in here to be like a husband to me. But I called for help. Then he ran off in a hurry. See? He left his coat here."

The captain's wife kept Joseph's coat with her. Later, the captain came home. Then she told him the same thing. The captain was very angry. He threw Joseph into jail.

But God was still with Joseph. God was good to him. The jail keeper liked Joseph. He put Joseph in charge of other people in jail. The jail keeper trusted Joseph. He did not have to worry. God helped Joseph do a good job. God helped Joseph take care of everything.

JANUARY 15

Two Strange Dreams

GENESIS 40

One day two new men were sent to jail. One was the man who took the king his drinks. He was a waiter. The other was the king's baker. They had made the king angry. That's why he put them in jail. Joseph was put in charge of them.

One night the baker and waiter both had dreams. The next morning Joseph came to see them. He could tell that they were upset. "Why are you sad today?" he asked.

"It's because of our dreams," they said. "There is no one to tell us what our dreams mean."

"God can tell what dreams mean," said Joseph. "Tell me what you dreamed."

The waiter said, "My dream was about a vine. There were three branches on it. The vine had buds. They turned into flowers. Then grapes grew. I held the king's cup. I put grape juice into the cup. Then I gave it to the king."

"Here is what your dream means," said Joseph. "The three branches mean three days. Three days will pass. Then the king will let you out of jail. You will get to give him drinks again. You will see the king. Please tell him about me. See if you can get me out of jail, too. I did not do anything wrong. I should not be here."

Now the baker saw that the waiter's dream was good. So he told Joseph his dream, too. "Three baskets of bread were on my head," he said. "The top basket held bread for the king. But birds came and ate the bread up."

"Here is what your dream means," said Joseph. "The three baskets mean three days. Three days from now, the king will hang you. You will die, and the birds will eat your body."

Three days went by. It was the king's birthday. So he had a party. He took the waiter and the baker out of jail. He gave the waiter his old job back. But he hanged the baker. It went just the way Joseph said it would. But the waiter didn't tell the king about Joseph. He forgot.

The King's Dreams

GENESIS 41

Two years passed. One night the king of Egypt had a dream. He dreamed that he stood by the Nile River. Seven fat cows came up out of the river. They ate the plants that grew by the river bank. Then seven ugly, thin cows came out of the river. They ate up the seven fat cows.

The king woke up from his dream. But he went back to sleep and had another dream. Seven good, fat heads of wheat grew up. They grew on one stem. Then seven thin heads of wheat came up. The thin wheat ate up the fat wheat. The king woke up again.

The next morning the king was upset. He called for the men who could do magic. He called for his wise men. He told them his dreams. But no one could tell him what they meant.

Then the waiter remembered Joseph. He said to the king, "I remember now. You were angry with me and the baker. You sent us to jail. In jail we had dreams. There was another man in jail. He told us the meaning of our dreams. Things happened just the way he said they would."

So the king called for Joseph. Joseph shaved. He put on clean clothes. Then he came to the king.

"I had a dream," said the king. "No one can tell me what it means. I heard that you can tell what dreams mean."

"I can't," said Joseph. "But God can."

So the king told Joseph about the fat and thin cows. He told Joseph about the fat and thin wheat.

Joseph said, "Both of your dreams mean the same thing. God is showing you what he is going to do. The seven fat cows and the fat wheat are the same. They mean seven years. Lots of food will grow in those seven years.

"The seven thin cows and the thin wheat are the same. They mean seven more years. No food will grow then.

"So first this land will have seven years with enough food. Then there will be seven years of no food. This will happen right away. So you should find a wise man. Put him in charge of Egypt. Save food that grows in the good years. Then later the people can eat the food they saved."

The king liked Joseph's idea. He said, "God has told this to you. You are the wisest of all. So you will be in charge of my palace. Everyone will obey you. I will be the only one greater than you. You'll be in charge of all the land of Egypt."

The king took his own ring off his

finger. He put it on Joseph's finger. He gave Joseph fine clothes. He gave him a gold chain to wear around his neck. He let Joseph ride in a chariot. There were men who ran in front of Joseph's chariot. They called out, "Make room!" The king even chose a wife for Joseph.

Now Joseph was 30 years old. He took many trips around Egypt. For seven years, plenty of food grew. So Joseph told the people to gather the food. They saved it in their cities. They saved it for the time when no food would grow.

Joseph made the people save lots of wheat. There was so much, it was like sand by the sea. In fact, they stopped counting how much they had. They could not even measure it.

Now Joseph and his wife had two sons. Joseph said, "God has let me forget my troubles." So he called his first son Manasseh. Joseph said, "God has sent good things to me." So he called his next son Ephraim.

But one day the seven good years were over. No food would grow. All the other lands ran out of food. But there was still food in Egypt. That's because they had saved it.

Joseph let people buy wheat.

Even people from other lands came to buy wheat. That's because their fields grew no crops.

JANUARY 16

Visitors from Canaan

GENESIS 42

No crops of grain were growing in the land of Canaan. That's where Joseph's father and brothers and their families lived.

Joseph's father, Jacob, heard that Egypt had wheat. So he talked to his sons about it. "Why are you just looking at each other?" he asked. "Go to Egypt and buy some wheat for us."

So 10 of Joseph's brothers went to buy wheat. Jacob would not let Benjamin go with them. Benjamin was the only other child of Rachel. Jacob was afraid that something bad might happen to Benjamin.

It wasn't long before Joseph's brothers got to Egypt. They went to see the man in charge. He was the one who sold the wheat. He was Joseph.

Joseph's brothers bowed to him. Joseph knew who they were right away. But he acted as if he didn't know them. "Where are you from?" he asked in a mean voice.

"We are from Canaan," they said. "We came to buy some food." They had no idea that this man was Joseph!

Joseph remembered his dreams from long ago. He said, "I think you came to trick us! You came to see how you can take over this land!"

"Oh, no!" they said. "We just came to buy food. We are all brothers. We are good people. We tell the truth. We are not here to trick you."

"Yes, you are," said Joseph.

But they said, "There used to be 12 of us. Our youngest brother is back in Canaan with our father. One of our brothers is gone."

"Just as I said. You are here to trick us!" said Joseph. "This is how I will test you. I won't let you leave until your youngest brother comes. One of you must go and get him. The others have to stay here in jail. I'll find out if you're telling the truth or not." Then Joseph put them all in jail.

The Test

GENESIS 42

Three days went by. Then Joseph told his brothers, "Only one of you must stay. The rest of you may go home. Take wheat with you. But bring your youngest brother back here. That way I'll know you told the truth."

The brothers began to talk to each other. "This is what we get for being mean to Joseph long ago. We saw how upset he was. He asked us to be kind to him. But we didn't listen."

Reuben said, "I told you not to hurt Joseph. But you wouldn't listen. Now we are paying for what we did."

They didn't know Joseph could understand every word they said. When Joseph talked, he spoke in the language of Egypt. Another person had to tell his brothers what he said.

But Joseph did know what they were saying. He had to turn his face away from them. He was starting to cry. In a minute, he turned around. He chose Simeon to stay in jail. And he let the others go home.

Joseph told his helpers to do three things. They had to fill his brothers' bags with wheat. They had to put each brother's money back in his bag. They had to give his brothers food for the trip back.

Joseph's helpers followed his orders. Then his brothers put their bags on their donkeys' backs. They started home.

That night Joseph's brothers stopped to rest. One of them wanted to feed his donkey. So he opened his bag to get some wheat. That's when he saw his money in the bag. "My money has been given back to me!" he said. "It's right here in my bag!"

They all looked at each other. They began to shake with fear. "What is God doing to us?" they asked.

But they kept on going home. When they got there, they told Jacob about their trip.

"This man is in charge of all the land," they said. "He spoke in a mean voice. He said we had come to trick him! He told us to bring our youngest brother to Egypt. Then he will know we are telling the truth about our family."

They began to open their bags and dump the wheat out. And they saw each brother's money in his own bag! They were scared!

Jacob said, "Joseph is gone. Simeon is in jail in Egypt. Now you want to take Benjamin back with you. Everything is going wrong!"

"I will take care of Benjamin," said Reuben. "Trust him to me."

"No," said Jacob. "He can't go with you. Joseph is dead. Benjamin is Rachel's only son who is left. What if something happened to him? I would be sad for the rest of my life."

No More Wheat
GENESIS 43

Time passed. Jacob's family ate up all their wheat. Still no food was growing in their land. So Jacob called his sons. "Go back to Egypt," he said. "Buy some more food for us."

"We can't do that," said Judah. "The man told us we must bring our youngest brother next time. We'll go back if you'll let Benjamin come, too. But if Benjamin can't come, we won't go."

"Why did you tell him about Benjamin?" asked Jacob.

"He asked us about our family," they said. "We just answered his questions. How could we know he'd want to see Benjamin?"

"Send Benjamin with me," said Judah. "We must go right away. If we don't, our families will die of hunger. I promise I will bring him back safely to you. We've waited so long to go to Egypt! We could have been there and back two times by now."

"All right," said Jacob. "Then take some of the best gifts we have. Give them to this man. Take some honey and spices and nuts. Take two times as much money with you. Maybe it was put back into your bags by mistake. And take Benjamin, too."

So they took Benjamin and the money and the gifts. They headed for Egypt.

Dinner at Joseph's House
GENESIS 43

Joseph's brothers went quickly to Egypt. They went to see Joseph.

Joseph saw Benjamin there with them. So he called his chief servant. "These men will eat with me at noon today," he said. "Take them to my house. Make dinner for us."

The servant led the brothers to Joseph's house. When they saw where they were going, they were afraid. "This is because our money was in our bags," they said. "This man is going to make us his slaves. He will take our donkeys, too."

They stopped in front of Joseph's house. There they talked to Joseph's servant. "We were here before to buy food," they said. "We stopped to rest on our way home. That's when we found our money back in our bags. We don't know who put it there. But we have brought the money back with us."

"Don't worry," said the servant. "God must have put your money back in your bags. I got the money you paid before."

Then the servant took Simeon out of jail. He took Simeon to his brothers. And he took them all into Joseph's house. He brought water so they could wash up. He fed their donkeys.

Joseph's brothers got their gifts ready. They had heard that Joseph would be there for dinner.

When Joseph got there, his brothers gave him their gifts. They bowed to him.

Joseph asked, "How is your father?"

"He is fine," they said.

Joseph looked around. He saw Benjamin. "Is this your youngest brother?" he asked. Then he talked to Benjamin. "May God bring good things to you," he said. This was his own brother. Rachel was their mother. It was good to see him.

Joseph felt like crying. So he hurried to his own room and cried. Then Joseph washed his face and came back out. He told the servants, "Bring our food!"

Joseph ate by himself. The brothers ate together in a group. Other people from Egypt ate there, too. But they sat in a different group. The people of Egypt never ate with God's people.

Now each of Joseph's brothers had a place to sit. They were seated in the order of how old they were. The one born first was the first to be seated. Then came the second, and the third, and so on. Benjamin was last. They all looked at each other. They were surprised.

Then the servants gave them dinner. But the servants gave Benjamin five times more than anyone else. So they ate and drank at Joseph's house.

A Silver Cup
GENESIS 44

Joseph gave orders to his servant. "Put wheat in the men's bags. Give them as much as they can carry. Put their money back in their bags, too. Then get my silver cup. Put it in the bag of the youngest brother." So the servant did what Joseph told him.

The next morning Joseph's brothers got the bags of wheat. They put them on their donkeys. Then they headed home.

Soon after they had gone, Joseph called his servant. "Go catch up with those men right away," he said. "Tell them that I was kind to them. Ask them why they were mean to me. Ask why they took my silver cup."

So the servant chased after Joseph's brothers. At last he found them. He said just what Joseph told him to say.

"Why would we take a cup?" they asked. "Last time we were here, we found money in our bags. But we brought it back. If one of us has the cup, you may kill him. Then you may take the rest of us to be slaves."

"All right," said Joseph's servant.

They all took their bags down off their donkeys. They opened the bags. The servant began with the oldest brother. He looked in his bag first. Then he went to the second brother. He looked in every brother's bag. He came to Benjamin's bag last. That's where he found the cup.

All the brothers were very upset. They put their bags back on their donkeys. They headed back to Joseph's house.

When they saw Joseph, they bowed. "What did you do?" said Joseph. "Didn't you know that I would find this out?"

"There is nothing we can say," said Judah. "We can't prove that we didn't do it. We are your slaves."

"No," said Joseph. "I will only take the one who had the cup. He will be my slave. The rest of you may go home."

Judah said, "Please don't be angry with me. But I promised that I would bring the boy home again. If I don't bring him back, our father will die. Please let me be your slave instead. Let the boy go back home."

Telling the Secret

GENESIS 45

Joseph couldn't stand it anymore. He sent everyone but his brothers out of the room. Then he told them who he really was. "I am Joseph!" he said. He cried out loud. Even the people outside the room heard him. They told the people at the king's house about it.

"Is my father still alive?" Joseph asked.

Joseph's brothers could not say a word. They were afraid.

"I am Joseph, your brother!" he said. "You sold me to be a slave. I was taken to Egypt. But don't worry about it now. God sent me here so I could save many lives. God put me in charge here. There will be five more years without food. So go back and bring your families to live here. Tell our father that God made me the ruler of Egypt."

Then Joseph hugged Benjamin and cried some more. Benjamin cried and hugged Joseph, too. Then Joseph kissed all of his brothers. And they talked together.

The king soon heard that Joseph's brothers were in Egypt. So he told Joseph, "Bring your brothers' families here to live. You can have the best land. Take carts with you so their children and wives can ride. Bring your father, too. Don't worry about bringing anything else. You can get whatever you need when you get here."

So Joseph gave his brothers some carts. He gave them food for their trip. He gave new clothes to each of them. But he gave five sets of clothes to Benjamin. He gave 300 pieces of silver to Benjamin, too.

Joseph sent his father 20 donkeys with packs on their backs. The packs were full of wheat, bread, and other food. They carried all kinds of good things from Egypt.

As his brothers were leaving, Joseph called out to them. "Don't fuss and fight on the way!" he said.

So Joseph's brothers went to Canaan loaded with gifts. They told Jacob, "Joseph is alive! He is the ruler of Egypt!"

Jacob could hardly believe it. But they told him all about their trip. They showed him all the gifts. Then he said, "I believe it now! Joseph is alive! I will go and see him again!"

JANUARY 18

Moving to Egypt
GENESIS 46–47

Jacob got his family together. They set out for Egypt. One night on their trip, God called, "Jacob!"

"I'm here," said Jacob.

"Don't be afraid to go to Egypt," said God. "I will turn your family into a big nation there. I will be with you."

So off they went to Egypt. The women and children rode in carts. They brought their sheep and cows along, too.

Joseph had told them to go to a place called Goshen. Joseph rode in his chariot to meet them there. When Jacob saw Joseph, he hugged him and cried. "Now I can die in peace," he said. "I know that you are alive!"

Then Joseph spoke to his brothers.

"I'm going to talk to the king about you. He will ask you what kind of work you do. Tell him that you take care of sheep. That way he will let you live in Goshen. The people of Egypt don't like sheep farmers."

Joseph took five of his brothers to see the king. The king asked, "What kind of work do you do?"

"We take care of sheep," they said. "We would like to live in Goshen."

The king told Joseph, "Give your family the best land in Egypt. Let them live in Goshen. Maybe some of your brothers are very good with sheep. So you can put them in charge of my sheep, too."

Then Joseph took his father to see the king. "How old are you?" asked the king.

"I am 130 years old," said Jacob. Then Jacob prayed for God's best for the king.

Joseph let his brothers and their families live in Goshen. He gave them as much food as they needed.

Now people began to run out of money. They couldn't pay for the food Joseph gave them. So they traded their sheep and cows for the food. But the next year they ran out of sheep and cows. So they traded their fields for food. Then they ran out of fields. So they sold themselves as servants.

That's the way Joseph got money and sheep and cows for the king. He got fields and servants for the king. The people were just glad to have food to eat.

Jacob's Last Words
GENESIS 47–49

Jacob, who was called Israel, knew he would die soon. He had lived 17 years in Goshen. He was 147 years old. He called for Joseph. "Promise you won't make my grave in Egypt," he said. "When I die, take my body back to Canaan."

"All right," said Joseph. He promised.

Later, a message came to Joseph. "Your father is sick." So Joseph took his sons, Manasseh and Ephraim, with him. They went to see Jacob.

Jacob heard that Joseph was there. So he sat up in his bed. He told Joseph about God's promise. "God told me he'd make my family into a big nation. He told me he'd give me the land of Canaan. You and your sons are part of my family. So your sons will have part of Canaan, too."

Jacob could hardly see. But he saw that someone was with Joseph. "Who is with you?" he asked.

"These are my sons, Ephraim and Manasseh," said Joseph.

"I want to pray for God's best for them," said Jacob.

So Joseph brought them close to

him. Jacob hugged and kissed them. "I never thought I'd see you again," he told Joseph. "Now I have even seen your children."

Jacob put his right hand on Ephraim's head. He put his left hand on Manasseh's head. Then he prayed for them. "God was my shepherd all my life. He was the angel who kept me safe. I pray that he will do good things for these boys. I pray that he will make their families great."

Then Jacob called all of his sons. "Come close around me," he said. "Reuben, you were the strongest. But you are like waves of water. You will not be the strongest anymore.

"Simeon and Levi, your tools are swords. You killed men because of your anger. You will go here and there in the land.

"Judah, you are like a lion cub. Kings will come from your family. Your brothers will say good things about you.

"Zebulun, you will live by the sea. You will be a place where ships stay. Ships will be safe there.

"Issachar, you are like a lazy donkey. It likes to lie down between the packs. You will work for other people.

"Dan, you are like a snake by the road. It bites at the heels of the horse. It makes the rider fall.

"Gad, robbers will fight with you. But you will fight them back.

"Asher, your food will be the best. It will be good enough for a king's table.

"Naphtali, you are like a deer that runs free. It has pretty fawns.

"Joseph, you are like a tree with lots of fruit. I pray for God's goodness for you. It's greater than the goodness of the old mountains. You are the prince of my sons. You have stayed strong with God's help.

"Benjamin, you are like a wolf that catches its food."

This is how Jacob, called Israel, prayed for his 12 sons. Now the families of Jacob's sons go by these 12 names. These are the family groups, or 12 tribes, of Israel.

Then Jacob told them, "I'm going to die soon. Make a place for my body in Canaan. Use the same cave where Abraham's and Sarah's bodies are. That's where Isaac's and Rebekah's bodies are, too. And that's where Leah's body is."

After this, Jacob, who was called Israel, pulled his feet into his bed. Then he died.

A Trip to the Cave
GENESIS 50

Joseph cried when his father died. Then he talked to the king. "My father made me promise to take his body to Canaan. So let me take his body to a cave there. Then I will come back."

"Go ahead," said the king. "Keep your promise."

So Joseph went back to Canaan. The leaders of Egypt went with him. Joseph's brothers went, too. But they left their children, sheep, and cows in Goshen.

They stopped at a place near the Jordan River. There they had seven days of crying. The people who lived nearby saw all the crying. They said, "This is a sad time for Egypt's people."

Jacob's sons put his body in a cave. It was where Abraham's and Sarah's bodies were. Then they all went back to Egypt.

Now Joseph's brothers were afraid. They said, "Joseph might still be angry with us. It's all because we sold him many years ago." So they sent Joseph a message. "Before our father died, he told us something. He said we should tell you to forgive us. So we ask you to forgive us."

Joseph cried when he heard the message.

Then Joseph's brothers came and bowed to him. "We will be your servants," they said.

But Joseph was kind to them and said, "Don't be afraid. You meant to hurt me. But God planned for good things to come from it. Many lives have been saved because of what happened. So don't be afraid. I will take care of you and your families."

Joseph lived 110 years. He even had great-grandchildren.

Before he died, he called his brothers. "Promise me something," he said. "When you leave Egypt, take my bones with you." They promised. Sometime later, Joseph died.

From Egypt to the Promised Land

A Mean King

EXODUS 1

As time went by, all of Joseph's brothers died. But they had children. And their children had children. So the sons of Jacob really did become a big nation. Jacob's other name was Israel. So the nation was called Israel. The people of this nation were called the children of Israel. Sometimes they were called God's people. And sometimes they were called Jews.*

> *NOTE: The children of Israel were not called Jews until a much later time. But in this Bible they will be called Jews from now on. Or they may be called Jewish people or God's people. Then you will always know who these people are. They are the family that started with Abraham, Isaac, and Jacob.*

Now a new king came into power in Egypt. He didn't know about Joseph. "Look at these Jewish people," he said. "There are so many of them! They are stronger than we are. We have to do something. If we don't, their group will grow even bigger. What if we have a war? They will join our enemies. They will fight us. They might leave our land."

So the king put masters over God's people. He made them do hard work. He made them build cities to store things in. But the more work they did, the more their families grew.

The people of Egypt were afraid of the Jews. They made them work very, very hard. They made the Jews' lives unhappy. The Jews had to build with bricks. They had to work hard in the fields. The people of Egypt were very mean to them.

Now two Jewish women were like nurses. They helped other Jewish women when they had their babies. The king gave them orders. "If the Jews' babies are boys, kill them," he said. "If the babies are girls, let them live."

But these two women believed in God. They knew he did not want them to kill the baby boys.

So the king called for them. He said, "Why do you let the boy babies live?"

The two women said, "Our Jewish women have their babies fast. The babies are born before we get there to help."

So God was good to these two women. He gave them children, too. That's because they obeyed God. They thought it was more important to obey God than to obey the king.

There were more and more of God's people. So the king gave his people an order. "Throw the Jewish boy babies into the Nile River."

The Princess and the Basket

EXODUS 2

One Jewish mother hid her baby boy. She hid him for three months. Then he was too big to hide anymore. So she took a basket. She painted tar on it to keep out the water.

Then the mother put the baby in the basket. She put the basket at the edge of the Nile River. She set it among the tall water plants. The baby's sister stayed a little way off.

She watched to see what would happen.

The princess went down to the Nile River that day. Her servant girls were with her. They walked along the edge of the river.

The princess saw the basket among the water plants. She told one of her servant girls to get it.

When the princess opened the basket, she saw the baby. He was crying. The princess felt sorry for the baby. "This is a Jewish baby," she said.

Then the baby's sister spoke to the princess. "Shall I go find a Jewish woman? She could take care of the baby for you."

"Yes," said the princess. So the baby's sister went and got the baby's mother.

The princess told her, "Take care of this baby for me. I'll pay you for it."

So the baby's mother took him home. She took care of him for the princess. He grew from a baby to a young boy. Then one day his mother took him to the princess.

The boy became the son of the princess. She called him Moses. His name sounds like the Jewish word that means "pull out." The princess said, "I pulled him out of the water."

Running Away

EXODUS 2

Moses grew up to be a man. One day he went where the Jews were working. He knew they were his own people. He watched how hard they worked.

Then Moses saw a man from Egypt beating a Jewish man. Moses looked around. Nobody was watching. So he killed the man from Egypt. He hid the body in the sand.

The next day Moses went out again. He saw two Jewish men fighting each other. He turned to the man who started the fight. "Why are you hitting your neighbor?" he asked.

"Who said you could be our prince?" the man answered. "Do you think you will kill me? I know you killed the man from Egypt."

Moses got scared. "People must know about what I did!" he thought.

The king had heard about it. He tried to kill Moses. But Moses ran

away from the king. He went to a land called Midian. He sat down by a well there.

In a little while, seven girls came to the well. Their father was a priest in Midian. They came to the well to give their sheep some water.

But some shepherds came over to the well. They pushed the girls away.

Moses stood up. He came over and made the shepherds move back. Then he got water for the girls' sheep.

The girls went back to their father, Jethro. "How did you get home so early today?" he asked.

"A man from Egypt was at the well," they said. "He saved us from the shepherds. He got water for our sheep, too."

"Where is he?" asked Jethro. "Why did you leave him there? Ask him to come and eat with us."

Jethro asked Moses to stay with them. And Moses said he would. Jethro let his daughter marry Moses. Sometime later, Moses and his wife had a baby boy.

While Moses was away, the king of Egypt died. The Jews cried to God. They cried because they had to work so hard for Egypt's people. God heard them. He remembered the promise he had made to Abraham, Isaac, and Jacob. So God watched over his people. He cared about what was happening.

Fire!

EXODUS 3

Moses took care of Jethro's sheep. One day he took them far across the desert. He came to Horeb Mountain. It's sometimes called God's Mountain. God came to Moses there. He showed himself as fire that was burning on a bush.

Moses saw the fire. He also saw that the bush didn't burn up. So Moses thought, "This is strange. Why doesn't the bush burn up? I'll take a closer look."

God saw Moses walk closer. So God called to him from the bush. "Moses! Moses!"

"I'm here," said Moses.

"Don't come any closer," said God. "Take off your shoes. You're standing on land that is special. It's just for me." Then God said, "I'm the God of your family from long ago. I'm Abraham's God, Isaac's God, and Jacob's God."

Moses hid his face when he heard this. He was too scared to look at God.

"I've seen how unhappy my people are," said God. "I've heard them crying in Egypt. Their masters are hard on them. And I care about how they are hurting. So I have come to save them. I have come to take them out of Egypt. I'll take them to a good, big land. It's a land that's rich. Plenty of food grows there.

"So I want you to go to Egypt," said God. "I'm sending you to the king. You'll bring my people out of Egypt."

"But who am I?" asked Moses. "I'm not strong enough to go to the king. How can I bring the Jews out of Egypt?"

"I'll be with you," said God. "Bring my people out of Egypt. Then you will worship me on this mountain. And you will know that God really sent you."

"Let's say I go to the Jews," said Moses. "I tell them God sent me to them. What if they ask what God's name is? Then what will I say?"

"The name is I Am Who I Am," said God. "You'll say I AM sent you. Tell them that I'm the Lord. I'm Abraham's God. I'm Isaac's God. I'm Jacob's God. This will be my name forever. It's the name parents will teach their children to call me.

"Now go to the leaders of the Jews," said God. "Tell them these things. They'll listen to you. Then all of you must go to the king. Tell him that the Jews' God talked to you. Ask the king to let you travel into the desert for three days. Ask him to let you give gifts to the Lord your God.

"But I know the king of Egypt," said God. "He won't let you go unless someone strong makes him. So I'll hit Egypt with troubles. Then he will let you go.

"When my people leave, they'll go with their hands full. Ask the people of Egypt for silver, gold, and clothes. Put these on your children. Then you will leave with the riches of Egypt."

The Snake

EXODUS 4

"What if the Jews don't believe me?" asked Moses. "What if they won't listen to me? God, what if they say that you never came to me?"

"What are you holding in your hand?" asked God.

"A stick that I use for walking," said Moses.

"Throw it down," said God.

So Moses threw his stick on the ground. It turned into a snake. Moses ran away from it.

"Reach out for it," said God. "Pick it up again by its tail."

Moses reached out. He picked up the snake. It turned back into his walking stick.

"Do this. It will show the people that I came to you," said God. "Now put your hand inside your coat."

Moses put his hand inside his coat. When he took his hand out, it was white like snow. It was covered with a skin sickness.

"Now put your hand back inside your coat," said God.

Moses put his hand back inside his coat. When he took his hand out, it was well again.

"They might not believe the first wonder," said God. "But they will believe the second one. Or they might not believe at all. Then dip out some water from the Nile River. Let it flow onto the ground. It will turn into blood on the ground."

Then Moses said, "I've never been good at talking to people. I haven't gotten any better even after you've talked to me. I'm too slow."

"Who gave people their mouths?" asked God. "Who makes people able to hear or see? Don't I do that? So go. I'll help you talk. I'll teach you what to say."

"Please, God," said Moses. "Send somebody else."

Then God became angry at Moses. "How about Aaron, your brother? He can talk well. He is already on his way here. He will be glad to see you. You'll talk to him and tell him what to say. I'll help both of you. He will be like a mouth for you. You'll give him my words. Take your walking stick with you. You can do wonders with it."

Then Moses went back to Jethro. Moses said, "Let me go back to Egypt. I'll see if any of my family are still alive."

"All right," said Jethro. "I hope everything goes well."

So Moses took his walking stick and went back to Egypt. His wife and sons went with him. They rode on a donkey.

God said, "I gave you power to do wonders. Show them to the king. But I'll make his heart hard. He won't let my people go. You'll say that God's people are like his first son. You'll say to let them go so they can worship. Tell the king that if he says no, his first son will die."

Then God told Aaron, "Go to the desert. Meet Moses there."

So Aaron met Moses at God's Mountain. Aaron kissed Moses. Then Moses told Aaron what God wanted him to say. He told about the wonders God told him to do.

Moses and Aaron went to Egypt. They called the leaders of the Jews together. Aaron told them everything God had told Moses. He showed the wonders to the people. They believed him. They learned that God cared about them. They learned that God saw how unhappy they were. So they bowed down and worshiped God.

Hay Bricks

EXODUS 5–6

Then Moses and Aaron went to see the king. They told him what the Jews' God said. God's words were, "Let my people go. I want them to go to the desert. I want them to have a holiday for me."

"Who is the Jews' God?" asked the king. "Why should I obey him? I don't know him. So I won't let the people go."

"The Jews' God came to us," said Moses and Aaron. "So let us take a trip to the desert. We'll be gone for three days. We will worship God by giving him gifts there. If we don't, he might make us sick. Or we might get hurt."

"Look!" said the king. "There are lots of people in the land. You are just trying to keep them from working!"

Then the king talked to the work bosses. "Don't give the people any more hay to make bricks. Tell them to get their own hay. But they still have to make just as many bricks. They don't want to work. That's why they're asking me if they can go. So make the work harder for them. Then they won't listen to these lies."

The work bosses told the people what the king said. Then the Jews had to look for hay. It took time. They had trouble making as many bricks as they did before. The work bosses beat them. They said, "Why didn't you make as many bricks today?"

Then the Jewish leaders went to the king. "Why are you doing this?" they asked. "The bosses don't give us hay. But they want us to make just as many bricks. They beat us. But we are not to blame."

"You just don't want to work!" said the king. "That's why you keep asking me to let you go worship your God. Get back to work. You won't get any hay. But you have to make just as many bricks."

The Jewish leaders saw they were in trouble. So they went to Moses and Aaron. Moses and Aaron were waiting for them.

The leaders said, "God will judge you for this! You made the king hate us! We'll all be killed!"

Moses talked to God. "Why are you bringing us trouble? Why did you even send me here?" he asked. "I went to the king. But now he is giving your people a hard time. You haven't saved them at all."

"Now you'll see what I'm going to do," said God. "The king will let the Jews go. My strong hand will make him do it. He will send you out of this land."

Then God said, "I'm Abraham's God. I'm Isaac's God and Jacob's God. I promised to give them the land of Canaan. I have heard my people cry. I remember my promise. So tell them that I am the Lord. I'll take you out of this land. I'll set you free. You will be my people. I will be your God. Then you'll know that I am the Lord your God. I'll take you to the land I promised to the Jews. I am the Lord."

Moses told the Jews what God had said. But they didn't listen to him. Their hearts were too sad and worried.

God told Moses, "Go to the king. Tell him to let the Jews leave this land."

"The Jews won't listen to me," said Moses. "So why would the king listen to me? I don't even talk very well."

Snakes and Blood
EXODUS 7

God talked to Moses. "It will seem to the king that you're like God. Aaron will go with you. Say whatever I tell you. Aaron will talk to the king. I will show many signs and wonders. But the king won't listen to you. Then I'll send trouble to Egypt. And I'll bring my people out."

So Moses and Aaron obeyed God. Moses was 80 years old. Aaron was 83.

God said, "The king will tell you to do a wonder. So tell Aaron to throw down the stick he uses for walking. It will turn into a snake."

Moses and Aaron went to the king. Aaron threw his walking stick down. It turned into a snake.

Then the king called his wise men. He called his magic men. Each man threw down his walking stick. The sticks turned into snakes. But Aaron's walking stick ate up their walking sticks.

The king got angry and wouldn't listen. His heart got hard. He would not let the Jewish people leave the land.

God talked to Moses again. "Go see the king in the morning. Wait by the Nile River to meet him. He will go out to the water."

These were God's words for the king. "Let my people leave this land. Let them go worship me in the desert. You don't listen to me. So I'll show you I am the Lord."

Then God told Moses to say this. "I'll hit the river water with my walking stick. It will turn into blood. All the fish will die. The river

will smell bad. The people of Egypt won't be able to drink the water."

Then God said, "Tell Aaron what to do. Tell him to hold his walking stick over the water. Hold it over the rivers and ponds. The water will turn into blood. Blood will be everywhere. It will even be in stone jars and wooden pails."

So Moses and Aaron did what God said. The water turned into blood. The fish died. The river smelled bad. Blood was everywhere. The people of Egypt couldn't drink the water.

But the king's magic men did the same thing. The king didn't care about God. His heart got hard again. He wouldn't listen. It was just like God had said it would be. The king turned around and went back into his palace. He didn't even think this was important.

All the people of Egypt dug wells by the river. They were looking for water to drink.

JANUARY 23

Frogs, Bugs, and Flies
EXODUS 8

A week later God told Moses, "Go back. Go to the king. Tell him to let my people go." God said to tell the king, "If you don't, I'll send frogs. The Nile River will be full of frogs. Frogs will get into your palace.

Frogs will be in your bedroom. Frogs will get on your bed. Frogs will get in all the houses. They'll get on all the people. Frogs will even be in your ovens and bowls."

God said to tell Aaron, "Hold out your hand. Hold your walking stick over the rivers and ponds. There will be frogs all over Egypt."

So Aaron did. Up came the frogs. They went over all the land.

But the king's magic men did the same thing. They made frogs come out, too.

The king called Moses and Aaron. "Pray to God," he said. "Ask him to take the frogs away. Then I'll let your people go."

"Tell me when," said Moses.

"Tomorrow," said the king.

"All right," said Moses. "Then you'll know there's nobody like God. The frogs will leave. They will only be in the river."

Moses and Aaron left. Then Moses prayed to God, and God answered him. The frogs died all around. Frogs died in the houses. Frogs died in the yards. Frogs died in the fields. People made piles of dead frogs. It made the whole land smell terrible.

The king saw that the frogs were dead. So he got angry. He let his heart get hard again. He wouldn't listen to Moses and Aaron. It was just like God had said.

So God talked with Moses again. He said to tell Aaron, "Hold your walking stick out. Hit the dust on the ground. The dust will turn into tiny biting bugs that fly."

So Aaron hit the dust with his walking stick. The dust turned into tiny biting bugs. They flew all over the people and the animals.

Now the king's magic men tried to do this, too. But they couldn't. They went to the king. "God is doing this," they said.

But the king didn't care. He wouldn't listen to Moses. It was just like God had said.

Then God talked with Moses again. "Get up early tomorrow morning. Meet the king when he goes out to the water. Talk to him."

These were God's words for the king. "Let my people go. They must worship me. If you don't let them go, I'll send flies. Lots of big flies will come everywhere in Egypt. Flies will fill the houses. Flies will cover the ground. But I won't send flies where the Jews live. Then you'll know I am the Lord. I'll treat your people and my people differently. This will all happen tomorrow."

That's just what happened. There

were so many flies that they looked like big, black clouds. Flies flew into the king's palace. Flies flew into people's houses. Flies messed up the land.

Then the king called Moses and Aaron. He said, "I'll let the people worship your God. But they must do it here in my land."

"That wouldn't work," said Moses. "The people of Egypt don't like the way we worship. They'll give us a hard time. We have to travel for three days. We have to go into the desert. That's where we'll worship God."

"I'll let you worship God in the desert," said the king. "But don't go very far. Pray for me now."

"I'll pray when I leave you," said Moses. "The flies will go away tomorrow. But make sure you don't lie to us again. This time you'd better let us go."

Then Moses left. He prayed to God. And God got rid of the flies. There wasn't even one left.

But the king still didn't think God was important. He didn't let God's people go.

Boils and Hail

EXODUS 9

God talked to Moses again. "Tell the king to let my people go." God told Moses to say, "If you don't, I'll make your animals sick. Your horses and cows will get sick and die. Your donkeys and camels will get sick and die. Your sheep and goats will get sick and die. But the animals that belong to my people won't die."

"I will do this tomorrow," said God.

The next day many of the animals in Egypt died. The king sent men to find out about the Jews' animals. He found out that none of them had died. But the king still didn't care. He let his heart be hard. He wouldn't let God's people go.

Then God called Moses and Aaron. "Get some dust left from a fire. Take it to the king. Toss it up into the air. The dust will go all over the land. It will make hurt places called boils on everyone."

So Moses and Aaron got some dust left from a fire. Then they went to see the king. They tossed the dust up into the air. Boils began growing on everyone. The king's magic men couldn't even stand up. The boils were on them, too.

But the king didn't care. He let his heart get hard. He wouldn't listen to Moses and Aaron. It was just as God had told them.

So God talked to Moses again. God said to get up early in the morning. He said to go tell the king, "Here's what God says. Let my people go to worship me. Or else I will send terrible trouble to your land. Then you will know that nobody on earth is like me.

"I could have already wiped you off the earth. But I saved you so I could show my power. People will tell about me all over the world.

"You're still against my people. So tomorrow I will send hail out of the sky. It will be stronger than any storm your land has seen. Bring everyone inside. Bring the animals inside, too. Any person or animal that is still in the fields will die."

Some of the leaders believed what God said. They went quickly to bring their servants and animals inside. But others didn't pay any attention to Moses. They left their servants and animals out in the fields.

Then God told Moses what to do. "Hold your hand up toward the sky," said God. "Hail will fall all over the land."

So Moses held his hand and his walking stick up toward the sky.

Then God sent thunder. Hail fell down on the land. Lightning flashed back and forth. It was a terrible storm. It was more terrible than any storm Egypt ever had. Hail tore leaves and branches off of trees. It beat down anything growing on the ground. But hail did not fall where God's people lived.

The king called Moses and Aaron. "I have done wrong," said the king. "God is right. Pray to him. Tell him to stop the thunder and hail. Then I'll let your people go."

"I'll leave the city," said Moses. "Then I'll hold my hands up to pray to God. The thunder and hail will stop. Then you will know that God owns the earth. But I still don't think you care about God."

Now the barley plants were growing well. The flax plants had blooms. But the hail broke down all the flax and barley plants. The wheat had not grown as much. So it was not hurt.

Moses and Aaron left the city. Moses held up his hands to God. The thunder stopped. The hail and rain stopped.

The king saw how the storm had stopped. But he didn't care about God. He let his heart get hard again. He wouldn't let God's people go. It was just like God had said.

Locusts and Darkness
EXODUS 10

"Go back to the king," God told Moses. "I've made his heart hard. That's so I can show my wonders. Then you can tell your families what I've done. You'll know that I'm the Lord."

So Moses and Aaron went back to

the king. They told him that God said these words. "How long will you let yourself be proud? Let my people go worship me. If you don't, I'll send big grasshoppers to your land. There will be so many of these locusts that they'll cover the ground. They'll eat whatever the hail left in your fields. They'll even eat the trees. They'll go into all the houses. There will be more locusts than your people have ever seen."

Then Moses turned around and walked out.

The king's men said, "How long will Moses bother us? Let his people go worship their God. Can't you see that the land of Egypt is lost?"

So the king sent for Moses and Aaron. "Go and worship your God," he said. "But tell me who will go with you."

"Young people and old people will go," said Moses. "We will take our children. We'll take our sheep and cows. We are going to have a holiday for God."

"You think I'll let you take the women and children? No way!" said the king. "You are planning to do something bad. Only the men can go." Then the king sent Moses and Aaron away.

So God told Moses, "Hold out your hand. Locusts will come all over the land. They'll eat anything that grows in the fields."

So Moses held his hand and his walking stick out. Then God sent a wind from the east. It blew over the land all day and night. By the next morning, there were locusts all over everything. There had never been so many locusts. There will never be that many again. There were so many that the ground was black with them.

The locusts ate everything that the hail didn't break. They ate the plants in the field. They ate the fruit on the trees. There was nothing green left when they finished eating.

The king quickly called Moses and Aaron. "Forgive me," he said. "I've done wrong. Pray to God. Ask him to take these locusts away."

So Moses left. He prayed to God. Then God made a strong wind blow from the west. The wind blew the locusts into the Red Sea. There was not one locust left. But the king let his heart get hard again.

Then God told Moses what to do. "Hold your hand up to the sky," said God. "Darkness will come. It will be so dark that the people will feel it."

Moses held his hand up toward the sky. Darkness came. It covered the land for three days. Nobody could see anybody else. Nobody could go anywhere. But God's people had light where they lived.

The king called Moses. "Go worship God," he said. "You may even take the women and children. But leave your sheep and cows here."

"We must take our sheep and cows with us," said Moses. "We'll have to use some of them to worship our God. We won't know which ones until we get there."

The king was angry. His heart was hard. He would not let them take their animals. So he said, "Get out of here! Don't let me see you again. Or you'll die!"

"All right," said Moses. "I won't come back."

Getting Ready for God to Pass Over

EXODUS 11–12

But God told Moses what would happen. "I'll send trouble to this land one more time. Then the king will send all my people away. Tell my people to go see their neighbors. Tell them to ask for silver and gold."

So Moses told the king about it. "God says he will go through Egypt. It will happen in the middle of the night. That's when the first son in each family will die. This will happen to the king. It will happen to the servants. It will even happen to the animals.

"People of Egypt will cry out loud. They will cry louder than they have ever cried before. But no Jews will cry. Dogs won't even bark where the Jews are. Then you'll know that the Jews are God's people. You'll know he is taking care of them.

"Your leaders will bow to me. They'll say to take the people and go! That's when I'll leave." Moses was very angry. He turned and left the king.

God had told Moses that the king wouldn't listen. His heart was too hard.

Then God told Moses and Aaron what to do. He said, "Call this the first month of the year. Tell everyone that the tenth day is special. On that day each family should get a lamb to eat. But let's say a family is too small to eat a whole lamb. Then they should share with a neighbor.

"Keep the lamb for 14 days. That night, kill the lamb. Paint some of its blood around the door. Paint it on the sides and top.

"That same night, cook the lamb meat. Make flat bread with no yeast in it.

Don't eat the meat raw. Don't cook it in water. Cook it over a fire. Don't save any food. If there is some left, burn it.

"Here's how to eat it. Tuck your robe into your belt. Wear your shoes. Hold your walking stick in your hand. Eat in a hurry. It is God's Pass Over. I will pass over you on that night.

"That night I will go through Egypt. I will kill the first son of every family. It will even happen to the animals. This is because of the gods that Egypt worships. But the lamb's blood will be around your doors. I will see the blood. Then I will pass over your houses. Nothing will hurt you.

"You should remember this time from now on. It will become a special holiday for God. Every year at this time, you'll eat flat bread. Eat it for seven days. You may cook your food. But don't do any other work. On this special day, eat inside your houses. And don't break any of the bones when you cook the lamb."

So Moses called the leaders of God's people. He told them what God had said. Moses said, "Your children will ask you what this holiday means. Then you tell them that this is the time of Pass Over. It's when God saved us from Egypt."

The leaders bowed down. They worshiped God. Then they did what Moses and Aaron told them.

In the middle of the night, God went through Egypt. The first son of each family died. The first son of the king died. The first sons of the people in jail died. Even the first of the animals died.

The people of Egypt woke up that night. They began to cry. Somebody in every house had died.

That night the king called for Moses and Aaron. He said, "Get out! Leave Egypt! Take your sheep and cows and all your people. And pray for me."

The people of Egypt told God's people to leave right away. "Leave now, or all of us will die!" they said.

So God's people took the batter for their bread. It didn't have yeast in it. They put it in their bowls and wrapped a cloth around it all. They carried it on their shoulders.

They also went to the people of Egypt. They asked for silver and gold. God made the people of Egypt think well of his people. So they gave God's people whatever they wanted.

That night God took his people out of Egypt. There were 600,000 (six hundred thousand) men. They walked. Then there were the women and children. Other people went with them, too. They took their animals with them. They took batter with them so that they could bake flat bread, too.

God's people had lived in Egypt for 430 years. But on that night, he took them out of Egypt. So every year the Jews are to remember that night. They are to worship God for what he did.

Chased by the Army!

EXODUS 13–15

Now there was a short way to get out of Egypt. But it went through another land. People from that land could have started fighting God's people. "Then my people might go back to Egypt," said God. So God took his people a different way.

God took his people down a road through the desert. The road led to the Red Sea.

Moses took Joseph's bones with him. Long ago Joseph had talked to his family about that. He made them promise to take his bones when they left.

God went ahead of his people. He led them with a tall cloud during the day. At night he led them with a tall cloud of fire. That way they could travel day or night. The cloud was with them all the time.

God told Moses to have his people make a camp. He said,

"Camp by the sea. Then the king will think the people are lost. He will think they don't know where they're going. I'll make his heart hard again. Then I'll show my power. The people of Egypt will know I am the Lord."

So God's people obeyed him. They camped by the sea.

Now Egypt's king saw that the Jews had really left. He said, "What did we do? We let those people leave Egypt! There's no one to work for us anymore!"

So the king got in his chariot. He called out his army. Lots of chariots went with him. Six hundred of them were the best chariots in Egypt.

The king was angry. His heart was hard again. He chased God's people. He caught up with them at the sea.

God's people looked up. They saw the army coming after them. They were scared! They called to God. Then they cried to Moses. "Did you bring us out here to die? Didn't we tell you to leave us alone in Egypt? It was better to be slaves in Egypt than to die here!"

But Moses said, "Don't be afraid. Stay where you are. You'll see how God will save you. You'll never see those people of Egypt again. God will fight for you. You just need to be still."

Then God talked to Moses. "Tell the people to go on," he said. "Hold your walking stick up. Reach your hand out over the sea. The water will move back. Then the people can walk across the sea on dry land.

"I'll make the army of Egypt chase you through the sea. Then I'll show my power," said God. "The people of Egypt will know that I am the Lord."

God's angel had been going ahead of his people. Now the angel went behind them. The tall cloud went behind them, too. It came between the army of Egypt and God's people. All night the cloud made it dark on the army's side. But it made it light on the side of God's people. So all night Egypt's army stayed away from God's people.

Then Moses held his hand out over the sea. All night God made a strong wind blow from the east. Sea water moved back on two sides. Wind dried out the land in between.

Then God's people walked across the sea on dry land. A wall of water stood on their right. A wall of water stood on their left.

Now the army of Egypt began to chase God's people. The horses and chariots went down into the sea. They began to cross on the dry land, too.

But God looked down from the tall cloud and the fire. He made the wheels of the chariots come off. The people from Egypt couldn't keep going.

The army men said, "Let's get out of here! God is fighting for his people. He is fighting against Egypt!"

Then God told Moses, "Hold out your hand again over the sea. The water will come back into place. It will flow over Egypt's army."

Morning was coming. The sun was just starting to come up. Moses held his hand out over the sea. The water flowed back into place.

The army of Egypt tried to run away from the water. But God trapped them in the sea. Water covered the army and their chariots. No one was left. God had saved his people from Egypt. Bodies of dead army men lay beside the sea.

God's people saw how he had saved them. They saw how special and wonderful God was. They trusted him. They trusted Moses, too.

Moses and God's people sang this song to God.

"I will sing to God.
He is great!
He threw the horse and its rider into
    the sea.
God has saved me.
I will cheer for him.
I will tell how great he is.
God is a fighter!
His name is the Lord.
He threw the army of Egypt into
    the sea.

Deep water covered them up.
They sank like rocks.

"Your right hand is strong, God.
Your right hand won over the enemy.
Your breath blew the water until it
    piled up.
Waves stood up like a wall.
Deep water became walls
in the middle of the sea."

Moses' sister Miriam picked up
a tambourine. She led the women.
They played tambourines, and they
danced. Miriam sang this song.

"Sing to God.
Tell how great he is.
He threw the horse and its rider
    into the sea!"

JANUARY 27

Making a Fuss for Food

EXODUS 15–16

Moses led God's people. From the
sea, they went into the desert. They
traveled for three days. But they
couldn't find any water.

At last they came to a place with
water. But the water tasted bad.
The people began to fuss at Moses.
"What are we going to drink?" they
asked.

Moses called to God. So God
showed Moses a branch from a tree.

Moses threw the branch into the
water. The bad water turned into
good, sweet water.

Then God told his people
something very important. "Listen
carefully to my voice," he said. "Do
what's right. Hear me. Obey what I
tell you to do. Then I won't let you
get sick. You won't get sick like the
people of Egypt. I am the Lord. I
make you well."

God's people traveled on. They
came to a place with 12 springs of
water. There were 70 palm trees
growing around it. So they made
their camp there for a while.

Then they traveled on. But in the
desert, they started making a fuss
again. They were mad at Moses and
Aaron. "We wish we had died in
Egypt!" they said. "We had lots of
meat there. We could eat as much as
we wanted. But you have led us out
here to the desert. You'll make us
die of hunger out here."

Then God told Moses, "I'll send
bread to the people. It will rain
down from heaven. Every day the
people can go out and get the bread.
But only as much as they can eat
that day. I'll see if they will obey
me. On the sixth day, they can bring
in two times as much. It will be
enough for the next day, too."

Moses and Aaron told the people
what God said. "You'll see God's
power in the morning," they said.

"He heard how you were making a fuss. You're not fussing against us. You're fussing against God."

Moses told Aaron, "Tell the people to come to God. He has heard them making a fuss."

So Aaron began to talk to the people. While he was talking, they looked out across the desert. The cloud was bright with God's greatness.

God said to Moses, "Tell the people they will eat meat tonight. Tomorrow morning they'll eat bread. Then they'll know that I am the Lord."

That evening fat little birds called quail flew in. They were all over the camp. The next morning dew covered the ground. Then the dew dried up. It looked like bits of ice covered the ground. But it wasn't ice. It was thin flakes of bread.

"What is it?" the people asked.

"It's the bread God sent you," said Moses. "Take two quarts for each person in your tent."

So the people picked up the bread. They measured it. Each person had as much as he needed.

"Don't keep any for tomorrow," said Moses.

But some of the people didn't obey. They saved some of it for the next day. The next day it had worms in it. It smelled bad. That made Moses mad.

Every morning people picked up as much bread as they needed. The bread melted off the ground when the sun got hot.

The people picked up two times as much on the sixth day. That's because the next day was a day for resting. Moses told the people what to do. "If you want to bake it, bake it. If you want to boil it, boil it. Save what's left over. Eat it tomorrow."

So the people saved what was left over. The next morning it didn't have worms. It didn't even smell bad.

"Bread won't be on the ground today," said Moses. "So you can eat what is left over. For six days every week, you'll pick up bread. The next day will be for resting."

But some people went out to get bread the next day. The bread wasn't there.

"How long will you not obey me?" asked God. "On the sixth day I give enough bread for two days. I want you to rest the next day."

The people called the bread manna. *Manna* means "what is it?" The bread was white. It tasted like honey cakes.

Moses told Aaron, "Put some manna in a jar. Keep it so our families will remember this time."

So Aaron put some manna in a jar, and they kept it.

God's people ate manna for 40 years. Then they came to the land God had promised them.

Water from a Rock

EXODUS 17

God's people left the desert. They went wherever God told them to go. At one camp there was no water to drink. The people fussed at Moses. "Give us some water," they said.

"Why are you fussing at me?" said Moses. "You're testing God."

But they were thirsty. So they kept fussing at Moses. "Why did you bring us here?" they asked. "We're going to die of thirst. Our children will die. Our animals will die."

So Moses cried to God. "What am I going to do? These people are ready to kill me."

"You go on ahead of the people," said God. "Take some of the leaders with you. Carry your walking stick. I'll stand by the rock at Horeb. Hit the rock, and water will flow out of it. Then the people can drink."

So Moses did what God told him to do. He called the place Testing and Fussing. That's because the people had made a fuss there. That's where they tested God. They had said, "Is God with us or not?"

Then an enemy army came out to fight against God's people. Moses called for Joshua. Moses told him, "Choose some men. Take them out to fight. I'll stand on the hill tomorrow. I'll hold the walking stick that God has used before."

So Joshua took some men out to fight. Moses and Aaron and Hur went up the hill. They watched from the top. When Moses held his hands up, God's people would win. When he put his hands down, the enemy would win.

Moses' hands got tired. So Aaron and Hur pulled a big rock over to Moses. Moses sat on it. Then Aaron stood on one side of Moses. Hur stood on the other side. They held Moses' hands up until the sun set. So Joshua and his men won the fight.

Then Moses piled up rocks and made an altar. He named it "God Is My Flag." Moses said, "These people shook their fist at God. So God will always fight against them."

JANUARY 28

Jethro's Good Idea

EXODUS 18

The father of Moses' wife was named Jethro. He heard what God was doing for Moses. He heard how God brought his people out of Egypt.

Moses had sent his wife home to

Jethro. She had taken their two sons with her. Now Jethro brought Moses' sons and his wife to him in the desert. Jethro had sent a letter to say he was coming.

Moses went out to meet them. He took them to his tent. Then Moses told Jethro all about what had happened. He told him about the king of Egypt. He told how God was taking care of his people.

Jethro was happy to hear this good news. He said, "Praise God. He saved you from Egypt. Now I know he is greater than any other god." Jethro worshiped God. Then Aaron and the leaders came to eat dinner with Jethro.

The next day Moses went to work. He was a judge. He would listen to people who did not agree with each other. He would tell them who was right and who was wrong. From morning until evening he judged people.

Jethro watched Moses. Then he said, "What are you doing? Why are you the only judge for all these people? It takes you all day."

"The people want me to tell them what God wants. So I tell them," said Moses.

"This isn't good," said Jethro. "You're going to get too tired. It's too much work. You can't do all this by yourself. Let me give you an idea. Teach the people how to live. But choose some men to help you. These should be men who follow God. They should be men you can trust. They can be the judges of the easy problems. They can bring the hard problems to you. That way you'll be able to do this hard job. And the people will be taken care of."

So Moses did what Jethro said. He chose some leaders. They were judges for the people. They took care of the easy problems. But they took the hard problems to Moses.

Then Moses said good-bye to Jethro. And Jethro went back home.

Thunder and Lightning on the Mountain

EXODUS 19

God's people traveled into the Sinai Desert. They made their camp at the bottom of the mountain.

Then Moses went up the mountain to talk to God. God called to Moses from the mountain. God said to tell his people, "You saw what I did to Egypt. I took you out. It was like you rode on eagles' wings. Now obey me. Then you will belong to me. You will be very special to me. The whole earth is mine. But you will be a special kingdom."

So Moses went back. He told the leaders what God said. They answered, "We will do what God says."

Moses went back up to talk to God. He told God what the people had said.

Then God told Moses what he was going to do. "I'm going to come to you in a big cloud. The people will hear me talking to you. Then they will always trust you."

God said, "Tell the people to get ready. Tell them to wash their clothes. Two days will pass. Then I'll come down on the mountain. All the people will see how I come. Mark out a line around the mountain. Tell them to be careful. They should not go up the mountain. They should not even touch the bottom of it. If they do, they'll die."

Moses went back down the mountain. He told the people what God said. So they washed their clothes and got ready.

Two days passed. The next morning they heard loud claps of thunder. They saw bright flashes of lightning. A big cloud came down over the mountain. There was a very loud horn sound. Everybody shook.

Then Moses went to the bottom of the mountain. The people followed. Smoke came up from the mountain. God had come down in fire. The smoke puffed up from the mountain. It looked like smoke from a big fireplace. The mountain shook hard. The horn sounded louder and louder. Then Moses talked to God. And God's voice talked to Moses.

God came down to the top of the mountain. He called for Moses to come up to the top. So Moses climbed up the mountain.

God said, "Go tell the people to be careful. They shouldn't dare to come up to see me. If they do, they'll die."

"You said to mark a line around the mountain," said Moses. "The people can't come up."

"Go down and get Aaron," said God. "Bring him here with you."

So Moses went and told the people to be careful.

JANUARY 29

Ten Rules
EXODUS 20; 23

God told the people, "I am the Lord your God. I took you out of Egypt. I saved you from being slaves."

Then God gave them 10 important rules.

1. Don't have any other gods.
2. Don't worship idols.
3. Treat God's name as the most important name of all. Use it for the right reasons.
4. Remember the worship day. Keep it special. God worked six days to make the earth. The next day he rested.
5. Treat your father and mother like important people and obey them. Then you'll live a long time in the land I'll give you.
6. Don't kill.
7. Have sex only with your wife or husband.
8. Don't steal.
9. Don't lie.
10. Don't want things that belong to someone else.

All the people saw the lightning. They heard the horn and the thunder. They saw the smoke over the mountain. They shook. They were afraid. They stayed back. "You talk to us," they told Moses. "We'll listen to you. But don't let God talk to us. We might die!"

"Don't be afraid," said Moses. "God is testing you. He wants you to worship him. Then you won't sin."

So the people stayed back. Moses went up toward the big, dark cloud where God was.

God said to tell his people, "You saw it. I talked to you from heaven. Don't make any other gods. Don't make gods of silver or gold.

"Pile up rocks for an altar to me. But don't build it with tools. Give your gifts to me there. I'll come to places where my name is worshiped. I'll come and bring good things.

"I'm sending an angel ahead of you," said God. "He will guard you as you travel. He will bring you to the land I want you to have. Listen to him. Don't turn against him. He has my name. He is taking my place for me. Listen to him, and do what he says. Do what I say. Then I'll be against your enemies.

"There are other people in the land. But I want you to have the land. My angel will get rid of other people," said God. "Don't worship their gods. Don't live like they do. Get rid of their idols. You worship the Lord your God. Then I'll take sickness away. Your food and water will be good. You'll have lots of children. And I'll let you live a long time.

"I'll make your enemies afraid of you," said God. "They'll turn and run. But I won't do it all at once. If I did, no one would be in the land. Wild animals would come live there. There would be too many for you. So I'll get rid of your enemies a little at a time. Someday there will be enough of you to live in the whole land.

"Don't let your enemies live in the land with you. They might get you to sin against me," said God. "You'll want to worship their gods."

On the Mountain with God

EXODUS 24

Then God told Moses, "Come up to see me. Bring Aaron, his sons, and the 70 leaders. They will stand back and worship. You, Moses, may come all the way up to me. But the people can't come up."

Moses told the people what God had said. He told them all God's laws.

The people said, "We'll do everything God says."

Then Moses wrote down what God had said.

The next morning Moses got up early. He piled rocks at the bottom of the mountain. That made an altar. He put 12 stone posts up. They were for the 12 family groups named for Jacob's sons.

Then Moses sent young men to offer gifts on the altar. Moses read from the Law Book. The people said, "We'll do what God said. We'll obey."

Then Moses took Aaron and his sons. He took the 70 leaders up to see God. They saw a street under God's feet. It looked like it was made of beautiful, blue stone. It was clear like the sky. God didn't hurt these leaders. They saw God, and they ate a meal together.

God told Moses, "Come up to me on the mountain. I'll give you a chart made of stone. I wrote my laws on this stone chart for the people."

Moses took Joshua with him. They went up on the mountain. Moses told the leaders to wait for them. He told Aaron and Hur to be judges while he was gone.

The cloud covered the mountain. Moses went up. God came down. God's people looked at the cloud. It looked like a burning fire on top of the mountain.

The cloud was on the mountain for six days. The next day God called to Moses from the cloud. So Moses climbed up and went into the cloud. He stayed there 40 days and 40 nights.

JANUARY 30

The Worship Tent

(The Tabernacle: *TAB-ur-nack-ul*)

from EXODUS 25–31

"Make a worship tent for me," said God. "Make it just the way I tell you to. My people should give gifts for this tent. They can give gold, silver, and other metal. They can give blue, purple, and red yarn. They can give goat hair and ram skins and wood. They can give oil for light. They can give beautiful stones.

"Tell them to make a special box from wood. It will be the Ark of My Word. Cover the inside and outside of the box with gold. Put gold rings on the side. Then put poles into the rings. You can use the poles to carry the box. Inside the box, place the stone charts with my words on them.

"Make a gold cover for the Ark. Make two gold beings with wings. Put one on each end of the cover. They should face each other. Their wings should go up over the cover. I will meet with you between these beings. I'll tell you what I want my people to do.

"Make a gold table with poles to carry it. Make gold plates and dishes, jugs, and bowls.

"Make a gold lamp stand with six branches going out. Make seven gold lamps for it.

"Make the worship tent out of cloth," said God. "Hang blue, purple, and red cloth around the tent for walls. Hang up sheets made from goat hair. Put a cover made of ram skins over the tent. On top of this, put a cover of goatskins. Make a frame with silver bases. The tent can hang over the frame.

"Blue, purple, and red cloth will hang inside the tent. It will make a room at the end of the tent. This room will be called the Most Holy Place. That's where the Ark of My Word will go. The Holy Place will be on the other side of the tent.

"Build an altar for the worship tent. Make it square. Tell the people to bring olive oil. Burn the oil in the lamps to make light. Keep the lamps lit all night long.

"Tell Aaron and his sons that they'll serve me," said God. "They will serve in the worship tent. They will be priests. They'll wear robes, long shirts, and belts. They'll wear caps with long cloths wound around them. Their clothes will be gold, blue, purple, and red.

"Make a special vest for Aaron. On the front, put 12 beautiful stones. Write the names of the 12 family groups on the stones. Aaron will wear this into the Holy Place. He will have the names of Jacob's 12 sons over his heart.

"Put gold bells around the bottom of Aaron's robe. Make a small gold sign to go on Aaron's cap. Put these words on it: Special to God."

God finished telling Moses about these things. Then he gave Moses two stone charts. God's finger wrote the laws on these.

The Gold Calf

EXODUS 32

Now God's people had been waiting for Moses. He had been on the mountain a long time. So they went to Aaron. They said, "We don't know what's happened to Moses. So make us a god. This new god can lead us."

"Bring me the gold ear rings you're wearing," said Aaron.

So the people brought their gold ear rings to Aaron. He melted the gold. He made it into a fake god. It was an idol that looked like a calf.

The people said, "This is our god. This god took us out of Egypt."

Aaron saw that the people liked the idol. So he built an altar for it. He said, "Tomorrow we will have a holiday for our god."

The people got up early the next morning. They gave gifts to the idol on the altar. They ate and drank at a wild party.

God told Moses, "Go back down the mountain. Your people have done wrong. They turned away from me. They made an idol. They are worshiping it. These people won't listen to me. Leave me alone. I'm angry at them. I'm going to get rid of them. Then I'll make your family into a great nation."

"Don't be angry," said Moses. "The people of Egypt will hear about it. They'll say that God took the Jewish people out of Egypt. They'll say that now he is killing them in the mountains. Remember Abraham and Isaac and Jacob. You made a promise to them. You said that their families would be a nation. You said there would be as many people as stars in the sky. You said you'd give them a special land forever."

So God didn't get rid of his people.

Moses went back down the mountain. He carried the two stone charts. God's writing was on the front and back of the charts.

Joshua was with Moses. He heard noise coming from the camp. He said, "It sounds like war!"

"It doesn't sound like people winning," said Moses. "It doesn't sound like people losing. It sounds like singing."

They got closer to the camp. Then they saw the gold idol. They saw the people dancing. Moses got very angry. He threw down the stone charts. They broke into pieces at the bottom of the mountain.

Moses tore down the gold idol.

He put it in the fire and burned it. Then he ground it up until it was like powder. He tossed it into the drinking water. He made the people drink it.

Moses turned to Aaron. "Why did you lead God's people into sin?" he asked.

"Don't get angry," said Aaron. "You know how these people are ready to do wrong. They told me to make gods for them. They didn't know what happened to you. So I told them to give me their gold ear rings. They did. I threw the gold into the fire. Out came this gold idol!"

Now Moses saw that everything was out of control. People were acting wild. Moses knew their enemies would make fun of them. So Moses went to the front of the camp. "If you're for God, come stand with me," he said.

People from the family of Levi came to stand with Moses. Moses told them, "Here's what God says. Go through the camp. Kill anyone who does not want to follow God."

So they went through the camp. They killed about 3,000 people. These were people who would not follow God.

The next day Moses said, "You people have sinned. I'm going back to see God. Maybe I can get God to forgive your sin."

So Moses went back to see God. He said, "These people have sinned badly. They made gold gods. But please forgive them. If you don't, take my name out of your book."

"I'll take out the names of people who sinned," said God. "You go and lead them. Take them to the land I told you about. I'll send my angel ahead of you. But someday they'll be in trouble for what they did."

Then God made the people sick. It was because of the gold idol they made.

JANUARY 31

Moses Sees God's Back
EXODUS 33

God said, "Move on now. Take my people to the land I promised them. I'll send an angel ahead of you. I'll drive out the people who live in that land now. The land is very good. You'll find plenty of food there. It's as if milk and honey flow out for people. But I won't go with you. Your people won't listen to me. If I went with you, I might get rid of them."

God's people were sad to hear this.

Now Moses had a special tent outside the camp. He called it the meeting tent. People who wanted to ask God something would go there. When Moses went there, people would stand in their tent doors. They would watch Moses go into the tent. Then the tall cloud would come down in front of the tent. It would stay there while God talked to Moses. The people would see the cloud. Then they would worship at their tents.

God talked to Moses as a friend. They talked together. Then Moses would come back to camp. But Joshua, his helper, wouldn't leave the meeting tent.

Moses told God, "You tell me to lead the people. But you don't tell me who will go with me. You said that you know me. You said that you know my name. So if I make you happy, teach me. Teach me your ways. So I can know you. Remember that we are your people."

"I'll go with you," said God.

"If you don't go with us, don't send us," said Moses. "When you're with us, people know we're yours. That's what makes us different from other nations."

"I'll do what you've asked," said God. "I'm happy with you. I know you as a friend."

"Now," said Moses, "show me who you are. Show me your greatness."

"I'll show you all my goodness," said God. "I'll tell you my name:

The Lord. I'll be kind to the people I choose. But I can't let you see my face. Anyone who sees my face will die."

Then God said, "You can stand on a rock near me. My greatness will pass by. When it does, I'll put you in a crack in the rock. I'll put my hand over you. After I pass, I'll move my hand off. Then you can see my back. But I can't let you see my face."

Two More Stone Charts
EXODUS 34

"Make two stone charts," God told Moses. "Make them like the first ones that you broke. I'll write the same words on them. Be ready tomorrow morning. Come up the mountain to me. Don't let anyone else come with you. Nobody should be anywhere on the mountain. Not even cows or sheep."

So Moses made two stone charts. Early the next morning, he went up the mountain. Then God came down to the mountain in the cloud. He moved in front of Moses.

Then God told Moses his name. He said, "I am the Lord, the kind and loving God. I am not in a hurry to get angry. I have more than enough love. I keep my promises. I keep on loving thousands of people. I forgive sin. But I don't let people get away with doing wrong. I pay them and their families back for doing wrong."

Right away Moses bowed down to the ground. He worshiped God. "If you are happy with me, go with us," he said. "I know we don't listen to you. But forgive us. Let us keep being your people."

"I'm making a special promise to you," said God. "I'll do wonders for your people. I'll do wonders nobody in the world has ever seen. Your people will see the great work I do.

"But you must obey what I tell you. I'll send the people out of the land you're going to. So don't make any deals with those people. If you do, they'll get you into trouble.

"Don't let your children marry their children. They would teach your children to worship their idols. Tear their idols down. Tear their altars down. Don't worship any other god. I want you for myself."

Moses was on the mountain with God for 40 days and 40 nights. All that time, he didn't eat or drink. He wrote the Ten Rules on the stone charts.

Then Moses came back down the mountain. He brought the stone charts with him. He didn't know that his face was shining. It was because he had talked with God.

Aaron and the people saw Moses coming. His face was shining. They were scared to get close to him. But Moses called them. Aaron and the leaders went near. Then all the people came near, too. Moses told them what God had said.

Then Moses put a thin cloth over his face. When he talked with God, he took it off. When he came back to the people, his face shone. So he put the cloth back over it again.

Rich Gifts and Hard Work
from EXODUS 35–40

Then Moses told the people to bring gifts for God. These were gifts God wanted for making the worship tent. Gold and silver and other metal. Blue, purple, and red yarn. Goat hair and ram skins and goat skins. Wood and olive oil and beautiful, shiny stones.

Moses said, "I want people who are good at making things. Come and make what God wants for his worship tent. Make the covers. Make the bases and posts. Make the ark box and lamp stand. Make oil for the light. Make clothes for the priests."

So everyone who wanted to work came. Men and women came. They brought gifts. They brought rings and pins and ear rings and arm bands and necklaces. They brought yarn and animal skins. They brought gold and silver.

Moses said that God chose one man to be a special worker. "God filled him with his Spirit. God made him good at art. He knows how to work with gold and silver. He knows how to cut and set stones. He knows how to work with wood. God has made him to be a good teacher.

"God made another man good at working with cloth. He can sew. He is a good teacher, too. So these men can work on the tent. And they can teach others how to help them."

Moses told the people how to build the worship tent. So they began working.

But people kept bringing their gifts every morning. At last the workers said, "The people have brought more than enough."

So Moses said, "Don't bring anything else." Then people stopped bringing their gifts.

The workers kept building the worship tent. They made the covers and the bases and the curtains. They made the ark box and the table and the lamp stand. They made the altars and the oil and the washing bowl. They made the clothes for the priests. They did everything just the way God told Moses to do it.

When they were finished, they set the worship tent up. They put the ark box in it. They put the altars and lamp stands in it. They put the table and the washing bowl inside. They set it up just the way God had told Moses to.

Then the cloud came down on the worship tent. God's greatness filled it. No one could go in. Not even Moses.

More Travels

LEVITICUS 8–10

Then Moses brought Aaron to the front of the worship tent. All the people gathered to watch. Moses put the long shirt on Aaron. He put the belt around him. He put the robe and vest on him. He put the cap on Aaron's head. Then he put oil on Aaron's head. This showed that Aaron had special work to do for God.

Moses put long shirts on Aaron's sons, too. He put belts on Aaron's sons. He gave them their caps.

They gave gifts to God on the altars. They gave a bull and two rams.

Moses told Aaron, "Cook the meat at the front of the tent. Eat it there. Stay at the front of the tent for seven days and nights. Do what God wants, because this is what God told me."

So Aaron and his sons stayed there. Seven days and nights passed.

Then all the people came to the front of the worship tent. Aaron lifted up his hands. He prayed for God to bring good things to his people. Then Moses and Aaron went into the tent.

When they came out, God's greatness was there. All the people saw it. Fire came from God. It burned up the meat that was on the altar. The people shouted with joy. They bowed down with their faces to the ground.

But two of Aaron's sons did not obey God. They put fire in their offering bowls. It was fire that God had not told them to use. So fire came from God and burned up Aaron's two sons.

Moses talked to Aaron. He said that God told him these words. "I will show myself as special to people who come to me. People will worship and obey me."

Aaron did not say anything.

Aaron had two other sons who were helping him. Moses spoke to Aaron and his other sons. "Don't drink wine when you go into the worship tent. You have to teach the people God's rules."

Camping under the Flags
from NUMBERS 1–3; 8

God told Moses, "Count the people. Count all the men who are 20 years old or older. They can be in the army."

So Moses counted the people. One man from each family group helped him count. But they didn't count the people from Levi's family group. God had put them in charge of the worship tent. They would take it down when the people traveled. They would set it up where the people stopped.

God said to Moses, "Get Levi's whole family group. Take them to Aaron. They will help him at the worship tent. They'll work there. They can start working when they turn 25 years old. They must stop working there when they turn 50."

God said, "The people will camp around the worship tent. Each family group will camp under its own flag."

So Judah's family group camped east of the tent. So did the family groups of Issachar and Zebulun. When they traveled, the family group of Judah led them. They went first.

Reuben's family group camped south of the tent. So did the family groups of Simeon and Gad. Reuben's group led them. They followed the families camped on the east.

The family group of Levi would come next. They would bring the worship tent.

Ephraim's family group camped west of the tent. So did the family groups of Manasseh and Benjamin. Ephraim's group led them. They followed the group of Levi.

Dan's family group camped north of the tent. So did the family groups of Asher and Naphtali. Dan's group led them. They followed families that camped on the west.

That's the way they traveled. Each group camped under its flag. The people traveled with their own family group.

FEBRUARY 2

Silver Horns

NUMBERS 10

"Make two silver horns," said God. "Use them to call the people together. Use them to tell the people to start traveling. Sometimes both horns will blow. Then the people should get together in front of the worship tent. Sometimes they'll hear one horn. Then only the leaders should come.

"There's a time when one blow of the horn will sound. Then the family groups to the east should start traveling. Then another blow will sound. That means the groups on the south should start out. But make a different sound on the horn to call people together.

"You might have to fight against an enemy. You should also blow the horns then. Aaron's sons will blow them. Then God will save you from your enemies. Blow the horns when you have holidays, too. You will be showing your joy."

It was the second year after the Jews left Egypt. It was in the middle of spring. The cloud lifted up from the worship tent. So God's people started traveling.

Now Moses' wife had a brother. Moses told him, "We're going to the land God promised. Come with us. We'll be good to you. God has promised to give us good things."

"No," said the brother. "I'll go back to my own land."

"Please don't go," said Moses. "You know the desert. You know the good places to camp. So come with us. We'll share the good things God gives us."

So they left the mountain. They traveled for three days. And God's cloud was with them.

God's cloud covered the worship tent when it was set up. All night it looked like fire. When the cloud moved, the people moved. Wherever the cloud stopped, the people camped. If the cloud stayed there, the people stayed there.

Sometimes the cloud stayed a few days. Sometimes it stayed for only a night.

The people of Levi would carry the ark box. When the special box started out, Moses would say, "Please get up, God! Send your enemies running here and there." When the Ark came to camp, he said, "Come back, God. Come to your people, who are too many to count."

Piles of Quail

NUMBERS 11

Now the people made a fuss about how hard their life was. God heard them, and he got angry. Then fire came from him. It burned part of the camp at the edge.

The people cried to Moses. Moses prayed to God. Then the fire stopped burning. So they named that place "Burning."

Now some of the people wanted different food. "We wish we had meat to eat," they said. "We remember the fish we had in Egypt. We got it free! We ate cucumbers and melons. We had leeks and onions and garlic. But now we don't even like to eat. We don't see any food but this manna!"

The manna would come every night when the dew came. The people would cook the manna in pots. Or they would make cakes out of it. It tasted like it was made with olive oil.

Moses heard all of the people fussing at the doors of their tents. God was very angry at them.

Moses was upset. "Why did you send me this trouble?" he asked God. "What did I do to make you unhappy with me? You've made me lead all these people. They're a heavy load. Am I their father? Where can I get meat for them? They keep telling me to get some meat! I can't take care of them by myself. Is this the way it's going to be? Then just let me die right now."

God said, "Bring the 70 leaders to the worship tent. They can stand there with you. I'll come and talk with you. Then I'll take some of the Spirit that is upon you. I'll put the Spirit upon them, too. They'll help you carry this heavy load.

"Tell the people to get ready," said God. "Tell them I'll give them meat. Tomorrow they'll eat it. But they won't eat it just for one or two days. They won't eat it just for five, ten, or twenty days. They'll eat it for a whole month. They'll eat it until it comes out their noses. They'll eat it until they hate it. It's because they turned against God. They made a fuss about having to leave Egypt."

"There are 600,000 (six hundred thousand) men," said Moses. "You say you'll give them meat. But let's say we killed all the sheep and cows. That wouldn't be enough meat for a whole month! What if we caught all the fish in the sea? That still wouldn't be enough!"

But God said, "Am I not strong enough to do this? Just watch. See if what I say comes true or not."

So Moses told the people what God said. He took the 70 leaders to the worship tent. Then God came down in the cloud. He talked with Moses. He took some of the Spirit that was upon Moses. He put it upon the 70 leaders. Then the leaders began speaking messages from God.

Now two men had stayed in the camp. They were leaders. So the Spirit came upon them, too. They started speaking messages from God right there in camp.

A young man ran to tell Moses about it. "Two men are telling God's plans in camp!" he said.

Joshua was Moses' helper. He had been Moses' helper since he was young. He said, "Moses, stop the two men!"

But Moses said, "I wish all people could speak messages from God. I wish God would put his Spirit upon all of them."

Then Moses and the leaders went back to camp.

God sent a wind to blow from the sea. It blew small birds called quail into camp. There were lots of quail. They piled up three feet high. They covered the ground. The people gathered baskets full of quail.

But while the people ate, God got mad at them. He made them get sick. People who had made a fuss about the food died.

FEBRUARY 3

Miriam Gets Sick

NUMBERS 12

Moses' sister, Miriam, and their brother, Aaron, started making a fuss. They fussed at Moses because of the wife he married. "Does God talk only to Moses? Hasn't he talked to us, too?" they said.

Now Moses did not think he was the greatest. He did not think he was the most important.

God spoke to Moses, Aaron, and Miriam. "I want all three of you to come to the worship tent," he said.

So they went to the worship tent. God came down in the tall cloud. He came right to the front. He called for Aaron and Miriam. They stepped closer.

"Listen," said God. "There are people who speak for me. I talk to them in dreams. But it's not this way with Moses. I talk right to him. I don't talk in dreams or riddles. He

78

sees my shape. So why doesn't it scare you to fuss at him?"

God was angry with Aaron and Miriam. God left. The cloud went up from the tent. Miriam was left standing there with a bad skin sickness. Her skin had turned as white as snow.

Aaron turned around and saw her. He said to Moses, "Please don't be angry at us! We have been foolish. Don't let Miriam die!"

Then Moses cried to God, "Please make Miriam well!"

God said, "Make her live outside the camp for a week. Then she can come back."

So Miriam stayed out of the camp for a week. That week the people didn't travel. After that, Miriam came back. She was well. Then the people traveled again.

A Look into the New Land

NUMBERS 13

God's people camped in a desert. There God told Moses, "Choose some men. Send them into the land of Canaan. It's the land I'm going to give my people. Tell the men to look around the land."

So Moses chose 12 leaders. Moses told them, "Go into the hill country. Find out what the land is like. Find out if the people are strong or not. Find out what kind of towns they

live in. See if the towns have walls. See if they are like forts. Look at the ground. See if it's good for growing food. Find out if trees grow there. Try to bring back some fruit from the land."

So the 12 men set out. They looked all around the land. They found a

valley where grapes were growing. They cut off a branch of grapes. It had one bunch of grapes hanging from it. They got some pomegranates and figs, too. They put these fruits on a pole. Two of the men carried the pole with the fruits.

After 40 days the 12 men came back to Moses. They told him about the land. They showed him the fruit. "It's a good land," they said. "It will be easy to grow food there. There's more than enough for everyone. It's as if milk and honey flow out for people. But the people who live there are strong. The cities are very big. They are like forts."

Caleb told the men to be quiet. He said, "We should go into the land. We should take it. I'm sure we can do it."

"We can't fight those people," said the other men. "They are stronger than we are. Those people are very big. We felt like grasshoppers next to them."

Scared of the People

NUMBERS 14

That night God's people cried. They fussed at Moses and Aaron. "We wish we had died in Egypt!" they said. "Or we wish we would die in this desert! Why is God taking us into this land? The people there will kill us. They'll take our wives and children to be theirs. It would be better to go back to Egypt!"

The people even said, "Let's choose another leader. Let's go back to Egypt."

Moses and Aaron bowed down in prayer in front of the people.

Joshua and Caleb were two of the 12 men who looked around Canaan. They said, "The land is very good. If God is happy with us, he will lead us there. It's a land where milk and honey seem to flow out for the people. God will give us the land. Just don't turn against God.

"We'll win over those people," said Joshua and Caleb. "Don't be scared of them. God is with us."

But people talked about killing Joshua and Caleb.

Then God's greatness came over the worship tent. God said to Moses, "How long will this go on?

How long will these people treat me as nothing? I've shown them wonders. But they choose not to believe me. I'll send a great sickness upon them. I'll get rid of them. Then I'll make your family into a nation. Your family will be stronger and greater than they ever were."

"But nations in Canaan have already heard about you," said Moses. "They heard that we have seen you. They heard that you lead your people with a tall cloud in the day. They heard about the cloud of fire at night. What if you get rid of your people? Then these nations will say you couldn't lead your people. So you killed them in the desert.

"Show these nations you are strong. Just like you said," Moses told God. "You said you do not get angry in a hurry. You have more than enough love. You forgive sin. You do bring trouble to people for doing wrong. But your love is great. So forgive your people's sin. You forgave them before."

"I will forgive them," said God. "Just as you asked me to do. But not one person who saw my wonders will go into Canaan. They saw the wonders I did in Egypt. They saw the wonders I did in the desert. But they didn't obey me. They tested me. So they won't get to see the new land.

"But Caleb is different," said God. "He follows me with his whole heart. So I'll bring him into the land I promised my people.

"My people must turn around tomorrow," said God. "They must go back into the desert. They must head back toward the Red Sea.

"They said they would die in the desert," said God. "So they will. Everyone who is 20 years old or more will die. They won't get to go into the Promised Land. Only Caleb and Joshua will get to go. My people said their children would be taken by their enemies. But the children will get to enjoy that land.

"You'll be shepherds in the desert for 40 years," said God. "That's one year for each day you looked at the Promised Land. I, the Lord, have said this. So you can be sure I'll do it."

Now the 10 men who made everyone afraid got sick. They died. They were the men who had looked at the new land. But Joshua and Caleb did not get sick or die.

Moses told all God's people what God had said. They cried and cried.

The next morning they headed for God's Promised Land. "We sinned," they said. "We'll go into the land and take it now."

"It won't work," said Moses. "You're not obeying God. Don't go. God won't be with you, because you turned away from him. You'll be killed if you go in now."

The people didn't listen. They kept going. They headed to the hill country. But Moses didn't go with them.

Then their enemies came down from the hills. They jumped out at them and chased them far away.

A Crack in the Ground
NUMBERS 16

Now a man named Korah got mad at Moses. Two of Korah's friends got mad at Moses. They got about 250 other men mad at Moses, too.

All these men got together. They went to see Moses and Aaron. They said, "You've gone far enough! God is with each one of us. So why are you so special? Why do you think you can lead us?"

Moses put his face down to the ground. Then he said to the men, "Tomorrow morning God will show which man he chooses. Bring offering bowls with you. Put fire in them. God will choose the man who is special.

"It's you who have gone far enough! You're not going against Aaron and me. You're going against God."

So the next morning Korah and all his followers came together.

They went to the front of the worship tent. Then God's greatness came down in front of them.

God told Moses, "Move away from these other men. I'm going to get rid of them."

Moses and Aaron bowed with their faces to the ground. "God," they said. "Don't be angry with all the people. Only one man has sinned."

So God said, "Tell people to move away from Korah's tent. Tell them to move away from the tents of his two friends."

Moses told them. So the people moved away.

Moses said, "Now you'll know God has sent me. You'll know that what I've done hasn't been my idea. Let's say these men die like most men do. Then God hasn't sent me. But what if God does something new? What if the ground opens up and swallows them? Then you'll know these men didn't think God was important."

Right away a big crack opened in the ground. Korah and his two friends fell in. Their tents and families fell in. Everything they owned fell in. Then the ground closed up again.

All God's people saw it. They began running around and screaming.

Then fire came from God. It burned up the 250 men who were mad at Moses.

But the next day all the people fussed at Moses. "You killed God's people," they said. They got together and went toward the worship tent.

All of a sudden, the cloud came down. It covered the worship tent. God's greatness was there.

Moses and Aaron ran to the front of the worship tent. God said, "Move away from these people. I'm going to get rid of them."

Moses and Aaron bowed with their faces to the ground. Moses told Aaron, "Hurry! Take your offering bowl. Put fire from the altar in it. Go to the people. Try to make up for what they've done. God is angry. He's sent a bad sickness."

So Aaron did what Moses told him. The sickness had started. Many people were dying. But Aaron stood between the dead people and the living people. Then the sickness stopped. But 14,700 (fourteen thousand, seven hundred) people had already died.

The Walking Stick That Grew Flowers

NUMBERS 17

God told Moses, "Get 12 walking sticks from the people. Get one from the leader of each family group. Write each man's name on his walking stick. Get one from Aaron and write his name on it. Put the sticks in the worship tent. Set them in front of the ark box. I will choose one man. His walking stick will get flowers on it. Then the people will stop being mad at you."

So Moses got the 12 walking sticks. He put them in front of the ark box.

Moses went back into the worship tent the next day. He looked at the walking sticks. Aaron's stick had grown flowers on it. Then almonds had grown on it.

Moses brought the walking sticks out. He showed the people. Then he gave the leaders their own walking sticks back.

Finding More Water

NUMBERS 20

God's people traveled to the Zin Desert. Miriam died there.

There wasn't any water in the Zin Desert. The people got together against Moses again. They said, "We should have died when the others died. Why did you bring us out here? There's no wheat here. There are no figs or grapes. There's not even water to drink!"

Moses and Aaron went to the worship tent. They bowed with their faces to the ground. God's greatness came.

God told Moses, "Get your walking stick. You and Aaron call all the people together. Talk to the rock. Water will flow out of it. Then the people can drink. Their cows and sheep can drink, too."

So Moses got the walking stick. He and Aaron called all the people together in front of the rock.

Moses said, "Listen! Do we have to get water from this rock for you?"

Then Moses hit the rock two times with the walking stick. Water flowed out. The people and their sheep and cows drank.

But God had said just to talk to the rock. He told Moses and Aaron, "You did not trust me. You did not treat me like the most important one. So you won't get to lead these people into Canaan."

Then Moses sent a message to the king of Edom. "You know we are having hard times. The people of Egypt were mean to us. But we cried to God. He heard us. He sent an angel and took us out of Egypt.

"Now we are on a long trip. We are at the edge of your land. We would like to go through your land. We won't go through fields. We won't drink water from your wells. We will just go on the road. We won't turn right or left. We will just pass through your land on our way."

The king of Edom sent an answer. "We will not let you pass through our land. Don't even try or we will fight."

Moses sent another message. "We'll just stay on the main road. We won't drink any of your water. We won't let our animals drink your water. We just want to pass through. We don't want anything else."

The king of Edom sent another answer. "We will not let you pass through."

Then the army of Edom came out to fight. The army was big and strong. So God's people turned back. They traveled to Hor Mountain.

God told Moses, "Here's where Aaron will die. Take Aaron and his son Eleazar up the mountain. Give Aaron's special clothes to Eleazar. Eleazar will take Aaron's place."

So Moses did what God said. Then Aaron died on top of the mountain. Moses and Eleazar came back down. All the people cried, because Aaron had died.

The Snake on a Pole

NUMBERS 21

God's people traveled toward the Red Sea. They could not go through the land of Edom. So they went around it. But it took a long time. The people began to fuss about it.

"Why did you bring us out here to die?" they asked. "There's no bread out here. There's no water here. We hate this food we're eating."

Then God sent snakes into the camp. They bit people. Lots of people died.

The people called to Moses. "We sinned. We fussed at God and at you. Pray to God. Ask him to take the snakes away."

So Moses prayed.

God said, "Make a metal snake. Put it on a pole. People who get a snake bite can look at it. Then they won't die."

So Moses made a metal snake. He put it on a pole. People with snake bites looked at it. Then they didn't die.

God's people traveled to many places. Then they came to another land. Moses sent the king a message. "We want to pass through your land. We won't go into any of your fields. We won't drink any of your water. We'll just go on the road. We'll just pass through your land."

The king wouldn't let them pass through. He called out his whole army. He went out into the desert to fight God's people.

But God's people fought back. They won. They took lots of land and many cities. Then they made their home there.

Still another king sent his army to fight God's people. God told Moses, "Don't be scared of the king. I've given his army and his land to you."

So God's people fought the king's army. God's people won. They took his land.

An Angel and a Donkey

NUMBERS 22

Then God's people traveled to Moab. They made their camp by the Jordan River.

Now the people of Moab were afraid of God's people. They had heard what happened to the kings from some other lands. They said, "These people will eat us like an ox eats grass."

The king of Moab sent a letter to a man named Balaam. It said, "Some people have come from Egypt. They are living near me. Come and pray for bad things to happen to them. I know they are too strong for me. Maybe then I can fight them and win. Maybe I can make them leave my land. I know that when you pray for good things to come, they do. When you pray for bad things to come, they do."

The king's men took the letter to Balaam. Balaam told them, "Stay here for the night. Then I'll tell you what God says to do." So the men stayed with Balaam that night.

But God came to Balaam. God said, "Who are the men staying with you?"

"The king of Moab sent them with a letter," said Balaam. "It's about people who came from Egypt. The king wants me to pray that bad things will come to them."

"Don't go with these men," said God. "You'd better not pray for bad things for these people. These people are to get good things."

Balaam went to the men the next morning. He said, "Go back home. God won't let me go with you."

So the men went back to the king. "Balaam wouldn't come with us," they said.

Then the king sent more men. These were more important men than the first men. They told Balaam these words from the king. "Come see me. Don't let anything stop you. I'll pay you well. I'll do whatever you say. Just come and pray for bad things for these people."

"The king of Moab might pay me well," said Balaam. "Let's say he gives me a palace full of gold and silver. I still can't do something God said not to do. But stay here tonight. I'll see what God says."

God came to Balaam again. He

said, "You can go with them. But only do what I tell you to do."

The next morning Balaam got up. He put a saddle on his donkey. He started out with the men to go see the king of Moab.

But God was angry with Balaam. God's angel stood in the road to stop him.

Balaam was riding on his donkey. Two servants were with him. But only the donkey could see the angel in the road. The angel was holding out a sword. So the donkey left the road and went into a field. Balaam beat his donkey. He made her get back on the road.

The road got narrow. It went between two grape fields. There was a wall on each side of the road. The angel stood in the road again. The donkey saw the angel. So she moved very close to one of the walls. Balaam's foot was pushed against the wall. So he beat his donkey again.

Then the angel stood in a very narrow place in the road. There wasn't any room for the donkey to turn around. She saw the angel. So she just lay down with Balaam on top of her.

Balaam was very angry. He beat his donkey with his walking stick.

Then God made the donkey able to talk. She said, "What did I do? Why did you beat me three times?"

"You made me look like a fool!" said Balaam. "If I had a sword, I'd kill you!"

"But I'm your own donkey," said the donkey. "You ride me all the time. Did I ever do this to you before?"

"No," said Balaam.

Then God made Balaam able to see the angel. Balaam saw that the angel held his sword ready. Balaam put his face to the ground.

"Why did you beat your donkey three times?" asked the angel. "I came here to stop you. You are taking chances by going with these men. Your donkey saw me. She tried to turn back three times. If she hadn't, I would have killed you. But I would have let her go."

"I sinned," said Balaam. "I didn't know you were in the road. If you're not happy with me, I'll go home."

"Go on with the men," said the angel. "But say only what God tells you to say."

So Balaam went on to see the king.

The king heard that Balaam was coming. So he went to meet him. "I sent you an important letter," he said. "I wanted you to hurry and come. Why didn't you come? I can pay you very well."

"I'm here now," said Balaam.

"But I can say only what God tells me to say."

From These Mountains of Rock

NUMBERS 23

The next day the king of Moab took Balaam with him. They went to a high place. They could look out over the land. They could see part of the camp of God's people.

"Build seven altars," said Balaam.

The king did. They put their gifts on the altar. The gifts were bulls and rams.

"Now stay here," said Balaam. "I'll go off by myself. Maybe God will talk to me. I'll tell you what he says."

So Balaam went off by himself. Then God talked to him.

Balaam went back. He told the king what God told him to say.

Balaam said, "King from the east mountains, you brought me here. You asked me to say that bad things will come to these people. But I can't. God has not planned bad things for them. I see them from these mountains of rock. I look down on them. I see that they are not like the other nations. There are more of them than you can count. I hope I will be right with God like they are!"

"What have you done?" asked the king. "I wanted you to say that God will send bad things. But you have prayed for good things!"

"I have to say what God says," said Balaam.

"Come to a different place," said the king of Moab. "You'll see all the people from there. Then you can say that bad things will come to them."

So the king took Balaam to a field on a mountain. He built seven altars there. He put gifts on the altars.

Balaam said, "You stay here. I'll go off by myself to see what God says."

So Balaam went off by himself. Then God told him what to say.

Balaam went back to the king of Moab. He told the king what God said.

"Get up, King. Get up and listen! God isn't a man. He doesn't lie. He doesn't change his mind. He doesn't say he will do something and then not do it. He doesn't make a promise and not keep it. He tells me to pray for good things. He has planned good things for his people. I can't change that."

"Don't pray for bad or good!" said the king.

"Didn't I tell you?" said Balaam. "I told you I would say what God tells me."

"Let me take you to a different place," said the king. "Maybe God will let you tell about bad things when you are there."

So the king of Moab took Balaam to the top of another mountain. He could see the desert from there. They built seven altars.

Balaam Tries Again

NUMBERS 24

Now Balaam had been trying to hear from God. He had been using witches' ways. But this time he didn't. He understood that God planned good things for his people. So Balaam looked out at the desert. When he saw God's people, God's Spirit came on him. He spoke these words.

"The people of God have beautiful tents. They look like gardens by a river. They look like cedar trees by the water. Their king will be great. Their kingdom will be great. People who pray for good things for them will get good things. People who pray for bad will get bad things themselves."

Then the king of Moab was very angry at Balaam. He hit his hands together. "I called you to say bad things will happen," he said. "These people are my enemies. But you have prayed for good things three times! I was going to pay you a lot of money. God has kept you from getting your pay."

"Didn't I tell your men?" asked Balaam. "You could give me a palace full of silver and gold. But I can say only what God tells me to say. Before I go home, I'll tell you what will happen.

"A very special person will come from these people. He will be like a star. He will win over his enemies. God's people will get strong."

FEBRUARY 7

With All Your Heart

from NUMBERS 26–33; DEUTERONOMY 1–11

Now God told Moses to count the men. He said to count men who were 20 years old or older. They had counted the men who lived many years ago. Now they found that all those men had died. God had said that they'd die in the desert, and they did. Only Caleb and Joshua and Moses were still alive.

Moses told God, "Choose someone to lead after I die. Then your people won't be like sheep with no shepherd."

God said, "Take Joshua. The Spirit is in him. Put your hand on him. Bring him in front of all the people. Tell them he will be in charge. Then they'll obey him. They must follow him."

Moses did what God told him. Joshua stood in front of all the people. Moses put his hands on him. Moses told the people that Joshua would be their leader.

Then God told Moses what he wanted his people to do. "Cross the Jordan River. Push out everyone who lives in the land of Canaan. Get rid of their idols. Get rid of their worship places. Make the land your own. Live there. It's the land I'm giving you. Give each family group a part of the land.

"You must push all the people out of that land. If you don't, they will bring trouble to you. Then you will be the ones who are hurt."

Then Moses talked to the people. "God has led us in the desert for 40 years. He has brought good things to us. God has been with us. We have not needed anything.

"Now hear the laws I'm going to teach you. Obey them. Don't add to them. Don't take away from them. Then other nations will see that you are wise.

"I won't get to go across the Jordan River," said Moses. "I'll die in this land. But you'll go across. Don't forget the promise that you and God made. Look for him and obey him. He is a kind God. He won't leave you or forget you.

"Hear this, people of God. Only the Lord is our God. Love him with all your heart. Love him with all your soul. Love him with all your strength.

"Put these laws in your hearts. Teach them to your children. Talk about them when you sit down at home. Talk about them when you walk outside. Talk about them when you go to bed at night. Talk about them when you get up in the morning.

"God led you for 40 years in the desert," said Moses. "He gave you manna for food. Now you know that people don't just live on bread. They live on every word God says.

"In the desert, your clothes didn't wear out. Your feet didn't even get sore.

"God is taking you into a good land. It has rivers and pools of water. It has valleys and hills. It grows wheat, vines, figs, and olives. It has honey. There is iron in the rocks. You can dig in the hills and get copper.

"You might say that you got these for yourself. That you're rich because of your own power. That you're rich because your hands are strong. But don't forget God. He is the one who makes you able to get riches.

"Don't say that God brought you here because you're so good. No. God is getting rid of the other people because they're so bad. God promised this land to his people.

"See? Today I'm giving you two ways to choose from. One will bring good. One will bring bad. If you obey God's rules, good will come to you. If you don't obey, you'll be in trouble."

Rules about Worship
from EXODUS 22–23; 31; 34–35; LEVITICUS 16; 18–20; 23–24; 26; NUMBERS 28–29; DEUTERONOMY 5; 12–18; 26

Here are some of the rules God gave his people.

I am the Lord your God. I brought you out of Egypt. I will be your only God.

Don't make idols. Don't bow down to them or worship them.

Don't worship me the way other people worship their gods. They do terrible things to worship their gods. They even kill their children as gifts to their gods.

You will go into your new land. You'll get rid of the enemies. Then God will choose a place of worship. That's where you'll bring your gifts for God.

Don't do what the enemies in the land do. Don't follow witches' ways. Don't follow bad spirits. God hates these things.

You may hear a prophet, a person who tells God's plans. What if he says, "Let's follow other gods"? Then don't listen to him. The Lord your God is the one to follow.

You must speak well of God's name. When you say it, say it with wonder. Don't say bad things about God.

Give God the first of the fruit you grow. Give him the first cows and sheep that are born. Put the fruit in a basket. Then take it to the priest. He will set it down before God. Then bow to God. Show your joy for what God has given you.

Make the seventh day of the week special. You can work for six days. But the next day should be special to God. You shouldn't work on that day. That's because God made the earth and space in six days. The next day he rested.

Have a Pass Over holiday every year. This is a holiday in the spring. At this holiday, remember the time you left Egypt. Eat flat bread. Do it because that's what you ate when you left Egypt.

Every year have a holiday called the Holiday of Weeks. Start it seven weeks after you begin to cut your wheat. This is a holiday for the early summer. It's for the first fruit that comes from what you planted. Bring God a gift of your new wheat.

Every year have a Horn Holiday. It will be in the fall. Everyone get together. Don't work on that day. Play the horns to worship God.

Every year have a Day of Paying for Sins. It will be in the fall. Don't eat anything on that day. Don't work. The priest will kill a bull and a goat. Then he will put his hands on a live goat. He will say what the sins of the people are. Then take the goat out of the camp. Leave it there as a gift to God. Do this every year to pay for the people's sins.

Every year have a Tent Holiday. It will be in the fall. It will last seven days. It's for the time when you gather in your crops. On the first day, get the best fruit from your trees. Get palm tree branches and other branches. Show your joy to God for seven days. Live in tents for these seven days.

Other Rules

from EXODUS 21–23; LEVITICUS 19; 24; NUMBERS 35; DEUTERONOMY 5; 15–16; 19; 24–25

Choose judges for each city. They should be fair when they judge people. Do what the judges say. Treat them as important people.

Don't pay someone to be unfair. Don't pay someone to lie. Don't pay someone to do wrong. Be fair to people from other lands. Be fair to children who have no fathers. Be kind to women who have no husbands.

Don't lie. Don't copy others who are doing wrong.

Fathers won't pay for what their children do wrong. Children won't pay for what their fathers do wrong. Each person must pay for what he did wrong himself. He must pay with his life.

What if a person kills someone? If he planned to do it, he should die. But what if he did not plan to do it? Somebody may want to kill him for what he did. So he should go to a special city. There he will be safe until the people decide if he did wrong.

What if somebody kidnaps someone else? He should die.

What if somebody hurts someone else? Then what he did should be done to him. A broken bone for a broken bone. An eye for an eye. A tooth for a tooth.

Don't steal.

A robber must pay back whatever he takes. Let's say he steals an ox or a sheep. What if he kills it or sells it? Then he has to pay back five oxen for the ox. He has to pay back four sheep for the sheep. What if he still has the ox or the sheep? Then he pays back two oxen for the ox. He pays back two sheep for the sheep.

Let's say someone digs a pit and doesn't cover it. What if an ox or a donkey falls into it? Then he has to pay for the animal that died.

Let's say someone starts a fire. It may get out of control and burn somebody's wheat. What if it burns the whole field? Then the person who started it pays for what burned.

What if somebody lets his animals eat from another person's field? He has to pay for what they ate. He has to give the best crops from his field.

Do right for the people who work for you. They may be poor. They may be people from other lands. That doesn't matter. Pay them every day before the sun goes down. They need what you pay them.

Let's say someone borrows something from you. Then don't make him pay back more than he borrowed.

Let's say one of God's people is poor. He lives in your town. Then freely give him whatever he needs. Don't let your heart get hard against him. Give him enough. Then God will give you good things. So open your hands to give to the poor.

Don't steal. Don't lie. Don't trick others into believing something that's not true.

Rules about Sickness and Food

from LEVITICUS 11; 13;
DEUTERONOMY 14

A person might get a sickness that others could catch. Then that person should live by himself. He should live outside the camp. He should call out, "Not clean! Not clean!" But if he gets well, he should go see the priest. The priest will look at him. The priest will say if he is well or not.

Here are some animals you may eat. You may eat the ox, sheep, goat, deer, and gazelle. You may eat the antelope. But don't eat camels or rock badgers or rabbits or pigs.

You may eat sea animals that have fins and scales. But if they don't have fins and scales, don't eat them.

Don't eat eagles, vultures, ravens, owls, or gulls. Don't eat hawks, ospreys, storks, herons, or bats.

Don't eat any insects unless they hop on the ground. They must have bending legs for hopping. So you may eat locusts, crickets, and grasshoppers.

Don't eat weasels, rats, or lizards. Don't eat anything you find that's already dead.

Don't eat any kind of blood. Blood is very important and special. The life of any being is in its blood. Don't eat the fat of cows, sheep, or goats.

FEBRUARY 9

Rules for Treating People Right

from EXODUS 22–23; LEVITICUS 19; 23–24; DEUTERONOMY 5; 22–24

When you gather crops, leave some in the field for the poor people. Leave it for people who come from other lands.

Let's say you walk through your neighbor's grape field. You may eat all the grapes you want. But don't carry any out of the field with you. You may go into your neighbor's wheat field. You may eat some of the grain. But don't cut down his wheat. Don't take it out of the field.

Be kind to your father and mother. Then you'll live a long life. God will bring good things to you. Obey your father and mother.

Stand up when an old person is with you. Be kind to old people.

Be kind to women whose husbands have died. Be kind to children whose mother and father have died.

Someone from another land may choose to live with you. He should follow the same laws your people follow. Treat him like one of your own people. Love him as you love yourself. Remember that you were strangers one time in Egypt.

Don't say bad things about people who can't hear. Don't put something in the way of someone who can't see.

Don't tell bad things about other people. Don't put somebody's life in danger. Don't hate other people. Don't try to get back at someone who has done you wrong. Love your neighbor as you love yourself.

Let's say you find something that belongs to someone else. It may be his ox or his sheep. It may be his donkey or his coat or something else. Take it back to him.

Don't want things that your neighbor has. Don't try to get what your neighbor has.

Rules about War

DEUTERONOMY 20

Let's say you go to war. You see horses and chariots. You see a big army coming to fight against you. Don't be afraid. God is with you. He will help you win.

You might march up to a city far away. Then offer peace to the people in the city. If they say they want peace, they can work for you.

But if they won't make peace, fight them.

There are cities nearby. They are in the land God is giving you. Fight these cities and get rid of the people. If you don't, they'll teach you to worship their gods. Then you'll sin.

Moses' Song

from DEUTERONOMY 30–32; 34

Moses said to God's people, "All of this isn't too hard for you. God's word is very close to you. It's in your mouth. It's in your heart. You can obey it.

"Today I'm showing you what to choose from. Choose between life and death. Choose between the good and the bad. Choose life. Then you and your children can live. You can love God. Listen to him. Stay with him, because God is your life."

Then Moses told the people, "I'm 120 years old. I can't lead you anymore. But God will go ahead of you. Joshua will go with you. God will help you win over your enemies. Don't be scared of them. God will go with you. He will never leave you. He will never forget about you."

Then God told Moses, "It's time for you to die. Get Joshua. Bring him to the worship tent."

So Moses took Joshua to the worship tent. Then God came there in the tall cloud. The cloud stayed over the front of the tent.

God spoke to Joshua. "Be strong. Be brave. You will take the people into the Promised Land. I will be with you."

Then God told Moses, "These people will forget me. When they do, I'll be angry with them. They'll have hard times. They'll say that this happened because I was not with them. So write down this song. Teach it to the people. They can remember this song."

So Moses wrote the song down. Then he taught it to the people.

Listen, sky. I will talk.
Listen, earth, to the words I say.
My teaching will come down like
    rain.
It will be like rain on new grass.

I'll tell about God's name.
Praise God's greatness!
He is like a Rock for us.
Everything he does is right.
He keeps his promises.
He doesn't do anything wrong.

Remember the old days.
Ask your fathers. They'll tell you.
God gave his people milk and
    wheat and grapes.
But they began to worship idols.
They forgot God.

So God was angry.
"I'll turn my face away," he said.
"I'll send trouble to them."
But God will be kind
    to people who serve him.
God will win over his enemies.
He will save his land and his people.

Moses told the people, "Think about everything I told you. Tell your children to obey God's laws. The law isn't just words. It's your life. So obey the law. Then you'll live a long time in God's Promised Land."

That day God told Moses, "Go up on the mountain. It's the one across from Jericho. You will die on this mountain. You won't be able to go into the Promised Land. But you may look at it. You can see it from the mountain."

So Moses climbed up the mountain. God showed him the Promised Land. Then Moses died. His grave is in a valley. But nobody knows just where it is.

Moses was 120 years old when he died. But he could still see, and he was still strong.

God's people cried when Moses died. There has never been another prophet like Moses. God talked with him in a special way. Moses did many wonders. Nobody else ever showed as much of God's great power.

Hiding on the Roof
JOSHUA 1–2

God told Joshua, "Moses is dead. Now get ready to go across the Jordan River. You'll go into the land that I'm giving my people. I'll give you the land you walk on. This is what I promised to Moses. Nobody will be able to come against you all your life. I will never leave you. I will never forget about you.

"So be strong. Be very brave. Be careful to obey the laws Moses gave you. Think about the laws day and night. Then you'll do what they say. You'll do a good job in whatever you do.

"So be strong. Be brave. Don't be scared. Don't give up because you think it won't happen. God will be with you wherever you go."

Joshua sent two men across the Jordan River. He told them, "Look around the land. Take a careful look at the city of Jericho."

So the two Jewish men went across the river. They went into the city of Jericho. They went to stay at a house there. The house belonged to a woman named Rahab.

But somebody told the king of Jericho, "Some Jewish men came here tonight. They came to look around our land."

So the king sent a message to Rahab. It said, "Send me the men who came to your house. They are here to look around our whole land."

But Rahab had let the men hide up on her roof. They were hiding under some plants. When Rahab heard the message, she said, "Yes. The men did come here. I didn't know where they came from. They left before the city gate was to be closed for the night. I don't know where they went. But if you hurry, you might catch them."

So the king's men left to chase Joshua's men. The city gate closed behind them.

Then Rahab went to talk to the men on her roof. "I know God has given this land to you," she said. "Our people are afraid. We heard what God did at the Red Sea. We heard how you won over other kings. So nobody here is brave anymore. Your God is the God in heaven and on earth.

"I've been kind to you," said Rahab. "So promise me something. Promise you'll save my life. Save my father and mother. Save my brothers and sisters."

The men said, "Don't tell what we're doing. Then we'll be kind to you. We'll save you when God gives us this land."

"Go into the hills," Rahab told them. "The men chasing you won't find you there. Hide there for three days. Then you can go home."

"Tie a red rope in your window," the men said. "Then bring all your family into this house. That way we can save you. But if you tell on us, we won't save you."

"All right," said Rahab.

Rahab's house was part of the city wall. So she let the men climb out her window. She helped them down the wall with a rope. Then she tied a red rope in her window.

The men went into the hills. They stayed there for three days. After that, they went back to camp. They told Joshua everything that had happened. "We know God will give us the land," they said. "All the people there are afraid of us."

The River Stops Flowing
JOSHUA 3–5

Three days passed. Then Joshua sent men through the camp. They told the people, "You've never come this way before. So watch for the ark box. The priests will carry it. You should follow. Then you'll know which way to go."

Joshua told the people, "Get ready. Tomorrow God will do some wonderful things."

Then Joshua told the priests to get

the ark box. So the priests took the ark box and started out.

God told Joshua, "Today  I'll start making you great. That way the people will know I'm with you. I'll be with you as I was with Moses. Tell the priests to take the ark box to the river. Tell them to stand in the river."

So Joshua told the people, "Come and listen. Here's how you'll know that God is with you. The priests will step into the river with God's ark box. Then the river water will stop flowing. It will stand up in a pile."

Now the river was very deep at this time. But the priests stepped into the river. Then the water stopped flowing. It piled up at a town far away.

The priests stood in the middle of the river. It was dry there now. The people crossed the river, walking on dry ground.

Then God told Joshua, "Choose 12 men, one from each family group. Tell them to get 12 rocks from the middle of the river. Carry them with you. Set them down where you camp tonight."

So Joshua chose 12 men. They got the rocks. Joshua said, "Your children will ask what these rocks are for. Then you'll tell them what happened today."

The priests were still standing in the middle of the river. They waited until everybody was across. Then God said, "Tell the priests to come out."

The priests carried the ark box out of the river. They stepped up onto the bank of the river. Right away the water flowed back into the river. It got very deep, like it was before.

God's people traveled to some flat land. They camped there. They set up the rocks from the river. That day the people saw that Joshua was an important leader. Joshua became as important to them as Moses had been.

Now the kings of the land heard what happened. They heard that God dried up the river. They heard that God's people crossed on dry ground. So they were afraid.

Fourteen days passed. Then it was time to have the Pass Over holiday. So God's people had their holiday. The next day they ate food grown in the Promised Land. After that, God did not send any more manna to eat.

Now they came close to the city of Jericho. Joshua looked up. He saw a man standing in front of him. The man was holding out a sword.

Joshua walked up to the man. "Are you for us or against us?" asked Joshua.

"I'm not for you or against you," said the man. "I'm the captain of God's army. That's why I've come."

Then Joshua put his face down to the ground. "What message do you bring me?" he asked.

"Take your shoes off," said the man. "You are standing on a special, holy place."

So Joshua did what the man said.

Falling Walls!

JOSHUA 6

The people of Jericho kept the gates to their city closed up. They didn't want God's people to come in. So nobody went out of the city. Nobody went into the city.

God told Joshua, "I'm giving you the city of Jericho. Take your army. March around the city one time every day. Do that for six days. Seven priests should carry horns. They should walk in front of my ark box.

"On day seven, march around the city seven times. The priests should blow their horns. Then they should make a long blow on the horns.

When the people hear the horns, they should shout. The city wall will fall down. Your people can go right in."

So Joshua told the people God's plan. "Go ahead!" he said. "March around the city. Let the guards and priests go in front of the ark box."

So the guards marched out. Then the priests with their horns marched out. Then the priests carrying God's ark box went out. Then the other guards went out. The priests started blowing their horns.

But Joshua told the people, "Don't say a word. Wait until I tell you to shout. Then you can shout."

So they went around the city once. Then they went back to camp. They stayed there that night.

Early in the morning, they marched around the city again. Then they went back to their camp. They did the same thing for six days.

Day number seven came. They got up early. They marched around the city again. But this time, they went around seven times. Then the priests sounded a long blow on their horns.

Joshua called, "Everybody shout! God is giving you this city. But save Rahab and everyone in her house as we promised. She hid two of our men. And don't take things from the city for yourselves."

So the horns blew, and the people

shouted. Then the wall of the city fell down. Joshua and his men went right into the city.

Joshua called the men who had stayed at Rahab's house. "Go save Rahab," he said.

So they went to Rahab's house. They brought out Rahab and her family.

Joshua's army burned the whole city. Then Joshua said, "No one should build this city again. If people try, bad things will happen to them."

God was with Joshua. Everyone in all the land heard about him.

Who Stole the Gold?

JOSHUA 7

Now one man took some things from Jericho. These things were to be given to God. So God was angry at his people.

Then Joshua sent men to look at the city of Ai.

The men came back and said, "It's small. Just send a few men to take the town."

So Joshua didn't send the whole army. A group of men went against the town. But the people of Ai chased them off. They chased them to the valley of stone cutting. Some of God's people got killed. God's people started getting scared.

Joshua went in front of God's ark

box. He lay down with his face to the ground. He stayed there all day. The leaders did the same thing, too.

Joshua prayed. "God, why did you bring us here to kill us? The other nations will hear about this. They'll come and fight us. They'll kill us all."

"Stand up!" said God. "Why is your face to the ground? My people have done wrong. They took some things I told them not to take. That's why they can't win against their enemies. You'll have to get rid of what they took. If you don't, I can't be with you."

Then God told Joshua, "Call the family groups. Tomorrow morning they will come before me. I'll get rid of the person who stole these things."

So the family groups came out early the next morning. God pointed to the family group of Judah. Out of that family group, God pointed to one man.

Joshua said to that man, "Tell me what you did. Don't hide it."

"It's true," said the man. "I sinned. I saw a beautiful coat in Jericho. I also found silver coins and a block of gold. I wanted them. So I took them. I hid them in the ground under my tent."

Joshua sent some men to the tent. They found the things the man had taken. They brought them to Joshua.

Then God's people took the man, his tent, and everything he had. They went to a valley. They killed the man and set fire to everything he had. The people piled rocks over everything. They called this the Sad Valley.

The Fight at Ai

JOSHUA 8

Then God told Joshua, "Don't be scared anymore. Don't give up. Take your whole army. Go out to fight the city of Ai. I'm giving that city to you."

So Joshua chose some of his best men. He told them his plan. "Listen," he said. "You go behind the city. But don't go very far. Then be ready. I'll take the main army. We'll come up to the city to fight.

"The men of the city will come out to fight," said Joshua. "We will run from them, and they'll chase us. When they have all left, that's when you should go into the city. God will give it to you. Then set the city on fire."

The first group of men went out that night. Joshua and the rest of the men stayed in camp.

Early the next morning Joshua called the men together. He led them out. They marched to Ai. By that night they were in the valley by the city.

The king of Ai saw them there. So the next morning he led his men out. Joshua and his men began to run away toward the desert. The men from the city chased them. They left their city open.

Then God told Joshua, "Hold out your spear."

So Joshua held out his spear. That was the sign his other men were waiting for. They were behind the city. They saw Joshua's spear, and they ran into the city. They took it and set fire to it.

Then the men from the city looked back. They saw smoke going up from their city. Joshua and his men began to fight them. And God's people won.

Stale Bread and Worn-Out Shoes

JOSHUA 9

Now all the kings of the land heard about God's people. The kings got together to fight God's people.

But the people of Gibeon didn't want to fight. So they played a trick on God's people. They put old, worn-out bags onto donkeys. The men put on worn-out shoes. They wore old clothes. They carried dry, stale bread. And they went to see Joshua.

They said, "We come from a land far away. We want to make a deal with you."

God's people said, "We don't know you. Maybe you live close to us. Then God wouldn't want us to make a deal with you."

"We'll serve you," they told Joshua.

"Who are you?" asked Joshua. "Where do you come from?"

"We are from a land far away," they said. "We heard about your God. So our leaders told us to come to you. They told us to make a deal with you. This bread was hot when we left home. But see? It's dry and stale now. The bags on our donkeys were new. But now they're old and worn out. We traveled so far our clothes and shoes wore out."

Some of Joshua's men took a look. They saw the old bread and the worn-out bags. They could see the worn clothes. But they didn't ask God about it.

Then Joshua and the leaders made a deal with the men. They promised not to fight them.

Three days passed. Then God's people found out that these men lived nearby. So God's people traveled to their city. But they didn't fight. They had promised not to.

"We won't fight them," they said. "But they will have to be our servants. They'll have to carry our wood and water." So God's people kept their promise.

Joshua went to the men of Gibeon. "Why did you lie to us?" he asked. "Now you'll have to be our servants."

"We heard about your God," they said. "We were afraid of you. So we lied to you. Do whatever you think is right."

So Joshua made them carry wood and water for God's people.

Sun and Moon Stand Still
JOSHUA 10; 13–14

The kings of the land heard what had happened. They heard that the people from Gibeon made a deal with Joshua. So the kings got together to fight Gibeon. That's because Gibeon was an important city.

Then the people of Gibeon sent a message to Joshua. "Come fast! Save us! The kings from the hills are trying to fight us."

So Joshua took his army to Gibeon. God told Joshua, "Don't be afraid. I'll make you win."

Joshua and his army marched all night long. The kings and their armies were surprised to see God's people. God made the kings' armies get mixed up. They began running away.

God's people chased the kings' armies. Then big hail stones fell from the sky. God sent hail down on the enemy armies.

That day Joshua prayed, "Let the sun stand still. Let the moon stand still."

The sun did stand still. The moon stopped moving across the sky. The sun and moon stopped until God's people won the fight.

The sun didn't move in the sky for about a day. There was never another day like that before or after. That was a day when God answered a special prayer. God really was fighting for his people. So Joshua won and took all the land in the hill country.

Joshua gave land to the family groups of God's people. Each family group got a different part of the land.

Then Caleb went to see Joshua. He said, "Remember what God told Moses about you and me? I was 40 years old. Moses chose me to check out the land of Canaan. I came back and said we could take the land. The other men with me were afraid. But I followed God with my whole heart. So Moses said that the land I walked on would be mine.

"God has kept me alive for 45 years since then. Today I'm 85 years old! I'm just as strong now as I was

then. I can fight as well now as I did then. So please give me the land God promised me."

Then Joshua prayed for God to bring good things to Caleb. And he gave Caleb the land God promised him.

The One We Will Serve
JOSHUA 23–24

A long time passed. God's people lived in peace. Joshua grew old. Then he called the leaders together. "I'm old," he said. "You've seen everything God has done for you. God fought for you and pushed the nations out of this land.

"So be strong. Be careful. Obey everything the law tells you to do.

"Some other nations still live in this land. Don't worship their gods. Keep following the Lord your God. Don't marry people from other nations. If you do, God won't push them out of the land. Then these nations will trap you.

"I'm going to die soon. You know that God has kept all his promises. If you don't keep your promise and obey him, he will be angry. Then you'll die. And none of God's people will be left in the land.

"So today, choose the one you will serve. Will you serve the gods of other nations? My family and I will not do that. We will serve God."

The people said, "We'll never leave God. We won't worship other gods. We will serve God, too. He saved us. He did great wonders."

"All right," said Joshua. "You know what you've said. You choose to serve God. So throw away any idols you may have. Love God with your whole heart."

"We will serve God," said the people. "We will obey him."

Joshua set up a big stone under an oak tree. "See this?" he said. "This stone will help you remember what you said. It heard everything God told us."

When Joshua was 110 years old, he died. His grave is in the hill country.

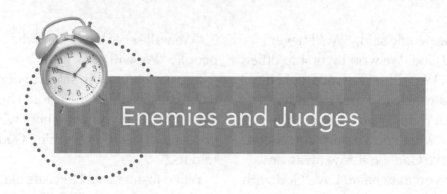

Enemies and Judges

Idol Worship

JUDGES 2

God's people followed God as long as Joshua lived. But then Joshua died. After a time, all the leaders died. Their children grew up to become men and women. But they didn't know God.

Then God's people began to worship idols. They worshiped the gods of the nations around them. They forgot God. That made God angry.

So when they went out to fight, God was against them. Their enemies would come into the land in secret. They would steal things from God's people. Then they would leave quickly. The people were very upset.

So God gave the people leaders to help them. The leaders were also called judges. They would save God's people from their enemies. But soon God's people stopped listening to the judges. They began to worship idols again.

God saved his people as long as each judge lived. God felt sorry for the people. So he was kind. But when the judge died, the people worshiped idols again.

Then God got very angry at the people. "They haven't kept the special promise we made together," he said. "So I'll stop pushing out the enemy nations. These nations will test my people. I'll see if they will follow me or not."

A Fat King

JUDGES 3

God left some enemy nations in the land. He used them to train his people to fight. But God's people married people from other nations. Then God's people began to worship the fake gods from these nations.

Now the king of Aram brought his army in. He became king of the land. He took charge of God's people.

But God's people called to God for help. So God chose a judge for them. His name was Othniel. He was Caleb's younger brother. God's Spirit was upon him.

This judge helped the people fight the king. God helped them win. So God's people lived in peace for 40 years. But then Othniel died.

God's people began to sin again. So God let King Eglon take over the land. God's people had to serve this king for 18 years.

At last God's people called to him for help. So God sent them another judge. He was a left-handed man named Ehud.

God's people sent their tax money to King Eglon. They chose Ehud to take the money.

Now Ehud had made a sword with two edges. It was one and a half feet long. He tied it to his right leg under his clothes.

Ehud took the tax money to King Eglon. This king was a very fat man. He was sitting in a room on his roof. It was cool up there.

The judge gave the tax money to the king. Then the judge told the king, "I have a secret message. It's only for you."

So the king said, "Quiet!" He sent all his helpers out of the room. Now the king was sitting by himself.

Ehud walked up to the king. "I have a message from God," said the judge.

The king stood up. Then Ehud reached with his strong left hand. He pulled the sword out from under his clothes. He pushed the sword into the king's belly. Even the handle sank in. The king's fat belly closed up over it. So Ehud didn't pull the sword out.

Ehud locked the doors and went out another way.

Later, the king's servants came back. But they found that the doors were locked. So they said, "He must be going to the bathroom."

The servants waited and waited. But the king didn't open the doors. At last the servants got a key. They unlocked the doors. They found that King Eglon was dead.

While they were waiting, Ehud had run away. He went to the hill country. There he blew a horn. Then some of God's people came to him from the hills.

"Follow me," said Ehud. "God has saved you from your enemy." So the people followed their judge.

That day God's people started fighting their enemies. And they won. Then God's people lived in peace for 80 years.

Another judge led the people after Ehud. His name was Shamgar. He picked up a stick used for leading oxen. All by himself he killed 600 enemy men with it.

A Woman Wins a Fight

JUDGES 4

After Ehud died, God's people started sinning again. So God let King Jabin take control of them. His army captain was named Sisera. He had 900 chariots made of iron. He was very mean to God's people. So they cried to God for help.

Now there was a woman who told God's plans. Her name was Deborah. She was the judge for God's people. She would sit under a palm tree. So the tree was called Deborah's Palm Tree. People with problems came to see Deborah there. She told them who was right and who was wrong.

One day Deborah called for a man named Barak. He came to see her. "God wants you to lead the army," she said. "He wants you to fight Sisera. God is going to help you win."

"I'll go if you'll go, too," said Barak. "But if you don't go, I won't go."

"All right," said Deborah. "I'll go. But you're not doing it the way God wants. So you won't get to be the great winner. A woman will win this fight."

Then Deborah went with Barak and the army. They went to Tabor Mountain.

Sisera heard about this. He got his 900 chariots and his fighting men. He took them to the river.

"Go!" said Deborah to Barak. "God will help you win today. God has gone ahead of you!"

So Barak took his army down the mountain. Then God helped them fight.

God's people were winning. So Sisera, the captain of the enemy army, left his chariot. He began running away. Barak chased the army. All of the enemy army was killed.

But Sisera ran to a tent. It belonged to a woman named Jael. She ran out to meet him. "Come in," she said.

Sisera went inside. She let him lie down. She put covers over him.

"I'm thirsty," he said. "Could I have some water?"

Jael got some milk and gave him a drink. Then she covered him up again.

"Stand at the tent door," he told her. "Someone might come by and ask you if I'm here. Say no."

Sisera was very tired. So he went to sleep. Jael was very quiet. She went over to Sisera. And she killed him.

Barak came by the tent. He had been chasing Sisera. Jael went out to meet him.

"Come in," she said. "Sisera is in here."

Barak went into the tent. There he saw that Sisera, the captain of the enemy army, was dead.

After that, God's people lived in peace for 40 years.

God Chooses Gideon

JUDGES 6

God's people began to sin again. So God let people from Midian take control of the land. They were very strong and mean. God's people would plant seeds in the fields. But the people from Midian would come into the land. They would get rid of the crops. They didn't leave anything alive. They didn't even leave sheep or cows or donkeys.

The people from Midian were like a large number of grasshoppers, or locusts. There were too many people and camels to count. They made God's people poor.

God's people called for God to help them. So God sent them a prophet, someone who tells God's words. The prophet told the people what God said. "I took you out of Egypt. I saved you. I took you to a new land and pushed out your enemies. I told you not to worship their gods. But you didn't listen to me."

One day God's angel came and sat under an oak tree. That's where Gideon was. He was working on the wheat crop. He was trying to hide it from the people of Midian.

"God is with you, strong fighter," said the angel.

"Then why has all this happened?" asked Gideon. "Our fathers tell us about God's great wonders. But God has left us."

"Go," said God. For the angel was really God. "You are strong. Save your people from the people of Midian. I'm sending you."

"How can I save them?" asked Gideon. "My family is not strong. And everyone in my family is more important than I am."

"I'll be with you," said God. "You'll win over the people of Midian."

"Are you really choosing me?" asked Gideon. "Then show me it's really you here talking to me. Please stay here. I'm going to get a gift for you."

"I'll wait for you," said the angel.

Gideon went to get a gift. He put some meat in a basket. He put the juice from the meat in a pot. He made flat bread. Then he took the food to the angel under the tree.

"Put the meat and bread on this rock," said the angel. So Gideon did.

The angel was holding a stick used for walking. He put the tip of the stick on the meat and bread. A fire started. It burned up the meat and bread. Suddenly the angel was gone.

Then Gideon knew it was God's angel. "God!" said Gideon. "I've seen your angel's face!"

"It's all right! Don't be scared," said God. "You won't die."

Then Gideon built an altar to God there. He called it "God Is Peace."

That night God talked to Gideon again. "Your father built an altar to a god. That god is not real. His name is Baal. Tear the altar down. Then build an altar to God."

So Gideon took 10 servants with him. They tore down the old altar. Then they built a new one to God. They did this at night. That's because Gideon was afraid of his family. He was afraid of men from the town, too.

The next morning men from the town saw it. "Who did this?" they asked.

Somebody told them, "Gideon did it."

So they told Gideon's father, "Bring your son here. He tore Baal's altar down. So he should die."

But Gideon's father said, "Are you fighting for Baal? If he is a god, he can fight for himself."

Now the enemy armies got together. They camped in a valley. But God's Spirit came upon Gideon. Gideon blew a horn. Fighters from God's people came to help him.

Then Gideon said to God, "Will you really save us? Prove it to me this way. I'll put sheep wool on the ground. If you'll save us, make the wool wet. Leave the ground dry. Then I'll know you'll save us."

Gideon got up early the next morning. He picked up the wool. It was wet. A whole bowl full of water came out. But the ground was dry.

Then Gideon told God, "Don't be mad at me. Let me ask you one more thing. I want to put the wool on the ground again. This time make the wool dry and the ground wet."

The next morning the wool was dry. The ground was wet.

A Night Fight

JUDGES 7

Now the enemy army camped in a valley. Gideon and his men camped near a small river.

God told Gideon, "You have too many men. I don't want them to say they saved themselves. I don't want them to say they won because they're so strong. So tell them that anyone who is scared may go home."

Gideon told his men to go home if they were scared. So 22,000 (twenty-two thousand) of them went home.

"You still have too many men," said God. "Take them down to the water."

So Gideon took his men to a small river. He let them get a drink there.

"Watch them drink," said God. "Some men will put the water in their hands. Then they'll lap it up like a dog. Other men will get down on their knees. They'll drink the water right from the river."

Gideon watched. Three hundred men lapped water out of their hands. The others got on their knees.

God said, "Take the 300 men who lapped water. Let the others go back to their tents. I'll save my people with 300 men."

Now Gideon and his men were in the hills. The enemy camp was down in the valley.

That night God told Gideon, "Go down into the camp. Take your servant. Listen to what the people are saying. Then you won't be afraid to fight."

So Gideon took his servant down the hill. The valley was full of enemy men. There were more camels than you could count. They were like sand on the beach.

Gideon and his servant walked very quietly. They went to the edge of the enemy camp. Then they listened.

They heard a man talking to his friend. "I dreamed about bread," said the man. "A big round loaf rolled into our camp. It hit our tent so hard, the tent fell down."

"That dream is about Gideon!" said the other man. "God is going to let Gideon win!"

Gideon heard all this. He worshiped God. Then he went back to his camp. He called to everyone, "Get up! God is going to let us win!"

He made his men get into three groups. He gave each man a horn. He gave each man a jar. In each jar was a stick with fire burning on it.

"Watch me!" said Gideon. "I'll lead. You follow. Do what I do. I'll blow my horn. Then you blow yours." Gideon told his men to shout these words: "For God and for Gideon!"

They went down into the valley. They came to the enemy camp. The enemy army had just changed guards.

All of a sudden, Gideon blew his horn. He broke his jar. The other men blew their horns. They broke their jars. They shouted, "A sword for God and for Gideon!" Then they just stayed where they were.

But the enemy army didn't stay. They were afraid, so they shouted and ran. They even began fighting against their own men. Then Gideon's men chased them.

Enemies and Judges
JUDGES 10–12

A man named Tola became the next judge of God's people. His grandfather's name was Dodo. Tola led God's people for 23 years.

The next judge was Jair. He led God's people for 22 years. Jair had 30 sons. They rode on 30 donkeys.

After these judges died, God's people sinned. They worshiped idols of Baal and other gods that were not real. They forgot the real God. So God was angry at them. He let enemies control the land again. God's people were having terrible trouble.

Then they called for God to help them. "We have sinned," they said. "We have forgotten you. We have worshiped Baal idols."

God said, "Didn't I save you from your enemies before? But you forgot about me. You worshiped idols. So I won't save you anymore. Ask your other gods to help you. If you're in trouble, let them save you."

"We have sinned," said the people. "Do whatever you want with us. Just save us now." Then they threw their idols away and began following God. So God couldn't stand their sadness anymore.

The enemy army came out to fight. So God's people gathered to fight, too. They began to talk to each other. "Whoever leads our fight will be our leader," they said.

Now there was a man named Jephthah. He was a strong fighter. He was the leader of a group of men. They often got into trouble.

Some of God's people went to Jephthah. "Come with us," they said. "Be our leader."

So Jephthah went with them. He sent a message to the enemy king. "Why did you come to fight us?"

The king sent a message back. "Your people took my land many years ago. Now I want it back. So give it back in peace."

Jephthah sent a message back to the king. "God's people did not take your land. They came out of Egypt. They traveled. They tried to pass through your land. But your king wouldn't let them. In fact, your king marched out to fight God's people. So God gave your land to his people."

Jephthah went on, "We'll keep whatever God gave us. Besides, God's people have lived in your land for 300 years."

Then Jephthah asked, "Why didn't you take it back before? I didn't do anything wrong to you. But you're doing wrong. You are trying to fight against me. So let God be the judge between us."

This time the king didn't listen to Jephthah's message. So Jephthah took his men out to fight. God made Jephthah win.

Jephthah led God's people for 6 years. Then he died.

The next judge was Ibzan. He had 30 sons and 30 daughters. He led God's people for 7 years. Then he died.

The next judge was Elon. He led for 10 years. Then he died.

The next judge was Abdon. He had 40 sons and 30 grandsons. They rode 70 donkeys. This judge led for 8 years. Then he died.

Going Home

RUTH 1

There were some hard years in the times of the judges. Sometimes food wouldn't grow. Then there was not enough to eat. So some families moved to other lands for a while.

One man left Judah. He moved with his wife and family to the land of Moab. He had two sons. His wife's name was Naomi. After they moved, the man died. Naomi had to take care of her sons.

When Naomi's sons were old enough, they got married. One married a young woman named Orpah. One married a young woman named Ruth. But about 10 years later, both of Naomi's sons died. So Naomi was left alone with Orpah and Ruth.

One day Naomi heard there was food in Judah. That's when she decided to go back home.

So Naomi and Orpah and Ruth packed up. They got ready to go back to Naomi's home. Then they started down the road to Judah.

But Naomi turned to Orpah and Ruth. "Go back home," she said. "I pray that God will be kind to you. I hope he will help you find new husbands." Then Naomi kissed Orpah and Ruth good-bye.

Orpah and Ruth cried. "We want to go with you," they said.

"No," said Naomi. "Go back home. Why do you want to come with me? I don't have any other sons to be your husbands. This is a sad time for me. God must have turned against me."

Orpah and Ruth cried again. Then Orpah kissed Naomi. She said good-bye and went home. But Ruth kept hugging Naomi.

"Look at Orpah," said Naomi. "She is going home. You should go back with her."

"Don't tell me to leave you," said Ruth. "I'll go where you go. I'll stay where you stay. Your people will become my people. Your God will be my God. I'll die where you die. My grave will be by yours. I won't leave you as long as I live."

Naomi could see that Ruth really wanted to go with her. So she didn't ask her to go back anymore.

Ruth and Naomi traveled to the town of Bethlehem. When they got there, people began talking about them. "Is that Naomi?" they asked.

"That was my name," said Naomi. "But God has sent me trouble. So call me Mara, for God has made my life sad. When I left here, I was full. But I'm coming back with nothing."

In the Grain Fields
RUTH 2

Now Naomi's husband still had family in Bethlehem. One of the men in the family was named Boaz.

One day Ruth told Naomi, "Let me go out today. I'll go to the fields. The workers are picking grain. I'll pick up some of the grain that's left over."

"All right," said Naomi. "Go ahead."

So Ruth went to the fields. She started picking up grain that was left over. She was working in Boaz's fields. But she didn't know it.

About that time, Boaz came back from town. He called hello to his workers. They called back to him.

Then Boaz talked to the man in charge of the workers. "Who is that young woman over there?" he asked.

"That's the woman who came back with Naomi," he said. "She is from Moab. She asked us if she could gather grain that was left over. So we let her go into the fields. She worked hard all morning. She rested for just a little while."

Boaz went over to talk to Ruth.

"You can stay right here in my field," he said. "Don't go anywhere else. Follow along after my servant girls. I told my workers not to bother you. If you get thirsty, drink from our water jars."

Ruth bowed down. "I'm not even from this land," she said. "So why are you being so nice to me?"

"I heard about what you did for Naomi," said Boaz. "You left your family. You left your land. You came here to live with people you didn't know. You've been good to Naomi. So I hope God brings good things to you."

"I hope I keep making you happy," said Ruth. "You've made me feel much better. You've been kind to me. But I know your servant girls are more important than I am."

When it was time to eat, Boaz called to Ruth. "Come and eat over here. Here's some bread for you."

Ruth sat down with the other workers. Boaz gave her some cooked grain to eat. Ruth ate as much as she wanted. She still had some left over.

When Ruth went back to the field, Boaz talked to his workers. "Let her get the grain wherever she wants. Even if she gets it from around the piles you gathered. Don't make her feel bad about it. In fact, pull some grain out of the piles for her. Leave

it for her to pick up. Don't get mad at her."

So Ruth gathered grain there until evening. Then she beat the grain. She threw away the part that wasn't good for eating. She had gathered just a little more than half of a bushel.

Ruth took the grain back to town. When Naomi saw it, she said, "Where did you go? Whose field did you work in?"

"I worked with Boaz today," said Ruth.

"I pray that God brings him good things!" said Naomi. "Boaz is being kind to us! My husband was from his family!"

"Boaz told me to stay with his workers," said Ruth. "He told me to work in his fields until they're finished."

"It's good to go with his servant girls," said Naomi. "In somebody else's field, you might get hurt."

So Ruth worked with Boaz's servant girls. She gathered barley and wheat until the work was done. All that time she lived with Naomi.

A Night in the Barn
RUTH 3

One day Naomi told Ruth, "You should have a husband. You need someone who can take care of you.

Here's our law. Your husband has died. So someone in his family should marry you. Boaz is from your husband's family. You've been working in his field.

"Boaz will work in the barn with the grain tonight. So wash up," said Naomi. "Put on some perfume. Get dressed in your best clothes. Then go to the barn.

"Don't let Boaz see you," said Naomi. "He will eat and drink. Watch him. See where he lies down to rest. Then go over to him. Take the covers off his feet. Then you lie down, too. Boaz will tell you what to do after that."

"All right," said Ruth. "I'll do whatever you want."

So that night Ruth went to the barn. She did just what Naomi had told her to do.

Boaz ate and drank. He was feeling good. There was a big pile of grain on the floor. Boaz went around it to the other side. He lay down there.

Ruth was very quiet. She walked over to Boaz. She took the covers off his feet. Then she lay down, too.

Late in the night, Boaz woke up. He turned over. He saw someone lying by his feet. It was a woman. "Who are you?" he asked.

"I'm Ruth," she answered. "You are from my husband's family. Would you take care of me?"

"God will bring good things to you," said Boaz. "This is the kindest thing you could do for me. You didn't try to get younger men to like you. They might have been rich or poor. But you didn't go after them. So don't be afraid. I'll do what you're asking me. Everybody knows you're a good person."

Boaz went on, "You're right. I'm from your dead husband's family. But there is also another man from your husband's family. By law, he gets to marry you first if he wants. So stay here for the rest of the night. In the morning, I'll ask him. If he wants to marry you, then he can. But if he won't, then God knows that I will. So just stay here until it's morning."

Ruth stayed in the barn until early morning. She got up while it was still dark.

Boaz said, "Don't let anybody know you were here. Now hold out your coat."

Ruth held her coat out. Boaz filled it with grain. He helped tie it around her. Then she went back to Naomi's.

"What happened?" asked Naomi.

Ruth told Naomi everything. She showed Naomi the grain Boaz gave her.

"We'll wait now," said Naomi. "We'll wait to hear what happens. Boaz will find out what he needs to know today."

A Deal at the City Gate

RUTH 4

That same morning Boaz went to the city gate. He sat down. Soon the other man in Naomi's family came by.

"Hello, friend!" called Boaz. "Come sit down by me."

So the man went over and sat by Boaz.

Boaz asked 10 town leaders to sit with them. He said to the man next to him, "Naomi came back from Moab. She is selling land that once belonged to our family. I thought I should tell you. That way you can buy it if you want to. If you don't want it, I'll buy it. By law, you get to choose first."

"Then I'll buy it," said the man.

"Ruth, the woman from Moab, comes with the land," said Boaz. "When you buy the land, you have to marry her."

"Then I can't buy the land," said the man. "You buy it yourself."

Back then, people made a deal this way. One person would take his shoe off. He would give it to the other person. So that's what the man did.

Then Boaz told all the people listening, "You see this. Today I'm buying the land from Naomi. And Ruth will be my wife. You saw the deal we made."

Then the people said, "We saw it. We pray that God will give you children. We pray that you'll have a good family."

So Boaz married Ruth. Later, God gave them a baby boy.

The women of the town were happy for Naomi. "Praise God," they said. "Now you have a family again. We hope everyone hears about Boaz. Ruth loves you, and now you have a grandson! He will cheer you up when you are old."

Naomi held the baby in her lap. She helped take care of him. The women said, "Naomi now has a boy in her family."

They named the baby Obed. He grew up and became Jesse's father. Jesse grew up and became King David's father.

FEBRUARY 18

A Message from an Angel

JUDGES 13

God's people started doing wrong things again. So God let enemies take over. For 40 years, enemies were in charge of the land.

Now there was a husband and wife who had no children. One day God's angel came to the woman. He said, "You are going to have a baby boy. He is going to be special to God. Make sure you don't drink wine. And don't cut the boy's hair.

God wants him to save his people from their enemies."

The woman went to find her husband. "A man came from God to see me," she said. "He looked like an angel. He was wonderful. But I didn't ask where he came from. He didn't tell me his name. He told me I'd have a baby boy. He said not to drink wine. The boy will be special to God."

Then the husband prayed. "Please, God, send this man back to us. Let him teach us how to bring up our boy."

God heard the man pray. So God's angel came back to the woman.

The woman was in the field. But her husband wasn't with her. So she ran to tell him. "That man is here again!" she said.

The husband ran back with his wife to the field. He saw the man. "Are you the man who talked to my wife?" he asked.

"Yes," said the angel.

"What should we do with our boy?" asked the husband. "What rules should we give him?"

The angel said, "Your wife must do what I said. She can't drink wine. She should do just what I told her."

"Stay here," said the husband. "We want to cook some meat for you."

"I won't eat your food," said the angel. "But you can give a gift for God."

The man didn't know that this really was an angel. He asked, "What's your name? We want to think of you when our boy is born."

"Why are you asking for my name?" asked the angel. "It is too great. You wouldn't understand it if I told you."

So the man offered a gift of goat meat and grain. He put it on a rock.

Then a wonderful thing happened. Fire came to burn the meat and grain. Then the angel went up to heaven in the fire.

The man and woman watched. They put their faces down to the ground. The angel didn't come back. So they knew it was God's angel.

"We'll die!" said the man. "We've seen God!"

"But God took our gift," said his wife. "God told us these things. So he couldn't have wanted to kill us."

The man's wife did have a baby boy. They named him Samson. He grew up. God brought good things to him. And God's Spirit started working in him.

FEBRUARY 19

Honey from a Lion

JUDGES 14

One day Samson went to a town. There he saw a young woman. She was not one of God's people. She was from the enemy's people. But Samson wanted to marry her. He told his father and mother, "I want her to be my wife."

"Why don't you marry someone from our people?" they asked. "Do you have to go to the enemy?"

"She is the one I want to marry," said Samson.

Samson's mother and father didn't know that this was God's plan. God was making a way to come against these enemies.

Samson took his mother and father to town. While they were there, Samson walked by a grape field. Suddenly a young, roaring lion jumped out at him.

Then God's Spirit came upon Samson. God's Spirit made Samson strong. He killed the lion just by using his hands. He didn't tell his mother or father what he'd done. He went on to talk to the woman he liked.

Later, Samson went back to marry the woman. He stopped to see what had happened to the lion's body. A lot of bees lived among the lion's bones. There was honey there, too. Samson took some in his hands. He ate it as he traveled.

Samson met up with his mother and father. He gave some of the honey to them. They ate some of it.

But Samson didn't tell them where he got it.

Samson's father went to visit the woman Samson would marry. Then, like most grooms, Samson had a party. Thirty young men were there with him.

"I have a riddle for you," Samson said. "I'll give you seven days to find the answer. Let's say you guess the answer. Then I'll give you 30 sets of everyday clothes and 30 sets of fancy clothes. But what if you don't guess it? Then you have to give me all of the clothes."

"Tell us the riddle," they said.

"Food came out of the eater. The sweet came out of the strong," said Samson.

Three days passed. But they couldn't guess the answer to the riddle.

At last they went to Samson's wife. "Tell Samson to give you the answer," they said. "If you don't, we'll burn you and your whole family. Why did you ask us here anyway? We'll all have to give clothes to Samson. It's like robbing us."

So Samson's wife went to him, crying. "You don't love me," she said. "You told a riddle. But you didn't tell me the answer to it."

"I didn't even tell my father and mother," said Samson. "So why should I tell you?"

Samson's wife cried every day. She kept asking Samson about the riddle. So at last, on the seventh day, Samson told her. Then she went and told the 30 men.

The sun had not gone down yet. So the 30 men went to Samson. They said, "There is nothing sweeter than honey! There is nothing stronger than a lion!"

"You got the answer from my wife," Samson said. "That's the only way you could know the riddle."

Then God's Spirit came upon Samson. He had great power. He went to another enemy town. He killed 30 men there and took their clothes. Then he gave their clothes to the 30 men who answered the riddle.

Samson was very angry. He went back home to live with his father and mother. After he left, his wife married one of his friends.

Fighting with a Jaw Bone
JUDGES 15

Days passed. The time came for the wheat to be gathered in.

Samson went to see his wife. But her father wouldn't let him go into her room. "I thought you didn't like her anymore," he said. "So I let your friend marry her. Look. Her younger sister is even prettier than she is. Why don't you marry her sister?"

"I'll pay my enemies back for this," said Samson. "I'll get them this time!"

Samson left. He caught 300 foxes. He put them in pairs. In each pair, he tied the two foxes' tails together. He tied a stick to their tails. He set fire to the sticks. Then he put the foxes in the enemies' fields.

The wheat that had been gathered was in the fields. So the fields caught on fire. All the wheat burned. The grape fields burned, too. So did the fields of olive trees.

The enemies saw their fields burning. They asked, "Who did this to us?"

"Samson did," someone said. "He did it because his wife married his friend."

So the enemies set his wife's house on fire. She and her father died.

"Now I won't stop until I pay you back," said Samson. So he killed many of the people. Then Samson went to a cave and stayed there.

The enemies got an army together. They camped around the land of Judah.

The men from Judah wondered what was happening. "Why are you coming to fight us?" they asked.

"We came to get Samson," said

the enemies. "We want to pay him back for what he did."

So 3,000 men went from Judah to Samson's cave. "These enemies are in charge of our land," they said. "Don't you know that? Why are you making them angry?"

"I just did to them what they did to me," said Samson.

"We have come to take you to them," said the men.

"Just promise me that you won't kill me," said Samson.

"All right," they said. "We'll only tie you up. Then we'll take you to the enemies."

They tied Samson up with two new ropes. Then they led him away.

The enemies saw Samson coming. They shouted and ran toward him. Then God's Spirit came upon Samson. He got very strong. The rope could not keep him tied. He broke the rope.

Samson picked up a jaw bone from a dead donkey. He began fighting. He killed 1,000 men.

Samson said, "I piled them up with a donkey's jaw bone. With a jaw bone I killed 1,000 men."

Then Samson threw the jaw bone away. People began to call that place Jaw Bone Hill.

Now Samson was very thirsty. So he cried to God. "You helped me win," he said. "Now will I die of thirst?"

Then God opened up a place in the ground. Water came out from it. So Samson drank the water. He felt better.

FEBRUARY 20

Samson's Secret

JUDGES 16

One day Samson went to the city of Gaza. He liked a woman there. So he went to her house. But someone told the people he was there. So they went to the city gate, which was closed. There they waited for Samson. They waited all night. They said, "We'll kill him in the morning."

But Samson left in the middle of the night. He pulled on the gate's doors and posts. He tore them off. He put them on his shoulders. And he took them up to the top of a hill.

Time passed. Samson met a woman named Delilah. He fell in love with her.

The enemy leaders went to Delilah. "See if you can trick Samson," they said. "Trick him into telling you what makes him so strong. Then we can catch him and tie him up. If you'll do this, we'll pay you."

So Delilah asked Samson, "What's

your secret? What makes you so strong? How could someone catch you and tie you up?"

"Tie me with seven new strings from a bow and arrow. Then I won't be the strongest man anymore," said Samson.

So the leaders brought seven bow strings to Delilah. They hid in the room. Delilah tied Samson up. Then she called, "Samson! The enemies are here!"

Samson popped off the bow strings. It was easy for him. It was as if the strings had touched fire. The strings broke in two. So nobody found out Samson's secret.

But Delilah said, "Samson, you made me look dumb. You didn't tell the truth. Please tell me how someone can tie you up."

"Tie me up with new ropes," said Samson. "They must be ropes that nobody has used before. Then I won't be the strongest man anymore."

So the enemies hid in the room. Delilah tied Samson up with new ropes. Then she called, "Samson! The enemies are here!"

Samson popped the ropes off his arms.

"You're just playing with me," said Delilah. "You're not telling me the truth. Now tell me how someone can tie you up."

"Take the seven braids in my hair," said Samson. "Tie them into the loom you make cloth on. Make sure it's tight. Then I won't be the strongest man anymore."

So Delilah waited until Samson was asleep. Then she tied his braids into the loom. She made sure it was tight. She called, "Samson! The enemies are here!"

Samson woke up. He got up. His hair stayed in the loom. But it pulled up the loom and the cloth, too.

"How can you say you love me?" asked Delilah. "You won't tell me your secret. This makes three times you've made me look dumb."

Delilah begged Samson every day. At last Samson couldn't stand it anymore. So he told her his secret. "Since I've been born, I've been special to God. I'm not supposed to shave my hair off. If I do, I won't be the strongest man anymore."

Delilah knew Samson was telling the truth this time. So she sent a message to the enemies. "Samson told me everything. You can catch him now."

The enemies came back. They brought the money to pay Delilah.

Delilah let Samson fall asleep. His head was in her lap. Then a man came and shaved off Samson's braids. He was not strong anymore.

Delilah called, "Samson! The enemies are here!"

Samson woke up. He thought,

"I'll get free like I did before." But there was one thing he didn't know. God had left him.

Then the enemies caught Samson. They poked his eyes out. They locked him up in jail. They tied him up. They made him work hard. But Samson's hair started growing back.

Now the leaders of the enemies got together. They gave a party for their god, who wasn't real. They were feeling good. They shouted, "Bring Samson out here. Let him give us a show."

So they brought Samson out of jail. He did things to make them cheer and laugh.

Then they took Samson over by some big posts. The posts held up the building.

A young man was holding Samson's hand. Samson told him, "I want to rest against the posts. Move me over so I can feel them."

The building was full of people. All the enemy leaders were there. Three thousand people were on the roof. They were watching Samson's show.

Samson prayed, "God, remember me. Make me strong one more time. Let me get back at these people for hurting my eyes."

Samson reached out to the posts. He put his right hand on one post. He put his left hand on the other. He said, "I'll die with my enemies!"

Then Samson pushed as hard as he could. The building fell down on everyone. Samson killed more people when he died than when he lived.

Samson's family went to get his body. They took it with them and put it in a grave. Samson had been the judge of God's people for 20 years.

A Sad Prayer and a Happy Answer
1 SAMUEL 1–2

There was a man who lived in the hills. He had two wives. One had children. The other didn't. The one who didn't was named Hannah.

Every year the man from the hills took a trip. He and his family went to the worship tent. There they would worship God.

The wife with children kept trying to bother Hannah. She would pester Hannah until Hannah cried. Then Hannah wouldn't eat.

Hannah's husband would say to her, "Why are you crying? Why are you so sad? Eat something. Am I not more important to you than 10 children?"

One time after they ate, Hannah got up. She was very sad. So she went to the worship tent to pray.

She cried to God. She asked God for a baby boy. She promised she would let her son serve God.

At that time, Eli was the priest. He was at the door of the worship tent. He was sitting in a chair. He watched Hannah. She was thinking her prayer. Her mouth was moving. But she wasn't talking out loud.

Eli thought Hannah was drunk. So he said, "Throw your wine away! How much longer will you go on getting drunk?"

"I'm not drunk, sir," said Hannah. "Don't think I'm sinning. I'm just very sad. I was praying to God."

"Then you can go home feeling better," said Eli. "I pray that God will give you what you asked for."

So Hannah went and ate. She didn't look sad anymore.

The next morning the family got up early. They worshiped God. Then they went back to their home in the hills.

God remembered Hannah's prayer. She had a baby boy. She named him Samuel. In the language of God's people, the name sounded like some other words. These words were, "I asked God for him."

Hannah's husband went to the worship tent that year. But Hannah didn't go with him. "I'll go when the baby is older," she said. "I'll take him with me. I'll give him to God. He can live there and serve God all his life."

"All right," said her husband. "If that's what you think is best."

So Hannah stayed home. Samuel grew a little older. Then Hannah took him to the worship tent. She took him to Eli, the priest.

"I'm the woman who was praying here," said Hannah. "I prayed for this boy. God gave me what I asked for. So I'm giving my boy, Samuel, to God now. My son will serve God all his life."

Then Samuel worshiped God at the worship tent.

Hannah prayed. "My heart is full of joy. I'm strong in God. He saved me. No one is right and good like God. Don't brag, because God knows. He can tell if what you do is right or not. The one who had no children now has seven. But the one with lots of children is sad.

"God makes people die or live," said Hannah. "He makes people rich or poor. He makes people great or lowly. He helps people who need help. He lets them sit with princes. Other people look up to them.

"God will take care of his people," said Hannah. "But sinful people will live in the dark. People who are against God will be broken. God will judge all the earth."

Then the family went back home. But Samuel stayed to serve God at the worship tent.

Samuel's mother made him a new

robe every year. She and the boy's father came to the worship tent once a year. That's when she brought the robe to Samuel.

Eli prayed for good things for Samuel's mother and father. "I pray that God will give you children," he said. "They'll take Samuel's place, because you gave him to God."

God was kind and loving to Hannah. She had three more boys and two girls.

Eli's Bad Sons

1 SAMUEL 2

Now Eli's sons were bad priests. They didn't obey God. People would bring gifts to the worship tent. The gifts were for God. But the law said priests could have some of the meat.

The meat would boil in a big pot. Then the priest's servant would stick a fork into the pot. He would pull meat out for the priest.

But Eli's sons wanted meat that wasn't cooked yet. So they asked for it before it went into the pot. They said, "Give it to us. If you don't, we'll take it from you ourselves."

To God, this was a great sin. Eli's sons acted as if people's gifts to God were not important.

Now Eli was very old. He heard about what his sons were doing. He heard about their sins. So Eli asked them, "Why are you doing these terrible things? God's people are talking about what you do. What they're saying is not good. If you sin against someone else, God may help you. But when you sin against God, who will help you?"

But Eli's sons did not listen to him.

Samuel grew bigger. Everyone liked him. God was happy with him, too.

One day a man came to visit Eli. He was a prophet, a man who told God's plans. He gave Eli this message from God. "Didn't I show you I was God? I took my people out of Egypt. I chose men to be priests. Why don't you act like people's gifts to me are important? You think your sons are more important than I am. You let them take the best parts of the meat.

"When people think I'm important, I do good things for

123

them. But I won't help people who turn against me. No one in your family will live to grow old. Your two sons will die on the same day. That will be a sign for you. I will choose another priest. He will do what I want."

A Voice at Night

1 SAMUEL 3

Now Samuel served God. Eli was in charge. At that time, God didn't talk to very many people face to face.

Eli's eyes could not see very well. One night he lay down where he always did. The lamp was still giving light. Samuel was sleeping in the worship tent. That's where God's ark box was.

Then God called to Samuel.

"I'm right here," said Samuel. He ran over to Eli. "I'm right here," he said again. "You called me."

"I didn't call you," said Eli. "Go back to bed."

So Samuel went back to bed.

God called again. "Samuel!"

Samuel got up again. He went to Eli. "I'm right here," he said. "You called for me."

"I didn't call you, son," said Eli. "Go back to bed."

Samuel didn't know God yet. God had never talked to him or shown him anything.

God called Samuel again.

Samuel got up and went to Eli. "I'm right here," he said. "You called for me."

Then Eli knew that God was calling Samuel. "Go back to bed," said Eli. Then Eli told Samuel to say these words if God called again. "I'm your servant. I'm listening, God."

So Samuel went back to bed.

Then God came and stood there. He called, "Samuel! Samuel!"

"I'm your servant," said Samuel. "And I'm listening."

"I'm getting ready to do something," said God. "It's something that will surprise people. I will do what I told Eli I'd do. I said I'd judge his family. It's because he knew the bad things his sons were doing. But he didn't stop them."

Samuel lay down. In the morning, he opened the worship tent doors. He was scared to tell Eli what God had said.

But Eli called for Samuel. "What did God tell you?" he asked. "Don't hide what he said."

So Samuel told Eli everything God had said.

"He is God," said Eli. "Let him do what he thinks is good."

Samuel grew up. God was with him all the time. God made sure that people listened to Samuel. All the people saw that Samuel was

God's prophet. He saw God's plans and told about them.

Bad News

1 SAMUEL 4

God's people marched out to fight their enemies. But the enemy army won. So God's people went back to camp.

"Why did God let us lose?" asked the leaders. "Let's take the ark box with us next time. It can save us from the enemies."

So they went and got God's ark box. Eli's two sons went, too. When the ark box got to the army camp, everyone shouted. They shouted so loud that the ground shook.

The enemy army heard the shout. "What are the Jewish people shouting about?" they asked.

They found out that God's ark was in the Jews' camp. Then they were scared. "A god is in the Jews' camp," they said. "Now we're in trouble! We've never faced anything like this before. Who will save us? These gods made all kinds of trouble for Egypt. We must be strong! If we're not, they'll win. Then we'll have to serve them. Be strong men, and fight!"

So the enemy army went out to fight God's people. The enemy army won. They killed lots of men. They took God's ark.

Eli's two sons died in the fight. One man ran to town to tell what had happened.

Eli was sitting in his chair. He was beside the road at the town gate. He was waiting for some news. He was afraid of what might happen to the ark box.

The man got to town. He told everyone what had happened. Everyone in town began to talk and cry about it. They made lots of noise.

Eli heard them. "What's the matter?" he asked. Eli was 98 years old. His eyes couldn't see anymore.

The man went over to Eli. "I just came from the fight," he said.

"What happened?" asked Eli.

"The enemy army won," said the man. "Many of our men were killed. Your two sons are dead, too. The enemies took God's ark."

When Eli heard about the ark box, he fell back. He fell off his chair and broke his neck. He was very old and fat. He had led God's people for 40 years.

The wife of one of Eli's sons heard the news. She was going to have a baby. She heard that the enemy army took God's ark. She learned that her husband was dead and Eli had died, too. She was so scared that she had her baby right then.

The women helping her told her

not to worry. They said she had a baby boy. But she didn't say anything. She named him Ichabod. The name means "no greatness." She said, "God's greatness has left his people."

Trouble for the Enemies

1 SAMUEL 5

The enemy army took God's ark box to a city in their land. They put it in their idol's worship house. Their idol's name was Dagon. They put God's ark by the idol.

The next morning they saw that Dagon had fallen. The idol was in front of God's ark! It was on its face on the ground. So they set Dagon back up.

But the next morning it was the same. Dagon was on the floor in front of God's ark! Dagon's head was broken off. His hands were broken off. They lay at the door. Only his body was left.

Then God sent trouble to the people of the city. He made them get sick. They got big, sore bumps on their bodies.

The people said, "We can't let this ark box stay here. It's the Ark of the Jewish people's God. It's making trouble for us and our god." So they got all the enemy leaders together.

"What can we do with this ark box?" they asked.

"Move it to another city," the leaders said.

So they moved it. But then God sent trouble to that city. The people were very scared. They were getting big, sore bumps now. So they sent God's ark to a third city.

But the people of that city saw the ark box coming. "They're bringing the Ark here to kill us!" they cried. Some of their people were already dead. Some had the big, sore bumps.

The Ark in the Cart

1 SAMUEL 6–7

Seven months passed. "What will we do with this ark box?" asked the enemies. "How can we send it back where it came from?"

The enemy priests thought of an answer. "Send the Ark of the Jewish people's God back," they said. "But send a gift with it. Then you'll get well."

"What gift should we send?" the people asked.

"Make five bumps of gold," said their priests. "Make five gold rats. That's because we have five leaders in our land. Sore bumps and rats are bringing us trouble. Send the gold rats and bumps to the Jewish people's God. Maybe he will take our troubles away. Don't let your hearts get hard. The king of Egypt did that. Then Egypt had to send the Jewish people away.

"Now make a new cart," said the priests. "Get two cows. Make sure the cows have never worked together before. They must also have babies. Put the baby cows in a pen. Put the mother cows in front of the cart to pull it. Put God's ark on the cart. Put a box beside the Ark with the gold things in it. Then send the cart off.

"Watch the cart," said the priests. "Let's say it goes back to the land of the Jews. Then we'll know God brought us these troubles. But what if it doesn't go back? Then we'll know these troubles just happened. God didn't send them."

So that's what the people did. They put the cows in front of the cart to pull it. They put the baby cows in a pen. They put God's ark on the cart. They put the box of gold things next to it.

The cows went right down the road. They didn't go to the right. They didn't go to the left. They were mooing all the way. They went right back to the land of the Jews.

Some of God's people were gathering wheat. They were in a valley. They looked up and saw God's ark box coming. They were very happy.

The cart went to a field. It stopped next to a rock. So the people cut up the wood that made the cart. Then they burned it on an altar. The cows became the meat on the altar. It was a gift for God.

The priests for God's people took God's ark box. They put it on a big rock. They put the other box on the rock, too. It had the gold rats and gold bumps in it. They gave other gifts to God there, too.

The enemy leaders had been watching all this. After they saw what happened, they went back home.

Then some of God's people looked into the ark box. So God made them die. The rest of the people cried. It was hard on them. "Who can come and stand where God is?" asked the people. "Where will the Ark go now?"

They sent a message to another town. "The enemies sent God's ark back. Come and get it. Take it to your town."

The people from the other town came and got it. They took it to a house on a hill. They got someone to guard it. That's where God's ark stayed for 20 years.

Fighting with Thunder

1 SAMUEL 7

God's people cried. They tried to find out what God wanted.

Samuel, God's prophet, talked to the people. "Are you coming back to God?" he asked. "Are you loving him with your whole heart? Then get rid of the idols you worship. Follow only God. Serve him. Then he will save you from your enemies."

So the people put their idols away. They began serving only God.

Then Samuel called all of the people together in one place. "I'll pray to God for you," he said.

The people came together. They went without food all day. They told God about their sins. "We've done wrong," they said.

Now their enemies heard that all of God's people were in one place. So they came to fight against them.

God's people were scared. "Don't stop praying for us," they told Samuel. "We need God to save us from our enemies."

So Samuel prayed to God for the people. God answered Samuel. Samuel was giving a gift on the altar. The enemies were coming close to fight. But God spoke in a loud voice. It sounded like a clap of thunder in a storm.

Their enemies got scared. They began running this way and that. Then God's people ran out to fight them. God's people won.

Samuel got a stone. He set it up and called it "The Help Stone." He said, "God has helped us so far."

As long as Samuel lived, God worked against their enemies.

Samuel was a judge for God's people all his life. When people would disagree, he'd say who was right. Samuel traveled around to judge the people. He was a judge in the city where his home was, too. He built an altar there to God.

Saul, the First King

Give Us a King!

1 SAMUEL 8

Now Samuel got old. He told his sons they could judge God's people. But Samuel's sons weren't like Samuel. They were not fair. People would pay Samuel's sons. Then his sons would not tell the truth. They would judge those people to be right. His sons would judge other people to be wrong.

The leaders came to Samuel. "You're old now," they said. "Your sons don't judge the way you do. So choose a king for us. All the other nations have kings."

Samuel wasn't happy about this. So he asked God about it.

"Listen to the people," said God. "They're not turning against you. They're turning against me as their king. They're doing what they have always done. They are forgetting me. They're following fake gods. So listen to them. But tell them what

will happen. Tell them what a king will do."

So Samuel told the people what God had said. "Here's what a king will do," he said. "He will make your sons work with his horses and chariots. They'll have to run in front of his chariots. Some will have to be captains in the army. Some will have to work in his fields. Some will have to make spears to fight with. Your daughters will have to cook and bake for him. They'll have to make perfume for him.

"A king will take your best fields to be his own. He will take some of your grain and wine. He will take some of your servants. He will take your best cows, donkeys, and sheep. You'll have to serve him. Then you'll cry to God. You'll want to get rid of your king. But God won't answer you."

The people would not listen to Samuel. They said, "No! We want a king. Then we'll be like the other

129

lands. A king can lead us. He can lead us out to fight!"

Samuel told God what the people had said. Then God said, "Get a king for them."

So Samuel said he would. Then he told the people to go home.

Looking for Lost Donkeys

1 SAMUEL 9

Now there was a young man named Saul. People said good things about him. No other young man was quite like him. He was a head taller than the other young men.

Saul's father had donkeys. One day his donkeys got lost. So he told Saul, "Go look for our donkeys. Take a servant with you."

Saul looked all over the hill country. But he didn't find them there. So Saul and his servant went to another place. But they didn't find the donkeys. They went through the land of Benjamin's family group. But they didn't find any donkeys.

Saul and the servant went to one more place. Saul said, "We'd better go home. My dad will worry about us more than about the donkeys."

But the servant said, "A prophet lives near here. He sees and tells God's plans. Everyone looks up to him. Whatever he says comes true. Maybe he can tell us where to find the donkeys."

"What can we give him?" asked Saul. "We have no more food in our bags. We didn't bring any gift with us."

"I have some silver," said the servant. "I can give it to the prophet. That way he will tell us which way to go."

"All right," said Saul. "Then let's go."

Saul and his servant walked up the hill to town. Some girls were coming from the town. They were going to get water at the well.

"Is the prophet here?" Saul asked.

"Yes," they said. "He just came to town today. But hurry. The people are giving gifts on the altar today. He will be going there to eat. People won't eat until he gets there. He has to pray for what they are giving. Then people will eat. So go now. You should be able to find him."

Saul and his servant went into the town. Right then, Samuel was coming toward them. He was on his way to the altar.

Samuel knew about Saul. God had said the day before, "I'm sending a man to you. He will come about this time tomorrow. Put oil on

130

his head. Choose him to be my people's king. He will save them from their enemies."

Now Saul was coming into town. God told Samuel, "Here's the man I told you about. He will be my people's king."

Saul came up to Samuel at the gate. "Could you tell me where the prophet's house is?" he asked.

"I'm the prophet," said Samuel. "Go up ahead of me to the altar. You are to eat with me today. Tomorrow morning I'll tell you what's in your heart. Then you may go home. Don't worry about the donkeys. Your father found them. All God's people want you to be king."

"Why are you saying that to me?" asked Saul. "My father's family is the smallest. All the other families are more important than we are."

But Samuel took Saul and his servant with him. He gave them the best seats. About 30 people were there.

Samuel talked to the cook. "Remember the piece of meat I told you to save? Bring it here."

So the cook brought the meat. He gave it to Saul.

"This meat was saved for you," said Samuel. "Eat it. It was saved for this special time." So Saul ate with Samuel.

After dinner they went back to town. Samuel took Saul up on the roof of his house. They talked for a while. Then Saul spent the night at Samuel's house.

The sun began to come up the next morning. Samuel called to Saul, "Get ready. It's time to go. I'm going to send you home."

So Saul got ready. Then Saul and Samuel went outside. They went to the edge of town.

Samuel said, "Tell your servant to go on. I want you to stay here for a while. God has a message for me to give you."

So the servant went on ahead.

Long Live Our King!

1 SAMUEL 10

Samuel took out a small jar of oil. He put some oil on Saul's head. Then he kissed Saul. He said, "God has made you king of his people. As you travel today, you'll meet two men. They'll say that the donkeys were found. They'll say that your father is worried about you.

"Then go to the big oak tree," said Samuel. "You will meet three men there. One will carry three young goats. One will carry three loaves of bread. One will carry a jug of wine. They'll say hello to you. They'll give you two loaves of bread. Take the bread.

"Then you'll come near a town," said Samuel. "A parade of prophets will come down the hill. They'll play harps, tambourines, flutes, and lyres. They'll tell God's messages. Then God's Spirit will come on you. You'll have power. You'll tell God's messages, too. You will change. You will be different. After this, do whatever you need to do. God is with you.

"Go on ahead of me. I'll come to see you next week. Then I'll tell you what to do," said Samuel.

So Saul left Samuel. And God changed Saul's heart. Everything happened just the way Samuel said it would. The parade of prophets met Saul. God's Spirit came upon him. He had power. Then he told God's messages along with the prophets.

People saw Saul with the prophets. They asked, "What happened to Saul? Is he a prophet, too?" So that became a saying. People would say, "Is Saul a prophet, too?"

Saul's uncle asked, "Where were you?"

"We went to look for the donkeys," said Saul. "But we couldn't find them. So we went to see Samuel."

"What did Samuel tell you?" asked his uncle.

"He said the donkeys had been found," said Saul. But he didn't tell his uncle about being the king.

Now Samuel called God's people together. He told them that God said, "I took my people out of Egypt. I saved you from your enemies. But now you've turned against me. You have asked for a king to rule you. So now you must come and stand in front of me."

All the family groups came near. God picked the family group of Benjamin. So the families from the group of Benjamin came near. God picked Saul's family. At last God picked Saul.

But no one could find Saul. They asked God, "Is Saul here yet?"

"Yes," said God. "Saul is hiding behind the boxes and bags."

The people ran over to the bags. They pulled Saul out. He stood up. He was tall. His head and shoulders were above everyone else.

"See this man?" said Samuel. "God chose him to be your king. There's no one else like him."

"Long live our king!" the people shouted.

Samuel told the people the rules of having a king. He wrote the rules down. Then he sent the people home.

Saul went home too. Brave men went with him. God had worked in their hearts.

There were some men who did bad things. They said, "How can Saul save us?" They hated Saul and didn't bring gifts to him. But Saul didn't say anything about it.

Hiding

1 SAMUEL 13

Saul was 30 years old. He was the king of God's people for the next 42 years. He had a wife. He also had three sons and two daughters.

Abner was the leader of Saul's army. Their fathers were brothers. So they were cousins. Saul led 2,000 men. One of his sons, Jonathan, led 1,000 men.

Jonathan took his men to fight one small enemy camp. But the rest of the enemy army heard about it. So they got together to fight Saul.

Then Saul sent men through the land. They blew horns and told about the fight. "Saul fought the enemy army," they said. "Now these enemies hate us." So the people came together to follow Saul.

Now the enemy army had 3,000 chariots. They had 6,000 chariot drivers. They had as many army men as sand by the sea.

The enemies hadn't let God's people make any tools. The enemies said, "They might make swords or spears!" So God's people even had to buy farm tools from the enemy. Now it was time to fight. But none of God's people had swords. Only Saul and Jonathan had swords.

The men with Saul were so afraid, they were shaking. They knew that they were in trouble. They hid in caves and bushes. They hid behind rocks. They hid in wells.

Samuel had told Saul to wait seven days for him. Samuel was going to offer gifts to God before the fight. He was going to ask God to help Saul's army. But when Samuel didn't come, Saul's men started leaving him.

So Saul said, "Bring me the things to offer to God." Then Saul offered the gifts on the altar.

Right after that, Samuel came. "What did you do?" asked Samuel.

"My men were leaving," said Saul. "You didn't come when you said you would. The enemy army is ready to fight us. I thought that it would come. And I hadn't asked for God's help. So I had to offer the gifts to God myself."

"That was not wise," said Samuel. "You did not wait for me. You have not obeyed God. If you had, your family would have been kings forever. Now your kingdom won't last. It's because you have not obeyed God. God has found a man who obeys him. God has chosen this man to lead his people."

Then Samuel left. Saul counted his men. There were only about 600.

Jonathan Climbs up a Cliff

1 SAMUEL 14

One day Jonathan had an idea. He told it to a young man who was his helper. "Let's go where the enemy is," said Jonathan.

Jonathan didn't tell his father he was going. So no one knew Jonathan had left.

"Maybe God will help us," said Jonathan. "Nothing can keep God from saving us. He can save us if there are lots of us. He can save us if we're a small group."

"Do whatever you think," said his helper. "Go on. I'm with you all the way."

They walked through a mountain pass. Cliffs were on each side. One cliff was on the north. One cliff was on the south.

"Come this way," said Jonathan. "We'll cross over here. We'll let the enemies see us. They may say that we should wait and they'll come over to us. Then we'll stay. We won't go over to them.

"But they may tell us to come and fight. Then we'll climb up. That will be a sign that God will help us win."

So they let the enemies see them.

"Look!" said the enemies. "It's the Jewish people! They're coming out of the caves where they were hiding." They called out to Jonathan and his helper. "Come up here! We'll show you who is in charge!"

"Follow me," said Jonathan to his helper. "God will help us win."

So Jonathan climbed up with his hands and feet. His helper followed. Then Jonathan began to fight the enemies. His helper came right behind him. They killed about 20 men.

Then God made the ground shake. The whole enemy army got scared. Now Saul's guards were watching. They saw the enemy army running away from them.

Saul said, "Bring everybody together. Let's see who is missing."

So Saul's army came together. Jonathan and his helper were missing. But Saul saw the enemies running here and there. So he led his army out to fight.

They found that the enemies were fighting each other. The enemies didn't know what was going on. There was a lot of panic.

The Jews who were hiding heard about it. So they came out to fight. And God saved his people.

Honey on a Stick

1 SAMUEL 14

God's people were having a hard time that day. It's because Saul made them promise not to eat anything.

They couldn't eat until that evening when the battle was over.

The whole army went into the woods. There they found honey on the ground. But nobody ate any. They had promised not to eat.

Jonathan had not heard about the promise. So he dipped his walking stick into the honey. He ate some. He felt stronger right away.

"Your father made us promise not to eat," said an army man. "That's why we're so tired."

"My father is making trouble for us," said Jonathan. "See how much stronger I feel after eating some honey? It would have been better for the men to eat. We could have killed even more enemies."

The men were very tired and hungry. They took the enemies' sheep and cows. They killed some right there and ate the meat. They even left the blood in the meat.

Someone said, "Look! They're sinning. They're eating meat with blood still in it."

"Bring the sheep and cows here," said Saul. "Eat the meat here. But don't leave the blood in it." Then Saul built an altar to God for the first time.

"Let's fight the enemies at night!" said Saul.

"Whatever you want," said the men.

"Let's ask God about it," said the priest.

So Saul asked God, "Should we fight? Will you help us win?"

But God didn't answer Saul.

So Saul said, "All you leaders, come here. Somebody must have sinned today. Whoever did will die, even if it's Jonathan, my own son."

Nobody said anything.

"You men stand over there," said Saul. "Jonathan and I will stand here."

"Whatever you want," said the men.

Then Saul prayed to God. They threw lots, which is like rolling dice. It showed that Jonathan was to blame.

"What did you do?" asked Saul.

"I just ate a little honey," said Jonathan. "Are you going to kill me for that?"

"Yes," said Saul.

But his men said, "Does he have to die? He helped us win against the enemy army. We can't let you kill him. He had God's help in the fight today."

So the men saved Jonathan. He was not killed.

After that, Saul stopped chasing the enemy army. Then the enemies went back to their own land.

As long as Saul was king, he would always fight enemies.

Sometimes Saul would see a man who was strong or brave. Then he would put that man in his army.

Why Do I Hear Sheep?

1 SAMUEL 15

Samuel went to King Saul. Samuel said, "God says to fight the enemy people of Amalek. God brought his people out of Egypt. But the people of Amalek were mean to God's people. So this will pay them back. Kill them all. But don't take anything that belongs to them."

So Saul got his army together. They marched out to fight the people of Amalek and killed them. But Saul kept the king of Amalek alive. He kept the best sheep and cows. The army men kept everything that looked good to them. They got rid of what looked bad.

Then God told Samuel, "I'm sad. I'm sad because I made Saul king. He does not obey me."

Samuel was upset. He prayed to God all night. He got up early the next morning. He went to see King Saul.

But Saul wasn't there. Someone said, "Saul is building a big stone monument. He is building it to make his name great."

Samuel went and found Saul.

King Saul said, "I hope God brings good things to you! I did what God said."

"Then why do I hear sheep?" asked Samuel. "Why do I hear cows?"

"My men brought them back," said the king. "We kept the best to give to God. But we got rid of everything else."

"Stop!" said Samuel. "I'll tell you what God told me last night."

"All right," said King Saul.

"Once you didn't think you were so great," said Samuel. "God chose you to be king. God gave you a job. God said to get rid of the enemy people of Amalek. Did you obey? You didn't get rid of everything."

"I did too," said Saul. "I killed the enemy people of Amalek. I brought their king back. It was the men who took sheep and cows. They took them as a gift for your God."

But Samuel said, "Obeying is better than giving a gift. Turning away from God is sin. Being proud is like worshiping idols. You have turned against God. So he is turning against you."

"I have sinned," said King Saul. "I was afraid of the people. So I let them do what they wanted. Please forgive me. Come back with me so I can worship God."

"No," said Samuel. "I won't go with you."

Samuel turned around to walk

away. But King Saul took hold of his robe. It tore.

Samuel said, "God has torn your kingdom from you today. God will give it to somebody better than you. God is great. God doesn't lie, and he doesn't change his mind. He is not a man."

"I have sinned," said Saul. "Please show me that I'm important to you. Please come back with me. I want to worship your God."

So Samuel went with King Saul. The king worshiped God.

Then Samuel said, "Bring the enemy king."

They brought the enemy king to Samuel. Samuel killed him.

Then Samuel left. And King Saul went back home. Samuel never went to see Saul again. But Samuel cried about Saul.

Choosing the Next King

1 SAMUEL 16

God spoke to Samuel. "How long will you be sad about Saul?" he asked. "Put oil in your jar. Go to see Jesse in Bethlehem. One of his sons will be the next king."

"How can I get a new king?" asked Samuel. "Saul will hear about it. Then he will kill me."

"Go to Bethlehem to offer a gift to me," said God. "Ask Jesse to come

too. Then I'll tell you what to do. Put oil on the man I show you."

So Samuel went to Bethlehem. The people of the town met him. He asked them to come offer gifts to God. He asked Jesse and his sons to come too.

Samuel saw Jesse's first son. "This must be the one God chose," he thought.

But God said, "Don't choose someone by his looks. Don't choose by how tall he is. I don't look at people the way you do. People only see what others look like. I see what's in their hearts."

Jesse called his next son. "He is not the one God chose," said Samuel.

Jesse called his next son. "He is not the one God chose," said Samuel.

Soon seven of Jesse's sons had come. "God didn't choose any of these young men," said Samuel. "Are these all the sons you have?"

"My youngest son is not here," said Jesse. "He is out taking care of the sheep."

"Go get him," said Samuel. "We won't do anything until he gets here."

So they went and got David. God said, "He is the one."

So Samuel put oil on David's head. Then God's Spirit came upon David. God's Spirit gave David power.

But God's Spirit had left Saul. A bad spirit had come on Saul instead. Saul's servants told him, "A bad spirit bothers you. Why don't you get somebody who plays the harp? He can play when the bad spirit bothers you. Then you'll feel better."

"All right," said Saul. "Find someone who plays the harp. Bring him here."

"I've seen one of Jesse's sons," said a servant. "He can play the harp. He is brave and is a good fighter. He knows how to talk to people. He is good looking, and God is with him."

So Saul sent a message to Jesse. "Send David here."

Jesse got some bread and wine. He put all of this on a donkey. He got a young goat. He sent his son David to Saul with these gifts.

Saul liked David. So David began to serve Saul. Sometimes David carried Saul's heavy armor.

Saul sent another message to Jesse. "I'm happy with your son. Please let him stay here to serve me."

David played his harp when the bad spirit bothered Saul. Then Saul would feel better. The bad spirit would leave.

MARCH 1

The Giant

1 SAMUEL 17

Now the enemy army came out to fight. The men made their camp on a hill.

So Saul got his men together. They made their camp across the valley.

A winning fighter was in the enemy camp. His name was Goliath. He was more than nine feet tall! He wore a hard metal helmet on his head. He wore very heavy metal armor. He wore a metal guard on the front of each leg. He carried a long, thin, pointed spear on his back. Another spear had a sharp point that weighed 15 pounds. A man went in front of Goliath, carrying a big shield.

One day Goliath stood up. He shouted at God's people. "Choose a man to come out and fight me. If he kills me, we'll be your servants. But if I kill him, you'll be our servants."

Goliath came out every morning and evening for 40 days. Saul and all God's people were afraid.

Now Jesse was very old. His three oldest sons were in Saul's army. His son David was Saul's helper. He'd be with Saul for a while. Then he'd go home for a while to care for his father's sheep.

One day Jesse called David. "Here's some grain and 10 loaves of bread," he said. "They are for your brothers. Hurry to the army camp. Take these 10 blocks of cheese to the captain. Find out how everyone is doing. Then come back and tell me."

David set out early in the

morning. He left his sheep with another shepherd. Then he went to the army camp.

Now the men were taking their places to fight. They were shouting their war cry. So David went to the man who kept the food. He left the bread and grain and cheese there. Then he ran to where his brothers were. He said hello.

Just then, Goliath came out. He shouted at God's people, just as he always did. David heard him.

Then God's people ran from Goliath. They were very scared. "Look how he keeps coming out!" they said. "The king will pay lots of money to anyone who kills him. The king will also let that man marry his daughter. His family won't have to pay taxes."

So David talked to some men close by. He asked, "Is that really what the king will do?"

The men told David again that the king would do this.

David's oldest brother heard him talking to the men. He got mad at David. "Why are you here?" he asked. "Who did you leave the sheep with? I know how proud you are. I know your heart is full of sin. You just came here to watch the battle!"

"What did I do now?" asked David. "Can't I even talk?" Then David turned to some others. He

asked the same question. They gave the same answer.

Somebody told King Saul what David was asking. So Saul sent for David.

"Nobody should be scared of Goliath," said David. "I'll go fight him."

"You can't go fight Goliath," said Saul. "You're just a boy. Goliath has been a fighter for years."

"I've been taking care of my father's sheep," said David. "When a lion or bear took a sheep, I chased it. I hit it and took the sheep back. When it came after me, I killed it."

David went on. "I've killed lions and bears. This man Goliath will be just like them. He has come against God's army. God is alive and well. He saved me from the lion and the bear. He will save me from Goliath."

"Go on, then," said Saul. "I pray that God will be with you."

Then Saul gave David his own heavy metal armor. He put his metal helmet on David's head. He gave David his sword. Then David tried to walk around. But he wasn't used to the heavy armor.

"I can't wear these," said David. "I'm not used to them." So he took them off.

David picked up the stick that he used for walking. He went to a brook. He took five smooth stones from the water. He put them into his shepherd's bag. Then David took his sling in his hand. He would use it to throw the stones. He walked toward Goliath.

Goliath came closer and closer to David. Goliath's helper carried his big shield in front of him. Goliath took a good look at David. He could see that David was only a boy. He could see that David was good looking. Goliath hated David.

"Do you think I'm a dog?" asked Goliath. "Do you come against me with sticks?" Then he asked his fake gods to do bad things to David. "Come over here," he said to David. "I'll let the birds and animals eat you up."

"You come against me with a sword," said David. "But I come against you in the name of the Lord. Today God will give you to me. I'll hit you. You'll fall down dead. Then I'll cut off your head!

"Today the birds and animals will eat your army," said David. "Then everybody in the world will know there is a God. He doesn't save by swords and spears. The fight is God's. He will help us win!"

Goliath came closer. David ran out to meet him. David got a stone from his bag. He swung his sling around. The stone flew out. It went right into the front of Goliath's head. Goliath fell down with his face to the ground.

David ran to Goliath. He pulled out Goliath's sword. He killed Goliath and cut off his head. David took Goliath's sword and spear. He put them in his own tent.

The enemies turned and ran away. God's people shouted and ran after them. God's people won the battle.

MARCH 2

A Friend, a Spear, and a Wife

1 SAMUEL 18

Saul's son Jonathan became David's good friend. He loved David as much as he loved himself. From that day, David lived at Saul's palace. He didn't go back home.

Jonathan and David made a promise to be special friends. Jonathan took off his own robe. He gave it to David. Jonathan also gave David his long shirt and his belt. He gave David his sword and his bow for shooting arrows.

David was good at whatever job Saul gave him. So Saul made David the leader of many men in the army. That made the people happy. The leaders of the army were happy too.

The army came back home after Goliath was killed. Women came out of all the towns on the way. They met King Saul and his men. They danced and sang happy songs. They played music and shook tambourines. "Saul killed thousands," they sang. "But David killed tens of thousands."

The women's song made Saul mad. "They said David killed tens of thousands," said Saul. "They said I only killed a few thousand. David has everything. Now all he needs is to be king." From then on, Saul watched David. He was angry because the people liked David best.

The next day a bad spirit came on Saul. It was strong. So David played the harp for Saul.

All of a sudden, Saul threw his spear at David. Saul thought, "I'll pin David to the wall." But David ducked. That happened two times.

Saul was scared of David. That's because God was not with Saul anymore. God was with David.

So Saul made David the leader of 1,000 men. Then he sent them out to fight. But David won every time, because God was with him. All the people loved David.

Saul told David, "I'll let you marry my older daughter. Just keep serving me and fighting with the army." Saul wanted David to get killed in the battle.

"How could I marry a princess?" asked David. "I'm not from an important family."

So Saul let his older daughter marry someone else. But Saul's daughter Michal loved David. Somebody told Saul about it. Saul was very happy to hear this news. "I'll let Michal marry David," he said. "Then the enemies will kill him."

Saul told David, "You have another chance. You can still be in my family."

Saul even made a plan with his servants. "Tell David that I like him. Tell him all my servants like him. Ask him to marry Michal."

So Saul's servants told David.

"Only important people can be in the king's family," said David. "I'm poor. Nobody knows who I am."

The servants went back and told this to Saul. Saul said, "Tell David he can pay to marry my daughter. All he has to do is kill 100 enemy men." Saul hoped the enemy men would kill David instead.

The servants told David what

Saul had said. Then David was glad he could be in the king's family. He took his men with him. He killed 200 enemy men. So Saul let Michal marry David.

Then Saul saw that God was with David. Saul also saw that his daughter loved David. So Saul was even more scared of David. Saul was David's enemy for the rest of his life.

David kept going out to fight, and he kept winning. Soon everyone knew who David was.

Michal's Trick

1 SAMUEL 19

King Saul told Jonathan and his servants to kill David. But Jonathan loved David. So he told David, "Be careful. My father is going to try to kill you. You should go hide. I'll talk to my father about you. I'll let you know what he says."

Jonathan told his father good things about David. "Don't hurt him," said Jonathan. "He hasn't hurt you. He has done good things for you. He put his life in danger to kill Goliath. God won for his people. You liked that. So why should you hurt David? Why kill him for nothing?"

Saul listened to Jonathan. "I won't kill David," Saul promised.

Jonathan told David what his father had said. So David went back to live with Saul's family.

One day a bad spirit came on Saul again. So David played the harp for Saul. Suddenly, Saul threw his spear at David. He tried to pin David to the wall. David ran. The spear went into the wall.

That night Saul sent some men to David's house. They watched the house all night. They were going to kill David the next morning.

But David's wife, Michal, told him about it. "You'd better get away tonight," she said. "If you don't, they'll kill you tomorrow." Michal helped David climb out a window. So David got away.

Then Michal put a stone idol in David's bed. The idol was shaped like a person. Michal pulled the covers over it. She put goats' hair where David's head would have been.

The next morning the men came to get David. Michal said, "He is sick."

They went and told Saul. But Saul sent the men back. He said, "Bring him to me anyway. I'm going to kill him."

So the men went into David's bedroom. They found the stone in David's bed. They found the goats' hair where his head would have been.

"Why did you trick me?" Saul asked Michal. "Why did you let my enemy get away?"

Michal said, "David told me to let him go. He said he didn't want to have to kill me, too."

David ran away to Samuel. He told Samuel what King Saul had done. Then David and Samuel went to another town together.

Now someone told Saul where David was. So the king sent some men to go get David. But they met up with Samuel. He was with a group of prophets. They were speaking God's messages.

God's Spirit came upon Saul's men. They began speaking God's words too.

Somebody told Saul what had happened. So he sent some more men. But the same thing happened to them. So Saul sent some more men. The same thing happened to them.

At last Saul went himself. Then God's Spirit came upon King Saul, too. Saul spoke God's words. He even took off his robe. The king spoke God's words all day and night. Samuel was standing right there with him.

The Arrow

1 SAMUEL 20

David went to find Jonathan. "What did I do?" David asked Jonathan.

"How did I hurt your father? Why is he trying to kill me?"

"He will never kill you," said Jonathan. "You won't die. See? My father always tells me what he is going to do. So why would he keep this a secret? He would tell me."

David said, "Your father knows we're friends. He knows it would hurt you if you knew. I'm sure I'm just a moment away from death."

"I'll do whatever you want," said Jonathan.

"There's a new moon tomorrow," said David. "That's when I'm supposed to eat with the king. But I'll hide in the field instead. Your father might miss me. So tell him I had to go home. If he says that's all right, then I'm safe. But if he gets angry, I'm in trouble. That means he wants to hurt me."

David went on. "Now, who will tell me if your father gets mad?"

"Let's go into the field," said Jonathan. So they went out to the field together.

"I'll find out my father's plans," said Jonathan. "If he is going to hurt you, I'll let you know. Then you can get away and be safe. I pray that God will be with you. Just like he was with my father. But be kind to me so I won't get killed. Be kind to my family, too."

Then David and Jonathan promised to be kind to each other.

"No one will sit in your chair tomorrow," said Jonathan. "People will miss you. The day after tomorrow, hide by the big rock. I'll shoot three arrows to the side of the rock. Then I'll send a boy to get the arrows.

"I might say to the boy that the arrows are on this side. That will mean you're safe," said Jonathan. "You can come back. Or I might say to him that the arrows are far away. That will mean you should leave. But remember. We're friends forever."

So David hid in the field. The next day King Saul sat down for dinner. His place was by the wall. Jonathan sat across from him. Abner sat by Saul. But no one sat in David's chair. Saul didn't say anything about it.

The next day came. Still no one sat in David's chair. Saul asked Jonathan, "Why isn't David here? He didn't come yesterday or today."

"He had to go home," said Jonathan.

Then Saul got angry at Jonathan. "You son of a sinner!" he said. "I know you're on David's side. But you'll never be king as long as he is alive! Now bring him here. He has to die!"

"Why?" asked Jonathan. "What did he do?"

Saul became angry and threw his spear at Jonathan. He tried to kill him. So Jonathan was sure that his father planned to kill David.

Jonathan was very angry. He left the table. He wouldn't eat anything. He was sad about the way his father treated David.

The next day Jonathan went to the field. A little boy went with him. "Go find the arrows I shoot," said Jonathan.

So the boy ran. Jonathan shot an arrow into the field. The boy ran to where it landed. Jonathan called, "The arrow is far away. It is past you." Then he called, "Hurry and go fast! Don't stop!"

The boy picked up the arrow and ran back to Jonathan. He didn't know this was a message for David. Jonathan gave his bow and arrows to the boy. "Take these back to town," he said.

The boy left. Then David came out from behind the big rock. He bowed three times to Jonathan. He put his face to the ground.

Then David and Jonathan hugged each other. They both cried. But David cried the most.

"Go in peace," said Jonathan. "We've promised to be friends. God knows about our promise."

So David left. Then Jonathan went back home.

Goliath's Sword

1 SAMUEL 21; Psalm 56:1-4, 13

David went to the town of Nob. He went to a priest there. The priest was afraid of David. "Why did you come by yourself?" he asked.

"The king sent me to do a secret job," said David. "I told my men to meet me somewhere else. What do you have to eat? I need five loaves of bread. I'll take anything you can give me."

"I don't have any plain bread," said the priest. "But there is some special, holy bread here."

"We are on a special job," said David.

So the priest gave him the special bread.

"Do you have a spear or sword here?" asked David. "I was in a hurry. So I didn't bring mine."

"Goliath's sword is here," said the priest. "Take it if you want it. It's the only sword here."

"There is no other sword like that one," said David. "I'll take it."

Now one of Saul's shepherds was there that day. He saw David.

Then David ran away. He knew he had to get away from Saul. He went to Gath in the enemy's land. The king of Gath had servants. They said, "Isn't this David? He is the one the song is about.

"The song says that Saul killed a few thousand. But David killed tens of thousands."

David heard what they said. So he was afraid of the king of Gath. David wrote this song in Gath.

Be kind to me, God.
Men are chasing me.
All day these proud men fight.
I will trust in you when I am
    afraid.
I praise your word.
I trust in God.
I will not be afraid.
What can people do to me?

I can walk with God.
He gives light to my life.

Then David acted like he had gone crazy. He made marks on the doors at the gate. He did it with his finger nails. He let spit run out of his mouth and down his beard.

The king of Gath said, "See that? David is crazy! Don't bring him to me. Do I need more crazy men here? Did you bring him here so I could watch him? Does he have to come into my house?"

Taste and See

PSALM 34:1-10

The king of Gath sent David away. Then David wrote this song.

I will always tell how wonderful
    God is.
My lips will always praise him.
My soul will tell how great God is.
Let everyone who has problems
    hear and be glad.
Praise God with me.

People shine with joy when they
    love God.
Their faces never look like they
    feel bad.
I called God, and he heard me.
God saved me from all my
    troubles.
God's angel stays around people
    who love God.
He saves them.

Taste and see. God is good.
Good things come to people who
    trust him.
People who love him have all they
    need.
Lions might get hungry and weak.
But people who look to God have
    every good thing they need.

Come, My Children

PSALM 34:11-22

Come, my children, and listen to me.
I will teach you to love God.
If you want to love life,
    then don't say bad things.
If you want to have many good days,
    don't lie.

Turn away from sin. Do good.
Look for the way of peace.

God watches over
    people who do what's right.
God listens to them.
But God turns his face away
    from people who sin.
Nobody will remember them.

People who do right cry to God, and
    he hears.
He saves them from all their troubles.
God is near people who have
    broken hearts.
God saves people who are sad.

A person who does what's right
    might see lots of trouble.
But God saves him
    from all his troubles.
God takes care of him.
None of his bones will be broken.

Sin will kill bad people.
The enemies of God's people
    will not be saved.
But God saves his people.

MARCH 5

Saul's Shepherd Tells

*1 SAMUEL 22; 1 CHRONICLES 12;
PSALM 142*

David ran away to a cave. His
brothers heard where he was. They
went to meet him. People who

didn't like King Saul went with David. He was their leader. There were about 400 men.

David wrote this prayer.

I cry out loud to God.
I tell him my troubles.
My spirit gets weak inside me.
But you still know my way, God.
People have set a trap for me.
No one seems to care about me.
There is no safe place.

So I cry to you, God.
I say, "You are a place to be safe."
Listen to my cry.
I need you very badly.
Save me from those who chase me.
They are too strong for me.
Set me free from my jail so I can
   praise you.

Then people who do what's right
   will come around me.
They'll come because you are good
   to me.

The men with David were brave and ready to fight. They were good at using a spear and shield. They were as brave and strong as lions. They were as fast as deer on the mountains.

Other men came to be with David. They came to the cave where he went to hide. David went out to meet them. "Did you come to help me?" he asked. "If you did, I'm ready to work with you. But if you came to catch me, you're in trouble."

Then God's Spirit came on one of the leaders. He said, "We are with you, David! We want you to win. We want your helpers to win. Your God will help you!"

David went to the king of Moab. "Will you let my father and mother stay with you?" David asked. "May they stay until I find out what God wants?"

The king said yes. So David's father and mother stayed in the land of Moab. David stayed in the cave.

But a prophet named Gad said, "Don't stay here. You should go back to the land of Judah."

So David left. He went to a forest in Judah.

Now Saul found out where David was. Saul was sitting under a tree on a hill. All his leaders stood around him. Saul said, "Listen! Will David give you fields? Will he make you leaders? Is that why you've made plans against me? Nobody tells me when Jonathan makes a deal with David. Nobody cares about me."

One of Saul's shepherds was

there. He had seen David with the priest in Nob. He said, "I saw David at Nob. The priest gave him bread and Goliath's sword."

Then Saul sent for the priest. The priest came. All the priests of Nob came with him.

"Why did you make plans against me?" asked Saul. "You gave David bread and a sword. David has turned against me."

"I don't know anything about this," said the priest. "I just know that David is your servant. He is a leader. He is in your family. Everyone says he is an important person."

"You'll die!" said Saul. Then Saul told his guards, "Kill the priests."

But they wouldn't. That's because the priests served God.

Then Saul turned to the shepherd. "You kill them," said Saul. So the shepherd killed the priests. Then he killed everyone in the town of Nob.

But one man got away. He ran to David. He told David that Saul had killed the priests.

"I should have known this would happen," said David. "I saw Saul's shepherd in Nob. I should have known he'd tell Saul. So I'm the one to blame. Stay with me. Don't be afraid. He may want to kill you, but he wants to kill me, too. You're safe here."

The Bragger
PSALM 52

Then David wrote this song.

Why do you brag about sin all day?
You are in sad shape.
You say words that are sharp like a
    knife.
You trick other people.
You love sin and not good.
You love lies and not the truth.
You love words that hurt.
I'm sure God will bring you down.
He won't let you live in peace.
God's people will see it.
They will be afraid.
They will laugh and say,
"Here is the man who did not
    trust God.
He trusted his riches.
He grew strong by hurting others!"

But I'm like an olive tree.
I grow strong in God's house.
I trust in God's love forever.
His love never ends.
I will praise him forever
    for what he has done.
I will trust in his good name.
I will cheer for him
    with all his people.

MARCH 6

Hiding Places
1 SAMUEL 23; PSALM 63

Now someone told David, "The enemy is fighting in a town close by.

They are taking grain from the barns."

David asked God, "Should we go fight the enemies?"

"Go ahead," said God. "Save the town."

But David's men said, "We're afraid."

So David asked God again. God said, "Go ahead. You'll win."

Then David took his men into town. They fought against their enemies, and they won.

But someone told Saul where David was.

"Now God is giving David to me," said Saul. "David is in a town with gates and bars. It's like he is in jail!" So Saul called out his army.

David found out that Saul was planning to fight him. So David prayed. "Saul plans to come here," said David. "He plans to get rid of the town because of me. Will Saul really come here?"

"Yes," said God.

"Will the people hand me over to Saul?" asked David.

"Yes," said God.

So David and his men left. They moved here and there.

Saul found out that David was gone. So he didn't go after him.

David stayed in desert hiding places. Saul kept looking for him. But God didn't let Saul catch David.

David wrote these words.

God, you are my God.
I look for you.
My soul is thirsty for you.
It's like being in a dry land
   where there is no water.

I have seen you in the worship
      place.
I saw your power and greatness.
Your love is better than life.
So my lips will praise you.
I will praise you as long as I live.
I will lift up my hands
   to show that your name is great.
My soul will be happy,
   the same way it is when I eat
      good food.
My mouth will praise you with
   songs.

I think of you when I go to bed
   at night.
You are my helper.
So I sing in the shadow of your
   wings.
My soul hugs you, and your right
   hand holds me.

David was staying in the Ziph Desert. He found out that Saul was coming after him.

But Jonathan went to see David there. He said, "Don't be scared. Saul won't hurt you. You'll be the king of God's people. I'll be the next highest leader. My father knows that."

David and Jonathan promised to be friends. Then Jonathan went back home. David stayed in Ziph.

Now the people of Ziph went to see Saul. "David is hiding close to us," they said. "So come whenever you want. We'll catch him for you."

"You care about me," Saul said. "I hope God is good to you. Go and find out where David is. He is tricky. Find out where his hiding places are. Come back and tell me. Then I'll go with you. I'll track David."

So the people of Ziph went ahead. Saul followed.

David was now in another desert. He stayed there, because he heard that Saul was after him. But Saul found out where David was. So Saul went to that desert too.

Saul traveled along one side of the mountain. David and his men traveled along the other side. They were in a hurry to get away from Saul. Saul and his men were getting closer and closer.

Then a man came to Saul with a message. "You'd better come quick! Enemies have come into our land. They're robbing us!"

So Saul stopped chasing David. He had to fight the enemy army instead.

Then David went to live in the En-gedi Desert.

A Chance to Kill the King

1 SAMUEL 24; PSALM 57

Saul finished fighting the enemy. Then someone told him, "David is in the En-gedi Desert." So Saul started chasing David again. He went to the Rocks of the Wild Goats. There he looked for David.

Saul and his men passed some sheep pens. Then they came to a cave. Saul had to go to the bathroom. So he went inside the cave. It was the same cave where David and his men were hiding. They were at the back of the cave.

David's men said, "God is giving your enemy to you today!"

David quietly cut off a piece of Saul's robe. But then David felt bad about it. He said, "I shouldn't  have done that to Saul. He is the king God chose." So David wouldn't let his men hurt Saul.

Saul left the cave. In a few minutes David came out of the cave too. He called out to Saul, "My king!"

Saul turned around to look. David bowed with his face to the ground.

"People tell you I want to hurt you," said David. "Why do you believe them? God gave me a chance to catch you today. You can see that. Some of my men told me to kill you.

But I saved you. I said that God chose you to be king, so I wouldn't hurt you. See? I cut off a piece of your robe. But I didn't kill you."

David went on, "I haven't done anything wrong. But you hunt me. You want to kill me. I pray that God will judge who is right here. There is an old saying that bad people do bad things. I'm not bad, so I won't hurt you."

Then David asked Saul, "Who are you chasing anyway? A dead dog or a tiny bug? I pray that God will save me from you."

Saul said, "Is that you, David?" And Saul cried.

"You're a better person than I am," said Saul. "You were good to me. But I've been mean to you. God gave you a chance to kill me today. But you didn't do it! People don't let their enemies get away. So I hope God will pay you back with good things. I know you'll be king. Now promise that you won't kill my family."

So David promised. Then Saul went back home. David and his men went back to their hiding place in a cave.

David wrote,

Be kind to me, God.
I come to you for safety.
I will be safe in the shadow of your
    wings
  until trouble is gone.
I call to God Most High.

He saves me.
He is mad at the ones who chase me.

God sends his love.
He keeps his promises.

Lions are all around me.
I lie down with hungry animals.
They're really people who hurt
    other people.
Their words hurt just as much as
    sharp swords.

But you are great, God, above the sky.
Shine your strong power over all
    the earth.

My enemies put out a net to trap me.
I was tired from being upset and sad.
They dug a deep pit where I would
    walk.
But they fell into it.

My heart will stay with you, God.
I will sing and make music.
Wake up, my soul!
Wake up, harp!
I will wake up the day.

MARCH 7

The Man Whose Name Means "Fool"

1 SAMUEL 25

Now Samuel died. All God's people cried for him. They put his body in a grave.

David moved to a desert near the town of Carmel. A rich man lived in Carmel. He had 1,000 goats and 3,000 sheep. His name was Nabal, and his wife's name was Abigail. She was smart and beautiful. But Nabal was rude and mean.

It was the time of year for cutting the sheep's wool off. David heard that Nabal was cutting sheep wool. So he sent 10 young men to Nabal. David said, "Tell Nabal hello for me. Tell him we pray for good things for him and his family. Then tell him that his shepherds were with us for a while. We were good to them. He can ask them about it. Then ask Nabal to give us whatever he can."

So David's men went to Nabal. They told him what David had said.

"Who is David?" said Nabal. "Lots of people are leaving their masters like he did. Why should I give bread and water to him? I have meat for my workers. Why should I give it to David? I don't even know where his men come from."

David's men went back. They told David what Nabal had said.

"Get your swords!" said David.

The men put their swords on. David put his sword on. Then David set out for Nabal's house with 400 men.

Back at Nabal's house, a servant told Abigail what happened. "Nabal was rude to David's men. But David's men were good to us. We were in the fields near them. They were around us like a wall. We were safe. See if there is something you can do about this. We're in trouble now. Nabal is such a rude man. Nobody can talk to him."

Abigail didn't wait. She got 200 loaves of bread and two bags of wine. She got meat from five sheep ready to cook. She got five baskets of grain. She got 100 raisin cakes and 200 fig cakes. She put all this onto donkeys. Then she sent her servants ahead with these gifts. She followed them, but she didn't tell Nabal.

Abigail rode through the mountain valley on her donkey. She saw David and his men coming down the mountain. She met them.

David had just been saying, "It was no use. We watched over Nabal's sheep in the desert. We were good to him. But he has been mean to us. I'll kill him and his men!"

Abigail saw David. She got off her donkey. She bowed down with her face to the ground. She was at David's feet. She said, "Blame only me. Let me talk to you. Hear what I'm saying. Don't listen to Nabal. He is a rude man."

Then Abigail said that Nabal's name meant "fool." She said, "And he is a fool."

Abigail told David, "God kept you from killing Nabal and his men.

Now I've brought a gift. Give it to your men. Please forgive our wrong. God will make you the king because you fight God's battles."

"Praise God," said David. "He sent you here. You are very wise. So I pray that God will bring you good things."

Then David took the gifts Abigail had brought. "Go back home in peace," he said.

So Abigail went home to Nabal. He was having a party fit for a king. He was feeling good and very drunk. So Abigail didn't tell him what she had done.

The next morning Abigail told Nabal everything. Then Nabal's heart stopped working right. He lay as still as a stone. Ten days later, he died.

David heard that Nabal had died. He said, "Praise God. He paid Nabal back for being mean. And he kept me from doing the wrong thing."

Then David sent a message to Abigail. He asked her to marry him.

Abigail bowed with her face to the ground. "I'm ready to serve David," she said. She quickly got on her donkey. Her five servant girls went with her. Then she married David.

David had another wife too. But Saul had told David's first wife, Michal, to marry someone else.

In Saul's Camp at Night

1 Samuel 26

The people of Ziph went to Saul. "We know the hill where David is hiding," they said.

So Saul took his men to the Ziph Desert. They were going to look for David there. They camped by the road on the hill.

Now David was in the desert. He found out that Saul had followed him there. So David secretly went to Saul's camp. He saw Saul and Abner lying down. Saul was in the middle of the camp. His men were sleeping all around him.

"Who will go with me into the camp?" asked David.

"I will," said one of David's men.

So that night, David and the other man went quietly into Saul's camp. They went up to Saul. He was sleeping. His spear was sticking into the ground by his head. Abner and the other men were sleeping around Saul.

"This is the day!" said the man with David. "God is giving your enemy to you. I can kill him with one blow. Let me pin him to the ground!"

"No," said David. "He is the one God chose to be king. If we kill him, we're to blame. God will get him. He will die from old age or in a fight.

But I'm not going to be the one who kills him. Let's take his spear and jug of water. They're close to his head. Then let's get out of here."

So David took Saul's spear and jug of water. Then the two men left. Nobody saw them. Nobody knew about it. Nobody woke up. God had made them sleep deeply.

David went across to the top of the hill. It was far enough away that Saul couldn't get him. Then David yelled to Abner. "Abner! Don't you have an answer for me?"

"Who is there?" asked Abner. "Who is calling?"

"Are you a man?" asked David. "Why didn't you guard your king? Somebody came to kill him. This doesn't look good! You and the whole army should die! You didn't guard your king. Just look! Where is the king's spear? Where is the jug of water that was by his head?"

Saul knew David's voice. He said, "Is that you, David?"

"Yes, my king," said David. "Why are you chasing me? What did I do wrong? Listen to me. Maybe God sent you against me. Then I hope God will forgive me. But maybe men talked you into chasing me. Then I hope God sends them bad things. They have chased me away. You're hunting me like you'd hunt birds in the mountains. But I'm not important. I'm like a tiny bug to

you. The king has come to hunt a tiny bug!"

"I have sinned," said Saul. "Come back to me. You thought my life was important today. So I won't try to hurt you anymore. I've been a fool. I've done a great wrong."

"Here's your spear," said David. "Send a young man over here to get it. God will bring good to people who do what's right. God will bring good to people who keep following him. God gave you to me today. But I wouldn't kill the one God chose as king. I think your life is important. So I hope God thinks my life is important. I hope he saves me from my troubles."

"I hope God gives you good things," said Saul. "You'll do great things. I'm sure you will win."

Then David left, and Saul went back home.

MARCH 9

David Moves to Enemy Country

1 SAMUEL 27–29; 1 CHRONICLES 12

Now David thought, "One day Saul will kill me. What could be better for me than moving to enemy country? That way Saul will stop looking for me here. I'll get away from him."

So David and his 600 men moved to enemy country. They lived in the city of Gath. David's two wives were with him there.

Somebody told Saul that David was in Gath. So Saul didn't look for him anymore.

David wanted to live in a small town. So he talked to the enemy king of Gath. The king gave him the town of Ziklag.

Other fighters came to live near David. They helped him fight. They used bows and arrows. They could shoot arrows with their right or left hand.

David and his men would go out to fight. They would win. They were fighting other enemies. But the king of Gath thought they were fighting King Saul and David's own people. He thought, "David's people, the Jews, will hate him. He will have to serve me forever." So the enemy king trusted David.

One day the king of Gath got his army together. They marched out to fight Saul's army. The king told David, "Come and help us fight."

"Then you'll soon see what a help we can be to you," said David.

"Good!" said the king of Gath. "You can be my guard for life."

So David and his men marched together with the enemy army. They marched out to fight Saul.

But the enemy leaders asked, "What about these Jewish people?"

"This is David!" said the king.

"He has been with me more than a year. He has done nothing wrong."

But the army leaders were angry. "Tell David to go back," they said. "He can't fight with us. He might fight against us. He might want Saul to like him again."

So the king spoke to David. "I would be happy for you to go with me. You haven't done anything wrong since I met you. But the leaders don't think you should go with us. So go back. Don't do anything to make the leaders mad."

"What did I do?" asked David. "Why can't I fight with you?"

"You've been good to me. You're as good as an angel," said the king. "But the leaders say you can't go with us. So take your men. Leave as soon as it is light in the morning."

Saving Wives and Children
1 SAMUEL 30

It took David and his men three days to get home. But while they were gone, some enemies had come. They had set fire to the town of Ziklag. They had taken all the women and children away. They had taken David's wives, too.

David and his men cried out loud. They cried until they couldn't cry anymore. David's men began to talk about killing David. They were angry because their wives and children were gone. David knew he was in trouble.

But David felt better thinking about God. He asked God, "Should we go after these enemies? Will we catch them?"

"Go after them," said God. "You will catch them. You will win back your families."

So David and his 600 men set out. They came to a brook, and 200 men stayed there. They were too tired to cross. But David and 400 men kept going.

David's men found a man from Egypt in a field. They took him to David. He hadn't eaten anything for three days and three nights. So they gave him part of a fig cake and two raisin cakes. They gave him some water to drink. After he ate, he felt stronger.

"Where are you from?" asked David.

"I'm from Egypt," he said. "I'm a slave. My master left me here because I got sick. We had been out to fight. We set Ziklag on fire."

"Can you take me to your master's army?" asked David.

"Promise you won't kill me," said the man. "Promise you won't give me back to my master. Then I'll take you to them."

So the man led David to where the enemy army was. David could see them all across the land. They were eating and drinking. They were having a party. It was because they took so much from the towns they robbed.

Then David and his men began to fight the enemy. They fought all evening and all the next day. They kept on fighting until it was evening again, and David's men won.

Some of the enemies rode off on camels. But nobody else got away. David got back everything the enemy army had taken from Ziklag. He got his wives back. He got all the people, young and old. He got all the boys and girls. He got all the things and the sheep and cows. He got back everything else the enemies had taken.

They traveled back to the brook.

That's where the 200 tired men waited. They came out to meet David and all the people. David asked how they were.

Some of the men with David were mean. They said, "These men didn't go with us. They can have their wives and children back. But we won't share the other things we got."

"God gave these things to us," said David. "So you can't keep them just for yourselves. God took care of us. He helped us win. So those who stayed behind get as much as you do. All of us will share what we got." That became a rule with all the Jews.

The Witch

1 SAMUEL 28

Now the people David lived with went to fight Saul's army.

When Saul saw the enemy, he was scared. So he asked God about the fight. But God didn't answer him.

King Saul called his servants. "Go find a witch," he said. "I want to ask what will happen in the fight."

"There's a witch in Endor," said his servants.

Now Saul had told all witches to leave the land. So he dressed up as another man. He took two men with him. That night he went to see the witch.

"Talk to a spirit for me," said Saul. "Call up the one I ask for."

"You know what Saul did," said the woman. "He sent all the witches out of the land. You're just trying to trick me. You'll get me killed!"

"No," said Saul. "Nothing bad will happen. I promise."

"Then who do you want to talk to?" she asked.

"Call up Samuel for me," said Saul.

Now Samuel was dead. But he showed himself to the witch. She cried out loudly and said to the king, "You've tricked me! You're Saul!"

"Don't be scared," said Saul. "What do you see?"

"I see a spirit coming up from the ground," she said.

"What is he like?" asked Saul.

"He is an old man," she said. "He is wearing a robe."

Then Saul knew it was Samuel. He bowed down with his face to the ground.

"Why did you bother me?" asked Samuel. "Why did you bring me here?"

"I'm in a lot of trouble," said Saul. "The enemy is out to fight me. God won't answer me. So I'm asking you what to do."

"Why do you ask me?" said Samuel. "God is your enemy now. God has done what he said he would do. He has taken your kingdom away from you. He is giving it to David. It's all because you didn't obey God. Tomorrow you and your sons will be where I am. Your army will lose the fight."

Then Saul fell to the ground. He was full of fear and didn't feel very strong. He hadn't eaten all that day and night.

The witch went over to Saul. She could tell he was very upset. "Look here," she said. "I did what you asked. I put my life in danger to do it. Now please listen to me. Eat some food. Then you'll be strong enough to leave."

"I won't eat," said Saul.

But Saul's men told him to eat, too. At last he said he would eat. He got up from the ground and sat on the bed.

The woman cooked some meat and baked flat bread. She gave it to Saul and his men. They ate. Then they left while it was still night.

The Day the Enemy Won
1 SAMUEL 31; 2 SAMUEL 4:4

The enemy army began fighting God's people. God's people began running away. Many of them died on Gilboa Mountain. The enemies pushed on to get to Saul and his sons. They killed Saul's son Jonathan. They killed two other sons also.

There was a lot of fighting around

Saul. Men with bows and arrows shot him. He was hurt badly.

Saul called to the man who carried his armor. "Kill me with your sword. If you don't, the enemies will hurt me more."

But the man was scared. He wouldn't kill Saul. So Saul decided to fall on his own sword, and he died. When the man saw this, he decided to fall on his sword too. He died with Saul. So Saul, his sons, and his men died that same day.

God's people saw that their army had run away. They saw that Saul and his sons were dead. So they left their towns and ran away too. Then the enemies came and lived in their towns.

The next day the enemies came to Gilboa Mountain. They came to take clothes and things from the dead people. There they found Saul and his sons. They cut off Saul's head. They took off his armor. Then they took Saul's armor to their idol's worship house.

Saul's son Jonathan had a son who was five years old. His name was Mephibosheth. The news came that Jonathan and Saul had been killed. So the woman who took care of the boy picked him up and ran. She was in such a hurry that she dropped the boy. He fell and hurt his feet very badly. From then on, he couldn't walk.

David, the Singing King

Sad News for David

2 SAMUEL 1

Now David had been out fighting an enemy army. He won. So he went back home to Ziklag. Three days later, a man came from Saul's army. He had dust on his head. His clothes were torn. He bowed down to David.

"Where did you come from?" asked David.

"I got away from Saul's camp," said the man.

"How is it going there?" asked David.

"Saul's army ran away from the fight," the man said. "Lots of them were killed. Saul and Jonathan died too."

"How do you know?" asked David.

"I was on Gilboa Mountain," said the man. "Saul was leaning on his spear. He was almost dead. Enemy chariots were coming. Saul saw me and called me to come. He asked me who I was. I told him I was from the land of his enemies.

"Then Saul asked me to kill him. He said he was hurt very badly. So I killed him, for I knew he would die anyway. I took his crown and his arm band. I've brought them to you."

Then David and his men cried. They didn't eat any food until evening.

David asked the man, "Where did you come from?"

"I live in your land," said the man. "But my family is from the land of your enemies."

"Weren't you afraid to kill the king God chose?" asked David.

Then David told one of his men, "Kill this man."

So he killed him. That's because the man had killed the king that God chose.

Then David wrote and sang a sad song about Saul and Jonathan. He said all people in Judah should learn it.

"Oh, God's people,
    the strong ones died on the
        mountain.
Don't tell our enemies,
    because they might be glad.
Jonathan's bow didn't turn away
        from the fight.
Saul's sword did its work.

Saul and Jonathan.
They were loved when they were
        alive.
They died together.
They were faster than eagles.
They were stronger than lions.
So cry for Saul, you women.

These strong ones died in the fight.
Jonathan died on the mountains.
I cry for you, Jonathan my brother.
You were a very special friend.
Your love was wonderful to me.
The strong ones have died!"

MARCH 12

A Marching Sound in the Tree Tops

2 SAMUEL 2; 4–5; 1 CHRONICLES 11–12

Time passed. One day David asked God a question. "Should I go back to the land of Judah?"

"Yes," said God.

"What town should I go to?" asked David.

"Go to Hebron," said God.

So David moved to Hebron with his two wives. He also took his men and their families.

There was lots of fighting between Saul's men and David's men. The war lasted a long time. David and his men got stronger. Saul's army got weaker.

Now one son of Saul still lived. He was made king. One day two army leaders went to his house. It was the middle of a hot day. Saul's son was resting in bed. The two leaders went inside. They acted as if they were bringing some wheat. Instead, they killed Saul's son with a sword. They cut off his head. Then they ran away.

The two men ran to David. They said, "Here's the head of the son of Saul. Saul was trying to kill you. Today God has paid him back."

"God saved me from all my troubles," said David. "A man once thought he was bringing me good news. He told me Saul was dead. I had him killed. But you are sinful men. You killed a man who did nothing wrong. You killed him in his house in his bed. So you should die!"

Then David ordered his men to kill them, and they did.

Now all the people who followed Saul's son turned to David. They chose David to be their king. So

David was the king of all God's people. It was just as God had promised. David was 30 years old when he became king. He was the king for 40 years.

All the fighting men from the army came to David. They said he was their king too. They stayed for three days in Hebron and visited David.

Other people brought David donkeys and oxen carrying food. People brought more than enough flour. There were cakes of figs and raisins. There were cows and sheep and wine and oil. Everyone was very happy.

Then David and his army went to fight some enemies. The enemies lived in Jerusalem. They said, "You'll never get into this city. Even people who can't see or walk could keep you out!" They really thought David couldn't get in.

David talked to his men. "The man who leads today will be my army leader," he said.

Joab led the fight. So he became the leader of David's army. David and his men took the city from the enemies.

Then David lived in Jerusalem. Everyone called it David's City. David made the city bigger. He became great because God was with him.

Now Hiram was the king of Tyre. He sent David logs of wood from cedar trees. He sent builders who built with wood and rock. They built a palace for David. David knew that it was God who had really made him king. He knew that God had made his kingdom great. He knew that God was being good to his people.

The enemies also heard that David was now king. So their army went to look for him.

David found out that the enemies were coming. He went to meet them with his army.

These enemies had already started fighting people in Giants' Valley. David asked God, "Should we go out and fight them? Will you help us win?"

"Yes," said God. "I'll help you win."

So David and his army went out to fight, and they won. "Waves break on the shore," said David. "And God broke out on our enemies with our fighting."

The enemies had left their idols there. So David told his men to set the idols on fire and burn them.

But the enemies came to fight the people in the valley again. So David asked God about it.

God said, "Don't go right in front of them. Go around behind them. Listen for a marching sound in the tree tops. That means God is going ahead of you. Then jump out at the enemies in front of the trees. God will fight the enemy army."

David did what God told him to do. His army won.

Everybody knew who David was. God made all the nations afraid of David.

On the Wings of the Wind
2 SAMUEL 22; PSALM 18

David wrote this after God saved him from all of his enemies.

I love you, God.
You make me strong.

God is like a strong rock to me.
He is like a fort around me.
He saves me.
He is like my guard.
I pray to God.
I want to praise him.

When everything was going wrong,
    I asked God for help.
God heard me.

Earth's mountains shook.
God was angry.
Smoke and fire came from him.
God opened heaven and came
    down.
His feet stood on dark clouds.
He flew on the wings of the wind.
Darkness was his blanket around
    him.
Dark rain clouds were a tent for him.

But he was so bright that the clouds
    moved away
    with hail and flashes of lightning.
God's voice sounded like loud
    thunder.
He made his enemies run
    by shooting lightning at them.
God's breath can open the way
    to the valleys in the sea.

God reached down and saved me.
When everything seemed lost,
    God helped me.
He was happy with me.

God, you keep my light shining.
You make dark turn into light for me.

God does nothing wrong.
What he says is right.
He watches over people who trust
    him.

MARCH 13

The Ark Comes Back
2 SAMUEL 6; 1 CHRONICLES 13; 15–16; PSALM 105:1-3; 96:1-8

David talked to the army leaders. "We didn't pray as we should have when Saul was king. So let's bring God's ark box back," said David.

Everyone said this was a good idea. So David went to get the ark box. Many people went with him. They put the Ark on a new cart.

Oxen pulled it. Two men walked in front of the cart. David and the others were showing their joy. They were playing harps and lyres and tambourines. They were playing cymbals and horns.

Now the cart came to a farm work place. The oxen tripped. One man put his hand on God's ark box. He wanted to keep it from tipping over. But God was angry that he touched it. So the man died right there.

Then David was angry. He was afraid of God. He said, "How can we bring God's ark to our city?"

So David didn't take the Ark to Jerusalem. Instead, he took it to a house in Gath. It stayed there for three months. God brought good things to the family that lived in the house. It was all because the Ark was there.

Somebody told David that good things were happening to the family. God's ark was at their house.

So David called the priests. He said, "You are going to bring the Ark here. You didn't bring it last time.

That's why God got angry at us. We didn't ask God how to bring the Ark. Only priests can carry the Ark. That's the way God wants it done."

So the priests put poles through the rings in the Ark. Then they carried the Ark with the poles on their shoulders. That's the way Moses had told them to carry it.

David told some of the people to be singers. He told them to sing happy songs. He told them to play harps and cymbals and horns. So they chose men to play the music. One man led the singing. He was good at leading singers.

Then David and the leaders went to get the Ark. They were all wearing special robes. They all brought the Ark into the city. There was shouting. There was music from horns and cymbals and harps.

David's wife Michal was watching from a window. God's ark was just coming into the city. King David was jumping and dancing. But in her heart, Michal was upset with him.

The leaders put God's ark into the tent David made for it. They offered gifts to God on the altar. David prayed for good things to come to the people. Then he gave each person a loaf of bread. He also gave each person a date cake and a raisin cake.

Then David talked to the priests who led the music. He told them to thank God with this song.

Give thanks to God.
Call his name.
Tell the nations what he has done.
Sing praise to him.
Tell about the wonderful things he
	has done.
Enjoy his name. It's the best.
Let people who trust God show
	their joy.

They also praised God with this song.

Sing a new song to God.
Sing to God, all the earth.
Praise his name.
Every day, tell about how he saves.
Tell about the wonderful things he
	does.
God is great.
He should be praised more than
	anyone else.
The fake gods of the nations are
	only idols.
But our God made all of space.
Greatness and light are with him.
He is strong and powerful.
Tell how great his name is.

All the people said, "Yes!" They said, "Praise God!"

David left the Ark with the priests. He told them to help take care of it each day. He chose men to watch the gates. Some men were there to offer gifts on the altar. Some were there to give thanks to God. Some were there to make music.

Then the people went home. David went to his palace.

But Michal went out to meet David. She was mad. "You really thought you looked great today, didn't you!" she said. "You took your kingly robe off right in front of the servant girls. You were like a proud fool!"

"I was doing it in front of God!" said David. "He chose me to be king. He didn't choose your father or anyone from your family. So I'll show my joy in front of God. I'll be even more foolish! I'll act like I'm not important, even to myself! But these servants will treat me like an important person."

So Michal didn't have any children the rest of her life.

MARCH 14

Jonathan's Son
2 SAMUEL 9

There was a man who had been a servant in Saul's family. David wanted to see him. So he came to the palace.

"Is anybody from Saul's family still alive?" asked David. "Is there someone I can be kind to because of Jonathan?"

"There is Jonathan's son," the servant said. "He can't walk."

"Where is he now?" asked David. The servant told him.

So David sent for Jonathan's son. His name was Mephibosheth. He came to see David. He bowed down.

"Don't be scared," said David. "I'm going to be kind to you."

Mephibosheth bowed down and said. "I'm just like a dead dog. Why should you think about me?"

"Your father, Jonathan, was my best friend. I'll give you all the land that Saul, your grandfather, owned. I'll always let you eat at my table."

David called Saul's servant. "I have given Mephibosheth all the land that Saul owned," he said. "You and your family will take care of that land. Gather the crops that grow. That way, Mephibosheth can have enough to live on. He will eat at my table."

"I'll do whatever you want," said the servant.

So Mephibosheth ate at David's table. He was like a part of David's family. Mephibosheth had a little boy. Saul's servant and his family helped them.

A Palace and a Tent
2 SAMUEL 7; 1 CHRONICLES 17

David was sitting in his palace. Nathan the prophet was there. David said, "Look at this. I'm living in a palace. But God's ark box is out there in a tent."

"Do whatever you're thinking," said Nathan. "God is with you."

That night God spoke to Nathan. God said to tell David, "Don't build a house for me to live in. One of your children will be king after you. He will build a worship house for me. I will never stop loving him. Your family and your kingdom will last forever."

Nathan told David everything God had said.

Then King David prayed to God. "You've shown me these things," said David. "So I've been brave enough to pray to you. Lord, you are God! There is no one like you. I can trust your words. You've promised good things to me! Now bring good things to my family. Then we'll be able to serve you forever. You have spoken. There will be good things for me forever!"

A Rude King
2 SAMUEL 10; 21:15-17;
1 CHRONICLES 19

An enemy army came to fight God's people again. So David went out to fight with his men. But he got very tired.

Now one of the enemy's men said he'd kill David. This man had a new sword. The sharp end of his spear weighed over seven pounds.

But another man saved David. He killed the man with the big spear.

Then David's men made a promise to him. "You'll never go to fight with us again. You might get killed."

Time passed. The king of Ammon died. His son became king. David thought, "I'll be kind to him. His father was always kind to me." So David sent a group of men to see the new king. They told him David was sorry that his father had died.

But the leaders of Ammon talked to their king. "Is David being kind by sending these men? They're here to check out our land. Soon King David will try to take our land for himself."

So the king took David's men. He shaved off half their beards. He cut their clothes in half across the middle. Then he sent them home.

Now somebody told David what had happened. So David sent a message to the men. He told them, "Stay at Jericho until your beards grow back. Then come home."

The leaders of Ammon began to see what they had done. They had been rude to David. So their king paid for chariots to come from other lands. Chariot drivers came too. Another enemy king came with his army. They all got ready to fight David's army.

David heard about this army. So he sent Joab and his men out to fight against it.

Now enemies were near the city. Enemies were in the country, too. So Joab led his best men out into the country to fight. The rest of his men went with his brother. They went to fight Ammon near the city.

"If the enemy I fight is too strong, come save me," said Joab. "If the enemy you fight is too strong, then I'll come save you. Be strong. Be brave. We'll fight for God's people. God will do what he thinks is best."

So Joab began fighting. The enemy army in the country ran away from them. The army of Ammon saw them run away. So they ran away too.

Now the army in the country called more men to help them. David found out about it. So he sent his army out to fight them again. But the army ran away again.

Then the people from that land made peace with David. They didn't help the army of Ammon anymore.

On the Palace Roof

2 SAMUEL 11

It was spring. David sent his army to fight the army of Ammon. Joab led them, but David stayed in Jerusalem.

One evening David couldn't sleep

and took a walk on the palace roof. From his roof, he saw a beautiful woman. So David asked someone who she was.

"It's Bathsheba," someone said. "She is Uriah's wife."

Then David sent someone to get Bathsheba. She came, and David loved her. He slept with her as if she were his wife. Then she went home again.

Later, Bathsheba found out she was going to have a baby. It was because David had slept with her like a husband would. Bathsheba sent a message to tell David about the baby.

Then David sent a message to Joab. It said, "Send Uriah to me."

So Joab sent Uriah to David. David asked him how the fight was going. He asked how Joab was doing. He asked how the rest of the men were doing. Then David said, "Go home and rest now." He hoped Uriah would sleep with Bathsheba. Then it would look like the baby was Uriah's, not David's. David even sent a gift with Uriah.

But Uriah didn't go home. He slept at the palace door with the servants.

Someone told David, "Uriah didn't go home."

So David asked Uriah, "Didn't you travel a long way? Why didn't you go home?"

"All the fighting men are staying in tents," said Uriah. "They are camped out in the fields. How could I go home? How could I eat and drink? How could I sleep with my wife? No! I could never do that!"

"Then stay here again today," said David. "Tomorrow I'll send you back to the fight."

So Uriah stayed. David asked Uriah to come eat and drink with him. David made him get drunk. But Uriah still didn't go home to sleep. He slept by the servants.

The next morning David wrote a letter to Joab. He told Uriah to take the letter to Joab. The letter said, "Put Uriah in a place where the fight is hardest. Then pull your men back. That way, Uriah will get killed."

Now Joab's men were fighting a city. So Joab put Uriah where the fight was hardest. The men of the city came out to fight. They killed some of Joab's men. Uriah was one of them.

Joab called a man to take a message to David. Joab told the man, "Tell the king about the fight. The king may get angry. He may ask why we were so close to the city. Or he may ask if we didn't know they'd shoot arrows at us. Then tell the king that Uriah is dead too."

So the man left to take David the message. He told David what Joab had said. "The enemies were too strong," he said. "They came out of the city to fight. But we pushed them back to the city gate. Then they shot arrows from the wall. Some of our men were killed. Uriah was killed too."

"Tell Joab not to be upset," said David. "Sometimes people die in fights. So keep fighting against the city. Tear it down."

Bathsheba heard that Uriah had been killed. She cried for him for a while. Then David sent for her. She came to his palace, and David married her. Sometime later, she had a baby boy. But all of this had made God very unhappy.

The Poor Man's Sheep

2 SAMUEL 12; PSALM 51

God sent the prophet Nathan to see David. Nathan told David, "Once there were two men. They lived in the same town. One man was rich. The other man was poor. The rich man had lots of sheep and cows. But the poor man had just one little pet lamb.

"The poor man's lamb was his children's pet. It ate his food. It drank out of his cup. It slept in his lap. To the man, it was like his own child.

"One day a friend came to visit the rich man. The rich man needed some meat for dinner. But he didn't want to use his own sheep. So he took the poor man's lamb and had it for dinner."

King David got very angry. "The rich man should die!" said David. "He should pay the poor man by giving him four sheep. He took the poor man's only lamb from him. He didn't feel sorry for the poor man at all!"

"You're that rich man!" said Nathan.

Then Nathan told David what God said. "I chose you to be my people's king. I saved you from Saul. I gave you his kingdom. If that had not been enough, I would have given you more. So why didn't you care about my laws? Why have you done this terrible wrong? You killed Uriah. You took his wife to be your wife. Now fighting will never leave your family. You acted as if I was not important."

"I've sinned against God," said David.

David wrote,

Be kind to me, God.
Show me your love that never stops.
Erase my sins because you are so
    kind.
Wash away all my sin, and clean my
    heart.

I know my sins.
I always think about them.

You are the one who has really been
hurt by this terrible sin.
I did wrong.
You are right when you say what's
good and what's bad.

I know I was a sinner
even when I was a baby,
even before I was born.
I know you want my heart to
be true.
You teach me to be wise.

Clean me, and I will be clean again.
Wash me, and I will be whiter
than snow.
Let me hear joy.
Let me be glad again.
Let my sad bones know joy again.
Hide your face from my sins.
Erase all my wrongs,
and make my heart clean, God.
Put a spirit within me
that stays true to you.
Don't send me away from you.
Don't take away your Holy Spirit.
Give me the joy that comes
from knowing that you save me.
Give me a spirit that wants to
follow you.
Then I will teach sinners your ways.
They will turn back to you.
Save me, God.
You are the God who saves me.
I will sing about how right you are.
God, open my lips, and my mouth
will praise you.

I would bring a gift,
but that's not what you want.
The gift you want is a heart
that's sorry about doing wrong.
You won't turn away a sorry heart.

"God has taken away your sin,"
said Nathan. "You won't die. But
you've made God's enemies make
fun of God. So your baby boy will
die." Then Nathan went home.

Bathsheba's baby did get sick.
David begged God to make the
baby well. David wouldn't eat any
food. He stayed in his palace. He lay
on the ground before God all night.

The older people of David's
family went to him. They begged
him to get up and eat. But he
wouldn't.

Seven days later, the baby died.
David's servants were scared to tell
him the news. They thought, "When
the baby was alive, David wouldn't
listen to us. What will happen if we
tell him the baby died? He may do
something bad."

But David saw his servants
whisper. He guessed that the baby
died. So he asked, "Did the baby
die?"

"Yes," they said.

David got up. He washed himself.
He changed clothes. Then he went
to the worship tent. He worshiped
God. After that, he went back to the

palace. He asked for some food, and he ate.

"What are you doing?" asked the servants. "You cried when the baby was alive. You went without food. Now the baby is dead. But you're getting up and eating!"

"Yes, I cried while the baby was alive," said David. "I thought maybe God would send his kind love. Maybe he'd make the baby well again. But the baby is dead now. So why should I go without food? Can I make him alive again?"

All this time Joab was still fighting Ammon. He was winning at the enemy city. So he sent a message to David. "Get all the army together. Come and take the city yourself. If you don't, I'll take it. Then it will be named for me!"

So David went to the city with his whole army. He took the enemy city. He took the enemy king's crown. It was gold and weighed 75 pounds. Beautiful stones were in the crown. David wore it.

David took lots of things from the city. He made the people who lived there work like servants. They had to work with saws and picks and axes. They had to make bricks, too.

The same thing happened to all the towns of Ammon. Then David took his army back to Jerusalem.

Brave, Strong Men

2 SAMUEL 23; 1 CHRONICLES 11

There were three strong men who led David's battles. One of them killed 800 men in one fight.

Then there was a second man. One time, the enemy army came against David's army. Everyone else ran away. But the second man stayed there to fight the enemy. He kept fighting until his hand got tired. His hand locked around his sword. God's people won the battle that day.

Then there was a third man. Once the enemy army came together in a field. David's army ran away. But this third man stayed right in the middle of the field. He kept fighting the enemy. God helped his people win.

Once David was staying near a cave. These three strong men came to see him there. An enemy group was camped in the valley. David was in his hiding place. The main part of the enemy army was at Bethlehem.

David wanted a drink of water very badly. "I wish someone would get water for me," David said. "I wish I had water from the well near Bethlehem's gate."

So the three strong men crept past

the enemy. They got water from that well. They took it to David.

But David wouldn't drink it. "I can't drink it," said David. "My men put their lives in danger to get it."

Now these three men had a leader. He had killed 300 men. So everybody knew who he was. He was as well known as David's three strong leaders.

There was another brave fighter, too. Once he killed two of the enemy's best fighters. Another time on a snowy day, he fought a lion. He killed it in a pit.

Another time this brave fighter killed a man from Egypt. The man was over seven feet tall. He had a huge spear. David's fighter only had a club. But he got the spear away from the tall man. He killed him with it.

People knew who the brave fighter was. He was as well known as the Three. David made him the leader of his own guards.

An Angry Son
2 SAMUEL 12–13

David still loved Bathsheba. He cheered her up after their baby died. Later, they had another baby boy. They named him Solomon. God loved Solomon.

David had other sons too. Two of them were Amnon and Absalom. Absalom hated Amnon. But he didn't say anything about it.

Absalom and Amnon grew up. One day Absalom was with his men. They were cutting wool off their sheep. So Absalom asked all the king's sons to come to a feast.

Absalom even went to King David. He said, "We are cutting the wool off our sheep. Would you and the other leaders like to come?"

"No, my son," said King David. "We would only get in the way."

"Then let Amnon come," said Absalom.

"Why?" asked the king.

Absalom kept asking for Amnon to come. So David sent Amnon and his other sons with Absalom.

Then Absalom talked with his men. He said, "Watch Amnon. He will drink and be full of wine. He will be feeling good. I'll tell you to strike Amnon. Then I want you to kill him. Don't be scared. I'm the one giving you this order. So be strong. Be brave."

Absalom's men did what he told them to do. They killed Amnon. Then the rest of David's sons got up. They got on their mules and rode away.

David heard that Absalom had killed all his sons. David was so sad he tore his clothes. He lay down on the ground. All his servants tore their clothes, too.

Then a man came with a message. "Not all your sons were killed," he said. "Only Amnon was killed. Absalom planned to do this for a long time. But your sons aren't all dead."

There was a watchman looking out from the city. He saw lots of people coming down the hill. They were on the west road. So he went to tell David. "I see men coming down the side of the hill."

"See?" said the man with the message. "What did I tell you? Your sons are coming."

Then David's sons came in. They were crying loudly for Amnon. David cried too. Even his servants cried.

Absalom ran away. He stayed away for about three years. David missed him every day. He wanted to go see Absalom, for he had gotten over Amnon's death.

MARCH 17

A Wise Woman and a Burning Field

2 SAMUEL 14

Joab knew that David wanted to see Absalom again. So Joab sent for a wise woman. He told her, "Pretend that you're crying because someone

died. Go see the king. Tell him a story." Then Joab told her what to say.

So the wise woman went to King David. She bowed down with her face to the ground. She said, "King David! Please help me!"

"What's the matter?" asked the king.

"My husband died," she said. "I was left with two sons. One day they got into a fight. One killed the other one. Now everybody wants to kill my other son. But he is all I have left."

"Go back home," said King David. "I'll give an order not to kill your son."

"Please let me say one more thing," the woman said.

"Go ahead," said King David.

"You're telling me the right thing to do," she said. "But aren't you pointing at yourself? You haven't let your son come back. God is not like that. He doesn't take life away from us. Instead, he plans ways for people to come to him.

"I thought I'd talk to you," said the woman. "I thought you might do what you should do. You're like God's angel to me. You can tell what's good and what's bad."

"I'm going to ask you a question," said King David. "Please don't keep the answer a secret."

"Go ahead," said the woman.

"Is Joab behind all this?" asked the king.

"Yes," said the woman. "Joab told me to do this. He told me what to say. He wanted to change things. You are as wise as God's angel. You know everything that happens!"

Then King David spoke to Joab. "All right," he said. "Bring Absalom back."

Joab bowed with his face to the ground. "Today I know that you like me," he said. "You said yes to what I asked."

Then Joab went to find Absalom. He brought Absalom back to Jerusalem.

But King David said, "Absalom must live in his own house. He can't come see me."

So Absalom lived in his own house. He didn't go see King David.

Now everyone said Absalom was the best-looking man around. From time to time his hair would grow

too heavy for him. Then he'd cut it and weigh it. It would weigh about five pounds.

Absalom lived in Jerusalem for two years. All that time he didn't see his father, King David. At last Absalom called for Joab. He wanted to send Joab to King David. But Joab wouldn't come. So Absalom called for Joab again. But Joab still wouldn't come.

Then Absalom called in his servants. "Joab's field is next door to mine," said Absalom. "There is barley growing in his field. Go set his field on fire."

So Absalom's servants burned Joab's field.

Then Joab went to see Absalom. "Why did you burn my field?" he asked.

"I told you to come see me," said Absalom. "I want you to go to the king for me. Ask him why he brought me here. It would have been better to leave me where I was. I want to see the king. Have I done wrong? If I have, then he can be the one to kill me."

So Joab went to see King David. He told him what Absalom said. Then King David called for Absalom.

Absalom came and bowed down before the king. Then David kissed his son Absalom.

Absalom Takes Over

2 SAMUEL 15

Time passed. Absalom bought a beautiful chariot and got horses. He got 50 men to run ahead of him wherever he went.

Absalom would get up early every morning. He would go to the road that led to the city gate. There he'd stand.

People would come into the city to see the king. Some of them would have a problem. They would want to ask the king about it. He could tell them what to do.

Now Absalom would meet them at the gate. He'd call to these men, "Where are you from?"

They would tell him. Then he'd say, "I know that you are right. But there is no one in the city to judge this case. Who will make me the judge? I'll make sure that everyone is treated right."

So people came to Absalom. They'd start to bow to him. But he'd shake their hand and kiss them. That's how he treated everyone who came to see the king. So all the people loved Absalom.

Four years went by. One day Absalom went to see King David. "I made a promise when I lived far away," Absalom said. "I asked God to bring me back to Jerusalem. I promised that I'd worship God in Hebron."

"Then go," said King David.

So Absalom went to Hebron. But he sent men with a secret message to all the people. It said that they were to listen for horns to blow. Then they were to call out, "Absalom is the king in Hebron."

Absalom asked 200 men from Jerusalem to come with him. But they didn't know what was going on.

Now David had a special helper. This man helped David make wise plans. Absalom asked this man to come with him. So more and more people were on his side.

One day a man brought a message to King David. It said, "God's people are following Absalom."

Then David called together the leaders in Jerusalem. "Let's go!" he said. "We have to leave. If we don't, we won't get away from Absalom. He will come after us. Then he will kill us and everyone in the city."

"We're ready," said the leaders. "We'll do whatever you want."

So King David left Jerusalem. He took his family with him. All the people followed.

Everyone in the country cried as they saw them passing by. They crossed a valley and headed toward the desert.

The priests came too. They carried God's ark box. They set it down. A priest offered gifts to God on an altar. All the while, people were leaving Jerusalem.

King David told one of the priests, "Take God's ark back into the city. God may be kind to me. Then he will bring me back to see his ark box again. But maybe God is not happy with me. Then he can do whatever he wants with me."

David told the priest to take his son with him. He said to take another priest and his son, too. David said, "I'll be at the river crossing in the desert. I'll wait to hear from you. You can let me know what's happening."

So the two priests took the ark box and their sons. They went back into Jerusalem.

David went up Olive Mountain. He was crying as he went. He had covered his head. He didn't wear any shoes. All the people covered their heads too. They all cried.

Now somebody told David, "Your special helper is with Absalom." So David prayed, "Make my helper tell Absalom the wrong thing."

David came to the top of the mountain. People used to worship God there. David's friend Hushai met him there. Hushai had torn his own clothes. He had put dust on his head.

David said, "Go back to the city. Tell Absalom you'll serve him. You can work against my helper, who is now with my son. He will tell Absalom what to do. But you can make his ideas sound like they're no good.

"The priests with the ark box are in the city, too," said David. "Tell them the news you hear at the palace. Then they will send their sons to tell me what's going on."

So David's friend Hushai went back to Jerusalem. He got there just as Absalom arrived.

Throwing Rocks at the King
2 SAMUEL 16; PSALM 3

David went on. Soon he saw Mephibosheth's servant. He was waiting for David. He had a line of donkeys with him. They carried a big load. They had 200 loaves of bread. They had 100 raisin cakes and 100 fig cakes. There was also a bag of wine.

"Why did you bring these things?" asked David.

"So your family can ride on the donkeys," said the servant. "The people can eat the bread and cakes. And the wine is for them to drink in the desert."

"Where is Mephibosheth?" asked David.

"He stayed back in Jerusalem,"

the servant said. "He thinks he will get back the kingdom of his grandfather Saul."

"Then you can have everything that belonged to him," said David.

"I bow to you," said the servant. "I want you to be happy with me!"

Now David and the people came close to a town. A man from Saul's family came out of the town. He yelled bad things about David. He threw rocks at David and the guards around him.

"Get out of here," called the man. "You're a killer! You're good for nothing! God is paying you back for killing Saul's family. God is giving your kingdom to Absalom. God is getting rid of you!"

One of David's army leaders spoke to David. "This man is as good as a dead dog! Why let him talk to you like that? Let me go take off his head!"

"You and I don't think alike," said David. "What if God has told him to say that? Then who am I to stop him?"

Then David talked to all his leaders. "My own son is trying to kill me," said David. "I'm sure this man is too. Leave him alone. Let him say bad things. Maybe God has

told him to. God will see how sad I am. Then maybe he will pay me back with good things. He may do it because this man is saying bad things."

So David and the people kept on going. The man from Saul's family was on the hill across the way. He kept saying bad things and kept throwing rocks. He even threw dirt at them.

At last the king and his people got to where they were going. They were very tired, so they stopped to rest.

David wrote,

Many people are against me, God.
They say, "God will not save him."
But you are like my guard.
You lift me up.

I call out loud to God,
    and he answers me.
I can lie down and sleep.
I know I will wake up again
    because God keeps me safe.
I will not be afraid,
    even if 10,000 (ten thousand)
        people are against me.
Come! Save me, God!

All this time, Absalom and his men were in Jerusalem. The man who had been David's special helper was there too. Then Hushai, David's friend, went in to see Absalom. He was doing just what David told him to do.

"I hope King Absalom lives a long time," said Hushai.

"Are you turning against your friend David?" asked Absalom. "Why didn't you go with him?"

"I'll stay with the one God chose," said Hushai. "I'll stay with the one all the people chose. I'll be your servant."

Who Has the Best Idea?

2 SAMUEL 17

Now people thought the words of David's special helper were like God's words. David had thought that. Now Absalom thought that too.

So Absalom talked to the man who had been David's helper. "Tell us what we should do," said Absalom.

"You should take 12,000 (twelve thousand) men," said the helper. "Leave tonight to chase David. Fight him while he is tired. He will be weak. Scare him. The people with him will run away. Then I will kill King David. You can bring the people back. They'll follow you."

Absalom thought this plan was good. So did all the leaders.

"Call Hushai," said Absalom. "Let's hear what he says."

Absalom told Hushai what the helper said. "Should we do that?" he asked. "What do you think?"

"It's not a good idea," said Hushai. "You know your father, David. You know the men with him. They're all mighty fighters. They're mean. They're like a mother bear whose cubs are taken away.

"Your father has done lots of fighting," said Hushai. "He won't camp out with the other men. I think he is hiding right now. He may be in a cave. He may be somewhere else. What if he jumps out at your men first? People will say that Absalom's men were killed!

"Your brave fighters have hearts like lions," said Hushai. "But even they will be scared. For everyone knows your father is a mighty fighter. They know his men are very brave.

"So here's what I say," said Hushai. "Gather all the fighting men together. There will be as many as sand on the beach. You can lead them out to fight. We'll fight David wherever we find him. We'll jump on him like dew falling on the ground. We'll kill him and his men.

"Let's say your father hides in some city," said Hushai. "Then we'll bring ropes. We'll tie them to the walls of the city. We'll drag the walls down into the valley. Not a stone will be left."

"That's the best idea!" said

Absalom. All his men said so, too. That's because God was working to make the helper's ideas seem bad. That way, Absalom would be in a lot of trouble.

Then Hushai went to the two priests. He told them what he told Absalom. He said to send a message to David right away. He said to tell David, "Don't stay at the river crossing tonight. Cross over. If you don't, they'll catch you."

Now the priests' two sons were staying close by. They couldn't go into Jerusalem. There was too much danger. A servant girl was to take them messages. Then they'd take them to King David.

But a young man saw the priests' sons. He went and told Absalom about it.

So the priests' sons left in a hurry. They went to another town. A man there had a well in his yard. They climbed into the well to hide. The man's wife put a cover over the well. She threw grain over the cover. Nobody knew they were hiding there.

Absalom's men came looking for the priests' sons. They came to the house. They asked the woman, "Where did the priests' sons go?" She told them they had crossed the river.

Absalom's men looked around. But they didn't find anybody. So they went back to Jerusalem.

Then the two sons came out of the well. They took their message to King David. "Cross the river right away," they said. Then they told him about the man who used to be his helper. They told about his idea to chase David and kill him.

So David and the people with him crossed the Jordan River. By the time morning came, everyone was across.

Now the helper saw that Absalom didn't like his idea. So the helper got on his donkey. He went back to his own town. He went to his house and killed himself.

Then Absalom and his men also crossed the Jordan River.

David and his people camped near a town. Some men brought them mats to sleep on. Other people brought bowls and pots. They brought wheat and barley flour. They brought beans, honey, sheep, and cheese. They took these to David and his people. They said, "You must all be hungry and thirsty and tired."

MARCH 20

At the Oak Tree
2 SAMUEL 18

David got his army together. He said, "I'll march out with you to fight."

"No," said his men. "You shouldn't go with us. What if we

have to run away? What if we get killed? They don't care about us. You are equal to 10,000 (ten thousand) of us. They will be looking only for you. It's better for you to help us from here."

"I'll do whatever you think is best," said David.

So David's men marched out. David stood beside the town gate as they went past. David told his army leaders, "Be careful with Absalom. He is my son."

The army marched out to a field. But the fighting began in the forest. It moved all over the country side. More men died because of the forest than because of swords. More than 20,000 (twenty thousand) men were killed that day, and David's men won.

Now Absalom was riding on his mule. He met up with some of David's men. The mule ran under some thick oak tree branches. Absalom's head got caught in them. But his mule kept running and left him hanging in the air.

A man who saw him told Joab, "I just saw Absalom! He was hanging in an oak tree!"

"You saw Absalom?" said Joab. "Why didn't you kill him? I would have paid you with silver."

"You could have put 25 pounds of silver in my hands. But I wouldn't have killed him," said the man. "He is the king's son. I heard the king say to be careful with Absalom. The king finds out about everything. I would have put my life in danger."

"I won't wait for you then," said Joab. He picked out three long knives. He stuck them in Absalom's heart. Absalom was still hanging in the oak tree. Ten of Joab's men got around Absalom and killed him.

Joab blew his horn. His fighters stopped chasing Absalom's men. They took Absalom's body down. They threw it into a pit in the forest. They piled rocks on top of it.

All the while, Absalom's men were running home.

Absalom didn't have any sons. He had thought no one would remember him. So he had built a big monument to make himself look important. This stone post was in the King's Valley. Absalom had named it after himself. It's still called Absalom's Post.

A priest's son told Joab, "Let me go tell the news. I'll tell King David that God saved him from his enemies."

"Not today," said Joab. "You can

bring news to the king another day. But not today. The king's son is dead."

So Joab called another man. "Go tell the king what you saw," said Joab.

The man bowed to Joab. Then he ran to tell the king.

The priest's son said, "Please let me run behind him. I want to go, no matter what happens."

"Why?" asked Joab. "This is not news that will make the king happy."

"I want to go anyway," said the son.

"Then go," said Joab.

So the priest's son ran. He went a different way. He passed the other man.

Now David was sitting by the city gate. The watchman went up to his post at the top of the wall. He looked out over the wall and saw a man coming. He was alone, and he was running. So the watchman told David about it.

"He is by himself," said David. "So it must be good news."

The runner came nearer and nearer. Then the watchman saw another runner. "Look!" he called. "Here comes another runner. He is alone too."

"He must have more good news," said David.

"The first man runs like the priest's son," said the watchman.

"He is a good man," said David. "He will bring me good news."

The son ran up to the gate.

"Everything is all right!" he said. He bowed down with his face to the ground. "Cheer for God! He let you win over your enemies!"

"Is Absalom all right?" asked David.

"There was a lot going on," said the priest's son. "I didn't know what was happening."

"Wait here," said David.

Then the other man ran up to the gate. "Good news!" he said. "God has saved you from your enemies!"

"Is Absalom all right?" asked David.

"I hope all your enemies die like Absalom!" said the man.

David began to shake. He went up to the room over the gate. He cried. He kept saying, "My son Absalom! My son, my son, Absalom! I wish I could have died instead of you! Absalom, my son, my son!"

MARCH 21

King David Goes Back Home

2 SAMUEL 19–20

Someone told Joab, "King David is crying for Absalom."

The army had been glad they won. Then they heard that King David was crying for Absalom. So they became sad. The army went into the town quietly. They were like men who felt bad because they lost.

King David kept crying, "My son Absalom! Absalom, my son, my son!"

Joab went to see King David. "You've made your whole army feel bad," said Joab. "We just saved your life today! We just saved your family! But it looks like we're not important to you. It looks like you wish Absalom was alive and we were dead. Now go out and see your men. Cheer them up. If you don't, they won't fight for you again. That will be the biggest problem you've ever had."

So King David got up. He went out and sat at the gate of the city.

The men heard that David was sitting at the gate. So they all went to see him there.

While this was going on, the people who had followed Absalom began fussing. "King David saved us from our enemies," they said. "But he has left the country. It's all because of Absalom. We chose Absalom to be our king. But now he is dead. Shouldn't we ask King David to come back?"

Then David sent a message to the priests. "Tell the leaders I've heard what the people are saying. Will you be the last ones to bring me back?"

Everybody wanted David to be king again. So they sent him a message. "Come back. Bring all your men with you."

So King David headed back. He got to the Jordan River. Some men from Judah had come to the river. The servant from Saul's family was with them. They hurried to help the king's family across the river.

A man came across the river to the king. He had thrown rocks at David before. But now he bowed down with his face to the ground. "Please don't be angry at me," he said. "Forget the bad things I said when you left. I know I sinned. But today I'm coming to be the first to meet you."

"We should kill this man," said Joab's brother. "He said bad things about you."

"You don't think like I do," said David. "Should we kill people today? I know I'm king today." Then David promised the man who had thrown rocks, "You won't die."

Mephibosheth, Saul's grandson, came to meet King David too. He hadn't washed his feet or clothes since David left Jerusalem. He hadn't trimmed his hair.

"Why didn't you come with me?" asked King David.

"I was going to go with you," said Mephibosheth. "You know I can't walk. So I was going to ride my donkey. But my servant tricked me. He lied to you about me. But you're like God's angel to me. So do what you think best. I was from Saul's family. I should have died. But instead you let me eat at your table.

So I have no right to ask you for anything else."

"That's all I need to know," said David. "I'll let you have half of the land. Your servant will have the other half."

An old man came out to see King David too. The man was 80 years old. He and his friends had brought food to the king before.

"Come across the river with me," said King David. "Live in Jerusalem with me. I'll take care of you."

"I won't live many more years," said the old man. "I can't tell you what's good and bad. I can't even taste what I eat and drink. I can't hear very well. I'd just be in your way. I'll cross the river with you. Then I'll go back home. That way, I can die in my own town. But, look! Here's my son. He could go with you."

"Then your son will go with me," said David. "I'll do whatever you'd like me to do."

So everybody crossed the Jordan River. King David hugged the old man. He prayed for God to give the man good things. Then the man went back home.

Now there was a man named Sheba who liked to cause trouble. He called out, "We don't follow David! Everybody go to your own homes!"

So many people left King David to follow Sheba. But the people from Judah followed King David.

The Angel at the Barn
2 SAMUEL 24; 1 CHRONICLES 21

Satan came against God's people. He tried to make David do wrong. Satan tried to get David to count the men in the army. So David called Joab and the other army leaders. "Count the number of men in the army," he said. "I want to know who fights for us."

"I hope God gives you lots of men," said Joab. "All the men in the land will fight for you. Why do you need to list them? It's wrong."

But King David was the boss. So Joab and the leaders listed the men. It took them nine months and twenty days. They counted one million one hundred thousand men. But Joab didn't count men from Levi or Benjamin. He didn't think it was right.

Now King David's order to count the people was wrong to God. "I have sinned," said David. "Please take my sin away."

David's prophet was named Gad. God told Gad, "Go to David. Tell him I'm letting him choose one of these three things. He can have no food grow for three years. He can have his enemies win for three months. Or he can have three days of a terrible sickness through the whole land. You choose which one you want."

"I'm very upset," David told Gad. "Let God send the sickness. God is loving and kind. Let him be in control. But don't let the enemy be in control."

So God sent sickness, and 70,000 (seventy thousand) people died.

Now God's angel was on the way to Jerusalem. But God was very sad at what was happening. He told the angel, "Stop! That's enough!"

The angel was standing at a farmer's work place. David looked up and saw the angel. The angel was between earth and heaven. His sword was out. It was pointing to Jerusalem. So David went toward the work place.

The farmer was working. His four sons were with him. He turned around. He and his sons saw the angel too. His sons went to hide.

Then David walked up. The farmer bowed down with his face to the ground.

David said, "Sell me your work place. I want to build an altar to God here. Then he will stop this sickness."

"Take my barn for free," said the farmer. "Do whatever you want with it. I'll even give you the oxen to offer as a gift to God. I'll give you the wood. I'll also give you wheat to offer to God as a gift."

"No," said King David. "I'll pay you for it. I won't take something that's yours and give it to God. I won't give God something that cost me nothing."

So King David paid 15 pounds of gold. He bought the farmer's work

place. He built an altar there and offered gifts to God. Then God stopped the sickness.

MARCH 22

A House for God

(A Temple for God)

1 CHRONICLES 22; 28

David stood at the farmer's work place. He said, "God's worship house will be built here."

David chose men to cut stone. He got iron for making nails for the gate doors. He got cedar logs.

"My son Solomon is young," said David. "He hasn't done many things yet. And the worship house should be wonderful. It should be great. It should be something all nations know about. So I'll get things ready now."

Then David called Solomon. David told his son to build the worship house for God. David said that he had wanted to build a house for God. But God didn't want him to. God had told David, "You have killed too many people in wars. But your son Solomon will rule in a time of peace. There will be rest. Enemies won't come against Solomon. He will build a house for my name. A kingdom will come from his family. The kingdom will last forever."

"So, my son," said David, "build God's worship house. I pray that

God will make you wise. Then you'll obey all God's laws. If you do, things will go well. Be strong. Be brave. Don't be afraid. Don't give up.

"I've gathered many things you can use to build the worship house," said David. "I have gold, silver, iron, and stone. You can get more. There are men to cut stone. There are men to work with wood. There are men to work with gold and silver. There are more men than you can count. So get to work. I pray that God will be with you."

Then David told all the leaders to help Solomon. "God is with you. There is peace now," he said. "Work at following God. Build the worship house for God. Then you can put the ark box in it."

David gave Solomon the plans for building the worship house. These were plans that God's Spirit had told David. "God made me understand every part of the plan," said David.

Gifts

1 CHRONICLES 29

David talked to the leaders of God's people. He said, "I am giving lots of gold and silver for God's house. Now, who else will give to God today?"

Then the leaders gave gifts for the worship house. They gave a lot of gold and silver. They gave tons of metal and iron. They gave beautiful, shiny stones. The people were happy that their leaders were giving. David was happy too.

David praised God. He said,

"We praise you, God.
You are God forever and ever.
You are great and strong.
You own everything in heaven and
    earth.
You are ruler over everything.
Riches and greatness come from you.
Now, we thank you, God.
We praise your name."

Then David told everyone, "Praise your God." So everyone bowed down before God and King David.

The next day they offered many gifts on the altar. Then they ate and drank. They were very happy. They said Solomon would be their king.

Songs for Times of Trouble

My Shepherd

PSALM 23, by David

The Lord is my shepherd.
I am like his sheep.
I won't need anything.
He takes me to green fields
   so I can lie down.
He brings me to quiet water.
He makes me strong again.
He leads me in the way that is right
   because of who he is.
Sometimes I am in danger.
I'm like a sheep in a valley
   full of shadows.
I may be in danger.
But I will not be afraid
   because you are with me.
You make me feel safe.

You set a table for me
   even when my enemies are
     around.
You make me feel special.
My cup flows over.
I have more than I need.

I know that love and good things
   will be with me all my life.
I know I will live with God forever.

Be Still

PSALM 46, by Korah's Family

God is like a safe place to be.
He is strong.
He is our helper when there is trouble.
So we will not be afraid.
Even if the earth shakes.
Even if the mountains fall into the
     sea.
Even if the oceans roar and make
     huge waves.

"Be still and know that I am God.
Nations will call me great.
The earth will call me great."

God has all power, and he is with us.

A High Rock

PSALM 61, by David

Hear me call, God.
Listen to me pray.

185

I call to you from the ends of the
    earth.
I call to you when my heart gets tired.
Lead me to the rock that is higher
    than I am.
You are like a place where I can be
    safe.
You are like a strong tower.
I want to live with you forever.
I want to be safe under your wings.

Let the king live a long time.
May he rule and be near you forever.
Send your love to keep him safe.
And keep your promises to him.

Then I will sing praise to your name
    forever.
I will keep my promises to you
    every day.

Strong and Loving

PSALM 62, by David

I can rest only in God.
He is the one who saves me.
He is like a fort.
Nothing can shake me.

How long will sinful people fight?
They smile at lies.
They may say good things with
    their mouths.
But they say bad things in their
    hearts.

I trust in God.
He saves me.

He is like a fort.
Nothing can shake me.
I am safe with him.
Oh, people, always trust God.
Tell him everything in your hearts.
You are safe with God.

Since I Was Young

PSALM 71

I am safe with you, God.
Don't let me feel like nothing.
Listen to me and save me.
Be like a rock I can hide behind.
Save me from sinful people.

You alone are my hope, God,
    since I was young.
I have trusted you
    since I was young.
I have counted on you
    since I was born.
I will praise you forever.
I talk about how great you are all
    day long.

My enemies talk about me.
They wait and plan to kill me.
They say, "God forgot him.
Let's chase him and catch him.
No one will save him."
Don't be far away, God.
Come fast to help me.
Get rid of my enemies.

But I will always have hope.
What you have done for me
    is more than I can measure.

You have been my teacher since
    I was young.
I still tell about
    the wonderful things you do.
Don't forget me when I am old,
    even when I have gray hair.
Let me tell children about your power.

You are right, God.
You have done great things.
Who is like you, God?
I have had many troubles.
But you will give me life again.
You will care about me.

I will praise you with the harp.
Because you keep your promises, God.
My lips will shout with joy
    when I sing praise to you.
My voice will tell about
    all the right things you do.

MARCH 24

I Will Remember

PSALM 77, by Asaph

I cried to God for help.
I looked for God when I was upset.
I held out my hands to him at night.
But my soul would not feel better.

I remembered you, God.
I thought about you,
    and my spirit felt helpless.

You kept me from closing my eyes.
I was too upset to talk.

I thought about the days that came
    before this.
I thought about years of long ago.
I remembered my songs in the
    night.
My heart thought.
My spirit asked,
    "Will God forget me forever?
Will he never show his love to me
    again?
Doesn't he keep his promises?
Does he forget to be kind?
Has his anger kept his kindness
    away?"
Then I thought,
    "I will remind God of how he
        took care of us."
    I will remember your wonders
        from long ago.
    I will think of the great things
        you did.

Your ways are best, God.
You are the God who does
    wonders.
You saved your people with your
    strong arm.

The water saw you and splashed.
Clouds spilled their rain.
Your thunder was heard in the
    wind.
Your lightning lit up the world.
The earth shook.
Your path went through the sea.
But no one saw your footprints.

A Whole Heart

PSALM 86, by David

Hear me, God, and answer me.
I'm poor, and I need you.
Keep my life safe,
    because I am all yours.
Be kind to me, God,
    for I call to you all day long.

Teach me your way, God.
I will follow you.
Give me a heart that is all yours.
Then I'll cheer for you, Lord my God.
I will praise you with all my heart.
I will always tell how great you are.
Your love for me is great.
You are a kind God.
You do not get angry quickly.
You have plenty of love.
You keep your promises.
Make me strong, and save me.
Give me a sign of your goodness, so
    that my enemies will see it.
Then they will not know which way
    to go.
You have helped me, God.
You cared about me.

Under His Wings

PSALM 91

The person who lives safe in God
    Most High
    will rest in God's shadow.
God has all power.
I will talk about God.

I will say, "He is like a fort to me.
He is my God, and I trust him."

God will save you from traps.
He will save you from sickness that
    takes your life.
He will cover you with his feathers.
You will be safe under his wings.
His promises will guard you.
You will not be afraid of night.
You will not be afraid of danger in
    the day.
You will not be afraid of sickness.
A thousand people may fall down at
    your side.
Ten thousand may fall at your right
    hand.
But nothing bad will come near you.
You will only see it with your eyes.
You will see what happens to sinful
    people.

You can let God be like a safe house.
Live under his tent, and you won't
    be hurt.
Trouble will not come close to you.
God will tell his angels about you.
He will tell them to keep you safe.
They will lift you up in their hands.
You will not hit your foot on a stone.

God says, "I will save people who
    love me.
I will keep them safe because they
    trust in me.
They will call me, and I will answer.
I will be with them in trouble.

I will save them.
They will be important to me.
I will please them by giving them a
    long life.
I will show them how I save them."

The Deep Earth in His Hand

PSALM 95:1-7

Come!
Let's sing with joy to God!
Let's shout out loud to the one who
    saves us.
Let's come to him, giving thanks.
Let's worship him with music and
    song.

The Lord is our great God.
He is the great King above all gods.
The deep earth is in his hands.
The mountain peaks belong to him.
The sea is his. He made it.
His hands made the dry land.

Come!
Let's bow down in worship.

Let's bow before God our Maker.
He is our God.
We are the people of his field.
We are the sheep he takes care of.

Wake Up the Morning

PSALM 108, by David

My heart will stay with you, God.
I will sing.
I will make music with all my soul.
Wake up, harp!
I will wake up the morning.
I will praise you, God.
Your love is higher than the sky.
Be praised above the sky.
Show your greatness over all the
    earth.

Help us with your strong right
    hand.
Then the people you love will be
    saved.
God spoke from his home.
"I will measure out the land.
It is my helmet.
It is my washing bowl.
I toss my shoe on it.
I shout over it."

Help us win over our enemies.
People's help isn't good for
    anything.
We will win with God's help.
He will get rid of our enemies.

189

My Eyes Look Up

PSALM 121

My eyes look up to the hills.
Where does my help come from?
My help comes from God.
He made heaven and earth.

God will not let you trip and fall.
He watches over you.
He never goes to sleep.

God is the shade at your right hand.
The sun won't hurt you in the
     daytime.
The moon won't hurt you at night.

God will keep you safe.
God will watch over you when you
     go out.
He will watch over you when you
     come in.
He will watch over you now and
     forever.

Show Me the Way

PSALM 143, by David

Hear my prayer, God.
Help me because you do what is right.
You keep your promises.
Please don't judge me.
No one is as good as you.

The enemy chases me.
He pushes me to the ground.
So my spirit is not strong anymore.
My heart is afraid.

I hold my hands out to you.
My soul is thirsty for you.
Answer me quickly, God.
Don't hide your face.
If you do, I will be like a person
     who is lost.
When the morning comes,
     let me hear about your love that
          does not end.
Show me the way I should go.
Save me from my enemies.
You are a safe place where I can hide.
Teach me to do what you want,
     for you are my God.
I pray that your good Spirit
     will lead me on smooth ground.

Save my life, God,
     because of who you are.
Bring me out of this trouble,
     because you do what's right.
Your love never fails.

Shoot Your Arrows

PSALM 144, by David

Praise God.
He teaches my hands to fight.
He is my loving God.
He saves me.
He is a guard for me.
I go to him to be safe.

God, why should you care about
     people?
People are like a breath of air.
Their days are like shadows that fade.

Open the sky, God, and come down.
Touch the mountains and make
   them smoke.
Send flashes of lightning out.
Shoot your arrows and make your
   enemies run.
Reach down your hand and save me.
Save me from strangers who lie.

Then our young sons will be like
   healthy plants.
Our daughters will be beautiful,
like posts that make a palace
   pretty.
We will have thousands of sheep in
   our fields.
Our oxen will be strong.
No one will break through our walls.
There will be no trouble in our
   streets.

Then the people will be happy.
Good things come to people
   when God is their Lord.

Songs about Good and Bad

A Tree by the Water

PSALM 1

Good things come to people
who don't do what bad people
tell them to do.
They don't follow sinful people.
They don't make fun of others.
They are happy to follow God's way.
Day and night they think about
what God says.

They are like trees growing by the river.
They give fruit at the right time.
Their leaves never dry up.

Everything they do turns out good.

It's not this way for sinful people.
They are like dust that the wind
blows away.
So they will not stand before God.
They will not be with good people.

God watches over people who do
what's right.
But the path of sinful people will
not last.

Like Strong Mountains

PSALM 36, by David

Sinful people don't think God is
important at all.
They are too proud to see their
own sin.
Their words are lies.
They don't do what is wise or what
is good.
Even when they lie in bed at night,
they plan to do wrong things.

God, your love is as great as all of
space.

192

Your promises reach up into the sky.
The right things you do are like
    strong mountains.
The way you are fair is like a deep
    sea.
God, you care for people and
    animals both.
Your love never ends.
It is greater than the greatest riches.
Some people are great. Some are not.
But all are safe in the shadow of
    your wings.
You have plenty in your house to
    feed them.
You let them drink from your
    wonderful rivers.
We see light because of your light.

Keep loving the people who love you.
Don't let proud people come
    against me.
Sinful people fall down.
They get thrown down, and they
    can't get up.

Like the Sun at Noon

PSALM 37:1-11, by David

Don't worry because of sinful
    people.
Don't wish you were like people
    who do wrong.
They will dry up like grass.
They will die like green plants.

Trust in God, and do what's good.
Live and enjoy being safe.

Be glad in God.
Then he will give you
    what your heart really wants.

Choose to always follow God.
Trust him, and he will help you.
He will make the right things you do
    shine like the sunrise.
He will make your good ways
    shine like the sun at noon.

Be with God, and be still.
Be quiet and wait for him.
Don't worry when sinful people
    get away with doing wrong.

Keep away from anger, and don't
    worry.
It only leads to sin.
Sinful people will not get God's
    riches.
But people who trust God will get
    all God has for them.

Some day sinful people will be gone.
Even if you look for them, you will
    not find them.
But God's people will always have
    his riches.
They will enjoy peace.

"Here I Am"

PSALM 40:1-10, by David

I was still, and I waited for God.
He heard my cry.
My trouble was deep like a pit.

He lifted me out.
He lifted me out of the mud.
He put my feet on a rock.
It was a strong place for me to stand.
God gave me a new song to praise
    him.
Lots of people will see this.
Then they will trust in God.

God will bring good things to people
    who trust in him.
Lord my God,
    you have done many wonderful
        things.
No one can even count
    the things you planned for us.

You didn't want me to bring you a gift.
Instead, you wanted me.
So I said, "Here I am.
There are words about me in your
    book.
I am happy to do what you want me
    to do, God.
Your way is in my heart."

I talk about how you keep your
    promises.
I talk about how you save me.
I don't hide your love and your truth.

Riches

PSALM 49, by Korah's Family

Listen, everybody.
I will tell a riddle with my harp.

Why should I be afraid of bad days?
Why should I be afraid of sinful
    people?
They trust in their riches.
No person can save another person.
No person can pay God to save him.
There is not enough money to buy
    a life.
Money can't help anyone live
    forever.

Wise and foolish men will all die.
They'll leave their riches behind.
People don't live here forever,
    even if they are rich.

This is what happens
    to people who trust in
        themselves.
They die just like sheep do.
Their graves will be far away
    from their big houses.
But God will save my life.
He will take me to be with him.

So don't be surprised when people
    get rich.
They won't take anything with them
    when they die.
People may say great things about
    them.
But when they die, it won't matter.

God Shines

PSALM 50, by Asaph

God is the Strong One.
He is the Lord.

He calls the earth from the sunrise
to the sunset.
God shines from his city, Zion.
Zion is a place that is good and
beautiful.
God comes, and he is not quiet.
A fire goes before him.
A storm roars around him.
He calls heaven and earth.
He can see who is right and who is
wrong.
He says, "Bring me the people
who promised to be mine."

"Hear me, my people, and I'll speak.
I am your God.
I don't blame you for what you
give me.
But I don't need bulls from your
barns
or goats from your pens.
Every forest animal is mine.
I own the cows on the hills.
I know every bird in the mountains.
The animals in the fields are mine.
If I were hungry, I would not tell you.
The world and everything in it is mine.
Give thanks to me.
Keep your promises to me.
Call on me when you are in trouble.
I will save you.
Then you will show how great I am."

But to sinful people God says,
"Why do you talk about my rules?
You hate my ways and don't obey
my words.

You help robbers.
You go along with foolish people.
You use your mouths to say sinful
things.
You use your voice to lie.
I have been quiet.
So you think I am just like you.
But if you forget God, no one will
save you.
The people who give thanks show
love for me.
They are getting ready for me to
save them."

My Feet Almost Tripped

PSALM 73, by Asaph

It's true! God is good to his people.
He is good to people whose hearts
are sinless.

But my feet almost tripped.
I nearly fell, because I wanted to be
like the proud people.
I saw that sinful people get rich.
They seem to have no troubles.
They are healthy and strong.
They don't have problems like most
people have.
So they wear pride like a gold band
around their necks.
Their hearts are hard.
There is no end to their bad plans.
They make fun of people.
Their voices are full of hate.
They want to boss everyone around.
They say that heaven belongs to them.

They say the earth is theirs, too.
People who follow them believe
what they say.
They say, "How could God know?"

That is what sinful people are like.
They don't have any cares.
They keep getting rich.

So have I kept my heart clean for
nothing?
I've had trouble every morning.

I tried to understand this, but it was
hard.
It was hard until I talked to God.
Then I knew what would happen
to sinful people.

God, I know you put their feet
on ground they can't stand up on.
You will tear them down all of a
sudden.
You will wipe them away with fear.
You will stand up, God.
Then their good life will be just a
dream.

But I'm always with you.
You hold my right hand, and you
lead me.
Some day you will take me to
greatness.
Who else do I have in heaven?
Only you.
And all I want on earth is you.
My body and my heart may get sick.
But God makes my heart strong.

He is mine forever.
It's good to be near God.
That's where I go to be safe.
God, I will tell about the things
you do.

MARCH 28

Even the Sparrow

PSALM 84, by Korah's Family

The place where you live is
beautiful, God!
My soul wants to be
with you.
You are the
living
God.

Even the sparrow has a home with
you.
The swallow has a nest, too.
She can raise her baby birds at a
place close to you.
You are the Lord Who Has All Power.
You are my King and my God.

Good things come to people who
live in your house.
They always praise you.

Good things come to people who
are strong in you.
They set their hearts on following you.
You make the valley flow with water.
Rain makes pools of water there.

One day in your house is better
     than a thousand days anywhere
          else.
I would rather be a door keeper in
     God's house
     than live with sinful people.
The Lord God is like a sun.
He is like a shield.
He makes people important.
He does not keep anything good
     from those who do what is right.
Good comes to people who trust
     you, God.

Every Morning

PSALM 90, A Prayer That Moses Wrote

God, we have lived with you
     ever since you made people.
You were God before the mountains
     were born.
You were God before you made the
     earth.
Forever and ever you are God.

The way you see it,
     a thousand years are like a day.
They're like only part of a night.
People don't last long.
They are like the new morning
     grass.
It grows up in the morning,
     but by evening it's dry.
We are afraid of your anger.
You see our secret sins in your light.
We live 70 years, or 80 if we are
     strong.

But we see lots of trouble and
     sadness.
Our years pass fast, and then we fly
     away.
Teach us to use our years doing
     what's right.

Be kind to the people who serve you.
Every morning, fill us with your
     love that never ends.
Then we'll sing with joy as long as
     we live.
Make us glad for as many days as
     we have been sad.
Show our children how great you
     are.
Be kind to us.
Let good things come from the work
     we do.

Morning and Night

PSALM 92

It's good to praise God.
It's good to make music to your
     name, Most High God.
In the morning, it's good to tell
     about your love.
At night, it's good to tell
     how you keep your promises.
It's good to make music on the harp.

You make me glad by what you do,
     God.
Your works are great,
     and your thoughts are deep.
Fools do not understand them.

Sinful people spring up like grass.
They may grow for a while.
But they will be torn down forever.

You are praised forever, God.
I know your enemies will die.
All sinful people will run away.

People who do what's right will
    grow like palm trees.
They will grow as tall as cedar trees.
They will grow in God's palace.
They will still grow fruit when they
    are old.
They will stay fresh and green.
They will say, "God is right.
There is no sin in him."

Even in the Dark

PSALM 112

Praise God!

God brings good things to people
    who look up to God.
They enjoy his commands.

Their children will be a success.
God brings good things to the
    families of people who do right.
Riches are in their houses.
Even in the dark, light will shine
  for people who do what's right.
They are kind and good.
They give to others. They are fair in
    business.
Those who do what's right will
    always be remembered.

They are not afraid of bad news.
Their hearts will keep on trusting
    God.
One day they will win over their
    enemies.

They give to poor people.
They will always do what's right.
They are strong.
Others treat them like important
    people.

Sinful people will see it.
They will be angry.
    Other people will forget them.
Their wishes will turn into nothing.

Eyes That Can't See

PSALM 115

You are great, God, not us.
It's because of your love. You keep
    your promises.

Why do nations say, "Where is their
    God?"
Our God is in heaven.
He does whatever he wants.
But their idols are made of silver
    and gold.
They are made by people's hands.
Idols have mouths, but they
    can't talk.
They have eyes, but they can't see.
They have ears, but they can't hear.
They have noses, but they can't smell.
They have hands, but they can't feel.

They have feet, but they can't
    walk.
They can't even make a sound.
People who make them will be like
    them.
People who trust in them will also
    be like them.

If you think God is the most
    important,
    you should trust him.
He is your helper and your guard.

God remembers us.
He will bring good things
    to everyone who looks up to him.
It doesn't matter if they are great or
    small.

The highest of all space is God's.
But he gave the earth to people.
We are the ones who praise God.
We cheer for him now and forever.

Praise God!

Songs of Joy

From Children's Mouths

PSALM 8, by David

Lord, our Lord,
  your name is great all over the
    earth!

Your greatness is higher than the sky.
You plan for children and babies to
    praise you.
Then your enemies are quiet.

I see the sky that you made with
    your hands.
I see the moon and stars that you
    put up there.
Then I wonder why you even think
    about people.
I wonder why you care about us.
But you made us only a little lower
    than the beings from heaven.
You made us important to you.

You put people in charge of
    everything you made.
They rule over sheep and cows and
    all the wild animals.

They rule over birds in the sky and
    fish in the sea.

Lord, our Lord,
  your name is great all over the
    earth!

God Teaches Me

PSALM 16, by David

Keep me safe, God.
I come to you to find a safe place.

I said to God, "You're my Lord.
Without you, I have nothing good."

I am happy with God's people.
People who don't put God first have
    more and more trouble.

God teaches my heart even at night.
So I am glad.
I will rest safely.
You won't leave me in the grave.
You show me how to live.
You fill me with joy, because you
    are near me.

But the greatest pleasure will be to
live with you forever.

God's Way

PSALM 19, by David

The sky shows how great God is.
Every day it tells about God.
Every night it shows what he is
like.
No matter what language people
speak,
they can understand what the
sky tells.
All over the world, people can see it.

God has made the sky a tent for
the sun.
The sun is like a groom getting
married.
He comes out of his tent.
The sun is like a happy winner
running a race.
It rises at one side of the sky
and travels to the other side.
Nothing can hide from the heat
of the sun.

God's way is the best.
It keeps us strong.
We can trust God's rules.
They make foolish people wise.
God's commands are right.
They fill our hearts with joy.
God's commands shine clearly,
giving our spirits light.
God's rules are sure and right.

They are more special than gold.
They are sweeter than honey from
the honeycomb.
Good comes to those who obey
God's rules.

Keep me from choosing to sin.
Then I will do what's right and not
what's wrong.

I want everything I say and think
to make you happy, God.

The Great King

PSALM 24, by David

The earth and everything in it
belong to God.
The world and everyone in it belong
to him.
He made the land and set it on
the sea.

Who can live with God?
Only people who don't have sin in
their hearts.
People who put God first.
God will send good things to
them.

Lift up your heads, you gates.
Open up, you doors.
Then the Great King can come in.
Who is this Great King?
God! He is strong and full of
power.
He is the Great King.

Tell about God

PSALM 29, by David

Tell how great and strong God is.
Worship God.
Think of how beautiful he is, how
    special, how holy.
He is the best.

God's voice thunders over the sea.
His voice is great and full of power.
His voice is so strong, it breaks
    cedar trees in pieces.
His voice strikes like a flash of
    lightning.
It makes the desert shake.
It twists oak trees.
In God's house everyone calls out,
    "God is Great!"
God sits on his throne.
He is the King forever.
He makes his people strong and
    gives them peace.

A New Song

PSALM 33:1-11

Let those who do what's right sing
    with joy to God.
Praising God fits you.
Praise him with the harp.
Make music to him on the lyre that
    has 10 strings.
Sing a new song to God.
Play your best and shout with joy.

God's word is right and true.
You can trust him in all he does.
God loves what is right and good.
The earth is full of his love.
His love never comes to an end.

The sky was made by God's word.
The stars were made by breath from
    his mouth.
He brings the sea water together.
He keeps the deep water in store
    houses.
All the earth should be filled with
    wonder for God.
All people should know how special
    he is.
He said a word, and the world was
    made.
The plans of God's heart will always
    come true.

Who Is Strong?

PSALM 33:12-22

A nation can be happy
    when God is their Lord.

The people God chose can be
  happy.
These people are the ones God
  chose for his own.
God looks down from heaven and
  sees everyone.
He made their hearts,
  so he understands everything
  they do.

A big army does not save a king.
A fighter does not win just because
  he is strong.
A horse cannot save anyone, even if
  it's strong.
God watches over people who love
  him.
They trust him to give them what
  they need.

We wait for God.
He is our guard. He helps us.
Keep us in your love that never
  ends, God.
We trust you to bring us what is good.

Where the Sun Rises

PSALM 65, by David

God, we will keep our promises
  to you.
You hear us pray.
We were sad because of our sins,
  but you forgave us.
The people you choose are happy.
People everywhere hope in you,
  even those on the far seas.

People who live far away talk about
  your wonders.
You bring glad songs from the
  places where the sun rises
  and sets.
You take care of the land.
You water it and make it ready
  to grow crops.
Your rivers are full of water.
You soak the fields and make
  them flat.
You make dirt soft with rain.
You make good crops grow
  and give us plenty of food.
Carts spill over with more than we
  need.
The hills look glad, and sheep fill
  the fields.
Crops of grain cover the valleys.
They all shout and sing for joy.

Come and See

PSALM 66:16-20

Come and listen, if you love God.
Let me tell you what he did for me.
I called out to him.
I praised him.
If I had kept sin in my heart,
  God would not have listened.
But I know that God listened.
He heard me pray.
Cheer for God!
He did not turn away my prayer!
He did not keep his love away
  from me!

The Thunder of the Water

PSALM 93

God is King!
Greatness is like a robe he wears.
He is strong.
The world stays where God put it.
It cannot be moved.

You became King long ago.
You have lived forever.
The seas lift up their voice.
The seas lift up their pounding waves.

God is stronger than the thunder of
     the waters.
God is stronger than the waves of
     the sea.

Shine!

PSALM 94:1-15

God, you are the one who pays
     sinful people back
   for what they do.
Stand up, Judge of the earth.
Pay the proud what they should get.
How long will sinful people be happy?
They brag and hurt your people,
     God.
They kill and say, "God doesn't care."

Listen, you fools!
When will you become wise?
God made your ears.

So, of course, God hears.
God made your eyes.
   So, of course, God sees.
God is mad at the nations.
   So, of course, God pays people
     back for the wrong they do.
God teaches.
   So, of course, God knows
     everything.
He knows what people think.

People are happy when they obey
     you, God.
They are happy when you teach
     them your ways.
You save them from days of trouble.
God will not turn away from his
     people.
He will never leave his children.
He will say what's right and wrong.
All the people whose hearts are
     right will follow what he says.

His Lightning

PSALM 97:1-7

God is King.
Let the earth be glad.
Let lands far away by the sea show
     their joy.

Clouds and darkness are around
     God.
His kingdom is built on what is
     right and fair.
Fire goes ahead of him.
It gets rid of his enemies on every side.

His lightning lights up the world.
The earth sees it and shakes.
Mountains melt like wax in front
   of God.
The sky shows how right he is.
All people see how great he is.

People who worship idols seem like
   nothing.
Worship God!

Make Music!
PSALM 98

Sing a new song to God.
He has done wonderful things.
His right hand saves.
He shows the nations how right he is.
He remembered his love.
He kept his promises to his people.

Shout to God with joy.
Sing happy songs with music.
Make music to God with the harp.
Make music with horns.
Shout with joy before God, the King!

Let the sea and everything in it
   shout out.
Let the world and all who live in it
   sing out.
Let rivers clap their hands.
Let mountains sing together with joy.
Let them sing to God.
He comes to judge the earth.
He will judge people by what is
   fair.

The King
PSALM 99:1-5

God is the King.
He sits in the King's chair between
   the heavenly beings.
Let the earth shake!
God is great in his city of Zion.
He is great over all the nations.
Let them praise his great and
   wonderful name.
God is holy. He does no wrong.

The King is strong.
He loves what's fair and right.
Treat God as the most important one.
Worship at his feet, for he is holy.
The Lord our God never does wrong.

His Sheep
PSALM 100

Let all the earth shout to God
   with joy.
Worship God and be glad.
Come to him with songs of joy.
Know that the Lord is God.
He made us.
We are his people.
We are like sheep from his field.

Go through God's gates giving
   thanks.
Go into his palace with praise.
Give thanks to him.
Cheer for his name, because God
   is good.

His love lasts forever.
He always keeps his promises.

APRIL 1

As High As the Sky

PSALM 103, by David

I say to my soul, "Cheer for God!"
Everything in me, praise his holy
    name!
Don't forget the good things he has
    done.
He forgives all your sins.
He makes you well from every
    sickness.
He saves your life.
He is loving and kind to you.
He answers your wishes with good
    things.
When you grow old, you feel young
    again.
You feel strong, like the eagle.

God does what is right and fair.
He is full of love and kindness.
He does not get angry quickly.
Love flows out of him.
He won't always blame us.
He won't be angry forever.
He doesn't pay us back for our sins,
    even though that's what should
        happen.
God's love is as high
    as the sky is above the earth.
He has moved our sins away from us
    as far as the east is from the west.

God is loving and kind to people
    who worship him.
He is like a father
    who is loving and kind to his
        children.
He remembers that we're made out
    of dust.
His love is always with people who
    worship him.
He is good to their children's children.

Cheer for God, you angels.
You are the strong ones who do
    what he says.
Cheer for God, everything
    everywhere in his kingdom.

Earth, Sea, and Moon

PSALM 104

Cheer for God, my soul!

The Lord my God is very great.
Wonder and greatness are like
        clothes on him.
He wraps himself in light.
He rolls out the sky like a tent.
He puts his upstairs rooms in the
    rain clouds.
He makes his chariot from clouds.
He rides on wings of wind.
Winds take his messages.
Flames of fire serve him.

God put the earth where he wanted it.
It can never be moved.
The waters were above the mountains.

But they rushed away when they
heard his thunder.
They flowed over the mountains
into valleys.
They went where God told them to
go.
He drew a line they cannot cross.
They will never cover the earth
again.

God makes springs of water flow
into rivers.
They give water to all the animals in
the field.
Wild donkeys drink.
Birds make nests by the water.
They sing in the tree branches.
God waters mountains from his
upstairs rooms.
He makes grass grow for cows.
He makes plants grow for people to
use.
Food comes up from the earth.
Then people can make wine
and oil.
People can make bread so they'll
be strong.
God's trees have plenty of water.
The stork makes its home in the
pine trees.
Wild goats live in the high
mountains.
Badgers hide in the rocks.

The moon shows the seasons.
The sun knows when to go down.
God brings the darkness.

Then forest animals come out to
look around.
Lions roar for food.

They look for the food God gives
them.
When the sun comes up, they creep
away.
They go back to their dens and lie
down.
That's when people go off to work.
They work until evening.

You have made so many things, God!
You made them all by your wisdom.
The earth and the deep, wide sea
are full of living things you made.
There are too many to count.
There are all kinds of living things.
Some are big, and some are small.

They all look to you, God.
They look for food from you
when it's time to eat.
You open your hand and give it to
them.

Then they are full.
But when you hide your face,
    they are afraid.
When you take their breath away,
    they die and turn into dust again.
When you send your Spirit,
    new life begins.
You make things on the earth new.

May God's greatness last forever.
May God show his joy
    when he sees what he has made.
He looks at the earth, and it shakes.
He touches mountains, and they
    smoke.

I will sing to God all my life.
Cheer for God, my soul!
Praise God!

APRIL 2

Sunrise to Sunset

PSALM 113

Praise God!

You servants of God, cheer for his
    name.
Praise his name now and forever.
His name should be praised from
    sunrise to sunset.

God is great over all nations.
His power is great above the sky.
Who is like God?
He sits on the King's chair in heaven.

He bends down to look at the sky
    and the earth.

God helps poor people.
He takes them to sit with princes.
He gives children to the woman
    who thought
    she would never have any.
He makes her happy in her home.

Praise God!

Hiding in My Heart

PSALM 119:1-16

Good things come to people who do
    what's right.
They keep God's rules. They obey him.
They look for God with all their hearts.
They don't do wrong.
You have told us your rules, God.
We should obey all of them.
I wish I would always do what you
    want me to do.
Then I would never feel bad.
I will praise you with a heart that's
    right.

How can a young person keep
    doing what's right?
By following your word, God.
I look for you with all my heart.
Don't let me turn away from your law.
I have hidden your word in my
    heart so I won't sin against you.
I'm glad to follow your rules.
I will not forget your word.

With All My Heart

PSALM 119:33-48

Teach me to follow you, God.
Help me understand.
Then I will obey you to the end.
I will obey with all my heart.
Lead me in your ways,
  because that's what makes me
    happy.
Don't let me be selfish.
Turn my eyes away from things that
  waste my time.

Send me your love that never ends,
  God.
Save me like you promised.
Then I will answer the people who
  make fun of me.
I'll have an answer
  because I trust what you say.
I will obey you forever and ever.
I will be free,
  because I look for what you want
    me to do.
I will tell kings about your rules.
I will not feel bad,
  because I am happy with your
    rules.
I love them and think about them.

More Special than Gold

PSALM 119:65-72

Do good to me just like you said,
  God.
Teach me what I need to know.

Teach me to choose wisely.
I believe in your rules.
In the past I did what was wrong,
  but now I obey you.
You are good, and what you do is
  good.
Proud people lie about me.
Their hearts are hard.
They have no feelings.
But I keep your laws with all my
  heart.
It was good for me to have trouble,
  because I learned your rules.
Your law is more special to me
  than thousands of pieces of
    silver.
It is more special to me
  than thousands of pieces of gold.

Foggy Eyes

PSALM 119:81-96

My soul gets weak,
  because I want so much for you
    to save me.
My eyes are foggy,
  because I have looked so long for
    your promise.
I say, "When will you cheer me
  up?"
I feel like I'm in a cloud of smoke.
But I don't forget your rules.
How long do I have to wait?
When will you pay people back for
  doing wrong?
Proud people try to make me fall.
Help me.

People are mean to me for no reason.
They almost got rid of me.
But I didn't turn away from your rules.
Save my life by your love.
Then I will obey you.

Your word and your promises last
     forever, God.
I am happy with your law.
If I had not been,
   I would have died in my trouble.
I will never forget your commands,
   because you saved my life.
Sinful people wait to get rid of me.
But I will think about your rules.
Even the best things go only so far.
But your rules last forever.

Sweet Words

PSALM 119:97-112

I love your law so much!
I think about it all day.
Your rules make me wiser than
     my enemies.
I understand more than my
     teachers do.
I understand more than the
     leaders do.
That's because I think about your
     rules.
I stay away from sin.
Your words taste so sweet!
They are sweeter than honey in my
     mouth.

Your comands teach me to
     understand.
So I hate everything that is wrong.

Your word is like a lamp
   that shows my feet where to go.
It is like a light for my path.
I may put my life in danger.
But I won't forget your law.
Sinful people set traps for me.
But I will not leave your ways.
Your rules will be my gift forever.
They fill my heart with joy.

My Guard

PSALM 119:113-128

I hate people who say one thing
   and then say a different thing.
They can't make up their minds.
But I love your law.
I can go to you to be safe.
You are my guard.
The words you say give me hope.
Get away from me, you sinful
     people.
I want to obey God!
Hold me, God. Then I'll be safe.
I will always follow your rules.
You are so great!
I shake when I think about it.
I wonder at your laws.

I have done what is right and fair.
Don't leave me alone with my
     enemies.
Make sure I'm all right.

Don't let proud people boss me
    around.
Show me your love.
Teach me your rules.
It's time for you to do something,
    God.
People are not obeying your law.
I love your law more than gold.
I know that all your commands
    are right.

Before Sunrise
PSALM 119:145-160

I call you with all my heart.
Answer me, God. Then I'll obey you.
Save me. Then I'll keep your laws.

I get up before sunrise,
    and I cry for help.
My eyes stay open all night
    so I can think about your
    promises.
Hear my voice because of your love.
Many enemies are coming
    against me.
But I don't turn away from you.

I don't like people who don't
    obey you.
See how I love your ways.
Save my life, God, by your love.

Where God's People Go
PSALM 122, by David

I was glad with the people who
    said, "Let's go to God's house."
Our feet stand at your gate, Jerusalem.

Jerusalem is a city with buildings
    close together.
That's where God's people go.
They go there to praise God's name.
That's where the judges sit.

Pray for Jerusalem to have peace.
"I pray that people who love you
    will be safe.
I pray that there will be peace in
    your city.
I pray that there will be safety
    around your towers."
Then my family and friends will
    be safe.
I will pray for good things to come
    to Jerusalem.

Out of the Hunter's Trap
PSALM 124, by David

Men came to fight us.
They were angry with us.
God was on our side,
    or they would have eaten us alive.

211

Our troubles would have covered
us like deep water.
They would have taken us away.

Praise God.
He did not let them get us.
We got away like a bird gets out of
the hunter's trap.
The trap broke, and we got away.
Our help is in God's name.
He is the Maker of heaven and
earth.

You Made Me Bold

PSALM 138, by David

I will praise you, God, with all my
heart.
I will sing your praise.
I will bow down toward your
worship house.
I praise you for your love.
I praise you for keeping your
promises.
You made your name and your
word to be the greatest.
You answered me when I called.
You made me bold and gave me a
brave heart.

I may have trouble.
But you save my life, God.
You hold out your hand to stop
my angry enemies.
God will do what he planned
for me.
God, your love lasts forever.

In the Secret Place

PSALM 139, by David

God, you know me.
You know when I sit down and
when I get up.
You know what I'm thinking.
You know when I go out and when
I lie down.
You know all my ways.
Even before I say a word, you know
it all, God.

You go behind me and in front of me.
You put your hand on me.
It's wonderful.
But it's too much for me to
understand.

Where can I go to get away from
your Spirit?
Where can I run to get away from
you?
I could go up into space, but you are
there.
I could make a bed in the deep
places below.
But you are there.
I could fly on the morning's wings.
I could land far beyond the sea.
But even there, your hand will
lead me.
You right hand will hold on to me.

I might say, "I know the darkness
will hide me."

But darkness is not dark to you.
Darkness is like light to you.

You made every part of me.
You put me together inside my
    mother.
I praise you, because the way you
    made me is wonderful.
Everything you do is wonderful.
I know that for sure.
My body was not hidden from you.
It was not hidden when you made
    me in the secret place.
You saw my body before it had a
    shape.
You planned all my days.
You wrote them in your book,
    even before I had lived one of them.

What you think about is so
    important to me, God!
I can't count all the things you
    think.
If I could, they would be more than
    pieces of sand.
When I wake up, I am still with you.

Look into me, God.
Know what's in my heart.
Test me, and know what I think about.
See if there is anything bad in me.
Lead me in the way that lasts forever.

Wonderful Love

PSALM 145, by David

I will bow before you, my God the
    King.

I will praise you every day.
I will worship your name forever.

No one can understand how great
    God is.
God is loving and kind.
He does not get angry quickly.
He is full of love.
God is good to everyone.
He is kind to everything he made.

God keeps all his promises.
He treats everything he made with
    love.
He holds up everyone who falls.

God is right in everything he does.
He is loving.
He is near everyone who calls to him.
He gives good things to people who
    look up to him.
He hears their cry and saves them.
God watches over people who love
    him.
But he gets rid of sinful people.

My mouth will cheer for God.
Let everyone praise his name forever.

Praise Him!

PSALM 148

Praise God from heaven high above.
Praise him, all you angels.
Praise him, armies of heaven.
Praise him, sun and moon.
Praise him, you stars that shine.

Praise him, you high heavens.
Let everything God made praise
   him.
He said the word, and they were
   made.
He set them in their places forever.

Praise God from the earth.
Praise him, you great sea life.
Praise him, you deep ocean.
Praise him, lightning and hail.
Praise him, snow and clouds and
   storm winds that do what he says.
Praise him, you mountains and hills.
Praise him, fruit trees and cedar
   trees.
Praise him, you wild animals and
   cows.
Praise him, small animals and birds
   that fly.
Praise him, kings and all nations,
   princes and all you rulers.
Praise him, young men and women,
   old men and children.

Let them all praise God.
His name should be most important.
He is greater than the earth and sky.
He gave his people a strong king.
He is the one they cheer for.
They are close to his heart.

Praise God.

Dancing
PSALM 150

Praise God in his mighty heavens.
Praise him for the powerful things
   he has done.
Praise him for how great he is.
Praise him with horns and harps.
Praise him with tambourines and
   dancing.
Praise him with flutes and with
   cymbals that crash.

Let everything that lives praise God!

All Kinds of Songs

Chariots and Horses

PSALM 20, by David

I pray that God will answer you
　　when you are sad.
I pray that God will guard you and
　　send you help.
I pray that he will remember the
　　worship gifts you gave him.

I pray that God will give you what
　　you wish for.
I pray that he will make your plans
　　work out.
I pray that we'll shout and be glad
　　when you win.
I pray that we'll wave our flags in
　　God's name.
I pray that God will give you what
　　you ask for.

God answers his people from heaven.
He saves them with his great power.
Some people trust in horses.
Some people trust in chariots.
They will fall.

But we trust in God.
We will stand strong.

Good and Right

PSALM 25:1-14, by David

I lift my soul to you, Lord.
I trust in you, my God!
Don't let sinful people win.
People who trust in you will feel good.
But sinful people won't feel good
　　for anything.

Show me the way I should live, God.
Lead me and teach me.
It is you, God, who saves me.
You give me hope all day long.

Remember your love for me.
Don't remember what I have done
　　wrong.
Remember me by how much you
　　love me,
　　because you are good, God.
Forgive my sins because of who
　　you are.
You will teach people who love you

215

how to choose your way.
You share your plans with people
who love you.
You give them your promises.

Not like a Horse

PSALM 32, by David

People are happy when their sins
are forgiven.
Their sins are erased.
People are happy when God throws
away the list of their sins.

When I kept quiet about my sins,
I felt terrible.
I cried all day.
Day and night, God, you tried to get
me to listen.
My strength melted away
like it does on a hot summer day.
Then I told you about my sins.
I didn't hide them.
I said, "I will tell God about my sins."
Then you forgave me.

So everyone who loves you should
pray to you.
You are like a place for me to hide.
You keep me from trouble.
You give me songs about how you
save me.

God says, "I will teach you how you
should live.
I will watch over you.
Do not be like the horse or mule.
It doesn't understand at all.

It has to be led by a bit in its mouth.
It won't move without a harness
and long reins."
People who do bad things have
many troubles.
But the people who trust God
will have God's love around them
forever.

Everyone who obeys God should
be glad.
Show your joy in God.
Sing if your heart is sinless.

Like a Deer

PSALM 42, by Korah's Family

My soul is like a deer that is thirsty
for water.
My soul is thirsty for the living God.
When can I meet with God?
My tears are all that I have for food
day and night.

Why are you sad, my soul?
Why am I troubled inside?
I will trust in God.
I will praise him,
because he
saves me.

Deep water
calls
when the
waterfall roars.
I feel like waves have splashed
over me.

God sends his love every day.
At night he sends his song.
It's a prayer to God.

I say to God, "Why did you forget
    me?
Why must I go around crying,
    held back by my enemies?"
My body hurts as my enemies
    tease me.
They say, "Where is your God?"

Why are you sad, my soul?
Why am I troubled inside?
I will trust in God.
I will praise him, because he
    saves me.

Proud Eyes

PSALM 101, by David

I will sing about your love, God.
I will sing about how fair you are.
I will be careful to live a life
    without sin.

I will walk in my house with a
    sinless heart.
I won't let my eyes see anything bad.

I hate what people do when they
    don't love you.
I won't let them near me.
I will stay away from people who
    sin in their hearts.

Some people might tell lies about
    their neighbors.

But I will tell those people to be
    quiet.
I will not stay around anyone
    who has a proud look and a
    proud heart.
I will look for people I can trust.
I'll let them live with me.

No one who lies will live in my house.
Every morning I will find all the
    sinful people.
I will not let them live in God's city.

APRIL 6

How to Begin to Be Wise

PSALM 111

I will thank God with all my heart.
I will praise him with people who
    do what is right.

What God does is great and
    powerful.
He is good and kind.
He is fair and right.
He gives food to people who trust
    him.
He remembers his promises forever.
You can trust his way.
God's name is special. It's the best!

Treat God as the most important one.
That's how to begin to be wise.
Everyone who obeys God
    understands.
Praise God forever.

More than the Guard

PSALM 130

I cry to you, God. Hear my voice.
Be kind to me.
If you kept track of our sins,
    no one could be good enough
        for you.
But you forgive. So we look up
        to you.

I wait for God
    more than guards wait for the
        morning.

Hope in God,
    because God's love never
        ends.
He can save his people from
        their sin.

Like a Well-Fed Baby

PSALM 131, by David

My heart is not proud, God.
I don't worry about things
    that are too big for me to
        understand.
I don't worry about things
    that are too wonderful
        for me.
My soul is still and quiet
    like a well-fed baby with its
        mama.
Put your hope in God now and
    forever.

Do Not Trust Princes

PSALM 146

My soul, praise God.
I will cheer for him all my life.
I will sing praise to him as long as
        I live.

Don't trust the leaders of the land to
        save you.
They are only people.
When they die, their plans become
        nothing.

But good things come to people
    who let God be their helper.
Their hope is in God.
He is the one who made heaven and
        earth and sea.
He is the Lord.
He always keeps his promises.
He takes care of people who are not
        treated right.
He gives food to people who are
        hungry.
He helps people who can't see
    so they're able to see again.
He lifts up people who feel pushed
        down by trouble.
He loves everyone who does what's
        right.
God watches over strangers.
He cares for children who have no
        fathers.
He takes care of women who have
        no husbands.
But he gives sinful people trouble.

God is King forever.

Cheer for God!

For the King

PSALM 45, A Love Song by Korah's Family

My heart is happy about telling my
poems to the king.
My voice is like a pen that belongs
to a good writer.

King, you are the best of all men.
God will bring good to you forever.
Hang your sword by your side.
Ride out for truth and for what is
right.
Ride out and win.
Do wonderful things.
Let your sharp arrows shoot your
enemies.
Let the nations fall before you.

You will be king forever.
You will be fair when you rule your
kingdom.
You love what's right and hate
what's wrong.
So God has made you great.
He has let joy flow over you.
Your robes smell sweet with perfume.
Music from beautiful palaces makes
you happy.
Many princesses are with you.
The queen is at your right hand.
She is dressed in gold.
Listen and think about it, princess.
Forget about your home far away.

The king is so happy with your
beauty.
Look up to him.
People will bring you gifts.
Rich people will want to meet you.

The princess is bright and beautiful
in her room.
Her gown is made of gold.
She is led to the king in her
beautiful gown.
Her friends follow her with joy.
They are glad to go to the king's
palace.

Your sons will grow up to rule
many lands.
People will remember you.
All nations will praise you forever.

Clap!

PSALM 47, by Korah's Family

Clap your hands, all you people.
Shout to God with joy.
God, the Lord Most High, is
wonderful.
He is the great King of all the earth!
He puts other nations under us.
He chose to give us a good land to
live in.
We are his people, and he loves us.

Sing praises to God.
Sing praises to our King, sing
praises!
God is the King of all the earth.
Sing a song of praise to him.

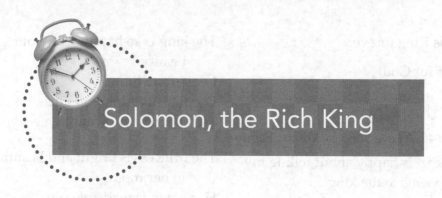

Solomon, the Rich King

Who Will Be the Next King?

1 KINGS 1

King David was very old. He stayed cold all the time. He was cold even when he was in bed under the covers.

"You need somebody to take care of you," said his servants. "Let us find a young woman. She can lie down by you. She will keep you warm that way."

So they looked all over the land. They found a beautiful woman. They took her to the king. She took care of him. But she wasn't like his wife.

Now David had a son named Adonijah. He was born after Absalom. Adonijah was handsome. And David never stopped him from doing whatever he wanted. David never asked, "Why are you acting that way?"

Adonijah said, "I'll be the next king." So he got some chariots and horses. And he got 50 men to run in front of him. Adonijah talked with Joab, the army leader. He talked with a priest. They agreed to help him become king.

But another priest, whose name was Zadok, didn't go along with Adonijah. The prophet Nathan didn't go along with him either.

Adonijah offered gifts to God at a big stone altar. He asked his brothers to come. They were King David's sons. But he didn't ask Nathan or his brother Solomon to come.

Bathsheba was Solomon's mother. Nathan went to see her. "Did you know that Adonijah is saying he is the king? David doesn't know it," said Nathan. "I'll tell you how you can save your life. You can save Solomon's life too.

"Go to King David," said Nathan. "Ask him if he said Solomon would be king. If he did, ask why Adonijah is saying he is the king.

"I'll come and see David while you're there," said Nathan. "I'll tell him that what you say is true."

So Bathsheba went to the king's room. The young woman was taking care of him. Bathsheba bowed in front of him.

"What do you want?" asked David.

"You promised that Solomon would be king," she said. "But Adonijah is saying he is the king now. He has offered gifts to God. He asked all your sons to come. But he didn't ask Solomon to come. Everybody is waiting for you to say who the next king will be. If you don't, Solomon will be in trouble when you die. Adonijah will be mean to Solomon and me."

Then Nathan got there. He went in and bowed down to David. "Did you tell Adonijah he could be king?" asked Nathan. "Today he offered gifts on the altar. He asked your sons to come. But he didn't ask Solomon. He didn't ask Zadok the priest. And he didn't ask me. Did this happen because you didn't say who would be the next king?"

"Tell Bathsheba to come here," said David.

So Bathsheba came back.

"I promise I'll do what I said I'd do," said David. "Solomon will be the next king." Then David said, "Tell Zadok to come here."

Zadok came. David said, "Take Solomon. Let him ride my mule. Blow the horns and shout, 'Long live King Solomon!' Then let him sit on my throne. He can rule as king instead of me. I chose him to be king of God's people."

So Zadok and Nathan took Solomon. They let him ride King David's mule. Zadok poured oil on Solomon's head. This showed that God wanted Solomon to be the next king. Then they called out, "Long live King Solomon!"

All the people came behind them. Some played flutes. They showed their joy. Their noise shook the ground.

Now Adonijah and his friends heard the sound. Joab, the army leader, heard the horns. "What does that mean?" he asked.

Just then a man came in.

"You are a good man. You must be bringing good news," said Adonijah.

"No," said the man. "David made Solomon the king. Zadok and Nathan are with him. They put oil on him, showing that God wants him to be king. People are shouting with joy. That's what all this noise is about.

"What's more, Solomon is sitting on David's throne," said the man. "All the leaders said they hope God makes Solomon even greater than David! Then King David worshiped God as he lay in bed. He praised God for letting him see the next king."

Adonijah's friends were scared. They got up and left. Adonijah was afraid of Solomon, too. He went to the altar in the worship tent.

Someone told Solomon, "Adonijah is afraid of you. He is at the altar. He is asking God to make you promise not to kill him."

Solomon said, "If Adonijah is a good man, then he won't die. But if he is a bad man, he will die."

Solomon sent some men to the altar. They brought Adonijah back. He bowed low in front of Solomon.

Solomon did not hurt Adonijah. Solomon just said, "Go home."

The First Days of King Solomon

1 KINGS 2–3:16

David knew he was going to die. So he told Solomon what to do. "I am going to die soon," said David. "So be strong. Be a man. Do what God wants. Follow his laws. Then good will come from what you do. And God will keep the promise he made to me. God said that our family should live the right way. We should follow God no matter what happens. Then people from our family will be the kings of God's people forever."

Then David died. His body was put in a grave. The grave was in a special part of Jerusalem called the City of David.

Samuel wrote a book about what happened in David's time. Nathan wrote a book about David. Gad wrote about David. They wrote about how he ruled. They wrote about his power. They also wrote about the other kingdoms and lands.

Then Solomon became king. God made Solomon great. He was greater than any king God's people had ever had.

Now Solomon made a deal with the king of Egypt. Then he married the king's daughter. The king of

Egypt gave his daughter a city for a wedding present.

Solomon took his new wife to the City of David. Solomon would soon build his palace there. He would build a worship house. He also would build a wall around Jerusalem.

God's people were offering gifts to God at altars in different high places. They couldn't go to the worship house because it wasn't built yet.

Solomon loved God. He showed it by living the way David lived. But Solomon did wrong by offering gifts at different high places too.

Then Solomon talked to the leaders of the people. They all went to a high place called Gibeon. God's worship tent was there. Inside the tent was a special altar. So Solomon went there and offered a thousand gifts to God.

That night God came to Solomon in a dream. "Ask me for whatever you want," God said.

"You have been very kind to me," said Solomon. "You were kind to my father, David, because he followed you. He followed you no matter what happened. He did what was right because his heart was right.

"Now you have let me be the king," said Solomon. "But I'm like a child. I don't know how to be a king. There are more of your people than anyone can count. Who is wise enough to rule your people? Make me wise enough to be their king. Help me understand what's right and what's wrong."

God was glad to hear Solomon ask to be wise. "You didn't ask for a long life," said God. "You didn't ask for riches for yourself. You didn't ask for your enemies to die. You asked to be wise. So I'll give you what you asked for. You'll be wiser than anyone who ever lived. You'll be wiser than anyone else ever will be.

"I'll also give you things you didn't ask for," said God. "I'll make you rich. I'll make you great. No other king will be like you while you are alive. Follow my way of doing things. Obey my laws like your father did. Then I'll let you live a long life."

Solomon woke up. He knew God had talked to him in a dream. He went back to Jerusalem and stood in front of God's ark box. He offered gifts to God. Then he gave a big dinner party for his leaders.

One day two women came to King Solomon. One said, "We live in the same house. I had a baby there. Three days later, this other woman had a baby. We were all by ourselves in the house. In the night, she rolled on top of her baby, and he died. So she took my baby while I was sleeping. She put her dead baby by me. The next morning I saw that the baby was dead. But then I looked carefully at him. I saw that it wasn't my baby!"

"No!" said the other woman. "The one that's alive is my baby! The dead baby is hers."

"No!" said the first woman. "The dead baby is yours. The one that's alive is my baby!" They started fighting with each other in front of King Solomon.

King Solomon said to one woman, "You say that your baby is alive." He said to the other woman, "But you say it is your baby that's alive."

Then the king asked for a long blade.

Someone brought a sword to the king.

"Cut the baby in half," said King Solomon. "Each woman can have half."

The real mother loved her baby. She cried out, "Please don't kill the baby! Give him to the other woman."

"Cut him in half!" said the other woman. "I won't have him, and you won't have him."

"Don't kill the baby," said Solomon. "Give the baby to the first woman. She wants him to live. She is his mother."

The people heard what Solomon had done. They thought the king was wonderful. God had made him wise and fair.

King Hiram Helps
1 KINGS 5; 2 CHRONICLES 2

Solomon told men to start building a worship house. He also told them to build a palace for him.

King Hiram from Tyre heard that Solomon was now king of Israel. So he sent some men to see Solomon. Hiram had always been King David's friend. Now he wanted to be friends with Solomon.

Solomon sent a message back to Hiram. It said, "My father, David, could not build a worship house. That's because he had to fight the enemy so much. But now we don't have any more enemies. So I'm going to build a worship house.

"You sent cedar logs to David for his palace," said Solomon. "Now please send some cedar logs for building a worship house. It is going to be a great house. Our God is greater than any other god. People really can't build a house good enough for him. Even the heavens can't hold him. But this worship house will be a place to pray. It will be a place to offer our gifts to God.

"Send someone who can work with gold and silver," said Solomon. "Send someone who can work with metals. Send someone who can work with red, purple, and blue yarn. Send someone who can draw pictures on wood and metal. They can work here with my workers.

"Send me some logs from different kinds of trees," said Solomon. "I know your men can cut logs very well. I can send men to help your workers. I want enough logs to build a large worship house. I'll give your workers wheat, barley, wine, and olive oil."

King Hiram wrote back to Solomon. He said, "God loves his people. So he has made you their king. Praise God. He made the earth and sky. He made you to be King David's wise son. You will build the worship house.

"I'm sending a good worker to you," said King Hiram. "He knows how to work with silver and gold. He can work with metals and yarn. He can draw pictures on wood and metal. He can make any kind of picture you want. He will work with your workers.

"So send the wheat and barley," said King Hiram. "Send the olive oil and wine. Then we'll cut the logs you want. We'll put them on flat boats. We'll send them down to you on the sea."

So Hiram and Solomon made a deal. The two kings became friends. Every year Hiram sent wood to Solomon. Solomon sent wheat, barley, oil, and wine to Hiram.

Solomon got 30,000 (thirty thousand) men. They took turns going to Hiram's land to help work. They would work on Hiram's land for a month. Then they would work at home for two months.

The Worship House

1 KINGS 6–7; 2 CHRONICLES 3–4

Solomon began building the worship house. He built it on Moriah Mountain. That's where David had seen an angel. David had bought a farmer's work place there.

The main room in the worship house was covered with gold. There were pictures of palm trees and chains on the gold. Beautiful stones were in it. The tops of the rooms and the doors were gold. Even the nails were gold.

The inside of the worship house was cedar wood. There were narrow windows. There were rooms on the sides.

At the back of the worship house was a special room. It was called the Most Holy Place. That was where God's ark box would stay.

Two tall figures were made for this room. They were heavenly beings about 15 feet tall. They were made of olive wood. Their wings were opened out. The wing of one figure touched one wall. The wing of the other figure touched the other wall. The wood figures were covered with gold.

There were pictures on the worship house walls. They were pictures of heavenly beings, palm trees, and flowers.

King Hiram's worker came to work for Solomon. He was a special worker who could make beautiful things from metal.

He made big, tall posts for the worship house. He made a big, metal altar shaped like a box.

He made a huge, round bowl for priests to wash in. It held about 17,500 gallons of water. It was called the Sea. He made figures of 12 bulls. The Sea sat across their backs. Then the special worker made 10 other bowls with stands. They were smaller than the Sea, but they were still big. Each one held about 230 gallons of water.

The Sea and the 10 bowls were put in a big yard. There were several yards around the worship house.

There was a gold altar inside the worship house. There was a gold table. There were 10 gold lamps on stands. There were other gold lamps, tables, bowls, and dishes.

King Solomon made sure all the work was done well. It took seven years to build the worship house. But at last it was finished.

Solomon Bows and Prays
1 KINGS 8; 2 CHRONICLES 5–7

King Solomon called all the leaders of God's people to come. It was time to bring the Ark to the worship house.

The priests carried the ark box. They carried the worship tent and the things in it. Solomon and all the people gathered in front of the Ark. They put sheep and cows on the altars. This was their gift to God.

Then the priests put the Ark in the worship house. They put it in the Most Holy Place. It went under the two big gold figures. The Ark had the two stone charts in it. Moses had put these in the ark box. Nothing else was in it.

The priests came out of the Most Holy Place. Then some of the priests played horns. Others sang. Some played cymbals, harps, and lyres. They all cheered for God. They sang, "God is good. His love lasts forever."

Then a cloud filled the worship house. The priests couldn't even do their work. That's because the cloud was there. God's greatness filled the worship house.

Solomon talked to God. "God, you said you would live in a dark cloud. But I built this great worship house for you, God. It's a place where you can live forever."

Then Solomon turned around to see all of God's people. He prayed for good things to come to them. "Praise God," he said. "He has kept his promise to David, my father. David wanted to build this worship house. But God chose me to build it. Now it has been built. I have put God's ark box in the worship house."

Solomon bowed down. He held his hands out toward heaven. "There is no God like you," he said. "You promised to love people who follow you. You've kept your promise.

"Even the highest heavens can't hold you," said Solomon. "So I know this worship house can't hold you! Watch over this worship house day and night. Hear us when we look toward this worship house and pray."

Solomon got up. He talked to the people in a loud voice. "Praise God! He promised he would give us rest. He has kept his promise. I pray that God will be with us. I pray that he will give us what we need each day. Then everybody in the world will know that he is the only God. Love him with your whole heart. Live the way he says to live. Obey his rules."

Then fire from heaven came down on the altar and burned up the offerings. God's greatness filled the worship house. The people saw it. They put their faces to the ground. They worshiped God for seven days. They thanked him. "God is good," they said. "His love lasts forever."

They offered gifts on the altar. The priests blew their horns.

For the next seven days they had a special holiday for God. After that, the people went home happy. They all were glad about the good things God had done.

Look for Me

1 Kings 9; 2 Chronicles 7

One night God came to Solomon. God said, "I heard you when you prayed. Let's say there's no rain for a long time. Or grasshoppers come and eat the crops. Or the people get sick. Then my people should stop thinking they're so great. They should pray. They should look for me. They should be sorry for what they've done wrong.

"Then I'll hear them from heaven," said God. "I'll forgive them. I'll make their land well again. I will watch over my people. I will hear their prayers, for I chose this worship house. It is a special place for me. My name will be here forever.

"Now how about you, Solomon?" asked God. "Live the way I tell you just as your father, David, did. Obey me. Then your family will rule forever.

"But what if you don't obey me?" said God. "What if you worship fake gods? Then I'll take my people out of this land. This worship house may look great now. But if you don't obey me, people will ask what happened to it. And the answer will be that my people didn't obey me. That's why I sent trouble to them."

Riches for a Wise King

1 KINGS 4; 9–10; 2 CHRONICLES 1; 9

God made Solomon very wise. He could understand so much, it was like all the sand on the beach. It couldn't be counted. He was wiser than all the wise men of the East. He was wiser than the wise men of Egypt. All the nations knew about him.

Solomon wrote 3,000 wise sayings. He wrote 1,005 songs. He wrote about big trees and little plants. He taught people about animals, birds, fish, and snakes.

People from all around the world came to hear Solomon's wise words. Kings had heard how wise he was. So they sent people to see him.

Every year Solomon got about 25 tons of gold. He made 200 big gold shields. He made 300 small gold shields. He put them in the Forest Palace.

Solomon made himself a throne of gold and ivory. Six steps went up to it. A lion figure stood at each side of the chair. One lion figure stood at the end of each step. That made 12 lions on the steps. No other kingdom ever had anything like this.

All of Solomon's cups were gold. Nothing was made of silver because it had little value then. It was just like rocks. Solomon was richer than any other king.

Everybody wanted to hear Solomon, because he was so wise. Everyone who came brought him gifts. They brought him silver and gold. They brought clothes and swords. They brought spices and horses and donkeys.

Solomon had 1,400 chariots. He had 12,000 (twelve thousand) horses. He had to have 4,000 pens for his horses.

Solomon also built ships. Hiram sent men who knew about the sea. They sailed with Solomon's men on the ships. They went to sea and brought back 16 tons of gold. They brought back silver and ivory. They brought back apes and baboons.

While Solomon was king, God's

people were at peace. They were happy.

The queen of Sheba heard about Solomon. She heard that he obeyed God. So she came to see Solomon. She wanted to see just how wise he was. She had many hard questions to ask him.

The queen brought a long line of camels with her. They carried spices, gold, and beautiful stones.

The queen of Sheba asked Solomon many questions. Solomon answered every question. There was no question too hard for him.

The queen saw how wise Solomon was. She saw his palace. She saw the food he ate. She saw how his leaders sat around him. She saw his servants in their beautiful robes. She saw the people who brought his drinks. She saw the gifts he offered to God at the worship house. It was more than she had dreamed.

"What I heard about you is true," she said. "I didn't believe it until I saw it for myself. What I see is much more than what I heard. You are wiser and richer than what I was told.

"Your people must be very happy," she said. "Your leaders must be happy to hear your wisdom. Praise goes to your God. He has been happy with you. He made you the king of his people. He did it so you could be fair and right."

King Solomon gave the queen of Sheba everything she wanted. Then she went back home.

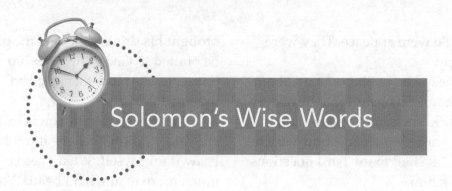

Solomon's Wise Words

Listen and Learn

PROVERBS 1

These are King Solomon's wise sayings.

These sayings will teach people the
wise way to think.
They'll help you do what's right
and fair.
They'll make fools become wise.
They'll help young people know
and choose what's good.
So if you're wise, listen and learn
even more.

Treat God as the most important one.
That gets you started to know
what's right.
The person who hates what's wise is
a fool.

What Is Wise Thinking?

PROVERBS 8

Wise thinking calls out to everybody.

"Listen. Choose to learn from what
I say.
Choose wise thinking instead of
silver.
Knowing is better than having gold.
Nothing you want can be better
than being wise.

"Thinking what's wise and doing
what's wise go together.
People who think God is important
hate what's bad.
Wise thinking hates pride and
bragging.
Rulers make good laws when their
thinking is wise.
If you look for wise thinking, you'll
find it.
Wise thinking brings riches and
greatness.

"Now listen to what's wise, my
children.
If you find wise thinking, you find
life and make God happy.
But if you don't find wise thinking,
you get hurt."

230

Hidden Riches

PROVERBS 2; 3:17-24

My child, listen to what's wise.
Try to understand. Ask for help with
    all that you need to
    know.
Then you'll understand how to look
    up to God.
You'll find out how to know God.

You'll understand what's right and
    fair.
Your heart will be wise.
It will feel good to know.
Choosing the right way will keep
    you safe.

Wise thinking saves you from bad
    people.
They trick people. They enjoy doing
    wrong.

Wise thinking saves you from
    sinning with sex.
Some people try to talk you into
    this.
But that leads to death.
So do what good people do. Do
    what's right.
It feels good to do what is wise.

My child, always choose wisely.
Wise thinking will help you be
    safe.
You won't be afraid when you lie
    down.
You will have a good night's sleep.

Early Morning Light

PROVERBS 4

My children, listen to your father.
I'll teach you what's right.
Don't forget my teaching.
When I was a boy,
    my father
    told me,
"Take my
    words
    into
    your
    heart.

Obey me, and you'll live.
Wise thinking will keep you safe. So
    love it.
Get understanding, even if it costs
    a lot.
Know that being wise is important.
Then wise thinking will make you
    important."

Listen, my child. Do as I say,
    and you will live many years.

Remember what you learn.
It's important for your life.
Don't live the way bad people do.
They can't sleep until they've done
    something bad.

The way right people live is like
    early morning light.
It shines brighter and brighter until
    it's day.
But the way sinful people live is like
    the darkness of night.

They don't even know what makes
   them fall.

More than anything, be careful of
   what you let into your mind.
Look ahead. Think about what you
   should do.
Follow the ways that are sure and right.
Stay away from things that are sinful.

Looking Up to God

PROVERBS

You can begin to be wise by looking
   up to God.
If you're wise, good things will
   come to you.
If you make fun of wise thinking,
   you'll be in trouble. 9:10-12

Caring about God will make your
   life long.
But being sinful will make your life
   short. 10:27

Looking up to God brings life.
It keeps people from the traps of
   death. 14:27

Looking up to God teaches people
   to be wise.
Knowing you're not so important
   comes before being important. 15:33

Good things come to people who
   always look up to God.

But some people won't let
   themselves care about God.
They are headed for trouble. 28:14

Trusting

PROVERBS

Trust in God with your whole heart.
Don't count on the way you understand things.
Always remember to let God be
   in charge.
Then he will show you what
   to do. 3:5-6

Let God be in charge of whatever
   you do.
Then your plans will work out for
   good. 16:3

Fools don't want to understand.
They just want to say what they
   think. 18:2

God's name is like a strong tower.
People who do what's right can run
   to him.
They can be safe there. 18:10

Foolish people bring trouble on
   themselves
and then are angry at God. 19:3

How can anybody know what to do?
God shows people what to do. 20:24

People who trust in themselves are
   foolish.
But those who are wise are safe. 28:26

Being afraid of people is like being
    in a trap.
But people who trust God will stay
    safe. 29:25

God's Care

PROVERBS

God is watching everywhere.
He sees both bad people and good
    people. 15:3

People make plans.
But God says yes or no. 16:1

We can make plans.
But God decides what we'll do. 16:9

No wise thinking or planning
    can win against God. 21:30

People get their horses ready for
    battle.
But God decides who wins. 21:31

Don't brag about what you'll do
    tomorrow.
You don't know what will happen
    then. 27:1

Wise People and Fools

PROVERBS

It's better to meet an angry bear than
    a person acting foolish. 17:12

Wise thinking is too much for a
    fool.

When he is with leaders, he has
    nothing to say. 24:7

Honey is sweet to your taste.
Wise thinking is sweet to your soul.
You have hope if you think
    wisely. 24:13-14

A wise saying doesn't belong in
    the mouth of a fool.
It's as useless as a leg that won't
    move. 26:7

A dog goes back to where it threw up.
And a fool does foolish things
    again. 26:11

Understanding and Knowing

PROVERBS

A fool is happy to sin.
But a person who understands is
    happy to be wise. 10:23

Wise people think about what they
    should do.
Fools lie. 14:8

Foolish people believe anything.
Wise people think about what they
    do. 14:15

God made ears that hear and eyes
    that see. 20:12

Wise people remember what they
    learn.
A fool asks for trouble. 10:14

A wise person looks for good things to know.
But a fool takes in foolish things like he takes in food. 15:14

It's not good to move too fast and miss your way. 19:2

There is gold. There are many beautiful red stones of great value.
But there aren't many lips that say wise things. 20:15

Things to Do

PROVERBS

Some people make fun of others.
If you tell them they're wrong, they'll make fun of you.
If you tell sinful people they're wrong, they'll be mean to you.
But tell wise people they're wrong, and they'll love you.
Teach wise people, and they'll be wiser.
Teach people who do what's right, and they'll learn more. 9:7-9

Fools think their way is right.
But those who are wise listen to others. 12:15

A wise child listens to what his father says.
But a person who laughs at others doesn't listen. 13:1

Don't talk to foolish people.
They'll make fun of the wise things you say. 23:9

You can trust a friend to tell you what's wrong.
But an enemy will pretend everything's all right. 27:6

Iron rubbed against iron becomes sharper.
One person makes another person wiser. 27:17

You may tell someone he is wrong.
What if you tell him many times, but he won't change?
All of a sudden, he will get into trouble.
And there won't be any way to get out of it. 29:1

APRIL 13

Being Trained to Do What's Right

PROVERBS

Nations get into trouble when no leaders tell them what's right.
But nations win when many leaders say what's right. 11:14

Your plans will work if you have helpers who tell you what's right.
Find people to guide you if you're going to war. 20:18

People who are wise have lots of
    power.
People who know a lot get stronger
    and stronger. 24:5

Don't be mad when God shows you
    you're wrong.
God shows these things to people
    he loves.
He is like a father showing his
    children what's right and
    wrong. 3:11-12

Listen when someone shows you
    what's right.
That shows you how to live.
People who don't listen lead others
    to do wrong. 10:17

Let's say you love to be shown
    what's right.
Then you love knowing.
But let's say you hate to be shown
    what's right.
That's dumb! 12:1

Some people don't listen when
    they're told they're wrong.

They grow poor and feel like
    nothing.
Some people listen when they're
    told they're wrong.
Others treat them like they're
    important. 13:18

Some people don't correct their
    children
    for doing what's wrong.
They show that they don't love their
    children.
Some people show their children
    what's right and wrong.
They show that they love their
    children. 13:24

Show your children how to do right,
    not wrong.
Then there's hope for them. 19:18

Teach your children the right way
    to live.
Then they will live that way when
    they grow older. 22:6

Make sure that your children get into
    trouble when they do wrong.
It may save them from bigger
    trouble later on. 23:13-14

A child who is corrected for doing
    wrong becomes wise.
But a child who is not corrected
    makes his mother look bad. 29:15

Show your children how to do right,
    not wrong.

Then they'll bring you peace.
They'll make you happy. 29:17

Right and Wrong

PROVERBS

We feel happy when we remember
people who do right.
But bad people's names seem to rot
away. 10:7

The pay for people who do right is life.
The pay for people who sin is
trouble. 10:16

People who do right can look
forward to joy.
But a sinful person can look forward
to nothing. 10:28

The right ways of good people save
them.
But the bad ways of bad people trap
them. 11:6

When bad people die, their hope is
gone.
Their power didn't get them
anywhere. 11:7

God saves people who do right.
He lets trouble come to people
who sin. 11:8

God is happy to help good people.
But God judges people who plan
bad things. 12:2

People cheer for others who are wise.

But they hate people who think
wrong things. 12:8

People who please God by doing right
are like bright shining lights.
But bad people are like burned-out
lights. 13:9

Troubles chase after bad people.
But good things come to godly
people. 13:21

People who do right make their
nation great.
But sinful people make a nation
look bad. 14:34

Bad things may happen to people
who do right.
These things may happen seven times.
But in the end, the people will still
be strong.
Trouble tears down people who do
wrong. 24:16

Everybody is glad when people
who do right win.
People hide when bad people get
power. 28:12

Sin grows when bad people win.
After a while, the bad people will lose.
People who please God by doing
right will see it happen. 29:16

People who do right don't like bad
people.
Bad people don't like people who
do right. 29:27

Fools laugh at the thought of saying
they're sorry.
But people who do right want the
best for others. 14:9

Good things don't come to people
who hide their sin.
Kind love comes to people who say
they're sorry. 28:13

Good Things and Greatness

PROVERBS

Bad things come to families of bad
people.
But good things come to families
who please God.
God is not happy with people who
make fun of others.
God loves people who make others
feel important.
Others will speak well of wise people.
But God will make fools look like
they're no good. 3:33-35

God doesn't let people who please
him go hungry.
But he doesn't give bad people what
they want. 10:3

When a storm passes over, bad
people are gone.
But people who do right stay
safe. 10:25

You can be sure of this.

Bad people will get paid back for
what they've done.
But people who do right will go
free. 11:21

People who look for what's good
find what's good.
People who look for what's bad
find what's bad. 11:27

Some people pay back bad for good.
Trouble will never leave their
family. 17:13

God sees families that sin.
He brings terrible things to bad
people. 21:12

Some people want to do what's right.
They look for love that doesn't end.
They find a life full of greatness and
all that's right. 21:21

If you plant sin, you grow trouble. 22:8

Snow does not fit summer time.
Rain does not fit the time to gather
crops.
Greatness does not fit a fool. 26:1

Plans of the Heart

PROVERBS

The things people do might seem
right to them.
But God sees why they do these
things. 16:2

Even children show what they're
like by how they act.

You can tell they are good if what
they do is right. 20:11

God looks inside people to see their
spirits.
He sees what they are thinking. 20:27

When you look into water, you can
see your face.
When you understand someone's
heart, you see what that person
is really like. 27:19

God is far away from people who
do wrong.
But God hears the prayers of people
who do right. 15:29

God likes it when people do what's
right and fair.
He likes it better than any gifts they
could give him. 21:3

Tricking People

PROVERBS

Sinful people go around saying bad
things.
They wink to show they're not
telling the truth.
They give secret signs with their feet
or fingers.
Their hearts plan to trick others.
They always make people fuss with
each other.
So trouble will come to these people
all of a sudden.

There won't be any way out
of it. 6:12-15

Good people are guided by truth.
But sinful people's lies get them into
trouble. 11:3

Some people look at what they want
to buy.
"It's not any good!" they say.
But after they buy it, they brag
about it. 20:14

Don't eat with people who don't
want to share.
Don't even think about wanting
their special food.
They're the kind of people who
worry about what it costs.
They'll tell you, "Eat. Drink."
But they don't really mean it.
You'll throw up what you ate.
The good things you said about
their food won't mean
anything. 23:6-8

Shiny paint covers a pot
made from clay.
Words that are too
good may hide
a sinful heart. 26:23

Some people don't care if they hurt
others.
They may try to hide what they're
really like.
They may sound great, but don't
believe them.

Their hearts are full of bad things.
Lies hide their hate.
But their sin will show up one
   day. 26:24-26

Keeping Promises

PROVERBS

Keep your promises.
Write them on your heart.
Then God and people will speak
   well of you.
They will be happy to hear your
   name. 3:3-4

Many people say they will never
   stop loving.
But who can find someone who
   keeps all his promises? 20:6

Don't trust someone who doesn't
   keep his promises.
That's as bad as having a hurting
   tooth.
It's as bad as walking on a foot that
   you broke. 25:19

Love, Hate, and Caring

PROVERBS

Hate brings fussing.
But love covers all wrongs. 10:12

Be happy to eat vegetables where
   there is love.

That's better than eating meat where
   there is hate. 15:17

Some people laugh at poor people.
The people who laugh show they
   don't think much of God.
Some people are glad when bad
   things happen to others.
The people who are glad will get
   into trouble. 17:5

Don't be happy when your enemy
   gets into trouble.
God will see you. He won't be
   happy with you.
And he will stop being angry at
   your enemy. 24:17-18

Give food to your enemy if he is
   hungry.
Give water to your enemy if he is
   thirsty.
God will bring good things to you
   for doing this. 25:21-22

Good things come to kind people.
But trouble comes to mean
   people. 11:17

People who do what's right take
   care of their animals.
When bad people try to be kind,
   they're still mean. 12:10

Worry makes a person feel bad.
A kind word makes him feel
   better. 12:25

Self-Control and Pride

PROVERBS

If you find honey, then eat just
enough.
If you have too much, you'll get
sick.
Don't go to your neighbors' house
too often.
They might stop liking you. 25:16-17

Someone who can't control himself
is like a city with broken-down
walls. 25:28

A fool shows all his anger.
But a wise person controls
himself. 29:11

People get proud. They think
they're the best.
Then others treat them like they're
not important.
But people become wise when they
make others feel important. 11:2

It's better not to think you're
the best, even if you have a
servant. 12:9

Some people act like they're rich.
But they are poor.
Other people act poor.
But they are rich. 13:7

Thinking you're the best only starts
fights.

But listen to what others tell you.
That will make you wise. 13:10

God is not happy with people who
think they're the best.
You can be sure they'll get in
trouble. 16:5

Thinking you're the best comes
before you get into trouble.
A bragging spirit comes before you
get into trouble. 16:18

Can anybody say,
"I've kept my heart clean.
I have not sinned"?
No one can say that. 20:9

Eyes that show pride are sinful.
A heart that thinks it's the best is
sinful. 21:4

People who are proud make fun
of others.
They act like they're the best. 21:24

It's not good to eat too much honey.
It's not good to try to get people to
say you're great. 25:27

Lazy people think they're wise.
They think they're wiser
than seven people who give good
answers. 26:16

Let somebody else say good things
about you.
Don't say those things yourself. 27:2

You heat silver in a pot. You heat
 gold in a fire.
That's how you test silver and gold
 to see if they're spotless.
But people get tested when
 others say good things about
 them. 27:21

Anger, Waiting, and Selfishness

PROVERBS

Anger is mean. Loud anger is too
 much.
But nobody can control people who
 want what others have. 27:4

A heart full of peace gives you life.
But wanting what others have
 makes your bones rot. 14:30

Don't wish to be like sinful people.
Sinful people have no hope for
 better things tomorrow.
People who do wrong will not last
 long. 24:19-20

People start fights when they want
 more and more things.
But good things come to people
 who trust God. 28:25

People are trapped when they make
 a promise to God in a hurry.
Later, they may not do what they
 said. 20:25

Good comes from the plans of
 people who think and act
 carefully.
But people who get in a hurry
 become poor. 21:5

Do you see somebody who is in a
 hurry to talk?
There is more hope for a fool than
 for that person. 29:20

Wise people look up to God.
 They stay away from sin.
But fools get angry easily.
 They're not careful. 14:16

A person who waits quietly
 understands many things.
But a person who gets angry too fast
 is a fool. 14:29

Be happy to control your anger.
That's better than controlling a
 whole city. 16:32

People who get angry too fast will
 get in trouble.
You might get them out of trouble.
But you'll have to do it again. 19:19

Don't make friends with people
 who get angry too fast.
You might learn to act like them.
Then you'll be trapped. 22:24-25

People who laugh at others get
 whole cities mad.
But wise people get others to stop
 being mad. 29:8

Eating and Drinking Too Much

PROVERBS

Because of wine, people make fun of others.
Because of beer, people start fights.
People who sin because of wine and beer are not wise. 20:1

Don't get together with people who drink too much wine.
Don't get together with people who eat too much food.
These people become poor.
They get sleepy and lazy.
In the end, they have no good clothes. 23:20-21

Who has trouble? Who is sad?
Who gets in fights? Who keeps talking about what's wrong?
Who gets hurt for nothing? Whose eyes stay red?
It is the people who drink too much wine.
Don't keep looking at wine when it's red.
Don't keep looking when it is bright in the cup.

Don't keep looking when it feels smooth in your mouth.
It will bite you and poison you like a snake.
You'll see strange things.
You'll get mixed up.
You'll be like someone sleeping in a ship at sea.
You'll say, "They hit me. But I didn't get hurt.
They beat me up, but I didn't feel it!
When will I wake up?
I want to have another drink." 23:29-35

Staying with the One You Marry

PROVERBS 5; 6:20-35; 7:6-27

My son, sometimes a woman leaves the person she marries.
She wants to live with someone else.
The way she talks is as smooth as oil.
But she will end up turning sour.
She is like a sharp sword with two edges.
She leads right to the grave.
She doesn't care about how to have a good life.

Stay away from a person like this.
Don't even go near her house.
If you do, you'll give her control.
Then you'll cry at the end of your life.
Your body will be all used up.

You'll say, "I hated being told I was wrong.
I wouldn't obey my teachers.
I wouldn't listen to them.
Now I'm in big trouble. Everybody sees it!"

Stay with your own wife.
It's like drinking water from your own well.
Should you give your body to other people?
That's like letting your water flow down the street.
Keep your body to yourself.
Never share it with strangers.
I pray that you'll be happy with the one you married.
Always be filled with wonder because of that person's love for you.
Don't go with someone who wants to sin.
Don't take someone else's wife.

God sees what people do.
Their sin traps them.
The wrong they do ties them up tight.
They'll die because they didn't control themselves.
They'll go wrong because they chose foolish things.

So obey your father.
Don't forget what your mother teaches you.

Let their teaching be something special you keep.
Let it be like a gold band to wear around your neck.
It will be something you want to wear forever.
Their teaching will guide you when you walk.
Their teaching will watch over you when you sleep.
Their teaching will lead you when you're awake.
It's like a light that shows you where to go.
Their teaching may show you you're wrong.
It may tell you to control yourself.
It will keep you from a person who wants to sin with sex.
It will keep you from believing her smooth talk.
Don't wish for another man's wife because she looks beautiful.
Don't let her trap you with the look in her eyes.
She will make you have no more value than a loaf of bread.
She will eat up your life.

Can you put fire in your lap without being burned?
Can you walk on hot coals and not burn your feet?
That's what it's like when someone sins with sex.
The person who does it will get into big trouble.

A man is not wise to have sex with someone else's wife.

He hurts himself.

He won't feel good about himself anymore.

Everyone will stop saying good things about him.

The one that the other person married will be angry.

He will get back at the one who took his wife.

Nothing will make him forget it.

I looked out my window.

I saw a young man who didn't know much.

He didn't know how to choose right from wrong.

He was walking down the street.

He was walking near a woman's corner.

He walked toward her house.

It was evening.

The sun was going down.

Night was coming.

This woman came out to see him.

She was dressed to make him look at her.

She planned to trick him.

She was loud. She never did do what anybody told her to.

She wouldn't stay home.

She walked the streets. She went to the parks.

She waited at all the corners.

This woman held onto the young man. She kissed him.

Her face showed that she didn't care.

The woman said her husband was gone on a long trip.

The young man followed her.

He was like an ox walking off to be killed.

He was like a deer stepping into a trap.

He was like a bird flying into a net.

He didn't know that it would be the end of his life.

So listen to me, my son.

Don't turn your heart to the way that kind of woman lives.

Don't walk on her roads.

She has torn down many people.

She is like a freeway that leads to a grave yard.

She will lead you to death.

The Words We Say

PROVERBS

A fool's words get him into trouble.

But a wise person's words keep him safe. 14:3

A wise person's mind tells his mouth what to say.

His words teach people. 16:23

My child, I'll be glad if you have a wise heart.

I'll show my joy when you say
 what's right. 23:15-16

The words of people who do what's
 right are rich like silver.
But a sinful heart is no good. 10:20

Sinful people get trapped by their
 sinful words.
But a person who does right gets
 out of trouble. 12:13

People who please God think about
 what they're going to say.
But sinful people rush to say bad
 things. 15:28

Saying the right things makes
 everyone happy.
A word said at the right time is
 good. 15:23

Wise people are called good thinkers.
Happy words help people learn. 16:21

Kind words are like honey.
They are sweet to the soul.
They keep our bodies well. 16:24

Good words said at the right time
 are like gold apples on silver
 plates. 25:11

Some people are too loud early in
 the morning.
They may say good things, but it
 sounds bad to their
 neighbors. 27:14

Too many words lead to sin.
But people who stay quiet are
 wise. 10:19

People who tell the truth are safe.
But people who tell lies will be
 found out. 10:9

A wise person knows things but
 doesn't show off.
A fool talks a lot and says foolish
 things. 12:23

People who are careful of what they
 say guard their lives.
But people who talk without thinking
 will get into trouble. 13:3

People will think a fool is wise if he
 stays quiet.
They'll think he knows a lot if he
 doesn't talk. 17:28

It's foolish to answer before you listen.
It shows you're not wise. 18:13

Be careful of what you say.
Then you'll stay out of trouble. 21:23

A kind word will take away anger.
But a mean word will bring anger. 15:1

Saying too many nice things to a
    neighbor
sets a trap for that neighbor. 29:5

Some people tell other people's secrets.
But people you can trust keep
    secrets. 11:13

A sinful person starts fights.
A person who talks about others
    turns friends into enemies. 16:28

A fire goes out if there's no wood
    to burn.
Fussing stops when nobody says
    bad things about others. 26:20

Foolish people say bad things about
    their neighbors.
A wise person keeps quiet. 11:12

Foolish words cut like a sharp sword.
But wise words take the hurt
    away. 12:18

Bad people look for bad things to say.
Their words burn like fire. 16:27

The north wind brings rain.
Words that hurt bring angry
    looks. 25:23

Starting a fight is like breaking a
    dam.

So stop before you get into a
    fight. 17:14

People who like to make a fuss like
    to sin. 17:19

It's good to stay away from fights.
Fools are quick to fuss with others. 20:3

It's better to be poor than to lie. 19:22

Some people get rich by telling lies.
But those riches will fade like smoke.
They will be a trap that leads to
    death. 21:6

APRIL 18

Fighting and Hurting
PROVERBS

What happens to people who get
    rich by stealing?
Their own lives are taken away. 1:10-19

Let's say a good person follows a
    bad person.
The good person is like clear water
    that gets mud in it. 25:26

Rocks are heavy. Sand makes a big
    load.
A fool daring you to do wrong is the
    biggest load. 27:3

Don't plan to hurt your neighbor.
He lives near you and trusts you.
Don't blame people when they
    haven't hurt you. 3:29-30

Don't say, "I'll get even with you for being mean to me."
Wait for God. He will take care of things. 20:22

God hates six things.
No, seven things are hateful to him.
1. Acting like you're better than others.
2. Telling lies.
3. Killing people who haven't done anything wrong.
4. Planning sin.
5. Hurrying to do what's wrong.
6. Getting others into trouble with your lies.
7. Starting fights in the family. 6:16-19

Be happy to have a bite of dry bread in peace.
That's better than a big dinner with fighting. 17:1

Some people are angry at what others did to them.
Their hearts are harder than the walls of a fort.
Fussing keeps friends apart like a gate with iron bars. 18:19

Some people fight about things that are none of their business.
They're like people who pull a dog's ears. 26:17

Telling the Truth
PROVERBS

People who plan sin have hearts full of lies.
But people who bring peace have hearts full of joy. 12:20

Telling the truth is like giving a kiss. 24:26

Some people trick others.
They say, "I was just joking."
They are like crazy people who shoot at you. 26:18-19

God doesn't like it when people lie about how big something is.
He doesn't like it when people lie about how much it weighs. 20:10

Money that people get the wrong way will get used up.
Money that people earn a little at a time will make more money. 13:11

If people lie to get food, it might taste sweet.
But it ends up like stones in their mouths. 20:17

People who want more and more bring trouble to their families. 15:27

Sinful people will take money to keep quiet.
They'll keep quiet instead of saying what's true. 17:23

A person who tells the truth says
what really happened. 12:17

A person who lies about what
happened will get into
trouble. 19:9

A person who lies will laugh at
what's fair. 19:28

Some people let a sinful person go.
But they put the good person in jail.
God hates both of these things. 17:15

Don't treat people who do wrong as
if they're right.
Don't treat people who do right as if
they're wrong. 18:5

Being Rich and Poor

PROVERBS

Use your riches to show God he is
the most important to you.
Give him the first part of everything
you earn.
Then your barns will be full.
There will be no more room.
Your wine will fill your tubs. 3:9-10

People who trust in riches will get
into trouble. 11:28

A person's riches may save his life.
But a poor person is not even in
danger. 13:8

If you're poor, be happy and look
up to God.

That's better than being rich and
having problems. 15:16

What good is money in a fool's hand?
He won't spend it to learn things.
He doesn't even want to be wise. 17:16

Rich people's riches are like a fort
to them.
They think riches will keep them
safe. 18:11

Rich people and poor people are
alike.
God made them all. 22:2

Rich people rule over poor people.
People who borrow money serve
people who lend it. 22:7

Don't get all tired out trying to get
rich.
Be wise. Control yourself.
Riches don't last.
They seem to grow wings.
They seem to fly into the sky like
birds. 23:4-5

When you're full, you don't want
honey.
But when you're hungry, even foods
you don't like taste good. 27:7

Be happy to be poor and right.
That's better than being rich and
wrong. 28:6

People in a hurry to get rich will get
into trouble. 28:20

Being Kind and Giving

PROVERBS

Do good when you can.
Let's say you have something your
    neighbor needs.
Don't say, "Come back tomorrow,
    and I'll give it to you
    then." 3:27-28

One person gives without worrying
    about it.
He gets even more.
Another person holds on to what
    he has.
But he grows poor. 11:24

A person who gives a lot will get
    a lot.
A person who makes people
    feel good will feel good
    himself. 11:25

A good person saves things for his
    grandchildren. 13:22

When people are kind to the poor,
    they lend to God.
God will pay them well for what
    they've done. 19:17

Some people don't listen when poor
    people cry.
Someday those people will cry,
    and no one will listen. 21:13

Some people brag about giving but
    never give.

They are like clouds and wind that
    don't bring rain. 25:14

People who give to the poor will
    have all they need.
People who don't help the poor will
    have trouble. 28:27

People who are mean to the poor
    don't care about God.
But people who are kind to the poor
    do care about God. 14:31

Working Hard or Being Lazy

PROVERBS

Look at the ant, you lazy person.
Think about what the ant does.
    Be wise.
The ant doesn't have a king to tell it
    what to do.
But it stores up its food in the
    summer. 6:6-8

If you are lazy, you'll grow poor.
If you keep working, you'll get
    rich. 10:4

What does a sour drink do to your
    teeth?
What does smoke do to your eyes?
That's how lazy people seem
    to the people they work for. 10:26

People who work will have enough
    food.

But people who dream all day are
  not wise. 12:11

People who keep working will be in
  charge.
Lazy people will end up being
  servants. 12:24

All hard work brings good things.
But if all you do is talk, you'll grow
  poor. 14:23

Lazy people don't get their fields
  ready to plant.
So when it's time to gather crops,
  there's nothing to gather. 20:4

Do you see any people who do a
  good job?
They will get to do their jobs for
  kings. 22:29

I passed a lazy man's field.

Weeds were everywhere.
The stone wall was broken down.
I thought about what I saw,
  and I learned something.
You sleep a little. You sleep a little
  more.
You fold your hands to rest.
Then you grow poor.
It's as if a robber came. 24:30-34

A door turns to open.
A lazy man turns over in bed. 26:14

Take care of a fig tree.
Then you will eat its fruit.
Take care of your boss.
Then good things will come
  to you. 27:18

Work hard, and you'll have plenty
  of food.
Don't chase dreams, or you'll grow
  poor. 28:19

Wise people save some of the nice
  things they have.
But fools use up everything they
  have. 21:20

My child, did your neighbor borrow
  money from someone?
Did you say you'd pay it back if he
  couldn't?
Then try to get free from this trap.
Go and beg your neighbor to set
  you free.
Don't let yourself sleep.
Get free like a deer gets free from a
  hunter.
Get free like a bird gets free from a
  trap. 6:1-5

Some people say they'll pay for
  what another person borrowed.
But that will bring trouble.
You're safe if you don't make that
  promise. 11:15

All about People

PROVERBS

A wise child makes Father happy.
A foolish child makes Mother sad. 10:1

A wise servant will rule over the
    family's foolish children.
The wise servant will be treated like
    one of the family. 17:2

Grandchildren are like a crown to
    grandmothers and grandfathers.
Children are proud of their mothers
    and fathers. 17:6

Gray hair is like a bright crown.
You get it by doing what's right. 16:31

Strength makes a young person great.
But gray hair makes an old person
    great. 20:29

Have you seen a beautiful woman
    who is foolish?
It's like seeing a gold ring in a pig's
    nose. 11:22

A good wife is like a crown to her
    husband.
But a foolish wife makes him rot
    from the inside out. 12:4

A wise woman takes care of her
    family.
But a foolish woman tears her
    family apart. 14:1

A man who finds a wife finds
    something good.
God is bringing good things
    to him. 18:22

A foolish child hurts his father.
A wife who makes a fuss is like
    water dripping in the sink. 19:13

Mothers and fathers give their
    children houses and riches.
But God gives their children wise
    people to marry. 19:14

Be happy to live on the corner of
    the roof.
That's better than living with
    someone who makes a fuss. 21:9

Be happy to live in the desert.
That's better than living with
    someone who gets angry
    a lot. 21:19

A fussy wife is like rain that keeps
    dripping.
Trying to stop her is like trying to
    stop the wind.
It's like trying to hold oil in your
    hand. 27:15-16

A king is great when he rules lots
    of people.
But what if he has no one to rule?
Then he is not a king. 14:28

A king is glad when he has a wise
    servant.

But he is angry when he has a
    foolish servant. 14:35

Kings are glad to hear people tell
    the truth.
A person who tells the truth is
    important to them. 16:13

When a king's face gets bright with
    a smile, that means you'll live.
When he likes you, it's like a cloud
    bringing spring rains. 16:15

A king's anger is like a lion's roar.
Whoever makes the king angry
    gives up his life. 20:2

When a king judges, his eyes can tell
    what's wrong. 20:8

A king stays safe if he is always
    loving and keeps his
    promises. 20:28

God is in charge of the king's heart.
God makes it do what he wants.
He turns it as he pleases like he
    turns rivers. 21:1

Love a heart that does not sin. Talk
    kindly.
Then the king will be your friend. 22:11

When you eat with the king, look at
    all the food.
Don't let yourself eat too much.
Don't keep wanting his rich food.
That kind of food tricks you. 23:1-3

Look up to God and the king.
Don't go along with people who
    don't obey.
God and the king will get rid of
    them. 24:21-22

God can hide how he does things.
    That shows God is great.
A king tries to find out things.
That shows the king is great. 25:2

Take the dirt out of silver.
Then you have something the silver
    worker can use.
Take sinful people away from the
    king.
Then he will do what's right. 25:4-5

Don't make yourself look important
    when you're with the king.
It's better for the king to make you
    look important.
That's better than looking foolish in
    front of great people. 25:6-7

Some rulers are mean to helpless
    people.
These rulers are like lions that roar.
They are like bears that jump on
    people. 28:15

When a ruler listens to people
    who lie,
    all the leaders become sinful. 29:12

A king who is fair to poor people
    will rule for a long time. 29:14

Friends

PROVERBS

People who do right say helpful things to their friends.
But sinful people lead their friends to do wrong. 12:26

Being around wise people makes you wise.
Being around fools hurts you. 13:20

A friend will love you all the time.
Brothers and sisters help you through hard times. 17:17

Some people think they have many friends.
But the real friend is the one who stays closer than a brother. 18:24

Don't wish you could be like people who sin.
Don't even want to be with them.
They plan to do mean things.
They talk about making trouble. 24:1-2

A person who leaves home is like a bird that leaves its nest. 27:8

Sweet smelling perfume makes you feel happy.
Friends make you happy too.
They tell you what's right. 27:9

Don't forget your friends.
Don't forget your father's friends.
Be happy to get help from a neighbor who lives close by.
That's better than going to a family member who lives far away. 27:10

People who help robbers are enemies to themselves.
They don't dare tell the truth to the judge. 29:24

Wise people see danger coming.
They go somewhere to be safe.
But foolish people keep going.
They get into trouble. 22:3

People who do wrong are headed for traps.
People stay out of trouble when they are careful. 22:5

Live so that people will say good things about you.
That's better than being rich.
Be happy when people look up to you.
That's better than having silver or gold. 22:1

253

You may fuss with your neighbors.
But don't tell their secrets to anyone
     else.
If you do, people may say that you
     talk too much.
Then people will never say good
     things about you again. 25:9-10

Being Brave and Full of Hope

PROVERBS

Don't be afraid of trouble that
     comes all of a sudden.
Don't be afraid of trouble that sinful
     people have.
God is the one you can trust.
He will keep you from being
     trapped. 3:25-26

Trouble makes sinful people feel
     very bad.
But people who do right have a safe
     place.
They have a safe place even if they
     face death. 14:32

The lazy person says, "There's a lion
     outside!"
He says, "I'll be killed in the
     street." 22:13

If you can't handle trouble, you're
     not very strong. 24:10

People who do wrong run away,
     even if nobody is chasing them.

But people who do right are as
     brave as a lion. 28:1

You're happy when you get what
     you want.
But fools don't like to turn away
     from sin. 13:19

Don't let yourself want what sinful
     people have.
Always think about how wonderful
     God is.
Then many good days will come
     to you.
You will always have hope. 23:17-18

Happy and Sad

PROVERBS

Each person has sad times.
And each person has happy times
     that nobody else quite
     understands. 14:10

Even while you're laughing, your
     heart can be sad.
Happy feelings can turn into sad
     feelings. 14:13

When you're happy, your face
     shows it.
But a sad heart makes your spirit
     feel unhappy. 15:13

A happy heart can make you feel well.
But a sad heart makes your bones
     feel dried up. 17:22

You can keep going when your
body is sick.
But how do you deal with
sadness? 18:14

Someone might sing songs to a sad
person.
That's like taking away his coat on a
cold day.
It's like putting salt on a sore place and
making it hurt even more. 25:20

People who do wrong are trapped
by their own sin.
But people who do right can sing
and be happy. 29:6

Looking happy gives people joy.
Good news gives people good
health. 15:30

Good news might come from far
away.
It's like cold water coming to thirsty
people. 25:25

Wise Words from Agur

PROVERBS 30:18-19, 24-33

There are four things I don't
understand.
How an eagle flies in the sky.
How a snake crawls over a rock.
How a ship sails on the tall
waves.
And how a man loves a woman.

Four things are very small,
but they are very wise.
Ants are not very strong.
But they store up food in the
summer time.
Rock badgers are not very strong.
But they have homes among the
rocks on the hills.
Big grasshoppers called locusts
don't have a king.
But they move out together like
an army.
Lizards can be held in your hand.
But they can also climb into
kings' palaces.

Four things are very grand when
they move along.
The lion, who is one of the strongest
animals.
He doesn't run away from
anything.
The rooster, who has a proud walk.
A billy goat.
And a king who has his army
around him.

Have you been a fool?
Have you tried to make yourself
look great?
Have you planned something
wrong?
Then stop and cover your mouth
with your hand.

When you shake milk up, you make
butter.

When you hit your nose, you bring
blood.
When you get someone angry, you
start a fight.

Wise Words of King Lemuel

PROVERBS 31:1-9

Here is what King Lemuel's mother
told him.

Kings should not drink wine.
Rulers should not want beer.
They might drink it and forget
their own laws.
They might not treat poor people
right.

Speak up for people who can't talk
for themselves.
Stand up for the rights of people
who are poor.
Be a fair judge, and speak up for
poor people.

A Good Wife

PROVERBS 31:10-31

Who can find a wife who is good?
She is better than riches.
Her husband trusts her.
He has everything he could want.
She brings good things into his life,
not bad things.

She chooses what she needs to make
yarn and threads.

Her hands are ready to work.
She is like the ships that bring
things to market.
She brings her food from far away.
She gets up while it's dark
to get food ready for her family.
She thinks about buying a field.
Then she buys it.
She buys seeds and plants them
with her own money.

She works hard.
Her arms are strong.
She makes money at what she does.
Even late at night, she is working.
She makes yarn with her fingers.
She gives to poor people.
She is not afraid when it snows.
Her family has good, warm clothes.
People say good things about her
husband.
He is a leader in the town.
She makes clothes and sells them.
She makes belts to sell to the stores.

She is strong. She feels good about
what she can do.
She is not worried about the days
that will come.
She says wise things.
She teaches. You can believe what
she says.
She takes care of her family. She is
not lazy.

Her children stand up and say good
things about her.

Her husband does too. He cheers for
   her.
"Lots of women do good things," he
   says.
"But you are better than all of them."

Just acting nice can trick people.

Being beautiful doesn't last forever.
But you should cheer for a woman
   who worships God.
She has worked hard, so give her a
   gift.
Let people praise her for what she
   has done.

Solomon's Thoughts

Solomon's Song

Song Of Songs

The king's bride said, "Kiss me.
Your love is better than wine.
Your perfume smells sweet.
Your name is sweet like perfume.
It's no wonder that all the girls love
   you!
But take me with you. Hurry!
King, take me to your room."

"We are happy with you," said the
   king's friends.
"We will praise your love more than
   we praise wine."

"I'm dark like Solomon's tents,"
   said the bride.
"I am beautiful.
Don't keep looking at me because
   I'm dark.
I'm dark because of being in the sun.
My brothers were mad at me.
They made me work in the fields.
I couldn't take care of my own field.

Tell me, my love, where you take
   your sheep.
Where do you let them rest at noon?"

"Follow the sheep tracks," said the
   king.
"Take your goats to the shepherds'
   tents.
I think you are like a young girl horse.
You're like a horse that pulls the
   king of Egypt's chariot.
Your ear rings make your face beautiful.
Beautiful stones hang on strings
   around your neck.
They make your neck beautiful.
But we will make gold ear rings
   for you.
We will put silver on them."

"The king was at his table," said
   his bride.
"My perfume smelled sweet.
The one who loves me is like a
   sweet smell.
He is like flowers from the field."

"You are beautiful," said the king.
"Your eyes make me think of doves."

"You are good looking," said his
    bride.
"You are fun and nice."

"Our house is made of cedar wood,"
    said the king.
"The top part is made of wood from
    fir trees."

"I'm like a rose," said his bride.
"I'm like a lily from the valley."

"You are like a lily among the
    weeds," said the king.
"That's what you're like among
    the other girls."

"You're like an apple tree in the
    forest," said his bride.
"That's what you're like among the
    other young men.
It makes me happy to sit in your shade.
I like your fruit. It's sweet.
You took me to a big dinner party.
Your love is like a flag over me.
It says I belong to you.
Give me raisins and apples to eat.

I need them to be strong,
    because love is making me feel
    weak.
The king puts his arm around me
    and hugs me.
Girls, I tell you this.
Don't let your heart love until the
    right time.

"Listen! Look! Here comes the one
    who loves me!
He is coming across the mountains
    and hills.
He makes me think of a deer.
Look! Now he stands behind the wall.
He is looking through the window."

The king said, "Get up, my beautiful
    one.
The winter is gone now.
It has stopped raining.
Flowers are growing all over the earth.
It's time to sing!
You can hear doves cooing.
Fruit is growing on the fig trees.
Flowers are growing on the vines.
You can smell their sweet smell.
So get up, my beautiful one.
Come with me!

"You make me think of a dove,"
    said the king.
"You're like a dove hiding in the
    mountains.
Let me see your face and hear your
    voice.
Your voice is so sweet.

Your face is so beautiful."

"The king loves me," said his bride.
"He belongs to me, and I belong to
    him.
Who is coming from the desert?
Look! It's King Solomon's cart.
He has 60 fighting men with him.
Each one has a sharp sword.
King Solomon made his cart from
    wood.
He made its posts out of silver.
He made the bottom out of gold.
He covered its seat with purple cloth.
Come and see, girls!
Look at King Solomon!
He is wearing the crown.
It's the crown his mother put on his
    head.
She gave it to him at his wedding.
That's the day joy filled his heart."

"You are beautiful," said the king.
"Your eyes make me think of doves.
Your hair makes me think of goats
    coming down the mountain.
Your teeth make me think of clean,
    white sheep.
Your lips make me think of a red
    ribbon.
You have a beautiful mouth.
Your neck makes me think of a
    beautiful tower.

"So come with me, my bride.
You stole my heart with one look
    from your eyes.
Your love is wonderful!

It's better than wine!
You make me think of a garden.
You make me think of a fountain in
    a garden."

"Wake up, north wind," said the bride.
"Come here, south wind.
Blow on my garden.
Send its sweet smell all around.
Bring the one who loves me.
Bring the king to his garden."

"Here I am at my garden," said the
    king.

"Eat and drink," said their friends.
"Drink all you want, because you
    love each other.
Oh, bride, how is the one you love
    better than others?"

"His face seems to shine," said the
    bride.
"You would pick him out among
    10,000 (ten thousand) others.
His hair is wavy and as black as a
    raven.
His eyes make me think of doves by
    the river.
His lips make me think of lilies that
    smell sweet.
His arms make me think of gold.
He is very good looking.
He loves me. He is my friend."

"You are beautiful," said the king.
"When you come, it's like the sun
    coming up.

You are as pretty as the moon.
You are as bright as the sun.
You are as wonderful as the stars."

"Love is strong," said his bride.
It's like a fire that burns.
Water can't put it out.
Rivers can't wash it away.
No one can buy it."

Nothing New

ECCLESIASTES 1

These are the words of the Teacher,
Solomon the king.

"Nothing! Nothing!" the Teacher says.
"It's good for nothing!"

What good is all the work people do?
People live.
People die.
But the earth
    stays
    forever.
The sun
    comes
    up.
The sun goes
    down.
Then it comes up again.
The wind blows south and then north.
It keeps going around and around.
All the rivers rush to the sea.
But the sea never fills up.
And water keeps filling the rivers.

All of it makes me more tired than I
    can say.
Everything that's been done will be
    done again.

There's nothing new in the world.
Can anybody say, "This is new"?
It was already here a long time ago.
It was here before we lived.

I'm the Teacher. I was the king of
God's people. I worked hard to
study and find out things. I saw
what a hard time people have. I saw
everything they do. It seems like
they're doing it for nothing. It's like
chasing the wind.

> Things that are bent can't be
>   made flat again.
> You can't count something that's
>   not there.

I thought about it. "See? I have grown
wise. Wiser than any king before
me." So I worked to understand
what it means to be wise. I also tried
to understand how fools think. But I
learned that this was like chasing the
wind, too. When you're wise, you
see many sad things. The more you
know, the more sadness you see.

Chasing the Wind

ECCLESIASTES 2

So I said, "I'll look for things that
make me feel good." But that ended

up being good for nothing. I said, "Laughing is silly. What good does it do to make yourself feel good?"

I tried cheering myself up with wine. I tried thinking like a fool. But I couldn't.

I wanted to find out what's really good to do. So I started doing things. I built houses for myself. I planted fields and fruit trees. I made gardens and parks. I made pools of water for watering new trees.

I bought slaves to work for me. I got lots of cows and sheep. I got silver and gold. I got land and singers. I got women to love me. I became greater than anyone who ever lived.

I got whatever I wanted.
I was happy doing all that work.
That was the good that came from
    my work.
When it was done, I looked at it all.
I had worked hard to get it.
But it was not good for anything.
It was like chasing the wind.
I really hadn't gotten anything.

So I thought about being wise.
I thought about being a fool.
Being wise is better than being a fool.
The wise man can see and understand.
The fool can't. It seems like a fool
    walks in the dark.

I thought, "I know what will
    happen to the fool.

The same thing will happen to me.
So what good is being wise?"
I thought, "This is no good."
People won't remember the fool.
But they won't remember the wise
    person either.
The wise person will die just like
    the fool will.

I hated the things I had worked to get. I knew I'd just have to leave them behind. The next king will get them. Who knows? Maybe he will be wise. Maybe he will be a fool. But he will be in charge of everything I worked for. It's too bad.

What do people get for all their work? They get hurt. They get sad. Even at night, their minds can't rest.

The best thing to do is eat and drink. Be happy in your work. This comes from God. If you don't have God, how can you enjoy anything?

A Time for Everything
ECCLESIASTES 3

There's a time for everything.
There's a season for everything
    people do.

A time to be born, and a time to die.
A time to plant, and a time to pull
    plants up.
A time to kill, and a time to heal.
A time to break, and a time to build.
A time to cry, and a time to laugh.

A time to throw stones, and a time
    to gather them.
A time to hug, and a time not to hug.
A time to hunt, and a time to give
    up the hunt.
A time to keep things, and a time to
    throw things away.
A time to tear, and a time to mend.
A time to be quiet, and a time to talk.
A time to love, and a time to hate.
A time for war, and a time for peace.

I saw what God did. He made
everything beautiful in its own time.
He lets us think about things that
last forever. Even then, we can't
know the beginning or the end.

I know the best thing we can do.
We'll be happy as long as we can.
We'll eat and drink and be happy in
our work. That's God's gift to us.

I know everything God does will last
forever. Nobody can add anything to it.
Nobody can take anything away from
it. God planned it this way. He did it so
people will look up to him in wonder.

So I saw that the best thing is to
enjoy work. Nobody can tell what
will happen after that.

APRIL 25

Two Are Better than One

ECCLESIASTES 4

I looked again. I saw people being
hard on each other.

I saw that people work to get
what their neighbors have. That's
no good. It's like chasing the wind.

Fools are lazy and get in trouble.
They're happy to have one hand full
    and have peace.
They think that's better than having
    two hands full with work.
They think that's like chasing the wind.

I saw something else that's not good.

There was a person all by himself.
He didn't have a son or a brother.
But he worked and worked.
He wasn't happy with what he had.
"Who am I working for?" he asked.
"Why am I keeping myself from
    enjoying my life?"
That's a sad way to live.

Two are better than one.
They can get a lot more for their work.
When one falls down, the other
    picks him up.
But it's sad if there's nobody to help
    him up.
Two can lie down together and stay
    warm.
But how can one stay warm by himself?
An enemy can win over one.
But two can fight back.
It's like tying three strings together.
Three together is not easy to break.

Be happy to be a poor but wise
young person. That's better than
being an old king who is a fool.

Riches

ECCLESIASTES 5

Be careful when you go into God's
worship house. Go in to listen.

Don't be too quick to talk.
Don't be in a hurry to say things
    to God.
God is in heaven. You are on earth.
So you should say just a few words.
When you say too many words, you
    talk like a fool.

Keep your promises to God. Be
happy to keep your promise.
Sometimes it's better not to make
a promise. Don't make one if you
aren't going to do what you said.
Don't let your words make you sin.
Don't say, "I didn't mean it." Why
should you make God angry at you?

People who love money never have
    enough of it.
This is not good either.
You may get more things.
But then more people come to you.
    They want to help you use
    things up.
So what good are things to the one
    who owns them?
All that person can do is look at
    them.

Workers may eat a lot or a little.
But they sleep well.

Rich people have more than enough.
But they can't sleep.

People are born with no clothes.
They leave the world that way too.
They don't take anything from their
    work with them.
They can't carry anything in their
    hands.
People leave the way they came.
What do they get for chasing the
    wind?

Then I saw that it's good to get
riches and health from God. He
lets us enjoy them. He wants us to
be happy with the days he gives
us. They're a gift from God. So
we hardly think about our days.
That's because God keeps
us glad.

Good and Bad Days

ECCLESIASTES 6–7

People work to have things for
    themselves.
But they never think they have
    enough.
Be happy with having what you see.
That's better than wanting what you
    can't see.

Be happy when people think good
    things about you.
That's better than having sweet
    perfume.

A wise person knows how to cry.
Fools only like to do what feels good.
Be happy to listen when wise people
say you're wrong.
That's better than listening to fools.

Paying someone to do wrong turns
wise people into fools.
It turns their hearts away from God.

The end is better than the start.
It's better to wait quietly than to brag.
Don't get angry too fast. That's for
fools.

Don't say, "Why were the good old
days better?"
It's not wise to ask questions like that.

Being wise is a good thing.
It's like getting a gift from your
mother and father.
It helps people.
Being wise is like having a safe
place to stay.
Money can help you stay safe too.
But being wise is better.
Being wise saves the life of the wise
person.

Be happy when days are good.
But think when days are bad.
God made both good and bad days.
So you can't find out much about
what's going to happen.

Try to be wise without being too
hard on yourself.

But don't do too many wrong
things. Don't be a fool.

Being wise gives power to the wise
person.
That person is stronger than 10
leaders in a city.

There's nobody on earth who
always does right.
There's not one person who never
sins.
Don't listen to everything people say.
You might hear your helper say bad
things about you.
You know you've said bad things
about others.

I tried to understand.
I tried to find out wise things.
I tried to understand how foolish
sin is.

"Look!" the Teacher says. "Here's
what I found out.
God made people to be right and
good.
But people went looking for their
own way of doing things."

A Bright Face
ECCLESIASTES 8

Wise thinking makes your face look
happy.
It changes your face from looking sad.

Obey the king. You promised God you would. Don't be in a hurry to leave the king. Don't take the side of what's wrong. Don't try to do bad things. The king does what he wants. People obey him. So who can tell him, "You shouldn't say that"?

Obey the king. Then you won't get
    hurt.
Wise people know
    the right
    time to do
    things.
They know
    the
    right
    way.
There's a
    right time for everything.
There's a right time,
    even if your troubles are hard on
      you.

Nobody knows what will happen
    tomorrow.
Nobody can hold back the wind.
Nobody can keep from dying.
Sin doesn't let sinners get away.

I was trying to learn about everything. Here's what I saw. Some people boss others around. But they are hurting themselves.

Let's say the judge says someone did wrong. Then that person should get in trouble. It should happen quickly. If it doesn't, everyone will choose to do wrong.

A bad person might do wrong things 100 times. That person might live a long time anyway. But I know it's still better to obey God. Sinful people don't obey God. So they'll have trouble.

There's something else that's not good. Sometimes people who do right get treated like sinners. Sometimes people who sin get treated like people who do right. That's not good.

So I say, "Enjoy life." There's nothing better than to eat, drink, and be happy. Then you'll be happy when you work. You'll be happy all your life.

Enjoy
ECCLESIASTES 9

Anybody who is alive has hope. A live dog is better than a dead lion.

Enjoy living with the one you married, the one you love. Enjoy that person all your life.

Do what your hands find to do. Do it with all your might.

Fast people don't always win the
    race.
Strong people don't always win the
    fight.
Wise people don't always get food.
Smart people don't always get rich.

Good workers are not always the
    people everyone likes.
Time passes for all of them.
Things just happen to all of them.

I saw something happen one time.
What I saw told me about wise
people. It made me think. Once
there was a little town. Not many
people lived there. But a strong king
came to fight against the little town.
His army stood in a circle around
the town. The king and his army
tried to get in. They tried to break
down the gate and the walls.
    Now a poor but wise man lived in
the town. He is the one who saved the
town. He saved it by being wise. So I
said, "It's better to be wise than strong."
    But nobody remembered the man.
People don't think much of a poor
man's wise thinking. They don't
listen to what he says.

Listen to the quiet words of a wise
    person.
That's better than listening to shouts
    from the king of fools.

A Sharp Ax

ECCLESIASTES 10

Dead flies make perfume smell bad.
A little foolish thinking hurts wise
    thinking.
Fools don't know anything,
    even when they're out for a walk.

They show everybody how foolish
    they are.

If your boss gets angry at you, don't
    give up.
Be full of peace. That can make up
    for mistakes.

If you dig a pit, you may fall in.
If you break down a wall, a snake
    might bite you.
If you cut stones from hills, you
    might get hurt.
If you chop wood, you might be in
    danger.

You need to be very strong if your
    ax isn't sharp.
Being wise is like having a sharp ax.
It helps you do your job well.

A wise person says kind, loving words.
But the words of fools get them into
    trouble.
At first their words are foolish.
The words end up being crazy.
The fool talks and talks and talks.

Fools get tired from their work
They can't even get to town.

Be sorry if your king acts like a
    young child.
Be happy if your king is great.
Be sorry if your leaders eat before
    it's time to eat.
Be happy if your leaders eat at the
    right time.

They eat to grow strong, not to get
　　drunk.

Lazy people have houses with roofs
　　that sag.
Lazy people don't work. So their
　　houses leak.

Don't say bad things about the king.
Don't even think bad things about
　　him.
A little bird might tell what you
　　said.

Light Is Sweet

ECCLESIASTES 11

You don't know where the wind
　　goes.
You don't know how babies are
　　made in their mothers.
You can't understand God's work.

Plant seeds in the morning.
Plant more seeds in the evening.
You don't know which will
　　grow best.

Light is sweet, and it's good to see
　　the sun.
No matter how long people live,
　　they should enjoy life.
But they should know that there
　　will be hard days.
There will be lots of them.

Be happy while you're young.
Do what you would like to do.
But know that God will judge you
　　for what you do.

Never an End

ECCLESIASTES 12

God made you.
Remember him while you're young.
That's before you have hard times.
You'll have days when you say, "I'm
　　not happy."
Remember God before you die.
Your body will go back to the
　　ground.
Your spirit will go back to God.

"Nothing! Nothing!" the Teacher says.
"It's good for nothing!"

The Teacher was wise. He taught
the people what he knew. He
thought about things. He tried to
find out many things. He wrote
many wise sayings.

　　The Teacher looked for just the
right way to say things. The things
he wrote were right and true.

　　There's never an end to how
many books people can make. And
too much study makes people tired.

Now you've heard it all.
Let's hear the end.
Treat God as the most important one.
Obey him.

This is what everybody is to do,
because God will judge what
we do.
God will even judge the things
we hide.
He will know if they are good
things or bad things.

Enemies

1 KINGS 11

King Solomon loved the princess from Egypt. But he loved lots of women from other nations, too. God had said not to marry people from these nations. But Solomon married them anyway. He had 700 wives. Each of them was a princess. He had 300 more women at the palace who were like wives. None of these was a princess.

All of Solomon's wives turned him away from God. They talked him into worshiping their fake gods. So Solomon did not love God with his whole heart. He built places to worship the fake gods.

God got angry at Solomon. "You have not kept loving and obeying me," said God. "So I'll take your kingdom away from you. But I won't do it while you're alive. That's because your father, David, loved me with his whole heart. I'll take most of the kingdom away from your son. But I'll let him lead a small part of the kingdom. That's because David served me."

So God brought in an enemy. His name was Hadad. Years ago Joab had killed the men in his city. Hadad was a boy then. He ran away to Egypt, where he met Egypt's king. The king of Egypt liked Hadad. He gave Hadad a house to live in. He gave him land and food. Hadad married the queen's sister.

Now Hadad heard that David had died. So he went back to the land of God's people. He became Solomon's enemy.

God gave Solomon another enemy. His name was Rezon. He had run away from his master. Other men had followed him. They all made trouble.

Then Jeroboam turned against Solomon. He had been one of Solomon's leaders. He did good work. So Solomon put him in charge of lots of workers.

One day Jeroboam was leaving the city of Jerusalem. A prophet named Ahijah met him.

Ahijah was wearing a new coat. But Ahijah tore his new coat into 12 pieces. He said, "Take 10 pieces, Jeroboam. God told me that he is taking the kingdom away from Solomon. God is giving 10 parts of it to you. Your part will be called Israel. If you obey God, Jeroboam, he promises to be with you.

Solomon's family will keep the small part that's left. Solomon's part will be called Judah."

Then Solomon tried to kill Jeroboam. But Jeroboam ran away to Egypt. He stayed there until Solomon died. Then he heard that Solomon's son Rehoboam was the new king. So Jeroboam came back from Egypt.

Bad Kings

One Nation Turns into Two Nations

1 KINGS 12; 2 CHRONICLES 10–11

Jeroboam and many other people went to see King Rehoboam. "When Solomon was the king, he was very hard on us," they said. "Make things easier for us. Then we will serve you."

"Come back in three days," said the king.

So Jeroboam and the people left.

King Rehoboam asked the older leaders what he should do. They had helped King Solomon with questions, too.

"Be the people's servant," said the older leaders. "Give them a good answer. Then they will serve you forever."

But King Rehoboam didn't like what the older leaders said. He went to the young men. They had grown up with Rehoboam. They were serving him now. "What should I say?" asked the king.

The young men told the king to say these words. "My little finger is big. It's bigger than the middle of my father's body. My father was hard on you. But I'll be harder. My father hurt you with whips. But I'll hurt you with big spiders that can bite you."

Three days passed. Jeroboam and the people came back.

King Rehoboam had an answer for them that was not kind. He didn't listen to the older leaders. He listened to the young men. He said, "My father was hard on you. But I'll be harder. He hurt you with whips. But I'll hurt you with spiders that can bite you."

"Then we won't be your people!" everyone said. And they went home.

King Rehoboam sent a man to try to make Israel serve him. But the people threw rocks at the man. They killed him. Rehoboam got away in his chariot. He went back to Jerusalem in Judah.

After that day, Israel and Judah were two different nations.

God's words to Jeroboam long ago came true. Jeroboam became king of the 10 family groups in the north. They called their nation Israel.

Rehoboam, son of Solomon, was still king. But he had just a small part of the kingdom. He had the family groups of Judah and Benjamin. They called their nation Judah.

When Rehoboam got to Jerusalem, he called out his army. He marched out to fight Israel. He wanted them to be in his kingdom again.

Now God gave a message to a prophet. God told him to go to Rehoboam and say these words. "God says to go back home. Don't fight. God made Israel leave Judah."

So Rehoboam and the army of Judah went back home.

In Israel, Jeroboam began thinking. "The worship house is in Jerusalem," he said. "My people will have to go there to worship. Then they'll turn back to King Rehoboam. And they'll kill me."

So Jeroboam made two gold cows for people to worship as idols. He showed them to his people. "It's too hard for you to go to Jerusalem," he said. "So these are your gods. They took you out of Egypt."

Then he put one gold cow in the town of Bethel. He put the other one in the town of Dan. The people sinned. They went to worship the idols.

Jeroboam also got people to be priests. But God did not say they could be priests. Only people from the family group of Levi could be priests. Jeroboam also started a holiday for the fake gods. He made altars and gave gifts to the idols.

Then the real priests from the family of Levi left Israel. They went to the city of Jerusalem in Judah. It was all because Jeroboam had let other people be priests.

People who loved God with their whole heart went to Judah. They let Rehoboam, son of Solomon, be their king. They helped make his kingdom strong.

APRIL 29

Jeroboam's Son

1 KINGS 13–14

One day King Jeroboam was standing by his altar in Bethel. A prophet came to him from Judah.

The prophet shouted to the king of Israel. He told the king what God said. "A king will be born in Judah. His name will be Josiah. He will kill the bad priests who work here. He will burn their bones on this altar." The prophet said, "God will give a sign showing his word is true. The altar will break apart. Dust from old fires will flow out."

King Jeroboam was very angry and held his hand up. He pointed to the prophet. "Catch that man!" he shouted.

Suddenly Jeroboam's hand bent over like a dry leaf. The altar broke apart, and dust from old fires flowed out.

"Pray for me," called King Jeroboam to the prophet. "Pray that my hand will be well again."

So the prophet prayed for King Jeroboam. Then his hand got well again.

But King Jeroboam would not change. He kept making people priests. They were people God did not choose. The king said anybody who wanted to be a priest could be. This sin led to Jeroboam's troubles. It led to losing his whole kingdom.

Now Jeroboam's son got sick. Jeroboam told his wife, "Make yourself look like another woman. Then nobody will know you are the queen. Go see Ahijah the prophet. He is the one who told me I would be king. Take 10 loaves of bread with

you. Take some cake and honey. Ahijah will tell you about our son."

So the queen dressed like someone else. Then she went to see Ahijah.

Now Ahijah was old and could not see. But God had told him, "Jeroboam's wife is coming today. She is going to ask you about their sick son. When she comes, she will pretend to be somebody else." Then God told Ahijah what to tell her.

Ahijah heard the queen walk up to the door. He said, "Come in, Jeroboam's wife. Why do you pretend to be somebody else?"

Then Ahijah said, "I have bad news for you. Tell Jeroboam what God says. He says that he chose Jeroboam to be his people's leader. He gave Jeroboam the kingdom. But Jeroboam has not been like David. David obeyed God. He did what was right. Jeroboam has done more wrong than anybody before him. He has made other gods. He has made idols out of metal. He has made God angry. He has turned away from God.

"So God is going to bring trouble to your family. Dogs will eat those from your family who die in the city. Birds will eat those who die in the country.

"Now go back home," said Ahijah. "When you step into the city, your son will die. The people will cry.

They'll put his body in a grave. But he is the only one who will have a grave. No one else in your family will have a grave. Only your son has any good in him.

"God will choose another king for Israel," said Ahijah. "Today. Yes. Now. God will send trouble to Israel. Your people will be like a water plant. God will pull up your people by the roots. He will send them away from this land he gave them. He will send them here and there across the river. It's all because they made him mad by making idols. God will give Israel up because of Jeroboam's sins."

Jeroboam's wife went back home. As soon as she stepped into her house, her son died. They put his body in a grave. Everyone cried for him.

Egypt Comes to Fight
1 KINGS 14; 2 CHRONICLES 11–12

Rehoboam still ruled in Jerusalem. He built forts. He stored food and olive oil and wine in them. He sent shields and swords to all the cities. He made his cities strong.

Rehoboam had many sons. One was named Abijah. Rehoboam said Abijah would be king after him. He sent his other sons to live in different cities. And he got wives for them.

But Rehoboam forgot about God's law. He did what was wrong. He didn't think about what God wanted. Then his whole nation sinned. The people made other places of worship, which God did not want. They did the bad things that other nations did.

So the king of Egypt came out to fight them. He brought 1,200 chariots. He brought 60,000 (sixty thousand) horse riders. He brought a big army. He took Judah's forts. Then he marched to Jerusalem.

A prophet went to Rehoboam and the leaders. He told them what God said. "You left me. So I'm leaving you to the king of Egypt."

Then Rehoboam and the leaders said, "God is right in doing this to us."

God saw that now they were making him the important one. So God told the prophet, "They are making me the important one. So I won't get rid of them. I'll save them soon. But they will have to serve the king of Egypt. They'll see how it is to serve another king. They'll see that it's better to serve me."

The king of Egypt fought against Jerusalem. He took the riches that were in the worship house. He took the riches that were in the palace. He took it all. He even took the gold shields Solomon had made.

So Rehoboam made shields out of

other metal. He gave some shields to the guards at the worship house. He gave some to the guards at the palace. They went to the worship house with Rehoboam. They carried their shields with them.

There was still some good in Judah. Rehoboam had said that God was the most important. So God was not angry at him anymore. But Israel and Judah were at war with each other all the time.

Rehoboam was king for 17 years. Then he died. His son Abijah became the next king.

APRIL 30

Judah and Israel Fight

1 KINGS 15; 2 CHRONICLES 13

Abijah was king of Judah now. His army kept fighting Israel. Abijah took 400,000 (four hundred thousand) men out to fight. King Jeroboam of Israel took 800,000 (eight hundred thousand) men out to fight.

Abijah stood up on a mountain. He called, "You people of Israel, listen to me. God made David's family to be kings. But Jeroboam turned away from David's family. Now you are planning to come against God's kingdom.

"You are a big army," called Abijah. "You have your gold cow idols with you. But God's priests have left you. You've made other people into priests.

"We have not left God," said Abijah. "Our priests are from Levi's family group. That's the way God said it should be. We are obeying God. But you have left God. So God is with us. God is our leader. His priests will blow their horns to start the battle. Don't fight God. You won't win."

While Abijah was talking, Jeroboam's men had crept up. When Abijah's men turned around, they saw Jeroboam's men from Israel. The men of Israel were fighting the men of Judah. They were fighting them in back and in front. So the men of Judah called to God. The priests blew their horns. The battle began.

God made Abijah and his men from Judah strong. They won. Israel's army ran away. Judah's army won because they trusted God.

Abijah still didn't love God with his whole heart. He sinned like his father had done. But God gave him a son to be king after him. That was because he was from David's family. David had obeyed God. There was only one time when he had not obeyed. That was when he took Bathsheba from her husband and had him killed.

Good King Asa

1 KINGS 15; 2 CHRONICLES 14–15

Abijah was king for only three years. He died, and his son Asa became king. Then the land of Judah had peace for 10 years.

Asa was a good king. He did what was right. He took down the idols. He took down the other worship places. He told the people to think about what God wanted. He told them to obey God. So his kingdom had peace.

King Asa built forts in Judah. "Put walls around the towns," said King Asa. "Build towers in them. Put gates in the walls. Make bars for the gates. This is our land. We obey God. He is letting us have peace."

King Asa of Judah had an army of 300,000 (three hundred thousand) men. They had big shields and swords. He had more than 200,000 (two hundred thousand) men with small shields, bows, and arrows. They were all brave fighters.

Back in Israel, King Jeroboam died. He had been Israel's king for 22 years. Then his son Nadab became king of Israel. But King Nadab did bad things. He sinned just like his father.

Now a man named Baasha wanted to kill King Nadab. One day King Nadab was with his army. He was fighting against a city. And Baasha killed him. Then Baasha made himself king of Israel. Nadab had been king for just two years.

King Baasha killed all of Nadab's family. That made the prophet Ahijah's words come true. God had said no one would be left from Jeroboam's family. That's because Jeroboam made his people sin. That had made God angry.

But Baasha was not a good king. He sinned just like Jeroboam had.

Back in Judah, Asa was still king. But an army from Cush came to fight Asa. Asa led his army out to the valley to meet them.

Then Asa called to God. "There's nobody like you, God," he said. "You help people who are not strong. Help us. We trust you to help us. We fight this big army in your name. You are our God. Don't let men win against you."

So God fought the army from Cush. They ran away. Asa and his army chased them. Asa and the army from Judah won.

The army from Judah tore down the cities around the south edge of Judah. They took sheep, goats, camels, and other things. Then they went back to Jerusalem.

Now God's Spirit came upon a man who went to see Asa. He said, "King Asa and people of Judah, listen! When you are with God, he is with you. Look for him. Then you will find him. But don't leave him. If you do, he will leave you. Be strong now. Don't give up. God will bring good things to you."

Then Asa was brave. He took down all the idols in the whole land. He fixed God's altar at the worship house. He loved God with his whole heart. He obeyed God all his life.

Lots of people from Israel had moved to Judah. They saw that God was with King Asa.

King Asa called the people of Judah together. They put meat on the altars. The meat was a gift to God. They all said they'd love God with their whole heart. They said they'd kill anyone who wouldn't obey God. They promised with a loud shout.

Then there was lots of shouting. Horns blew. All of the people were happy about their promise. They looked for God, and they found him. So God gave them peace.

Making a Deal

1 KINGS 15–16; 22; 2 CHRONICLES 16–17

Now King Baasha of Israel started fights with Judah. He began building a fort at Ramah. Then people couldn't go in or out of Judah.

There was some silver and gold left in the worship house. There was some left in the palace. Asa gave it to some leaders. They took it to the king of another land. It was the land of Aram.

"Let's make a deal," they told the king of Aram. "We're giving this silver and gold to you. Forget your deal with Baasha and Israel. Then he will stop fighting us."

So the king of Aram made a deal with King Asa of Judah. Then the army of Aram went to fight Israel. They took many of the towns in Israel.

King Baasha heard about it. He stopped building the fort at Ramah. He and his army left.

Then King Asa told everyone to take Ramah apart. They took away the stones. They took away the wood. They used them to build walls around two other towns.

Now a prophet came to King Asa in Judah. The prophet's name was Hanani. He said, "You did not trust God. Instead, you trusted the king of Aram. Remember the army from Cush? It was a big, strong army. But you trusted God, and God helped you win.

"God looks all around the earth," said Hanani. "He looks for people who love him with their whole heart. He makes them strong. You were not wise to make a deal with Aram. So now Judah will have to fight."

King Asa got angry at Hanani. He was so angry, he put Hanani into jail.

Sometime later, King Asa got sick. He got a sickness in his feet. It was very bad. But he didn't ask God to help him. He only asked the doctors. So Asa died.

The people put Asa's body in a grave in Jerusalem. They made a big fire to show how great he was.

Asa's son Jehoshaphat became the next king of Judah. He was a good king. He did what was right. He made forts and sent army men to the forts.

God was with King Jehoshaphat. King Jehoshaphat tried to do what God wanted. So God let him control the land. Many people brought him gifts. He became very rich. People talked about how great he was.

King Jehoshaphat followed God's ways. He got rid of places for worshiping idols. He sent men to teach in different towns. They took God's Book of the Law with them.

All the other lands around were afraid of God. So they didn't fight with Judah. Even Israel didn't fight with Judah.

Some nations brought gifts to Jehoshaphat. Some brought him silver. Some brought him goats and rams. So Jehoshaphat grew more and more powerful. He had a big army, too.

Trouble in Israel

JOSHUA 6; 1 KINGS 16

Now the prophet Hanani had a son named Jehu. He was a prophet, too. God sent Jehu to King Baasha in Israel.

Jehu told King Baasha what God said. "I made you the leader of my people. But you sinned just like Jeroboam. You made my people in Israel sin. You made me angry. So I'm going to get rid of you and your family. They will be like Jeroboam's family. Dogs will eat the ones who die in the city. Birds will eat the ones who die in the country."

Sometime later, King Baasha died. His son Elah became the next king of Israel.

There was a leader in Israel

named Zimri. He was in charge of half of the chariots. Zimri made plans to kill King Elah.

One day King Elah was at his house. He was getting drunk. Zimri came into the house and killed King Elah. Then Zimri became the king of Israel.

Right away, King Zimri killed all of Baasha's family. That made Jehu's words come true. Baasha's family died like Jeroboam's family. That's because they had sinned. They had made idols to worship. They had led the people of Israel to sin.

Now Israel's army was in its camp. They heard that Zimri had killed King Elah. So they said Omri would be the next king. Omri was the leader of the army. They marched to the town where Zimri was. They began fighting against it.

Zimri saw that Omri's army had taken over the city. So Zimri went into the palace. He set it on fire, and he died in the fire. It all happened because he had sinned. He had done what was wrong.

Then the people of Israel made two groups. One group wanted Tibni to be king. The other group wanted Omri to be king. Omri's group was stronger. So Omri became the king of Israel.

King Omri bought a hill. He built a city on the hill. He named the city Samaria.

But King Omri was a bad king. He sinned more than anybody before him. Doing wrong didn't matter to him.

King Omri had a son named Ahab. Ahab married a woman named Jezebel. She was the daughter of the king of another land.

When Omri died, Ahab became the king. Nobody before was quite as bad as Ahab. He did terrible, sinful things. His wife, Jezebel, got him to sin even more.

King Ahab worshiped idols. He began to worship the fake god called Baal. He built a worship house for Baal. He set up an altar for Baal. He did many things to make God angry. He did more bad things than any kings before him.

Now during this time a man built the city of Jericho back up. This happened when Ahab was king. Long ago God had talked to Joshua about Jericho. God had told him what would happen to anyone who built Jericho again. It happened just as God had said. The man's oldest son died when he started building it. His youngest son died when he put the gates in. That's what God had said would happen.

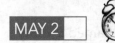

No Rain, No Food

1 KINGS 17

Now there was a man named Elijah. He was a prophet who served God. One day he went to King Ahab in Israel. He said, "It's not going to rain for many years. It won't rain until I say it will rain."

Then God told Elijah, "Go east. Hide by the brook there. Drink water from the brook. I have told the birds to bring you food."

So Elijah obeyed God. He stayed by the brook. Big, black birds called ravens brought food to him. They brought bread and meat every morning and every evening. Elijah drank water out of the brook.

But the brook dried up. There was no water, because there hadn't been any rain.

Then God told Elijah, "Go into town. A woman lives there whose husband has died. I've told her to give you food."

So Elijah went to the town. A woman was picking up sticks at the gate. Elijah asked, "Would you bring me some water?"

The woman went to get some water. Elijah called, "Please bring me some bread, too."

"I don't have any bread," said the woman. "I have just a little bit of flour in a jar. I have just a little

bit of oil in a jug. I'm going to use these sticks to build a fire. I can cook some food for my son and me one more time. Then we'll die."

"Don't be afraid," said Elijah. "Cook your food. But bring a little bread for me first. Then make something for you and your son to eat. God says that you won't use up the flour in the jar. You won't use up the oil in the jug. You won't use it up until God sends rain."

So the woman made bread for Elijah. Then she had enough flour and oil every day. She could make enough food for her family and Elijah. The jar didn't run out of flour. The jug didn't run out of oil. It happened just like God said it would.

Time passed. One day the woman's son got sick. He got sicker and sicker until he stopped breathing.

The woman cried to Elijah. "Are you angry at me?" she asked. "Are you trying to make me sorry for my sin? Are you trying to kill my boy?"

"Give him to me," said Elijah. He carried the boy up the stairs. Elijah went to his own room. He put the boy on his bed. He began to pray, "God! Why did you let this boy die? Why did you let this happen to his mother?"

Then Elijah lay across the boy. He did that three times. Then he called, "God, please give this boy's life back!"

God heard Elijah. The boy came

back to life! Elijah carried him back down the stairs. He handed him to his mother. "Look!" he said. "Your son is alive now!"

"Now I know you're a prophet," said the woman. "I know that your words are true because they're from God."

MAY 3

Fire on Carmel Mountain

1 KINGS 18

Three years had passed since the rain stopped. God told Elijah, "Go to King Ahab. I'm going to make it rain."

So Elijah went to see King Ahab.

No food was growing. There was not much to eat. It was very bad in Samaria.

King Ahab called for Obadiah. He was in charge of Ahab's palace. "Go look all over the land," said Ahab. "Look in the valleys. Look for the brooks. See if you can find grass for our horses and mules. Maybe we can keep them alive. Then we won't have to kill any of them."

King Ahab sent Obadiah through part of the land. Ahab went to look through the other part.

Obadiah believed in God. Queen Jezebel had killed many of God's prophets. But Obadiah had saved 100 prophets. He had hidden 50 of

them in one cave. He had hidden 50 more in another cave. He had given them food and water.

Now Obadiah was walking along, and he met Elijah. Obadiah knew Elijah. So he bowed down. He said, "Is that really you, Elijah?"

"Yes," said Elijah. "Go tell King Ahab that I'm here."

"Do you want to get me killed?" asked Obadiah. "What have I ever done to you? King Ahab has looked everywhere for you. Now you tell me to say that Elijah is here. What if God's Spirit takes you somewhere else? What if I tell King Ahab you're here? Then what if you're not here when he comes? King Ahab would kill me for that."

Obadiah went on, "I've worshiped God ever since I was a boy. Do you know what I did when Jezebel killed the prophets? I hid 100 of them. I brought food and water to them. But now you want me to tell Ahab you're here. I know he will kill me!"

"I'll be here," said Elijah. "I promise. I must talk to King Ahab today."

So Obadiah found King Ahab. Then King Ahab went to see Elijah. Elijah was there.

"Is that you, you trouble maker?" asked King Ahab.

"I didn't make trouble," said Elijah. "You made trouble. Your

281

father's family made trouble. You turned away from God. You worship Baal idols. Now call the people of Israel together. Come to Carmel Mountain. Bring Baal's 450 prophets. Bring the other 400 prophets who worship other idols."

So Ahab got the people together. He called the idols' prophets together. They all went to Carmel Mountain.

Then Elijah talked to the people. "How long will it be before you choose?" he asked. "Follow the Lord, if he is God. But follow Baal, if Baal is God."

The people didn't say anything.

"I'm the only prophet of God left," said Elijah. "But here are 450 prophets of Baal. Give us two bulls. The other prophets can choose which bull they want. They can kill it. They can put the meat on their altar. But they can't set it on fire.

"Then I'll get the other bull ready," said Elijah. "I'll put its meat on my altar. But I won't set it on fire. Then you call for Baal. I'll call for God. The one who answers by sending fire must be God!"

"That's good!" said the people.

"You go first," said Elijah to Baal's prophets. "Call for Baal's help. Don't start the fire yourselves."

So they chose a bull. They killed it and put it on the altar. Then they called, "Baal! Answer us!"

Baal's prophets called from morning until noon. But there was no answer.

At noon Elijah said, "Call louder! You're sure Baal is a god, aren't you? Maybe he is thinking. Maybe he is busy. Maybe he has gone on a trip. Maybe he is sleeping. You'll have to wake him up!"

So they called louder and louder. They even cut themselves. That's what they always did. They were bleeding. They kept this up until the evening. But there was no answer.

At last, Elijah told the people, "Come here." So they came.

Elijah took them over to an old altar. It had been built to worship God. Elijah got 12 stones. Each stone stood for a family group of God's people. Elijah built up the altar with these stones.

Then Elijah dug a small pit all the way around the altar. He put wood on the altar. He put the bull meat on the wood. Then he said, "Fill four big jars with water. Put the water all over the meat and the wood."

So the people did.

"Do that again," said Elijah. So they did.

"Do that one more time," said Elijah. So they did.

The water went all over the altar.

It flowed down the altar into the pit. Water filled the pit.

Then Elijah prayed. "God, show that you are God in Israel. Show that I'm your servant. Show that I'm obeying you. Answer me, God. Let these people know that you are God."

Then fire came down from God onto the altar. It burned up the meat. It burned up the wood. It burned up the stones. It burned up the dirt. And it burned up the water in the pit!

The people were watching. They bowed down with their faces to the ground. "The Lord is God!" they shouted. "The Lord is God!"

"Catch Baal's prophets!" said Elijah. "Don't let them get away!"

So the people held onto Baal's prophets. They took them into the valley. They killed them there.

"Go!" said Elijah to King Ahab. "Eat. Drink. It sounds like it's going to rain."

King Ahab left. But Elijah went back up Carmel Mountain. He bent down and put his head between his knees.

"Go look out to the sea," he told his servant.

His servant went and looked out to the sea.

"I don't see anything," said his servant.

Elijah told him to go back and look again. So he went again, but he saw nothing. Elijah sent him back again. He went, but he saw nothing. The servant ended up going to look seven times.

The last time he looked, the servant said, "I see something. It's a cloud. It's small, like a person's hand. It's coming up from the sea."

"Go tell Ahab to get in his chariot," said Elijah. "Tell him to leave before rain keeps him from riding."

The sky got dark with clouds. Wind started blowing. Heavy rain started coming down. Ahab left to go into the city.

Then God's power came upon Elijah. He tucked his coat into his belt and ran. He passed Ahab. He ran all the way to the city.

MAY 4

Afraid in the Desert
1 KINGS 19

King Ahab told his wife, Jezebel, what had happened. He told how Baal's prophets had been killed. So Jezebel sent a message to Elijah. "I promise I'll kill you! By this time tomorrow, you'll be dead!"

283

Elijah got scared. He ran away. He left his servant in town. Elijah ran away into the desert. He went as far as you could go in a day.

Then Elijah saw a broom tree. He sat down under it. He prayed that he'd die. "This is too much for me, God," he said. "Just let me die."

Elijah lay down there, and he went to sleep.

Suddenly an angel came. He touched Elijah and woke him up. "Get up," said the angel. "Eat something."

Elijah looked around. He saw some bread. He saw a jar of water. So he ate the bread. He drank some water. Then he lay back down.

God's angel came to Elijah again. He touched Elijah. "Get up," said the angel. "Eat some more, or your trip will be too hard for you."

So Elijah got up. He ate and drank. Then he felt stronger. That was all he ate. But he was strong enough to travel for 40 days and 40 nights.

At last Elijah got to Horeb Mountain. That was the mountain of God. Elijah spent the night in a cave there.

Then God spoke to Elijah. "Why are you here, Elijah?"

"I have worked hard for you, God," said Elijah. "But your people have turned away from you. They broke your altars. They killed your prophets. I'm the only prophet left. Now they're trying to kill me."

"Go stand on the mountain," said God. "I'm going to pass by."

A strong wind blew. It was so strong, it broke rocks. But God was not in the wind.

The earth began to shake. But God was not in the shaking earth.

A fire came. But God was not in the fire.

Then Elijah heard a soft, quiet voice.

Elijah pulled his coat over his face. He stood at the opening to the cave.

Then God spoke. "Why are you here, Elijah?"

"I've worked hard for you, God," said Elijah. "But your people have turned away from you. They tore your altars down. They killed your prophets. I'm the only prophet left. Now they're trying to kill me."

"Go back," said God. "Make Jehu king of Israel. Make Elisha the next prophet after you."

Then God said, "I have saved 7,000 people for myself in Israel. They do not worship Baal or follow him."

So Elijah left. He found Elisha. Elisha was plowing a field. He had lots of oxen pulling the plow. Elijah walked up to Elisha. He put his coat over Elisha's shoulders.

Elisha left the plow. He ran after

Elijah. "I have to kiss my mother and father good-bye," he said. "Then I'll come."

"All right," said Elijah.

So Elisha went back. He killed some of the oxen. He burned the plow. He cooked the meat. He gave it to people to eat. Then he left to go with Elijah.

King Ahab Fights a War

1 KINGS 20:1-22

Now the king of Aram got his whole army together. He got 32 other kings to go with him. They got their horses and chariots ready. Then they all marched out to fight against Israel. They marched to the city of Samaria.

The king of Aram sent a message to King Ahab. "I want to have your silver and gold. I want to have your best wives and children."

King Ahab sent a message back. It said, "All right."

Then the king of Aram sent another message. "Tomorrow I'll send my leaders into your city. I'll take everything that looks good to me."

King Ahab called his leaders together. He said. "The king of Aram is asking for trouble. First he asked for my wives and children. He asked for silver and gold. I told him yes."

"Don't give him anything more," said the leaders.

So King Ahab sent a message back. "I'll give you what you asked for the first time. But I can't give you anything else."

Then the king of Aram sent another message. "Only dust will be left when I'm done with your city."

King Ahab sent a message back. "You haven't even started to fight! You shouldn't brag as if you'd already won!"

The king of Aram and his leaders were in their tents. They were drinking when the message came. The king of Aram said, "Get ready to fight!" So his army got ready to fight the city of Samaria.

Then a prophet came to King Ahab. The prophet told the king what God said. "Look at this big army. I'm going to give it to you. You will win. Then you'll know that I'm God."

"Who should fight?" asked Ahab.

"God says the young leaders will fight," said the prophet.

"Who will start the fight?" asked Ahab.

"You will," said the prophet.

So Ahab called his young army officers. There were 232 of them. Then Ahab got the rest of the army together. There were 7,000 of them. He sent them out at noon.

Now at noon, the king of Aram

285

was in his tent. The 32 other kings were in their tents. They were getting drunk.

The king of Aram had men watching the city of Samaria. They sent him a message. "Men are coming from the city!"

"Catch them!" said the king of Aram.

So the men from Aram went to catch the young officers. But the young officers killed them. Then the army of Aram began running away. And the king of Aram got away on a horse.

But King Ahab and his army chased them. He caught up with them. A fight began. King Ahab and his army won.

The prophet came back to King Ahab. He said, "Make your army stronger. Make your city stronger. The king of Aram will come back to fight. He will come back next spring."

 MAY 5

The Enemy Comes Back

1 KINGS 20:23-43

The leaders of Aram told their king, "Israel's gods are hill gods. That's why they won. If we fight on flat ground, we'll win. Get more men for your army. Get more horses and chariots. Then we can fight Israel on flat ground."

The king of Aram thought his leaders were right. So he did what they said. The next spring he went back to fight against Israel.

The army of Israel came to meet the army of Aram. The two armies made their camps. The army of Israel camped on one side of the valley. They looked like two small groups of goats. The army of Aram camped on the other side of the valley. There were so many of them that they covered the ground.

The prophet came back to King Ahab. The prophet told the king what God said. "The people of Aram think I'm just a hill god. They don't think I'm a god of valleys, too. So I'm going to give their army to you. You'll win. Then you'll know I'm God."

The armies camped near the valley for a week. At the end of the week, they began fighting. The army of Israel was winning. Lots of enemy men ran away to a city. But the wall of that city fell. It fell on 27,000 (twenty-seven thousand) enemy men.

The king of Aram had run to that city too. He was hiding in a room there. His officers told him, "We've heard that Israel's kings are kind. Let's give up and go to King Ahab. Maybe he won't kill us."

So the officers of Aram went to King Ahab. "The king of Aram will be your servant," they said. "Please don't kill him."

"Is he still alive?" asked King Ahab. "He will be like a brother to me!"

The officers of Aram thought this was good. "Yes!" they said. "He is like a brother to you!"

"Bring him here," said King Ahab.

The king of Aram came out. King Ahab asked him to come up into his chariot.

"I'll give cities to you," said the king of Aram. "They're the cities my father took from you. Then Israel may sell things in my cities. I'll let them do it, because my father sold things in your cities."

"It's a deal," said King Ahab. "I'll let you go free."

So they made a deal. Then the king of Aram was set free.

Now God spoke to another prophet. God told him what to say. So the prophet told a man, "Hit me." But the man wouldn't do it.

The prophet said, "You didn't obey God. So a lion will kill you."

The man left, and a lion did kill him.

The prophet went to another man. "Please hit me," he said. So the man hit him. The prophet got hurt.

Then the prophet pulled his head band down over his eyes. He went to the road. He waited for King Ahab to pass by.

As King Ahab went by, the prophet called to him. "I went into battle," he said. "Someone brought a man over to me. This man was part of the enemy's army. I was told to watch this man. I was told not to let him get away. If he got away, I'd have to give my life for his life. Or I'd have to pay with silver. But I was busy with the fight. The man got away."

"Then you are to blame," said King Ahab. "You were told what would happen if you let the man go."

Then the prophet pulled up his head band. King Ahab saw that he was one of God's prophets.

The prophet told Ahab what God's message was. "The king of Aram should have died. But you set him free. So you will give your life for his life."

King Ahab was angry when he heard this. He went off to his palace.

King Ahab and the Grape Field

1 KINGS 21

Time passed. There was a grape field next to King Ahab's palace. It belonged to a man named Naboth.

King Ahab told Naboth, "I want your grape field. I want to make it into a vegetable garden. So let's make a deal. I'll pay you for your grape field. Or I'll give you a better field for it."

"No," said Naboth. "This field has belonged to my family for many years. My father gave it to me. I will not give it to you."

King Ahab went home. He was sad and angry. He lay down on his bed. He wouldn't eat anything.

Jezebel, his wife, came in. "Why are you sad and angry?" she asked. "Why won't you eat anything?"

"Naboth won't sell me his grape field," said Ahab. "I even said I'd trade him another field for it."

"You're the king of Israel!" said Jezebel. "Is this how a king acts? Get up! Eat something! Don't worry. I'll get the grape field for you."

Jezebel wrote some letters. She signed King Ahab's name. She put his special seal on them. Then she sent them to the leaders of Naboth's city. Here's what the letters said.

Have a big dinner party. Let Naboth sit where the important people sit. Then get two mean men. Let them sit on the other side of the table. Have them tell everyone that Naboth said bad things about God. They should tell everyone that Naboth said bad things about the king, too. Then take Naboth out. Kill him by throwing rocks at him.

This is just what the leaders did. They had their party. The two mean men came. They lied about Naboth. Then they dragged Naboth outside and killed him. After that, they sent a message back to Jezebel. It said, "Naboth is dead."

Jezebel went to King Ahab. "You can have that grape field now," she said. "Naboth is dead."

So King Ahab went out to take the grape field.

Then God told Elijah, "Go see King Ahab. He has gone down to take Naboth's grape field."

God told Elijah what to say to Ahab. These were God's words. "You killed a man. You took his field. You will die where Naboth died. Dogs will lick up your blood! Yes! Your blood!"

Elijah went to King Ahab. King Ahab said, "So! It's my old enemy! You found me!"

"Yes," said Elijah. "It's because

you sinned. God says he is bringing you trouble. No one in your family will live. You've made God angry. You've made God's people in Israel sin.

"Let's talk about Jezebel, too," said Elijah. "Dogs will eat her up. Your family will be like Jeroboam's family. Dogs will eat the ones who die in the city. Birds will eat the ones who die in the country."

Now King Ahab was very upset. He tore his clothes. He didn't eat. He walked around quietly.

God said to Elijah, "See what Ahab is doing? He is showing that he is sorry. So I'm not going to bring terrible trouble while he is alive. I'll bring it on his son."

MAY 6

The Prophet Who Told the Truth

1 KINGS 22

King Ahab talked to his leaders in Israel. "The city of Ramoth belongs to Israel," he said. "But the king of Aram has it. We aren't doing anything to get it back."

King Jehoshaphat from Judah was visiting King Ahab. So King Ahab asked him, "Would you fight with us at Ramoth?"

"Yes," said King Jehoshaphat. "I'll go, my people will go, and my horses will go. But first, you'll have to ask God about it."

So King Ahab got his prophets together. There were about 400 of them. "Should we fight Ramoth or not?" Ahab asked.

"Go and fight," they said. "God will help you win."

Now, both kings had their king's robes on. They sat on their thrones by the gate. All of Ahab's prophets were telling them what would happen. They were saying the kings would win.

One prophet was named Zedekiah. He had made some iron horns. He showed them to the kings. He said, "You will win with these. You will get rid of Aram!"

"Don't you have any prophets from God?" asked Jehoshaphat.

"There is one man we could ask," said Ahab. "His name is Micaiah. But I hate him. He always tells me bad things."

"You shouldn't say that," said Jehoshaphat.

So King Ahab called for one of his leaders. "Go get Micaiah," he said. "Bring him here."

The leader went to get Micaiah. He said, "All the other prophets are saying Ahab will win. You should say the same thing. Give a good answer."

"I can only say what God tells me

to," said Micaiah. He went to see King Ahab.

"Should we fight Ramoth or not?" asked Ahab.

"Go ahead," said Micaiah.

"How many times do I have to ask?" said Ahab. "Do I have to make you promise to tell the truth?"

So Micaiah told the truth. "I saw your army in my mind," he said. "They were running here and there. They were all over the hills. They were like sheep with no shepherd. God said that these people have no master. He said to let them go home. He said to let them have peace."

"See?" said Ahab to Jehoshaphat. "I told you he always says bad things will happen."

Micaiah said, "Hear what God says. I saw God sitting on his throne in heaven. All the armies of heaven were around him. Some were on his right. Some were on his left. And God asked who could get Ahab to fight Ramoth and die. One being said one thing. Other beings said other things.

"At last a spirit came up to God," said Micaiah. "Ahab, this spirit promised to get you to fight. God wanted to know how the spirit would do it. 'I'll get Ahab's prophets to lie,' said the spirit. God said that plan would work. He told the spirit to go and do it.

"So God is getting your prophets to lie," said Micaiah. "God plans terrible trouble for you, Ahab."

Then Zedekiah, one of Ahab's prophets, walked up and hit Micaiah's face. "God's Spirit was in me," said Zedekiah. "How did he get to you?"

"You'll find out on the day you hide," said Micaiah.

"Take Micaiah away," said King Ahab. "Throw him in jail. Don't feed him anything but bread and water. Leave him there until I'm back safe from this fight."

"If you stay safe, God didn't talk through me," said Micaiah. "Everybody remember what I said!"

Then King Ahab and King Jehoshaphat went to Ramoth to fight.

Ahab told Jehoshaphat, "You wear your king's robe. I'll dress like someone else. That way, nobody will know who I am."

So King Ahab dressed in other clothes. Then the two kings and their armies went out to fight.

Now the king of Aram had 32 chariot leaders. He gave them orders. "Only fight with King Ahab," he said. "Don't fight with anybody else."

The chariot leaders saw King Jehoshaphat. "That's King Ahab!" they thought. So they started to fight him.

But Jehoshaphat shouted. The men saw that he wasn't King Ahab. So they stopped chasing him.

Then a man shot an arrow. He was not really trying to shoot any special person. But the arrow hit King Ahab. It hit him in a place between the pieces of his heavy armor.

"Turn around!" called King Ahab to his chariot driver. "I'm hurt! Take me away from the battle!"

The battle lasted all day. King Ahab watched, leaning over in his chariot. His blood ran down onto the chariot floor. He died that evening.

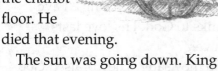

The sun was going down. King Ahab's fighting men called out, "Go back home, everybody!"

The people put their king's body in a grave in Samaria. They washed his chariot in a pool there. The dogs licked Ahab's blood up. It happened just like God said it would.

King Ahab's son Ahaziah became the next king of Israel. He was a bad king too. He was just like his father and mother. He worshiped the idol of Baal. He made God angry, just like Ahab had done.

Facing the Enemy

2 CHRONICLES 19–20

Now Jehoshaphat, king of Judah, got home safely from the fight at Ramoth. Then the prophet Jehu went to his palace to see him.

"God is angry at you," said Jehu. "It's because you helped King Ahab. Is it right for you to help sinful people? Is it right to love people who hate God? But there is some good in you. You got rid of idols. You are trying to obey God."

Then King Jehoshaphat went to the towns of Judah. He got the people to obey God again. He chose judges for the cities. "Be careful when you judge," he told them. "Remember that you're not judging for people. You're judging for God. He is with you when you say what's right and what's wrong. So make God the most important one. He is fair and right."

King Jehoshaphat also chose priests from the family of Levi. "Keep serving God no matter what," he told them. "Look up to God. Serve him with your whole heart. Tell the people not to sin. If they don't sin, God won't be angry. Be brave. Do your job well, and God will be with you."

One day some men came to see King Jehoshaphat. "A big army is coming this way!" they said. "They're coming to fight us!"

Jehoshaphat was surprised and afraid. He told all the people not to eat. They all came together to pray for God's help. People came from every town.

Jehoshaphat prayed with them in front of the worship house. "God, you are the God who is in heaven. You're the King of all kingdoms. You are strong. Nobody can stand up against you. You gave your people this land. We built a worship house here for you. We said, 'We'll come here if we get in trouble. We'll call out to you in our trouble. You will hear us and save us.'

"But now an army is coming against us," said Jehoshaphat. "We are not strong enough to win the battle. We don't know what to do. We are waiting for you to tell us."

All the men stood there. All the women stood there. All the children and little babies were there, too.

Then God's Spirit came on one of the men. "King Jehoshaphat! All you people! Listen!" he said. "Here's what God says. 'Don't be scared. Don't give up. The fight isn't yours. It's God's.'

"God says to march out to meet the enemy army tomorrow. They'll be coming up the Ziz Pass. You'll find them at the end of the valley in the desert. You won't have to fight.

Just stand there and watch. You'll see how God saves you.

"So God says not to be afraid. He says not to give up. Go out tomorrow. Face the enemy. God will be with you."

King Jehoshaphat bowed down. All the people bowed and worshiped God. Then some of them stood up. They began cheering loudly for God.

Early the next morning the army of Judah headed for the desert. King Jehoshaphat said, "Listen, people. Trust in God. He will save you. Believe his prophets. You will win."

Jehoshaphat talked to the leaders. Then he chose singers to sing to God. They praised God. Then they led the army. They sang, "Give thanks to God. His love lasts forever."

So they sang. They praised God. Then God began to work out his plan against the enemies. The enemies began to fight each other. They killed each other.

Sometime later, God's people came to the place where the enemy army was. All they saw were dead bodies. None of the men from the enemy army had lived.

Jehoshaphat and his men found riches at the enemy camp. They found lots of clothes and other things. There was so much that it took three days to gather it all.

God's people got together in the valley. They cheered for God. Then they went back home. They were very happy because God had won. They went into the worship house. There they played harps and horns.

Now the other nations heard what happened. They heard that God had been the one to fight for his people. The other nations were afraid. So Jehoshaphat's kingdom of Judah lived in peace.

Sometime later, Jehoshaphat made a deal with Ahaziah. He was the king of Israel. He was a bad king like his father, Ahab. But both kings built some ships to share. These ships were for bringing things to buy and sell.

Then a prophet came to Jehoshaphat. He said, "You made a deal with Ahaziah. So God will get rid of what you built."

Later, the ships crashed. They couldn't sail anywhere.

Orders from the King

2 KINGS 1; 3:1-3

Now in Israel, King Ahaziah fell and got hurt. So he sent some of his men to the idol of Baal. He said, "Ask Baal if I'll get well."

But God's angel went to Elijah. He said, "Go out and meet the king's men." These are the words God's angel told Elijah to say. "Is there no God in Israel? Is that why you're going to see Baal? The king will never get out of bed. He will die there!"

So Elijah went out and met the men. He gave them God's message. The men went back to the king.

"Why did you come back?" asked King Ahaziah.

"A man met us," they said. "This man told us to come back. He said you won't get out of bed. You'll die there!"

"What was this man like?" asked the king.

"He wore clothes made of animal skin," they said. "He had a belt on."

"It was Elijah!" said the king. Then he sent an army captain and 50 men to get Elijah.

Elijah was sitting on a hill. The army captain said, "The king orders you to come down!"

"If I'm a prophet, let fire come down from heaven," said Elijah. "Let it burn you up with your 50 men!"

Then fire came down from God. It burned up the captain and his 50 men.

So the king sent another captain. He sent 50 more men with him.

The captain said, "The king orders you to come down! Right now!"

"If I'm a prophet, let fire come

down from heaven," said Elijah. "Let it burn you up with your 50 men!"

Then fire came down from God again. It burned up the captain and his 50 men.

So the king sent another captain. He sent 50 more men with him.

This captain went to Elijah. He fell down in front of Elijah. "Please think of my life," he said. "Think of the lives of these 50 men. We are your servants. Fire killed the first two captains. It killed all their men. Please be kind to us!"

Then God's angel came to Elijah. He said, "Go with this captain. Don't be afraid." So Elijah went with the captain to see King Ahaziah.

Elijah told the king what God said. "Why did you want to ask Baal if you'd live? Isn't there a God in Israel? Because you did this, you'll never get out of bed. You will die!"

King Ahaziah died. He did not have a son. So his brother Joram became the next king. Joram was a bad king. He did not stop sinning.

A Chariot and Horses of Fire

2 KINGS 2

God was going to take Elijah to heaven. Elijah and Elisha were leaving a town.

"You stay here," said Elijah. "God is sending me to Bethel."

"I won't leave you," said Elisha.

So they went to Bethel together.

The prophets that lived in Bethel went to Elisha. "God is taking Elijah to heaven today," they said. "Did you know that?"

"Yes," said Elisha. "But don't talk about it."

Then Elijah told Elisha, "You stay here. God is sending me to Jericho."

"I won't leave you," said Elisha.

So they went to Jericho together.

The prophets that lived in Jericho went to Elisha. "God is taking Elijah to heaven today," they said. "Did you know that?"

"Yes," said Elisha. "But don't talk about it."

Then Elijah told Elisha, "You stay here. God is sending me to the Jordan River."

"I won't leave you," said Elisha.

So they walked on together. Soon they came to the Jordan River. Fifty prophets followed them. They stood back a little way to watch.

Elijah took his coat off. He rolled it up. Then he hit the water with it. The water moved back. Some of it went to the left, down the river. Some of it went to the right, up the river. Elijah and Elisha walked across the river on dry ground.

Then Elijah said, "I'm going soon.

Is there something I can do for you first?"

"I want to have your spirit," said Elisha. "I want two times as much as you have."

"You've asked something hard," said Elijah. "But if you see me go, you'll have it. If you don't see me go, you won't have it."

They walked along, and they talked. All of a sudden, horses of fire appeared. They pulled a chariot of fire. It went between Elijah and Elisha. Then a wind came, turning around and around. It took Elijah up to heaven.

Elisha saw it. He cried, "My father! Israel's horses and chariots!"

Elisha didn't see Elijah anymore. He tore his own coat apart. Then he picked up Elijah's coat. It had fallen from Elijah.

Elisha walked back to the Jordan River. He hit the water with Elijah's coat. He said, "Where is Elijah's God?"

The water moved apart for him. Elisha walked across on the dry ground.

The prophets from Jericho were watching. "Elijah's spirit is upon Elisha now," they said.

They went to Elisha and bowed down. "We have 50 men," they said. "Let's get them to look for Elijah. Maybe God's Spirit took him to a mountain or valley."

"No," said Elisha.

But the prophets kept asking him. At last Elisha said, "All right. Send the men to look."

So they sent the 50 men to look for Elijah. They looked for three days. They didn't find him anywhere. So they went back to Elisha in Jericho.

"I told you not to go," said Elisha.

Now the men of Jericho went to Elisha. "Our town is built in a good place," they said. "But our water is bad. The land won't grow crops."

"Bring me some salt in a new bowl," said Elisha.

So they brought it to him. Elisha went to the spring where the water for the town came from. He threw the salt into the water. He said these words from God. "I have made this water good. It won't ever be bad again. Now it will make crops grow."

From then on, the water of Jericho was good.

Elisha left Jericho. He walked toward Bethel. As he walked along, boys came out of the town. They made fun of Elisha. "Go on, you bald head!" they called. "Go on, you bald head!"

Elisha turned and looked at them. He promised that something bad would happen to them. Then two bears came out of the woods. The bears hurt 42 of those boys.

Elisha went on to Carmel Mountain. Then he went back to Samaria.

Oil to Sell

2 KINGS 4:1-7

One day a prophet died. His wife went to Elisha, crying. "My husband is dead," she said. "You know how much he loved God. But he owed some money. The man he owed it to wants to take my two boys. He wants to make them his slaves."

"What's in your house?" asked Elisha.

"Nothing," she said. "There is just a little oil."

"Go to your neighbors," said Elisha. "Ask them for jars that have nothing in them. Ask for lots of jars. Then go into your house with your sons. Close your door. Fill each jar with oil."

So the woman left. She did what Elisha said. After their door was

closed, her boys brought the jars to her. She put oil from her jar into the other jars. At last all the jars were full. She said, "Bring me another jar."

"There aren't any more jars," said her sons.

Then no more oil came from her jar.

The woman went to tell Elisha that they were finished.

"Now go and sell the jars of oil," said Elisha. "Pay the man the money your husband owed him."

A Room on the Roof Top

2 KINGS 4:8-37; 8:1-2

One day Elisha went to a town called Shunem. A rich woman lived there. She asked Elisha to come for dinner. Every time Elisha went through Shunem, he ate there.

The woman told her husband, "Elisha is a prophet. Let's make a little room on our roof. Let's put a bed and table in it. Let's put a chair and lamp in it. Elisha can stay there when he comes."

One day Elisha came. He went into his room. He lay down on the bed. He had a servant named Gehazi. He asked Gehazi, "What can we do for this woman?"

"Her husband is old," said Gehazi. "And she doesn't have a son."

"Call her," said Elisha.

Gehazi called the woman. She came and stood at the door.

"You'll have a son at this time next year," said Elisha.

"Don't be silly," she said.

Later, she found out she was going to have a baby. The next year she had a baby boy. It happened just like Elisha said it would.

The boy grew older. One day he went out to the field to see his father. "My head hurts!" cried the boy.

"Take him back to his mother," his father told a servant.

The servant picked up the boy. He carried him to his mother.

The mother held the boy in her lap. But at noon he died. She took him up the stairs to Elisha's room. She closed the door.

Then she called her husband. "Send a servant here with a donkey," she said. "I need to go see Elisha."

"Why?" asked her husband. "It's not a holiday or a worship day."

"That's all right," she said.

She put the saddle on the donkey. She told her servant to lead the donkey. "Don't go slowly unless I tell you to," she said.

She found Elisha at Carmel Mountain. Elisha saw her coming. He sent Gehazi to her. "Look! There's the woman from Shunem!" said Elisha. "Run down and ask her if everything is all right."

Gehazi went and asked her. "Yes," she said. "Everything is all right."

When she got to Elisha, she held onto his feet. Gehazi started to push her away.

"Leave her here!" said Elisha. "She is very sad. But God hasn't told me why."

"Weren't you the one who said I'd have a son?" she cried.

Then Elisha turned to Gehazi. "Take my walking stick," he said. "Run to her house. Don't stop to say hello to anyone you meet. Don't stop for anyone who says hello to you. Lay my walking stick on the boy's face."

"I'm not leaving you," said the woman. So Elisha got up and went with her.

Gehazi got to the woman's house first. He laid Elisha's walking stick on the boy's face. But nothing happened.

Gehazi went back to meet Elisha. He told him, "The boy is still dead."

Elisha got to the house. He went up to his room. He went in alone and shut the door. He saw the boy on his bed. So he prayed to God. Then he got on the bed too. He lay down on the boy. He put his mouth to the boy's mouth. He put his eyes on the boy's eyes. He put his hands on the boy's hands.

The boy's body got warm. Elisha got up. He walked around the room.

Then he got on the bed again. He lay down on the boy again.

The boy sneezed. He sneezed seven times and opened his eyes.

Elisha called Gehazi. "Call the woman," he said.

Gehazi called her. She came. Elisha said, "Here's your son."

The woman bowed down at Elisha's feet. Then she took her son and left the room.

Sometime later, Elisha talked to the woman again. "Take your family to another land," he said. "God is sending a time when no food will grow. There won't be much to eat. This will go on for seven years."

So the woman did what Elisha said. She moved to another land. She stayed there for seven years.

Death in the Soup

2 KINGS 4:38-44

Elisha went to a town where people had no more food. Crops weren't growing in the land. Elisha met with a group of prophets there.

Elisha told Gehazi, "Put a big pot on the fire. Cook some soup for these men."

One man went out to the fields. He looked for something to make the soup taste good. He found a vine growing wild. Some kind of fruit was on the vine. So he picked the fruit. He filled his coat with it and took it back.

Nobody knew what kind of fruit it was. But the man cut the fruit up. He put it into the pot.

The men started to eat the soup. "There's death in this soup!" they said. "It's poison!" So they couldn't eat the soup.

"Bring me some flour," said Elisha. He put the flour into the soup pot. "You can eat it now," he said.

The soup wasn't bad anymore.

A man came to see Elisha. He brought Elisha 20 loaves of bread. It was made from the first grain crop he had grown.

"Give it to the people," said Elisha. "Let them eat it."

"This won't feed 100 people!" said Gehazi.

"Give it to them anyway," said Elisha. "God says they'll eat it. They'll even have food left over."

So the man gave it to the people. They ate it, and they had leftovers. It happened just like God said it would.

An Ax on the Water

2 KINGS 6:1-7

The prophets told Elisha, "Our meeting house is too small. Let's go to the Jordan River to get logs. Then let's build a new meeting place. We can live there."

"Go ahead," said Elisha.

"Please come with us," one man said.

"All right," said Elisha. So he went with them.

They started cutting down trees at the river. But the sharp iron top

of one man's ax fell off. It fell into the river. "Oh no!" cried the man. "That's not my ax! It belongs to someone else!"

"Where did it go?" asked Elisha.

The man showed Elisha where it fell into the water.

Elisha cut a stick. He threw the stick into the water. It landed where the ax fell in.

Then the heavy iron top of the ax came up. It lay there on top of the water.

"Pull it out," said Elisha.

The man did.

Water That Looked Red
2 KINGS 3

Now Joram was the king of Israel. Jehoshaphat was the king of Judah.

King Joram sent a message to King Jehoshaphat. "Would you come and help me fight the country of Moab?"

"Yes," said Jehoshaphat. "I'll go with you. My people will go. My horses will go. What road should we take?"

"We should go through the desert," said King Joram.

So both kings headed out with their armies. The king of Edom and his army went with them.

They marched around for seven days. Then they ran out of water.

"What's happening?" asked King Joram. "Did God get us together so Moab could win?"

"Is there a prophet of God with us?" asked Jehoshaphat. "He could ask God what to do."

One of the leaders said, "Elisha is here. He used to be Elijah's helper."

"God will give him a message for us," said King Jehoshaphat.

So the three kings went to see Elisha.

"Why are you asking me?" said Elisha to King Joram. "Why don't you ask your father's prophets?"

"Because God got us together so Moab could win," said Joram.

Elisha said, "I wouldn't even look at you if Jehoshaphat weren't here. But I care about King Jehoshaphat. Now bring me someone who plays the harp."

The harp player came. He began

to play music. Then God gave Elisha these words to say. "Here's what God says. Dig long ditches in this valley. You won't see any rain. There won't be any wind. But the valley will fill up with water. You and your animals can drink it."

Then Elisha said, "This is easy for God. He will also let you win over Moab. You'll win over every fort. You'll win over all the important towns. You'll cut down all their trees. You'll close up their springs of water. You'll throw rocks in their fields."

So they dug the long ditches. The next morning water rushed into the valley. It filled the ditches.

Now all the men of Moab had come out to fight. There were young men and old men. They got up early in the morning. They looked out where the three kings were camped.

The sun was shining on the water in the valley. That made the water look red. It looked like blood.

The men of Moab said, "Look at the blood! The kings must have killed each other. Let's go take their things!"

So the men of Moab went down into the camp. Then the army of the three kings rushed out. They began to fight. The men of Moab ran away.

The three kings took their army into Moab. They won over all the cities. They covered the good fields with rocks. They closed up the springs of water. They cut all the trees down.

The king of Moab saw that he was losing. So he got 700 men together. He led them against the king of Edom. But he didn't win.

The king of Moab was very angry at the three kings. At last the three kings went back home.

MAY 11

The King Whose Insides Came Out

2 CHRONICLES 21

Sometime later, King Jehoshaphat died. His son Jehoram became the next king of Judah. But Jehoram married the daughter of Israel's King Ahab. Jehoram was a bad king, just like the kings of Israel. He sinned, and he led God's people in Judah to sin.

The king of Edom turned against Jehoram. So Jehoram took his army to fight Edom.

Edom's army got in a circle around Jehoram's army. But Jehoram and his army got away during the night.

Then one day Jehoram got a letter from Elijah! The letter told what God said to Jehoram.

You are not like your father, Jehoshaphat. Instead, you are like

Ahab. You have led your people to sin. Now God is going to bring trouble to the people of Judah. He will bring terrible trouble to your family. You will get sick. You'll be so sick that your insides will come out.

Soon God sent enemy armies against Jehoram. They came into Judah to fight. They took everything in Jehoram's palace. They even took Jehoram's family. They only left his youngest son. His name was Ahaziah.

King Jehoram got sick, just like Elijah said. He had lots of pain. His insides came out, and he died. Nobody was sorry he had died. So they didn't build a fire to show he was great. They did put his body in a grave. But it wasn't with the other kings.

Jehoram's son Ahaziah became the next king of Judah.

About that time, Obadiah the prophet spoke. He told what God said about the land of Edom.

Bad News for Edom

OBADIAH

Here's what God showed Obadiah.

"Edom, you will not be important.
Nations will hate you.
You are proud. You believed a lie.

You live in the rocks up high in the
    mountains.
You say that nobody can bring you
    down.
You may fly like an eagle.
You may have your nest up in the
    stars.
But I will bring you down from
    there," says God.

"What if robbers came to you?
What if they came at night?
They would only take what they
    wanted.
What if people came to pick your
    grapes?
They would leave some on the vine.
But all your riches will be taken
    away.
Your friends will trick you.
They will be stronger than you.
They'll plan to trap you, and you
    won't know it.

"I'll get rid of Edom's wise men,"
    says God.
"You hurt others.
So you will be torn down forever.
You just stood there while enemies
    took riches from God's people.
You shouldn't look down on God's
    people when they're in trouble.
You shouldn't be happy when bad
    things happen to them.

"God's day is coming close for
    everyone.

Whatever you did will be done
     to you.
You'll get paid back for what
     you did.
But on Zion Mountain, my people
     will be saved.
It will be a special place, good and
     right.
It will belong to my people.
My people will be like a fire.
But Edom will be like dry grass.
The fire will burn the dry grass.
No one from Edom will be left,"
     says God.

What Elisha Saw

2 KINGS 6:8-23

The king of Aram went out to fight
against Israel. He talked to his army
officers. Then he said, "We'll camp
at this place."

But Elisha told King Joram of
Israel where Aram's army was. He
said, "Don't go there. That's where
the army of Aram is camped."

Every time Aram's army moved,
Elisha knew where they went. He
would tell King Joram.

The king of Aram got very angry.
He talked to his officers about it.
"Which of you is telling King Joram
where we are?"

"None of us," said one officer.
"It's Elisha who is telling where we
are. He even tells King Joram what
you say in your bedroom!"

"Then go find Elisha," said the
king of Aram. "I'm going to catch
him."

So his men found out where
Elisha was. Then Aram's king sent
out lots of men. They rode out with
horses and chariots. They went to
get Elisha.

It was night when they got to
where Elisha was. So they got in a
circle around the city.

Elisha's helper, Gehazi, got up
early the next day. He looked out
and saw the army around the city.
He saw the horses and chariots.
"What are we going to do?" he
called to Elisha.

"Don't be scared," said Elisha.
"Our army is bigger than theirs."

Then Elisha prayed. He said,
"God, let Gehazi see."

So God let Gehazi see. He looked
out and saw another army all over
the hills. It was an army of horses
and chariots of fire.

The army of Aram began to come
toward the city.

Elisha prayed to God. He said,
"God, please make them so they
can't see." So God took away their
sight.

Then Elisha went to the army.
He said, "This isn't the road you're
looking for. This isn't the city you're
looking for. I'll take you there."
Then Elisha led them all the way to
Samaria.

Elisha prayed again. "God, now let them see," he said.

So God made them see again. They saw that they were in the city of Samaria.

Joram, the king of Israel, was in Samaria. He saw the enemy army in his city. "Should I kill them?" he asked Elisha.

"No," said Elisha. "Give them food and water. Let them eat and drink. Then send them back to their king."

So King Joram made a big dinner. The enemy army ate and drank. Then Joram sent them back to their king. After that, the army of Aram stopped fighting Israel.

MAY 12

The Rich Woman's Land
2 KINGS 8:1-6

Now the rich woman that Elisha knew moved back to Israel. Seven years had gone by. She went to King Joram. She asked for her land back.

King Joram was talking to Elisha's helper, Gehazi. Joram had asked, "Tell me about the great things Elisha has done."

So Gehazi was telling about the time a boy died. He told how Elisha made the boy live again.

Just then the rich woman came in with her son.

"Here she is," said Gehazi. "Here's her son, who came back to life."

King Joram asked the woman to tell him about it. She did. Then the king called in a leader. King Joram told him to make sure she got her land back.

Dipping into the River
2 KINGS 5

Now Naaman was the leader of the army in Aram. God had helped Naaman and his men win battles. So his king thought he was great.

Naaman was very brave, but he had a bad skin sickness. It made his skin white and sore. No one could make him well.

Some fighting men from Aram had gone to Israel to fight. They had found a young girl in Israel. They had brought her back to their land. Naaman's wife had taken her to be a servant.

The young girl went to Naaman's wife. "I wish Naaman would visit Elisha the prophet," the girl said. "Elisha is in Israel. He would make Naaman well."

Naaman went to his king. He told him what the girl had said.

"Then go see Elisha," said the king. "I'll send a letter with you to King Joram."

So Naaman went to Israel. He

303

took 750 pounds of silver. He took 150 pounds of gold. He took 10 sets of clothes. He also took the letter from his king. It said, "I'm sending Naaman to you. I want you to make him well."

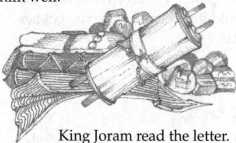

King Joram read the letter. He was very upset. "Why is the king sending this man to me? I'm not God!" he said. "I can't bring people back to life! The king of Aram is trying to start a fight!"

Elisha heard about it. So he sent King Joram a message. "Why are you upset? Tell the man to come and see me. He will find out that there's a prophet in Israel."

Naaman took his horses and chariots. He went to Elisha's house. He stopped at the door.

Elisha sent a man out to Naaman with this message. "Go to the Jordan River. Dip down into the river seven times. Then your skin will be well."

Naaman became angry. "I thought Elisha would come out and see me," said Naaman. "I thought he'd stand there and call on his God. I thought he'd wave his hand over my skin. I thought he'd make me well. We

have better rivers in our land. Can't I be made well if I dip in them?" Then Naaman left. He was very angry.

Naaman's helpers said, "What if Elisha said to do something great? Wouldn't you have done that great thing? All he said was to wash in the river. So why don't you do it?"

Then Naaman went to the Jordan River. He dipped himself in the water seven times. After that, his skin was like new.

Naaman and his helpers went back to see Elisha. He told Elisha, "Now I know that God is the only God. Please let me give you a gift."

"No," said Elisha. "I won't take anything from you."

Naaman begged him to take a gift. But Elisha wouldn't.

"Then let me take some dirt back home," said Naaman. "I will worship no one but God from now on. But there is one thing I have to do. My king goes to worship an idol. He takes me with him. He has to lean on my arm. So I bow when he bows. I pray that God will forgive me for this."

"Don't worry about it," said Elisha. "Go home in peace."

So Naaman left to go home.

Now, Naaman had only been gone for just a little while. Gehazi, Elisha's servant, began to think. He thought, "Elisha should have taken a gift. So I'll catch up with Naaman. I'll take the gift."

Gehazi ran after Naaman.

Naaman saw Gehazi coming. So Naaman got down from his chariot. "What's the matter?" he asked.

"Everything is fine," said Gehazi. "But Elisha sent me to catch up with you. He says to tell you that two young prophets just came. Please leave 75 pounds of silver and two sets of clothes for them."

"I'll be glad to," said Naaman. "But take more than that!"

Naaman gave Gehazi 150 pounds of silver. He gave him two sets of clothes. Then Naaman told two servants to carry the gifts for Gehazi.

Gehazi and the servants walked down the road. They came to a hill. Gehazi took the silver and clothes from the servants. Then he sent the servants back to Naaman.

Gehazi took the silver and clothes to the house. He hid them away. Then he went to Elisha.

"Where did you go?" asked Elisha.

"I didn't go anywhere," said Gehazi.

"I know Naaman got down from his chariot," said Elisha. "My spirit was with you when he went to meet you. This is not a time to take money. It's not a time to take clothes or fields. It's not a time to take animals or servants. Now you will have Naaman's skin sickness."

When Gehazi left, his skin had turned as white as snow.

MAY 13

A City with No Food

2 KINGS 6:24–7:2

Later, the king of Aram got his whole army together. They went into Israel. They camped around the city of Samaria. They wanted Samaria to give up. So they stayed there for a long time.

After a while the people in the city ran out of food. One cup of seeds cost two ounces of silver. A donkey's head cost two pounds of silver.

One day King Joram passed by the city wall. A woman cried out, "Help me!"

"How can I help you if God doesn't help you? Can I get food from the barn floor?" he asked. "Can I get a drink from the wine tub? What's wrong?"

"A woman I know had an idea," she said. "This woman said we would eat my son one day. Then we would eat her son the next day. So we ate my son one day. But then she hid her son."

King Joram was so upset that he tore his clothes. People watched him walk along by the wall. He said, "I'll kill Elisha for this!" Then he sent a message to Elisha.

Elisha was in his house. The leaders of Israel were sitting there with him. The message had not come yet. But Elisha said, "A killer is sending someone to kill me. Close the door. Don't let the servant in with the message. I hear King Joram's footsteps behind him."

Then the servant came with the message from the king. It said, "God has brought us this trouble. Why should I wait for him to do anything anymore?"

"Here's what God says," said Elisha. "Tomorrow at this time, it will be different. Seven quarts of flour will cost only one ounce of silver. Thirteen quarts of grain will cost only one piece of silver."

King Joram was leaning on an army officer's arm. The officer said, "How could that happen? Even if God opened heaven, it wouldn't happen."

"You'll get to see it," said Elisha. "But you won't get to eat it!"

The Sound of Horses and Chariots

2 KINGS 7:3-20

Four men were at the city gate. They all had skin sickness. They said to each other, "Why should we stay here? We'll die if we stay here. We'll die if we go into the city, too. Let's go to the enemy camp. Let's give up. They might let us live. If they kill us, that's all right. We would die here anyway."

The sun began to go down. The four sick men walked to the enemy camp. They came to the edge of the camp and looked around. No one was there.

God had sent the sound of horses and chariots. The enemy army had heard it. They said, "King Joram must have called another army! They're coming to help him!" So they ran away as the sun was going down. They left their tents, horses, and donkeys behind.

The four sick men went into one tent. They ate food and drank wine. They took silver and gold and clothes. Then they went and hid them. They came back to the camp. They went into another tent. They took more things and hid them.

Then they said, "This isn't right. We're keeping this good news to ourselves! Something bad will happen to us if we wait until morning. Let's go tell King Joram right away!"

The four men went to the gate. They shouted to the gate keepers. "We went to the enemy camp, but no one was there. They've left everything behind!"

The gate keepers shouted the

news to the people. Soon the news came to the palace.

It was night. But King Joram got up. He talked to his army men about it. "I know what happened," he said. "The enemies know we don't have any food. So they left their camp. They're hiding out in the country. They'll fight us when we go out there."

One army officer said, "Send some men out there to see. They might get killed, but they would die here anyway."

So the leaders got two chariots and some horses. They got some men to drive the chariots. King Joram told them, "Go out and see what happened."

The drivers followed the enemy army's tracks. They went all the way to the Jordan River. They saw clothes here and there. They saw tools here and there. It was like that all down the road. That's because the enemy had left in such a hurry.

The men went back and told King Joram about it. Then all the people went to the enemy camp. They took the things that were left behind.

So seven quarts of flour cost only one ounce of silver. Thirteen quarts of grain cost only one piece of silver. It happened just like God said it would.

King Joram put an army officer in charge of the gate. He was the man King Joram leaned on at Elisha's house. He had not believed what Elisha said. So Elisha told him that he would see it. But he wouldn't get to eat it. That's just what happened. There were lots of people going out of the gate. The crowd bumped into this officer. He fell down. The crowd ran over him, and he died.

MAY 14 ☐

A New King for the Land of Aram

2 KINGS 8:7-15, 25-29

Elisha went to the city of Damascus. It was in the land of Aram. The king of Aram was sick. But somebody told him that Elisha was in his land.

The king of Aram called for a man named Hazael. "Choose a gift," said the king. "Take it to Elisha. Tell him to ask God if I'll get well."

So Hazael chose some of the finest things in the city. It took 40 camels to carry them. Then Hazael took the gifts to Elisha.

"The king of Aram is sick," said Hazael. "He sent me to ask if he will get well."

"Tell him that he will get well," said Elisha. "But God has shown me that he will really die."

Elisha kept looking right at Hazael. Hazael began to worry. Then Elisha began to cry.

"Why are you crying?" asked Hazael.

"I know how you'll hurt God's people in Israel," said Elisha. "You'll burn their forts. You'll kill the people."

"How could I do that?" asked Hazael. "I'm about as important as a dog."

"God showed me what's going to happen," said Elisha. "You will become the king of Aram."

Hazael went back to the king.

"What did Elisha tell you?" asked the king.

"He said you would get well," said Hazael.

The next day Hazael got a heavy piece of cloth. He got it all wet. Then he put the cloth over the king's face. The king could not breathe. So he died. Hazael became the next king of Aram.

Now King Ahaziah of Judah got together with King Joram of Israel. They took their armies out to fight Hazael. King Joram got hurt in the fight. So he went back to Israel. King Ahaziah went to visit him.

Driving like a Crazy Man
2 KINGS 9

Now Elisha called for a young prophet. He said, "Hurry and take this oil to Ramoth. Look for Jehu there. Get him to leave his friends and come with you. Then take him into a house. Put this oil on his head to show that he will be king. Say that God chooses him to be Israel's king. Then leave the house and run. Don't stop!"

The young prophet went to Ramoth. He saw Jehu and some other army officers sitting there. "I have a message," he said.

"Who is it for?" asked Jehu.

"It's for you," said the young prophet.

So Jehu got up and followed him into the house. The prophet put oil on Jehu's head to show that he would be king. Then the prophet told Jehu these words from God. "I choose you to be Israel's king. Get rid of all of Ahab's family. Do it because his wife, Jezebel, killed so many of my prophets. I will pay back the family of Ahab now. Dogs will eat Jezebel. No one will put her in a grave."

Then the young prophet left the house and ran.

Jehu came out of the house. "Are you all right?" asked the army officers. "That young man was acting crazy. Why did he come here?"

"You know how prophets are," said Jehu.

"No," they said. "Tell us what happened."

"All right," said Jehu. "He told me that God chooses me to be Israel's king."

Then the men took off their coats. They put them on the steps. Jehu stood on the coats. Someone blew a horn. Everyone called out, "Jehu is the king!"

"I think you want me to be king," said Jehu. "So don't let anybody out of the city. Someone might go tell King Joram." Then Jehu made plans against Joram.

Jehu rode in his chariot to where King Joram was.

King Joram found out Jehu was coming. He sent a horse rider to meet him. "Ask him if he comes in peace," said King Joram.

So the horse rider rode out to meet Jehu. "The king asks if you come in peace," he said.

"Do you really want peace?" asked Jehu. "Then come with me."

A man was helping King Joram by watching from the city. He said, "The horse rider got there, but he isn't coming back."

So King Joram sent another horse rider out. He met Jehu. He said, "The king asks if you come in peace."

"Do you really want peace?" asked Jehu. "Then come with me."

The man watching from the city said, "The rider got there. But he isn't coming back. The chariot driver is driving like a crazy man. It must be Jehu."

"Get my chariot ready," said Israel's King Joram. Then King Joram rode out to meet Jehu.

King Ahaziah from Judah was visiting. He rode his chariot out there too.

"Jehu, do you come in peace?" asked King Joram.

"How can we have peace?" asked Jehu. "Your mother, Jezebel, led the people to follow idols and witches!"

Then King Joram turned around and drove away. He shouted to Ahaziah, "They've tricked us! They're against us!"

Then Jehu shot an arrow. It hit Joram between his shoulders. It hit his heart. Joram sank down in his chariot.

"Throw his body into the field," said Jehu. "It's the field Naboth used to have. I remember when we rode with Joram's father, King Ahab. God promised to pay Ahab back for killing Naboth. He promised it would happen here. God is keeping that promise today."

King Ahaziah from Judah saw what happened. He drove away. But Jehu chased after him. "Kill Ahaziah, too!" shouted Jehu.

Jehu's men hurt Ahaziah. But he got away.

Jehu went into the city. Jezebel heard about it. So she put make-up on her eyes. She fixed her hair. Then she looked out a window.

Jehu came in the gate.

Jezebel called, "Do you come in peace?"

Jehu looked up at Jezebel. Jehu called, "Who is on my side?"

Two or three men looked out of the window at Jehu. "Throw Jezebel out of the window!" called Jehu.

So they threw Jezebel out of the window. Then the horses rode over her.

Jehu went inside. He had something to eat and drink. "Someone go and take care of Jezebel's body," he said. "Put it in a grave. After all, she was a princess."

Some men went out to pick up Jezebel's body. But they couldn't find it. They only found her skull, her feet, and her hands.

They went to tell Jehu. Jehu said, "What God said has just come true. Elijah did tell God's words. He said that dogs would eat Jezebel's body."

Jehu Tricks the Idols' Prophets

2 KINGS 10–11:3; 2 CHRONICLES 22:7-12

Now Ahab had 70 sons. Jehu wrote letters to all the leaders. He wrote letters to people who helped Ahab's sons. He wrote, "You can make one of Ahab's sons your king. Then you'll have to fight for him so he can stay the king."

The people were very scared of Jehu. They said, "He fought two kings and won. So how can we win against him?"

So the people sent a message back to Jehu. "We serve you now. We'll do whatever you say. We won't choose another king. So do whatever you think you should do."

Then Jehu wrote another letter. "If you'll follow me, do this. Kill Ahab's sons."

So the people killed Ahab's sons. No one in Ahab's family was left. It happened just like God said it would.

Jehu's men also found King Ahaziah from Judah. They killed him and some of his family, too. Ahaziah had not been a good king. His mother, Athaliah, had taught him to do wrong.

Athaliah found out that her son Ahaziah was dead. So she made plans to kill the rest of his family.

But Ahaziah's sister found out that Athaliah was killing every prince. So she hid Ahaziah's baby, Prince Joash, in a bedroom. Then she moved him to the worship house. Her husband was a priest. She hid the little prince for six years. All that time, Athaliah ruled as queen.

Back in Israel, Jehu got all the people together. He said, "Ahab worshiped Baal a little bit. I will worship Baal a lot. So bring all the people who worship Baal here. I'll kill any worshiper of Baal who doesn't come."

Now Jehu was really tricking them. He planned to get rid of all those who worshiped Baal. "Let's all get together to worship Baal," said Jehu.

So all who worshiped Baal came. There were so many that they filled Baal's worship house.

Jehu put 80 men outside the worship house. He said, "Don't let anyone get away. If you do, you'll be killed."

Inside the worship house, Jehu talked to the people. "Make sure no one who worships God is here," said Jehu.

Then Jehu told the guards, "Kill all the people who worship Baal."

So they killed the people with their swords. Then they tore down Baal's worship house. The people began using it as a bathroom.

That's the way Jehu got rid of the fake god Baal. But Jehu didn't obey God with his whole heart. He didn't stop the worship of the gold calf idols. He sinned like Jeroboam.

Tricking the Queen
2 KINGS 11:4-21

Back in Judah, Athaliah was queen. But the priest was hiding little Prince Joash.

Six years went by. The next year the priest made a deal with the army officers. They went to all the towns. They got all the officers together. The officers came to Jerusalem.

The priest said, "Prince Joash will become the king."

All the officers promised to follow King Joash.

So the priest said, "Some of you watch the doors. Some of you watch the queen's palace. Some of you watch the gate. Some of you watch the yards by the worship house. Let only the worship leaders go into the worship house.

"You officers stand around the king. Hold your swords in your hands. Kill anybody else who comes into God's worship house. Stay by the king. Go wherever he goes."

So they did what the priest said. He gave the officers swords and shields from the worship house. They once belonged to King David.

Then the priest brought Joash out and put a crown on his head. The officers said he was the king now. They shouted, "Long live the king! Long live the king!"

Now Athaliah heard all the shouting. So she went to the worship house. There she saw the king. Officers stood by him. Horn players stood by him. People from all over sang praises. They blew horns and showed their joy.

Athaliah was so upset that she tore her clothes. She yelled, "You've tricked me! You've turned against me!"

"Bring her away from the worship house," said the priest. "Don't kill her here."

So she left with the army around her. She came to the Horse Gate at the palace yard. That's where they killed her.

King Joash was only seven years old. The priest made a promise. He said the people and Joash would belong to God.

The priest brought King Joash to the palace. King Joash sat on the king's throne. All the people showed their joy.

Joash was a good king. He did what was right. The priest was his teacher.

When Joash was a young king, the prophet Joel spoke.

Messages about Kings, Armies, and Idols

The Grasshoppers

JOEL 1

This is what God told Joel to tell his people.

Listen, people who live in this land.
Tell your children about this.
An army of big grasshoppers came
    and ate.
They tore down vines and fig trees.
They tore the bark off and threw it
    away.

Now fields are dry and torn up.
The wheat and barley crops are gone.
Even palm trees and apple trees
    are dry.
I'm sure that joy has dried up too.

Seeds dry up under the dirt.
Store houses are falling down.
Cows make loud noises as they go
    here and there.
They don't have a field to eat from.
Even the sheep have no food.

I call to you, God.
Fire has burned up fields and trees.
Even the wild animals want you.
Their rivers have dried up.

A Big, Strong Army

JOEL 2

There was never an army like this.
There will never be one like it again.

In front of the grasshoppers, the
    land is like the Garden of Eden.
Behind them, it's like a desert.
Nothing gets away from them.
They look like tiny horses running
    along.
They sound like chariots.
They jump over mountains.

Nations are afraid when they see
    this army.
Their faces turn white.
That's because the grasshoppers
    march like fighters.
They go over the walls and march
    in line.

They don't bump each other.
They march right on.
They go right through walls and
    still stay in line.
They run on the walls.
They go into the houses through the
    windows.

The earth and all of space shake in
    front of them.
The sun and moon look dark.
The stars don't shine.
God's voice sounds like thunder in
    front of his army.
There are so many in the army that
    they can't be counted.

"Even now you can come back to
    me," says God.
"Come back with all your heart."
God is kind and full of love.
He doesn't get angry very fast.
He doesn't want to send trouble.
Who knows? Maybe he will change
    his mind.
Maybe he will give you something
    good.

Blow the horn in God's city, Zion!
Make it a special day, a day when
    no one eats.
Call the older people together.
Get the children together.
Let the priests cry at the worship
    house.
Let them say, "Save your people,
    God."

Then God will want his land.
He will feel sorry for his people.
God will say to them,
"I'll send you wheat and new wine
    and oil.
The nations will never make fun of
    you again.

"I'll send the army from the north
    far away.
I'll push it into the sea.
Then the sea will smell bad."

Don't be afraid, my people.
Be glad. Show your joy.
God has done great things.
Don't be afraid, wild animals.
Fields are turning green.
Trees are growing fruit.
God sends you plenty of rain in
    the fall and spring.
It will be just like it was before.

"I'll pay you back for what the
    grasshoppers ate," says God.
"They were my great army that I sent.
But now you will have enough to eat.
You will get full and praise me.
I've done wonderful things for you.
My people will never be put down
    again.

"After the rain comes,
    I'll send my Spirit to flow out on
    all people.
Your children will tell my plans.
Your old men will dream dreams.

Your young men will have dreams
    even when they are awake.
My Spirit will flow out on all my
    servants.
Men and women will tell my plans.
I'll show you wonders in space.
I'll show you signs on the earth.
The sun will get dark.
The moon will look like blood.
That will happen before the Lord's
    great day comes.
Everyone who calls on God will be
    saved."

MAY 17

New Wine and Milk

JOEL 3

"Then I'll get all the nations together.
I'll judge them for sending my
    people here and there
    through the nations.

"Now why are you mad at me, you
    nations?
Are you paying me back for
    something I did?
If you are, then I will pay you back.
You took my silver and gold.
You sold the people
    and sent them far away from their
    homes.

"See? I'll bring them back
    from the places where you sold
    them.
I'll pay you back."

Get ready for war!
Wake up the fighting men!
Make your farm tools sharp.
Let weak people say they're strong!
Come together quickly, you nations.

Bring your fighters, God!
Many, many are in the Valley of
    Choosing.
That's because the Lord's day is near.
God will roar and thunder from
    Jerusalem.
But God will be a safe place
    for those who are his people.
"Then you will know that I live in
    Zion.
I'm the Lord your God.
Strangers will never fight Jerusalem
    again.

"New wine will drip from the
    mountains.
Milk will flow from the hills.
Water will run through all the valleys.
But the lands of God's enemies will
    be desert lands.
That's because of what they did to
    God's people.
But people will live in Judah
    forever.
It's all because I'll forgive them."

Turning Away

2 KINGS 12; 2 CHRONICLES 24

Joash was seven years old when he
became king of Judah. Time passed.

Joash thought he'd fix up God's worship house. He talked to the priests about it. "Gather money that's given at the worship house," he said. "Use the money to fix whatever needs to be fixed. Go to other towns to gather money for this, too. Do it right away."

But the priests didn't do it right away.

Joash had now been king for 23 years. And the priests still had not fixed the worship house.

"Why aren't you fixing up the worship house?" asked Joash. "Stop taking money for yourselves. Give it to someone who can fix the worship house."

One priest made a hole in the top of a large wooden box. He put it by the altar. A message went to all the people. 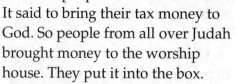 It said to bring their tax money to God. So people from all over Judah brought money to the worship house. They put it into the box.

People were glad to put tax money in the chest. They filled it up. They gathered lots of money that way. Then they paid workers to fix up the worship house.

The workers did good work. They worked hard. They fixed up the worship house. There was money left over. So it paid for worship house dishes. They were made of gold and silver.

Now the priest who taught Joash died. The priest had done many good things. So they put him in a grave with the kings.

Then other leaders came to see Joash. He began to listen to them. They worshiped idols. They turned away from God.

God sent prophets to the leaders. The prophets told the leaders to remember God. But the people wouldn't listen to the prophets.

Now the old priest who taught Joash had a son. His name was Zechariah. God's Spirit came on Zechariah. He came and talked to the people.

"These are God's words to you," said Zechariah. "Why don't you obey me? You turned away from me. Now things will not go well for you. You forgot me. Now I'll forget you."

But the people made plans against Zechariah. King Joash told them to kill Zechariah. So they found Zechariah in the yard of the worship house. They threw rocks at him. As he died, Zechariah said, "I pray that God will see this. I pray that he will pay you back for this."

The army of Aram came out to fight Joash. The army marched into the land of Judah. They killed leaders. They took things from the people. Then they sent everything to the king of Aram.

The army of Aram was small. But God made them win. That's because Joash and the people in Judah forgot God.

Then the army of Aram started to fight Jerusalem. King Joash gathered all the riches in Jerusalem. He took the gold in the worship house and the palace. He sent it to Aram's king. He paid the king to stop fighting. So the army of Aram left Jerusalem.

But Joash had been hurt in the fight. And now his own leaders turned against him. They were angry that he had killed Zechariah, the son of the priest. So the leaders killed Joash while he was in bed.

Joash had a son named Amaziah. He became the next king of Judah. He was a good king.

Arrows

2 KINGS 13

Now back in Israel, King Jehu died. His son Jehoahaz became Israel's next king. He was a bad king. He did what was wrong.

God was angry at his people in Israel. So he let the king of Aram rule over them.

Then the king of Israel asked for God's help. God listened. He saw how the king of Aram treated his people.

Israel had only 10 chariots left. They had only 50 horse riders. The king of Aram had gotten rid of the others.

King Jehoahaz died. His son Jehoash became Israel's next king. He was a bad king too. He kept sinning.

Now Elisha got sick. King Jehoash went to visit him. Jehoash cried.

"Bring a bow and some arrows," said Elisha.

So Jehoash brought a bow and some arrows.

Elisha put his hands on Jehoash's hands. "Open the window that looks east," said Elisha.

Jehoash opened the window.

"Now shoot an arrow out of it," said Elisha.

Jehoash shot an arrow.

"This arrow means you will win," said Elisha. "You will win over the army of Aram. You'll get rid of them."

"Now hold the arrows," said Elisha.

Jehoash held the other arrows.

"Hit the ground," said Elisha.

Jehoash hit the ground three times.

Elisha was angry. "You should have hit the ground five or six times. Now you will win over Aram just three times."

Later, Elisha died. His body was put in a grave.

Sometimes enemy robbers came into the land. They came every spring. One day some people were putting a man's body in a grave. All of a sudden they saw the robbers coming. So they threw the body into Elisha's grave. The body fell on Elisha's bones. All of a sudden, the man came back to life and stood up!

Judah and Israel Fight

2 KINGS 14; 2 CHRONICLES 25

Back in Judah, King Amaziah got his army together. He paid some men from Israel to fight with them.

One of God's prophets came to Amaziah. "Don't let the men of Israel fight with you," he said. "God has left Israel. You might be very brave when you fight. But you will not win if they are with you. It's God who helps you win or lose."

"What about the money I paid the army of Israel?" asked Amaziah.

"God can give you a lot more than that," said the prophet.

So King Amaziah sent the fighters from Israel home. That made them very angry at him.

King Amaziah led his army into the Salt Valley. They began to fight the enemy. They won.

But the men that Amaziah sent home began fighting his towns.

They killed lots of people. Then they took whatever they wanted.

King Amaziah brought the enemy's idols back with him. He worshiped them as if they were his own gods.

So God was very angry at King Amaziah. God sent a prophet to him.

"Why are you praying to these idols?" the prophet said. "They couldn't even save their own people from you!"

"Hush!" said King Amaziah. "Who said you could tell me what to do?"

Then the prophet said, "God plans to get rid of you. It's because you worship these idols and won't listen to me."

King Amaziah talked to his leaders. And he sent a message to King Jehoash in Israel. "Come out to fight us!"

Jehoash sent this message back. "You won your fight. So you are proud. You think you're great. You're like a weed that thinks it can marry a tree. But then a wild animal walks all over the weed. You'd better stay home. You're just asking for trouble."

Amaziah would not change his mind. God was working to tear him down because he worshiped idols.

So out marched the armies of Israel and Judah. They began to fight each other. Israel won. The army of Judah ran away.

Israel's King Jehoash caught Judah's King Amaziah. Jehoash took Amaziah back to Amaziah's own city of Jerusalem. Jehoash broke part of the wall down. He took all the riches in the worship house. He took all the riches in the palace. He took some people. Then he went back to Israel, leaving Amaziah with no riches.

Sometime later, King Jehoash died. His son Jeroboam the Second became Israel's king. He was a bad king. He did what was wrong.

The prophet Jonah lived while Jeroboam the Second was king.

The Storm

JONAH 1

God told Jonah, "Go to the big city of Nineveh. I see very sinful people there. Tell them they're in trouble."

But Jonah ran away. He went down to the sea. There he saw a ship that would be sailing soon. So he paid for a ride and got on the ship. Jonah was trying to run away from God.

The ship sailed out to sea. Then God sent a strong wind. A storm blew in.

The storm was bad. The sailors thought the ship would break apart.

They were scared. They prayed to their fake gods. Then they started throwing things into the sea. That would keep the ship from being so heavy.

But Jonah was down in the bottom of the ship. He was sleeping there.

At last, the captain of the ship woke Jonah up. "How can you sleep?" he asked. "Get up. Pray to your God. Maybe your God will see our trouble. Maybe we won't die."

"Let's throw dice," said the sailors. "Let's see who is to blame for this storm."

So they threw dice. The dice showed that Jonah was the one to blame.

"Who made all this trouble?" they asked Jonah. "Who are you? Where are you from?"

"I'm a Jewish man," said Jonah. "I worship God. He made the sky, the sea, and the land."

The sailors got very scared. "What did you do?" they asked. Jonah had already told them he was running away from God.

All this time, the waves tossed higher and higher.

"How can we make the sea quiet again?" asked the sailors.

"Throw me into the sea," said Jonah. "Then the sea will be quiet again. That's because I'm to blame for this storm."

The sailors began rowing. They tried to get the ship back to land. But they couldn't. The waves got higher and higher.

So they called to God. "Don't blame us for killing this man," they said. Then they threw Jonah into the sea.

The sea became quiet again. The sailors were afraid of God. They offered gifts to him. They made promises to him.

Now God sent a big fish to swallow Jonah. So there Jonah was, inside the fish. He was there for three days and nights.

Deep Water and Sea Weeds

JONAH 2

Jonah prayed to God from inside the fish.

"I was in a lot of trouble," said Jonah.
  "I went into the middle of the sea.
  All the waves rushed over me.

The water brought danger.
  Deep water came around me.
  Sea weeds waved around my head.
I dropped down to the very bottom
    of the mountains.
  The sea floor held me forever.
But you saved me from death, God.

"My life was coming to an end.
  But I remembered you.
  I prayed to you.

"People who worship idols
  give up your kind love.
I will sing a song of thanks.
  I will keep my promise.
  God is the one who saves."

Then God told the fish to spit Jonah out on dry ground.

The King's Order

JONAH 3

God spoke to Jonah again. "Go to the big city of Nineveh. Tell them what I will do because of their sin."

This time Jonah obeyed God. He went to Nineveh.

Nineveh was a big, important city. It took three days to walk around the city.

Jonah called out, "Nineveh has only 40 more days. Then the city will be destroyed."

The people believed God. They did not eat. They all dressed in old sack cloth. It showed how sad and upset they were.

The king of Nineveh heard what Jonah said. The king was sitting on his throne. But he got down from it. He sat in the dirt. He took his kingly clothes off. He put on clothes made from old sack cloth.

Then the king gave an order. "Don't eat or drink anything. Don't even let animals eat or drink anything. Put on plain clothes. Pray to God. Stop doing wrong. Stop hurting others and being mean. Maybe God will change his mind. Maybe he will be kind. Maybe he will stop being angry, and we won't die."

God saw what the people were doing. He saw how they had stopped sinning. So he felt loving and kind toward them. He didn't get rid of them.

The Vine

JONAH 4; 2 KINGS 14:25

God didn't send trouble to Nineveh. This made Jonah upset. He got angry.

"I knew this would happen," Jonah prayed. "That's why I ran away. I know you're a loving, kind God. You're not in a hurry to get angry. You have plenty of love for everyone. You change your mind about sending trouble. So just let

me die. It's better for me to die than to live."

"What right do you have to be angry?" asked God.

Then Jonah left Nineveh. He went to a place where he could see the city. He made a shady place to sit. He watched the city from there.

Now God made a vine grow up. It made shade for Jonah. Jonah was glad the vine was there.

But early the next morning, God sent a worm. The worm bit into the vine. So the vine dried up.

The sun moved high into the sky. Then God sent a hot wind. The sun beat down on Jonah's head. He got tired. He was so tired that he felt like dying. "It's better for me to die than to live," he said.

"What right do you have to be angry about the plant?" asked God.

"I have a right," said Jonah. "I'm so angry I could die."

"You cared about what happened to this vine," said God. "You were not even the one who took care of it. You didn't make it grow. It just came up in the night. Then it died just as fast as it came. But there are more than 120,000 (one hundred twenty thousand) people in Nineveh. They don't know which way is right. Shouldn't I care about them?"

Now Jeroboam the Second was still the king of Israel. The enemy had taken land from him. God told Jonah that Jeroboam would win his land back. So Jonah told Jeroboam. Then Jeroboam and his army did win the land. It happened just like God said it would.

Three Babies

Hosea 1–3

Hosea was another prophet who worked for God. He began telling God's words when Jeroboam the Second was Israel's king.

God told Hosea, "My people don't obey me. They don't stay with me. So marry a woman who won't stay with you. She will be like my people."

So Hosea married a woman named Gomer. They had a baby boy.

"Name your baby Jezreel," said God. "A king of Israel killed people in Jezreel Valley. So I will put an end to Israel there."

Sometime later, Hosea and Gomer had a baby girl.

God said, "Name your baby 'Not Loved.' I'm not going to show my love to Israel anymore. But I will show my love to Judah. I will save Judah. I won't save them by bows and arrows. I won't save them by swords and fights. I won't save them by horses and riders. I am their God, the Lord. And I'll save them by myself."

Then Hosea and Gomer had another baby boy.

God said, "The name of this baby will be 'Not My People.' The people in Israel are not my people anymore. I'm not their God. But Judah and Israel will come together again. Then the people will be called children of the living God.

"I'll place my people in the land and help them grow.
I'll love the one I called 'Not Loved.'
To those I called 'Not My People'
I'll say, 'Now you are my people.'
Then they'll tell me that I am their God."

Then God told Hosea, "Love your wife. Love her even though she loves other men. Love her like I love my people. I love them even though they love other gods."

So Hosea told his wife, "You will live with me. You must not love other men."

Hosea said, "The people of Israel will lose their king. They'll go many days without a king. Then they'll look for God again. They'll come back to his goodness in the last days."

The Bad Things Israel Did

HOSEA 4–6

Hear what God says against Israel.
"No one in the land keeps promises.
　No one knows that I am God.
People lie, kill, and steal.
　They leave their husbands and
　　wives.
So the land dries up.
　Birds, fish, and land animals die.

"The people's sins are like food to
　the priests.
　They are glad to see people do
　　wrong.
I'll bring trouble to the priests and
　the people for what they've
　done.

"The people ask their questions to
　an idol made of wood.
　They worship idols under the
　shady oak trees.

"The people of Israel don't care
　about me.
　They're like a cow that won't go
　where you lead.
So how can I lead them to green
　fields?
　How can they be my sheep?

"Israel and Judah saw that they
　were in trouble.
　They asked other kings to help
　them.

But other kings can't help.
So I'll be like a lion to Israel and
　Judah.
　I'll take them away. There will be
　no one to save them.
Then I'll wait for them to say
　they've done wrong.
　They will feel so bad, they'll look
　for me."

"Come," said Hosea. "Let's go back
　to God.
He broke us into pieces.
　But he will make us well.
He will give us new life after two
　days.
　He will bring us back to him on
　the third day.
　Then we can live with him.
So let's all learn to know God.
Let's really learn to know him.
He will come to us.
　It will be like spring rain
　coming to water the ground."

Their Hearts Are like Hot Ovens

HOSEA 7–8

God says to his people,
　"I start to make Israel well again.
　But then I see their sins.
They lie and take things.
They don't know
　that I remember the bad things
　they do.

"The king has a party.
The princes get drunk.
Then they begin to make fun of
people.
Their hearts are like hot ovens.
They plan to sin.

"My people in Israel are of no use.
They are like a pancake that doesn't
get turned over.
People from other lands take their
power.
But they don't know it.
Their hair is getting gray.
But they don't see it.
Their pride shows bad things about
them.
But after all this,
they still don't turn back to God.

"My people in Israel are like silly
doves.
It's easy to trick them.
They don't think.
They fly around, calling other lands
to come help them.
But I'll catch them.
I want to save them,
but they tell lies about me.

"Now Israel calls for my help.
The people say that I am their God.
But they don't want to do what's
good.

They make idols
with their silver and gold.
Throw away your gold cow idol,
Israel.
It's not God.
Break it into pieces."

MAY 21

Bad Weeds in a Good Field

HOSEA 10

Hosea said, "Israel was like a
growing vine.
But then they built places to
worship idols.
So now they will get into trouble."

God said to his people, "I told you
to plant what's right.
Then you'd grow a crop of my
love that never ends.
I wanted you to know that it's time
to look for me.
I wanted you to keep looking
until I'd bring what's good and
right.
But you planted sin.
You are like bad weeds in a good
field.
You trusted your own power.
You trusted in how many fighting
men you had.
But the battle will come against
your people.
All your forts will be torn down.
It's all because of your sin."

324

Like a Green Tree

HOSEA 14

"Israel, come back to God," said
    Hosea.
"Ask him to forgive you.
    Ask for his kind love.
We'll never call idols our gods.
    Idols are made with our own
      hands.
    But only you give kind love,
      God."

"I'll make my people well from
    their sickness of sin," says God.
    "I'll love them for free.
    My anger is gone.
I'll be like water on the morning
    grass for Israel.
    Israel will bloom like a lily.
Israel will be like a tall tree.
    Its roots will go down deep.
Israel will be great like an olive tree.
    Israel will smell good like a cedar
      tree.
Israel will grow flowers like a vine.
    Everyone will know who Israel is.
Do you really want idols anymore?
    I'm the one who will answer you.
    I'll take care of you."

Forts, Towers, and Rock-Throwing Machines

2 CHRONICLES 25:26-28; 26

In Judah, Amaziah was the king.
But he stopped obeying God. Then
some people made plans to kill him.
So King Amaziah ran away.

But men went after King
Amaziah. They found him and
killed him. They brought his body
back on a horse. They put it in a
grave.

Amaziah's son Uzziah became
the next king of Judah. He was
16 years old. He was a good king.
He did what was right. He looked
for ways to make God happy.
So God brought good things to
him.

God helped King Uzziah win
against his enemies. All nations
knew who King Uzziah was. He
had lots of power.

King Uzziah built towers in
Jerusalem. One was at the Corner
Gate. One was at the Valley Gate.
He made them like forts. He built
towers in the desert, too.

King Uzziah dug wells. He had
lots of cows. People worked in his
fields. He loved to grow things.

King Uzziah also made machines
in the city. They were placed on the
towers. They were used to shoot
arrows and throw rocks when their
enemies came.

King Uzziah had a good army.
The fighting men were very strong.
Uzziah gave them shields and
swords. He gave them metal coats
and metal hats. He gave them bows
and arrows.

God's Anger

AMOS 1–2

Amos was a shepherd. God talked to him. He saw things in his mind about Israel. He told what he saw. This happened when Uzziah was Judah's king. Jeroboam the Second was Israel's king.

Amos said, "God roars from his
    mountain.
  He is like thunder that comes
    from Jerusalem."

Here's what God says.
"I'm angry at the enemy lands.
  They tore up Israel.
They took my people out of their
    cities.
  They sold my people.
They didn't keep their promises to
    my people.
  They chased friends with swords.
They would not be kind or loving.
  They were angry all the time.
They did not control themselves.
  They killed people just to get
    more land.
So I'll burn down their forts.
  There will be strong winds and
    storms," says God.

"I'm angry at my own people in
    Judah, too.
  They haven't obeyed me.
They worship idols.
  Idols are not real gods.

So I'll burn down the forts of
    Jerusalem.

"And I'm angry at my people in
    Israel.
They sell good people for silver.
  They sell helpless people to get
    shoes.
They give poor people a hard time.
  They treat them like dirt.
  They won't be fair to them."

Paying for Sin

AMOS 3

"Israel, I chose only you
  out of all the people on earth.
So I will bring trouble to you
  for all your sins."

Two people don't walk together
  unless they agree to walk together.
A lion doesn't go roaring into a bush
  unless he is chasing something.
A bird doesn't get into a trap on the
    ground
  unless the trap is set to catch him.
A trap doesn't snap shut
  unless there's something to catch.
A horn doesn't blow in a city
  unless there's something to be
    afraid of.
A city is not torn down
  unless God makes it happen.

God doesn't do anything
  unless he tells his prophets.

"Listen to this," says God.
"I'll bring trouble to the people of
Israel for their sins.
I'll tear down their altars.
I'll tear down the winter house.
I'll tear down the summer house.
I'll tear down houses that have
ivory on them.
I'll tear down the big houses,"
says God.

MAY 22

You Didn't Come Back

AMOS 4

You women of Israel, listen.
You give poor people a hard time.
You tell your husbands, "Bring
drinks for us!"
God promises, "A time of trouble is
coming.
People from another land will take
you away.
They will throw you out of your
city.

"I let you go without food.
There wasn't enough bread
anywhere.
But you didn't come back to me,"
says God.

"I sent rain to one town.
I kept it from raining on another
town.
It rained on one field.
But another field dried up.

People went to other towns
looking for water. They never
got enough.

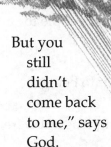

But you
still
didn't
come back
to me," says
God.
"I made the plants sick
in your gardens.
The leaves dried up and died.
Grasshoppers ate your trees.
But you still didn't come back to
me," says God.

"I sent sickness to people,
just like I did in Egypt.
I let your young men get killed in
fights.
I let the enemy take your horses.
I made you smell stinky army
camps.
But you still didn't come back to
me," says God.

God makes mountains, and God
makes wind.
God lets us know what he is
thinking.
He walks on the earth's high places.
His name is the Lord God Who
Has All Power.

Look for Good;
Look for God

Amos 5

Here's what God says.
"Look for me. Then you'll live.
  Don't look for other people to
    save you."

You turn being fair into being
    angry.
  You treat doing right as if it were
    not important.
You hate people who tell you that
    you're wrong.
  You hate people who tell the
    truth.
You run over poor people.

You built big stone houses.
  But you won't get to live in them.
You planted big, green grape fields.
  But you won't drink wine from
    your grapes.
That's because I know how many
    times you've sinned.

Look for what's good, not for what's
    bad.
  Then God will be with you.
Hate wrong. Love right.
  Be fair when you judge.
Maybe God will be kind to you.

"I hate your worship parties," God
    says.

"I can't stand it when you get
    together.
Take your noisy songs away
    from me!
  I won't listen to your music.
What I want is for you to be fair.
  I want you to do what's right,"
    says God.

The People's Pride

Amos 6

There's bad news for you people
    who don't care.
You lie down on beds made of
    ivory.
  You sit down on resting places.
You eat the best lamb meat.
  You eat the fat beef.
You play your harps.
You drink bowl after bowl of wine.
  You use the best creams for your
    skin.
But you're not sorry that God's
    people have sinned.
So you'll be the first ones to be
    taken away.
  Your parties will come to an end.

God has promised. Here's what he
    says.
  "I hate my people's pride.
I will give the city to its
    enemies.
I will give away everything in
    the city."

Grasshoppers, Fire, and a String

AMOS 7:1-9

Here's the picture God put in my mind. He was getting lots of big grasshoppers ready. Part of the crop from the field had been picked for the king. The rest was just coming up out of the ground. But the big grasshoppers called locusts ate everything off the land.

I cried, "God! Forgive your people! How can they live? Israel is such a small nation!"

So God said, "I won't make this happen."

Here's the next picture God put in my mind. God was sending fire. It dried up the sea. It ate up the land.

I cried, "Please stop, God! How can your people live? Israel is such a small nation!"

So God took it back. "I won't make this happen," he said.

Here's the next picture God put in my mind. God stood by a wall. It was straight. God was holding up a string. The string hung down to show that the wall was straight. God said, "Amos, what do you see?"

"I see a string you're checking the wall with," I said.

Then God said, "I am holding a string to check my people. I won't keep trouble from them any longer.

"The worship places for idols will be torn down. I will come against Israel with my sword."

The Basket of Fruit

AMOS 8

Here's the next picture God put in my mind. It was a basket of fruit, ready to eat. God asked, "Amos, what do you see?"

"I see a basket of fruit, ready to eat," I said.

"The time is ready for my people," said God. "I won't keep trouble from them any longer. When it happens, the worship songs will turn into crying."

Listen to this if you give poor people a hard time.

You say, "When will this worship
    day be over?
We want to sell our wheat."
You don't give people all they
    paid for.
  You cheat when you weigh what
    they're buying.
  You sell dirt mixed in with the
    wheat.
You buy poor people with your silver.
  You trade a pair of shoes for a
    poor person.

"The land will shake for this.
  The people will cry," says God.

329

"I'll make the sun go down. But it
    will only be noon.
  I'll turn your worship parties into
    sad times.
I'll make you wear clothes made out
  of old sack cloth.
  I'll make it feel like the end of a
    bad day.

"The time is coming when there
    won't be enough.
It's not that there won't be enough
    food.
It's not that there won't be enough
    water.
  It will be a time when no one
    hears God's words.
People will go from east to west.
  They'll go from north to south.
They'll look for God's word,
  but they won't find it.

"Then the beautiful young women
    will fall down.
The strong young men will fall
    down too.
They'll all be so thirsty for God's
    word
  that they will fall down.
  And they won't get up
    again."

Don't Tell Us

Amos 7:10-17

One of the priests talked to Amos.
"Get out of here, you prophet!" he
said. "Go back to Judah! Tell God's

words there. Don't tell us what God
says. This is a safe place for our
king. This is the worship house for
our kingdom."

  "Once I was not a prophet," said
Amos. "I wasn't even a prophet's
son. I was just a shepherd. And I
helped take care of trees. But God
said I should tell his words to Israel.
So listen!

"You say I should not tell you God's
    word.
  You say I should stop talking
    against Israel.
So here's what God says.

"Your wife will leave you and love
    other men.
  Your children will be killed by
    swords.
Your land will be given to other
    people.
  You'll die in a land where people
    don't worship God.
The people of Israel will be taken
    away by another nation.
  They will be taken out of their
    own land."

God Watches

Amos 9

I saw God. He was standing by the
altar.

God said, "Hit the posts that hold
  up the worship house.

Hit them so hard that the floors
    shake.
Pull the posts down on the people's
    heads.
    Nobody will get away.

"You are like enemies to me,"
    says God.

"But I won't get rid of all of my
    people," says God.
    "I will bring back David's
      kingdom, the kingdom of
      Judah.
I will fix the places where it is
    broken.
    I will build it up like it used to be."

"Someday I'll bring Israel back
    home.
    They are my people too.
They'll build up the cities again.
They'll plant grape fields.
    They'll drink wine.
They'll grow gardens.
    They'll eat fruit.
I'll bring the people of Israel back to
    their own land.
    They'll never be sent away again.
    This is the land I've given to
      them," says God.

Uzziah Becomes Proud
2 KINGS 14:29–15; 2 CHRONICLES 26

Now Jeroboam the Second died. His
son Zechariah became the next king
of Israel. Zechariah was a bad king
just like his father.

Zechariah was the king for just
six months. A man named Shallum
made plans to kill Zechariah.
Shallum had a fight with Zechariah
while the people were watching.
Shallum killed Zechariah. Then
Shallum became the next king of
Israel.

Shallum was the king for just one
month. Menahem had a fight with
him. Menahem killed Shallum. Then
Menahem became the king of Israel.
He was the king for 10 years. But he
was a bad king.

Back in Judah, Uzziah was still
the king. He had been a good king.
But he got lots of power. Then he
became proud. He went into the
worship house. He tried to offer a
gift on the altar.

But the high priest and 80 other
priests followed him. They were
very brave. They said, "This isn't
right. You're not allowed to offer
a gift on the altar. Only the priests
are supposed to do that. Leave
the worship house. You have not
obeyed God. So God will not take
your gift."

Uzziah held the offering bowl in
his hand. He was ready to give his
sweet smelling gift. He got very
angry. He began shouting madly at
the priests.

All of a sudden, Uzziah's

forehead turned white with a skin sickness.

The priests saw what had happened. They made him leave in a hurry. Uzziah wanted to leave fast anyway. That's because God had made him sick.

King Uzziah had the skin sickness until he died. He had to live in a different house. He had to stay away from the worship house.

While King Uzziah was sick, his son Jotham was in charge. Jotham took over the palace. He ruled the people.

Messages about What's Coming

The Ox Knows

ISAIAH 1

These are the pictures God put in Isaiah's mind. Isaiah was a prophet when Uzziah was king of Judah. When Isaiah saw the pictures, he heard God talk, too. And Isaiah told God's plans. Isaiah was still a prophet when Jotham was king of Judah. Later, Ahaz and Hezekiah were kings of Judah. Isaiah was still a prophet then.

Hear this, sky! Listen, earth!
God has talked.
"I trained my children.
    But they turned against me.
The ox knows who his master is.
    The donkey knows where its
        owner feeds it.
But my people don't know.
    My people don't understand."

The nation of Israel is sinful.
    The people have done wrong.
They are bad children.
    They have left God.

"Your gifts don't mean anything,"
    says God.
"I have more than enough gifts.
    That's not what makes me
        happy.
I can't stand it when you get
        together and sin.
    I hate your parties for me.
    They are like a heavy load for me
        to carry.
You hold out your hands to pray
        to me.
    But you hurt people.
    Make your hearts clean again.
Get rid of the wrong you do.
    Get it out of my sight.
Stop doing what's wrong.
    Learn to do what's right.
    Help people who have been put
        down.
Speak up for children who don't
        have fathers.
    Help women whose husbands
        have died.

"Come on. Let's think about this
        together.

333

Your sins may seem to be as red as
    blood.
    But you'll be made as clean as
        white snow.
Your sins may be as red as red can be.
    But you'll be made as clean as
        white wool.
Do you want to follow me? Do you
    want to obey?
    Then you'll eat the best food from
        your land.
But what if you won't follow me?
    What if you won't obey?
    Then you will be killed in battles."

See the city that used to obey God?
    Now that city has turned away
        from God.
The people there used to do what
    was fair and right.
    But now they don't.
So God says,
    "I'll pay them back for what
        they've done.
    I'll get rid of the sinful hearts.
    I'll get rid of what's wrong.
Then people will call you the City of
    What's Right.
    They'll call you the City That
        Always Obeys God."

Tunnels and Caves

ISAIAH 2

Here's what Isaiah saw about the
kingdom of Judah and the city of
Jerusalem.

In the last days,
    God will make his mountain the
        most important.
    That's where his worship house
        will be.
God's mountain will be high above
    the hills.
    All the nations will come to it.

The people will say, "Come on!
    Let's go to God's worship house.
He will teach us about his ways.
    That way, we can obey him."
God's word will come from
    Jerusalem.
    He will say who is right and who
        is wrong.
People will turn their swords into
    farm tools.
    They'll turn their spears into
        garden tools.
Nations won't fight each other
    anymore.

So come, you people of God.
    Let's live God's way.
    It's like walking in light.

God, the Lord, has all power.
    He is planning a day for everyone
        who is proud.
    It's a day for people who think
        they're great.
    Then they will see that they are
        not great.
Only God will be great on that day.
    The idols will be gone.

People will run away to caves.
　　They'll run to tunnels.
They'll be scared of God.
　　They'll be scared of his greatness.
　　He will get up to shake the earth.
Then people will throw their idols
　　away.
　　They'll throw them to the rats
　　and bats.

MAY 25

Don't Make Me the Leader!

ISAIAH 3–4

See God now. He has all power.
He will take all food and water away
　　from Judah and Jerusalem.
　　He will take away their leaders
　　and army captains.
　　He will take away their guides,
　　workers, and speakers.
Boys will become their leaders.
　　Children will rule over them.
People will be hard on each other.
Somebody will go find his brother.
　　He will say, "You have a coat.
　　So you be our leader.
　　Rule over this broken-down city!"
But his brother will say,
　　"I don't know what to do!
　　I don't have food or clothes at my
　　house.
　　Don't make me the leader!"

Jerusalem bends, and Judah falls.
What they do and say is against God.

They show their sin as if they
　　were in a parade.
　　They don't even try to hide it.
　　They are asking for trouble.

But tell people who do right that
　　things will go well.
　　They will enjoy the good things
　　that come to them.
　　These good things will come
　　because of what they've done.

God says,
"The women of Jerusalem are proud.
　　They walk along, holding their
　　heads high.
　　The way they look at people says
　　they want to sin.

"So God will make sores come on
　　their heads.
　　He will make them lose all their
　　hair."

　　On that day, God will take away
all their fine clothes. He will take
away head bands and beautiful
neck bands. He will take away ear
rings, arm bands, and belts. He will
take away sweet-smelling perfume,
finger rings, and nose rings. He will
take away pretty robes and coats.

There will be a stink instead of
　　sweet smells.
　　There will be ropes instead of belts.
There will be no hair instead of
　　beautiful hair.

There will be clothes made from
   old cloth sacks.
The men will die in the fighting.
   Everyone will sit on the ground
   and cry.

On that day, God will show his
beauty and greatness. People who
are left will be proud of their land.
Their hearts will be clean and right.
God will wash away their sin. He
will make his people clean.

Then God will make a cloud
over Zion Mountain. It will be a
cloud of smoke in the daytime. It
will be a bright fire at night. It will
keep people safe from the hot day.
It will be a safe place in storms
and rain.

God's Grape Field

ISAIAH 5

The one I love had a grape field.
   It was on a hill.
He dug the ground and took
   rocks out.
   He planted vines in it.
He built a tower where he could
   watch over it.
   He cut a tub out of rock.
   It was a tub to make wine in.
Then he waited for good grapes
   to grow.
   But the field only grew bad
   grapes.

"Now you people in Judah,
   think about me and my grape
   field.
What could I have done?
   I looked for good grapes.
   Why did my field grow bad ones?
I'll tell you what I'll do to my grape
   field.
   I'll tear its wall down.
   I'll make it a weed field."

The people of
   Israel are
   God's
   grape field.
The people
   of Judah
   are the garden
   he loves.
God looked for people
   who were fair.
   But all he found was killing.
God looked for people who did
   right.
   But all he heard were troubled
   cries.

There's bad news for people who
   get up early to drink.
   They stay up late getting drunk.
They play music at their parties.
   But they don't pay attention
   to God.

There's bad news for people who
   call bad things good.
   There's bad news for people who
   call good things bad.

336

They think dark is light and light
    is dark.
    They think sour is sweet and
        sweet is sour.

So God holds up a flag.
    He calls people who are far away.
They come fast.
    They don't get tired.
    They don't trip and fall.
They have sharp arrows.
    Their chariot wheels are like a
        fast-turning wind.
They roar like lions.
    They catch what they're hunting.
They take it away.
    No one can stop them.

MAY 26

Paying the Enemy to Leave
2 KINGS 15:17-35

Back in Israel, Menahem was king.
He was a bad king. He did what
was wrong.

Israel had an enemy. It was a
nation called Assyria. The king of
Assyria had his people come into
Israel to fight. King Menahem gave
them 37 tons of silver. He wanted
Assyria to leave Israel alone. He
wanted to keep being king.

King Menahem got the silver
from the people. Everyone had to
give silver for the king of Assyria.
So the people from Assyria left
Israel. They didn't fight. Instead,
they went back home.

Sometime later, King Menahem
died. His son became Israel's king.
He was a bad king. He did what
was wrong.

Now there was a leader named
Pekah. He took 50 men with him.
He killed the king at the palace.
Then Pekah became Israel's king.
But he was a bad king too. He did
what was wrong.

Uzziah was still the king in Judah.
But he died. His son Jotham became
Judah's king. He was a good king
just like his father, Uzziah. But the
people were doing wrong things.

A Burning Coal
ISAIAH 6

That same year, God put another
picture in Isaiah's mind. Isaiah
wrote down what he saw.

The year Uzziah died, I saw God
sitting in heaven. He was above others,
and he was great. His robe was so long
that it filled the worship house.

Beings from heaven were flying
above God. Each one had six wings.
The beings covered their faces with
two wings. They covered their feet
with two wings. They flew with two
wings. They called out to each other.
"Good and right and holy is God
Who Has All Power. His greatness
fills the whole earth."

The doors shook with their sound. Smoke filled the worship house.

"I'm in trouble now!" I cried. "My life is finished! My lips are dirty with sin. I live with people whose lips are dirty with sin. But now I've seen the King! I've seen God Who Has All Power."

Then one of the beings flew over to me. He had a burning coal in his hand. It had come from the altar in the worship house. He touched my lips with the coal. He said, "Look! This coal has touched your lips. Your sin is gone now."

Then I heard God speak. "Who will I send? Who will go for us?"

"I'm here," I said. "Send me!"

God said, "Go and tell my people this.
They will hear my words.
     But they won't understand.
They will see what I do.
     But they won't know what it
          means.
Make their hearts hard so they don't
          care about me.
     Make their ears dull.
     Close their eyes.
If you don't, they might see.
     They might hear.
     They might understand.
They might turn back to me.
     Then I would make them well."

"How long?" I asked.

God said, "Until the cities are torn
          down.
     Until I send everybody far away.
But my people will be like a tree
          that is cut down.
The bottom part of a tree is left.
     In the same way, there will be
          some people left in the land."

Lots of Power
2 CHRONICLES 27:1-6

Jotham was the king in Judah. King Jotham built back the Upper Gate at the worship house. He worked to fix part of the wall around the city. He built towns in the hills. He built forts and towers in the woods.

King Jotham also took his army out to fight. He won over the people of Ammon. So they paid him four tons of silver. They also paid him with lots of wheat and other grain.

King Jotham got lots of power. That's because he kept following God.

A Pile of Rocks
MICAH 1:1-9, 16

God put pictures and words in the mind of a man named Micah. This happened when Jotham was king of Judah. It happened when Ahaz and Hezekiah were kings too. The prophet Micah told what he saw about Israel and Judah.

Hear this, all you people.
Look! God is coming from where he
    lives.
    He comes down and walks on the
        high places.
The mountains melt under his feet.
    The valleys break.
They look like wax melting in a fire.
    They look like water running
        down a hill.
It's because of the wrong things
    God's people have done.
    It's because of Israel's sins.

"So I will turn the city of Samaria
    into a pile of rocks.
    I'll toss its stones into the valley.
The idols will be broken into
    pieces," says God.

I will cry because of this.
    I won't wear shoes or clothes.
I'll cry out like a wolf.
    I'll cry like an owl.
People from another nation will
    come into your land.
    They will carry your children
        away.

MAY 27

A Ruler Will Come

MICAH 4:6-7; 5:2, 4-5

God says what will happen in the
    last days.
"I will gather people who can't walk.

I'll gather people who have been
    taken from their land.
I'll turn them into a strong nation.
I will rule them from Zion Mountain.
    I will rule them forever.

"Bethlehem, you are a small town in
    Judah.
    But someone who will rule my
        people will come from you.
He comes from long, long ago."

He will lead God's people like a
    shepherd.
    He will lead in God's power.
    He will lead in God's great name.
God's people will be safe.
    People all over the world will see
        his greatness.
    He will bring peace.

What Does God Want?

MICAH 6:6-13

What should I bring when I worship
    God?
    Should I come with gifts?
Does God want cows and goats
    and oil?
    Should I give my first child for
        my sins?
No! God shows us what is good.
He wants us to be fair and to love
    kindness.
    He wants us to let him be the
        greatest.
    He wants us to walk with him.

Listen! God is calling the city.
    It's wise to make God's name the
        most important.
God says, "Listen to me when I say
        you're wrong.
    Am I supposed to forget the
        riches you stole?
    Am I supposed to let you get
        away with lying?
I'll bring you trouble."

God Will Be My Light

MICAH 7:7-8, 10, 16-20

This is what Micah said.
I'm watching for God. I'm hoping
        in him.
    I'm waiting for God, because he
        saves me.
    My God will hear me.

Maybe I fell, but I'll get up again.
    Maybe I sit in the dark.
    But God will be my light.

My enemies said,
    "Where is the Lord your God?"
I will see my enemies fall.
    They will be run over like mud in
        the street.

Nations will see. They'll feel bad.
    Their power will be taken away.
They'll put their hands over their
        mouths.
    Their ears won't be able to hear.
They'll shake in fear and turn to God.

Where is there another God like you?
    You forgive sins.
You don't keep being angry forever.
    Instead, you like to show your
        kind love.
You'll throw away our sins.
    It will be like throwing them into
        the deep sea.
You'll keep your promises to your
        people.
    You'll be kind to them.
It will be just like you promised a
        long time ago.

The Sign

2 KINGS 15:29; 16:1, 4-5;
ISAIAH 7:2-19, 23-25

Pekah was the king of Israel. But
the army of Assyria came into the
land. They won fights with many of
the cities. They took people away to
Assyria.

Back in Judah, Jotham was king.
But he died. Then his son Ahaz
became Judah's king. He was a bad
king. He made idols and worshiped
the fake god Baal.

Now the army of Aram got
together with the army of Israel.
They marched out to fight
Jerusalem in Judah. They didn't
win. But somebody told King Ahaz,
"The armies of Israel and Aram are
together." So King Ahaz and his
people were afraid. They were like
trees shaking in the wind.

God spoke to Isaiah. "Go see King Ahaz," he said. "Take your son with you. Meet Ahaz at the end of the Upper Pool's water pipe. It's on the road to the Washer Man's Field."

God said to tell Ahaz, "Be careful. Don't panic. Don't be scared. Don't give up. The kings of Aram and Israel are like 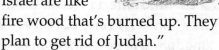 fire wood that's burned up. They plan to get rid of Judah."

Then God said this.

"It won't happen.
In 65 years, there will be little left of Israel.
So stand firm in what you believe.
If you don't, you won't stand at all."

God talked to Ahaz again. "Ask me to give you a sign," he said.

"I won't ask for a sign," said Ahaz. "I won't test God."

"Then God will give you a sign himself," said Isaiah. "There will be a young woman. She will never have slept with a man like a wife would. But she will have a baby. She will call her son Immanuel, which means "God Is with Us." He will grow old enough to know what's right and wrong. Then he will eat honey.

"Before that time, the nations of Israel and Aram will be torn down. Then God will bring the nation of Assyria against your land."

God will call for Egypt's army and Assyria's army to come. They'll come like flies from the river. They'll come like bees. They'll come and fill the valleys. They'll be around all the weeds and ponds.

Then weeds will grow where vines once grew. People will go there to hunt with bows and arrows. The hills that grew crops will grow weeds instead. Cows and sheep will run around on the hills.

A Long Name for a Little Baby

ISAIAH 8:1-8, 11-14, 18-20

Then God told me, "Get a big roll of paper. Use a pen to write on it. Write this name: Maher-Shalal-Hash-Baz." It means "Quick to Take Riches Won in a Fight."

Now my wife and I had a baby. God said, "Name the baby Maher-Shalal-Hash-Baz. That's because Assyria will fight Israel. Assyria will win. They'll take Israel's riches. This will happen before your baby can talk. It will happen before he can say, 'Mommy' or 'Daddy.'"

God spoke.
"My people have turned away
from me.
So enemies will come and fight them.
The enemies will be like water
flowing out of the river.
They will flow over all the land."

God told me not to act like the rest
of his people.
He told me not to be afraid of
what they're afraid of.
God has all power. He is good
and right and holy.
He will be a safe place.

I am Isaiah. Here I am. Here are the
children God gave me. We are like
signs from God.

People may say, "Get answers
from the spirit world. Talk to people
who talk to spirits." But shouldn't
you get answers from God instead?
Why ask dead spirits what will
happen to people who are alive? Go
to God's laws and words. If spirits
don't agree with God's Word, they
don't know anything.

A Great Light

ISAIAH 9:1-7

Someday, people who were sad will
be glad. Someday, God will make
Galilee great.

People walking in the dark see a
great light.

They're like people who are happy
to bring in their crops.
That's because you won over their
enemies.
You took away the people who
gave them trouble.
A child is born.
A son is given to us.
He will rule.
People will call him
Wonderful Guide, Powerful God,
Father Forever, Prince of Peace.
His kingdom will be a kingdom of
peace.
It will grow and will never end.
He will be a king from King David's
family.
He will keep the kingdom.
He will be fair and right forever.
God planned it, and he will work
hard to do it.

Like Getting Eggs
from a Nest

ISAIAH 10:5-27

"There's bad news for the people of
Assyria," said God.
"I'm sending them to go against
my people.
I'm doing it because my people
don't obey me.
I'll let the enemies from Assyria
take riches from my people.
But the enemies plan to do more
than that.

They want to get rid of my people.
They say that they won over nations
who followed idols.
So they think they'll win over
Judah and Israel, too."

But God will finish his plan
against Judah. Then he will say,
"I'll pay back the enemies for their
pride."
This is what the enemies say.

"We did this by our power.
We did this by our wise thinking.
We went to fight the nations.
We took their land and riches.
We are strong, so we took their kings.
It was like getting eggs from a
nest.
The nations were like little birds.
They didn't even make a sound.
They didn't even flap their wings."

Is the ax stronger than the person
who uses it?
Does the saw see itself as better
than the person who saws?
Can a stick control the person who
picks it up?
Can a club come against a person
by itself?
God is the most powerful.
He is called the Light of Israel.
He will be like fire.
He will get rid of forests and fields
that belong to the enemies.
There will be just a few trees left.
A child will be able to count them.

Then Israel and Judah won't trust
their enemies to help them.
They'll trust in God.
Right now there are many of God's
people.
But only a few will come back.

God says, "My people in Judah,
don't be afraid of your enemies.
These people from Assyria will fight
against you.
But I'll be angry at them."

Then God will take away the heavy
load of his people.

Making Slaves of God's People

2 CHRONICLES 28

Ahaz was Judah's king. He made
idols and worshiped Baal. So God
let the army of Aram win over
Judah. The people of Aram took lots
of God's people out of their land.

God's people from Israel also
came to fight God's people in Judah.
The people from Israel won. They
took people and riches from Judah
back with them to Israel.

This happened because Judah had
turned away from God.

Now there was a prophet named
Oded. He went to meet Israel's army
on its way home. He said, "God was

angry at Judah. So he let you win. But you killed them because of your anger. You're planning to make Judah's people into slaves. But haven't you done things against God, too? So listen! Send these people back home. God is angry at you, too!"

Some of the leaders talked to the army about it. "Don't bring Judah's people here," they said. "If you do, God will blame us. We've already done enough to make God angry."

So Israel's army sent Judah's people back home. The leaders sent back the things the army took. These leaders gave clothes back to the people of Judah who didn't have any. They gave the people shoes and food and drinks. They put oil on their hurt places to make them feel better. They let people who weren't strong ride on donkeys. They took the people of Judah back home.

Then Judah's king, Ahaz, asked the king of Assyria for help. That's because the army of Edom had come to fight. They had taken people away. They had taken over some cities, too. God let this happen because Ahaz led the people to sin.

So people from the nation of Assyria came to Judah. But they brought trouble instead of help. King Ahaz paid Assyria with riches from the worship house. But that didn't help.

Altars on Every Street Corner

2 KINGS 16:9-20; 2 CHRONICLES 28:22-27

Then the nation of Assyria went out to fight the nation of Aram. People from Assyria took control of the city of Damascus. They took all the people away and killed the king.

King Ahaz went to see the king of Assyria in Damascus. There he saw an altar. He called for one of his priests. He asked him to draw a picture of the altar. Ahaz wanted the priest to build one just like it. So the priest did. He finished it before King Ahaz got back home to Judah.

King Ahaz saw the new altar. He offered gifts of worship on it. Then he gave orders to the priest. "Offer all gifts to God on the new altar," he said. "But I'll use the old altar to get answers from God." Then King Ahaz moved the old altar.

King Ahaz moved lots of the things in the worship house. Then he offered gifts to the fake gods of Aram. He thought, "Aram's gods helped them. So I'll give gifts to their gods. Maybe they'll help me, too." But they brought him trouble instead.

Ahaz took away the tables and lamps from the worship house. He closed the worship house doors so no one could go there anymore. He built altars at all the street corners. He also built places to offer gifts to idols in every town.

All this made God angry.

Sometime later, King Ahaz died. His son Hezekiah became the next king of Judah.

Hezekiah was a good king.

A Branch

ISAIAH 11–12

The family of King David is like
 a tree.
 It was cut down.
But part of it will begin to grow
 again.
 A Branch will come up from the
 roots.
 It will grow fruit.
A new King will come.
God's Spirit will stay upon him.
 This is God's wise, understanding
 Spirit.
 This is God's guiding, strong
 Spirit.
 This is God's Spirit who knows
 and looks up to God.
The King will be glad to treat God
 like the most important one.

He will choose what's right for
 the poor.
 He will be fair to the poor.
 He will keep his promises.

The wolf will live with the lamb.
 The leopard will lie down with
 the goat.
The calf and lion will eat together.
 A little child will lead them.
The cow will eat with the bear.
 Their babies will lie down
 together.
 The lion will eat straw, like the ox
 does.
The baby will play close to the
 cobra's hole.
 The little child will touch the
 snake's nest.
Nothing will hurt anyone anywhere
 on my holy mountain.
The earth will be full of people who
 know God.
 It will be as full as the water that
 fills the sea.

Then the King from David's family will stand. He will stand like a flag for people. The nations will come to him. The place where he rests will shine with greatness.

God will bring back those of his people who are left. He will bring them back from enemy lands.

God will gather Judah's people from
 all over the earth.
Israel won't be angry at Judah.
 Judah won't be angry at Israel.
They will fight together against their
 enemies, and they will win.

Then God's people will say, "We
    praise you, God.
You were angry with us.
    But you're not angry anymore.
You have made us feel happy.
    We will trust you. We won't be
    afraid.
God is our power. He is our song.
    He saves us."

Everyone will say, "Thank God!
    Tell how great his name is!
Sing to God! He did great things!
    Tell everyone in the world!
Shout out loud! Sing for joy!
    God is great!"

The Beautiful Stone of the Kingdoms

ISAIAH 13:1-3, 19-22; 14:24-25, 28-30

Here's what God told Isaiah the
year King Ahaz died.

Don't be glad, you enemies.
    Judah may be broken.
    But the nation will become strong
    again.
The poorest people will find a place
    to stay.
    They will be safe when they lie
    down.

God promises, "It will be the way I
    planned.

I will mash the enemies flat.
I'll run over them on my mountain.
    I'll get them away from my people."

Here's what God says about Babylon.
Set a flag up on a hill.
I've called my fighters to come.
    They are glad to see me win.

Babylon is like the most beautiful
    stone of the kingdoms.
    Its people are proud that Babylon
    is so great.
So God will tear it down.
    Nobody will live there again.
    Shepherds won't even take their
    sheep there.
Instead, desert animals will stay
    there.
    Jackals will go into the houses.
Owls will live there.
    Wild goats will jump around.
Hyenas will yell there.
    Jackals will go into the palaces.
It will happen soon.
    Babylon won't last long.

A Son of the Dawn

ISAIAH 14:3-5, 12-15, 22-23

You were slaves. Babylon was mean to you. But God will set you free. Then you'll say this about Babylon's king.

"The mean man's end has come.
    His anger is over!
God broke his power.

"You have fallen from heaven!
    You were like a morning star.
    You were like a son of the dawn.
But you were thrown down onto the
        earth.
Once you tore nations down.
You said, 'I'll go up to heaven.
I'll sit there above God's stars.
I'll go up above the clouds.
I'll make myself like God!'
But you have been taken down to
        the grave."

"I'll come against Babylon," says
        God.
    "I'll make it a place for owls to
        stay.
    It will be a place of mud and
        weeds.
I will get rid of it," says God.

Getting the Dirt Out

2 KINGS 18:1-7; 2 CHRONICLES 29

Now Judah's king, Hezekiah, was a good king. He did what was right. He took the idols down and broke them.

Hezekiah trusted God. He kept following God no matter what. He obeyed God's laws. And God was with him. Everything Hezekiah did turned out right.

Hezekiah opened God's worship house again. He fixed the doors. He brought the priests back.

"Listen," said Hezekiah to the priests. "Take all the dirt out of here. Our fathers didn't keep following God. They did what was wrong. They closed these doors. They put out the lamps. They didn't offer any gifts to God here. So God was angry at us. That's why there has been so much war.

"But I'm going to make a promise to God," said Hezekiah. "That way, God will stop being angry at us. Stand before God. Serve him here."

So the priests and their families got to work. They cleaned out every part of the worship house. Then they told King Hezekiah they had done the job.

The next morning King Hezekiah got up early. He got the city leaders together. They went to the worship house. They offered gifts of meat on the altar. They asked God to forgive their sins.

Priests came with cymbals, harps, and lyres. They did what God had said to do long ago. Priests also got their horns ready.

King Hezekiah told them when to offer the gifts on the altar. Then they began singing. Priests played music.

When the gifts had been given, they all bowed down. They worshiped God. King Hezekiah ordered the priests to praise God with David's songs. So they sang David's songs. They were glad. They bowed their heads. And they worshiped God.

"You've told God you would obey him," said Hezekiah. "So bring your gifts to God's worship house."

All the people got to bring their gifts.

MAY 31

A Holiday

2 CHRONICLES 30–31

Then King Hezekiah wrote letters to all the people of Judah. He wrote to people in Israel, too. He asked everybody to come to the worship house in Jerusalem. He asked everyone to come for the Pass Over holiday. It had been a long time since everyone got together for the Pass Over holiday.

So the king's helpers took the letters all over the land.

The letters said,

"People of Israel, come back to God. Then he can turn back to you. Come to his worship house. Obey God. Then he will stop being angry at you. Your enemies will set your people free. God is kind and loving. He won't turn away from you. Just come back to him."

Many people laughed at the letters. They laughed at the people bringing the letters. But some people came to Jerusalem. God helped people in Judah agree to do what the king said. That's because the king was obeying God's word.

Lots of people came for the Pass Over holiday. It was also called the Flat Bread holiday. The holiday lasted a week. All of the people showed their joy. The priests sang to God every day. They played music, too. They praised God.

Then they all chose to keep the holiday going. So for seven more days they kept the Pass Over holiday. There was lots of joy in Jerusalem. It hadn't been like this since King Solomon's time.

The priests stood up. They prayed that God would bring good things to his people. God heard their prayer.

Then King Hezekiah gave the priests different jobs. He told the people to bring things for the priests. That way, the priests could use their time doing their work for

God. They could do what God's laws said they should do.

Right away, the people gave more than enough. They brought new wine and oil and honey. They brought the first of all the crops they grew. They brought some of their cows and sheep.

The king saw the piles of gifts people brought. He praised God. He prayed that good things would come to his people.

King Hezekiah asked the priests about the piles of gifts. They said, "We have more than enough to eat. It's all because God is being so good to his people. We have a lot left over."

So the king told people to make rooms to store things in. They made these rooms at the worship house. Then they brought the piles of gifts into the rooms.

King Hezekiah did what was good and right. He kept following God no matter what. He followed God with his whole heart. So God brought good things to Hezekiah.

A Dinner Party on the Mountain

ISAIAH 25:1-9

Lord, you are my God.
    I will tell how great you are.
    I'll cheer for your name.

You keep your promises.
    You have done wonderful things.
    You planned these things a long
        time ago.
You turned the city into a pile of
        bricks.
    You turned the fort into a pile of
        sticks.
The enemies' strong city won't be a
        city anymore.
    No one will ever build it again.
So people in strong nations will
        worship you.
    Cities of mean people will look
        up to you.
You've been like a safe place for
        poor people.
    You've been like a place to get
        away from storm and heat.
Mean people are like a storm
        beating a wall.
    They are like heat in the desert.
But you make them be quiet.
    A cloud's shadow makes the heat
        cool down.
    That's what you're like when you
        make mean people get quiet.

God will make a dinner party on
        Zion Mountain.
    There will be good food for all
        people.
It will be a party with wine.
    It will have the best meat and the
        best wine.
God will tear down the fear of death.
    God will get rid of death forever.

349

God will clean all tears away from
every face.
No one will say anything bad
about his people anymore.

That day they'll say,
"This is our God!
We trusted him, and he saved us.
Let's show our joy! Let's be glad
he saved us!"

Peace from God

ISAIAH 26:1-13

Then the people in the land of Judah
will sing this song.

You'll keep giving peace to people
who keep thinking about you.
They trust you.
Trust in God forever.
God the Lord is like a Rock.
He is strong, and he lasts forever.
He lets proud people know they're
not so great.

People who do right walk on a
flat road.
God makes their way smooth.
God, we obey your laws.
We wait for you.
We want everyone to know who
you are.
That's what our hearts really
want.
My soul wants you in the night.

My spirit wants you in the
morning.
You say what's right and wrong on
the earth.
That way, people learn what's
right.

God, you give us peace.
If we've done anything good,
it's because of what you've
done for us.
Lord, our God, other kings have
ruled over us.
But your name is the only name
we look up to.

Working in the Dark

ISAIAH 29:13-21

God says, "My people talk about
coming close to me.
They say good things about me.
But their hearts are far away
from me.
Their worship is only rules made
by people.
So I will surprise them.
I'll show them many wonders.
Wise people won't think they're so
wise anymore.
Smart people won't think they're
so smart anymore."
There's bad news for people who try
to hide their plans from God.
They work in the dark.

They think, "Nobody sees us.
 Nobody will know."
But they're getting it backward.
 It's as if the person who makes
 clay pots was just clay himself.
What if you made something?
 Could it say to you, "You didn't
 make me"?
Could a pot tell its maker,
 "You don't know anything"?

It won't be long until people who
 can't hear will hear.
 People who can't see will see.
Then people who know God is great
 will be happy again.
 Poor people will show that God
 makes them glad.
Mean people won't be around
 anymore.
 People who make fun of others
 will be gone.
 People who look for sin will be
 thrown out.
People who trick and lie and blame
 others will be gone.

Rain for the Gardens
ISAIAH 30:1-7, 15-24

"There's bad news for children who
 won't obey," says God.
"There's bad news for people who
 follow plans that aren't my
 plans.
 They make deals with other
 lands.

But my Spirit didn't tell them to
 do this.
 They are doing one sin after
 another.
They go to Egypt.
 But they didn't ask me if they
 should go.
They ask the king of Egypt to keep
 them safe.
 But his help is no good.
So I call Egypt the 'Do-Nothing.'"

Here's what God says.
"Stop doing wrong. Start doing
 right. Rest.
 That's what will save you.
Be quiet. Trust.
 That's what will make you strong.
 But you wouldn't do any of these
 things.
You said, 'No! We'll run away on
 horses.'
 So you will.
You said, 'We'll ride away on fast
 horses.'
 So the enemies chasing you will
 be fast.
A thousand people will run away,
 afraid of one person.
 If five people scare you, all of you
 will run!
At last, you'll be left alone.
 You'll be alone like a flag on top
 of a mountain."

But God wants to show you his
 kind love.

God is fair and right.
He will bring good things to
people who wait for him!

God will be so kind when you
cry for help! He will hear. He will
answer you right away.

God has let you have hard times.
But your teachers won't hide anymore.
You'll see them with your own eyes.
You'll hear a voice behind you. It will
say, "This is the way to go."

Then you'll get rid of your silver
and gold idols. You'll tell them, "Get
away from
here!"

God will
send rain for
your gardens.
You'll grow
good food.
You'll have
plenty. Your

cows will eat grass in wide fields.
You'll set out food for your oxen
and donkeys.

The Beautiful King
ISAIAH 33:2-6, 10, 17, 20-21, 24

God, be kind and loving to us.
We want you.
Be strong for us every morning.
Save us when we're in trouble.
Your voice sounds like thunder.
When people hear it, they run
away.

God is great. He lives up high.
He will bring what's fair and
right.
He is the one you can trust in these
days.
He saves. He is wise. He knows
everything.
Worshiping God is the way to
have riches from him.

"Now I'll come," says God.
"Now people will call me great."

You will see the beautiful king with
your own eyes.
You'll see a land that goes on a
long way.

Look at Zion. It's the city where we
had holidays.
You will see Jerusalem.
It will be a place to stay in peace.
It will never be broken down again.
God will be the Strong One there.
Nobody living there will say, "I'm
sick."
God will forgive the people's sins.

Shout with Joy
ISAIAH 35

The desert and the dry land will be
glad.
Flowers will grow.
The land will shout with joy.
Everything will see God's
greatness.

Make weak hands strong.
Make legs that shake stand
straight and still.
Tell people who are afraid,
"Be strong. Don't be scared.
God will come.
He will come and save you."

Then people who couldn't see will
see.
People who couldn't hear will hear.
People who couldn't walk will jump
like a deer.
People who couldn't talk will
shout with joy.
Water will flow in the desert.
Hot sand will turn into pools of
water.
Dry ground will turn into springs
of water.
Jackals used to lie down there.

But grass and water plants will
grow there now.

A wide road will be there.
It will be called the Way of What's
Right and without Sin.
People who sin won't get to travel
on it.
It will be a road for people who
follow God's ways.
Fools won't travel on it.
No lions will be on it.
No angry animals will get to it.
They won't even be there.
Only the people God has saved will
go there.
They will go on that road.
They'll sing as they go into God's
city of Zion.
They'll be glad.
Sadness will be gone.

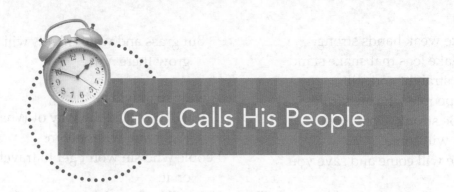

God Calls His People

Lions in the Land

2 KINGS 17

Back in Israel, Hoshea was the king. Israel was paying money to the king of Assyria. That kept Assyria from fighting them.

But then King Hoshea asked Egypt for help. So he stopped paying Assyria. When Assyria's king found out, he sent out his army. The people in his army went to fight Israel. They put King Hoshea in jail.

Assyria's army fought the capital city of Israel for three years. At last the people from Assyria took over the whole land. Then they took the people of Israel away. They made God's people live in cities far away. Then the people from Assyria took people from other nations. They sent them into Israel's land to live.

All this happened because Israel had stopped obeying God. God had said, "Don't worship idols." But they worshiped idols anyway. They

did wrong things in secret. They acted like the nations around them. And they made God angry.

God sent prophets to them. He said, "Stop doing wrong. Obey me."

But the people of Israel wouldn't listen. They had hard hearts. They didn't trust in God.

So God was very angry at Israel. That's why he sent them out of the land. Only Judah was left.

But Judah started doing the same things Israel had done. So God turned away from all his people.

Now people from other nations were living in Israel's land. At first they didn't worship God. So God sent lions into the land. The lions killed some people there.

Someone told the king of Assyria, "You sent people into Israel. But they don't know how to worship the God of that land. He sent lions into the land. The lions are killing people."

The king said, "Get one of the priests we took away. Send him back to live there. Tell him to teach the new people how to worship his God."

So they sent a priest back to the land of Israel. He taught the people how to worship God.

But the people made idols, too. They worshiped God. But they also worshiped idols.

God and his people had made a promise together. God said, "Don't worship any other gods. Don't bow down to them. I took you out of Egypt with my power. I am the one to worship. Bow down to me. Keep my laws. Don't worship other gods. Don't forget the promise we made together. Worship me, the Lord your God. I'm the one who will save you from your enemies."

But the people wouldn't listen.

JUNE 3

Trying to Scare God's People

2 KINGS 18:13-37; 2 CHRONICLES 32:1-19; ISAIAH 36

Now Hezekiah was still Judah's king. But the army of Assyria came in to fight Judah. They took all the forts.

So Hezekiah sent a message to Assyria's king. "I did the wrong thing. I'll pay you whatever you want if you'll leave our land."

So Assyria's king asked for 11 tons of silver. He asked for one ton

of gold. Hezekiah got the silver from the worship house and the palace. He took the gold off the doors of the worship house. He gave it to Assyria's king.

Now Hezekiah saw that Assyria planned to fight Jerusalem. So he asked his army for help. They blocked up all the springs of water outside the city. They fixed all the broken walls. They built towers. They even built another wall around the first one. They made lots of shields and tools to fight with.

Hezekiah chose army leaders. He told them, "Be strong. Be brave. Don't be afraid. Our power is greater than their power. They only have people. But we have God to help us fight."

So the people felt brave and sure of themselves.

Sometime later, Assyria's king sent his army leaders to Jerusalem. They took a message to Hezekiah. They stopped on the road to the Washer Man's Field. It was close to the Upper Pool.

The army leaders called for King Hezekiah to come. Hezekiah sent the man in charge of the palace. He also sent two other men.

Assyria's army leader said, "Our king asks why you're so sure of yourself. You say you have a plan. You say your army is strong. But this is just talk. You're turning against our king. Who are you trusting to help you?

"Look," said the army leader. "You're trusting in Egypt. But Egypt is like a broken walking stick. It will hurt the person who leans on it.

"You might say you are trusting your God," he said. "But Hezekiah is just lying to you. He is going to let you die of hunger.

"The king of Assyria wants me to ask you this. Don't you know what he did to people from other lands? Their gods couldn't save them. So how can your God save you? Don't believe Hezekiah. Make a deal with Assyria. How can you push back one of our army leaders? You can't push us back, even if Egypt helps you. Besides, God told us to fight this land. He told us to get rid of it."

Hezekiah's men said, "Talk to us in a different language. That way, the town's people won't know what you're saying."

"Were we sent only to Hezekiah?" said the leader from Assyria. "Shouldn't the people get to hear too? After all, they'll run out of food. Just like you."

Then he shouted so everyone could hear. "Listen to what the great king of Assyria says! Don't believe Hezekiah. He can't save you. Don't let him talk you into trusting God.

"Follow the king of Assyria!" he shouted. "Then each of you will have your own fig tree. Each person will have a well of water. I'll take

you to a land just like yours. There are grain fields and grape fields. There's wine and bread. There are olive trees and honey.

"Choose to live, not to die!" he shouted. "Hezekiah says, 'God will save us.' But your king is lying. No other nations' gods could save them from Assyria."

The leaders from Assyria tried to scare the people. They wanted to take over the city. They talked about God as if he were a fake god.

But the people kept quiet. King Hezekiah had told them, "Don't answer."

Hezekiah's men went back to him. They were so upset, they tore their clothes. They told Hezekiah what the men from Assyria had said.

JUNE 4

God Sends His Angel to Fight

2 KINGS 19; ISAIAH 37

King Hezekiah was upset. He tore his clothes too. He put on clothes made of old sack cloth. He went to God's worship house.

Then he sent his leaders and priests to Isaiah.

"Here's what Hezekiah says," they told Isaiah. "This is a day of trouble. Maybe God will hear what the men of Assyria said. They made fun of God. Maybe he will pay them back for that."

"Go back to King Hezekiah," said Isaiah. "Tell him that God says not to be scared. The men of Assyria lied about God. So their king is going to get a message. God will make him go back to his country. He will be killed there."

Then the king of Assyria got a message. It said the army of Egypt was coming to fight him. So he sent a letter to Hezekiah. The letter said, "Don't let your God lie to you. He says Assyria won't take over Jerusalem. But the gods of other lands couldn't save them."

King Hezekiah got the letter. He read it. Then he took it to the worship house. He laid it out before God. Then he prayed. "Lord God, you're the only God in the world. You made all of space. You made the earth. Listen, God. Open your eyes and see. Listen to the bad things the king of Assyria says about you.

"It's true that the people of Assyria tore up other lands," said Hezekiah. "But their gods were only wood and rock. Men made them. Now save us, God. Then everyone in the world will know you're the only God."

After Hezekiah prayed, Isaiah sent a message to him. "God says that he heard your prayer. Here's what he says against the king of Assyria.

"The people of Jerusalem laugh at you.
    They make fun of you as you run away.
Who have you said bad things about?
    Who did you shout against?
You are acting as if you're the best.
    But you have come against the Holy One!

"But I know about you.
    I know when you go places.
    I know how angry you are at me.
You talk against me.
    And I have heard your rude talk.
So I'll make you go back the same way you came.

"Here's a sign for you, Hezekiah.

"This year you'll eat whatever you can find.
    Next year you'll eat what grows from that.
But the next year, you'll plant seeds.
    You'll pick crops.
    You'll plant grape fields. You'll eat the fruit.
The land of Judah will grow.
    People will be left here.

"God wants to do this. He will work at it until it's done.
    Here's what he says about Assyria's king.

"He won't come into this city.
He won't even shoot an arrow
here.
He won't fight against it.
He will go back the same way he
came," says God.
"I'll stand up for this city.
I'll save it."

That night God's angel killed
185,000 (one hundred eighty-five
thousand) army men from Assyria.
The next morning the rest of them
got up. They saw all those dead
bodies. So Assyria's king took his
army home, and he stayed there.

A Shadow Moves Backward

2 KINGS 20:1-11; ISAIAH 38:1-20

King Hezekiah got sick. He was
dying. Isaiah went to see him. Isaiah
said, "Here's what God says. Get
everything ready. You won't get
well. You're going to die."

Hezekiah turned to the wall. He
prayed. "God, remember how I've
done what was right. I kept obeying
you no matter what," Hezekiah cried.

Isaiah was leaving when God
spoke to him. "Go back to Hezekiah.
Tell him that I heard his prayer. I
saw him cry. I will make him well.
I'll let him live for 15 more years.
I'll save him and this city from
Assyria."

So Isaiah told God's words to
Hezekiah.

"Is there a sign to show me that
this is true?" asked Hezekiah.

"This will be the sign," said
Isaiah. "The shadow on the stairs
will move 10 steps. Do you want it
to move forward or go back?"

"It's easy for the shadow to move
forward," said Hezekiah. "So make
it go back 10 steps."

Isaiah prayed to God. Then God
made the shadow go back 10 steps.

After King Hezekiah got well, he
wrote about it. Here's what he wrote.

I said, "I'm in the best part of my life.
Do I have to die?
I cried like a dove.
My eyes were not strong
anymore.
I looked up to the sky.
I'm upset. God, come and help
me!"

God has talked to me.
I'll let him be the greatest all my life.

I'll do it, because I've had this
    trouble.
You made me well again, God.
    You let me live.
It was for my good.
    That's why I had such hard times.
You showed me your love.
    You hid all my sins.

God will save me.
    We'll sing and make music in the
        worship house.
    We'll sing and make music all our
        lives.

JUNE 5

Riches

*2 KINGS 20:12-20; 2 CHRONICLES
32:27-33*

King Hezekiah was very rich. People
treated him like a very important
person. He built places to keep his
silver and gold and riches. He built
places to keep his spices and shields.
He built houses for storing grain and
wine and oil. He made pens for cows
and sheep. He built some towns, too.
Everything he did went well.

Now the king of Babylon sent
men to see Hezekiah. They took him
letters and a gift. They had heard
that Hezekiah had been sick.

Hezekiah showed the men
everything in his store houses. He
showed them his silver and gold. He
showed them his spices and oil.

He showed them his shields and all
his riches. There wasn't anything he
didn't show them.

Then Isaiah went to King
Hezekiah. He said, "Where did those
men come from? What did they say?"

"They came from a far-away
land," said Hezekiah. "It's called
Babylon."

"What did they see?" asked Isaiah.

"Everything," said Hezekiah. "I
showed them all my riches."

"Someday Babylon will take
away all your riches," said Isaiah.
"God says they won't leave a thing.
They'll even take some people from
your family. Your family will serve
the king of Babylon."

"Whatever God says is good,"
said Hezekiah. He thought, "At least
there will be peace while I'm alive."

While Hezekiah was king, he
made a pool and a tunnel. The pool
and tunnel helped bring water to
Jerusalem.

Sometime later, Hezekiah died.
All the people of Judah said good
things about him.

A Voice in the Desert

ISAIAH 40

Make my people feel better, says
    God.
    Tell them that their hard times are
        over.
    They've paid for their sin.

There's a voice calling.
"Make the way ready for the Lord.
Make it ready in the desert.
Make a flat road for God.
The valleys will get higher.
The hills will get lower.
The bumpy ground will get
smooth.
God will show how great he is.
Everybody in the world will see it."

A voice says, "People are like grass.
Grass dries up and dies.
People are like that.
People may seem special for a while.
But they're like flowers that grow
in a field.
Flowers dry up and fall.
Grass dies, and flowers fall.
But God's Word is not like that.
It will last forever."

God is like a shepherd taking care of
his sheep.
He holds the little lambs in his
arms.
He holds them next to his heart.
He carefully leads the sheep that
have babies.

Who measured the water in his hand?
Who planned where to put the
sky?
Who held earth's dust in a basket?
Who weighed the mountains and
hills?
Who knows what's in God's mind?

Who ever told him what he
should do?

Who is like God?
Is he like an idol?
A poor man picks a good piece of
wood.
Then he looks for somebody to
make an idol for him.
Someone puts gold all over it.

Don't you know?
God sits on the king's throne, above
the earth's circle.
The people are as small as
grasshoppers to him.
He rolls the sky out like a tent.

"Who is like me?" says God.
Look up at the sky.
Who made it all?
God did. He brings out each star,
one by one.
He calls each star by its name.
Not a star is missing, because of
God's great power.

My people, why do you say that
God doesn't see you?
Why do you say that he doesn't
care?
Don't you know? God lasts forever.
He made every bit of the earth.
He won't get tired.
No one will ever know how much
he understands.
Even young people get tired.

Even young
   people
   have
   trouble.
But God makes people
   strong again if they
   trust him.
They will be like eagles.
   Eagles fly high with strong
   wings.
God helps people run and not get
   tired.
   He helps them walk and not get
   worn out.

Don't Give Up

ISAIAH 41:8-16

"Israel, you're my servant.
   I chose you.
So don't be afraid. I'm with you.
   Don't feel so helpless that you
   give up. I'm your God.
I'll make you strong. I'll help you.
   I'll keep you strong with my right
   hand.

"Everybody who gets angry at you
   will feel no good.
People who turn against you will
   die.
I'm the Lord. I'm your God.
   I hold your right hand.
I tell you not to be scared, my
   little people.

I will help you myself," says God.
   "I will save you. I'm your Holy
   One.
You will have my joy.
   My great power will shine in you."

JUNE 6

God's Servant

ISAIAH 42:1-13

"Here's my servant. I keep him strong.
   Here's the one I chose. I'm happy
   with him.
I'll put my Spirit upon him.
   He will be fair to all nations.
He won't shout.
   He won't talk loudly in the streets.
He won't get rid of people who are
   hurt.
   He won't get rid of people who
   aren't strong.
He will keep his promises. He will
   be fair.
   He won't get tired or give up.
He will bring what's right and fair
   to the earth.
   People everywhere will trust in
   him."

Here's what God says.
"I am the Lord. I called you to do
   what's right.
   I'll hold your hand.
I'll take care of you.
   Through you, I'll keep my special
   promise to my Jewish people.

361

You'll also be a light for all people
who aren't Jewish.
You'll open eyes that can't see.
You'll free people who are in
jail.
You'll bring people out of the
dark.

"I'm the Lord. That's my name!
I won't give my greatness to
anyone else.
Praise belongs to me. I won't let
it go to idols.
See? I'm telling you about new
things.
I'm telling you before they
happen."

Sing a new song to God.
Sing praise to him from every
part of the world.
Sing, people who go to the sea.
Sing, people of the islands.
Let the desert sing out loud.
Let the towns be glad.
Let the people sing with joy.
Let them shout from the tops
of mountains.
Let them tell how great God is!
Let them cheer for him from the
islands.
God will march out like a strong
man.
He will work like a fighter.
He will shout for the fight.
And he will win over his
enemies.

Erased Sins

ISAIAH 43:1-7, 10-13, 25

Here's what God says.
"Don't be afraid. I'm buying you
back.
I named you. You are mine.
I'll be with you when you go
through water.
It won't rush over you.
I'll be with you when you go
through fire.
You won't be burned.
That's because I'm the Lord. I'm
your God.
I'm the Holy One. I have saved
you.
You are special to me.
I love you.
Don't be afraid. I'm with you.
I'll bring your children back.
I'll bring them from every part of
the world.
Bring all my people. I made them.
I made them to show how great
I am.

"No god was made before me.
There will never be one after me.
I am God. Yes, I am.
There is no other one who can
save you.
I showed you this. I saved you.
I told you.
It was me. It was not a strange
god with you.
You have seen it," says the Lord.

"You've seen that I'm God.
I am the one from long, long ago."

"I am the one who erases your sins.
Then I don't remember them
anymore."

Idols

ISAIAH 44:6, 9-28

"I, the Lord, say this.
I am the first. I am the last.
There's no other God but me."

People who make idols are
nothing.
The things they think are great
really aren't good for anything.
They make idols to be their gods.
But the idols don't do them any
good.
People who make idols are just
people.
They'll just end up looking like
fools.
The man who works with metal gets
his tools.
He works over the hot coals.
He hammers out an idol.
But he gets hungry and tired.
The man who works with wood
marks a line.
Then he cuts the wood there.
He makes it look like a man.
He makes it so it can sit in a
worship place.
The man cuts down trees.

People make a warm fire and cook
with half of the wood.
They make an idol out of the rest.

They bow down and pray to it.
They say, "You're my god. Save me."
But they don't understand.
The people aren't wise.
They don't stop to say,
"I used part of the wood for baking.
Should I make a hateful thing
from the rest?
Should I bow down to a wooden
block?"
The people can't save themselves.
They don't know to say, "Isn't
this wooden idol a lie?"

"Remember this, my people," said
God.
"I made you, and I won't forget you.
I blew your sins away like a cloud.
Come back to me, because I have
saved you."

You sky, sing with joy, because God
did this.
You earth, shout out loud.
You mountains, start singing.
You forests and trees, sing.
God has saved his people.
He shows how great and strong
he is.

God says, "Jerusalem will have
people living in it again.
Judah's towns will be built back up.
King Cyrus will do what I want.
He will say that Jerusalem can be
built back up.
He will say to build the worship
house again."

Making a Fuss
with the Maker

ISAIAH 45:9-13, 20, 22-25; 46:3-4

"There's bad news for people who
make a fuss with me, their Maker.
Those people are like a piece of a
broken pot.
Does clay talk to the person who
makes it a pot?
Does it say, 'What are you making?'
Does the thing you make tell you
that you don't have hands?

"Here's what I, your Maker, say.
Are you telling me what to do
with what I made?

I'm the one who made the earth and
its people.
My own hands rolled the sky
out wide.
I brought the stars together.
I will make Cyrus be a king.
I will make him do the right
thing.
He will build my city back again.
He will let my people go free.
I won't have to pay him to do it.

"People all over the world, come
to me.
Be saved, because I'm God.
There is no other God.
I have promised.
I tell the truth.
My words will come true.
You can be sure that everyone will
bow to me.
Every mouth will promise.
People will say that what's right
comes only from God.
They will say that strength comes
only from God."

All those who talked about God in
anger will come.
But they won't feel good for
anything.
God's people will be right.
They will show their joy.

"Listen, my people.
I've taken care of you since you
were born.

364

I'm the one who will keep taking
    care of you.
    Even when you're old.
    Even when you have gray hair.
I made you. I will carry you.
    I'll keep you strong. I'll save
        you."

Queen of the Kingdoms
ISAIAH 47:5-15

"Sit down and be quiet, Babylon.
People won't call you queen of the
    kingdoms anymore.
I was angry with my people.
    I let you take them to your land.
But you were not kind to them.
    You said, 'Our kingdom will
        always be the queen!'

"So listen.
    You think you're safe.
You say, 'There's no one like me.
    I'll never lose.'
But you will. You'll lose in one day.
    Your spells and magic won't save
        you.
You trusted in the bad things you
    did.
    You said, 'Nobody sees it.'
    You say, 'I'm the only important
        one.'
But trouble will come to you.
    You won't know how to make it
        go away.
It's something you won't see coming.
    Suddenly it will be upon you.

"So keep saying your magic spells.
    You've worked at these since you
        were children.
Maybe they'll work.
    Maybe you'll scare trouble away.
Some people tell what they think
    will happen by watching the
        stars.
    They can't even save themselves.
They can't give you a fire to make
    you warm.
    They can't do anything for you.
They keep following their own lies.
    Not one of them can save you."

Peace As Wide As a River
ISAIAH 48:1-7, 9-11, 17-18, 22

"Listen, Israel. Listen, Judah.
I told you about these things a long
    time ago.
    Then I suddenly did what I said
        I'd do.
I knew you didn't care about me.
    Your hearts were hard.
That's why I told you what would
    happen before it happened.
    Now you can't say, 'My idol made
        this happen.'

"Now I'll tell you new things.
    You haven't heard about them yet.
    So you can't say, 'I knew that.'
I waited to get angry with you.
    I waited because of who I am.
    I didn't want to leave you with no
        one to help you.

365

See? I took out the sin in you.
I tested you with hard times.
I did this because of who I am.
How could I let people say bad
things about me?
I will not let anyone else be called
the greatest.

"I'm the Lord, your God.
I teach you what's best for you.
I show you the way you should go.
I wish you had listened to my rules.
Then peace as wide as a river
would be yours.

"People who do wrong don't have
peace," says God.

A Picture on God's Hands
ISAIAH 49:1-6, 13-16

God called me before I was born.
He said, "You are my servant.
I'll use you to show how great
I am."

Now God says,
"It's not enough for you to bring
back my people.
I'll make you a light for people who
aren't Jewish, too.
That way, I can save people all
over the world."

Shout with joy, you heavens.
You earth, show your joy.
Sing, you mountains.

God cheers up his people.
He will be kind to the hurt ones.

But God's city said, "God left me.
God forgot me."

"Can a mother forget her baby?
Can she stop being kind to her
own baby?
Even if a mother might forget,
I won't forget you," said God.
"See? I drew your picture on the
inside of my hands.
I always see you."

Every Morning
ISAIAH 50

"I sold you because of your sins.
Wasn't I strong enough to save you?
Sure I was!
I can dry up the sea with my words.
I can turn rivers into a desert.
I can make the sky dark."

God taught me what to say.
He told me what to say to help
people feel strong.
He wakes me up every morning.
He wakes me up to listen. He is
teaching me.
I let people beat my back and pull
out my beard.
I let them make fun of me and
spit on me.

God helps me.
  I chose to follow him no matter
    what.
  I know he won't let me feel like
    nothing.
He stands up for me. He is close by.

People who don't trust God are like
    people in the dark.
  They should trust in God.
If you're trusting in yourself, you're
    asking for trouble.

Beautiful Feet

ISAIAH 52:7-10

People's feet are beautiful when
    they bring good news.
  They're beautiful when they bring
    peace.
  They're beautiful when they say
    you'll be saved.
  They're beautiful when they say,
    "Your God is King!"
Listen! The people who watch say it
    out loud.
  They shout together with joy.
God will come back to his city.
  They will see it happen!
Sing together, you broken-down
    walls of Jerusalem.
God has cheered up his people.
  He has saved Jerusalem.
He will show all the nations.
  The whole world will see how
    God saves!

Like a New Green Plant

ISAIAH 53

God's servant grew up with him.
  He was like a new green plant.
  He was like a stem pushing up
    out of the dry dirt.
He wasn't beautiful. He didn't seem
    great.
  His looks weren't anything to
    make us want to know him.
People didn't like him. They didn't
    want him around.
  He knew what it was like to be sad.
He knew what it was like to have
    trouble.
  We didn't treat him like a great
    person.

But we know he took our sickness.
  He felt our sadness.
We said God hurt him.
  We said God gave him trouble.
But he was hurt because of our sins.
  He was paid back for what we
    did wrong.
That brought us peace. But he paid
    for it.
  We get well, because he got hurt.
We are just like sheep. We ran away
    here and there.
  All of us did what we wanted to do.
God paid him back for the wrong
    things we did.

He had hard times. People hurt him.
  But he didn't say a word.

A sheep is quiet while the farmer
    cuts off its wool.
    He was quiet too.
They treated him like nothing.
    What they did to him was not fair.
They took him away.
    He was killed for my people's
    sins.
They put him in a grave as if he
    were a sinful person.
    He was in a rich person's
    grave.
He hadn't done anything wrong.
    He never lied to anybody.

It was God's plan to let this happen.
    He took the blame. He gave his
    life.
But he will see all who are his
    children.
    He will live a long time.
    He will do what God wants.
His soul will get sad and hurt.
    But then he will live again.
    He will know it was for good.
For many people, it will be just as if
    they'd never sinned.
    He will take the blame for their
    sins.
So I will say he is great.
He gave his life. He died.
    He was counted with the people
    who did wrong.
He took the sins of many people.
    He stood in their place.

Kindness That Lasts Forever

ISAIAH 54:1, 4, 7-10, 13

"Sing, my people, and shout with
    joy," says God.

"Don't be afraid.
    No one will make fun of you.
You'll forget that people made fun
    of you before.
    You won't remember how bad
    you felt.
I left you for a minute.
    But I'll bring you back with my
    great love.
I turned away from you in anger.
    But I'll care for you with my
    kindness.
    My kindness lasts forever,"
    says God.

"To me this is like the time of Noah.
    I promised that water wouldn't
    cover the earth again.
So now I promise not to be angry
    with you again.
    I'll never get mad at you again.
The mountains might shake.
    The hills might be torn down.
But my love lasts forever. It won't
    shake.
    I'm making a promise of peace.
    It won't be taken away from you."
This is what God says, and he cares
    for you.

God will teach all your children.
    And they will have great peace.

Trees Will Clap

ISAIAH 55

"Come, thirsty people.
  Come to the water.
Come, people who don't have money.
  Come and buy. Come and eat.
You can buy wine and milk.
  You don't need money. It doesn't
    cost a thing.
Why work and pay money for
    things that don't do you any
    good?
Listen. Come to me.
  Hear me so your soul can live.
I'll make a special promise that lasts
    forever.
  It's my love that will never end.
  That's what I promised to David."

Look for God while you can find him.
  Talk to him while he is near.
People who do wrong should stop
    living that way.
  They should turn to God.
God will be kind and loving to them.
  God will forgive them for free.

"My thoughts aren't your thoughts.
  My ways aren't your ways," says
    God.
"The sky is higher than the earth.
  And my ways are higher than
    your ways.
  My thoughts are higher than your
    thoughts.

The rain and snow come down from
    the sky.
  Before they go back, they water
    the earth.
They make things grow.
  That way, there are seeds for the
    farmer.
  Then there is bread for people
    to eat.
My word is like that.
  It will do what I want
    it to do.
You'll go out with
    joy and peace.
Mountains and
    hills will start
    singing right
    in front of you.
All the trees in the
    field will
    clap!
Pine trees
    will grow
    instead
    of weeds.
This will show everyone that God
    is the Lord."

A Prayer House
for All Nations

ISAIAH 56:1-7; 57:1-6, 11, 15-21

"Keep choosing what's fair and
    doing what's right.
I'll save you soon.
  Keep obeying no matter what."

Some people from other lands have chosen to follow God.
Don't let them say, "God will leave me out."

Here's what God says.
"People from other lands promised to serve me.
They promised to love my name.
They promised to worship me.
I'll bring these people to my good, holy mountain.
I'll make them happy in my prayer house.
My worship house will be called a prayer house.
It will be a prayer house for all nations."

People who do what's right die, and nobody thinks about it.
Good people who follow God die, but nobody knows why.
Nobody knows that these people die to be kept from bad things.
People who do what's right go into peace.
They rest when they die.

"You people who do wrong, come here!
Who are you making fun of?
You are sticking out your tongue.
Who are you making faces at?
You turn against God.
You lie.
You want things you shouldn't have.

You worship idols.
You have not remembered me.
Is it because I've been quiet for so long?
Is that why you don't think I'm important?"

Here's what God says.
"I live in a high place. I live in a good, holy place.
But I also live with people who know they're not great.
I live with people who are sorry for their sins.
I won't blame them forever.
I won't always be angry.
If I was, people would get weak.
Their breath, their spirit I made, would not be strong.
I was angry because they sinned.
I paid them back for what they did wrong.
I saw what people did, but I'll make them well.
I'll guide them and cheer them up.
I'll make their crying turn into praise.
Peace comes to people far away.
Peace comes to people near," says God.
"I'll make them well."
But people who do wrong are like tossing sea waves.
They can't rest.
Those waves bring mud up onto the land.
"There isn't any peace for people who sin," says God.

370

The One Who Fixes Broken Walls

ISAIAH 58:2-12

"My people ask me for answers that are fair," says God.
 "It seems like they want me to be near them.
'We went without food for a while,' they say.
 'We did it for you.
 Why didn't you see us?
We showed that we knew we were less important than you.
 Why didn't you listen?'

"You go without food.
 But then you do whatever you want.
 You are hard on the people who work for you.
You end up fussing and fighting.
 You hit each other.
You can't act that way and think I'll hear you.
Is that why I ask you to go without food?
 Is it to make yourself less important for just one day?
Is it just so you can bow your head?
 Is that what makes me happy?

"Going without food should help you obey me.
 It should help you start being fair.
 You should help people get free from their troubles.

You should share food with hungry people.
 You should give poor people a place to stay.
You should give clothes to people who need them.
 You should help your own families.
Then you'll be like the first morning light.
 You will get well fast.
You will live the right way.
 My greatness will guard you as you go.
You'll pray, and I will answer.
 You'll call to me for help,
 and I'll say, 'Here I am.'
I will always guide you.
 I'll give you what you need.
My people will build up the torn-down city.
I'll be called The One Who Fixes Broken Walls."

Like a Spider's Web

ISAIAH 59:1-7, 16-21

God's arm is not too short to save you.
 His ear is not too stopped up to hear you.
 It's your sins that keep you from God.
You are to blame for what you did.
 You have lied and said bad things.
Nobody tries to be fair.

Nobody tells the truth.
People just fuss a lot and tell lies.
They plan trouble.
So bad things happen.
It's like baby snakes coming out
of snake eggs.
It's like spinning a spider's web.
People do wrong things.
They are mean.
They think bad thoughts.

God looked at this. He was not happy.
Nobody was being fair.
God was upset that there wasn't
anyone to help you.
So he did it himself with his own
arm.
He will pay back his enemies for
what they did.
He will be angry at them.
Then people will treat God's name
with care.
From west and east they'll
wonder at his greatness.
The enemies might come in like
rushing water.
But God's Spirit will push them
back.

"This is the promise I make to
them," says God. "My Spirit is on
you. My words are in your mouth.
My Spirit and my words won't
leave your mouth. They won't leave
your children. They won't leave
their families from now on," says
God.

Get Up and Shine!

ISAIAH 60:1-3, 11, 19-22

"Get up! Shine! Your light is here.
God's greatness shines on you.
Nations will come to the light you
show.
Kings will come to your
brightness.
Your gates will always be open.
They won't ever shut, day or
night.
The sun won't be your light in the
daytime.
The moon won't shine on you.
God will be your light forever.
Sad times will be gone.
All your people will do what's right.
They'll have their land forever.
I'm God.
I'll do this quickly when it's
time."

God Chose Me

ISAIAH 61:1-3

God's Spirit is on me.
God chose me to teach good news
to poor people.
He sent me to care for people with
sad hearts.
He sent me to tell people in jail
they can be free.
He sent me to tell about God's
kind love.
He sent me to tell how God pays
people back for doing wrong.

He sent me to cheer up people
who cry.
He sent me to give them beauty.
He sent me to make them glad.
He sent me to help them praise.

The Wolf and the Lamb
ISAIAH 65:1-10, 17-25

"I show who I am to people who
don't ask for me.
People who don't look for me
find me.

"I hold out my hands to my people.
But they don't care about me.
They do wrong things.
They follow their own
daydreams.
They are like smoke in my nose.
They are like a fire that burns all
day.

"See? I won't stay quiet.
I'll pay them back for what they
did.

"Sometimes people find juice left in
grapes.
So they say, 'Don't get rid of them.
There's still some good in them.'
That's the way I'll be with my people.
I won't get rid of all of them.
I'll bring them back to their land.
There will be fields for their
sheep.

There will be a place for their
cows to rest.
That's what my people will have
if they look for me.

"Look! I'll make a new sky and a
new earth.
The old things will be forgotten.
People will never think about them.
Be glad. Show your joy forever.
Be happy about what I'll make.
I'll make Jerusalem bring joy to
people.
Its people will bring gladness.
There won't be crying anymore.

"There won't ever be a baby who
lives just a few days.
There won't ever be a man who
dies too soon.
People will think a 100-year-old
person is young.

"My people used to build houses.
But people from other lands lived
in them.
Now they'll live in the houses
they build.
They used to plant fields. But people
from other lands ate the food.
Now they'll eat food from the
fields they plant.
Trees live a long time.
My people will live a long time too.
They'll get to enjoy what they do for
a long time.
They'll work and have all they need.

373

Their children won't have hard
 times.
I'll bring good things for them and
 their families.
I'll answer before they ask.
 I'll hear while they're still talking.

The wolf and the lamb will eat
 together.
 The lion will eat hay like an ox.
 But the snake will eat dust.
Nothing will hurt anyone anywhere
 on my mountain," says God.

Like a Rushing Wind

ISAIAH 66

Here's what God says.
"Heaven is the throne where I sit.
 Earth is where I rest my feet.
Where could you build me a house?
 Where would I rest?
My hand made all these things.
 That's how they came to be,"
 says God.

"These are the kind of people I
 make great.

They're the people who don't
 think they are the best.
They're the people who care
 about what I say.
Be glad with Jerusalem, if you love
 the city.
I will give Jerusalem peace like a
 river.
 I'll give it riches like a river
 flowing over.
A mother cheers up her child.
 In the same way, I'll cheer you up.
 You'll be glad about Jerusalem."

See? God is coming with fire.
 His chariots are like rushing wind.
He will bring his anger hard and fast.
 God will judge all people.

"I'm getting ready to come. I will
get all nations together. They'll see
how great I am.

 "I'll send a sign to them. I'll send
people to islands far away. I'll send
them to lands where the people
have never heard about me. I'll send
them to people who never saw my
greatness. They'll bring my people
from all nations to Jerusalem. They'll
come on horses. They'll come in
chariots. They'll come in wagons.
They'll come riding mules and camels.

 "The new sky and new earth will
last," says God. "My people's name
will last. My family will last. All
people will come and bow to me,"
says God.

JUNE 12

A 12-Year-Old King

2 KINGS 21:1-15; 2 CHRONICLES 33:1-10

Hezekiah's son Manasseh became Judah's next king. He was 12 years old. But he became a bad king. He worshiped idols. He built altars to stars and worshiped them. He even put the altars in God's worship house.

Manasseh asked witches to help him. He did many wrong things. And God's people did what Manasseh did. So God got very angry with them.

God spoke to his prophets about it. "Manasseh has done terrible sins," said God. "He leads the people to sin. So I'm going to bring big trouble to Judah. I'll wipe them off the land. It will be like wiping dirt off a dish.

"I'll leave my people," said God. "Their enemies will take everything away from them. It's because my people are doing wrong. They are making me angry."

A Ring in the King's Nose

2 KINGS 19:36-37; 2 CHRONICLES 33:10-17

The king of Assyria was worshiping his idol one day. Two of his sons came in. They killed him with a sword. Then they ran away. Another son became the next king of Assyria.

Now Manasseh was Judah's king. God talked to Manasseh and his people. But they didn't listen. So God let the army of Assyria come into the land.

Assyria won the fight and took King Manasseh. They put a ring in his nose. Then they took him to Babylon.

King Manasseh was very upset. So he prayed to God. Now the king knew he was not the greatest. So when he prayed, God listened. God brought him back to Jerusalem. Then Manasseh knew that the Lord is God.

After that, Manasseh built back the outside wall of Jerusalem. He built it even higher than before. He put army leaders in all the forts.

Manasseh also got rid of the idols. He took the idol out of God's worship house. He threw all idols out of the city. Then he brought the altar back to the worship house. He gave gifts to God on it.

King Manasseh told all the people to serve God. They did. But they chose to worship God at the wrong places.

A Safe Place in Times of Trouble

NAHUM 1

Here's what God said about Nineveh, the main city of Assyria. God said this to Nahum by putting pictures in Nahum's mind.

God wants people to follow his way.
    He is God.
    He pays people back for doing wrong.
God doesn't get angry quickly. But he has great power.
    He won't let people get away with sin.
God's power is in the rushing wind.
    His power is in the storm.
    Clouds are the dust from his feet.
God dries up the sea.
    He dries up the rivers.
The mountains shake.
    The hills melt.

Who can stand up against God's anger?
    He lets his anger flow out like fire.
    Rocks break in front of him.

God is good.
    He is like a safe place in times of trouble.
He takes care of people who trust in him.
    But he will get rid of Nineveh.
    He will chase his enemies into the dark.

They may make plans against God, but he will stop them.
They'll be mixed up in the weeds.
    They'll be drunk from their wine.
    They'll be burned up like dry grass.

Someone has come from Nineveh.
    He makes bad plans against God.
    He tells people to do bad things.

God has told what's going to happen to you, Nineveh.
    "You won't have any people left.
    I'll get rid of your idols."

But look! Someone is bringing good news to God's people.
    He comes from the mountains.
    He is bringing news of peace.
So have your dinner parties for God, Judah.
    Keep your promises to God.
Sinful nations won't come to fight God's people anymore.

The Work of the Fighting Men

NAHUM 2:1-10

Someone will come to fight you,
    Nineveh.
    Guard your forts.
    Watch your roads.
    Get ready.
    Get as strong as you can be!

God will make his people great again.

The fighting men have red shields.
    They are dressed in red.
The metal chariots shine when they
    are ready to go.
    The men on horses rush around.
The chariots race through the
    streets.
    They rush back and forth.
They look like fire on sticks.
    They zip around like lightning.

The leader calls the army men he
    chose.
    But they trip as they go.
They hurry to the city wall.
    They put up their shields.
They open the dams on the river.
    And the palace falls down.
The people will be taken away.
    The slave girls cry like doves.
    They pound their chests.
Nineveh looks like a pool.
    Its water flows away.

"Stop!" the people cry.
    But nobody comes back.
Take the silver! Take the gold!
    There are store rooms full of
    riches.
The city is cleaned out.
    Hearts melt. Knees bend and fall.
    People shake. Faces lose their
    color.

The Nation That Made Slaves

NAHUM 3:2-7, 19

Whips crack!
    Wheels make noise on the
    streets.
Horses run, and chariots bump by.
    Men on horses rush by with shiny
    swords.
    Lots of people get hurt and die.
It's all because this nation made
    other people their slaves.
    This nation followed witches.

"I'm against you," says God.
    "I'll show the nations that you're
    not good for anything.
Everybody who sees you will run
    away.
    They'll say that Nineveh is torn
    down."

Everybody who hears about it will
    clap.
    That's because everyone knows
    how mean you are.

A Grave in the Palace Garden

2 KINGS 21:18-26; 22:1-2; 23:25-27

Now Judah's king Manasseh died. His grave was in the garden of his palace. His son Amon became the next king of Judah.

Amon was a bad king. He worshiped idols. He never did turn to God. The leaders killed him in his palace. His grave was in the garden too.

Amon's son Josiah became Judah's next king. Josiah was eight years old. Josiah was a good king. He did what was right. He followed God with all his heart and soul and might. That's the way Moses had said to follow God.

But God was still angry at the land of Judah. That was because of the bad things Manasseh had done. God said, "I will turn away from Jerusalem."

The Great Day of God

ZEPHANIAH 1:1-9

God spoke to Zephaniah while Josiah was Judah's king.

"I'll sweep everything off the earth," says God.
"I'll sweep away people and animals.
I'll sweep birds from the air.
I'll sweep fish from the sea.
There will only be piles of trash left.
That's all sinful people will have," says God.

"I'll hold my hand out against Judah.
I'll get rid of every last bit of the idols.
I'll get rid of people who bow down on their roofs.
They worship the stars.
They don't worship me," said God.
"They don't look for me.
They don't ask me what to do.
Be quiet in front of me.
My day is coming soon.
I'll bring trouble to people for what they did."

A Proud Land

ZEPHANIAH 2:3-10

Look for God, you people who know he is great.
Look for God, you people who obey him.
Try to do what's right. Show that you're not greater than others.
Maybe you'll stay safe when God shows his anger.

"I've heard the ugly way the people of Moab talk.
I've heard how they make fun of my people.

So Moab will be like Sodom.
  It will be a place where weeds grow.
  Salt pits will be there.
  It will be a desert forever.
My people who are still left will take
    Moab's riches.
  They'll get to have Moab's land.
That's what Moab gets, because its
    people were proud.
  They said bad things about my
    people," said God.
  "They made fun of my people."

Making Clean Hearts

ZEPHANIAH 3:1-2, 8-20

There's bad news for Jerusalem!
  People there give others a hard
    time.
They turn against God.
  Their hearts and lips are dirty
    with sin.
They don't obey anybody.
  They don't let anybody show
    them what's right.
They don't trust God.
  They don't come close to God.

"So wait for me," says God.
  "I'll get kingdoms together.
I'll let my anger flow out on them.
  All the world will burn in my anger.

"Then I'll make people's hearts and
    lips clean.

I'll do it so they can all call my
    name.
  They can all serve me together.
I'll take away people who are glad
    to be proud.
You won't ever brag again on my
    holy hill.
  I'll leave people here who know
    they're not great.
  They trust in my name.
The people of Israel who are left
    won't do wrong.
  They won't lie.
They'll get to eat and sleep.
  Nobody will make them afraid."

Sing and shout out loud, Israel!
  God has stopped bringing you
    trouble for your sin.
  God has sent your enemies away.
God is the King of Israel.
  He is with you.
  You'll never be afraid of getting
    hurt again.
On that day, people will tell Jerusalem,
  "Don't be afraid.
God is with you.
  He is strong. He can save you.
He will be happy with you. He will
    enjoy you.
  He will love you, and you'll rest
    quietly.
  He will show he is happy with
    you by singing."

"I'll take away the sadness you
    feel," says God.

"I'll pay back the people who
    gave you a hard time.
I'll bring your riches back.
    You'll see it with your own eyes."

Getting Rid of Idols

2 CHRONICLES 34:3-7

As King Josiah grew up, he followed
God. He got rid of idols. He got
rid of altars for idols. He got rid of
worship places for idols.

I'm like a Child

JEREMIAH 1:1-10, 13-19

These are Jeremiah's words. God
began talking to him when Josiah
was Judah's king.

    God spoke to me. "I knew you
before I made you inside your
mother. I chose you before you were
born," said God. "I chose you to be
a prophet. I chose you to tell my
words to the nations."

    "Lord God," I said. "I'm not
good at talking to people. I'm like
a child."

    "Don't say that you're like a
child," said God. "You have to go
where I tell you to go. You have to
say what I tell you to say. Don't be
afraid of people. I'm with you. I will
take care of you."

    Then God touched my mouth
with his hand. He said, "I've put my
words in your mouth. Now you can
tell the nations what I say. You can
tear them down. You can build them
back up, too."

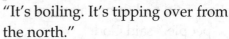

    Then
God asked,
"What do
you see?"

    "I see a
pot," I said.
"It's boiling. It's tipping over from
the north."

    "Trouble will boil out from the
north," said God. "It will come over
everybody living here in Judah. I'm
going to call the nations from the
north.

"Their kings will come here.
    They'll sit at Jerusalem's gates.
They'll fight against Judah's towns.
    I'll judge my people, because they
        turned away from me.
    They worshiped idols.

"Get ready!" said God. "Stand up.
Tell my people what I say. Don't
be scared of them, or else I'll scare
you.

    "I have made you like a fort," said
God. "You are like an iron post. You
are like a metal wall. You'll stand
against this whole land. You'll stand
against kings, leaders, priests, and
people. They'll fight you. But they
won't win, because I'm with you.
I'll save you."

A Bride's Love

JEREMIAH 2:1-5, 11-14, 17, 19, 27-28

God said to go and tell this to the people of Jerusalem.

"I remember how you obeyed me
    when you were young.
    You loved me like a bride loves a
    groom.
You followed me through the desert.
    My people were special and holy
    to me.

"What did your fathers find wrong
    with me?" asks God.
    "Why did they go so far away
    from me?
They followed idols that were no
    good.
    They became no good themselves.

"Look at the other nations.
    Do they change their gods,
        even though their gods aren't
        real?
But my people traded away their
    great God.
    They traded him for idols that
    were no good.

"My people did two wrong things.
First, they turned away from me.
    Then they chose to trust themselves.
I am like a river of living water for
    them.

But they are like a well they dug
    themselves.
It can't even hold water.
My people were not born to be slaves.
    Then why are armies taking them
    away?
My people, you are to blame.
    You turned away from me, the
    Lord your God.
Your own sin will bring you trouble.
    Think about it.
See the trouble that comes when
    you turn away from me?
You get in trouble.
    Then you ask me to come and
    save you!
So where are the idols you made?
    Let these fake gods save you."

Come Back

JEREMIAH 3:6-13, 22-25

Josiah was the king of Judah. God said, "Did you see what the people up north in Israel did? They worshiped idols. I thought they would come back to me, but they didn't. So I sent them out of their land.

"Judah saw it. But Judah didn't care. The people here worshiped idols too. Judah's people only acted like they were obeying me," says God.

"Come back, Israel," says God.
    "I won't frown at you anymore.

That's because I'm kind and
    loving," says God.
    "I won't be angry forever.
Just tell me that you know you sinned.
    You turned against me, the Lord
      your God.
You worshiped other gods.
    You didn't obey me," says God.

"Come back to me.
    I'll help you keep following me."

"Yes. We'll come back to you.
    You are the Lord, our God.
    We know you will save us.
We sinned against you, God.
    We did not obey you."

A War Cry

JEREMIAH 4:1-4, 13-14, 18-21

"Come back, if you will, Israel,"
    says God.
"Put away your idols.
    Don't do wrong anymore.
Promise. Be true and fair and right.
    Then God will bring good things
      to the nations.
    They'll call God great."

Here's what God says to Judah's
    people.
"Obey me. Do what's right.
    If you don't, I'll be angry."

Look! He is coming like clouds
    come.

His chariots come like a fast
    circling wind.
His horses are faster than eagles.
    This is bad news for us! We lose!
Oh, Jerusalem! Clean the sin out of
    your heart.
    Be saved.

"This happened because of the way
    you acted," says God.
    "This trouble came to you
      because of the wrong you did.
It is very sad! It hurts my heart!"

Jeremiah's heart was very, very sad.
"My heart pounds inside me," he
    said.
    "I can't stay quiet.
I heard the horn of the fighters.
    I heard the cry of the fight.
More and more trouble comes.
    Our enemies tear up the whole
      land.
My tents are torn down in one
    moment.
    All of a sudden, my house is gone.
How long will we see the flag of the
    army?
    How long will we hear the war
      horn?"

Where the Roads Cross

JEREMIAH 5:20-22; 6:10, 13-16, 22-23

"Tell this to my people," said God.
"Listen. You are foolish. You don't
    think.

You have eyes. But you don't look.
   You have ears. But you don't listen.
Shouldn't you treat me like someone
      important?" says God.
   "Shouldn't you shake with fear
      when I'm with you?"

"Who can I talk to? Who will listen?"
      asked Jeremiah.
   "How can I tell God's people
      what's going to happen?
Their ears don't listen.
They don't like what God is saying.
   It doesn't make them feel good."

"They are all wanting more and
      more things," says God.
   "The prophets and priests lie.
They think they can tape over the
      hurt places.
   They act as if things were not
      that bad.
They say, 'Peace. Peace.'
   But there is no peace.
Do they feel bad about the wrong
      things they do?
   No. They don't feel bad at all.
   Their faces don't even turn red
      when they sin.
So I'll bring trouble to them for
      what they've done," says God.

"Stand where the roads cross each
      other.
   Look down the roads.
Ask which is the good way.
   Then walk that way."

"Look! An army is coming.
   It's coming from the north.
A great nation is moving in from
      far away.
The people carry bows and spears.
   They are mean. They are not kind.
They ride their horses.
   It sounds like the sea's roar.
They come out to fight Jerusalem,"
      says God.

JUNE 16

A Message at the Gate
JEREMIAH 7:1-11, 18-19

God told Jeremiah to stand at the
gate of God's worship house. He
said to give the people this message.

   "Hear God's word, you people
of Judah. You come through these
gates to worship God. But God says
to change the way you act. Then he
will let you live here.

   "Don't trust lies. Don't just say,
'This is God's worship house! God's
worship house! God's worship
house!' Instead, do what's right. Be
kind to people from other lands.
Be kind to children who don't have
fathers. Be kind to women whose
husbands have died. Don't kill.
Don't worship other gods. Then I'll
let you live here in this land.

   "But you trust lies. You steal. You
kill. You leave the one you married.
You lie. You worship idols. Then

383

you stand in my worship house. You say, 'We're safe.' Are you safe to do all these bad things? Is this house a house for robbers? I've watched all this!" says God.

"The children go out and get wood. The fathers make a fire. The women make cakes. Then they use these things to worship idols. These people make me angry," says God.

"But I'm not really the one they're hurting," says God. "They're really hurting themselves. They're making themselves look bad."

The Belt in the Rocks
JEREMIAH 13:1-11, 15-17

Here's what God told me. "Go and buy a cloth belt. Put it around your middle. But don't let any water get on it."

So I bought the belt. I put it on.

Then God said, "Take the belt off. Hide it in the rocks."

So I hid the belt in the rocks.

Sometime later, God said, "Go back to get the belt you hid."

So I went back. I dug up the belt I hid. But it was all dirty and torn. It was no good.

God said, "This is how I'll get rid of Judah's pride. My people won't listen to me. They don't care about me. They worship idols. So they'll be like this belt. No good.

"A belt is tied around a person.

So I tied Israel and Judah to me," said God. "I wanted them to be my people. I wanted them to praise and worship me. I wanted them to let others know about me. But they haven't listened to me."

Listen to God. Think about this.
   Don't brag. Tell how great God is.
If you don't listen, I'll cry in secret,
      because you're so proud.
   God's people will be taken from
      their land.

The Potter's House
JEREMIAH 18:1-8, 11-12, 15, 17-23

God told Jeremiah to go and see the person who made clay pots. God said, "I'll give you my message there."

So Jeremiah went to the potter's house. The man was working with clay. But he messed up the pot he was making. So he made it into a different pot. He made it the way he thought was best.

Then God said, "Israel, don't you see? I can do to you what this potter does to clay. You are like clay in my hands. Stop doing wrong and start doing right. Then I'll change my mind. I won't bring the trouble I planned.

"Tell my people in Judah that I'm getting trouble ready for them. So stop doing wrong. Start doing right. But they'll say that they'll follow their own plans."

So here's what God says.
"A terrible thing has been done.
    My people have forgotten me.
    They worship idols.
So I'll turn my back on them when
        they're in trouble."

Then people said, "Come on! Let's get Jeremiah. We won't let him talk against us. Let's not listen to anything he says."

So Jeremiah said, "Listen, God.
    Hear what these people say.
Should you send me trouble for the
        good I've done?
    They set a trap for me.
Remember when I came to you.
    I spoke for them.
    I asked you to stop being angry
        at them.
But now take their food away.

Let fighting come.
They're trying to catch me.
    You know about their plans to
        kill me.
Don't forgive them.
    Don't let them get away with
        their sins."

The Clay Jar
JEREMIAH 19:1-4, 10-11, 14-15

God said, "Go see the potter. Buy a clay jar from him. Then go out to the valley near the Pot Gate. Take some leaders and priests with you. Tell them these words from me.

"Listen! I'm going to bring terrible trouble on this place. When people hear about it, their ears will feel hot. It's all because they turned away from me. They made this a place for idols."

Then God told me, "Break your jar while the leaders watch. Tell them that God says he will break this nation and this city. They will break like a pot that breaks and can't be fixed."

Then Jeremiah went to God's worship house and stood there. He told the people what the God of All Power had said. "Listen! I'm going to bring all the trouble I told you about. It's all because the people didn't care about me. They wouldn't listen to me."

The Stocks

JEREMIAH 20:1-13, 18

Now the leader at the worship house heard what Jeremiah said. So he took Jeremiah away. He had Jeremiah beaten.

Then this leader took Jeremiah to the Upper Gate at God's worship house. He put Jeremiah in stocks. Jeremiah's legs and hands were locked in holes in wooden boards.

The next day the man let Jeremiah go. Then Jeremiah said, "God's name for you is Fear on Every Side. God says he will make you afraid of yourself. You'll scare your friends.

"God says that you'll see your enemies kill your friends. He will give Judah to Babylon. Babylon will get all of Judah's riches. They'll take you and your family to Babylon. They'll take the friends you lied to. So you and your friends will die in Babylon."

Then Jeremiah asked God,
"Why was I ever born?
    I'll only see trouble and sadness.
    I'll end my days feeling no good.

"God, you talked me into this.
    You were stronger. You won.
All day everyone makes fun of me.
    It's because all I say is,
        'Trouble is coming.'
So your word gets me in trouble.

People say ugly, mean things to me.
What happens when I say that I
        won't talk about you anymore,
        God?
Your word burns my heart like fire.
    It's like a fire inside my bones.
    I can't stay quiet about it.
I hear lots of whispers.
    'Tell on him! Tell on him!'
All my friends wait for me to say
        something wrong.

"But God is like a great fighter.
    He is with me.
    So people who laugh at me
        won't win.
They'll end up looking no good.
God of All Power, you see people
        who do what's right.
    You look into their hearts and
        minds.
Pay them back for what they did.
    I'm giving my life to you.

"Sing to God!
    Cheer for God!
He saves poor people's lives.
    He saves them from mean people."

Finding a Book

2 KINGS 22; 23:1-20, 24;
2 CHRONICLES 34:8-33

Now Josiah was still Judah's king. He sent some men to God's worship house to fix it. "Go to the priest," he said. "Tell him to get the money the people have given. Use it to pay workers to fix the worship house. They can buy the wood and stone they need."

So the priest got the money. He gave it to men who worked on the worship house. The men did good work. They kept at it.

While all of this was going on, the priest found something. It was the book of laws God gave Moses. The priest went to one of the king's helpers. "I found the Law Book in the worship house!" said the priest.

The king's helper took the Law Book to King Josiah. "We are doing what you asked," he said. "We paid the money to the workers. Then the priest gave me a book." The king's helper read part of the book to King Josiah.

The king heard the words of the Law Book. Then he was so upset, he tore his robe. He told the leaders, "Go ask God about this book. God is very angry at us. It's all because our families from long ago did not obey his laws. They didn't do what this book says."

So the leaders went to Huldah, a woman who was a prophet. She lived in Jerusalem.

Huldah told them God's words for the king. "I'm going to get rid of this place and these people. They have turned against me. They worship idols. So I'll let my anger flow out on them."

Then she told them these words from God for the king. "You listened. Your heart was sad when you heard my laws. You knew you were not as great as I am. You tore your robe. You cried. I heard you. So you will live and die in peace. You won't see the trouble that's coming."

The leaders went back and told the king about this.

Then King Josiah called all the leaders together. He led them to the worship house. All the other people went too. There Josiah read all the words of the Law Book.

The king stood by a tall post. He promised to keep following God's laws. He promised to obey God with all his heart. He asked all the people to promise the same thing. The people did.

Then King Josiah told the priests to clean the worship house. He told them to take out everything made for idols. He burned the things they took out. He got rid of the priests who worshiped idols. He got rid of priests who worshiped the sun and moon. He got rid of priests who worshiped stars. He tore down their worship places.

There were wooden horses near the front of the worship house. Judah's kings had made them to worship the sun. They had made chariots to worship the sun too. King Josiah burned them all.

King Josiah got rid of people who talked to spirits. He did all this to follow God's laws. He told all the people to serve God. As long as Josiah lived, they followed God.

One day, Josiah was out burning down an idol's worship place. He saw a grave. "Whose grave is that?" he asked.

"It's the grave of a prophet," his men said. "Long ago, he said these things would happen. You have done what he said."

"Then leave the grave alone," said Josiah.

JUNE 18

A Holiday and a Fight

2 CHRONICLES 35

King Josiah made plans for the Pass Over holiday in Jerusalem. He chose priests to serve at the worship house. He said, "Put God's ark box in the worship house. Get ready to have the Pass Over holiday. Do it just like God told Moses to do."

King Josiah gave sheep and goats to all the people. The animals were offered to God as gifts. The other leaders gave cows to the people. The cows were also gifts to God.

The people who played music stood in the right places. The gate keepers stayed by their gates.

The Pass Over holiday lasted for seven days.

There had not been a Pass Over holiday like this since Samuel's time. No king ever had such a Pass Over as Josiah did.

Sometime later, Egypt's army went to fight Babylon. Then Josiah took Judah's army out to fight Egypt's army.

Neco was the king of Egypt. Neco sent a letter to Josiah. "I'm not mad at you," he said. "I'm not fighting you. I'm fighting Babylon. God told me to hurry. So stop getting in the way. If you don't, God will get rid of you."

But Josiah wouldn't stop. Josiah dressed like an army man. He went out to fight King Neco.

Josiah didn't listen to what God had told Neco to do.

Josiah got shot with an arrow in the fight. He told his army leaders, "Get me out of here. I'm hurt very bad."

So they took him out of his chariot. They put him in another chariot. They took him to Jerusalem. There, King Josiah died.

All of the people of Judah cried for their king.

Jeremiah wrote sad songs telling good things about King Josiah. People sing these songs to remember him.

Paying with Silver and Gold
2 KINGS 23:31-37; 2 CHRONICLES 36:1-5; JEREMIAH 22:13-17

Josiah's son Jehoahaz became Judah's next king. He was a bad king. He did what was wrong.

Jeremiah wrote about Jehoahaz. "Don't cry for the king who died. Instead, cry for the one who was taken away."

Here's what God says about Jehoahaz. "He won't come back. He will die in the land they took him to. He will never see this land again."

Jehoahaz was king for only three months. King Neco from Egypt put Jehoahaz in jail. Then King Neco made the people pay him silver and gold. Later, he took Jehoahaz to Egypt. That's where Jehoahaz died.

King Neco chose Josiah's son Eliakim to be the next king. He changed Eliakim's name. He called him Jehoiakim. Jehoiakim also had to pay silver and gold. He got it by making the people pay taxes.

Jehoiakim was a bad king too. He did what was wrong.

Then Jeremiah wrote these words.

"There's bad news for a king
    who builds big kingdoms by
    sinning.
He makes people work hard but
    doesn't pay them.
He says, 'I'll build a great palace
    for myself.
    I'll make big rooms upstairs.'
So he makes big windows.
    He covers the walls with wood.
    He paints the palace red.

"Does having a palace make you a
    king?
Your father had food to eat.
    He did what was right and fair.
    So good things came to him.
He cared about poor people.
    So good things came to him.
Isn't that how to show you know
    me?" asks God.
"But what you want is riches.
    You sin to get them.
You give other people a hard time."

Jeremiah Should Die!
JEREMIAH 26:1-16

Now when Jehoiakim was king of Judah, God said these words to Jeremiah. "Stand in the yard of the worship house. Tell the people what I say. Don't leave out one word. Maybe they'll listen. Maybe they'll stop doing wrong. Then I'll change my mind. I won't bring trouble on them."

These are the words God told Jeremiah to say. "Listen to me. Obey my laws. Listen to my prophets. I sent prophets to you over and over again. I sent them, even though you didn't listen. What if you still don't listen? Then I'll tear down this worship house. There will be nothing good left to say about this city."

Priests, prophets, and people heard what Jeremiah said. They came and took hold of him. All the people gathered around Jeremiah.

"You have to die!" they said. "Why do you say that God will tear down this worship house? Why do you say no one will be left in this city?"

The leaders of Judah heard about this. They left the palace and went to the worship house. They stood at the New Gate.

The priests and prophets and people said, "Jeremiah should die! He spoke against our city! You heard it with your own ears!"

Then Jeremiah said, "God sent me to speak against this city. Now change the way you live. Change the way you act. Obey God. Then he will change his mind. He won't bring trouble on you.

"I'm in your hands," said Jeremiah. "Do whatever you want with me. But if you kill me, you'll pay for it. I didn't do anything wrong. The truth is, God sent me to tell you these things."

Then everyone said, "Jeremiah shouldn't die. God sent him to speak to us."

JUNE 19

Like Wind in the Desert

HABAKKUK 1:1-13

Here's what God told the prophet Habakkuk.

Habakkuk asked, "God, how long
    do I call for help?
    I cry out, 'People are being so mean!'
Why do you let wrong things
    happen?
    There's fussing and fighting.
The law isn't doing us any good.
    Nobody is being fair.
Bad people are hurting good people."

God said, "Look at the nations.
    Watch and be surprised.
I'm going to do something during
    your life.
    You won't believe what I'm going
        to do.
    You wouldn't believe it even if
        somebody told you it would
        happen.
I'm giving Babylon power.
    They are mean.
        They act without thinking.
They move all over the earth.
    They take land that doesn't
        belong to them.

People are afraid of them.
They don't follow any law but
their own.
They are out to make themselves
look great.
Their horses are faster than leopards.
They are meaner than wolves in
the evening.
They come down like wind in the
desert.
They take people as if they were
sand.
They laugh at kings and rulers and
forts.
They take over cities.
They blow past like wind.
Then they go on.
They worship their own power."

Habakkuk said, "God, you are
forever.
You're the Holy One. We won't
die.
You are too good to look at bad things.
You can't stand what's wrong."

Bad News

HABAKKUK 2:2-3, 6, 9, 19-20

Then God said, "Write down what I
tell you.
Make it very clear.
What I say will come true at the
right time.
It really will happen.

"There's bad news for people who
steal things!

They get rich by tricking people.
How long must this keep going on?

"There's bad news for people who
get rich by doing wrong.
It puts their lives in danger.

"There's bad news for people who
tell wood, 'Come alive!'
They tell rocks, 'Wake up!'
But idols can't talk.
Can an idol guide you?
It's covered with silver and gold.
It does not have any breath.
But God is in his special, holy
worship house.
Be quiet for him, everybody."

Wow!

HABAKKUK 3:1-13, 16-19

Here's a prayer Habakkuk prayed.

God, I've heard of you.
I say, "Wow!" when I see what
you've done.
Do these things again.
Let us see them in our lifetime.

God's greatness covered the sky.
His praise filled up the earth.
His greatness was like the sun
coming up in the morning.
Light shone from his hand.
That's where his power hid.
He stood up and shook the earth.
The old mountains broke in pieces.
The old, old hills fell.

Were you angry at the rivers, God?
    You rode out with your horses.
You took out your bow.
    You asked for lots of arrows.
You broke the earth with rivers.
    The mountains saw you, and
        they shook.
Waves of water rushed by.
    The deep sea roared.
    Waves jumped up high.
The sun and moon stood still in
        the sky.
    They saw your arrows fly.
    They saw your sword shine like
        lightning.
You walked over the earth in anger.
    You shook up the nations.
You came out to save your people.
You threw out the leader of the land
        that did wrong.

I heard it. My heart beat very hard.
    My lips shook. My legs shook.

The fig tree may not have buds.
    There may not be grapes on the
        vine.
There may not be sheep or cows in
        the pen.
    But I'll be glad in God.
    I'll have joy because of God. He
        saves me.

God makes me strong.
    He makes my feet to be like a
        deer's feet.
    He helps me climb up high.

A Family That Obeyed

*2 KINGS 24:1-7; 2 CHRONICLES 36:5-7;
JEREMIAH 35:1-14, 18-19*

Jehoiakim was Judah's king when
Babylon's army marched into
Judah. The people of Babylon took
over the land. They let Jehoiakim
be the leader. But the king of
Babylon was his boss for three
years.

Then the army of Babylon came
back into the land. This time they
took King Jehoiakim. They put
chains on him. They took him to
Babylon. They took things from
God's worship house, too.

The king of Egypt didn't come to
fight anymore. Babylon had taken
all of Egypt's land.

While Jehoiakim was still king,
God spoke to Jeremiah.

God told Jeremiah, "Go to Recab's
family. Ask them to come to the
worship house. Take them to a side
room. Then give them some wine to
drink."

So Jeremiah went to Recab's
family. He took them to God's
worship house. He took them to
a side room. He set out bowls of
wine. He set out cups. Then he said,
"Drink some wine."

But they said, "We don't drink
wine. Our father said our family

should never drink wine. He told us not to build houses or plant fields. He told us we must always live in tents. We move from place to place. We are nomads. We obeyed.

"But then Babylon's army came into the land. So we said, 'Come on! We must go to Jerusalem to stay safe.' That's why we're here."

Then God told Jeremiah to say these words to the people of Judah. "Learn a lesson. Learn to obey me. Recab told his family not to drink wine. They obeyed him. But I talked to you over and over again. You still have not obeyed me."

These are the words God told Jeremiah to say to Recab's family. "You obeyed your father. You did everything he told you. So there will always be people in your family who serve me."

The King in the Winter House

JEREMIAH 36; 45

God told Jeremiah, "Get a roll of paper. Write on it everything I told you. Write what I said about Israel, Judah, and other nations. Maybe the people will hear about it. Maybe they'll stop doing wrong and start doing right. Then I'll forgive them."

So Jeremiah called his helper, Baruch. Jeremiah told his helper what to write. Baruch wrote it on the roll of paper.

Then Baruch said, "I'm sad and tired. I'm worn out. I can't rest."

God gave Jeremiah some words for Baruch. God said, "I'm going to tear down what I built. I'm going to pull up what I planted. So don't look for great things for yourself. I'm bringing trouble to everybody. But wherever you go, you will get away. You will live."

Then Jeremiah said to Baruch, "The leaders won't let me leave this place. I can't go to the worship house. So you go. Go on a day when people are giving up food to worship God. Read to the people from this roll of paper. God is very angry at them. So maybe they'll turn to God. Maybe they'll stop doing wrong."

Baruch went to the worship house. He read from the roll of paper.

Now one of the leaders heard Baruch read. He heard everything God had told Jeremiah to write.

The man went to the palace. He

told all the other leaders what he had heard.

Then the leaders sent someone to get Baruch. He came. The leaders said, "Sit down, please. Read this to us."

So Baruch read God's words to them, too.

They looked around at each other. They were afraid. They said, "We have to tell the king about this! Where did you get these words? Did Jeremiah give them to you?"

"Yes," said Baruch. "He told me what to write. So I wrote it on this roll of paper."

"Go hide somewhere," said the leaders. "Take Jeremiah with you. Don't let anybody know where you are hiding."

The leaders took the roll of paper. They put it in one of their rooms. Then they went to see King Jehoiakim. They told him about the roll of paper.

King Jehoiakim sent a helper to get the roll of paper. The helper brought it back and read it to the king. All the leaders were standing there too.

Now the king was in his winter house. Fire was burning in a pot in front of him. His helper would read part of the paper roll. Then the king would cut that part off with a knife. He'd throw it into the fire pot. At last the whole roll of paper was burned.

The leaders asked the king not to burn the paper. But the king wasn't afraid. His helpers weren't afraid. They wouldn't listen to the leaders.

The king ordered his men to get Jeremiah and Baruch. He told them to put Jeremiah and Baruch in jail. But God had hidden them.

Then God spoke to Jeremiah again. "The king burned up the first roll of paper," said God. "So get another roll of paper. Write the same things you wrote on the first paper."

God also gave Jeremiah these words for the king. "You burned the roll of paper. You asked why Jeremiah wrote about Babylon coming. You asked why he wrote about them tearing up your land.

"So none of your children will become king after you. Your body will be thrown outside. The day will be hot for you. The frost will come on you at night. I'll pay you for the wrong you've done. I'll do everything I said in the roll of paper. I'll bring every trouble, because you didn't listen."

Then Jeremiah gave another roll of paper to Baruch. Jeremiah told Baruch what to write. Baruch wrote it. He put in even more of God's words.

The King's Food

DANIEL 1

Now Babylon's army had come into Judah before. They had taken riches from God's worship house. They had taken some people back to Babylon too.

Nebuchadnezzar was the king of Babylon. He asked to see some of the people from Judah. He wanted to see some young men from the families of Judah's leaders. They had to be good-looking. They had to be good learners. They had to know a lot. They had to be good enough to help the king.

The king wanted these young men to learn about Babylon. They had to learn the language. They had to learn the stories of Babylon too.

The king gave them food and wine from his table. He wanted them to study for three years. Then they could be his helpers.

Daniel and three of his friends were in this group of young men. The man in charge changed their names. The name he gave Daniel was Belteshazzar. He named Daniel's friends Shadrach, Meshach, and Abednego.

But Daniel chose not to eat the king's food. He chose not to drink the king's wine. He wanted to keep himself right and good.

The man in charge liked Daniel and his friends. God had worked in the man's heart. But the man said, "I'm afraid of my king. He told me to give you this food. The other young men will look strong and well. But you won't. What will happen when the king sees that? The king will kill me."

"Just try it for 10 days," said Daniel. "Give us vegetables to eat. Give us water to drink. See how we look after that. Then you can choose which food is right for us."

So the man in charge did what Daniel asked.

After 10 days, Daniel and his friends looked stronger. They looked more healthy than the other young men. So they got to eat only vegetables.

God helped Daniel and his friends learn. God helped them know and understand all kinds of things. He helped Daniel understand all kinds of dreams.

Time passed. One day the young men were taken to see the king. King Nebuchadnezzar talked with them. He found that the best ones were Daniel and his friends. So they got to be the king's helpers.

Daniel and his friends were wise. They understood everything the king asked them about. They were 10 times wiser than all the king's magic men.

A Figure in a Dream

DANIEL 2

Now King Nebuchadnezzar began to have dreams. He would worry about them. He couldn't sleep.

So the king called all his magic men. He said, "I had a dream. It troubles me. I want to know what it means."

"Our king!" said the magic men. "Tell us what the dream is. Then we'll tell you what it means."

"You must tell me what my dream is," said the king. "Then tell me what it means. If you don't, I'll cut you into pieces. I'll tear down your houses. But if you tell me, I'll give you gifts. I'll make you great."

"First tell us the dream," they said. "Then we'll tell you what it means."

"You're just trying to get more time," said the king. "You plan to trick me. You hope I'll change my mind. But if you don't tell me my dream, you're in trouble. So just tell me my dream. Then I'll know you can tell me what it means."

"Nobody in the world can do that!" said the men. "No king ever asked magic men to do something like this. It's too hard. Nobody but the gods can tell you your dream. And the gods don't live with people."

This made the king very angry.

He ordered all the wise men to be killed. Daniel and his friends were wise men. So they were going to be killed too.

The captain of the guard started to look for the men so he could kill them. But Daniel was very wise. He talked to the captain. "Why did the king order this?" he asked.

The captain told Daniel what had happened. Then Daniel went to the king. He asked the king for a little time. He wanted to find out what the king's dream meant.

Daniel went back home. He told his three friends about it. He asked them to pray to God about this. They wanted help so they wouldn't be killed with the other wise men.

That night God showed Daniel a picture of the king's dream. God told Daniel what it meant. Then Daniel praised God.

"Praise God's name forever!
    He is wise. He has all power!
    He makes kings, and he gets rid
        of kings.
He gives wise people their wise
        thoughts.
    He shows people things that were
        hidden.
    He knows what's in the dark.
I thank you, God. I praise you.
    You made me wise and strong.
You showed me what we asked for.
    You showed us the king's dream."

Daniel went to the captain of the guard. He said, "Don't kill the wise men. Take me to see the king. I'll tell him about his dream."

So the captain took Daniel to the king. He said, "Here's a man from Judah. He can tell you what your dream means."

"Can you tell me what my dream was?" asked the king. "Can you tell me what it means?"

"No wise man or magic man can tell you," said Daniel. "But there is a God in heaven. He shows us things we don't understand. He is showing you what's going to happen. Here's your dream.

"You were lying down. You started thinking about things that are going to happen. God showed this to me. It's not because I am wiser than others. It's so you can know and understand this dream.

"You saw a big figure in front of you. It was huge and wonderful! Its head was gold. Its chest and arms were silver. Its middle was brown metal. Its legs were iron. Its feet were part iron and part clay.

"You saw a rock hit the figure on its feet. The feet broke. Then the iron, clay, brown metal, silver, and gold broke. They were like dry grass on a barn floor. The wind blew them away. Nothing was left.

"But the rock grew and grew. It became a huge mountain. It filled the earth.

"That was your dream. Now I'll tell you what it means. You are the greatest king. God gave you power and made you great. He put you in charge of people, animals, and birds. You rule over them. You are the figure's gold head.

"Another kingdom will come after you. It won't be as great. Then another kingdom will come. That's what the brown metal stands for. It will rule the whole world.

"Then another kingdom will come. It will be as strong as iron. Iron can break everything into pieces. This kingdom will break all the others.

"You saw that the feet and toes were iron and clay. So the next kingdom will have two parts. Part of it will be strong. Part of it will be weak. The people will not all agree. They won't stay together.

"Then God will set up a new kingdom. It will last forever. It will break down the other kingdoms. That's what the rock stood for. That rock was cut from a mountain. But it was not cut by people's hands. It broke the iron, brown metal, clay, silver, and gold.

"The great God just showed you what's going to happen. This dream is true. You can trust that it means what I said."

Then the king bowed to Daniel. He

said good things about him. He sent for a gift to give Daniel. He said, "I'm sure your God is the God of gods. He is the Lord of kings. He is the one who shows what's hidden. I know that's true, because you were able to tell my dream!"

The king gave Daniel many gifts. He put Daniel in charge of all Babylon. He put Daniel in charge of all the wise men.

Daniel asked the king to let his three friends help him. So the king let Shadrach, Meshach, and Abednego help Daniel rule. Daniel stayed on as one of the king's special friends.

JUNE 23

Like a Dead Donkey
JEREMIAH 22:18-22

Here's what God told Jeremiah about King Jehoiakim of Judah.

"People won't cry for him when he dies.
   His body will be dragged off like a dead donkey.
He will be thrown out of Jerusalem."

"Go and cry.
Nations who were your friends have been torn down.
I told you it would happen.
   But you thought you had no problems.

You said, 'I won't listen!'
That's the way you've been since you were young.
   You have not obeyed me.
Nations who were your friends will be taken away.
   You'll feel no good.
It's all because you did what was wrong."

Babylon
2 KINGS 24:8-20; 2 CHRONICLES 36:16; JEREMIAH 22:24-30; 37:1-2

Jehoiachin was Judah's next king. He was 18 years old. But he was a bad king. He did what was wrong.

Then God spoke about Jehoiachin. "If you were a ring, I'd pull you off my finger," said God. "I'll give you to the land of Babylon. You will die there. You will never come back to this land."

Jehoiachin is like something nobody wants.
   He will be taken to a land he doesn't know.
Oh, land, land, land!
   Hear God's Word.
Here's what God says.
"Write it down.
   Jehoiachin is like a man with no children.
He will not see good things in his life.
   None of his children will be kings."

Then Babylon's army marched to Jerusalem and fought against the city.

Jehoiachin and the leaders gave up. So King Nebuchadnezzar took them to Babylon. It happened just like God said it would.

Babylon took all the riches from God's worship house. They took the riches from the palace. They took them to Babylon. They put them in their idol's worship house. They took all the fighting men of Judah. They took all the artists. They took all the workers who could make things. They took 10,000 (ten thousand) people in all. They left only the people who were very poor.

King Nebuchadnezzar chose Zedekiah to be king of Judah. But he was a bad king. He did what was wrong. He would not obey God. The people turned away from God too.

God sent prophets to talk to his people again and again. God felt sorry for them. But the people made fun of God's prophets. They thought God's words were nothing. So God got angry at them. Then he sent them away from him.

The Figs

JEREMIAH 24

Now God showed me two baskets of figs. They were in front of God's worship house. Good figs were in one basket. Bad figs filled the other basket. They were not good to eat.

God asked me, "What do you see, Jeremiah?"

"Figs," I said. "The good ones are very good. But the bad figs are too bad to eat."

Then God spoke to me. God said, "I sent the people of Judah to Babylon. They are like good figs. They are good, so I will watch over them. Someday I'll bring them back to their land.

"I'll build Judah up," says God. "I won't tear the people down. They'll be like a plant that I put in the ground. I'll give them hearts that know me. They'll know I'm the Lord. They'll be my people. I'll be their God. They will come back to me with all their hearts.

"But Zedekiah and his leaders are like bad figs," says God. "So I'll make the other kingdoms hate them.

"People will make fun of Zedekiah and his leaders," says God. "People will say bad things about them. Wherever they go, there will be fighting. There will not be enough food. There will be sickness. This will happen until they are gone."

A Letter to Babylon

JEREMIAH 29:1-7, 10-13, 24-32

Jeremiah sent a letter to God's people in Babylon. In the letter were God's words.

"I, the Lord your God, want you to build houses. Move in. Plant gardens. Eat the food you grow. Get married. Have children. Let your children get married. Let them have children. Then there will be more and more people.

"Help the city you live in. Make peace. Pray for your city. Then things will go well there. That means things will go well for you, too.

"I'll come back for you in 70 years. I'll take you back to Judah. I'll keep my promise to bring you home. I know the plans I made for you," says God.

"I plan to bring good things to you," says God. "I plan to give you hope. I plan good things for the days that are coming. Then you'll pray to me, and I will listen to you. You'll look for me. You'll find me when you look with all your heart."

Now a man who was not a real prophet wrote some letters. He sent them to priests in Jerusalem. He wrote, "Crazy men acting like prophets should be stopped. So why didn't you stop Jeremiah? Jeremiah sent a letter to us in Babylon. He said we'd be here a long time. He told us to build houses and move in. He told us to plant gardens. He said to eat the food we grow."

A priest read the letter to Jeremiah.

Then God spoke to Jeremiah. He said to send another message to his people in Babylon. The words were about the man who was not a real prophet. "He lied to you. I didn't send him. I'll pay him back. He won't see the good things I'll do for my people."

Jeremiah Wears a Yoke

JEREMIAH 27:1-6, 9-11; 28

While Zedekiah was king, God spoke to Jeremiah. "Make a big wooden beam to go across your shoulders. It's a yoke like the ox wears when it plows the field. Wear it around your neck. Then send a message to the kings of the nations."

This was God's message. "I made the earth by my power. I made people and animals. I give the earth to anyone I want. So now I give your countries to Babylon. The king of Babylon will even be in charge of animals.

"So don't listen to the people who say this won't happen. They lie. Let

Babylon rule over you. Then I'll let you stay in your own land," says God.

There was a prophet named Hananiah. He told Jeremiah that this is what God says. "I'll make the king of Babylon leave you alone. In two years I'll bring back everything he took. I'll bring King Jehoiachin back. I'll bring back all the other people."

Then Hananiah took the yoke off of Jeremiah's neck. He broke it. He said that God told him these words. "This is the way I'll break Babylon's power. I'll break it in two years."

Some time passed. Then God told Jeremiah to go and tell Hananiah these words. "You broke a wooden yoke. So I'll put an iron yoke on you. All these nations will serve Babylon. King Nebuchadnezzar will even be in charge of wild animals."

So Jeremiah went to Hananiah. Jeremiah said, "Listen! God did not send you. You tell lies. So God says that you are going to die this year. It's all because you turned people against God."

Later that same year, Hananiah died.

Like a Hammer
JEREMIAH 23:25-32, 40

Now about the prophets.
"Some prophets lie. They say I sent them. Then they say, 'I had a dream! I had a dream!'

"How long will they keep doing this? They think their dreams will make people forget me. But my word is like fire. It's like a hammer that breaks a rock," says God.

"So I'm against those prophets," says God. "They take words from each other. They say the words are from me. I didn't send them. They are not doing any good.

"I'll pay people back for saying their words are my words," says God.

A Desert Forever
JEREMIAH 50:11-12, 31-32; 51:59-64

King Zedekiah asked one of his helpers to go with him to Babylon. Jeremiah wrote God's message to Babylon on a roll of paper. Then Jeremiah gave this message to the king's helper.

Here's God's message about Babylon.

"Right now the people of Babylon
    are glad.
    But someday they'll feel like
        nothing.
Babylon will be a desert.

"See? I'm against you.
    You are proud," says God.
"Now it's time to pay you back.

401

The proud one will fall.
Nobody will help Babylon up."

Jeremiah told the king's helper, "Read God's message out loud in Babylon.

"Let the people know that God will get rid of Babylon. People won't live there. Animals won't live there. It will be a desert forever," said Jeremiah.

"Then tie a rock to this roll of paper," said Jeremiah. "Throw it into the river. Say that this is the way Babylon will sink. Babylon won't come up anymore. It's because of the trouble God is bringing. Babylon will fall."

JUNE 25

The People Change Their Minds

JEREMIAH 34:8-22

King Zedekiah made a deal with all the people in Jerusalem. He said all the slaves could go free. So the people said they would let their slaves go free. And they did.

But later, the people changed their minds. They took their slaves back. They wouldn't let them go.

So God spoke to Jeremiah. "I made a promise to your families long ago," said God. "I took them out of Egypt. I said my people could be slaves for no more than six years. Then you would have to let them go free. But your families long ago didn't obey me.

"Not so long ago you acted like you were sorry. You did what was right. You set your slaves free. Now you changed your minds. You took your slaves back.

"You didn't obey me. You didn't let your slaves go free. They are my people. You are my people too. So I will set you free. You are free to die in fights. You are free to go without food, and free to get sick.

"I'll give King Zedekiah to the enemies in Babylon," says God. "I'll bring Babylon here to fight. I'll get rid of the cities in Judah. Nobody will be able to live here."

In the Wind Storm

EZEKIEL 1

Ezekiel was with God's people in Babylon. He wrote this from Babylon.

We had been in Babylon for five years. One day I was by the Kebar River. All of a sudden, I saw pictures in my mind. I saw heaven open up. I saw things about God.

I saw a wind storm. It came from the north. There was a big cloud. Lightning flashed. Bright light was all around the cloud. The very middle looked like fire and shining metal.

Four beings were in the fire. They were like men. But each one had four faces and four wings. Their legs did not bend. Their feet were like cows' feet. Their feet shone like shiny brown metal.

The beings had hands under their wings. Their hands looked like people's hands. Their wings touched each other. They moved straight ahead. They didn't turn at all.

Each being had a face like a man's face. Each one had a lion's face on the right side. An ox's face was on the left side. There was also an eagle's face.

The wings went out and up. Each being had two wings. Each wing touched the wing of the being beside it. Each being had two wings that covered its body.

The beings would go wherever their spirit went. They looked like burning coals of fire. Fire went back and forth between the beings. Lightning flashed from the fire. The beings went back and forth like lightning.

I watched them. Then I saw a wheel on the ground beside each being. Each wheel shone. Each one seemed to go into another wheel. Eyes filled the rims of the wheels.

The beings would move, and the wheels would move. The beings went up from the ground. Then the wheels went up. They would go wherever their spirit would go. The spirit of the beings was in the wheels.

A wide space was above the heads of the beings. The space shone. It looked like ice.

The beings moved. They sounded like water rushing and roaring. They sounded like God's voice. They sounded like a noisy army. Then they stood still and brought their wings down.

A voice came from the space above them. Above the space was something that looked like a king's chair. This throne was made of beautiful blue stone. Someone who looked like a man sat on the king's throne. His top half looked like shiny metal, full of fire. His bottom half looked like fire. Bright light was all around him. He looked like a rainbow in the clouds.

That's what God's greatness looked like. I put my face down to the ground when I saw it. Then I heard a voice.

JUNE 26

Eating Paper
EZEKIEL 2; 3:1-3

God said, "Stand up, Ezekiel. I'll talk to you."

The Spirit came into me while

God was talking. He pulled me up so I was standing. I heard God talk to me.

God said, "Ezekiel, I'm sending you. I'm sending you to the nation of Israel. The people turned against me. Their hearts are hard. Tell them, 'Here's what God says.'

"They might listen. They might not listen. But they will know that a prophet talked to them.

"Don't be afraid of them. Don't be afraid of what they say. You must tell them what I say, even if they don't listen. Don't be like them. Listen to what I tell you. Open your mouth. Eat what I give you."

Then I saw a hand. It held out a roll of paper for me. He unrolled the paper. It had writing on both sides. It had sad words and bad news.

God said, "Eat this roll of paper. Then go speak to my people."

So I ate the roll of paper. It was sweet like honey in my mouth.

Hard Hearts

EZEKIEL 3:4-11; 4:1-12, 16-17

Then God said, "Go to my people. Tell them my words. They speak your language. They understand your words. But they won't want to listen to you. That's because they don't want to listen to me. They have hard hearts. But I'll make you as strong as they are. I'll make your forehead as hard as stone. It will be harder than rock. So don't be scared of them.

"Listen," said God. "Think about what I'm saying to you. Go to your people here in Babylon. Talk to them. Tell them what I tell you to say. Tell them, even if they don't listen.

"Now get a clay writing pad," said God. "Draw a picture of Jerusalem on it. Make it look as if enemy ladders are going up to the walls. Draw enemy camps around it. Then get an iron pan. Use it for an iron wall. Put it between you and the city. Then look at it, as if you're fighting against the city. This will be a sign for my people.

"Then lie down on your left side. Lie there one day for every year my people in Israel sinned. Israel sinned for 390 years. So lie there for 390 days.

"After that, lie down again. This time, lie down on your right side.

Lie there for 40 days, because Judah sinned for 40 years. Turn your face toward Jerusalem, and speak against Judah. I'll tie you up with ropes. Then you can't turn over to your other side.

"Eat bread and drink water. Plan how much you'll eat and drink each day. Plan when you'll eat and drink. Bake your bread where people can see it.

"I'll take the food away from Jerusalem," said God. "The people will have to plan how much to eat. They'll have to plan how much to drink. They won't have enough. They'll get weaker and weaker because of the wrong they've done."

Three Piles of Hair

EZEKIEL 5:1-4, 8-13

"Get a sharp sword," said God. "Use it to shave your head and your face. Make three piles of hair. Burn one pile of hair inside the city. Take one pile of hair out of the city. Hit it with your sword. Throw the last pile up into the wind. This shows that I'll chase the people with a sword.

"Keep a few hairs. Put them in your robe. Throw some into the fire. Let them burn up. This shows that a fire will go out from there. It will go to all of Israel.

"Here's what God says. I'm against you, Jerusalem. I'll pay you back for the wrong you've done. It's all because of your idols. I won't feel sorry for you.

"Some of your people will die of sickness. Some will die of hunger. Some will die in fights. Some will leave. They'll go here and there through the world. Then I'll stop being angry. They'll know that I said this would happen. I am God. I have spoken."

It's the End!

EZEKIEL 6:1-10; 7:2, 20-21, 27

Then God told me to speak his words against Israel's mountains. "Mountains, I'm going to bring fighting. Towns will be torn down. Idols will be torn down. People will be killed.

"Some people will get away. But they'll have to live in other nations. Then they'll remember me and be sorry they did wrong. They'll know that I'm the Lord.

"Trouble! Trouble like you've never seen before is coming! It's the end! It's the end! It has come!

"They were proud of their beautiful gold rings and neck bands. They used their gold to make idols. So other nations will rob my people of their riches. I'll pay them back for the wrong they've done. Then they'll know I'm the Lord."

Pictures on the Walls

EZEKIEL 8

We had been in Babylon for six years. I sat in my house. The leaders of Judah sat there with me. God came to me there.

I looked, and I saw someone who looked like a man. The bottom half of him looked like fire. The top half looked like shiny metal. He held out something that looked like a hand. He took hold of my hair.

Then the Spirit picked me up. He held me between the earth and sky. He put pictures of Jerusalem in my mind. Then I saw God's greatness. It was the same as what I had seen before.

The Spirit said, "Look north."

So I looked, and I saw an idol.

"Do you see the terrible things they're doing?" he asked. "You will see things that are even more terrible."

He showed me where people go into the yard around the worship house. I saw a hole in the wall.

"Dig into the wall," he said.

So I dug into the wall. There I saw a door.

"Go in," he said. "Look at the bad things they are doing."

So I went in and looked. Pictures were drawn all over the walls. They

were pictures of crawling animals and idols. Seventy leaders of Israel stood in front of the pictures. They were worshiping the animals and idols.

"See what the leaders are doing in the dark?" he said. "They say that I don't see them. They say that I've left their land. You will see things more terrible than this."

Then he took me to the north gate of the worship house. I saw some women sitting there. They were crying for an idol.

"See this?" he said. "You'll see things more terrible than this."

Then he took me into the inside yard. At the door of the worship house, 25 men were worshiping the sun.

"See this?" he said. "Is this a small thing? They also do things that are hateful and mean. They are making me angry. So I won't feel sorry for them. I won't save them. I won't listen even if they shout in my ears."

The Man with the Writing Kit

EZEKIEL 9

Then I heard the Spirit call loudly, "Bring the city guards. Bring them with their swords."

I saw six men coming. There was another man with them. He wore linen clothes. He carried a writing kit. They came in. They stood by the altar.

Then God's greatness moved to the door of the worship house. God called to the man with the writing kit. God said, "Go through Jerusalem. Find people who are sad about Jerusalem's sins. Make a mark on their heads."

God talked to the other men. "Follow him," said God. "Don't touch people who have the mark on their heads. But kill everyone else. Don't feel sorry for them. Start at the worship house."

So they started with the leaders at the worship house.

I was left alone. I fell down on my face. I cried, "God! Are you going to get rid of all the people?"

"My people have many sins," said God. "I'll pay them back for what they've done."

Then the man with the writing kit came back. "I did what you told me to do," he said.

Turning Wheels

EZEKIEL 10:1-2, 6-18

Then I saw what looked like a king's chair. The throne was made of beautiful blue stone. It was above the living beings' heads.

God talked to the man with the writing kit. "Go under the beings where the wheels are. Pick up burning coals. Throw the coals here and there over the city."

I watched. The man went to where the living beings were. He stood beside a wheel. One being put his hand in the fire that was there. He put some fire into the man's hands. The man took it and went out.

Then I saw four shiny wheels by the beings. One wheel was by each being. Each wheel went through another wheel. The wheels went where the beings went.

The beings went where they were looking. Their whole bodies were covered with eyes. Even their backs and hands and wings had eyes. The wheels were full of eyes too. I heard that the wheels were called "turning wheels."

The beings held out their wings and went up. The wheels stayed beside them and went up too.

God's greatness left the front of the worship house. It stopped above the beings.

Picked Up by the Spirit

EZEKIEL 11:1-8, 16-25

Then the Spirit picked me up. He took me to the east gate of the worship house. I saw 25 men there.

God said, "These men plan bad things. They tell lies to people. They say that soon it will be time to build houses. So speak against them."

God's Spirit came to me. He gave me these words to say. "You killed many people. So I'll send you out of the city. You are afraid of fighting. But that's just what I'm going to bring."

I put my face down to the ground. I said, "God! Are you going to get rid of everybody?"

Then God said, "I sent some of my people far away. I sent them to other lands. Tell them that I'll bring them back to Israel.

"They'll come back and get rid of idols. I'll put a new spirit in them. I'll take away their hard heart. I'll put a soft heart in them. Then they'll obey my laws. They'll be my people, and I'll be their God."

The beings held their wings out. God's greatness went up from the city. It stopped over the mountains to the east.

Then the Spirit picked me up.

He took me back to the people in Babylon. The dream in my mind faded away. I told the people everything God had shown me.

Digging through the Wall

EZEKIEL 12:1-13, 16

Sometime later, God spoke to me. "You live with people who turn away from me. They have eyes to see with, but they don't look. They have ears to hear with, but they don't listen.

"So pack up your things like you're going away. Go out in the daytime. Let people watch you. Go to another place. Maybe they will understand.

"Dig through the wall. Take your things through the hole in the wall. Carry your things on your shoulders. Take them out as the sun goes down. Cover your face so you can't see the land. This will be a sign for the people."

So I did what God said. I packed my things. I took them out in the daytime. In the evening, I dug through the wall. I carried my things out as the sun went down. I carried them on my shoulders. The people watched.

The next morning, God spoke to me again. "Did my people ask you what you were doing? Tell my people in Jerusalem that they'll have to do this too. Another nation will take them away.

"The prince will carry his things on his shoulders. He will leave as the sun goes down. He will go through a hole in the wall. He will cover his face so he can't see the land. I'll bring him to Babylon. He will die there.

"But I'll save some of the people. They will be sorry in the lands where I send them."

The Baby No One Wanted

EZEKIEL 16

Then God said to tell Jerusalem, "You were like a baby that no one wanted. But I took care of you. You were mine. I made you beautiful. I gave you everything you needed. You had fine flour and honey and olive oil. Everyone knew who you were. You were like a queen.

"But you trusted in your beauty. You turned away from me. You made idols. You didn't remember how I saved you long ago.

"There's bad news for you! You made me angry. So I sent enemies to you. They took your country.

"You are like a wife who leaves her husband. She leaves him so she can love another man. You left me so you could love idols.

"So I'll give you to nations who worship idols. They'll throw rocks at you. They'll cut you with their swords. They'll burn your houses down. I'll pay you back for the wrong things you've done.

"But you'll remember what you did. You'll feel bad about it. I'll promise to be your God. And you'll know I'm the Lord. I'll forgive you. And you'll feel bad and be quiet," says God.

JUNE 29

An Eagle Plants a Cedar Tree

EZEKIEL 17

Then God said to tell his people this story. "A big eagle came to the land. He had strong wings. He had long feathers of many different colors.

"The eagle held

on to the top of a cedar tree. Then he broke the top of the tree off. He took it to a land where people buy and sell things. The eagle planted the tree there.

"Then the eagle got some seeds from your land. He planted them in good dirt. The seeds got lots of water. So they began to grow. They made a vine.

"The vine was low, but it grew wide. It grew leaves. The branches turned toward the eagle. The vine's roots grew down under it.

"Then another eagle came along. He had strong wings. He had lots of feathers.

"The vine's roots turned and grew toward the other eagle. Its branches turned toward him. The vine waited for him to water it. It forgot there was good dirt and lots of water where it was planted.

"The vine should make fruit. But it will be pulled up. The fruit will be pulled off. Then it will dry up."

God said to tell his people what this story means. "The king of Babylon is like the first eagle. He went to Jerusalem. He took away the kings and leaders. He took them to Babylon.

"Then he put a new king in charge of Jerusalem. He made the new kingdom low like the vine. It had to obey Babylon.

"But the new king turned against Babylon. He sent people to Egypt for help. Egypt is like the other eagle.

The new king asked Egypt for horses and an army. But Egypt's army won't help. Jerusalem's king promised to obey the king of Babylon. He didn't keep his promise. So he won't get away.

"I, the Lord God, will set a trap for him. He will get caught. I'll take him to Babylon. I'll pay him back for the wrong he has done.

"I'll save some of my people. They'll be like the top of the cedar tree. I'll plant my kingdom on a high mountain.

"I am God. I said it, and I will do it."

JUNE 30

Sour Grapes
EZEKIEL 18:1-25, 30-32

God said that there's a saying about Israel. "The fathers eat sour grapes, and the children taste it."

Then God said, "People won't say this anymore. That's because every person who lives belongs to me. Fathers belong to me, and children belong to me. Each person will get in trouble for his own sins.

"Let's say there's a good person.
He does what's right and fair.
He doesn't worship idols.
He stays with his own wife.
He doesn't give anyone a hard time.

He gives back what he borrows.
He doesn't rob anyone.
   He gives food to hungry people.
   He gives clothes to people who
      need clothes.
He keeps himself from doing wrong.
   He is fair.
He obeys my laws.
   He does what's right. He will live,"
      says God.

"But let's say his son is mean. He
kills or does something else bad,
even though his father didn't.

"He worships idols.
He leaves his wife for another woman.
He gives poor people a hard time.
He robs people.
He doesn't give back what he borrowed.
He does mean, hateful things.

"Will the son live? No. It's all
because he has done these terrible
things. He must take the blame for
what he has done.

   "But let's say this man has a son
too. His son sees what his father
did. So he doesn't do these things.

"He doesn't worship idols.
He stays with his own wife.
He doesn't give anyone a hard time.
He doesn't rob people.
He gives food to hungry people.
He gives clothes to people who
      need clothes.

He keeps himself from doing wrong.
He obeys my laws and follows me.

   "This man won't have to take the
blame for what his father did. He
will live. His father will die for his
own sin.

   "The person who sins will die.
The son won't be blamed for what
his father did. The father won't be
blamed for what his son did. Good
things will come to the man who
did right. The man who did wrong
will be blamed.

   "But let's say a sinful man
changes. He starts obeying my laws.
He starts doing what is right and
good. Then he will live. I won't
remember any of the wrong things
he has done. He will live, because of
the good he has done.

   "Am I glad to see sinful people
die? No. But I'm glad to see them
stop doing wrong. I'm glad to see
them live.

   "Now let's say a good man
changes. He turns away from the
right things. He starts doing wrong.
Then I won't remember the right
things he has done. That's because
he has not kept obeying me. So he
will be blamed for the wrong he has
done. He will die for it.

   "You might say that's not fair. But
listen. It's what you do that's not fair.
So change! Get rid of your sin. Get a
new heart. Get a new spirit. It doesn't

make me happy to see anyone die. Start doing right, and live!"

The Cooking Pot

2 KINGS 25:1-2; 2 CHRONICLES 36:11-13; JEREMIAH 52:1-5; EZEKIEL 24:1-6, 11-14

In Judah, King Zedekiah had promised to let Babylon rule his land. But then he turned against Babylon's king, Nebuchadnezzar.

So King Nebuchadnezzar marched out with his army to fight Jerusalem. They camped around the city. Then they started fighting.

Now Ezekiel had been in Babylon for nine years. One day God said,

"Write down this date. Today Babylon started fighting Jerusalem. Then tell these people a story. Say that this is what God says.

"There's bad news for Jerusalem.
Put a pot on the coals without
    anything in it.
Let it get hot, so the pot glows.
Let the dirt melt away.
    But it won't be clean.

"I tried to clean you from your sin. But you wouldn't get clean. You won't be clean until I've stopped being angry at you. I am God, and I have said this. You'll be judged for what you've done," says God.

Messages about Trouble for Judah

A Way to Live, a Way to Die

JEREMIAH 21

Back in Jerusalem, King Zedekiah sent two men to Jeremiah. They said, "Babylon is fighting us. Ask God about this. Maybe he will do something to make Babylon stop fighting."

Jeremiah said to tell King Zedekiah these words from God. "I'm turning this fight against you. The people are fighting you outside the city walls. But I'll bring them inside.

"I myself will fight against you with my anger," says God. "I'll kill people and animals in the city. They'll die of sickness.

"Then I'll give the people who are left to Babylon. I'll give King Zedekiah to Babylon," says God. "The king of Babylon will kill them. He won't feel sorry for them at all.

"I'm showing you two ways," says God. "One way is a way to live. The other way is a way to die. If you stay in the city, you'll die. But if you give up to Babylon, you'll live.

"I've planned bad things for this city," says God. "The king of Babylon will burn it down.

"These are my words for the king and his family," says God.

"Do what's fair every morning.
  Save people from others who are
    bringing them trouble.
  Help people who have been
    robbed.
If you don't, I'll be angry at you.
  It's all because you have done
    what's wrong.
I'll bring you trouble because of
    your sins."

The King's Palace

JEREMIAH 22:1-9; 34:1-7

God told Jeremiah to go to the palace and give them this message. "Hear what God says. Do what is

413

right and fair. Don't do wrong. Be careful to obey my rules.

"Then your kings will come through the palace gates," says God. "They'll ride their chariots and horses. Their leaders and people will be with them.

"If you don't obey, I promise this," says God. "The palace will turn into a pile of sticks and stones.

"You may be like the top of the
        mountain to me.
    But I'll make you like a desert.
    Nobody will live in the towns.
I'll send people to get rid of you.
    They'll bring their swords.
They'll cut down your beautiful
        wooden posts.
    They'll burn them in the fire.

"People from many nations will pass this city. They'll ask why God did this to the great city. The answer will be that it's because they turned against God. They worshiped idols."

Then God said to give King Zedekiah this message from God. "I'm getting ready to give this city to Babylon. King Nebuchadnezzar will burn it down. You won't get away from him. He will catch you. You'll see him with your own eyes. He will talk to you. Then you'll have to go to Babylon.

"But hear what God promises to you, Zedekiah. You won't be killed.

You'll die in peace. The people will say good things about you. They'll cry for you."

So Jeremiah told this to King Zedekiah. All this time, Babylon was fighting Jerusalem. Only two other forts were left in Judah. The people there were fighting too.

JULY 2

Jeremiah's Jail

JEREMIAH 32

Jeremiah had to stay in the guards' yard at the palace. King Zedekiah had made it Jeremiah's jail.

Zedekiah had said, "Why are you saying these things? You say that God is going to give us to Babylon. You say I won't get away. You say I'll be taken to Babylon. You say we won't win this fight."

Jeremiah said, "Here's what God told me. He said my cousin would come and say, 'Buy my field.' That's just what happened.

"I knew that's what God had said. So I bought the field. I paid my cousin seven pieces of silver for it. I signed the papers to own the field. I gave them to Baruch. The people sitting in the yard saw it.

"I told Baruch, 'Here's what God says. Take these papers. Put them in a clay jar. That way, they'll stay safe for a long time. Someday people will buy houses in this land again. They'll buy fields, too.'

"After that, I prayed.

"God, you made the earth and space with your great power. Nothing is too hard for you. You show your love to thousands of people. But you bring people trouble for the wrong they've done.

"Great, strong God, your name is the Lord of All Power. Your plans are great. You do powerful things. You see what people do. If they do good, you give them good things. If they do bad, you send them trouble. You did wonders in Egypt, and you still do wonders.

"See how the enemies fight against this city? There's sickness. There's not enough food. Babylon will take charge of this city. You told about it, and it has happened. But still, you told me to buy the field."

Then God said to Jeremiah, "I'm the Lord. I'm the God of all people. Nothing is too hard for me. I'm going to give this city to Babylon. They will take over. They'll come in and burn the city.

"Judah's people have done wrong," says God. "They've made me so angry, I'm getting rid of them. They wouldn't listen. They set up idols.

"But someday I'll bring my people back from other lands. I'll bring them here," says God. "I'll let them live safely here. They'll be my people, and I'll be their God.

"I'll give my people a heart that wants to obey me. They'll always obey me," says God. "We'll make a promise together. It will last forever. I'll never stop doing good for them. They'll never turn away from me. I'll be glad to be good to them.

"I've sent trouble to these people. But I'll also bring the good things I promised. Someday people will buy fields again. They'll buy in the towns and in the hills. I'll bring good days back again," says God.

Turning Sadness into Gladness
JEREMIAH 31:1-9, 15-17, 25-26

"I will be the God of all the family groups of Israel. They will be my people," says God.

Here's what God says.

"The people who live will see my
goodness.
I will give Israel rest."

God came to us before. This is what
he said.

"I loved you with love that lasts
forever.
I brought you to me with my love
and kindness.
I'll build you again.
You'll dance with joy again.
You'll plant fields and enjoy their
fruit again.
The people who watch will call
everyone to come.
They'll say,
'Let's go to Zion, God's city.
Let's go and see our God.'"

Here's what God says.

"Sing with joy!
Shout for the greatest nation.
Let everyone hear your praise.
Say, 'God, save your people.'
See? I'll bring them from all over
the earth.
Many, many people will come
back.
They'll come crying.
They'll come praying.
I'll lead them by rivers.
I'll lead them on a flat road.
They won't trip and fall, because
I'm their father."

Here's what God says.

"A crying voice comes from Ramah.
It sounds like Rachel crying for her
children.
She won't let anyone cheer her up.
Her children have died."

Here's what God says.

"Stop crying.
Good things will come to you
because of your work.
There is hope for the days that are
coming.
Your children will come back to
their land.
I'll make tired people feel like new."

After I heard these words from God,
I woke up. I looked around. I had
slept well.

A Wise King

JEREMIAH 23:5-6; 33:14-26

"Someday, I'll bring a wise King,"
says God.
"I'll keep the promise I made to
Israel and Judah.

"I'll make a Branch grow from King
David's family.
He will do what is fair and right.
Judah will be saved.
Jerusalem will be safe.

Israel will be safe too.
The Branch will be called the Lord
    Our Goodness."

God told Jeremiah, "Someone from David's family will always be king. Someone from Levi's family will always be a priest."

God spoke to Jeremiah again. "Can you stop day from coming? No. Can you stop the night time? No. Then no one can stop the promise I made to David. No one can stop the promise I made to the priests.

"I, the Lord your God, keep my promises to bring day and night. I made the laws that the sky and earth obey. So I won't turn away from my people. I will bring back good days for them. I will take care of them."

Little Ones and Big Ones
JEREMIAH 31:27-28, 31-40

"Someday I'll bring my people back," says God. "I watched over them before and sent them away. This time I'll watch over them and bring them back.

"The people of Israel and I will
    make a new promise together.
    The people of Judah and I will
    make a new promise.
It won't be like the promise I made
    before.

I took them out of Egypt.
I was like a husband to them.
    But they broke their part of the
    promise.

"Here's the new promise
    I'll make with them.
I'll put my laws in their minds.
    It will be as if I write them inside
    their hearts.
I'll be their God.
    They'll be my people.
They won't have to teach their
    neighbors.
    They won't have to say, 'Know
    God.'
That's because they'll all know me.
    Little ones and big ones will
    know me.
I'll forgive their sins.
    I won't remember their sins
    anymore."

God tells the sun to shine in the
    daytime.
    He tells the moon and stars to
    shine at night.
He makes the sea toss.
    He makes the waves roar.
He is the God Who Has All Power.
    That's his name.
Here's what he says.
"Will Israel stop being a nation?
    Only if these things stop.
Will I turn against Israel?
    Only if you can measure all of
    space.

Only if you can dig into the
middle of the earth.

"Someday Jerusalem will be built
again," says God.
"It will never be torn down
again."

A Sad Song

EZEKIEL 27:1-24, 26-27

One day God spoke to Ezekiel. He
said to sing a sad song for the city
of Tyre. People went to Tyre so they
could sail on the sea. Tyre's people
sold things to people in many lands.
But here is God's sad song.

"Tyre, you say you're beautiful.
You say there's nothing wrong
with you.
You lived on the high seas.
The people who built you made
you beautiful.
They built you with wood from
pine trees.
They used cedar trees too.
They used oak and other wood.
They used ivory.

They brought linen cloth from Egypt.
They used blue and purple cloth.
Sailors lived there.
All the sea's ships came to buy
and sell.

"You had an army of fighting men.
They hung their shields on your
walls.
They hung the helmets for their
heads on your walls too.
Men looked out over your walls to
watch for enemies.
Men looked out of the tall towers.

"You had lots of things for others
to buy. People traded silver, iron,
tin, and lead for things you had.
"People traded work horses, war
horses, and donkeys.
"People paid you with ivory and
black wood.
"People traded beautiful blue and
red stones. They traded linen cloth
and purple cloth.
"Even Judah and Israel traded
with you. They traded wheat and
sweets. They traded honey and oil
for the things you had.
"People traded blankets to go
under horses' saddles.
"People traded sheep, rams, and
goats for what you had.
"People traded spices, beautiful
stones, and gold.
"People traded beautiful clothes.
They traded colorful rugs.

"But the east wind will break your
ships into pieces.
It will happen in the middle of
the sea.
Everything on your ships will go
down into the sea."

Not a God

EZEKIEL 28:1-2, 6-19

God told Ezekiel what to say to
Tyre's king.

"Your heart is proud.
You say you're a god."
You may think you are as wise as a
god.
But you are a man. You're not a
god.
You think your wise thinking made
you rich.
So your heart is proud.

"I am God.
I'm going to bring other lands
against you.
It's all because you think you're
so wise.
I'll bring mean nations.
They'll fight you, and they'll win.
Then will you say that you're a god?
You'll see that you're only a man.
You're not a god.
I am God.
I say this will happen."

God spoke to Ezekiel again. God
said to sing a sad song about Tyre's
king. This was God's sad song.

"There was nothing wrong with
you.
You were wise and beautiful.
You were in Eden, God's garden.
You wore beautiful, shiny stones.
They were red, yellow, green,
white, blue, and pink.
You had gold.
It was ready for you when you
were made.
I chose you to be an angel guard.
You lived on God's special, holy
mountain.
You walked around the stones of
fire.
You had not done anything wrong.
Then one day something bad
happened.
You traded with people here and
there.
You became hurtful.
You sinned.
So I made you leave my mountain.
I threw you out, you angel who
guards.
Your heart grew proud because you
were so beautiful.
So I threw you down to the earth.
You were a terrible sight to kings.
You lied when you bought and sold.
You had many sins.
So I made fire come from you.
It burned you up.

419

The nations who knew you are
shocked.
Your end is terrible."

A Room under the Ground

JEREMIAH 37

Back in Judah, King Zedekiah sent a message to Jeremiah. It said, "Please pray to God for us."

Babylon's army was fighting Jerusalem. Then Egypt's army marched out to help Jerusalem.

The army of Babylon heard that Egypt's army was coming. So the ones who were fighting moved away from Jerusalem.

Then God gave Jeremiah this message for King Zedekiah. "The army of Egypt came to help you. But it will go back to Egypt. Then Babylon will come again to fight Jerusalem. The people will take over the city. They'll burn it down.

"Don't lie to yourselves," says God. "Don't think that Babylon will leave you alone. They won't!

"Let's say you won over the whole army of Babylon. Let's say that only hurt men were in Babylon's tents. They would still come and burn down this city," says God.

Now Jeremiah started to leave Jerusalem. He was going to go to the land he owned. He was going out through a city gate.

But the captain of the guard stopped Jeremiah. "You're leaving us and going to help Babylon!" he said.

"No, I'm not," said Jeremiah.

The captain wouldn't listen. He took Jeremiah to the city leaders.

The city leaders were angry at Jeremiah. They had him beaten. They put him in jail in a room under the ground. Jeremiah had to stay there a long time.

Then King Zedekiah asked guards to bring Jeremiah to see him. So Jeremiah was taken to the king's palace.

King Zedekiah asked him, "Did God tell you anything?"

"Yes," said Jeremiah. "You'll be given to the king of Babylon."

Then Jeremiah said, "Where are your own fake prophets? They told you Babylon wouldn't fight Jerusalem. What did I do wrong? Why am I in jail? Don't send me back to the jail under the ground. I'll die there."

So King Zedekiah said Jeremiah could stay in the guards' yard. He told the guards to give Jeremiah bread every day. He could have bread until the city ran out of bread.

A Muddy Well

JEREMIAH 38; 39:15-18

Jeremiah told people these words from God. "If you stay in the city, you'll die. You'll die fighting. You'll die of hunger. You'll die of sickness. But if you go out to Babylon's army, you'll live."

Some of the king's men heard what Jeremiah was saying. They told the king about it. "He should be killed," they said. "He is making our army feel bad. He is making the people feel bad too. He is not thinking about what's good for the people. He is thinking about what's bad for them."

"Take Jeremiah," said King Zedekiah. "Do whatever you want. I can't stop you."

So they took Jeremiah. They put him in a well in the guards' yard. They let him down into the well by ropes. There wasn't any water in the well. There was just mud at the bottom. Jeremiah sank down into the mud.

But a leader at the palace heard about it. He was from Cush. He went to see the king. The king was sitting at a gate.

"My king," said the man from Cush. "These men have been mean. They put Jeremiah into a well. He

will die there when we run out of food."

"Get 30 men," said the king. "Pull Jeremiah out of the well so he won't die."

So the leader from Cush got 30 men. Then he went to a room in the palace. He got some old rags and clothes. He tied ropes to them. He let them down into the well.

"Put these old rags and clothes under your arms," said the man from Cush. "That way, the ropes won't hurt your arms."

Jeremiah put the old rags under his arms. Then he put the ropes under his arms. The men pulled him up out of the well. Then Jeremiah stayed in the guards' yard.

King Zedekiah asked Jeremiah to come and see him again. They met at one of the doors to the worship house.

"I have something to ask you," said the king. "Don't keep any secret from me."

"If I answer you, you'll kill me," said Jeremiah. "Even if I tell you what to do, you won't listen."

But King Zedekiah promised, "I won't kill you. I won't give you to people who want to kill you."

So Jeremiah spoke these words from God. "If you give up to Babylon, you'll live. They won't burn the city down. But if you don't give up to them, you won't live.

Babylon will take over the city. The people will burn it down, and you won't get away."

"I'm scared of our Jewish people who are fighting with Babylon," said the king. "The army of Babylon might give me to them. Then they'd be mean to me."

"They won't give you to the Jewish people," said Jeremiah. "Obey God. Do what I tell you. Then things will go well. Your life will be saved. But God showed me what will happen if you don't obey.

"The women in the palace will be taken to Babylon's leaders. These women will say that your friends lied to you. They'll say your feet are stuck in mud and your friends have left you.

"Babylon will also take your wives and children. You won't get away. Then they'll burn down this city," said Jeremiah.

"Don't let anybody know we talked about this," said the king. "If you do, you might be killed. The leaders might hear about our meeting. They might ask you what you said to me. Tell them that you asked the king not to send you to jail."

The leaders did come to Jeremiah. They asked him about his talk with the king.

Jeremiah told them, "I asked the king not to send me to jail."

So the leaders didn't ask him anything else about it. No one had heard him talk with the king.

Jeremiah stayed in the guards' yard until Babylon took over Jerusalem.

God gave Jeremiah a message for the palace leader from Cush. "I'm getting ready to keep my promise about Jerusalem. You'll see it come true. But I'll save you. You won't die, because you trust in me."

Running Away at Night
2 KINGS 25:3-23; 2 CHRONICLES 36:17-20; JEREMIAH 39:1-14; 40:1-6; 52:6-27

Now Jerusalem ran out of food. There was nothing to eat.

Then Babylon's army broke through the city wall. The leaders of Babylon sat at the Middle Gate.

Zedekiah and his army saw the leaders of Babylon. So Zedekiah and his army ran away. They left the city at night. They went through the king's garden. Then they went through the gate between two walls. They headed for the Jordan Valley.

But Babylon's army chased them. They caught up with them.

King Zedekiah was taken to the king of Babylon. The king of Babylon killed his sons. Then he put out King Zedekiah's eyes. He put metal chains on Zedekiah and took him to Babylon. King Zedekiah was in jail there until he died.

The army of Babylon set God's worship house on fire. They burned down the palace and all the houses. They burned down every important building. They broke down all the city walls.

Babylon's army took the priests and leaders. They took them to the king of Babylon. He killed them.

Babylon's army broke the things at the worship house. They took all the metal to Babylon. They took the pots and dishes, too. They took the things that were gold or silver.

Babylon's army took some of the poorest people and the workers. But they left some of the poor people. These people didn't own anything. So the captain of Babylon's army gave them fields.

Then the people of Judah were taken away. They were taken to Babylon.

The king of Babylon chose Gedaliah to be in charge of Judah.

The king also gave his captain orders about Jeremiah. The king said, "Take care of Jeremiah. Don't hurt him. Do whatever he asks you to do."

So the captain took Jeremiah out of the guards' yard. Jeremiah was in chains. He was with the people being taken to Babylon.

The captain said to Jeremiah, "God told about this trouble. Now it has happened. God did what he said he'd do. God did this because these people sinned against him. They didn't obey God.

"I'm going to set you free now," said the captain. "You can come with me to Babylon if you want to. I'll take care of you there. But if you don't want to come, you don't have to. Look. The whole land is here. Go wherever you want."

Then the captain said, "Go to Gedaliah. He is in charge of Judah. Live with him, or live wherever you want."

Then the captain gave food to Jeremiah. He also gave him a present. Then he let Jeremiah go.

So Jeremiah got to go home. He got to stay with his own people who were left in Judah.

JULY 6

From a Queen to a Slave

LAMENTATIONS 1

Jeremiah wrote this sad poem.
The city is like a desert.
    Once it was full of people.
Now it's like a woman who has lost
        her husband.
Once the city was a great nation.
    It was like the queen of the land.
    Now it's like a slave.

The roads cry, because no one
     comes for the special holidays
     for God.
No one comes through the gates.

The enemies are in charge now.
     The enemies have peace.
It's all because of the people's sins.

Enemies Laugh

LAMENTATIONS 2:9, 14, 16-17, 20, 22

The city gates sank into the dirt.
     God broke the bars.
The king and princes were taken
     away.
     God's laws are gone.
The prophets don't hear from God
     anymore.

What your fake prophets saw was
     no good.
They didn't tell you that you had
     sinned.
What they told you was a lie.
     They led you the wrong way.

Your enemies open their mouths
     wide against you.
They laugh. They put their teeth
     together.
     They say, "We ate up Jerusalem!
This is the day we were waiting for.
     We lived to see this day!"

God did what he planned to do.
     He kept his promise.

It's what he said long ago.
He let the enemies win over you.
     He made your enemies stronger
     than you.

"God, look and think about it.
     Who did you ever treat like this?
You called trouble to come just like
     you'd call for dinner.
Nobody got away on the day God
     got mad.
I took care of my people.
     I watched them grow.
But the enemy has torn them down."

Great Love

LAMENTATIONS 3:21-27, 31-42, 49-50

I remember one thing.
     I have hope because of what I
     remember.

God has great love. So we are not
     lost.
     God's care never ends.
His care is new every morning.
     It's great the way he keeps his
     promises.
I tell myself, "God is what I want.
     So I will wait for him."

God is good to people who hope in
     him.
     He is good to people who look for
     him.
It's good to wait quietly for God to
     save you.

It's good for people to have hard
    times while they're young.

God doesn't leave his people
    forever.
  He might bring sadness.
But he will show his care, too.
  His love is great. It never ends.
He doesn't want to bring hard times.
  He doesn't want to make his
    people sad.

But God sees it when people put
    others down.
He sees when people don't give
    others what they need.
  God knows.
He sees when people aren't fair.
  God sees.

Who can make things happen if
    God hasn't planned it?
Both good times and trouble come
    from God.
Why should people make a fuss
    when God brings them trouble
    for sinning?

Let's look at how we act.
  Let's come back to God.
Let's lift up our hearts and hands
    to God.
  Let's say, "We sinned. We turned
    away from you.
  You have not forgiven us."

Tears will flow without stopping.
  Nothing can cheer me up until
    God looks down and sees me.

Summer Fruit
JEREMIAH 40:7-16

Some of Judah's army leaders and
their men were out in the country.
They heard that Babylon's king had
put Gedaliah in charge. So they
came to Gedaliah.

Gedaliah said, "Don't be afraid
to let the people of Babylon rule
over you. Move into the land. Do
what the king of Babylon says.
Then things will go well. I'll
stay here and talk to people who
come from Babylon. You go out
and bring in the wine. Gather the
summer fruit. Bring in the oil.
Store everything in jars. Live in
the towns."

Some Jews had moved to the
countries of Moab, Ammon, and
Edom. They heard that Gedaliah
was in charge. So they came back to
Judah too. They gathered the wine
and summer fruit. There was more
than enough.

Then some army leaders came
to Gedaliah. They said, "Ammon's
king is sending Ishmael to kill
you."

Gedaliah didn't believe them.

Johanan, one of the leaders, went
to Gedaliah alone. "Let me kill
Ishmael," he said. "Nobody will
know who did it. Why should he
kill you? Then all the Jewish people
will run away."

"No!" said Gedaliah. "Don't kill Ishmael. He would never kill me."

A Trick

JEREMIAH 41

Now Ishmael was from Ammon. He had been one of his king's leaders. He took 10 men and went to see Gedaliah. They ate together.

While they were eating, Ishmael killed Gedaliah. Then Ishmael and his men killed all the Jewish people there. They killed the men from Babylon who were there too.

The next day 80 men came to town. They came to offer gifts to God. They didn't know what had happened to Gedaliah.

Ishmael went out to meet the men. He was crying as he went. He told them, "Come and see Gedaliah."

So the men went into the city. Then Ishmael and his men killed them and threw their bodies into a well.

But 10 of the men said, "Don't kill us. We can give you wheat and barley. We have oil and honey. We hid it in a field." So Ishmael didn't kill them.

Ishmael took the rest of the people from town. He left with them to go to the land of Ammon.

Johanan and the other leaders heard what Ishmael had done. They got their men together and went to fight Ishmael. They found him near a big pool.

The people that Ishmael had taken saw Johanan. They were glad. They ran over to Johanan.

But Ishmael and eight of his men got away. They ran back to the land of Ammon.

Then Johanan took God's people and headed for Egypt. They wanted to get away from Babylon. Babylon's king had chosen Gedaliah and put him in charge. Now Ishmael had killed Gedaliah. So the people were scared of what Babylon's king might do.

Rocks in a Hole

JEREMIAH 41:17; 42:1-17; 43

Johanan and the people stopped near Bethlehem. They went to see Jeremiah. "Please listen to us," they said. "Pray to God for all of us. There were many of us. Now there are only a few of us. Ask God to tell us where to go. Ask him to tell us what to do."

"I hear you," said Jeremiah. "I'll pray to God. I'll tell you everything God says."

"We promise to do whatever God says," they said. "It may sound good to us, or it may sound bad. But we'll obey God."

Ten days later, God spoke to Jeremiah. So Jeremiah called all the people together.

God gave Jeremiah this message for the people. "Stay in this land. Then I'll build you up. I won't tear you down. I'm sad about the trouble I sent you. Don't be afraid of Babylon's king. I'm with you. I'll save you from him. He will give your land back to you."

"What if you say that you won't stay in this land? That would not be obeying God," said Jeremiah. "What if you say that you'll go live in Egypt?"

Jeremiah told the people what God said he'd do then. "If you go to Egypt, war will come to Egypt. Food won't grow there. You'll die there. Anyone who goes there to live will die. No one will get away."

Johanan and the leaders were proud. They said, "You're telling lies! God didn't say we shouldn't go to Egypt. You're just trying to give us to Babylon. You'll let them kill us. You might take us away to their land."

So Johanan and the people did not obey God. They went to Egypt. They made Jeremiah and Baruch go with them.

In Egypt, God spoke to Jeremiah. "Get some big rocks," said God.

"Dig into the clay in the road by the king's palace. Put the rocks in the hole and then cover them up. Be sure my people are watching.

"Then tell them this. I, the God of Israel,

will send for the king of Babylon. I'll put his throne right over these rocks. His tent will be right here. He will fight Egypt. He will kill some people. He will take some people to Babylon. He will burn down the idols' worship houses. Then he will go home, not hurt at all."

The Wives and Their Idols
JEREMIAH 44:1-7, 15-30

There were Jews living in other parts of Egypt. God spoke to Jeremiah about them.

"You saw the trouble I gave the towns of Judah," said God. "The people made me angry by worshiping idols. I told the people, 'Don't worship idols.' But they didn't listen. That's why the towns are piles of sticks and stones.

"Now why bring this same trouble to yourselves?" asked God. "Why make me angry?"

Now the men knew that their wives worshiped idols. Some of the women were even there to hear Jeremiah. It was a big group.

But the people said, "We won't listen to this. We'll worship the Queen of Heaven like we did in Judah. We had plenty of food then. We had no trouble. But we stopped worshiping the Queen of Heaven. Then we had trouble. People died in fights. People died of hunger."

The women said, "We worshiped the Queen of Heaven. Our husbands knew about it. They didn't stop us."

Then Jeremiah said, "Didn't God know what you were doing? At last he couldn't stand it anymore. That's why your land is a desert now. It's all because you turned against God. You did not obey him. You didn't obey his laws. That's why trouble came.

"So go ahead. Worship idols. But God promises this. No Jewish people in Egypt will call on his name again. God is going to bring them trouble, not good. Then you'll know if God's word or theirs will come true.

"Here's the sign that what I say is true," says God. "I gave your king, Zedekiah, to Babylon. Now I'm going to give the king of Egypt to his enemies."

Messages about God's Plans

They Don't Do What They Hear

EZEKIEL 33:21, 30-33

Ezekiel had been in Babylon for 12 years. He wrote this.

One day a man came to me from Jerusalem. He had gotten away. He told me, "Jerusalem has fallen!"

Then God spoke to me. "Ezekiel, your people talk about you by the walls. They talk about you at their doors. They say, 'Come and hear God's message.' So they come to you. They listen to you.

"But they don't do what they hear. They say they obey me. But their hearts want more and more things. They even sin to get more things. To them, you're just somebody who has a great voice. You're like someone who sings love songs. You're like someone who plays music. They hear your words. But they don't do them.

"Everything I said will happen.

Then my people will know a prophet has been with them."

Moving Back Home

EZEKIEL 36:16-19, 24-30, 33-38

God spoke to me. "Ezekiel, my people made their land bad by what they did. So I was angry at them. I sent them to other nations.

"I'll bring you out of the nations. I'll take you back to your own land. I'll clean you up from the bad things you did. I'll give you a new heart. I'll put a new spirit in you. I'll take away your stony, hard heart. Then I'll give you a soft heart.

"I'll put my Spirit in you. I'll get you to obey my laws. You'll live in the land I gave you. You'll be my people. I'll be your God. I'll save you from your sins.

"I'll give you more than enough grain. I'll give you fruit on your trees. I'll give you crops in your fields. This will keep you from

429

feeling like nothing among the nations.

"I'll let you move back into your towns. Piles of sticks and stones will be built back into cities. The desert land will be watered. It will grow food.

"Then the nations will know that I built this again. I planted this land again. I am the Lord. I said I'd do it, and I will.

"I'll answer the prayers of my people again. I'll give them big, growing families. The cities will be full of people. Then they'll know I'm the Lord."

A Valley Full of Bones
EZEKIEL 37

God was with me. His Spirit took me to the middle of a valley. The valley was full of bones. He took me back and forth around the bones. They were very dry.

God asked, "Ezekiel, can these bones live?"

"You are the only one who knows that, God," I said.

Then God said, "Talk to these bones."

These are the words God told Ezekiel to say. "Dry bones, hear God's word! Here's what God says to these bones. You'll live. I'll put muscles on you. I'll cover you with skin. I'll put breath into you, and

you will live. Then you'll know I'm the Lord."

So I talked to the bones. I said what God told me to say.

While I was talking, I heard a sound. It was like a rattle. The bones started coming together! One bone hooked onto another bone. Muscles and skin came on them. But there wasn't any breath.

Then God said to tell the breath, "Here's what God says. Come from the four winds, breath. Breathe into these dead bodies. Make them live."

So I said what God told me to say. Then breath went into the bodies. They came to life. They stood up. They made a big army!

God said that these bones show what the people of Israel are like. They say that their bones have dried up. They don't have hope anymore. They are lost. God told Jeremiah to give them this message. "I'm going to bring you back to Israel. I'll put my Spirit in you, and you'll live. I'll bring you back to your own land. Then you'll know that what I said is true."

God spoke to me again. "Ezekiel, get a stick. Write on it, 'Judah's stick.' Then get another stick. Write on it, 'Israel's stick.' Put the sticks together to make one stick. Make them look like one stick in your hand.

"People will ask what this means. Tell them I'm going to make Judah and Israel one nation. I'll gather my people from other nations. I'll take them back to their own land.

"I'll make them one nation in that land. One king will rule them. They won't ever be two nations again. They won't ever be two kingdoms again. They won't have idols. I'll save them from their sin. I'll clean up their hearts. Then they'll be my people, and I'll be their God.

"My servant will be their king. They will have one shepherd leader. They'll obey my laws. They will live in the land I gave to them. Their families will live there forever. My servant will be their prince forever.

"I will live with them. Then the nations will know that I make Israel special. I make Israel holy and clean."

JULY 9

The Big, Burning Oven
DANIEL 3

Now King Nebuchadnezzar made a gold idol in Babylon. It was 90 feet high and 9 feet wide. He set it up on wide, flat land. Then he called the leaders together to make it their god. So they came and stood in front of the idol.

The speaker called, "All people! Nations! People who speak different languages! Here's the rule. You will hear the music. Then you must bow down and worship the gold god. If you don't, you'll be thrown into a big, burning oven."

So the music played. There were horns, flutes, zithers, harps, and all kinds of music. When the people heard it, they all bowed down. They worshiped the gold idol.

Then some men who worshiped stars came up. They said bad things about the Jewish leaders. They spoke to the king.

"May our king live forever!" they said. "You made a law. Everyone who hears the music must bow down and worship. People who don't will be thrown into the burning oven. Some Jews are leaders here. But they aren't doing what you said. It's Shadrach, Meshach, and Abednego. They don't follow your gods. They aren't worshiping the gold god you set up."

The king was very angry. He called for Shadrach, Meshach, and Abednego. He asked, "Is this true? Don't you obey my gods? Don't you worship the gold god I set up?

"Now you will hear music," said the king. "Then you must worship the gold god I made. If you worship the god, everything will be all right. If you don't, I'll throw you into the burning oven. Then what god will save you?"

"King Nebuchadnezzar," said Shadrach, Meshach, and Abednego. "We don't need to tell you we're right. Our God can save us if we're thrown into the burning oven. Even if he doesn't save us, you should know this. We won't obey your gods. We won't worship the gold idol you set up."

The king was very angry. He stopped being nice to them. He gave an order to make the oven seven times hotter. He called for his strongest guards. He told them to tie up Shadrach, Meshach, and Abednego.

The three friends were wearing robes, pants, and hats. The guards tied them up. The king wanted the guards to move fast. So they threw the men into the burning oven.

The fire was burning very hot. It killed the guards. Shadrach, Meshach, and Abednego fell into the burning oven.

All of a sudden, the king jumped up. He was surprised. He turned to his helpers. "Didn't we tie up three men?" he asked. "Didn't we throw three men into the fire?"

"Yes," said his helpers.

"Look!" said the king. "I see four men walking around in the fire. They aren't tied up! Three of them are the men we threw in. The other one looks like a son of the gods."

Then the king went to the door

of the oven. He called, "Shadrach, Meshach, and Abednego! Servants of the Most High God! Come out!"

So Shadrach, Meshach, and Abednego came out. All the leaders gathered around them. The fire had not hurt the three friends at all. Their hair wasn't burned even a little bit. Their robes weren't burned. They didn't even smell like smoke.

"Praise the God of Shadrach, Meshach, and Abednego!" said the king. "He sent his angel. He saved his servants! They trusted him. They didn't obey me. They wouldn't worship another god. They even knew they might die for it. They worship no one but their God.

"So I'll make a new rule. Nobody will say anything bad about their God. People who do will be cut to pieces. Their houses will become piles of sticks and stones. That's because no other god can save people like this."

Then the king gave the three friends new jobs. Now they were even greater leaders in Babylon.

The Top of the Mountain

EZEKIEL 40:1–43:11; 44:1-2

We had been in Babylon for 25 years. It had been 14 years since Babylon took over Jerusalem. God was with me, Ezekiel. He took me to Israel by putting pictures in my mind.

God took me to a high mountain. Buildings were on the south side of the mountain. They looked like a city.

God took me to this city. There I saw a man who looked like shiny brown metal. He stood at a gate. He had a rope and a long ruler in his hand.

The man said, "Look with your eyes. Hear with your ears. Think about what I'm going to show you. That's why you are here. Tell the people of Israel everything you see here."

I saw a wall. It went all the way around the worship house. The ruler the man held was about 10 feet long. He measured the wall with it. The wall was 10 feet thick and 10 feet high.

Then the man went to the east gate. He went up the steps there. He measured the gate. It was 10 feet from front to back. There were places in the gate for guards to stand. The walls inside the gate had pictures of palm trees on them.

Then the man took me to the other gates. There was one on the north and one on the south. They were the same size as the east gate.

Then the man measured the yard. It was square. He took me all around the worship house. He measured every part of it.

Then the man took me to the east gate. I saw God's greatness coming from the east. His voice sounded like the roar of fast-moving water. The land glowed with his greatness.

This was the same picture I had seen in my mind before. It was like what I saw at the Kebar River. So I put my face down to the ground.

God's greatness went into the worship house through the east gate. Then the Spirit picked me up. He took me into the inside yard. God's greatness filled the worship house.

The man stood beside me now. I heard somebody talking to me. The voice came from inside the worship house. He said, "This is the place where I sit on my throne. This is where I rest my feet. Here's where I'll live among my people forever. My people will never treat my name like dirt again. They won't worship idols again.

"At one time they put their idols

433

in a room next to me. There was only a wall between us. That's when they treated my name like dirt. So I got angry at them. I got rid of them. Now let them get rid of their idols. Then I'll live with them forever.

"Tell the people of Israel what the worship house looks like. Write it down. Then the people will feel bad about their sins. And they can follow the plan of how the worship house is to be built."

The man took me back to the outside gate. It was the east gate. It was closed. God said, "This gate must stay closed. It must not open. Nobody can come in this way. It has to stay closed, because God has come through it."

The Deep River

EZEKIEL 47:1-12

Then the man took me back to the door of the worship house. I saw water flowing out from under the door. It flowed east.

The man took the long ruler. He went east. He measured 1,500 feet. Then he took me through water up to the top of my feet.

He measured 1,500 more feet. Then he took me through water up to my knees.

He measured 1,500 more feet. Then he took me through water up to my middle.

He measured 1,500 more feet. By now, the water was a river. I couldn't get across, because it was too deep. I'd have to swim. Nobody could cross this river.

"Do you see this?" asked the man. Then he took me back to the side of the river. I saw lots of trees on each side.

"This water goes to the Jordan Valley," he said. "It flows into the Dead Sea. Then the salt water there turns into fresh water. Lots of animals will live where the river goes.

"Lots of fish will be in the river. Men who fish will stand beside the river. They will throw out their nets. There will be many kinds of fish. But the swamps will still be salty. They will be there for the salt.

"Fruit trees will grow on both sides of the river. Their leaves won't dry up. That's because water from the worship house flows out to them. Their fruit will be for food. Their leaves will make people well."

JULY 11

The King Who Lived with Wild Animals

DANIEL 4

Now the king of Babylon wrote a letter. It said,

434

From King Nebuchadnezzar.

To people and nations from every language.

I pray that you will have plenty of everything!

It makes me happy to tell you about some wonders. These are wonders and signs that the Most High God did. He did them for me.

His signs are great!
His wonders are powerful!
His kingdom lasts forever.
He rules for all time.

I, Nebuchadnezzar, was home in my palace. I felt good about having plenty of everything. I felt rich. One night I was in bed. I had a dream that scared me very badly.

I asked all the wise men in Babylon to come. I wanted them to tell me what my dream meant. Magic men came. Men who worshiped stars came. I told them my dream. But no one could tell me its meaning.

At last, Daniel came. So I told him my dream. I said, "Daniel, the holy God's spirit is in you. No problem is too hard for you. So here's my dream. Tell me what it means.

"I was in bed. I saw a tree in the middle of the land. It was very tall. It grew big and strong. The top went all the way to the sky. It could be seen from anywhere in the world.

"The tree's leaves were beautiful. It had lots of fruit. There was food on it for everyone. The animals were safe in its shade. Birds lived in the branches. All animals got their food there.

"Then I saw a holy man. He came down from heaven. He called loudly, 'Cut down the tree. Cut off its branches. Take away its fruit. The animals and birds must run away. But leave the bottom part of the tree trunk. Leave its roots in the ground.'

"Then the holy one said, 'Let dew from the sky make him wet. Let him live with animals. Let him live with plants. Let his mind be changed into an animal's mind. Let him live this way for seven years.'

"The holy one said, 'This is so people will know that God is the king. He rules over people's kingdoms. He gives them to anyone he wants. He even puts lowly men in charge.'

"This is the dream I had. Now, Daniel, tell me what it means. My wise men can't tell me. But you can. The holy God's spirit is in you."

Then Daniel wondered about the dream. It was mixed up in his mind for a while. His thoughts scared him.

So I said, "Don't let the dream scare you. Don't let its meaning scare you."

"My king," said Daniel. "I wish the dream was about your enemies! But you are that tree! You have grown great and strong. Your greatness goes up to the sky. Your kingdom goes all over the earth.

"You saw a man come from heaven. You heard what he said about cutting down the tree. Here's what that means. Here's what the Most High God said would happen.

"You will be sent away from your people. You'll live with wild animals. You'll eat grass like a cow. The sky's dew will make you wet. Seven years will pass. Then you'll say that God is king over all kingdoms. He gives kingdoms to anyone he wants.

"But the bottom of the tree trunk was left. In your dream, the roots were left. That means you'll be king again. You'll say that God is the greatest king.

"So I have a good idea for you. Stop doing wrong things. Do what's right. Be kind to people who are having a hard time. Maybe then things will keep going well for you."

A year later, I was walking on my palace roof. I said, "This is the great Babylon that I built. I built it by my strong power. It shows how great I am!"

I had hardly stopped talking when I heard a voice. It came from heaven. "Here's what will happen to you, King. You will not be king anymore. You'll be sent away from people. You'll live with wild animals. You'll eat grass like a cow. Seven years will pass. Then you'll say that God is the king. You'll know that God gives kingdoms to anyone he wants."

Right away, it happened. I was sent away from my people. I ate grass like a cow. Dew from the sky made my body wet. My hair grew out like eagle feathers. My nails grew out like bird claws.

After seven years, I, Nebuchadnezzar looked up to heaven. My right mind came back to me. Then I praised the Most High God who lives forever. I treated him as the most important one. I spoke about his greatness.

His kingdom lasts forever.

People all over the world are like nothing.

God does what he wants with heaven's powers.

He does what he wants with earth's people.

Nobody can stop God.

TIME LINE

On the next 14 pages is a timeline.

The top part shows many Bible stories

and people you'll read about in the

Day by Day Kid's Bible. The bottom

part shows other interesting things

that were happening all around

the world at the same time.

WHEN THE WORLD WAS NEW

Adam
and Eve

Noah

Tower
of Babel

AROUND 2400 B.C.

Chariots are pulled by
donkeys in Sumeria

The Great Sphinx
and Cheops' Pyramid
are built in Egypt

Dogs are first
tamed in Egypt

Games in Egypt:
tug-of-war, tossing
leather balls stuffed
with grain

Abraham and His Family

Abraham travels

Isaac and Rebekah

Jacob and Esau

Joseph goes to Egypt

Joseph becomes a ruler in Egypt

AROUND 1890 B.C.

Mummies are made in Egypt

Water bottles are made of whole goat skins

People first keep chickens in Babylon

First trumpets are made in Denmark

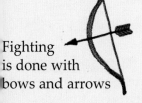

Fighting is done with bows and arrows

Horses are used to pull carts

Bible

FROM EGYPT TO THE PROMISED LAND

Baby Moses is born

God's people leave Egypt

Ten rules and a worship tent

Jericho falls

World

AROUND 1500 B.C.

First Chinese dictionary

Silk cloth is made in China

A song in Egypt talks about the Israelites, God's people

Strong ships are built close to the seas

ENEMIES, JUDGES, & KINGS

A GOOD KING

A GOOD KING
PART OF THE TIME

A BAD KING

Gideon,
Samson,
Ruth

Saul, the First King

David, the
Singing King

Solomon,
the Rich King,
builds the
worship house

AROUND 1000 B.C.

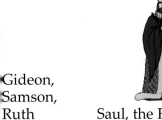

The Sun Pyramid
is built in Mexico

Cloth is colored
with purple dye
from snails
around the big
sea near Israel

People like to shoot
slingshots at targets

Bible

Bad Kings

A GOOD KING

A GOOD KING
PART OF THE TIME

A BAD KING

The kingdom of God's people becomes two kingdoms: Israel and Judah

PROPHETS

ISRAEL'S KINGS	Jeroboam	Nadab	Baasha	Elah	Om
JUDAH'S KINGS	Rehoboam		Asa		

AROUND 930 B.C.

World

Pinto Indians build huts of wood and reeds in California

Greek stories are written: "Iliad" and "Odyssey"

A favorite sport: hunting from chariots

MESSAGES ABOUT KINGS, ARMIES, AND IDOLS

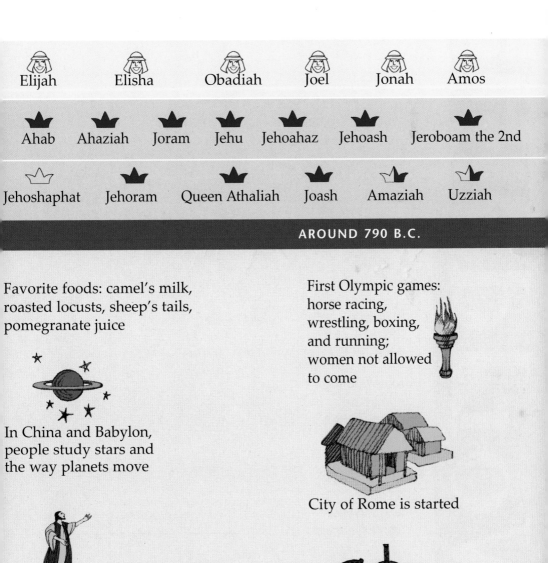

| Elijah | Elisha | Obadiah | Joel | Jonah | Amos |

| Ahab | Ahaziah | Joram | Jehu | Jehoahaz | Jehoash | Jeroboam the 2nd |

| Jehoshaphat | Jehoram | Queen Athaliah | Joash | Amaziah | Uzziah |

AROUND 790 B.C.

Favorite foods: camel's milk, roasted locusts, sheep's tails, pomegranate juice

In China and Babylon, people study stars and the way planets move

Singers travel from town to town

First Olympic games: horse racing, wrestling, boxing, and running; women not allowed to come

City of Rome is started

A favorite game in Europe: horseshoes

World Bible

MESSAGES ABOUT WHAT'S COMING

A GOOD KING

A GOOD KING
PART OF THE TIME

A BAD KING

PROPHETS	Hosea	Micah		Isaiah
ISRAEL'S KINGS	Zechariah	Menahem	Pekah	Hoshe
JUDAH'S KINGS	Jotham		Ahaz	

AROUND 750 B.C.

NOTE ABOUT THE BIBLE PROPHETS AND KINGS:

Most of the names are on this time line. But some prophets and kings were not around very long. So you won't see their names here.

Water clocks are used in Assyria to tell time

MANY MESSAGES FROM GOD

 Nahum
 Zephaniah
 Jeremiah
 Habakkuk

 Israel is taken captive
by the Assyrians (722 B.C.)

 Hezekiah
Manasseh
Josiah
Jehoahaz
Jehoiakim
Zedekiah

AROUND 600 B.C.

In Greece, people like songs
about fights and wars

Nebuchadnezzar
is king in Babylon

A big library is built
in Nineveh

Babylon defeats Assyria
(605 B.C.)

Bible

MESSAGES ABOUT GOD'S PLANS

PROPHETS Daniel Ezekiel   Zechariah

Judah is
taken captive
by the Babylonians
(605, 597, & 586 B.C.)

Jerusalem is
torn down

Maybe the
book of Job
was written
at this time

Zerubbab•
leads God'
people ba•
to Jerusal•
(538 B.C.)

World

AROUND 590 B.C.

Aesop's fables are told

Babylon is overthrown
by Persia, and Cyrus
becomes king (539 B.C.)

A ship sails around
Africa for the first time

Some children's games:
hopscotch, leapfrog,
hide-and-seek, tug-of-war

A TIME FOR SAVING GOD'S PEOPLE

Haggai

Malachi

The worship house in Jerusalem is built again

Esther becomes a queen in Persia

Ezra leads more of God's people back home

Nehemiah helps build the wall of Jerusalem back up

AROUND 450 B.C.

In Persia, men riding horses carry messages back and forth like mail

Alexander the Great begins ruling in Greece

Dams are built in India

Greek people study plants and make medicines from them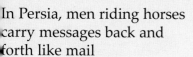

There are many plays in Greece, and many temples are built for fake gods

Pigeons are used to carry messages in Greece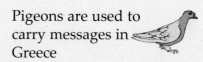

World Bible

The Old Testament is written in Greek

Greeks rule the country where God's people live

The Great Wall of China is built, 1,400 miles long

The first Roman coins are made

Paper is first made in Chi

The first stone bridge is built in Rome

Romans and Greeks play ball games, dice games, games on game boards

Streets are first paved in Rome

THE LIFE OF JESUS

When God's Son came

Jesus teaches
and does wonders

Jesus' best gift

AROUND A.D. 30

Rome rules the world

Greeks and Romans
like chariot races

Storytellers travel
from town to town

Herod the Great is put
in charge of the country
where God's people live

GOD'S KINGDOM GROWS

Peter and John teach,
Stephen and Philip preach

Paul travels

The Romans
learn to use
soap

The city of London is started

Bible

World

LETTERS TO GOD'S PEOPLE

Letters from Paul

James, Jude,
and Peter
write letters

John writes
about the future

AROUND A.D. 90

Nero becomes
ruler of Rome

Jerusalem and the worship
house are torn down

NOTE ABOUT THIS TIME LINE:

The number of years between the pictures is not always the same. There are more than 100 years between some of the pictures at the beginning. There are only a few years between some of the pictures at the end.

Nobody can say, "What did you do?"

Then I was back in my right mind. I became great again. My helpers and leaders wanted to meet with me. I went back to being the king again. In fact, I became even greater than I was before.

Now I, Nebuchadnezzar, praise the King of heaven. I say he is the greatest. Everything he does is right. All his ways are fair. He can make proud people feel like nothing.

A King Gets Out of Jail
JEREMIAH 52:31-34

We had been in Babylon for 37 years. Jehoiachin, Judah's king, was still alive there. There was a new king in Babylon. He let Jehoiachin out of jail. He was kind to Jehoiachin. He treated him better than the other kings.

Jehoiachin got to take his jail clothes off. He ate at the king's table the rest of his life. The king even gave Jehoiachin money to live on for the rest of his life.

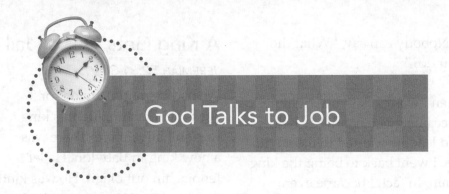

God Talks to Job

Trouble

JOB 1

Job lived long ago. Many people had told his story. At last someone wrote it down.

Once there was a man named Job. He lived in the land of Uz. He did what was good and right. No one could blame him for doing wrong. He obeyed God and stayed away from sin.

Job had seven sons and three daughters. He had 7,000 sheep and 3,000 camels. He had 1,000 oxen and 500 donkeys. He had lots of servants. Job was the greatest man in the East.

Job's sons took turns having big dinners at their houses. They would ask their three sisters to come for dinner. They would eat and drink.

Then Job would make sure they made things right with God. He would offer God a gift for each of them. He said, "They might have sinned. They might have said bad things about God." So Job offered a gift to say they were sorry. He did it so God would forgive them. That's what Job always did.

One day the angels came before God. Satan, the one who blames people, came with them.

"Where did you come from?" God asked Satan.

"I've been going here and there on the earth," said Satan.

"Did you ever think about Job?" asked God. "Nobody else in the world is like him. He does what is right and good. Nobody can blame him for doing anything wrong. He obeys me and stays away from sin."

"Do you think he obeys you for nothing?" asked Satan. "You are keeping him safe. You keep his family safe. You keep everything he owns safe. You send good things to him. His sheep and cows are all over the land. Send him bad times. Then he will say bad things about you."

"All right," said God. "You can do what you want with whatever he has. But don't touch Job."

438

Then Satan left.

One day Job's sons and daughters were having dinner together. They were at the oldest brother's house.

A man ran to Job with a message. "The oxen were working in the field. The donkeys were eating grass nearby. But robbers came and took them. They killed all your servants. I'm the only one who got away!"

This man had hardly stopped talking when another man came. "Fire came from the sky," he said. "It burned up the sheep and the servants. I'm the only one who got away!"

This man had hardly stopped talking when another man came. "Robbers came and took your camels," he said. They killed all your servants. I'm the only one who got away."

This man had hardly stopped talking when another man came. "Your sons and daughters were having dinner. All of a sudden a strong wind blew in. It came from the desert. It hit all four corners of the house. The house fell on top of them. They all died. I'm the only one who got away!"

Then Job got up. He tore the clothes he was wearing. He cut  off all his hair. He put his face to the ground. He worshiped God.

He said, "I had nothing when I was born.

I'll have nothing when I die.

God gave me what I had. He took it away.

Praise God's name."

Three Friends

JOB 2

One day the angels came before God again. Satan came with them.

"Where did you come from?" asked God.

"I've been going here and there on the earth," said Satan.

"Did you think about Job?" asked God. "There's no one in the world like him. He does what is right and good. He obeys me and stays away from sin. You talked me into letting him have hard times. There's no good reason for it. But Job is still good."

"Skin for skin!" said Satan. "People will give anything to stay alive. Hurt his body. Then he will say bad things about you."

"All right," said God. "Do what you want with Job. But don't kill him."

So Satan left. He made Job get sores on his body. They were on the bottom of his feet. They were on the top of his head. And they were all over his body. They hurt.

Job sat in dust from a fire. He took a piece of broken pot. He rubbed it across his sores.

His wife said, "Are you still going to be true to God? Say bad things about him and die!"

"That's a foolish thing to say," said Job. "Should we let God send us just good things? Shouldn't we let him send trouble if he wants?" So Job didn't sin by saying bad things about God.

Job had three friends, Eliphaz, Bildad, and Zophar. They heard what happened to Job. So they got together and went to see him.

The friends saw Job when they were still far away. But they could hardly tell that it was Job. They began to cry out loud. They were so sad, they tore their robes. They put dust on their heads.

Then they sat down on the ground with Job. They sat there for seven days and nights. Nobody said a thing. That's because they could see how much Job was hurting.

Crying Instead of Eating

JOB 3:1, 6, 16-17, 24-26; 4:1, 4-5; 5:8, 17-24; 6:1-3, 11-15, 26-30

Then Job talked.

"I should never have been born.
    My birthday shouldn't even be on
    the calendar.

If I hadn't been born, I wouldn't
    have this trouble.

"I'm crying instead of eating.
    Tears flow out of me like water.
I was afraid of this.
    Now it has happened.
I don't have any peace.
    I just have trouble."

Then Eliphaz said,
    "You said things to cheer people
        up.
Now trouble has come to you.
    You want to give up.
If I were you, I'd talk to God about
        this.
    I'd tell him what's happening.

"Good things come to people when
        God shows them they're wrong.
    So don't think God's training
        is bad.
He will save you from fights and
        robbers.
    He will save you from wild
        animals."

"If only I could weigh my trouble!"
        said Job.
    "It would weigh more than the
        sand by the sea.
I'm not strong. So what can I
        hope in?
    I can't help myself.

"A man who is sad should have
        his friends' help.

440

But I can't trust you.
Are you trying to tell me I'm wrong?
  Do you think my words are just
    hot air?
I think you'd sell your own friend.

"Have I said anything sinful?
  Don't I know what's right and
    wrong to say?
Things are still right between me
  and God."

Hot Air

JOB 8:1-6; 9:1-15, 19-20, 25-29, 32-35

Then Bildad spoke.

"How long will you talk like that?
  Your words are like hot air.
Does God do things that are not fair?
  Your children sinned.
    So God paid them back for their
      sins.
Look to God.
  Beg him for help.
Be good and right.
  Then he will help you."

"I know that's true," said Job.
  "But how can a person be sinless
    before God?
God's wise thinking is great. His
  power is great.
  Who can fight against God and
    not get hurt?
God moves mountains, and they
  don't even know it.

He tells the sun not to shine, and
  it doesn't.
He is the only one who can make
  the sky.
  He walks on sea waves.
He made all the stars to form
  pictures in the sky.
  God does wonders that no one
    can understand.
He passes by me, and I can't see him.
  Who would ask God, 'What are
    you doing?'

"So how can I make a fuss with God?
  What words can I say?
I couldn't answer his questions,
    even if I hadn't sinned.
I could only ask God to be kind to me.
Is this about power? God has the
    most power.
  Is this about being fair?
  Who can say God's not fair?
My words would blame me,
    even if I didn't sin.

"My days go by faster than a person
  can run.
  They slide past like paper boats.
  They fly like eagles diving down
    for food.
I might say, 'I'll forget about what's
  wrong.
  I'll smile now.'
But I'm still afraid of my troubles.
  I know you will blame me.
You already think I'm wrong.
  So why should I fight it?

"God is not a man.
So I can't answer him like I'd
answer a man.
I can't take him to a judge.
I wish someone would make peace
between God and me.
I wish someone could take God's
anger away from me.
Then I'd talk to him without
being afraid.
But right now, I can't."

Deeper Than the Deep Earth

JOB 11:1-5, 7-9, 12-16; 12:1-4, 7-16; 13:4-5

Then Zophar talked to Job.

"Someone has to answer you.
Do you think we'll listen to this
and be quiet?
You tell God that you're not wrong.
You say you haven't done
anything wrong.
I wish God would talk to you.
He would talk against you.

"Can you understand God?
Can you find out how great
God is?
God's ways are higher than all of
space.
They are deeper than the deep
earth.

God's ways are longer than the earth.
They are wider than the sea.
So how much do you know?

"Love God with your whole heart.
Stop sinning.
Then you can come to God.
You won't feel bad about it.
You won't be afraid.
You'll forget this trouble."

"You must be all people rolled into
one!" said Job.
"Wise thinking will die when
you die!
But I have a mind just like you do.
You're not more important than
I am.

"I'm right. I'm not to blame.
But you laugh at me.

"Ask animals about it. They'll teach
you.
Ask the birds. They'll tell you.
Talk to the earth. It will teach you.
Let the fish tell you.
They know God has done this.
He holds the life of every being in
his hand.
Older people are wise.
The longer you live, the more you
understand.

"Wise thinking and power belong to
God.
You can't build back what he
tears down.

You can't set free the person he puts
   in jail.
When God keeps the rain away, the
   land dries up.
When he sends lots of rain, it floods
   the land.
Power is God's. He is the one who
   wins.

"You are all good-for-nothing
   doctors.
I wish you'd all be quiet!
   That would be wise for you."

Being Angry at God

JOB 15:1-2, 8-9, 11-13, 17, 20-25;
16:1-3, 7, 10, 16-17, 19-21

Then Eliphaz spoke.

"A wise man wouldn't talk about
   these good-for-nothing ideas.
   He wouldn't fill himself with
   hot air.
Do you think you're the only one
   who is wise?
   What do you know that we don't
   know?
Aren't God's words good enough
   for you?
   Why are you so angry?
   You are being angry at God.

"Listen. I'll tell you how it is.
People who sin have trouble all
   their lives.
They give up thinking they'll get
   out of the dark.

Sadness and worry fill them with
   fear.
It's all because they shake their fists
   at God.
   They come against God, who has
   all power."

"Will you ever stop talking?" asked
   Job.
   "You all do a bad job of cheering
   a person up.
   Why do you keep fussing at me?

"God, you wear me out.
   You tore down my whole family.
People laugh at me.
My face is red because I've cried so
   much.
   But I haven't done anything mean
   or hateful.

"The one who sees it all is in heaven.
   The one who speaks up for me is
   my friend.
He talks to God for me while my
   tears flow."

Let God Test Me

JOB 31:5-7, 13, 18-40

"If I lied, then let God test me," said
   Job.
"God will know that I did nothing
   wrong.
   Did I turn away from God?
Did my eyes lead my heart?
   Did my hands do wrong?

"I was like a father to children who
had no fathers.
I helped women whose husbands
had died.
I gave clothes to people who needed
clothes.
I didn't use my power to hurt people.

"I didn't trust in gold.
My great riches were not my joy.
I didn't worship the sun or moon.
I wasn't glad when my enemies
had trouble.
I shared my food with many people.
My door was always open to
strangers.
I didn't hide sin in my heart.
I paid the people who worked in
my fields.

"I wish somebody would hear me.
Let God answer me.
Let him tell me what I did wrong."

That's all Job said.

Do I Have to Wait?

JOB 32:1-12; 33:1-3, 8-19, 23-28

Job's three friends stopped talking
to him. That's because Job kept
saying he was right.

But a young man named Elihu
got very angry at Job. He was angry
at Job's three friends, too. They
hadn't found any way to make Job
say he was wrong. Instead, Job had
told them they were wrong.

Elihu had waited to talk. That's
because the other men were older
than he was. Now he saw that they
didn't have much to say. So he got
angry. This is what he said.

"I'm young, and you're old.
So I didn't dare tell you what I
know.
But it's God who makes people wise.
It's not just old people who are
wise.

"I listened to you.
But nobody showed that Job is
wrong.
Listen to my words now, Job.
I tell the truth about what I know.

"You said you didn't sin.
I heard you myself.
You said your heart was clean, but
God was blaming you.

"I say you aren't right to talk like this.
God is greater than people.
So why do you fuss at him?
Why do you say he doesn't
answer people?

"God does speak. Sometimes he
speaks one way.
Sometimes he speaks another way.
People might not know he is
speaking.

He might speak in their ears in a
    dream at night.
He might scare them to keep them
    from doing wrong.
  He might scare them to save them
    from dying.
He might even send pain.

"But an angel may say, 'Save this
    person.
  I've found a way to pay for his
    sins.'
Then God makes everything right
    again.
Then the person will say that he
    sinned.
  But God didn't pay him back for
    the wrong he did.
God saved him.
  He will live now. He will enjoy
    the light."

Nobody Can Understand

*JOB 35:1-3, 6-8; 36:26-33; 37:1-10,
14-19, 23*

"You say that doing right does you
    no good," said Elihu.
  "You ask what good it does not
    to sin.

"What if you sin? What does that do
    to God?
  It's yourself you hurt when you
    sin.
  It's other people you help when
    you do what's right.

"God is great!
Nobody can understand how
    God sets out clouds.

He fills his hands with lightning.
  He tells it to go where he sends it.
God's thunder tells that a storm is
    coming.
  Even the cows can know it's
    coming.

"My heart beats hard when I hear it.
  Listen! Listen to his voice roar.
God lets his lightning come out of
    the sky.
  He sends it all over the earth.
Then his roar sounds.
  He thunders with his great voice.
He tells the snow, 'Fall on the earth.'
  He tells the rain, 'Fall hard.'
Then all people can know God's
    power.
  His rain stops people from working.
The animals have to stay dry.
  They stay in their dens.
The storm comes out of its room.
  The cold comes out of the
    blowing wind.

God's breath brings the ice.
The water freezes.

"Listen, Job.
Stop and think about God's
wonders.
God knows everything.
The land is quiet in the hot south
wind.
You are hot in your clothes.
Can you help God paint the sky?
Can you make it look hard like a
metal mirror?

"Tell us what to say to God.
We can't say anything, because we
don't know anything.
God is higher than we can reach."

JULY 16

God Talks from a Storm

JOB 38:1-12, 16-19, 22-29, 32-41

Then God talked to Job from a
storm.

God said, "Who is this?
Who is talking without knowing
what he is saying?
Get ready like a man.
I'll ask you questions now, and
you'll answer me.

"Where were you when I made the
earth?
Do you understand it? Then tell
me.

Who marked how big it would be?
What was the earth built on?
That's when the morning stars
sang.
That's when the angels shouted
with joy.

"Who closed the sea up behind doors?
I made clouds for the sea's clothes.
I told the sea, 'This is as far as you
come.
Here's where your proud waves
must stop.'

"Did you ever tell the morning what
to do?
Did you show the sunrise where
to start?

"Have you traveled to where the sea
starts?
Have you walked in the deep
places?
Have you seen the gates of death?
Do you understand how wide the
earth is?
Tell me if you know.

"How do you get to where the light
lives?
Where does the dark live?

"Have you gone into the place
where the snow is stored?
Have you seen where the hail is
kept?
I save it for times of trouble.
I save it for wars and fights.

"How do you get to where the
    lightning starts?
  How do you get to where the east
    wind starts blowing?
Who makes a road for the rain to
    follow?
  Who makes raindrops water the
    desert where nobody lives?
Does the rain have a father?
  Who is the father of ice and frost?

"Can you put the stars in their places?
  Do you know the laws of the
    earth and space?

"Can you call out to the clouds?
  Can you cover yourself with
    water?
Do you send out flashes of lightning?
  Do they tell you, 'Here we are'?

"Who made hearts wise?
  Who made minds understand?
Who is wise enough to count the
    clouds?

"Do you hunt for the lions' food?
  Do you bring them food when
    they lie in their dens?
Who gives birds food to eat when
    their babies are hungry?"

Do You Know?

JOB 39:1, 5, 9, 13-28

"Do you know when mountain
    goats have their babies?

Do you watch when a deer has
    her baby?" asked God.
"Who lets wild donkeys run free?
Will the wild ox serve you?

"The ostrich flaps its wings with
    joy.
  But its wings aren't as great as the
    stork's feathers.
She lays eggs on the ground.
  She lets them get warm in the
    sand.
Someone might step on them.
  But she doesn't think about that.
That's because God didn't make her
    wise.
  But she holds out her wings and
    runs.
  Then she laughs at horses and
    their riders.

"Do you make the horse strong?
  Do you put a flowing mane on his
    neck?
Do you make him jump like a big
    grasshopper?
  Do you make him scare people
    with his proud sounds?
He hits the ground with his hoof.
  He runs into the fight.
He is not afraid of anything.
  He doesn't run from swords.
He hears the war horn blow.
  Then he can't stand still.
He is ready to go into the fight.
  He smells the fight.
  He hears the captains shout.

"Does the hawk fly because you are
wise?
He holds out his wings and flies
south.
Does the eagle fly when you tell him
to?
Do you tell him to build his nest
up high?
He lives on a cliff. That's where he
stays at night.
A high rock is his fort."

Answer Me!

JOB 40

"Will you tell me what's right and
wrong?" asked God.
"You blame me. So answer me!"
"I don't feel good about myself,"
said Job. "How can I answer
you?
I will put my hand over my
mouth."

Then God talked to Job from the
storm.

"Get ready like a man should.
I'll ask you questions, and you'll
answer me.

"Will you tell me I'm not fair?
Will you blame me so that you
can make yourself right?
Do you have a strong arm like mine?
Can your voice thunder like mine?

Try to wear my brightness and
beauty.
Try to make my greatness your
clothes.
Look at proud people and make
them feel like nothing.
Give all sinful people a grave in
the dust.
Can you do these things?
If you can, I'll say your own hand
can save you.

"Look at the elephant.
I made him, just as I made you.
He eats grass like an ox does.
His legs are strong.
His belly muscles have power!
His trunk swings like a cedar tree.
His bones are like metal bars.
He is one of the best of all I made.
He lets me come near him.
All the wild animals play close by.
But he hides under the water
plants.
The river fills up and rushes by, but
he is not scared.
He is safe even if the water comes
up to his mouth."

An Animal That Is
Not Afraid

JOB 41

"Can you catch a leviathan with a
fish hook?" asked God.
"Can you make him be a pet, like
a bird?

Can you catch him with a spear?
  If you touch him, he will give you
    a fight to remember.
  You won't ever touch him again.
Nobody is strong enough to get him
    out of the water.
  So who can stand against me?
Who can say I owe anything to
    anybody?
  Everything under heaven is
    mine.

"I'll tell about the leviathan's legs.
  I'll tell how strong and beautiful
    he is.
Who can take his skin off?
  Who can try to ride him?
Who dares to open his mouth?
  It has rows of scary teeth inside.
When he breathes hard,
  he throws out flashes of light.
Fire flows out of his mouth.
  Smoke flows out of his nose.
His neck is strong.
  His chest is hard like a rock.
Strong people are scared when he
    stands up.
  They step back when he moves.
A sword doesn't hurt him.
  Iron is like dry grass to him.
Arrows don't make him run away.
  Stones are like nothing.
Sharp pieces of his hide stick out
    under him.
  It makes a trail when he goes
    through the mud.
He makes waves in the sea.

He makes deep water look like
    it's boiling.
He leaves a shining line behind him.
Nothing on earth is quite like him.
  He is an animal that's not afraid
    of anything.
He looks down on proud people.
  He is the king over all proud
    things."

Things Too Wonderful for Me

JOB 42

Then Job said these words to God.

"I know that you can do all things.
  Nothing can stop your plans.
You asked, 'Who talks without
    knowing what he says?'
  I talked about things I didn't
    understand.
  I talked about things too
    wonderful for me to know.

"I had heard of you, but now I have
    seen you.
  So I don't feel good about myself.
    I'm sorry."

Then God talked to Eliphaz. "I'm angry at you. I'm angry at your two friends, too. You didn't say what's right. But Job did. So go to Job. Give him bulls and rams. He will offer them to me as a gift. Job will pray for you. I'll listen to him. Then I won't pay you back for the wrong you've done."

So Eliphaz, Bildad, and Zophar did what God said. And God listened to Job's prayer.

Then God made Job rich again. God gave Job two times as much as he had before.

Job's brothers and sisters came to his house. His friends came. They ate with Job. They cheered him up. Each person gave Job a piece of silver. Each person gave him a gold ring.

God sent many good things to Job. God sent more than he had before. Job ended up with 14,000 (fourteen thousand) sheep and 6,000 camels. He got 2,000 oxen and 1,000 donkeys. He had seven sons and three daughters. His daughters were more beautiful than any other women.

Job lived a long time after this. He lived to see his grandchildren and his great-grandchildren. He died an old man.

JULY 18

Four Big Animals

DANIEL 7

Belshazzar was now king of Babylon. During the king's first year, Daniel had a dream. He was in bed at night. He saw pictures in his mind. So he wrote down his dream.

"I saw four winds from heaven. They made waves in the great sea. Then four big animals came out of the sea. They were all different from each other.

"The first animal was like a lion with eagle wings. The next animal looked like a bear. Another animal looked like a leopard with four wings and four heads. The last animal was terrible, scary, and strong. It had iron teeth and ten horns.

"I was thinking about the horns. Then I saw a little horn grow up with the others. It pushed three of the first horns out. This little horn had eyes like a person's eyes. It had a mouth. It talked proudly.

"I watched.
Kings' thrones were brought in.
    Then the God of All Time sat
        down.
His clothes were as white as snow.
    His hair was white like wool.
The throne he sat on burned with
        fire.
    It had burning wheels.
A fire river flowed out in front of
        him.
Thousands and thousands served
        him.
    Ten thousand times ten thousand
        stood in front of him.
The judge and his helpers sat down.
    Then the books were opened.

"In my dream, I kept watching. I saw someone like a person. He came with heaven's clouds. He went to see the God of All Time. He was given power and greatness. All people and all nations worshiped him. His kingdom will last forever. It will never end. It will never be torn down.

451

"I, Daniel, was upset. The pictures in my mind troubled me. I went up to someone who stood there. I asked him what the meaning of the special dream was.

"He told me the meaning. He said that the four big animals stand for four kingdoms. They will come on the earth. But God's people will get the kingdom. They will have it forever. Yes. Forever and ever.

"Then I wanted to know the meaning of the last animal. It was the most scary. I wanted to know about its 10 horns and the little horn.

"The man told me that the last animal is a different kingdom. It will eat up the whole earth. It will run over it.

"The man said that the 10 horns stand for 10 kings. They'll come from this kingdom. Then another king will come. He will be different from the others. He will take over three kings. He will talk against God. He will give God's people a hard time. He will try to change God's special days and laws. He will rule over God's people for a while.

"But the judge and his helpers will meet together. They'll take the different king's power away. They'll get rid of him forever. Then God will give the kingdoms to his people. He will give them the kingdoms' power and greatness.

His kingdom will last forever. All rulers will worship and obey God.

"This was the end of what I saw. I, Daniel, was very upset. My face lost its color. But I didn't say anything more about it."

A Ram and a Goat
DANIEL 8

Belshazzar had been king of Babylon for three years. Then I, Daniel, had another special dream. I saw myself in a city far away. I was beside a river. There I saw a ram with two long horns.

No other animal could stand against him. No one could save others from his power. He became great.

All of a sudden, a goat came from the west. This goat had a big horn between his eyes. He pushed the ram with two horns down to the ground. The goat with one horn became very great. Then his big horn broke off. Four horns grew where it had been.

Another horn came out of one of the four horns. It was small at first. But it grew until it reached the stars. Then the horn made itself as great as the Prince of the stars. It pushed down the special, holy worship house. It pushed truth down too.

Then I heard a special, holy angel talking. Another special, holy angel answered. "How long will it be before this dream comes true?"

He told me, "It will be 2,300 evenings. It will be 2,300 mornings. Then God's holy worship house will be special again."

I tried to understand the dream. Then I saw someone who looked like a man. I heard a man's voice. It said, "Gabriel, tell this man what the dream means."

He came close to where I stood. But I was scared. I fell down with my face to the ground.

"Son of man, understand this," he said. "This special dream is about the end of time."

Now I was sleeping deeply, but he touched me. He lifted me up to my feet.

He said, "I'll tell you what's going to happen. The dream is about the time when the end comes.

"The goat with long hair is the king of Greece. The big horn between his eyes is the first king. The four horns that grew up are four kingdoms. They won't be as strong.

"People will be against them. The people will get mean. Then another king will come. He will have a hard look on his face. He will be very good at planning lies. He will get very strong. He will win at whatever he does.

"This king will get rid of strong people and holy people. He will lie to get riches. He will think he is the best. People will think they're safe. But he will get rid of many of them. He will stand up against the Prince of princes. Then the king will be torn down, but not by people's power.

"The dream about the mornings and evenings is true. But close and lock up the dream. It's about what will happen a long time from now."

The Fingers That Wrote on the Wall

DANIEL 5

Now King Belshazzar had a great dinner for 1,000 leaders. They were in the palace. They ate, and they drank wine. The king told his servants to bring gold and silver cups. The cups were from the worship house in Jerusalem.

The servants brought in the gold and silver cups. The king and leaders drank wine out of them. The king's wives and other ladies drank wine out of them. While they drank, they cheered for their fake gods.

All of a sudden the fingers of a man's hand showed up. The fingers wrote on the wall by the lamp stand.

The king watched. His face lost its color. He was so scared, his knees shook and hit together. His legs got weak.

The king called for his magic men

to come. He said, "Read this writing. Tell me what it means. Whoever tells me gets to wear the purple clothes of kings. He gets to have a gold chain around his neck. He will be the number three ruler in my kingdom."

So all the king's magic men came in. But they couldn't read the writing. They couldn't tell the king what it meant.

Then King Belshazzar got even more scared. His face lost even more color. His leaders didn't know what to think.

The queen heard their voices. She came into the great hall where they had dinner.

"Live forever, my king!" she said. "Don't be scared! There is a man in this kingdom who is wise. He has the spirit of the holy gods in him. He is as wise as a god. Your father, King Nebuchadnezzar, put him in charge of the magic men. His name is Daniel. He knows and understands lots of things. He can tell the meaning of dreams, too. He can tell you what riddles mean. He can tell what to do about hard problems. Call for Daniel to come. He will tell you what the writing says."

So Daniel came to see the king.

"Are you Daniel?" asked the king. "Are you one of the people my father brought from Judah? I've heard that you are wise. My wise men came. But they couldn't tell me what the writing means. Now I've heard that you can tell what dreams mean. I hear that you know what to do about hard problems. So read this and tell me what it means. Then I'll give you purple clothes. I'll give you a gold chain for your neck. I'll make you the number three ruler in my kingdom."

"You can keep your gifts," said Daniel. "Or you can give them to somebody else. I'll read the writing for you. I'll tell you what it means.

"God gave power to your father, King Nebuchadnezzar. God made him great. People from every nation looked up to him. He killed whoever he wanted to kill. He saved whoever he wanted to save. He made some people great. He put some people down.

"But your father's heart became proud. Then he could not be king. God sent him away from people. God gave him an animal's mind. He lived with wild donkeys. He ate grass like a cow. Dew made his body wet. He lived that way until he said God is King. God rules over the kingdoms. He chooses their kings.

"You know all this, King Belshazzar. But you are still proud. You set yourself up against God. You brought in the cups from his worship house. You drank wine from them. Then you praised fake gods, which can't see or hear or understand.

"You didn't worship God," said Daniel. "He holds your life in his hands. So God sent the hand that wrote on the wall. These are the words.

"MENE, MENE, TEKEL, PARSIN

"Here's what the words mean.

"MENE means God has counted the days of your kingdom. He has ended it.

"TEKEL means you've been tested, and you weren't good enough.

"PARSIN means two other nations will share your kingdom. These are the Medes and the Persians."

Then King Belshazzar gave Daniel purple clothes to wear. He gave him a gold chain for his neck. He made Daniel the number three ruler in his kingdom.

That night King Belshazzar was killed. King Darius from the Medes' nation took over.

Daniel's Prayer and God's Answer

DANIEL 9

Now Darius was the king over Babylon. In his first year, I, Daniel, understood what Jeremiah had written. I understood that Jerusalem would stay torn down for 70 years.

So I prayed. I begged God. I didn't eat anything. I wore clothes made of old sack cloth.

I said, "Lord, you are a great, wonderful God. You keep your promise of love to everyone who loves you. You keep your promise to everyone who obeys you.

"God, you always do what's right. Today your people feel bad. You have sent us to many lands, near and far. It's all because we sinned against you.

"So the bad things written in your laws happened. You made the words come true against us. But we still didn't turn away from our sins. We didn't listen to your truth. So you brought this trouble on us. That's because you are right in all you do.

"God, you do what's good and right. So turn your anger away from Jerusalem. Jerusalem is your city. It's your holy hill. Now, God, hear my prayers. Be kind to your city.

"We don't ask you because we are right and good. We ask because you are kind. Listen, God! Forgive us! Hear and act! Do it because of who you are. Don't wait."

I was praying this to God. Then Gabriel flew to me. I saw him in the dream I had before.

Gabriel said, "Daniel, I came to help you understand. An answer was ready for you right when you began praying. I've come to tell you the answer. Good things are said about you. So think about the message. Understand this special dream.

"Seventy weeks are planned for your people and your holy city. Your people will stop their sin. They will make up for the wrong they've done.

"Know this and understand it. There will be a law made to build Jerusalem back again. Then the special ruler that God chose will come. The city will be built back up. But it will be built in a time of trouble.

"After this, the special ruler will be thrown down. He won't have anything. The next ruler and his people will tear down the city. The end will come like flood water. War will keep on going until the end. That ruler will set up something terrible in the worship house. Then God will get rid of him."

That was the end of Daniel's special dream.

Lions!

DANIEL 6

Now Darius chose 120 leaders for his kingdom. He chose three men to be in charge of them. Daniel was one of those three men.

Daniel did a very good job. So the king planned to put Daniel in charge of everyone.

The other leaders tried to find something wrong with Daniel. But they couldn't. Daniel was someone you could trust. He didn't do wrong. He did a good job with whatever he did.

At last the men said, "We'll never find anything wrong. Let's think of something that has to do with Daniel's God."

So the leaders went to the king. "King Darius, may you live forever!" they said. "We think you should make a law. Tell people to pray only to you for the next 30 days. Anyone who doesn't obey will be thrown into the lions' den. Write this law down. That way, it can't be changed. No one can change the laws of the Medes and Persians."

So King Darius wrote the law down.

Then the men went to see Daniel. They found him praying to God.

So they went back to the king. They said, "Didn't you make a law? Anybody who doesn't pray to you gets thrown to the lions."

"Yes," said the king. "The law can't be changed."

"Daniel isn't listening to you," they said. "He isn't obeying the law. He still prays to God three times every day."

Now the king was very upset. He thought hard about how to save Daniel. He tried everything he could until the sun went down.

Then the men went to the king again. "Remember," they said. "No law you make can be changed."

So the king gave an order for Daniel to be brought in. Then Daniel was thrown into the lions' den.

The king called to Daniel, "May your God save you!"

The king's men found a big stone. They put it in front of the opening into the den. The king marked it by pressing his ring in wax. He did the same with the rings of the other leaders. That was so no one could let Daniel out. No one could help him.

Then the king went back to his palace. He didn't eat anything that night. He didn't have anyone sing or dance for him. He couldn't sleep.

As soon as morning came, the king got up. He ran to the lions' den. He called to Daniel with a sad voice. "Daniel, could your God save you from the lions?"

"May you live forever, King!" Daniel called back. "My God sent his angel. He closed the lions' mouths. They didn't hurt me. That's

because I hadn't done anything wrong to God. And I haven't done anything wrong to you."

The king was very happy. He ordered his servants to take Daniel out of the den. They saw that he was not hurt at all. That's because he trusted God.

The king gave new orders. He called for the men who had blamed Daniel. He had them and their families thrown to the lions. The lions killed them before they touched the ground.

Then King Darius sent a letter to all his people.

"I pray that good things will come to you!

"I'm making a new law.
    All people must look up to Daniel's God.
    He is the living God.
    He lives forever.
    His kingdom will never end.
    He does wonders in the sky and on the earth.
    He saved Daniel from the lions' power."

JULY 21

Going Back Home

EZRA 1; 2:64-70; 3:1-3, 7-13; 4:1-5

Cyrus became the king of Babylon. The land was now called Persia. The first year Cyrus was king, God worked in his heart. God did this to keep the promise he made in his words to Jeremiah. God got Cyrus to make a law. Cyrus wrote it down.

"This is what I, Cyrus, King of Persia, say. God gave me all the kingdoms in the world. He chose me to build a worship house for him. It will be in Jerusalem in Judah. Any of God's people here can go back to Jerusalem. They can build God's worship house back up. The other people here will give them silver. They'll give gold and cows and other things."

Many people chose to go back to Jerusalem. God had worked in their hearts so they would want to go. They got ready to build God's worship house again. Their neighbors helped them. Their neighbors gave them gold and silver. They gave them cows and other things.

Then King Cyrus gave back the gold and silver dishes. These had been taken away from the worship house long ago.

There were 42,360 people who went back to Jerusalem. They took their servants. They took their horses, mules, camels, and donkeys. Singers went too.

They traveled back to God's worship house in Jerusalem. Then they gave gifts for building the worship house again. They started living in their own towns.

Seven months passed. The people had moved into the towns. Then they came to meet together at Jerusalem.

Zerubbabel and some other men built an altar. They were afraid of people from the lands around them. But they built the altar anyway. They offered gifts to God on it.

Then they gave money to the builders. They started building the worship house.

First they made the base for the worship house. When it was finished, they all praised God. They praised God like King David said to do long ago. They thanked God. They sang, "God is good. His love for his people lasts forever." Then all the people shouted praise to God.

Some of the older people cried. They remembered the worship house from long ago. So some of them cried out loud. Some shouted with joy. You couldn't tell the shouting from the crying. There was lots of noise. The sound could be heard far away.

Now the enemies heard about the people coming back. They heard that the worship house was being built again. So they went to Zerubbabel.

"Let us help you," they said. "We're looking for your God too."

But Zerubbabel and the people said, "No. This is for us to do. We'll do it alone. King Cyrus of Persia has told us to."

Then the enemies tried to make God's people give up. They tried to scare them. They paid people to work against Zerubbabel. That happened the whole time Cyrus was king.

A Message and a Dream
DANIEL 10:1-19

Cyrus had been king of Persia for three years. Then God gave Daniel a message about a big war. The meaning of the message came in a special dream.

Then I, Daniel, cried for three weeks. All that time I didn't eat any rich food. I didn't eat meat. I didn't drink wine. I didn't put any sweet-smelling cream on my body.

It was the first month. I stood by the Tigris River. There I saw a man in front of me. He wore linen clothes. He had a gold belt on. His body was like a beautiful stone. His face glowed like lightning. His eyes were like fire. His arms and legs shone like shiny brown metal. His voice sounded like a crowd of people.

I was the only one who saw this.

There were men with me, but they didn't see what I saw. They got scared anyway. They ran and hid.

So there I was alone. My face lost so much color that I looked as if I'd died.

Then I heard the man talk. I went to sleep. I slept deeply, with my face to the ground.

A hand touched me. It pulled me up on my hands and knees. I began to shake.

"Daniel," he said, "good things are said about you. Think about what I'm going to tell you. Stand up, because I've been sent to you."

So I stood up, shaking.

"Don't be afraid," he said. "You chose to try to understand. You chose to make God great instead of yourself. God heard your words from the first day. I came to answer you. But the prince of Persia stopped me for 21 days. Then Michael, a prince of leaders, came to help me. So now I'm here to tell you what will happen. These things will happen in days to come."

I put my face down to the ground. I couldn't say anything.

Then the man touched my lips. I opened my mouth. I began to talk. I said, "Sadness has come over me because of the pictures in my mind. There is no one to help. How can I even talk to you? I'm weak. I can hardly breathe."

Then the one who looked like a man touched me again. He made me stronger. "Don't be afraid," he said. "Good things are said about you. Be at peace! Be strong now. Be strong."

When he talked, I felt stronger. So I said, "Speak. You have made me stronger."

The North King and the South King

DANIEL 10:20–11:24; 11:36-45

"Do you know why I'm here?" asked the one who looked like a man. "Soon I'll go back. I'll fight the prince of Persia. The prince of Greece will come when I leave. But first I'll tell you what's in the Book of Truth.

"Michael is your prince. He is the only one who helps me against them. When Darius first became king of Persia, I chose to help Michael.

"Now three more kings will come in Persia. Then another will come. He will be a lot richer than the others. He will get power because he is so rich. He will get everyone to go against the kingdom of Greece.

"Then a strong king will come. He will rule with great power. He will do whatever he wants.

"After this king is gone, his kingdom will break up. It will be given to others. Then it won't have as much power anymore.

"The king of the South will get to be a strong leader. But one of his captains will be even stronger. He will rule a kingdom of his own.

"Time will pass. Then they'll become friends. The South king's daughter will go to the North king. They'll make a deal to help each other. But they won't keep their power.

"Then someone from her family will take her place. He will fight the North king and win. He will take idols and silver and gold from the people of the North. He will take these things to Egypt.

"Years later, the North king will come out to fight the South king. Then the South king will come out to fight the North king. They'll fight each other many times.

"Then a hateful person will take over. He will take the kingdom of God's people by lying to them and tricking them. He will plan to tear down forts. But this will happen only for a little while.

"This king will do what he wants. He will treat himself as the most important. He will say terrible things against the God of gods. He won't worship any god. Instead, he will say he is the greatest. He will like people who agree with him. He will let them rule over other people.

"Then the end time will come. The South king and North king will march out to fight. Many lands will fall, but some won't. He will put his tents up between the sea and the holy mountain. But his end will come. Then nobody will help him."

Shining like Stars
DANIEL 12

"Now Michael takes care of your people, Daniel. At that time, Michael will watch over you. It will be a time of trouble. There will be more trouble than there has ever been before. But your people will be saved. Everyone whose name is in the book will be saved.

"Many people who have died will wake up. Some will live forever. People who are wise will shine bright like the sky. People who lead others to do right will shine like stars. They'll shine for ever and ever.

"But, Daniel, close these words. Lock them up until the end comes. Many people will go here and there to learn and know."

Then I, Daniel, saw two others. One was on this side of the river. One was on the other side. One said to the man in linen clothes, "How long? How long until these surprising things happen?"

The man in linen was above the river. He held his hands up to heaven. I heard him promise, "It will be for a time, times, and half a time. It will be finished when the holy people's power is broken."

I heard this. But I didn't understand. So I asked, "What does all this mean?"

"Go on your way, Daniel," he said. "The words are closed up. They're locked until the end time. Sin will be cleaned out of many people's hearts. They'll be spotless. Sinful people will keep doing wrong. They won't understand. But wise people will understand.

"God brings good things to people who wait for the end. As for you, go on your way. You'll die. Then in the end you'll live again. You'll get God's gift for you."

A Letter to the King
EZRA 4:6-24

Now Xerxes became the king of Persia. So the enemies of God's people wrote a letter to him. This is what the letter said.

To King Xerxes.

You should know that the Jewish people are building Jerusalem again. They are building the walls around the city too.

If the city gets built again, the people won't pay taxes. We feel like we have to tell you these things. We don't want to see you have trouble. Look in all the old letters and laws. You'll see that this city always brings trouble. That's why it was torn down in the first place. If it's built again, you'll be left with nothing.

From your servants.

The king sent an answer back.

Hello.

We read your letter. I looked in the old letters and laws. I found that this city always brings trouble. Jerusalem had strong kings. Tell these people to stop building the city. It won't be built until I say so.

The enemies read the king's answer. Then they went to the Jewish people in Jerusalem. The enemies made them stop building the city.

So the work on the worship house in Jerusalem stopped. It didn't start again until the second year Darius was the king in Persia.

Who Told You?

EZRA 5

Now two prophets spoke in Jerusalem and all over Judah. One was Haggai. The other was Zechariah. God talked to them, and they told God's words.

Zerubbabel started working to build the worship house again. The two prophets were there, helping him.

The leaders of the people around there went to Zerubbabel. They said, "Who told you that you could build again? Who are these men doing the work?"

But God was taking care of his people. So nobody stopped them just then. The leaders from around there had to send a letter to King Darius. Then they had to wait for an answer.

Here's the letter that the leaders sent to King Darius.

To King Darius.

Hello.

You should know that we went to Judah. We went to God's worship house. The people are building it again. They are using big stones and wood. They are working quickly.

We asked them who told them to do that. We asked them what their names were. We wanted to let you know who was doing this. Here's what they told us.

They said that they serve the God of heaven and earth. They are building his worship house again. A great king of Israel built it long ago. But their people from long ago made God angry. So he gave them to Babylon's army. The army tore down the worship

house and took the people to
Babylon.

They told us that later,
King Cyrus said to build the
worship house again. He even
sent back the gold and silver
dishes. The people brought
them to Jerusalem, and they
started building. They have been
working on it all this time. But it's
not finished yet.

Now, please look back at the
old laws and letters of Babylon.
See if King Cyrus did tell them
to build this worship house. Let
us know what you learn about
this.

The Roll of Paper
EZRA 6:1-13

King Darius looked at the old laws
and letters. He found a roll of paper
with a message on it. It said,

A note to help everyone
remember.

King Cyrus made a law in
his first year as king. It was
about God's worship house in
Jerusalem. This is what it said.

Let the worship house be built
again. The king's money will help
pay for it. The gold and silver
dishes Babylon took will be given
back. They'll be put back in God's
worship house.

So King Darius sent a letter to the
leaders who lived around God's
people.

I want you to stay away from the
Jewish people. Don't bother them
while they build God's worship
house.

What's more, I want you to
help them. Pay for the building
with your land's tax money. That
way, the work won't stop. Give
them whatever they need. Give
them bulls, rams, lambs, wheat,
salt, wine, and oil. Give it to them
each day. Then they can give gifts
to God. And they can pray for the
king and his sons.

If anybody changes this law, he
is in trouble. He will be killed and
his house will be torn down. It
will be left as a pile of sticks and
stones. I hope God tears down
anyone who changes this law. I
hope he tears down anyone who
hurts the worship house.

I, Darius, have made this a law.
Let it be done.

So the leaders who lived around God's
people did what King Darius said.

A Pile of Sticks and Stones
HAGGAI 1

Darius had been king of Persia for
two years. Then God spoke to

Haggai the prophet. He told Haggai what to tell Zerubbabel, the leader of Judah. These were God's words.

"The people say that it's not time to build the worship house. But I ask you this. Is it time for you to live in nice houses? Should you do that while my worship house is a pile of sticks and stones?

"Think about what you do. You planted a lot of seeds. But you grew just a few crops. You eat. But you never have enough food. You drink. But you never get full. You wear clothes. But you don't get warm. You get money for working. But your money bags seem to have holes in them. That's because my worship house is a pile of sticks and stones. Each of you is busy with his own house.

"Think about what you do. Go to the mountains. Get wood there. Build my worship house. That will show you care about me," says God.

Then Zerubbabel and all the people obeyed God. They treated God as the most important one.

Then Haggai gave them another message from God. "I am with you," says God.

So God changed the people's hearts. Then they wanted to work on God's worship house. They started building it again.

Shaking the Earth
HAGGAI 2:1-9; ZECHARIAH 1:1-6

Then God spoke to Haggai again. "Tell Zerubbabel and the people to be strong. Work. I'm with you, just as I promised. My Spirit stays with you. So don't be afraid.

"Someday, I'll come and shake the sky. I'll shake the earth, the sea, and the dry land. I'll shake all the nations. This worship house will be greater than the first one. I will bring peace to this place," says God.

That same year God spoke to Zechariah the prophet. "I was very angry with your families from long ago," God said. "Come back to me. Then I'll come back to you. Don't be like your people from long ago. The prophets told them to turn away from sin. But they didn't listen. Where are they now? The messages I gave the prophets came true for them."

A Man on a Red Horse
ZECHARIAH 1:7-21

Zechariah wrote this about pictures he had in his mind.

I saw pictures in the night. I saw a man riding a red horse! He was among trees in a little valley. Red, brown, and white horses were behind him.

An angel was there, talking to me.

"What are the horses?" I asked.

"I'll show you," said the angel.

The man by the trees spoke. "They are the ones God is sending through the earth."

Then the riders of the other horses talked to the angel. "We went through the earth," they said. "We found rest and peace all over the world."

The angel said, "God, how long will it be before we have peace too? How long will you keep your kindness away from Jerusalem? You've been angry with Jerusalem for 70 years."

So God spoke kind words to the angel.

Then the angel spoke to me. "Tell people this word. God says that he wants Jerusalem for himself.

He was just a little angry with his people. But now he is very angry with the other nations. They made even more trouble.

"So God says he will go back to Jerusalem. He will be kind to Jerusalem. His worship house will be built again.

"His towns will also grow and have good times again. He will choose Jerusalem. He will cheer up his city."

Then I saw four horns in front of me. I asked the angel, "What are these?"

"These are the nations that sent my people away," he said.

Then God showed me four workers.

"What are they doing?" I asked.

"They are going to scare the horns," he said. "They'll destroy the nations that came to fight Judah."

A Wall of Fire

ZECHARIAH 2

Then I saw a man holding a ruler. "Where are you going?" I asked.

"I'm going to measure the city of Jerusalem," he said. "I'm going to see how wide and long it is."

Then the angel left. He was the one who had talked to me. Another angel came to meet him.

"Run!" said the other angel. "Say that the city of Jerusalem won't have walls. That's because there will be many people and animals in it."

"I'll be like a wall of fire for Jerusalem," says God. "I'll be its greatness."

"Come on! Come on! Run away from the north," says God. "I've sent you to the four winds.

"Come on, Jerusalem! Get away, my people who live in Babylon! Anyone who touches you touches the ones I love. I'll put out my hand against them.

"Shout! Be happy! I'm coming. I'll live with you," says God. "Many nations will come and be with me then. They'll be my people.

"Judah will be my place. I will choose Jerusalem. So everybody be still in front of me. I'm coming out of the place where I live."

New, Clean Clothes

ZECHARIAH 3

Then God showed me Joshua, the high priest. He was standing in front of God's angel. But Satan was standing there too. Satan was there to blame Joshua.

God told Satan, "I say you're wrong! I chose Jerusalem. This man has been saved from the fire."

Now Joshua was wearing dirty clothes. The angel said, "Take off the dirty clothes."

Then he told Joshua, "I have taken your sin away. I'll put new, clean clothes on you."

I said, "Put a clean hat on his head."

So they did. Then God's angel stood beside him.

God's angel told Joshua these words from God. "Obey me. Keep my laws. Then you'll rule over my worship house.

"Listen, Joshua. Listen, you helpers of Joshua. I'm going to bring my servant. See? I put a rock in front of Joshua. I'll write something on it," says God. "I'll take the sin of the land away in one day.

"Then each person will ask his neighbor to come over. They'll sit under the vine and the fig tree," says God.

JULY 25

A Gold Lamp Stand

ZECHARIAH 4; 5:5-11

The angel who talked with me came back. He woke me up. It was like waking up somebody who is asleep.

The angel gave me this message from God to Zerubbabel. "Your power doesn't come from being strong. It comes from my Spirit. Zerubbabel's hands started building the worship house. His hands will finish it."

The angel asked, "What do you see?"

"I see a gold lamp stand," I said. "There's a bowl on top. There are seven lights on it. Two olive trees are beside it. One is on the right side. The other is on the left side. What are they?" I asked.

"Don't you know?" asked the angel.

"No," I said.

"The seven lights stand for God's eyes. They look around all over the earth."

"What do the olive trees mean?" I asked.

"Don't you know?" asked the angel.

"No," I said.

"They are the two who are chosen to serve God," he said.

"Look up," he said. "See what's coming."

"What is it?" I asked.

"It's a basket," he said. "Think about it as if it's filled with people's sins."

The heavy metal cover of the basket was lifted off. A woman sat in the basket!

"Think about this as sin," said the angel. He pushed the woman back inside the basket. He closed the heavy cover.

Then I saw two women in front of me. They had wings that looked like a stork's wings. The wind was in their wings! They picked up the basket. They took it up into the sky.

"Where are they taking the basket?" I asked.

"To Babylon," he said. "They'll build a house for it there. That's where they'll put the basket."

Four Chariots

ZECHARIAH 6

Then I saw four chariots coming. They came from between two shiny, brown metal mountains.

Red horses pulled the first chariot. Black horses pulled the next one. White horses pulled the next one. Spotted horses pulled the last chariot. All the horses were very strong.

"What are they?" I asked.

"They are heaven's four winds," said the angel who was with me. "They stand in front of God. They are going out into the world. The black horses are pulling their chariot north. The white horses pull their chariot west. The spotted horses pull their chariot south."

The horses were pulling forward. They were ready to go through the whole earth.

"Go!" said the angel. "Go around the world."

So the horses headed out.

"Look!" the angel said. "The horses going north let God's Spirit rest in the north."

Then God told me this. "Get silver and gold from people who've just come from Babylon. Then make a crown out of the silver and gold. Put the crown on the high priest, Joshua.

"Tell Joshua what I say. I say that here is the man who is called the Branch. He will build God's worship house. He will sit on the king's throne. He will be a priest on the king's throne."

Then God said, "People will come from far away. They will help build the worship house. This will happen if you're careful to obey me."

Will It Surprise Me?

EZRA 6:14-22; ZECHARIAH 8:1-6, 12-17, 20-23

God spoke to me again. "I want my city. I'll come back and live in Jerusalem. It will be called the City of Truth. My mountain will be called the Holy Mountain."

Here's what God says. "Old people will sit in Jerusalem's streets. They'll have canes in their hands. Boys and girls will play in the streets.

"That might surprise people who come back," says God. "But will it surprise me?

"Seeds will grow," says God. "Vines will grow fruit. The land will make crops. Rain and dew will come from the sky. All of this will be for my people.

"I planned to bring trouble to you," says God. "Your people from long ago made me angry. I didn't feel sorry for you. But now I plan to bring good to you. So don't be afraid. Here's what you should do. Tell the truth. Be fair. Don't plan bad things against your neighbors. Don't love lies. Those are things I hate.

"Many people and many nations will come to Jerusalem. They will look for me," says God. "They will pray to me. People from all nations will hold on to one Jewish person. They'll ask to go with that person. 'We've heard that God is with you,' they'll say."

The leaders kept building. Good things came to them. They listened to the teaching of Zechariah and Haggai.

The people finished building God's worship house. Then they had a great holiday for God. They offered many bulls, rams, lambs, and goats to him.

They also had their Pass Over holiday. This was their Holiday of Flat Bread. All God's people who had come back home had this

holiday. It lasted for seven days.
God filled everyone with joy.

JULY 26

My Bow and My Sword

PSALM 44:1-8

Our fathers from long ago told us
what you did.
You planted your people in their
land.
You made your people grow
strong.
They didn't win the land by swords.
They didn't win by their strong
arms.
The power of your right hand won
for them.
The light of your face was on
them, and they won.
It's all because you loved your
people.

You are my King and my God.
It's by your name that we win.
I don't trust in my bow and arrow.
My sword does not make me win.
You make us win over our enemies.
We talk about how great God is all
day long.
We will praise your name forever.

Love That Lasts Forever

PSALM 107:1-31

Give thanks to God. He is good.
His love lasts forever.

Let the people that God saved say so.
He saved people from many lands.

Some people went here and there in
the desert.
They could not find a city to stay in.
They were hungry and thirsty.
Then they called to God, and he
saved them.
He led them on a road that did not
turn.
He led them to a city where they
could stay.
So let them thank God for his love
that lasts forever.
Let them thank him for the
wonderful things he does.
He gives thirsty people a drink.
He fills hungry people with good
things.

Some people sat in the dark.
They were in jail with chains on.
They had not obeyed God.
They did not think God was
important.
So they had to work hard.
When they fell, there was nobody
to help them up.
Then they called to God, and he
saved them.
He took them out of the dark.
He broke off their chains.
So let them thank God for his love
that lasts forever.
Let them thank him for the
wonderful things he does.

He breaks down metal gates.
He cuts through iron bars.

Other people sailed ships on the sea.
They took loads of things to sell
to other lands.
They saw the wonderful things God
did in the deep sea.
God spoke and brought a storm.
He made waves jump up high.
The ship tossed as high as the sky.
Then it went down deep.
The people were in danger.
Their boldness seemed to melt
away.
They tripped and fell as if they were
drunk.
Then they called to God, and he
saved them.
He turned the storm into a whisper.
He made the waves be quiet.
The people were glad when the sea
was still.
God took them to a safe place on
land.
So let them thank God for his love
that lasts forever.
Let them thank him for the
wonderful things he has done.

God's Right Hand

PSALM 118:1, 5-6, 8-16, 19-24, 28-29

Give thanks to God. He is good.
His love lasts forever.

While I was upset, I called to God.
He answered me and set me free.

God is with me.
I will not be afraid.
What can people do to me?
It is better to trust in God than to
trust in people.

All the nations came to fight me.
But I won in God's name.
They were like bees around me.
But they burned out like weeds
on fire.

They pushed me back, and I almost
fell.
But God helped me.
God makes me strong.
He saves me.
Shouts of joy come from the tents of
people who do what is right.
They say, "God's right hand has
done powerful things!"

Open the gates to what's right.
I will go in and give thanks to God.
People who do what is right may
go in.
I will thank you, God, because you
answered me.
You saved me.

There was a stone that builders
didn't want.
Now that stone holds up the
whole building.
God made this happen.
We think it's wonderful.
This is the day that God has made.

Let's show our joy and be glad today.

You are my God.
I will thank you.
I will treat you as the most important one.
Give thanks to God. He is good.
His love lasts forever.

Laughing and Joy

PSALM 126

Enemies had taken us away.
But God brought us back to Jerusalem.
It was like a dream.
We were full of laughing and joy.
God has done great things for us.
We are full of joy.

Give us what belongs to us, God.
Let it be like rivers in the desert.
People may go out crying, holding seeds to plant.
But they will come back with happy songs.
They will bring the crops they have gathered.

Like Olive Branches

PSALM 128

Good things come to people who walk in God's ways.
God's riches will come to you.

Your wife will be like a vine with fruit.
Your sons will be like olive branches.
They will be around your table.
The man who looks up to God will have these good things.

I pray that God will give you these good things all your life.
I pray that you will see Jerusalem grow.
I pray that you will live long enough to see your grandchildren.

I pray that God's people will have peace.

He Counts the Stars

PSALM 147

Praise God!
It is good to sing praise to our God.

God makes Jerusalem strong.
He brings back the people who were sent away.
He mends their broken hearts.
He takes care of their hurts.

He counts the stars and calls each one by its name.
Our God is great and strong.
There is no end to his understanding.

God takes care of people who know
they are not important.
But he lets sinful people fall to the
ground.

Sing to God and thank him.
Make music to God on the harp.
He makes clouds cover the sky.
He brings rain to the earth.
He makes grass grow on the hills.
He gives the cows their food.
He gives food to the young
ravens when they call.

A horse may be strong, but that's
not what makes God happy.
A man's legs may be strong, but
that's not what makes God
happy.
God is happy with people who love
him.
He is happy with people who
trust in his love.
He is happy when they know that
his love never ends.

Bow before God, Jerusalem.
Praise your God, Zion.
He makes your gates strong.
He gives good things to your
people.
He gives your land peace.
He brings you fine wheat.

God lays out the snow like wool.
He sends down the frost like dust
from a fire.

He throws down his hail like tiny
rocks.
Who can stand up against the icy
wind?
God sends his word, and the ice
melts.
He brings his light winds, and the
water flows.

God showed his word to Jacob.
He told his laws to Israel.
He didn't do this for any other
nation.
Other nations don't know his
laws.

Praise God!

Singing in Bed
PSALM 149:1-5, 9

Cheer for God!
Sing a new song to God.
Sing praise to him together with
everyone who loves him.

Let God's people show joy in their
Maker.
Let them praise him with dancing.
Let them make music to him with
the tambourine and the harp.
God is happy with his people.
He saves them.
So let them show their joy and sing
with joy in bed.

Praise God!

472

A Time for Saving God's People

God's Arrow

ZECHARIAH 9:9-17

Zechariah wrote these words.

Show your joy, Jerusalem!
See? Your king is coming to you.
He is right. He saves you.
He is kind and good.
He rides on a donkey.
It's a colt, a donkey's baby.
He will break the bow and arrow.
He will send peace to the nations.
He will rule from one sea to another.
He will rule over all the earth.
I have made a special promise to you.
I'll set you free.
I'll give you two times as much as
you had before.
I'll wake up the people of my city,
Zion.

Then God will appear over them.
God's arrow will flash like
lightning.
God will blow the war horn.
He will march out in storms in
the south.
God's people will tear down the
enemies.
Then God will save his people.
They'll shine in his land like shiny
stones in a crown.
They'll be beautiful.
Grain and new wine will make
them live and grow.

Coming Back

ZECHARIAH 10:4-12

"The stone that holds the building
up will come from Judah.
The peg that holds the tent up
comes from him.
The war bow comes from him.
Every ruler comes from him.
God is with them.
They'll fight their enemies.

"I'll make Judah strong.
I'll save my people.
I'll bring them back, because I care
for them.

It will be like I never turned away
    from them.
I'm the Lord their God.
    I'll answer them.
They'll be strong.
    Their hearts will be glad.
Their children will be happy to see it.
    Their hearts will show their joy in
    God.
I'll call for them.
    I'll bring them in.
I'll save them.
    There will be as many of them as
    before.
I may send them here and there in
    the nations.
    But even far away, they'll
    remember me.
They will live. Their children will live.
    And they will come back.
I'll bring them back from Egypt.
    I'll bring them from the North.
I'll bring them in.
    There won't be enough room for
    them.
I'll make them strong.
    They'll walk in my name," says
    God.

JULY 29

A Riddle

ZECHARIAH 11:4-17

God said, "Choose sheep. Put them
in the field. They will be like my
people. They will have trouble."

So I took care of the sheep. I
took special care of the ones who
had trouble. I got two sticks used
for walking. I named one stick
"Kindness." I named the other stick
"Together." Then I took care of
the sheep. I had to send three bad
shepherds away in one month.

But the sheep hated me. I got
tired of them. I said, "I won't be
your shepherd anymore. Let the
sheep die."

I broke my walking stick named
Kindness. The troubled sheep knew
it was God's word.

I told them, "Pay me if you think
you should. If you don't think you
should pay me, keep the money."

So they paid me. They paid 30
pieces of silver.

God told me, "Throw the money
to the potter." So I threw the silver
to the potter in God's house.

Then I broke my walking stick
named Together. That meant that
Judah and Israel weren't together
anymore.

Then God told me, "I'm going to
bring a shepherd for this land. But
he won't care about lost sheep. He
won't look for little ones. He won't
make the sick ones well. He won't
feed the strong ones. Instead, he will
eat the meat of the best sheep.

"There's bad news for the shepherd
    who is no good.

He leaves his sheep!
Let the sword hit him.
   Then he can't see or work."

Fire and a Fountain

ZECHARIAH 12:1-9; 13:1-2, 7-9

Here's what God says about Israel. He says, "I'm going to make Jerusalem like a cup. It will be like a drink that makes people dizzy.

"All nations in the world will come to fight Jerusalem. Then I'll make Jerusalem like a rock that won't move. Anybody who tries to move it will get hurt. I'll make the war horses panic. I'll make the riders go crazy," says God.

"I'll make Judah's leaders like a pot of fire. They'll be like a pot of fire in a wood pile! They'll be like a stick of fire in a hay stack. They'll take over people everywhere. But Jerusalem will stay where it is. It won't be hurt. I'll get rid of every nation that comes to fight Jerusalem."

"Then a fountain will open for my people," says God. "It will clean sin out of their hearts.

"I'll get rid of the idols from the land. Nobody will even remember them," says God. "I'll take away sin. I'll take away prophets who lie.

"Wake up, sword. Fight against my shepherd.

Fight against the one who is close to me!" says God.
"Hit the shepherd.
   Then the sheep will run here and there.
I'll take the ones who are left.
   I'll clean them up like silver.
   I'll test them like gold.
They'll call my name, and I'll answer them.
I'll say that they are my people.
   They'll say that I, the Lord, am their God."

A One-of-a-Kind Day

ZECHARIAH 14:1, 3-11, 20-21

God's day is coming. Then God will go out and fight the nations. His feet will stand on Olive Mountain. It's east of Jerusalem. Olive Mountain will break into two parts. A big valley will be made in the middle. Half of the mountain will move north. Half of it will move south. Then God will come. All the holy ones will come.

There won't be any light on that day. There won't be cold or ice. That day will be one of a kind. It won't have day or night. It's a day that God knows about. When night should come, it will be light.

Then water that brings life will flow out of Jerusalem. Half of it will flow to the sea on the east. Half of it will flow to the sea on the west. It will flow in summer and winter.

The Lord will be king of the whole earth. There will be only one Lord then. His name will be the only name.

Jerusalem will stay where it is. People will live in it. It will never be torn down again. Jerusalem will be safe.

People will write HOLY TO THE LORD on the horses' bells. Every pot in Judah will be holy to God. Everyone who comes to God's house will belong to him.

JULY 30

The King's Dinner Party

ESTHER 1

It was some time after God gave messages to Zechariah. There was now another king named Xerxes. He was king of Persia. His palace was in the city of Susa.

Xerxes had been king for three years when he had a big party. All the rich men and leaders came. All the army leaders and princes came.

The king showed the riches of his kingdom to everyone for 180 days. After that, the king had a dinner party. It was in the king's garden. All of the men of Susa came. There were some important men and some not-so-important men.

There were marble posts in the garden. White and blue cloth hung from the posts on white ropes. The floor was made from small tiles of stones that cost a lot. Silver and gold seats were all around.

Everyone got to drink wine from gold cups. Each cup was different from the others. There was plenty of wine. And the king  gave it out freely. The king told his servants to serve whatever the people asked for.

Queen Vashti had a dinner party for the women. It was in the king's palace.

Seven days passed. The king was feeling good from drinking so much wine. So he asked his servants to bring the queen in. He said she should wear her queen's crown. That way, everyone could see how beautiful she was. She was very pretty.

So the servants went to get the queen. But she wouldn't come.

That made the king very angry. He called his wise men. He asked them what to do. "What does the law say?" asked the king. "The queen has not obeyed my command."

One of the wise men said, "She has done wrong. This is bad for you and all your people. All the women will hear about this. Then they won't obey their husbands. They'll say, 'The queen didn't have to obey the king.' So they won't obey their husbands. There will be fussing and fighting.

"Make a law," said the wise man. "Say that the queen can never come see you again. Then choose a new queen. The new queen should be better than the old queen. That way, all the women will hear about this. Then they'll obey their husbands."

The king liked what the wise man told him. So he did it. He sent news out into all the kingdom. He said every man should rule his own house.

The New Queen

ESTHER 2

Later, the king cooled down. He wasn't angry anymore. He remembered the queen. He remembered what she did. He remembered the law he had made.

Then the king's helpers gave him an idea. "Let people look for beautiful young women in your land. Choose men to bring these women to the city of Susa. One of your helpers is in charge of the women. Let him take care of these young women. They can have special beauty care. Then you can

see which one you like best. She can be the new queen."

The king liked this idea. So he did it.

Now in Susa there was a Jewish man named Mordecai. He had come from a family of people taken from Jerusalem. He had a cousin named Esther. She was very beautiful. Her mother and father had died. So Mordecai was taking care of her. He treated her like his own daughter.

Many young women were coming to Susa. The king's helper was taking care of them. Esther was taken to the palace too. The king's helper liked Esther very much. He gave her special beauty care and special food. He gave her seven maids from the palace. He gave Esther and her maids the best place to stay.

Esther had not told anyone she was Jewish. Mordecai had told her not to talk about it.

Every day Mordecai walked around near the palace yard. He tried to find out what kinds of things were happening to Esther.

Now the beauty care for a young woman took 12 months. She had six months with special oils. She had six months with perfumes and make-up. Then she would go see the king. She could take anything she wanted with her.

The young woman would go see the king in the evening. The next morning, she would leave. Then she'd stay with the young women in another part of the palace. She wouldn't go back to the king unless he liked her. Then he might ask her to come back.

One evening, Esther's turn came. Everyone who saw Esther liked her. And the king liked her more than any other girl. So he put the crown on her head. He made her the new queen.

Then the king gave a great dinner party for Esther. All the rich men and leaders came. The king said that day would be a holiday everywhere. He gave gifts to people.

Now Mordecai kept sitting near the king's gate. There were two guards at the door. These guards got angry at the king. They made plans to kill him.

But Mordecai found out about their plans. He told Queen Esther. Queen Esther told the king. She said that Mordecai had found this out.

The king checked it out. He found out that this was true. So the two guards were killed. They were hanged on poles. All of this was written down in the king's book.

A Letter with Bad News

ESTHER 3:1-13

One day, the king called in a man named Haman. The king made Haman greater than the other leaders. The king said the leaders had to bow to Haman. So all the leaders bowed to him. But Mordecai wouldn't bow to Haman.

The guards at the gate asked Mordecai, "Why don't you obey the king?" Every day they asked him. But he still wouldn't bow. Mordecai had told the guards he was Jewish. So they told Haman about it. They wanted to see what he would think.

Haman was very angry. He thought killing Mordecai wouldn't be enough. So he looked for a way to kill all the Jewish people.

Haman talked to the king about it. "There are some people in your kingdom," he said. "They are different from all the other people. They don't obey your laws. That's not good. So you should make a law to get rid of these people. I'll pay you 375 tons of silver to do it."

So the king took his ring from his finger. He gave it to Haman. "Keep the silver," said the king. "But do whatever you want with these people."

Haman had the king's helpers write a letter in every language. They sent it all around the land. They signed it by marking it with the king's ring. The letter said to kill all the Jewish people. It said to kill everyone, young and old, even women and children. It told the day when they were to be killed.

If I Die

ESTHER 4

Now Mordecai heard about the law. So he tore his clothes. He put on clothes made of old sack cloth. He went through the city, crying. But he could only go up to the king's gate. That's because nobody wearing sack cloth could go in.

Jews all over the land were crying. Many of them wore clothes made of old sack cloth. They were going without food.

Esther's maids told her what Mordecai was doing. Esther was upset. She sent other clothes for him to wear. But he wouldn't wear them. So Esther called for one of her helpers. She asked him to find out what the trouble was.

Esther's helper found out. He told Esther that Mordecai wanted her to talk to the king.

Then Esther sent another message to Mordecai. "I can't go see the king about this. Everyone knows that you can't choose when to see the king. The king has to ask you to come. If you go without being asked, you'll be killed. There's only one way to go in if you aren't asked.

That's if the king holds out his gold rod to you. But it's been 30 days since the king asked me to come."

Mordecai sent a message back to Esther. "Don't think you're safe just because you live at the palace. If you're quiet, our people will be saved some other way. But you and your family will die. But who knows? Maybe the reason you became queen is so you can help our people now."

Esther sent a message back to Mordecai. "Get all the Jews in Susa together. Go without food for me. Don't eat or drink for three days. I'll go without food too. My maids will go without food. After three days, I'll go to the king. I'll go even if he hasn't called me. Then if I die, I die."

So Mordecai did what Esther asked.

Haman Brags

ESTHER 5

After three days, Esther put on the robes she wore as queen. She went to the inside hall of the palace. It was in front of the king's hall.

The king was sitting on his throne. He was facing the door to the hall. He saw Queen Esther standing there. He was glad to see her. He held out his gold rod.

Esther walked up and touched the end of the gold rod.

"What do you want, Queen Esther?" asked the king. "I'll give you whatever you want. I'll even give you half of my kingdom if you want."

"I have made a great dinner," said Esther. "Please come to my dinner. Bring Haman with you."

So the king called out, "Bring Haman right away. We will do what Esther asks."

So the king and Haman went to Esther's dinner. They drank wine. Then the king asked Esther, "What would you like to have? I'll give it to you. I'll even give you half of my kingdom if you want."

"Here's what I want," said Esther. "If you like me, come to dinner again tomorrow. Bring Haman with you. Then I'll answer your question."

Haman left very happy. But then he saw Mordecai. He saw that

Mordecai didn't stand up when he passed. He also saw that Mordecai wasn't afraid of him. So he got very angry. But he controlled himself. He went home.

Then Haman called his friends and his wife. He bragged about his riches. He bragged about how many sons he had. He bragged about how the king had made him great. He bragged about how important he was.

"That's not all," said Haman. "The queen asked the king to come to dinner. I'm the only other person she invited. She wants me to come with the king again tomorrow.

"But I can't really be happy about this," said Haman. "Not as long as Mordecai sits at the king's gate."

Haman's wife and friends said, "Set up a hanging pole. Make it 75 feet high. Tomorrow morning, ask the king to hang Mordecai on it. Then you can go to dinner with the king. And you can be happy."

Haman liked this idea. So he had the pole set up.

The King's Book

ESTHER 6

That night, the king couldn't sleep. So he told his servant to bring in his book. It was the story of what had happened since he became king. He asked his servant to read to him.

The servant read about the two guards. He read about their plan to kill the king. He read about how Mordecai had found out. He had told the king about it.

"What did we do to thank Mordecai?" asked the king.

"Nothing," said his servants.

"Who is out in the hall right now?" asked the king.

Now Haman had just come into the hall. He was going to talk to the king about hanging Mordecai.

"Haman is in the hall," said the servants.

"Bring Haman in," said the king.

So Haman came in.

"There's a man I want to thank," said the king. "What should I do to make him great?"

Haman thought, "Who would the king want to thank? Me!" So Haman said, "Bring one of your robes. Bring one of your horses. Choose a leader to put your robe on this man. Then the leader will lead the man on your horse. They'll go through the streets. The leader will shout. He will say that the king gladly makes this man great!"

"Go right away," said the king. "Get the robe and the horse. I want you to do this for Mordecai. He sits at my gate. Do everything you said."

So Haman had to get the robe and horse. He put the robe on Mordecai.

Then he led Mordecai on the horse through the streets. He had to call, "The king gladly makes this man great!"

After that, Mordecai went back to the king's gate. But Haman ran home. He was very upset and sad. He told his wife and his friends what had happened.

They said, "You can't work against Mordecai! You'll just have trouble!"

They were still talking about this when servants came. They were there to take Haman to Esther's dinner.

Who Dares to Do This?

ESTHER 7

Haman and the king went to Esther's dinner. They drank wine. Then the king asked Esther, "What do you want? I'll give you whatever you ask for. You can even have half of my kingdom if you want."

Then Queen Esther said, "Please save my life. That's what I want. Save my people. If you don't, we will be killed."

"Who is this enemy?" asked the king. "Where is the man who would dare to do this?"

"The enemy is this hateful man, Haman," said Esther.

Haman was very scared.

The king got up. He was very angry. He went out to the garden.

Haman saw that the king had made up his mind. The king knew what he'd do to Haman. So Haman stayed with Queen Esther. He begged her to save his life.

The king came back into the room. There he saw Haman, holding on to Esther's chair, begging her.

"Will you even try to touch my queen?" cried the king.

Then the servants pulled Haman away.

One servant said, "A tall hanging pole stands next to Haman's house. He was going to hang Mordecai on it. But Mordecai is the one who saved your life."

"Hang Haman on the pole!" said the king.

So they hung Haman on the pole he made for Mordecai. Then the king stopped being angry.

Fast Horses Carry the News

ESTHER 8:1-10, 14-17

That day, the king gave Haman's house to Esther. He gave Haman's land to Esther too. Then Esther told the king that Mordecai was her cousin. So the king called for Mordecai to come see him.

Now the king had taken his ring back from Haman. So he gave his ring to Mordecai. Then Esther put Mordecai in charge of Haman's land.

Esther bowed at the king's feet. She cried. She asked him to stop the killing of the Jews. The king held out his gold rod. Esther stood up in front of the king.

"Please write another law," she said. "Write a law that will stop the killing. How can I stand to see my people killed?"

"No law can be changed," said the king. "That's because it was written in my name. It was sealed with my ring. But you can write another law in my name. Write it to help the Jews. Do whatever seems best to you."

So Mordecai wrote a new law. It was written in every language. Mordecai wrote the law in the king's name. He sealed it with the king's ring. The law said that the Jews could fight back. They could kill anyone who tried to kill them.

Mordecai sent men through all the country. They rode the king's fast horses. They raced out of the city to tell everyone the new law.

Then Mordecai left the king. The king had given him blue and white clothes to wear. Mordecai also wore a big gold crown and a purple robe.

Then the city had a holiday. It

was a happy, joyful time for the Jews. All Jews who heard the king's new law were glad. So there were parties and dinners everywhere. In fact, lots of other people became Jews. That's because they were afraid of the Jews.

The Holiday

ESTHER 9:1-5, 12-14, 17-32; 10

Now the day came to kill the Jews. That's what the first law said. It was the day that the enemies of the Jews had wanted. But the second law said the Jews could fight back. So the Jews got together in every city. They got ready to fight people who would fight them.

Nobody could win against the Jews. All the other people were scared of them. Even the leaders helped the Jews. They were afraid of Mordecai. Mordecai was now an important man at the palace. People everywhere had heard about him. He got more and more power.

So the Jews killed their enemies that day. The king told Queen Esther about it. "Now what would you like to have?" he asked. "I'll give you whatever you want."

"Let the Jews keep fighting their enemies tomorrow," Esther said. "And get rid of Haman's sons."

So the king gave the order. The Jews fought against their enemies the next day. Haman's sons were killed too.

The day after that, the Jews rested. It was a day of big, happy dinners. That's why Jews make that day a holiday every year. It's a day when they give presents to each other.

Mordecai wrote all of this down. He sent letters to all the Jews in the land. The letter told them to have a two-day holiday. He told them to have big dinners. He told them to be happy. He told them to give gifts to each other. He told them to give gifts to poor people too.

They call these days Purim. That's because Haman and his friends had thrown the pur. It was like throwing dice. That's how they chose the day when they'd kill the Jews. So every family of Jews should remember this holiday every year.

Queen Esther and Mordecai wrote a letter. It said that Purim would be a holiday. Mordecai sent the letter to all the Jews in the land. It cheered up all the Jews.

Now the king made his people pay taxes. His kingdom was very big and great. The king was the boss. But Mordecai was the next man in charge. The Jews liked Mordecai. He worked to treat them right. He spoke up for them.

A Gift of Sick Animals

MALACHI 1:1-13

Sometime later, a prophet named Malachi talked to God's people. Here's what God told Malachi to say.

"I loved you," says God. "You ask me how I loved you.

"This is how. Esau was Jacob's brother," says God. "But I loved Jacob. I chose him. I turned Esau's land into a desert called Edom."

The people of Edom might say, "We were torn down. But we'll build this pile of sticks and stones back up."

Here's what God says. "They might build again. But I'll tear it down again. They'll be called the Sinful Land. The people make me angry. You'll see it for yourself. You'll say, 'God is Great. He is great even in lands outside of Israel.'

"A son looks up to his father. A servant looks up to his master. I am a father. Where is the praise my people should give me? I am a master. Where are the good things my servants should say about me?" asks God. "It's you priests who treat me like nothing.

"You ask how you have treated me like nothing.

"This is how. You offer me animals you don't want. You bring me the sheep that can't see. You bring me sick animals and animals that can't walk.

Just try to give those animals to your rulers. Would they be happy with a gift like that?" asks God.

"Now ask me to be kind and loving to you. Will I let you come to me? I'm not happy with you. So I won't let you give me your gifts," says God.

"My name will be great in all nations, east and west. Good, clean gifts and sweet smells will be given to me. My name will be great in all nations," says God.

"But you make my name sound bad. You talk about the table in my worship house. You say, 'It's dirty.' You talk about the food there. 'It's bad,' you say. Then you say that doing my work is too hard for you. You treat it as if it's not important," says God.

Promises

MALACHI 2:10, 13-16

One God made us. But we break the promise we made together with him. We do it by breaking promises to each other. Why do we do this?

You cry at the altar. You cry because God is not happy with your gifts. You ask, "Why?" It's because God has seen you break your promises. You did not stay with your wife. But you made a promise to her when you married her.

God made a husband and wife to be like one person. Your body and spirit are God's. Why did he make you to be like one person? It's because God wants children who care about what he says. So guard yourself. Don't break your promise to your wife.

"I hate it when you leave the one you married," says God. "I hate it when you are mean and hurtful."

So guard yourself. Don't break your promises.

A Land That Brings Joy

MALACHI 3:1, 5–4:6

"I'll send someone with a message," says God. "He will get the way ready for me. Then suddenly, the Lord you look for will come. He will come to his worship house. He will bring a message about the promise between you and me. He is the one you want.

"I'll come close to you to judge you. I'll speak against witches. I'll speak against people who don't stay with their husbands or wives. I'll speak against liars and people who don't pay their workers. I'm against people who are hard on women whose husbands died. They're hard on children who have no fathers or mothers. They're not fair to people from other lands. They don't care about me," says God.

"I'm the Lord. I don't change. So I've kept you around. You've turned away from me over and over again. You haven't kept my laws. But come back to me. Then I'll come back to you," says God.

"You ask how you can come back.

"I tell you that you rob me," says God.

"You ask how you rob me.

"This is how. You rob me by not giving to me. Trouble is coming to all of you in this nation. It's all because you're robbing me. Bring your gifts to me. Bring your offerings," says God.

"See for yourselves. I'll open the gates of heaven. I'll let good things flow out! You won't have room for all of it. I'll keep bugs from eating up your plants. Your vines will always have good fruit."

"You said bad things about me," says God.

"You ask what you said.

"You said that it does no good to serve me. You said that proud people get good things. You said that people who turn against me get away with it."

Then people who looked up to God talked to each other. God heard them. Their names were written on a roll of paper. These were names that God would remember.

"They'll be mine when I gather my riches," says God. "I'll save them like a man saves his son. You'll see. I don't treat good people and bad people the same.

"A day is coming. It will burn like a hot oven. People who do wrong will be like dry grass. That day will set them on fire," says God. "Nothing will be left for them.

"But it won't be that way for you who obey me. What's good and right will heal you. You'll go out dancing like a calf let out of its pen. You'll run over sinful people. They'll be like dust under your feet," says God.

"See? I'll send a prophet like Elijah to you. He will come before the Lord's great day comes. He will make fathers' hearts turn to their children. He will make children's hearts turn to their fathers."

AUGUST 3

The King Writes to the Teacher

EZRA 7

Artaxerxes had been the king of Persia for seven years. That's when Ezra left Babylon to go to Judah.

Ezra was a teacher. He knew God's laws very well. These were the laws God gave to Moses.

The king gave Ezra whatever he wanted. That's because God was with Ezra.

Other people went with Ezra. Some were priests and singers. Some were men who guarded the gates. Some were servants for the worship house. They all went to Jerusalem in Judah.

The king gave Ezra a letter.

From Artaxerxes, king of kings.
   To Ezra the priest and teacher of God's laws.
   Hello.

Any Jews in my kingdom may go with you. They may go if they want to. I'm sending you to ask about Jerusalem and Judah. Take silver and gold with you. Take it as a gift from me to your God. Take gifts from the people and priests. Buy bulls, rams, and lambs to offer to God. Offer grain and drinks, too. Give them on the altar at God's worship house.

Then you can take the rest of the silver and gold. Use it in the way you think is best. Do what you think God wants you to do with it.

Now I, King Artaxerxes, give orders. These are for the men who take care of my money. Give Ezra whatever he asks you for. He can have silver, wheat, wine, olive oil, and salt. Whatever gifts God wants, get them for Ezra to take to him. And do it fast. Why make God angry? You may not tax this group of people. You may not tax any workers at God's worship house.

Ezra, choose leaders and judges. Teach people who don't know God's laws. People who don't obey God's laws will be killed or put in jail. Or they might be sent out of the land. Everything they own might be taken away. The same will happen to people who don't obey me.

Praise God! He made the king's heart care about God's worship house. God has been kind to me in front of the king. He has been kind in front of the leaders of the land. So I got brave. I called leaders of God's people to go with me.

A Safe Trip

Ezra 7:8-10; 8:15-36

I, Ezra, got many people together at the river. We camped there for three days. I looked over all the people. I didn't find any people from Levi's family group. So I sent for some of them. I asked them to come and work at God's worship house. God was good to us. Many people from Levi's family came.

Then I said we should not eat for a while. That way, we could show that God was most important. We could ask God for a safe trip. I felt we couldn't ask the king to send guards along. We had told the king, "God is kind. He takes care of everyone who obeys him. But he gets angry at people who leave him."

So we did not eat while we prayed to God about this. He answered our prayer.

Then I chose 12 priests. I gave them the silver and gold offering. I said, "You are special to God. So are these gifts. Guard them carefully. They will go to God's worship house in Jerusalem."

Then we left from the river. We headed toward Jerusalem. God was with us. He kept us safe from enemies and robbers. So we got to Jerusalem. We rested there for three days.

God's people had started the trip in the first month. They got to Jerusalem in the fifth month. God was kind to Ezra. He had worked hard to study and teach God's laws.

Then they counted the silver and gold. Everything was there. They offered bulls, rams, lambs, and goats to God. They gave the king's letter to the leaders there. Then the leaders helped the people. And they helped with the worship house.

AUGUST 4

Sins As High As the Sky

EZRA 9–10:14, 44

The leaders came to me. They said, "God's people have mixed in with other nations. They've married women from other lands. Even leaders have done this."

I tore my shirt and coat. I sat down in shock. People gathered around me. Everyone was there who knew it's important to obey God's words. I sat in front of the worship house until evening.

Then I got up. I bowed down. I held my hands out to God, and I prayed.

I said, "God, I feel too bad about this to look at you. Our sins are piled higher than our heads. Our wrongs reach up to the sky. We've been the ones to blame since long ago. That's why we lost the fights. That's why we were taken to other lands. That's why other kings rule over us today.

"But now you have been kind and loving to us. You saved a few of your people. You brought us to your worship house. We are slaves. But you haven't left us alone. You made the kings of Persia kind to us. You are letting us build the worship house again.

"Now what can we say? We haven't kept your rules. You told us not to marry people from other nations. That's because they do wrong. But that's just what we did. You do what's right, God! Here we are. We are to blame. Because of our sin, we can't come near you."

Ezra was praying. He was crying on the ground in front of the worship house. A big crowd gathered around him. They began to cry too.

One man said, "We haven't obeyed God. We married women from nations that don't follow him. But we still have hope. Let's make a promise to God. Let's send all these women back to their lands. Get up. You can tell us if this is right to do. We'll do whatever you say. Be brave and do it."

So Ezra got up. He made the people promise to do what the man said. They all promised.

Then Ezra left the worship house. He went into a room. He didn't eat or drink anything. He was still sad. He was sad because the people didn't obey God.

Then a message was sent through all the land. It went to God's people who had lived in other lands. It called them to come to Jerusalem. At the end of three days, all the people were there. They sat in the yard in front of the worship house. It was raining. The people were upset because of the reason they were meeting. They were upset by the rain, too.

Ezra stood up. He said, "You haven't kept your promises. You married women from nations that don't follow God. Now tell God what you did. Be sorry. Then do what God wants. Stay away from people who don't follow him."

Everyone said, "You're right! We should do that. But there are lots of people here. It's raining. So we can't stay outside. This is something that will take more than a day. This is a big sin. So let our leaders say what to do. Then choose a day. Everyone who married a woman from another land can come here. Then we'll do what God wants."

That's what they did. They sent away women who worshiped the gods of their own land.

The Broken Wall

NEHEMIAH 1

These are the words of Nehemiah.

I was in the city of Susa in Persia. One of my brothers from Judah came to see me. I asked him about Jerusalem. I asked about God's people who were there.

He said, "The people are in trouble. People treat them like they're no good. Jerusalem's wall is broken down. Fire burned the city gates."

I sat down and cried. I cried and went without food for many days. I prayed to God.

Then I said, "Lord! Great, wonderful God. You keep your loving promises to people who obey you. Listen. Open your eyes. Hear my prayer. Yes, we have sinned. We did wrong to you. We didn't obey you.

"Remember what you told Moses. You said that if your people didn't follow you, you'd send them away. You'd send them to other lands. But if your people came back to you, you'd bring them back. You'd bring them back to the land you gave them.

"These are your servants, God. These are your people. You saved them with your great power. Listen to my prayer. Listen to the prayers of the people who love you. Be kind to me. May things go well."

Burned Gates

NEHEMIAH 1:11; 2–3:3, 8-16, 26, 28

I was the king's servant. I took drinks to the king. One day I took the king's wine to him.

The king had never seen a sad look on my face before. So he asked, "Why are you sad? You are not sick. Your heart must be sad."

I was afraid. But I told the king, "It's because of Jerusalem. It's the city where my people lived. It's a pile of sticks and stones. Fire has burned up its gates. That's why I look sad."

"What do you want to do about it?" asked the king.

I prayed to God. Then I answered the king. "If you're happy with me, let me go to Jerusalem. Let me build the city back up."

The king was sitting beside the queen. He said, "How long will this trip take? When will you be back?" He was glad to send me. So I told him a time.

Then I said, "I need to take letters to the leaders around here. The letters should tell what I'm doing. That way, the leaders will let me travel through their lands. I'll be safe.

"Would you write a letter to your forest keeper, too? Then he can give me wood to build the gates by the worship house. He can give me wood for the city wall. He can give me wood for a house to live in."

God was with me. So the king did what I asked. The king also sent army captains with me. He sent guards on horses, too.

I went to the leaders of the lands. I gave them the king's letters.

Two leaders who lived close by heard about this. Their names were Sanballat and Tobiah. They were upset that someone would come to help God's people.

I went to Jerusalem. I stayed there for three days. Then I went out into the city at night. I took a few men with me. I was the only one riding a horse.

Now I hadn't told anybody else what I was doing. But it's what God had put in my heart to do. I went out the Valley Gate. I went toward the Fig Well. I took a good look at the city walls. They had been broken down. The gates had been burned.

Then I went toward the Fountain Gate and the King's Pool. But there was no room for my horse to get through. So I went into the valley. I looked at the wall there.

At last I came back through the Valley Gate. The leaders didn't know what I had done. I hadn't told any of the Jews about this.

Then I told them, "Look at this problem. Jerusalem is a pile of sticks and stones. The gates have been burned down. Come on! Let's build the wall again. Then we won't look bad anymore."

I told them how God had been with me. I told them what the king had said.

They said, "Let's start building!" So they began.

Sanballat and Tobiah heard about this. They began making fun of us. "What are you doing?" they asked. "Are you turning against the king?"

"God will help us finish this," I said. "We are his servants. We will start building Jerusalem again. You don't own Jerusalem. You have no right to this city."

Priests built the Sheep Gate again. They built the wall to the Hundred Tower. They built as far as the next tower. Men from Jericho built the part next to that.

Other men built the Fish Gate again. They put doors and bars in it. Many men worked on the walls and gates. A gold worker helped. A perfume maker helped. They built Jerusalem up to the Broad Wall.

Some men fixed the wall across from their houses. They built back the Ovens Tower. One man's daughters helped him fix part of the wall.

The workers fixed the Valley Gate and the Fountain Gate. They fixed the wall by Siloam Pool and the King's Garden. They went as far as the House of the Heroes. They also fixed the wall across from the Water Gate.

The priests fixed the walls by the Horse Gate. Each priest fixed the wall in front of his own house.

AUGUST 6

Tools in One Hand, Swords in the Other

NEHEMIAH 4

Now Sanballat heard that we were building the wall again. He got very angry. He made fun of the Jewish people. He talked about us to his friends. He talked about us to the army of Samaria.

Sanballat said, "What are those weak Jews doing? Can they build their wall back? Can they give gifts to God again? Will they be done in one day? Can they make the stones

491

live? The gates are burned down. The city is just a pile of sticks and stones."

Tobiah said, "What do they think they're building? A fox could break the wall by jumping on it!"

Hear us, God! They hate us. Pay them back for this. They are making fun of the workers here.

We built the wall back up again. We got it half as high as we wanted. The people were working as hard as they could.

But Sanballat and his friends heard about it. They heard that the holes in the wall were being fixed. They were very angry. They made plans to come and fight Jerusalem. They planned to make trouble for us. But we prayed to God. Then we put men on guard to watch day and night.

Our people said, "The workers are getting tired. There are so many piles of sticks and stones! We can't build the wall."

Our enemies said, "We'll go in there with them. They won't know we're coming. We'll kill them. Then their work will end."

Some Jews lived near our enemies. They came to tell us what the enemies said. "They'll fight you wherever you turn," they told us.

So I put people behind the short parts of the wall. I sent them with their swords and bows.

Then I looked at everything. I stood up and talked to the people. "Don't be scared of our enemies," I said. "Remember God. He is great and wonderful. Fight for your families. Fight for your homes."

Our enemies found out that we knew about their plan. Then we all went back to work on the wall.

After that, half of my men did the work. The other half held swords and bows. The army captains stood behind the people who were building. People carried tools in one hand. They carried swords in their other hand. Each worker had his sword beside him while he worked. The man who had the war horn stayed with me.

I told the people, "There's lots of work to do. We're far apart from each other on the wall. So if you hear the horn, come to fight. Come wherever the sound of the horn is. God will fight for us!"

So we kept working. We started every morning when the sky first got light. We worked until the stars came out.

I told everyone, "Stay in the city at night. That way, you can be guards."

We never took our clothes off. We always carried our swords, even when we went to get water.

Money for Grain

NEHEMIAH 5

Now the people began fussing at each other. Some said, "We have big families. We have to get grain so we can make food."

Others said, "We need money to buy grain. Nothing will grow in the fields now. We give our fields and houses to our leaders. Then they lend us the money."

Others said, "The king taxes our fields. We had to borrow money to pay the tax. We borrow from our own leaders. We even had to sell our children as slaves to them."

I heard what they were saying. I got very angry. I thought about it. Then I talked to the leaders. "You're taking things from your own people!" I said.

Then I called a big meeting. "Our people have sometimes been taken to be slaves," I said. "They've been taken by people from other lands. Then we try to buy them back. But now you are selling your own people!"

The leaders were quiet. They couldn't think of anything to say.

"This is not right!" I said. "You should be afraid of God. I lend people money for grain. My men lend them money for grain. We don't ask them to give us their houses and fields. But you ask for their houses before you'll lend them money. This has to stop! Give their houses back. Give their fields back."

"We will," they said. "We won't ask them for anything else."

Then I called the priests. I made the leaders promise to do what they said. I shook out my robe. "May God shake out people who don't keep this promise. May God shake them out of his house."

Everyone said, "Yes!" Then they praised God. They did what they promised to do.

Now the king chose me to be the leader of Judah. The leaders before me had made the people pay a big tax. Their helpers had bossed the people around. But I loved God too much to do that. Instead, I kept working hard on the wall. All of my men worked. We didn't take land from anyone.

Every day I fed 150 Jews and Jewish leaders at my table. I could have asked for food like leaders do. But I never asked for food. That's because I saw that these people worked hard.

Remember me, God. I've done all this for your people.

493

Trying to Scare Nehemiah

NEHEMIAH 6

Sanballat and Tobiah found out that the wall was back up. There were no holes in it anymore. So they sent me a message. "Come meet with us in one of the towns."

But they were planning to hurt me. So I sent a message back to them. "I'm very busy. I can't come. I don't want this work to stop just for a meeting."

They sent me the same message four times. Every time, I sent back the same message.

Then Sanballat sent his helper to see me. He had a letter in his hand. It said, "We hear that you're planning a fight. You're going to fight against the king. That's why you're building the wall. We hear that people are going to make you their king. The king will hear about this. So come meet with us."

I sent this message back. "You are wrong. The things you say are not happening here. You're just making them up."

They were trying to scare us. They thought we would be too scared to work. Then the work wouldn't get finished.

But I prayed, "Make my hands stronger."

One day I went to see a man at his home. He said, "Let's go meet in God's worship house. Let's close the doors behind us. Men are coming to try to kill you. They'll be coming at night."

"Am I the kind of man to run away?" I said. "Should I go to the worship house to be safe? I won't!" I knew God hadn't told the man to say that. He was just trying to scare me. Tobiah and Sanballat had paid him to scare me. Then I'd look bad for running away.

Lots of leaders were sending letters to Tobiah. Tobiah was sending letters to them. The leaders would tell me what good things Tobiah had done. Then they'd tell Tobiah what I said. Tobiah even sent letters to scare me.

God, remember Tobiah and Sanballat. Remember what they've done. Remember the people who are trying to scare me.

Soon the wall was finished. Our enemies heard about it. Then they were afraid. They stopped feeling so good about themselves. They saw that God had helped us do this work.

Gate Keepers and Singers

NEHEMIAH 7:1-5; 11:1-2

Then I chose gate keepers and singers. I chose my brother to be in charge of Jerusalem. I chose another man to help him. I knew that this man always told the truth. He cared about God more than most men did.

I said, "Don't open Jerusalem's gates until the sun is hot. Tell the gate keepers to close the doors. Tell them to put the bars across. Choose some people to be guards."

Now the city was very big. It had lots of room. But there weren't many people who lived there. All the houses hadn't been built yet.

So God put a plan in my heart. I called the people to come sign up. That way, we knew who the families were. I found a list. It showed who had come back to Jerusalem first.

So the leaders came to live in Jerusalem. The other people threw lots, like rolling dice. That's the way they chose people to live in Jerusalem. The rest of the people stayed in their own towns.

Reading from Morning until Noon

NEHEMIAH 8

Then the people got together in front of the Water Gate. They told Ezra to bring out Moses' Law Book. It had God's laws for his people in it. So Ezra brought it out. He read it out loud. He read it from early morning until noon. All the people listened carefully.

Ezra stood on a high wooden stand. He opened the book. Everybody could see him, because he was so high up.

When Ezra opened the book, all the people stood up. Ezra praised God. The people held their hands up. They said, "Yes! Yes!" Then they bowed down with their faces to the ground. They worshiped God.

Then men from the family of Levi taught the people. They made the Law Book clear. They told the people what it meant.

All the people had been crying while they listened. But Nehemiah and Ezra talked to the people. "This is a special day to God. Don't cry," they said.

"Go and enjoy some good food," said Nehemiah. "Go have some sweet drinks. Share your food with others. This day is special to God. Don't cry. God's joy makes you strong."

So the people left to eat and drink. They had a joyful holiday. That's because they understood the words of the Law Book.

The next day the leaders came together. They stood around Ezra. They listened to God's laws again.

They learned that they were supposed to have a Holiday of Tents. It was to happen that month.

So they said, "Go to the hills. Get tree branches. Make tents out of them like the Law Book says to do."

So the people went out and got tree branches. They built branch tents. Some people made tents on their roofs. Some built tents in their yards. Some built tents by the Water Gate. Everyone built branch tents. They lived in them for the holiday. They were very happy.

Every day Ezra read from the Law Book. The holiday for God lasted seven days.

Remembering

NEHEMIAH 9; 10:29-32, 35-39

At the end of the month, the people got together. They went without food. They wore clothes made of old sack cloth. They put dust on their heads. They told God what their sins were. They said they were sorry. They read from the Law Book.

The men from Levi's family stood on stairs. They called to God with loud voices. They said, "Stand up and cheer for God! He lives forever and ever!

"Your great name is good! It is greater than anything we could say! Only you are God. You made the sky, the stars, and all of space. You made earth and sea and everything in them. You give life to everything. All of heaven worships you.

"You are the Lord God. You chose Abram. You made a special promise to him. You gave his family this land. You kept your promise, because you are right and good.

"You saw the trouble your people had in Egypt. You sent wonders against Egypt's king. You made your name great. Your name is still great today. You brought your people out of Egypt. You led them by a cloud in the daytime. You led them by a cloud of fire at night.

"You came to the mountain. You gave your people laws that are right. You gave them bread to eat. You gave them water to drink. You told them to take the land you had promised them.

"But your people were proud. They didn't care about you. They didn't obey you. But you are a forgiving God. You are kind and loving. You don't get angry very fast. Your love runs over. So you didn't leave them. You didn't leave, even when they made a gold calf idol.

"You didn't leave your people in the desert. You kept leading them. You kept them safe for 40 years. They didn't need anything. Their clothes didn't wear out. Their feet didn't even get hurt from walking.

"You gave your people kingdoms

and lands. Their families grew. There were as many people as there are stars. You took them to the land you promised them. They took over forts and fields. They got all kinds of good things. They got wells, olive fields, grape fields, and fruit trees. They ate until they were full. They enjoyed your goodness.

"But they turned against you. They forgot your laws. They killed your prophets, the ones who spoke your words. So you gave them to their enemies. Their enemies gave them trouble. Then they cried to you. You heard them from heaven, and you saved them.

"But then they did wrong again. So you let their enemies take over again. Then they cried to you. You saved them again and again.

"You told them to turn back to your laws. But they became proud. They didn't obey you. You waited for them to come back. You waited many years. You sent prophets to teach them. They didn't listen. So you gave them to other nations.

"But you didn't leave them alone. You didn't get rid of them. That's because you are a kind and loving God. You are great and strong and wonderful. You keep your loving promises.

"We're slaves now. We're slaves in the land you gave our people long ago. It's because of our sins.

We have to give the crops we grow to the king. He rules over us and our animals. He does whatever he wants with us. We have hard times.

"So we are making a promise. We are writing it down. We all promise to follow the Law of God.

"We promise not to marry people from lands around us.

"We will not buy things on the worship day. We won't buy on any day that's special to God.

"We will give part of what we make every year. We'll give it for the worship house. We'll bring the first of what we grow each year. We'll give it to God. We'll give the first of our cows and sheep to God.

"We'll fill up the store rooms at the worship house. We'll bring grain, wine, and oil.

"We won't forget God's worship house."

AUGUST 9

Closing the Gates
NEHEMIAH 13:4-11, 15-27, 30-31

Now there was a priest who had been in charge of the store rooms. These were at the worship house. But he was a friend of Tobiah's. He had given Tobiah a big room there.

I wasn't in Jerusalem at that time. I had gone back to Babylon. I had gone back to serve the king. Later, I asked the king if I could come back to Jerusalem.

That's when I learned about Tobiah's room at the worship house. I was very unhappy about this. I threw Tobiah's things out of the room.

I found out something else. People were supposed to give the priests and singers food. But the people weren't giving it. The priests and singers had to go back home. They had to work in their fields. They couldn't serve God at the worship house.

So I called the leaders together. "Why do you forget about the worship house?" I asked.

Then I saw people working on the worship day. They brought food into Jerusalem to sell. They were loading grain on donkeys. They brought in grain, wine, grapes, figs, and other food. But I told them not to sell food on that day.

Other men brought in fish and other things. They sold these on the worship day. I said, "What are you doing? You're making the worship day seem like nothing. Your families from long ago did the same thing. That brought us the trouble we're having now. You'll make God angry at us again."

So I gave an order. The city gates were to be closed on the worship day. They would close in the evening. They wouldn't open until the worship day was over. I put some of my men at the gates. Then nothing could be brought in on the worship day.

Sometimes a seller would spend the night outside the gate. But I said, "Why spend the night here? Don't do it again. If you do, I'll come and get you." They never came on the worship day again.

Remember me for doing this, God. Be kind to me, because your love is great.

I also saw men from Judah marry women from other lands. Half of the children didn't even know the language of Judah. I told these men they were wrong. I made them make a promise. They wouldn't let their children marry people from other lands.

I said, "Isn't that how Solomon sinned? There was no other king like him. God loved him. But even Solomon sinned. The women he married led him into sin. They were from other lands. Do you have to do this too? You aren't obeying God if you marry women from other lands."

I made priests get rid of everything that didn't please God. I gave each priest a job to do. I made sure that people knew when to bring their gifts.

Remember me and be kind to me, my God.

Singers on the Wall

NEHEMIAH 12:27-44; 13:1-3, 12-14

Now the day came to give the city wall of Jerusalem to God. It was time to say that God was in charge of it. It belonged to him. So people from the family group of Levi came to help. They led songs to give thanks to God. They played music with cymbals, harps, and lyres. The singers came together too. They had built towns for themselves around Jerusalem.

I told Judah's leaders to go on top of the wall. I chose two big groups of singers to give thanks. One group went on top of the wall to the right. Half of the leaders followed them. Ezra led them. They marched to the Fountain Gate. They went up the steps of David's City. Then they went to the Water Gate.

The next group of singers went the other way. I followed them on top of the wall. Half the people followed too. We went past the Ovens Tower to the Wide Wall. We went over the Fish Gate and the Hundred Tower. We went to the Sheep Gate. We stopped at the Guard Gate.

The two groups of singers gave thanks. Then they went to the worship house. I went too. Half of the leaders went. The priests went. They took their horns. The singers sang.

That day many gifts were given to God. That's because God had made the people very happy. The women and children showed their joy too. The happy sound could be heard far away.

Everyone brought their gifts of grain, wine, and oil. The gifts were put in store rooms.

We chose men to be in charge of the store rooms. These were men we could trust.

Remember me, God. Don't forget what I've done for your worship house.

Then Moses' Law Book was read out loud. All the people could hear it. They did what it said.

NEW TESTAMENT

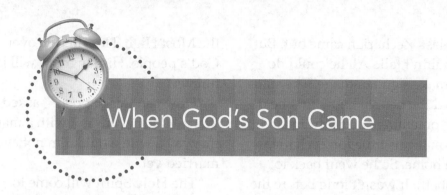

When God's Son Came

An Angel at the Altar

LUKE 1:5-25

Herod was the king of Judea. At that time, there was a priest named Zechariah. He had a wife named Elizabeth. They both obeyed God's laws. God saw that they were very good people. But they had no children, and they were growing old.

One day Zechariah was at the worship house. It was his turn to help with the worship. He left the people worshiping and praying outside. He went inside.

What Zechariah saw there surprised him. He saw an angel! The angel stood at the right side of the altar. Zechariah was afraid.

"Don't be afraid, Zechariah," said the angel. "God heard your prayer. Your wife, Elizabeth, will have a baby boy. You'll name him John.

"Your son will make you happy," said the angel. "In fact, many people will be happy when he is born. God will call him great! But he must never drink wine. He will be filled with the Holy Spirit as soon as he is born.

"John will help many people turn back to God. He will come before the Lord comes," said the angel. "He will have the spirit of Elijah. He will have the power of Elijah. He will help fathers show love to their children. He will help people who disobey so they'll want to obey. Then people will be ready for the Lord."

"How can I be sure that what you say about a son is true?" asked Zechariah. "After all, my wife and I are old."

"My name is Gabriel," said the angel. "I come from God. He sent me to tell you this good news. But you did not believe me. So now you won't be able to talk. You'll be quiet until the day this happens."

All this time, the people waited for Zechariah to come out. They began to wonder what was taking so long.

At last, Zechariah came out. But he couldn't talk. All he could do was make sign language. The signs helped the people know that he'd seen something special from God.

Soon it was time for Zechariah to go home. So he went back to Elizabeth. It wasn't long before the angel's words came true. Elizabeth was going to have a baby.

"God has done this for me," Elizabeth said. "God has been kind. I don't feel bad anymore about not having children."

A Message for Mary

LUKE 1:26-56

God sent the angel Gabriel with a message again. This time he sent Gabriel to the town of Nazareth.

Gabriel went to a young woman. She had never slept with a man the way a wife would. But she was going to be married to a man named Joseph. Her name was Mary.

"Hello!" said Gabriel to Mary. "You are very special. God is with you!"

Mary was afraid. She was not sure about this. She wondered what the angel meant.

"Don't be afraid," said Gabriel. "God is happy with you. You are going to have a baby boy. You are to name him Jesus. He will be great. He will be called Son of the Most High. He will rule over God's people. His kingdom will last forever."

"How can this happen?" asked Mary. "I've never slept with a man the way a wife would. I'm not even married yet."

"The Holy Spirit will come to you," said Gabriel. "God's power will come over you like a shadow. So the baby will be special. He will be holy. He will be God's Son.

"You know Elizabeth, who is in your family," said Gabriel. "She is going to have a baby too. You know how old she is. People thought she couldn't have a baby. But the baby has been growing inside her for six months. There is nothing that God can't do."

"I'm God's servant," said Mary. "Let this happen just the way you said it would."

Not long after that, Mary went to Elizabeth's house. Elizabeth lived in the hill country.

Mary went in to say hello. Right away the baby growing inside Elizabeth jumped.

Then the Holy Spirit filled Elizabeth. "God has been very good to you, Mary!" she said. "God will bring what's good to your child! I don't know what's so special about me. I don't know why my Lord's mother should come to visit me. But I heard your voice," said Elizabeth.

"And the baby inside me jumped for joy. You have God's riches. It's all because you believe God will do what he says."

"How great God is!" said Mary. "My spirit is happy with God. He saves me! He can tell that I know I'm not important. Now everyone will say God has been good to me. He has done wonderful, great things for me. His name is special and good. He is kind to everyone who looks up to him.

"God has done powerful things for many years," said Mary. "He sends proud people away. He brings down rulers. But he lifts up people who know he is the great one."

Mary stayed with Elizabeth for three months. Then she went back home.

Naming the Baby

LUKE 1:57-80

All of Elizabeth's friends and family were happy. They heard what God had done for her. They got together the week after the baby was born. They were going to give him his father's name, Zechariah.

But Elizabeth said, "No! We will call him John!"

"John?" they said. "None of your family has the name John." They used sign language for Zechariah. They asked him what he wanted to name the baby.

Zechariah asked for something to write on. Everyone was surprised when he wrote, "His name will be John."

Right then, Zechariah could talk again. He cheered for God. Friends and family were filled with wonder.

Then Zechariah was filled with the Holy Spirit. "Cheer for God the Lord!" he said. "The Lord has come to save his people. He is saving us through the family of David. It's just what he promised through the prophets long ago.

"My child, you will be called God's prophet. You'll see God's plans and tell about them," said Zechariah. "You'll go ahead of the Lord. You'll make a way ready for him. You'll let his people know how to be saved. You'll say this will happen when their sins are forgiven."

The news went out all over the hill country. People talked about what had happened. Everybody who heard about it wondered, "What will this child be? God is with him in a special way."

As time went by, John grew. He turned out to be strong in spirit. After he grew up, he went to live in the desert.

A Trip to Bethlehem

MATTHEW 1:18-25; LUKE 2:1-20

Here's what happened when it was almost time for Jesus to be born. First of all, his mother, Mary, was supposed to marry Joseph. But she found out she was going to have a baby. He would be God's Son.

Joseph didn't know the baby would be God's Son. He just knew this didn't seem right. Mary shouldn't have a baby before she got married. So he was going to tell her he wouldn't marry her.

Joseph thought about this for a while. Then God sent an angel to him in a dream.

The angel said, "Joseph, don't be afraid to let Mary be your wife. She will have a baby boy by the power of the Holy Spirit. You will name him Jesus. He will save his people from sin."

Everything happened just as Isaiah the prophet had said many years before: "There will be a young woman. She will never have slept with a man like a wife would. But she will have a baby. She will call him Immanuel, which means 'God with us.'"

Joseph woke up from his dream. He did just what the angel told him to do. He married Mary. But he did not sleep with her the way a husband would until her baby boy was born.

At that time, Caesar Augustus was the highest ruler. He made a law that everyone should be counted. So people had to go back to their own towns to be counted. These were the towns where their families from long ago had been born.

That meant Joseph had to leave Nazareth. He had to go to Bethlehem in the hill country. That's because he was from the family of King David. So Joseph went to Bethlehem to be counted. He took Mary with him.

While they were in Bethlehem, the baby was born. It was a boy. Mary wrapped him in warm cloth. But she had to put him in a feed box for animals. That's because there was no place to stay at the inn. The rooms were full.

There were some fields close to town. That night, some shepherds were out in the fields. They were taking care of their sheep.

God sent an angel to the shepherds. God's greatness shone all around them. They were afraid.

"Don't be afraid," said the angel. "I'm bringing you good news. Great joy is coming for all people. Today, in the town of Bethlehem, a baby was born. He is Jesus Christ the Lord, and he has come to save you. Here's how you can know it's him. You'll find him in a feed box."

All of a sudden many, many angels showed up. They all cheered for God. They said, "God in highest heaven gets the praise for this! Peace is coming to people who make God happy!" Then the angels went back to heaven.

"Something special happened in Bethlehem," said the shepherds. "Let's go see."

The shepherds hurried into town. There they found Mary and Joseph and the baby. The baby was in a feed box for animals.

Then the shepherds left to tell everyone what the angels said. People who heard it were surprised.

Mary thought deeply about everything that had happened. She kept it all in her heart like a special gift.

The shepherds went back to their fields. They cheered for God. They thanked him for what they had heard and seen. It was just the way the angel said it would be.

AUGUST 12

No More Waiting
LUKE 2:21-38

Eight days later, Mary and Joseph named the baby Jesus. That was the name the angel had given him.

Mary and Joseph had to do what God's law said. So they waited for a while. Then they took the baby to Jerusalem.

God's law said, "Every first-born boy must be God's." God's law also said to offer a gift of two doves or pigeons. So Mary and Joseph offered a gift to God. And they promised that the baby would belong to him.

A man named Simeon lived in Jerusalem. He was a good man. He loved and obeyed God. The Holy Spirit was with him.

Simeon had been waiting for someone special. This person would save God's people. The Holy Spirit had told Simeon he would see this special person. Before he died, Simeon would see the Promised One.

The Spirit told Simeon to go to the

worship house. That's when Joseph and Mary brought Jesus there.

Simeon held baby Jesus and praised God. "God, you promised this," he said. "Now you are letting me die in peace. I have seen the one who will save. All people will see him. He will be like a light, God. He will show you to people who are not Jewish. He will show how great you are to your people Israel."

Mary and Joseph were surprised at what Simeon said.

Simeon prayed for good things for Mary and Joseph. Then he said, "Many people in Israel will fall and rise. It will be because of this child. He will be a sign. Some people will speak against him. It will be easy to see what many people think. And your heart will feel like it's been cut open." He said this to Mary.

Another person was at the worship house. She was a woman prophet. Her name was Anna. She was very old. She had been married when she was very young. But her husband had died after seven years. After that, she had no husband. Now she was 84 years old.

Anna stayed at the worship house. She worshiped night and day. She prayed. Sometimes she even went without food to worship God.

Right at that moment, Anna came up to Mary, Joseph, and baby Jesus. She thanked God. And she talked about Jesus. She talked to everyone who was waiting to be saved.

AUGUST 13

Wise Men from the East

MATTHEW 2; LUKE 2:39-40

It was some time after Jesus had been born in Bethlehem. King Herod was ruling.

Wise men from the East came to Jerusalem. They began asking about Jesus. "Where is the child who was born to be King of the Jews? We saw a star in the east. It was his star. We have come to worship this baby king."

King Herod heard about their questions. He was upset. All Jerusalem was upset. So King Herod called the worship leaders and Jewish teachers together. He asked them where the Promised One was to be born.

They said he was to be born in Bethlehem. They said the prophet Micah wrote these words from God:

Bethlehem, you are a small town in
     Judah.
But someone who will rule my
     people will come from you.
He will lead my people like a
     shepherd.

King Herod called a secret meeting with the wise men. He

found out when they first saw the star. Then he told them to go to Bethlehem.

"Look carefully for this baby," he said. "When you find him, report back to me. Then I can go worship him too."

The wise men left the king. They followed the star. It went ahead of them and then stopped.

The wise men saw that the star was over a house. They were full of joy. They went into the house. There they saw the child Jesus. He was with his mother, Mary.

The wise men bowed down and worshiped Jesus. Then they opened their rich gifts. They gave him gold, sweet-smelling incense, and myrrh.

Now God talked to the wise men in a dream. He told them not to go back to King Herod. So they took another road back to their own land.

Then an angel of God came to Joseph in a dream. The angel said, "Get up. Take the child and his mother. Leave for Egypt. Stay there until I tell you to come back. King Herod will look for the child. He will try to kill him."

So Joseph got up. That night he took Mary and Jesus. They left for Egypt. They stayed there until King Herod died. That made the prophet Hosea's words come true. Hosea had said these words from God:

"He was my son. I took him out of Egypt."

After a while, King Herod saw that the wise men had fooled him. He was angry. So he gave orders to kill all the baby boys in Bethlehem. He killed any who were two years old or younger.

That made the prophet Jeremiah's words come true: "A crying voice comes from Ramah. It sounds like Rachel crying for her children. She won't let anyone cheer her up. Her children have died."

In time, Herod died. Then God sent an angel again. He appeared in a dream to Joseph in Egypt. The angel said, "You can take Jesus and Mary back home. The people who tried to kill Jesus are dead."

So Joseph took Jesus and Mary. They went back to Israel.

But Joseph heard that Herod's son was now the king. So Joseph was afraid to go back to Bethlehem. He was told in a dream to stay away from Bethlehem.

So Joseph and his family went to Galilee and lived there. They lived in a town called Nazareth. So the words of the prophets came true. They had said Jesus would be called a Nazarene.

Jesus grew up in Nazareth. He grew strong and wise. God's kind love was with him.

In the Big City

LUKE 2:41-52

Once a year, Joseph and Mary went to Jerusalem. They went for the Pass Over holiday. When Jesus was 12 years old, he went too.

After the special holiday for God, Joseph and Mary began the trip home. But Jesus stayed in Jerusalem.

Joseph and Mary didn't know that Jesus had stayed behind. They thought he was with their friends or their family. So they traveled for a whole day without him.

Then Joseph and Mary began to look for Jesus. They looked to see if he was with their family. They looked to see if he was with their friends. But they couldn't find him. So they went back to Jerusalem. They looked through the city for three days.

At last they found Jesus. He was in the worship house, sitting with the teachers. He was listening to them. He was also asking them questions. Everyone was surprised by how much he understood. They were surprised at his answers.

When Joseph and Mary saw Jesus, they were surprised too. Mary said, "Son, why have you done this to us? We've been worried. We've been looking for you."

"Why did you have to look for me?" Jesus asked. "Didn't you know I would be in my Father's house?"

They didn't understand what Jesus was talking about. But Mary thought about it. She kept these things as rich gifts in her heart.

Jesus went back to Nazareth with Joseph and Mary. Jesus obeyed them, and he grew. He grew taller. He grew wiser. He grew as a friend to God. He grew as a friend to people, too.

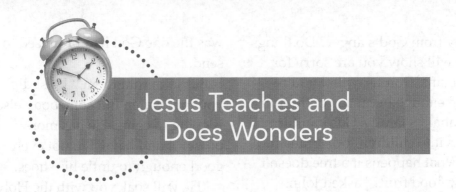

Jesus Teaches and Does Wonders

The Man Who Wore Camel's Hair

MATTHEW 3:1-10; MARK 1:2-6;
LUKE 3:1-14

Another Caesar was now the highest ruler of the land. He had ruled for 15 years. At this time, God sent word to Zechariah's son, John.

John was in the desert. He wore clothes made of camel's hair. He wore a leather belt. He ate honey and big grasshoppers called locusts. Many people went to hear him teach.

John went to the land around the Jordan River. He told all the people to be sorry for their sins. He told them to be baptized.

That's how the prophet Isaiah's words came true:

There's a voice calling in the desert. Make the way ready for the Lord. Make a flat road for him. The valleys will get higher. The hills will get lower. The bumpy ground will get smooth. God will show who he is. Everybody in the world will see how God saves.

Crowds of people came out to hear John. They came to be baptized in the river water too. Many of the people said they had sinned. They were sorry. So John put them under the water and brought them up again. He baptized them, and God forgave them.

John had this message for some of the Jewish leaders. "You're a pack of snakes! Who told you to get away from God's anger? Do things that will show you are sorry for your sins. Don't say that you're good enough because you're from Abraham's family. God can turn rocks into children for Abraham.

"What happens if a tree doesn't grow good fruit?" asked John. "It gets cut down. Then it gets tossed into the fire. So stop doing wrong and do good, or you'll be in trouble."

"What should we do?" asked the people.

"Let's say you have two coats," said John. "Share one with somebody who doesn't have a coat. Let's say you have food. Share it with someone who needs food."

Men who gathered tax money came to be baptized. They asked, "What should we do, Teacher?"

"Don't take more money than you should," he said.

Men from the army asked, "What should we do?"

"Don't make people give you money," John said. "Don't lie to get people in trouble. Be happy with the money you are paid."

Jesus at the River
MATTHEW 3:11-17; MARK 1:7-11;
LUKE 3:15-18, 21-23

People wondered if maybe John was the Promised One. Maybe he was the one God had promised to send.

But John told them, "I just dip you into water. But somebody else is going to come. He has more power than I have. I'm not even good enough to untie his shoes.

"He will soak you with the Holy Spirit," said John. "He will bring fire. He will gather what's good the way wheat is gathered into a barn. But he will burn up everything that's not good."

John told the people many other things. His words brought good news.

One day Jesus came to the Jordan River. He asked John to dip him under the water.

John tried to stop him. "You should baptize me in water," said John. "Instead, you want me to baptize you?"

"Yes," said Jesus. "Go ahead. It's a good thing to do. We should do everything that's right."

So John dipped Jesus into the water.

Jesus came up out of the water. Then he saw heaven opened. God's Spirit came down like a dove and landed on Jesus.

"This is my Son," said a voice from heaven. "I love him. I am very happy with him."

Jesus was about 30 years old.

Trying to Make Jesus Do Wrong

MATTHEW 4:1-11; MARK 1:12-13; LUKE 4:1-13

The Spirit led Jesus into the desert. That's where Satan tried to make Jesus do wrong.

Jesus went without food for 40 days and 40 nights. He was hungry.

Then Satan came to him. "Are you really God's Son?" he asked. "Then why don't you turn the rocks into bread?"

Here's what Jesus told Satan: "God's Word says that people don't live just by eating bread. They live by believing every word God says."

Then Satan took Jesus to Jerusalem. They stood on the tallest part of the worship house. "If you really are God's Son, jump off," said Satan. "God's Word says that his angels will keep you safe. God will tell them to lift you up in their hands. You won't even hit your foot on a rock."

But Jesus gave this answer to Satan: "God's Word also says not to test the Lord your God."

Then Satan took Jesus to a high mountain. He showed Jesus the riches of all the world's kingdoms. "I'll give all this to you," Satan said. "Just bow down and worship me."

"Get away from me, Satan!" said Jesus. "God's Word says to worship only the Lord your God. Serve only him."

Then Satan left, and angels came and took care of Jesus.

Who Is John?

JOHN 1:19-27

Now the Jews in Jerusalem sent some men to John. They were sent to ask John who he was.

"I'm not the Promised One," said John.

"Then who are you?" they asked. "Are you Elijah?"

"No," he said.

"Are you the Prophet?" they asked.

"No," he said.

At last they asked, "Who are you? What should we tell the men who sent us?"

John answered with some of the prophet Isaiah's words. He said, "I am a voice calling in the desert. I say to make a flat road for God!"

Some Jewish leaders were there. "Why do you dip people in water?" they asked. "You aren't the Promised One or Elijah or the Prophet."

"It's true that I baptize people in water," said John. "But there is someone here who will come after me. I'm not even good enough to untie his shoes."

The Lamb of God

JOHN 1:29-51

The next day, John saw Jesus coming. "Look!" said John. "It's the Lamb of God. He takes away the sin of the world! This is the man I was talking about.

"I told you a man would come after I did," said John. "He is greater than I am. He lived before I did. I didn't know him myself. But I came to dip people in water. I've been doing it to show God's people who he is."

Then John told what had happened. "I saw God's Spirit coming like a dove from heaven. It stayed on him.

"I wouldn't have known he was the one," said John. "But God sent me to dip people in water. He said I'd see his Holy Spirit come down and stay on a man. Then I'd know he was the one. He is the one who will baptize with the Holy Spirit.

"I saw it," said John. "So I know this is God's Son."

The next day John was there at the same place. This time two of John's followers were with him. One of them was Andrew.

John saw Jesus going by. So John said, "Look! It's the Lamb of God!"

Andrew and his friend heard what John said. So they followed Jesus.

Jesus turned around and saw them. "What do you want?" he asked.

"Teacher, we want to know where you're staying," they said.

"Come and see," said Jesus.

So they went with him. They saw where Jesus was staying. It was about four o'clock in the afternoon. They spent the rest of the day with Jesus.

At the end of the day, they left. Right away, Andrew went to get his brother. "We met the Promised One!" Andrew said. Then he took his brother to meet Jesus too.

Jesus took a good look at Andrew's brother. He said, "Your name is Simon. But I'm going to call you Peter, the rock."

Jesus wanted to go to Galilee the next day. He saw Philip and said, "Come with me."

Now Philip was from the same town as Andrew and Peter. Philip went to find Nathanael. Philip said, "We found the man Moses wrote about. He is the one the prophets wrote about too. His name is Jesus. He is from Nazareth."

"Nazareth?" said Nathanael. "Can anything good come from Nazareth?"

"Come and find out," said Philip. So Nathanael went with Philip.

Jesus saw Nathanael coming. "Here is a man who tells the truth," said Jesus. "There are no lies in him!"

"How could you know me?" asked Nathanael.

"I saw you before," said Jesus. "You were under the fig tree. It was before Philip came and got you."

"Teacher!" said Nathanael. "You are God's Son! You are the King of God's people!"

"Do you believe this because I saw you under the tree?" asked Jesus. "You'll see greater things than that. You'll see heaven open up. You'll see God's angels going up and down with me."

AUGUST 16

A Wedding Party

JOHN 2:1-11

Two days later, there was a wedding in Galilee. It was in the town called Cana. Jesus and his friends went. Jesus' mother went too.

But the people who were having the party ran out of wine. So Jesus' mother went to him. "They're out of wine!" she said.

"Why do you want me to take care of things like this?" said Jesus. "It's not time yet."

Jesus' mother talked to the servants. "Do whatever he asks you to do," she told them.

There were six big stone jars close by. The jars were there to hold water. The Jews used the water to wash their hands in a special way. Each jar could hold about 20 to 30 gallons of water.

"Fill those jars with water," Jesus told the servants.

The servants filled them all the way to the top.

"Now," said Jesus, "dip some of it out. Take it to the man in charge of the party."

The servants did just what Jesus said.

The man in charge took a drink. He didn't know it had been water. That's because it had turned into wine! But the servants knew!

The man in charge talked to the man who just got married. "Most people give everyone the best wine first," he said. "After a while, everyone has had too much to drink. So they bring out wine that's not as good. But you saved the best wine for now!"

This was the first wonder Jesus did. It showed how great he was. Then Jesus' followers believed in him.

The Money Tables

JOHN 2:13-25

It was almost time for the Pass Over holiday. So Jesus went to the worship house in Jerusalem.

Jesus found animals in the closed-in yards around the worship house. Men were selling cows and sheep and doves. Other men sat at money tables. They were changing money so that people from different places could buy things.

Jesus got some rope and made a whip. Then he chased out the sheep and cows. He tossed the money here and there. He turned the money tables over.

"Get these out of here!" he told the people who were selling doves. "How dare you turn my Father's house into a store!"

That made Jesus' followers remember a psalm: "I care so much for your house! I just have to do something about it."

But the Jews said, "Show us a wonder. Prove that you have the right to do this."

"Tear down this worship house," said Jesus. "I will bring it back again in three days."

"Three days?" said the Jews. "It took 46 years to build this worship house."

But Jesus was really talking about his body. His followers remembered this after he died and came back to life again. Then they believed the words God had told people to write down. And they believed the words Jesus said.

Many people saw Jesus at the Pass Over holiday. They saw the wonders he was doing. So they believed in him.

But Jesus didn't trust the people. He knew what was in their hearts.

A Night Visit

JOHN 3:1-21

There was once a Jew named Nicodemus. He was one of the leaders. One night he came to see Jesus.

"We know you are a teacher from God," he said. "Nobody can do the wonders you do unless God is with him."

"Here's the truth," said Jesus. "Nobody can even see God's kingdom without being born again."

"Born again?" asked Nicodemus. "How can a person be born again when he is already old? I'm sure he can't go back inside his mother."

"Here's how you get into God's kingdom," said Jesus. "You must be born of water and God's Spirit. A body is born from a body. A spirit is born from God's Spirit. Don't be surprised, but you have to be born again.

"The wind blows where it wants to," said Jesus. "You can hear the sound of the wind. But you can't see where it's coming from. You can't see where it's going. It's the same way with people born of the Spirit."

"How can that be true?" asked Nicodemus.

"You are a teacher of God's people," said Jesus. "Don't you understand? The truth is, we talk about things we know about. We tell what we've seen. But you people don't believe us.

"I told you about things of the earth," said Jesus. "You don't believe me. So will you believe if I tell you about heaven? Nobody has gone into heaven but the one who came from heaven. That's what I did."

Then Jesus told about the time when Moses put a metal snake up on a pole. It was when God's people were in the desert. People who had snake bites could look at it. Then they would live. Jesus said, "The Son of Man has to be lifted up too. Then everyone who believes in him will live forever.

"God loved the world very much," said Jesus. "He loved it so much that he gave his only Son. People who believe in him will not die. They will live forever.

"God didn't send his Son to blame the world," said Jesus. "He sent his Son to save the world. People who believe in him will not be blamed. But people who don't believe are blamed already. That's because they don't believe in God's only Son.

"Here's what people have to choose," said Jesus. "They have to choose between light and dark. Light is in the world. But people love the dark instead. That's because what they do is wrong. So they hate light. They won't come into the light. They are afraid that their sin will show up clearly.

"But people who live in truth come into the light. They want to show that they live with God's help."

The Groom
JOHN 3:22–4:3

Jesus and his friends went into the country. Jesus spent time with his friends there. Jesus also baptized people.

John was still dipping people in water too. He was at a place where there was lots of water. People kept coming to be baptized.

John's followers went to John. "Remember the man you told us about? He is the man who was at the Jordan River. He is dipping people in water too. Now everybody is going to him."

"A person has only what God gives him," said John. "I told you I'm not the Promised One. I was sent to make things ready for him.

"It's like two people who will get married. The bride will marry the groom. The groom's best friend waits for him. He is happy to hear the groom coming.

"That's the kind of joy I feel," said John. "Jesus has to become more and more important. I have to become less and less important.

"Jesus is from above," said John. "So he is above everything. I am from the earth. So I talk like a person from the earth. Jesus talks about things he has seen and heard. But nobody believes him.

"People who believe Jesus show that they know God tells the truth. The one God sent speaks God's words. There is no end to God's Spirit in him.

"The Father loves the Son," said John. "He gave everything to him. People who believe in him will live forever. But people who don't obey God's Son won't have the life that lasts forever. They live in God's anger."

Some people said Jesus was getting more followers than John. The Jewish teachers heard about it. They heard that Jesus was dipping people in water too. But it was really Jesus' followers who were baptizing people. When Jesus heard all this, he went back to Galilee.

Water from a Well
JOHN 4:3-42

Jesus was on his way to Galilee. He went through the land of Samaria. He was tired. So he stopped at a well and sat down.

It was about noon. Jesus' friends went to the town nearby to get lunch.

It wasn't long before a woman came to the well. She was coming to get water.

"Would you give me a drink?" Jesus asked her.

Now Jews don't like people from Samaria. So the woman said, "Why are you asking me for a drink? You are a Jew. I'm from Samaria."

"God has a gift for you," said Jesus. "If you knew who I am, you'd ask me for a drink. I would give you water that brings you life."

"You don't have anything to get water with," she said. "So where are you going to get this water? You're not greater than Jacob, are you? He dug this well. He drank water from it. So did his sons and his sheep and cows."

"People who drink this water get

thirsty again," said Jesus. "But they can drink the water I give and never get thirsty again. In fact, my water will turn into a fountain. It will be like a fountain of water inside them. It will become life that lasts forever."

"Then give me this water," said the woman. "That way, I won't get thirsty again. I won't have to keep coming back to this well."

"Go and get your husband," said Jesus. "Then come back."

"I don't have a husband," said the woman.

"That's true," said Jesus. "You've had five husbands. But the man you live with now isn't one of them."

"You're a prophet!" said the woman. "So what do you think? Here on this mountain is where my people worship. You Jews say we have to worship in Jerusalem."

"Someday you won't worry about where to worship," said Jesus. "But you people don't really know the one you worship. We Jews do know the one we worship. It's through the Jews that the world will be saved.

"Someday true worship will come from the spirit," said Jesus. "In fact, the time is already here. God is spirit. So worship must come from the spirit. It must be true. That's the way the Father wants it."

Then the woman said, "Someday the Promised One is coming. He will be able to tell us all about it."

"I am the Promised One," said Jesus.

About that time, Jesus' friends came back. They were surprised to see Jesus talking with this woman. But they didn't ask him why he was talking to her.

Then the woman left her water jar there. She went back to town. She told people, "Come with me! Come and see a man who knows everything I've ever done. Do you think he might be the Promised One?"

The people went with the woman to see Jesus.

Now Jesus' friends were trying to get him to eat something.

But Jesus said, "I already have food. It's food you don't know about."

"Do you think somebody gave him food?" his friends asked.

"Doing what God wants is like food to me," said Jesus. "Finishing his work fills me. You say that in four more months you can bring in the crops. But look! Look at the fields! They are ready. It's time to bring crops in now. People are like crops. They can be gathered and helped to find life that lasts forever.

"The planter and the one who

gathers are happy together. It's true," said Jesus. "One person plants and another brings in the crops. I'm sending you to bring in what you didn't plant. Other people have done the hard work. Now you can gather what they planted."

Lots of people from that town believed in Jesus. They believed because of what the woman told them. "Jesus knows everything I've ever done," she said.

The people asked Jesus to stay with them for a while. He stayed for two days. Many more people heard what Jesus had to say. They believed too.

They talked about it with the woman. "At first we believed just because of you," they said. "But now we have heard Jesus ourselves. We know he really did come to save us."

A Sick Son
JOHN 4:43-54

Jesus went back to the land of Galilee. The people there were glad to see him. They had been at the Pass Over holiday. They had seen the things he did there.

Jesus went to the town of Cana again. That's where he had turned water into wine.

Now a man who worked for the king lived nearby in Capernaum. He heard that Jesus had come to Galilee. So he went to see Jesus.

This man's son was sick. It looked like he wouldn't live much longer. So the man asked Jesus to come to Capernaum. He asked Jesus to make his son well.

"You people have to see wonders, don't you?" said Jesus. "Then you will believe."

"Please come before my son dies," said the man.

"You can go back to him," said Jesus. "He will live."

The man believed Jesus. He left to go home. On the way, his servants came and met him. They told him his son was alive.

"What time did he get better?" asked the boy's father.

"At one o'clock yesterday afternoon," they said. "That's when he wasn't hot with a fever anymore."

The father knew this was when Jesus said, "He will live." So the man believed in Jesus. Everyone who lived at his house believed too.

That was the second wonder Jesus did.

AUGUST 19

Jesus' Home Town
MATTHEW 4:12-17; MARK 1:14-15; LUKE 3:19-20; 4:14-30

John had been teaching in the desert. Something he said had made King Herod angry. John had told

Herod that he shouldn't marry the wife of Herod's brother. John told about other things Herod shouldn't have done. So Herod put John in jail.

Jesus heard about this. That was one reason he went back to Galilee. He went to live in the town of Capernaum. It was by Lake Galilee. So Isaiah's words came true:

The way to the Lake Galilee
is by the Jordan River.
People who lived in the dark
now see a bright light.
It is beginning to shine.
It shines on people living in
death's shadow.

Then Jesus started teaching. He said, "Turn away from your sins. Heaven's kingdom is near."

People everywhere started hearing about Jesus. He went to teach at their worship places. Everyone said good things about him.

Then Jesus went to Nazareth, his home town. That's where he grew up. The worship day came. Jesus went to the town's worship house. That's where he always went on the worship day.

Jesus stood up and got ready to read. Someone gave him the book of Isaiah. The words were on a long roll of paper.

Jesus unrolled it. He found a place to read from. This is what he read:

God's Spirit is on me.
He chose me.
He sent me to teach good news to
poor people.
He sent me to tell people in jail
they can be free.
He sent me to help people who can't
see so they can see again.
He sent me to help people who
have had a hard time.
He sent me to tell about a new time.
It's a time when God will save his
people.

Then Jesus rolled up the paper. He gave it back to the man who was helping. He sat back down. Everybody was watching him. "These words have come true today," he said.

The people had only good things to say about Jesus. But they were surprised at the way he talked. "This is Joseph's son, isn't it?" they asked.

Jesus said, "I'm sure you'll tell me this old saying. 'If you are a doctor, then make yourself well.' You heard about what I did in Capernaum. You'll want me to do the same things here. But here's the truth. People in a prophet's home town don't say good things about him.

"Remember when Elijah lived?"

521

said Jesus. "The sky stayed closed for three and a half years. There was no rain. No food grew. There were many women whose husbands had died. God sent Elijah to one of these women. But she was not Jewish.

"When Elisha lived, many people had a skin sickness," said Jesus. "But Naaman was the only one God made well. He was not Jewish."

Everyone was angry when Jesus said this. The people all stood up. They pushed Jesus out of town.

The town was on a hill. The people pushed Jesus right to the edge of the hill. They were going to throw him over the edge. But Jesus passed right through the crowd. He walked away.

Nets Full of Fish

MATTHEW 4:18-22; MARK 1:16-20; LUKE 5:1-11

Jesus stood by Lake Galilee. Many people stood around him. They were listening to Jesus teach God's Word.

Peter and some other men who had been fishing were there. They were washing their nets. They had left two boats at the edge of the water.

Jesus saw the boats. He got into one of them. It was Peter's boat.

Jesus asked Peter to row out on the lake. They went just a little way from the shore. Then Jesus sat down in the boat. He began to teach the people.

When Jesus finished talking, he turned to Peter. "Take the boat into deep water now," he said. "Then put your nets out. We can catch some fish."

"We fished all night," said Peter. "It was hard work, and we didn't catch anything. But if you say so, I'll put the nets out."

The men threw out their nets.

Right away, hundreds of fish swam into the nets. The nets got heavy with all the fish. The nets began to break.

Peter and the men in his boat needed help. They called for James and John in the other boat.

James and John brought the other boat to help. They filled both boats with fish. In fact, both boats were too full. It looked like they might sink. The men were very surprised to see all the fish.

Peter bowed down in front of Jesus. "You should leave me, Lord," he said. "I am sinful!"

"Don't be afraid," said Jesus. "You'll catch men after this. So follow me. I'll show you how to fish for men."

So they pulled their boats up onto the land. Then they followed Jesus.

Many Sick People

MATTHEW 8:14-17; MARK 1:21-34; LUKE 4:31-41

Jesus and his friends went back to Capernaum. The worship day came. Jesus went to the town's worship house. He started teaching there.

People were surprised. Jesus didn't sound like any other teacher of the Law. He sounded like he knew what he was talking about.

All of a sudden, a man in the town's worship house yelled. "Jesus of Nazareth! I know who you are! You are God's Holy One! What do you want here? Did you come to get rid of us?"

A bad spirit was in control of the man. So Jesus said firmly, "Hush! Come out of that man!"

The bad spirit made the man shake. Then the spirit came out with a loud yell.

The people were surprised. "What's happening here?" they asked each other. "This is a new teaching. Jesus talks like a man in charge. He even tells bad spirits what to do, and they obey!"

The news about Jesus soon went all over the place. People everywhere around Galilee heard about this.

Jesus and his friends left the town's worship house. They went to Peter and Andrew's house. James and John were with them.

Peter's wife's mother was at the house. She was in bed. She was very hot and very sick. Peter told Jesus about her.

Jesus went into the room where she was. He held her hand. Then he helped her get up.

Right away, she was well. She started taking care of her visitors.

After the sun set, many people came by the house. They brought sick people to Jesus. They brought people who were controlled by bad spirits. The whole town seemed to be coming to Peter's door.

People were sick in different ways. But Jesus made them well. He sent many bad spirits away from people. He would not let the spirits talk. That's because they knew who he was.

People from Everywhere

MATTHEW 4:23-25; 8:1-4; MARK 1:35-45; LUKE 4:42-44; 5:12-15

Jesus got up very early the next morning. He went to find a place to be alone. He wanted a place where he could pray.

Later, Peter and his friends went looking for Jesus. They found him at last. They said, "Everybody is looking for you!"

"Let's go," said Jesus. "Let's go to other towns near here. I can teach in other towns too. That's why I came."

So Jesus traveled all through the land of Galilee. He spoke in the towns' worship houses. He told the Good News about God's kingdom. He made people well. Even people to the north, in Syria, heard about Jesus.

People kept bringing sick friends and family to Jesus. Some people were hurting very badly. Some had bad spirits in control of them. Some people couldn't move. Jesus made them well.

Big crowds of people came to Jesus. They came from Galilee and the Ten Cities. They came from Jerusalem and from around the Jordan River. Many of them followed Jesus.

One day a man with a skin sickness came to Jesus. "You can make me well if you want to," he said.

Jesus felt kind and caring toward this man. So Jesus touched him. "I do want to," said Jesus. "Be well."

Right away the sickness went away. The man was well.

Then Jesus said, "Don't tell anyone about this. Go to the priest. Let him check your skin. Give the gifts you're supposed to give for getting well."

But the man went off and told about what happened. The news went all over the place. So Jesus couldn't go into the towns for a while.

But people still came to see Jesus from everywhere. They came to be made well.

A Hole in the Roof
MATTHEW 9:1-8; MARK 2:1-12; LUKE 5:18-26

Jesus went back to Capernaum. News went around that he was home. So crowds started coming to the house where he was staying.

So many people came that the house was full of people. There was no more room. There wasn't even room around the door outside. But Jesus taught the people right there.

Then four men walked up to the house. They were bringing a friend who couldn't move. They carried him on a mat.

But they couldn't get through the crowd. So they dug through the roof. They made a hole right above Jesus. Then they let the sick man down on his mat. He went right through the hole in the roof.

Jesus saw how much they believed. He told the sick man, "Your sins are forgiven."

Some teachers of God's laws were watching. They thought, "How can he say that? Only God can forgive sins."

Jesus knew just what they were thinking. He said, "Why are you thinking that? Is it easier to say, 'Your sins are forgiven'? Or to say, 'Get up, take your mat with you, and walk'? I have the right to forgive sins here on earth. You'll see."

Then Jesus looked again at the man who couldn't move. He said, "Get up. Take your mat with you. You can go home now."

The man stood up. He picked up his mat. Then he walked out with everyone watching him.

Everyone was very surprised. They praised God. They said, "We never saw anything like this before!"

AUGUST 21

A Party at Matthew's

MATTHEW 9:9-15; MARK 2:13-20; LUKE 5:27-35

Jesus walked out by the lake. Lots of people came to see him there. So he started teaching them.

Then Jesus saw Matthew.

Matthew was sitting at his tax table. He was a tax man. He took the tax money that people had to pay.

"Follow me," Jesus said to Matthew.

So Matthew followed Jesus. He even gave a big dinner party for Jesus. It was at his own house. Tax workers and many other people came to his party.

Some of the Jewish leaders came to the party too. But they didn't like tax men. These men took more money than they should. The leaders talked to Jesus' friends about it. "Why are you eating and drinking with these tax workers? They are sinners."

Jesus heard what the leaders said. "People who are well don't need a doctor," said Jesus. "Sick people do. Why don't you go and learn what this means? 'I want your kindness, not your gifts.' I didn't come to find people who are doing right. I came to find people who are doing wrong."

Then the leaders said, "John's followers go without food to worship God. They do it while they pray. The followers of the Jewish leaders do it too. But your followers eat and drink."

"The groom is with his friends," said Jesus. "Will his friends stop eating now? One day the groom will be gone. Then there will be days when they don't eat."

At the Pool

JOHN 5:1-15

Sometime later, Jesus went to Jerusalem for a Jewish holiday. Now in Jerusalem there was a gate called the Sheep Gate. Near the Sheep Gate there was a pool. Five covered sidewalks led to the pool.

Lots of sick people came to the pool. They thought the water could make them well when it bubbled. People who couldn't see came. People who couldn't move would lie down there.

One man hadn't been able to walk for 38 years. Jesus saw him lying by the pool. So Jesus asked him, "Do you want to get well?"

"Yes," said the man. "But no one will help me into the pool. The water bubbles. Then I try to get in. But somebody else always gets in first."

Then Jesus said, "Get up. Pick up your mat. Walk."

Right away, the man's legs got strong. He picked up his mat, and he walked.

Now this happened on a worship day. The Jewish leaders saw the man carrying his mat. They said, "This is a worship day. God's law says not to carry mats on a worship day."

"A man made me well," he said. "He told me to pick my mat up and walk."

"Who was this man?" asked the leaders. "Who told you to pick up your mat and walk?"

The man who had been made well didn't have any idea. He didn't know who had made him well. Jesus had quietly moved away. He had moved away into the crowd standing around the pool.

Later, Jesus saw the man at the worship house. Jesus said, "You are well now. Don't sin anymore. Not being able to walk is bad. But it's not as bad as what could happen if you keep sinning."

Then the man went and found the Jewish leaders. He told them that Jesus had made him well.

Father and Son

JOHN 5:16-47

The Jewish leaders got angry at Jesus. It was all because he made someone well on a worship day.

"My Father is always at work," said Jesus. "He is even working today. So I'm working too."

The leaders didn't like to hear this. So they tried to find a way to kill Jesus. They thought he didn't care about the worship day. What's more, he was calling God his own Father. He was making himself the same as God.

Jesus talked about himself. He said, "The Son can't do anything by himself. He only does what he sees his Father do. Whatever the Father does, the Son does too.

"The Father loves the Son," said Jesus. "He shows the Son everything he does. He will surprise you. He will show the Son even greater things than you've seen. The Father gives life to the dead. In the same way, the Son gives life too.

"The Father doesn't judge anyone," said Jesus. "He lets his Son judge. Then everyone will treat the Son like he is important. It's just like making the Father important. What if you don't treat the Son like he is important? Then you're not treating the Father like he is important. The Father is the one who sent the Son.

"Listen to me," said Jesus. "Believe the one who sent me. Then you'll have life forever. You won't be blamed. You have moved out of death into life. It's time for the dead to hear the Son's voice. Everyone who hears will live.

"Don't be surprised," said Jesus. "Someday, all people in their graves will hear the Son's voice. They'll come out of their graves. People who did good things will get up and live. People who sinned will get up and be blamed.

"You went to see John," said Jesus. "He told you the truth. John was like a lamp. He gave light for a while. You chose to enjoy his light. But I am able to tell about my Father better than John. The Father gave me work to finish. That's what I'm doing. My work shows that the Father sent me.

"The Father tells about me," said Jesus. "He sent me. You didn't hear his voice. You didn't see how he looks. His word doesn't live in you, because you don't believe me.

"You work hard at studying God's Word," said Jesus. "You think that's the way to have life forever. The same words you study tell about me. But you won't come to me to have life.

"It's not important that people cheer for me. But I know you," said Jesus. "I know God's love isn't in your hearts. I come to you in my Father's name. But you don't believe me. Other people come in their own names. You believe them. You want other people to cheer for you. But you don't even try to get God to cheer for you.

"Moses wrote about me," said Jesus. "But you don't believe what Moses wrote. So how can you believe what I'm telling you?"

On the Worship Day

MATTHEW 12:1-14; MARK 2:23–3:6;
LUKE 6:1-11

It was a worship day. Jesus and his friends walked through some wheat fields. His friends picked some of the wheat. They ate it because they were hungry.

Some Jewish leaders saw them. They said, "You can't pick wheat on a worship day. It's against God's law."

"Remember David and his friends?" asked Jesus. "They were hungry. So David went into the worship house. He and his men ate some of the special bread. It was bread for the priests.

"Maybe you remember reading the Law," said Jesus. "It says that priests work on the worship day. And God doesn't blame them. But I say that someone here is greater than the worship house.

"God's Word says that he wants your kindness, not your gifts," said Jesus. "If you knew what that meant, you wouldn't be mad. We didn't do anything wrong. People were not made for the worship day. Instead, the worship day was made for people. I am Lord of the worship day."

Another worship day came. Jesus went to the worship house. He began to teach there.

There was a man in the worship house. His right hand was small and twisted.

The leaders watched Jesus. They wanted to see what he would do. They wanted a reason to say Jesus did something wrong.

At last they asked Jesus a question. "Is it right to make people well on the worship day?"

Jesus said, "Let's say you have a sheep. It falls into a pit on the worship day. Wouldn't you pull it out? A person is a lot more important than a sheep. So it is right to do something good on the worship day."

Jesus looked at the man whose hand was small and twisted. "Stand up in front of everyone," said Jesus. Then Jesus turned to the people. "Should we do good or bad on the worship day? Should we save lives or kill on the worship day?"

Nobody answered. The people were all quiet.

Jesus looked around. He was very upset because their hearts were hard. They didn't care about God.

Then Jesus looked at the sick man. "Hold your hand out," he said.

So the man held his hand out. It reached out all the way now. It was all well.

But the people got very angry. They began talking to each other. They started planning to get even with Jesus. The leaders began making plans to kill him.

Crowds

MATTHEW 12:15-21; MARK 3:7-12

Jesus and his friends went to the lake. Many people from Galilee followed him. People came from across the Jordan River. People came from Tyre and Jerusalem and many other places. There was a huge crowd.

Jesus had made many people well. So the sick people kept pushing toward him. They wanted to touch him.

People controlled by bad spirits fell down before him. They called out, "You are God's Son!" But Jesus was very firm with them. He told them not to tell anyone who he was.

That made the words of Isaiah come true. Long ago Isaiah wrote, "Here is my servant. I chose him. He is the one I love. I'm happy with him. I'll put my Spirit on him. He will tell all nations what is right and fair. He won't fuss and fight. He won't cry out. People in the streets won't hear his voice.

"A person who is sad is like a bent plant," wrote Isaiah. "My servant won't hurt bent plants. A person who is glad is like a glowing candle. My servant won't blow out glowing candles.

"My servant will stand up for what's right," wrote Isaiah. "He will win. The nations will hope in his name."

Friends and Helpers

MARK 3:13-19; LUKE 6:12-19

Jesus went up on a mountain to pray. He spent all night there, praying to God.

In the morning Jesus called his friends. He picked 12 of them to be his special friends and helpers.

He chose Peter and his brother Andrew.

He chose James and his brother John.

He chose Philip and Nathanael.

He chose Matthew, Thomas, and Simon.

He chose another James, who was the son of Alphaeus.

He chose Judas, whose father's name was James.

Then Jesus chose another Judas,

called Judas Iscariot. He turned out to be an enemy.

Jesus took these men to a big, flat place. A large crowd of his followers stood there. People had come from all over the place. They were there to listen to Jesus.

Some people had come to be made well. People bothered by bad spirits were set free.

Everyone tried to touch Jesus. Power was coming from him. He was making everyone well.

Up the Mountain

MATTHEW 5:1-12; LUKE 6:20-23

Jesus saw how many people were coming to hear him. So he went up on the side of a mountain. There he sat down. His followers gathered around him. Then he began to teach them.

"God will bring good to people who know they need him. The kingdom of heaven belongs to them," said Jesus.

"God will bring good to people who cry. They will feel better.

"God will bring good to people who think others are more important. The earth will belong to them.

"God will bring good to people who are hungry for what's right.

They're thirsty for what's right. They'll be filled up.

"God will bring good to people who are kind. God will be kind to them.

"God will bring good to people whose hearts are clean. These people aren't dirty from sin. They'll get to see God.

"God will bring good to people who make peace. They'll be called God's children.

"God will bring good to people who get hurt for doing what's right. The kingdom of heaven belongs to them.

"God will bring good when people laugh at you. They might hurt you for doing good. They might lie about you because of me. But God has great gifts for you in heaven. So be happy. People also hurt the prophets who told God's words."

Salt and Light

MATTHEW 5:13-28; LUKE 6:24-26

"Watch out if you are rich," said Jesus. "That means you have your gifts already. Watch out if you have plenty of food now. You will go hungry. Watch out if you laugh now. You will end up crying. Watch out when people say good things about you. People said good things about prophets who lied.

"You're like salt here on earth," said Jesus. "But what if the salt stops being salty? Can it get salty again? No. It's not good for anything. It has to be thrown out. It's only good for walking on.

"You're like a light to this world," said Jesus. "You're like a city high on a hill. It's up where everyone can see it.

"People don't put a lamp under a bowl," said Jesus. "Instead, they put it out where it will shine. It lights up the house. So let your light shine where people can see it. They'll see the good things you do. Then they'll cheer for God your Father.

"Don't think I came to get rid of the Law. Don't think I came to get rid of what prophets wrote. I didn't come to get rid of these words," said Jesus. "I came to make the words come true. Even the smallest law is important. It will be important until everything happens the way God planned.

"What if people break the smallest law?" said Jesus. "They'll be the smallest in the kingdom of heaven. What about people who teach others to break God's laws? They'll be the smallest in the kingdom of heaven too.

"But people who obey God's laws will be great in heaven. So will people who teach others to obey," said Jesus. "You must be even better than your Jewish leaders. If you're not, you'll never get into heaven's kingdom.

"You've heard that the Law says not to kill," said Jesus. "You've heard that people who kill will pay for it. But I say this. Anybody who is angry with another person gets in trouble. Anyone who isn't kind answers to the judge. What if someone says, 'You fool'? He will be in danger of going to hell.

"Let's say you bring a gift for God to the altar. Then you remember that someone is angry at you," said Jesus. "Leave your gift there. Go and make peace with the person who is angry at you. Then come back and give your gift.

"Make peace quickly with a person who blames you for something. Do it before you get to the judge," said Jesus. "If you don't, the judge will give you to the officer. You might even be put in jail. You'll stay there until you've paid the last penny.

"You've heard, 'Don't have sex with someone you're not married to.' But I tell you not to even let your mind think about it. If you think it, you've done it in your heart."

An Eye for an Eye

MATTHEW 5:29-48; LUKE 6:27-36

"Is your eye making you sin?" asked Jesus. "Then it would be better not to have an eye. Is your hand making you sin? Then it would be better not to have a hand. You don't want to sin and be sent to hell someday.

"You've heard about someone who leaves his wife," said Jesus. "He is supposed to give her a divorce paper. I say, anybody who leaves his wife and marries another woman is sinning. He is sinning unless she left him first. Anybody who marries a divorced woman is sinning.

"You've heard that you're to keep the promises you made to God," said Jesus. "But I tell you just to say yes and mean 'yes.' When you say no, mean 'no.' Anything more than that comes from Satan.

"Don't make promises in heaven's name. That's where God sits to rule. Don't promise by the earth's name. It's the stool for God's feet.

"Don't promise by Jerusalem's name," said Jesus. "It's a great king's city. Don't promise by pointing to your own head. You can't even make your hair white or black.

"You've heard that if somebody hurts you, then you can hurt that person. But I tell you not to fight a sinful person," said Jesus. "What if somebody hits you on your right cheek? Then turn your left cheek to that person too. What if somebody takes your coat? Give that person your shirt, too. What if somebody makes you walk a mile with him? Go two miles instead.

"Give to people who ask you for something," said Jesus. "Don't say no to people who want to borrow something. Treat other people the way you want to be treated.

"You've heard that you're to love your neighbor and hate your enemy," said Jesus. "I say, love your enemies. Pray for people who hurt you. Then you will be children of your Father in heaven. Your Father makes the sun shine on all people, bad and good. He sends rain for people who do right and for people who do wrong.

"What if you love just the people who love you? What good does that do?" said Jesus. "Even sinners love people who love them. What if you're friendly just to people you like? How is that different from what other people do? Even people who don't believe in God do that.

"Let's say you lend money to some people," said Jesus. "You do it because you know they'll pay you back. What good does that do? Even people who don't believe in God do that. They lend money when they know they'll be paid back.

"Love your enemies," said Jesus. "Do good to them. Lend to them. Don't look for anything back. Then God will plan good things for you. You will be his children. God is kind to people who are not even thankful. He is kind to sinful people. So be kind like your Father."

Your Secret
MATTHEW 6:1-21

"Don't do good things just so people will see you. If you do, God your Father won't do good things for you," said Jesus. "Don't show off when you give. Some people give so that other people will say good things about them. The truth is, that's all the good that will come to them.

"Give to the poor," said Jesus. "Don't tell your left hand what your right hand does. That way, it will be a secret. Your Father sees things that are done in secret. So he will do good things for you.

"What about praying?" said Jesus. "Don't pray just so others will see you. Some people do that. The truth is, being seen is all the good that will come to them.

"Go to your room when you pray," said Jesus. "Close the door. Then pray to the Father you can't see. Your Father sees everything you do in secret. He will do good things for you.

"Don't just chatter away when you pray," said Jesus. "People who don't believe in the true God do that. They think their god hears them if they use lots of words. Don't be like them. Your Father knows what you need even before you ask.

"This is how you should pray," said Jesus.

"Our Father in heaven,
    your name is wonderful.
Bring your kingdom here to earth.
We pray that what you want
    will be done on earth
    like it is in heaven.
Give us the food we need each day.
Forgive us for our sin.
  Forgive us as we forgive people
    who sin against us.
Don't let anyone try to make us do
    wrong.
Save us from Satan, the enemy.

"Forgive other people when they treat you badly," said Jesus. "Then God your Father will forgive you, too. What if you don't forgive other people? Then your Father won't forgive you.

"You can choose to go without food to worship God," said Jesus. "But don't frown about it. Some people make faces. They're showing everyone that they're going without food. The truth is, that's all the good that will come to them.

"When you go without food, put sweet-smelling oil in your hair. Wash your face," said Jesus. "Then other people won't notice that you're going without food. But God will notice. He sees what you do in secret. He will do good things for you.

"Don't store up riches for yourself here on earth. Moths and rust tear down things on earth," said Jesus. "Robbers break in. They steal riches.

"Store up your riches in heaven," said Jesus. "Moths and rust can't tear things apart in heaven. Robbers can't break in and steal things. Your heart will care about the place where you keep your riches."

AUGUST 25

Birds' Food and Flowers' Clothes

MATTHEW 6:22-34; LUKE 6:37-38

"Your eye is like a lamp for your body," said Jesus. "If your eye is good instead of sinful, your body is full of light. If your eye is sinful, your body will be full of darkness. Light is supposed to be inside you. If there is darkness instead, then it's really, really dark!

"You can't follow two leaders at one time," said Jesus. "You'll hate one of them and love the other one. Or you'll obey one and not the other. You can't serve God and money, too.

"So I tell you not to worry," said Jesus. "Don't worry about what you'll eat or drink. Don't worry about what you'll wear. Life is much more important than food. Your body is much more important than clothes.

"See the birds in the air?" said Jesus. "They don't plant food. They don't bring in crops. They don't save food in barns. God your Father feeds them. You're more important than birds. Can anybody make his life last an hour longer by worrying?

"Why worry about clothes?" said Jesus. "Look at the flowers in the field. They don't work. They don't make their own clothes. King Solomon had beautiful clothes. But his clothes weren't as wonderful as one of these flowers. That's the way God dresses the grass in the fields. The grass is here today and gone tomorrow. So God will give you clothes too, won't he?

"Your faith is so small!" said

Jesus. "Don't worry. Don't say, 'What will we eat? What will we drink? What will we wear?' People who don't believe in God worry about those things. But your Father in heaven knows what you need. Put God first in your life. Then he will make sure you have everything you need.

"Don't worry about tomorrow," said Jesus. "Tomorrow can worry about itself. Each day has enough trouble of its own. Why add tomorrow's worries to today?

"Don't blame people for what they do," said Jesus. "Then you won't be blamed for what you do. Forgive people. Then you will be forgiven.

"Give, and good things will come to you in return," said Jesus. "You will get plenty. God will shake it up. Then he will push it down to make room for more. God will give you so much! It will run over and flow out onto your lap. God will be fair to you. He will give to you the same way you give to others."

The Dust and the Log

MATTHEW 7:1-14; LUKE 6:39-42

Then Jesus told his followers a story. "Can a blind man lead another blind man? Wouldn't they both fall into a hole? The learner is not greater than his teacher. But when he has learned everything, he will be like his teacher.

"Why point at a bit of dust in someone's eye? You don't even see the big log in your own eye. How can you say, 'Let's get that dust out'? You have a log in your own eye," said Jesus. "First get rid of the log in your eye. Then you'll see clearly. You'll be able to get rid of the other person's dust.

"Don't give dogs something special that is for God," said Jesus. "Don't give beautiful pearls to pigs. If you do, they'll run over them. They'll mash them under their feet. Then they'll run over you, too.

"Ask, and God will give you what you ask for," said Jesus. "Look for him. Then you'll find him. Tap on his door. He will open it for you. Everybody who asks, gets. The person who looks for God finds him. The door opens for the person who taps on it.

"Let's say your son asks you for bread," said Jesus. "Will you give him a rock? What if he asks you for a fish? Will you give him a snake? You know how to give good gifts to your children. So, of course, your Father in heaven gives good gifts when you ask.

"Treat people the way you want them to treat you. This is the whole message of the Law and the prophets.

"Go in through the small gate," said Jesus. "There is a wide gate and a wide road. But people who take the wide road will be in trouble. Many people follow the wide road. There is also a small gate and a narrow road. This road leads to life. Only a few people find it."

Good Fruit and Bad Fruit
MATTHEW 7:15-29; LUKE 6:43-49

"Watch out for prophets who lie," said Jesus. "They may pretend to be sheep. But inside, they are mean wolves. You will know them by the way they act. What they do is like bad fruit.

"People don't pick grapes from weeds," said Jesus. "They don't pick figs from weeds. Good trees make good fruit. Bad trees make bad fruit. A good tree can't make bad fruit. A bad tree can't make good fruit.

"Trees get cut down if they don't make good fruit. They get burned up," said Jesus. "So you will know trees and people by their fruit. You can tell what they are like by what they do.

"Good things happen when good people are around," said Jesus. "That's because they have good stored up in their hearts. But bad things happen when bad people are around. That's because they have sin stored up in their hearts. People's words come from their hearts first. Then the words come out of their mouths.

"Just calling me 'Lord' won't get people into God's kingdom. People must do what my Father wants," said Jesus. "Many people will say, 'Lord, we spoke in your name. We sent away bad spirits in your name. We did wonders in your name.'

"But I'll tell them, 'I never really knew you. Get away from me. You do wrong things. Why do you call me "Lord"? You don't do what I tell you.'

"Some people hear me and obey," said Jesus. "They are like the wise man. He built his house on a rock. Rain came down, and rivers got high. Wind roared and beat on his house. But his house didn't fall down. It stood safe on the rock.

"Some people hear me, but they don't obey," said Jesus. "They are like the foolish man. He built his house on sand. Rain came down, and rivers got high. Wind roared and beat on his house, and it crashed down."

People were surprised to hear what Jesus was teaching. He sounded like he knew what he was talking about. He didn't sound like any teachers they knew.

The Captain's Servant

MATTHEW 8:5-13; LUKE 7:1-10

There was once a Roman army captain who lived in Capernaum. He had a servant who was very special to him. But his servant got very sick. He was so sick, he was almost dead.

Now Jesus had gone back to Capernaum. The captain heard that Jesus was in town. So he sent some Jewish leaders to meet with Jesus. He sent them to ask Jesus to come to his house. He wanted Jesus to make his servant well.

When these leaders came to Jesus, they begged him to help. "The captain is a good man," they said. "He loves our nation. He even built our town's worship house. So you should help him. You should make his servant well."

Jesus went with the leaders. But the captain had sent some friends to Jesus too. They met him on his way to see the captain. They gave Jesus another message.

The message said, "Lord, don't bother to come. I'm not good enough for you to come to my house. That's why I didn't come to you myself. I'm not good enough to see you. Just say the word. Then I know my servant will be well again.

"You see, I know about being in charge," the message said. "I have a boss to obey. And I'm the boss of many other men. I tell one to come, and he comes. I tell another one to go, and he goes. I tell my servants, 'Do this' or 'Do that.' And they do what I tell them."

Jesus was surprised to hear this. He looked at the crowd following him. He said, "I haven't seen such great faith in the land of Israel before.

"People will come from the east," said Jesus. "People will come from the west. They'll eat a big dinner with Abraham in God's kingdom. Isaac and Jacob will be there. But other people will be thrown out into the dark. They will cry out there."

Then Jesus sent word to the captain. "You believed I would make your servant well. I will do just what you believed."

At that moment, the captain's servant got well. The friends he had sent to Jesus went back home. They saw that the captain's servant was well.

Getting a Son Back

LUKE 7:11-17

Jesus and his friends headed toward a town called Nain. A big crowd was with them. They came up to the

537

town gate. People were coming out of the town through the gate. The people were carrying a dead man.

The dead man was the only son his mother had. The man's father had died some time before. Many people were there with his mother.

Jesus saw the dead man's mother. "Don't cry," he said. His heart was very sad for her.

Jesus touched the long box that held the body. The people who were carrying it stood still.

Jesus said, "Young man, get up."

The man who had been dead sat up. He began to talk. So Jesus gave him back to his mother. He was alive!

Everyone was surprised. They praised God. They said, "This man Jesus is a great prophet. God is here helping his people."

The news about Jesus went quickly all over the land.

What Did You Come to See?

MATTHEW 11:1-19; LUKE 7:18-35

Now John, the one who baptized people, had some followers. They told John what Jesus was doing. So John asked two of them to go to Jesus. He told them to ask Jesus a question. "Are you the one we've been waiting for? Or should I look for someone else?"

At that time, Jesus was making many sick people well. He was sending many bad spirits away. He was making many people see again.

So Jesus said, "Go back to John. Tell him everything you've seen. Tell him everything you've heard. People who couldn't see before can see now. People who couldn't walk before can walk now.

"People with skin sickness are well," said Jesus. "People who couldn't hear before can hear now. Dead people are coming to life again. Poor people are hearing the Good News. Good things will come to people who keep following me."

So John's followers went back to tell John.

Then Jesus talked to the people about John. "What did you go out to the desert to see? Did you go to see plants blown by the wind? If not, what did you think you would see? Did you think you'd see someone dressed in fine clothes? No. People who wear fine clothes are in palaces.

"So what did you go to see in the desert? Did you go to see a prophet? Yes," said Jesus. "But John is more than a prophet. He is the one Malachi wrote about. Malachi wrote that God would send someone with a message. That person would help people get ready for me.

"Here on earth there is nobody greater than John. But in God's kingdom, even the smallest is greater than John.

"The Law and the prophets told about all that was to happen until John came. John is the prophet like Elijah who was supposed to come. Hear this if you have ears," said Jesus.

People listened to what Jesus said. They said that God's way was the right way. Even men who took tax money said this. They had been baptized by John.

Some Jewish leaders had not been baptized by John. So they wouldn't take what God had planned for them. They said they knew all about the Law already.

"What are these people like?" asked Jesus. "They are like children who sit in the market place. They call to each other. They say, 'We played the flute for you, but you didn't dance. We sang a sad song, but you didn't cry.'

"John came and didn't eat bread or drink wine," said Jesus. "So you say a bad spirit controls him. I come, and I do eat bread and drink wine. So you say, 'This man eats too much. He is a drunk. He is a friend of tax men. He is a friend of sinners.' But I say being wise is what's right. You can see that by watching a wise person."

Perfume

LUKE 7:36-50

There was a Jewish leader named Simon. He asked Jesus to come to dinner at his house. So Jesus went. He sat down at Simon's table.

Now there was a sinful woman in town. She heard that Jesus was having dinner at Simon's house. So she went there. She took a beautiful stone jar with her. The jar was filled with sweet-smelling perfume.

The woman went into the house. She stood close to Jesus, at his feet. Then she began to cry. Her tears dripped on Jesus' feet. They made his feet wet. So she wiped his feet with her long hair. Then she kissed Jesus' feet. She let perfume flow out of the jar onto his feet.

Simon saw this. He said to himself, "Jesus can't really be a prophet. If he was, he would know this is a sinful woman."

Jesus said, "Simon, I want to tell you something."

"Tell me, Teacher," said Simon.

"Two men borrowed money from another man," said Jesus. "One man borrowed 500 pieces of money. The other man borrowed 50 pieces. The time came to pay the money back. But they couldn't pay it back. The man who let them borrow the money said that was OK. 'I won't make you pay me back,' he said. Now, which man will love him more?"

"The man who borrowed the most money," said Simon. "He would be the most thankful. He would love him more."

"You're right, " said Jesus. Then he turned to the woman. "See this woman?" he said to Simon. "She wet my feet with her tears. She wiped my feet with her hair. She kissed my feet. She put perfume on my feet too.

"You didn't even give me water to wash my feet. You didn't welcome me with a kiss when I came," said Jesus. "You didn't put oil on my head.

"This woman has lots of love," said Jesus. "She had many sins. But they have been forgiven. Some people haven't been forgiven for very much. So they don't love very much."

Then Jesus said to the woman, "Your sins are forgiven."

Now other people at Simon's house began to talk among themselves.

"Who is this man?" they asked. "He even forgives people's sins."

Jesus talked to the woman. He said, "Go in peace. Your faith has saved you."

A Pack of Snakes
MATTHEW 12:22-37; MARK 3:20-30; LUKE 8:1-3

Jesus went from town to town. He taught the Good News about God's kingdom. His 12 special friends went with him. Some women went with him too. Jesus had made many of them well.

Mary Magdalene was with Jesus. Seven bad spirits had come out of her. Joanna was with Jesus. Her husband was in charge of King Herod's whole house. A woman named Susanna was with Jesus. There were many others. These women spent their own money to help Jesus. They helped him and his friends get things they needed.

Jesus and his friends went to eat. A crowd began to gather around. It got so crowded, Jesus and his friends couldn't eat.

Then some people brought in a man controlled by bad spirits. He couldn't see, and he couldn't speak. Jesus made the man well. Then he could see and talk.

The people were surprised. They said, "Could Jesus really be the one God promised to send?"

The Jewish leaders heard about this. They said, "Jesus gets power from the prince of the bad spirits. That's how he sends spirits away."

Jesus knew what they were thinking. Jesus said, "What if a kingdom fights against itself? It can't last long. What if a city or a family fights against itself? It will be torn down. What if Satan sends Satan away? Then he fights against himself. How could his kingdom last?

"You say my power comes from bad spirits," said Jesus. "You say that's how I send bad spirits away. Then how do your people send bad spirits away? I send bad spirits away by God's Spirit. That means that God's kingdom has come.

"If you're not with me, you're against me," said Jesus. "You can choose to work with me. If you don't, you choose to work against me.

"People will be forgiven for every sin. But what if they say the Holy Spirit is a bad spirit? They won't be forgiven. Anybody who speaks against me will be forgiven. But anybody who speaks against the Holy Spirit won't be. Not now. Not ever." Jesus said this because of what they said. They said he was controlled by a bad spirit.

Then Jesus said, "Make a tree good. Then its fruit will be good. Or make a tree bad. Then its fruit will

be bad. The fruit shows what kind of tree it is.

"You're just a pack of snakes!" said Jesus. "You're full of sin. So how can you say anything good?

"The mouth says what comes from the heart. Good things come from good hearts," said Jesus. "Sin comes from sinful hearts. Someday God will judge the world. People will have to tell why they said words without thinking. You'll be made clean from sin because of your words. Or you'll be dirty with sin because of your words."

Jesus' family heard about what he said. So they went to take charge of him. They said, "He must be out of his mind."

AUGUST 28

Wanting a Sign

Matthew 12:38-50; Mark 3:31-35; Luke 11:24-32

Some Jewish leaders and teachers came to Jesus. They said, "We want to see you do a wonder. It will be like a sign to us."

"Only sinful people ask for a wonder," said Jesus. "The only sign they'll see is the sign of Jonah. Jonah spent three days and nights inside a big fish. In the same way, I'll spend three days and nights in the earth.

"Someday, people from Jonah's

time will be with the people of today. It will happen when God judges everyone," said Jesus. "Then they'll blame the people of today for what they have done. People from Nineveh heard what Jonah said. They were sorry for what they'd done. They stopped doing bad things. But someone more important than Jonah is here now.

"The Queen of Sheba will be with the people of today. It will happen when God judges everyone," said Jesus. "Then she will blame the people of today for what they have done. She came from far away. She listened to Solomon. She heard the wise things he said. But someone more important than Solomon is here now.

"A bad spirit comes out of a person," said Jesus. "Then it goes through dry places. It tries to find a place to stay. But it might not find a place to stay. So it says, 'I'll go back to the place I left.'

"What if the place it left is empty?" asked Jesus. "Then this spirit will go and get seven other spirits. They're even more sinful. They go and live in the person. Then the person is in even bigger trouble. That's how it's going to be with these sinful people."

There was a woman in the crowd. She called out to Jesus. "God will be good to the mother who has you for a son."

Jesus turned to her. "God will be good to people who hear and obey God," he said.

Jesus was talking to the people. Jesus' own mother and brothers came and stood outside. They wanted to talk to Jesus. So someone went in and told Jesus. "Your brothers are outside," he said. "They want to talk to you."

Jesus pointed to his followers. "Here's my family," he said. "My Father is in heaven. People who do what my Father wants are my brothers. They are my sisters and my mother."

The Cup and the Dish
LUKE 11:37-46, 52

One of the Jewish leaders asked Jesus to eat with him. So Jesus went. Jesus didn't wash the same way the leader did before he ate his meal. That surprised the leader.

Jesus said, "You leaders are like a cup and dish. You clean the cup and dish only on the outside. But inside yourselves, you're sinful. That's foolish. God made you on the outside. But he also made you on the inside. Give what you can to the poor. Then you will really be clean.

"How sad it will be for you leaders," said Jesus. "You give God a small part of what you earn. You even give him one out of every 10 garden plants. But you don't think about what's right. You don't think about God's love. You should think about fairness and about loving God. Then think about giving one out of every 10 pieces of your money, too.

"How sad it will be for you leaders," said Jesus. "You want to sit at the most important places. You want people to think you're the most important people.

"How sad it will be for you," said Jesus. "You're like graves that aren't marked with stones. People walk over them without even knowing it."

One of these men knew a lot about the Law. He talked to Jesus. "Teacher, we feel put down when you say these things."

"You know a lot about the Law," said Jesus. "It will be sad for you. You give people all kinds of laws. It's very hard for people to do them all. You won't even lift a finger to help them.

"How sad for you who know about God's law," said Jesus. "It's like you took away a key. It's the key to knowing. You don't try to learn and know. And you don't let other people learn and know."

From the Roof Tops

LUKE 11:53–12:12

Now the Jewish leaders began to talk very sharply against Jesus. They asked him many questions. They were just waiting for him to say something wrong. They wanted to trap him with his own words.

But thousands of people were gathering. The people in the crowd were pushing and even stepping on each other.

Then Jesus began to talk. First he talked to his followers. He said, "Watch out! What the leaders say and do isn't right.

"One day people will know everything that has been hidden. Things you said in the dark will be told in daylight. You may have whispered in someone's ear," said Jesus. "You may have said it in a room inside a house. But what you said will be shouted from the roof.

"Don't be afraid of people who can kill your body. After that, they can't do anything else," said Jesus. "I'll tell you who you should be afraid of. Be afraid of the one who can do more. He can kill the body. He can also throw you into hell. Yes, he is the one to be afraid of.

"You can buy five sparrows for two pennies," said Jesus. "They don't cost much, but God doesn't forget any of them. God knows all about you, too. He even knows how many hairs are on your head. So don't be afraid. You're more important than many sparrows.

"Tell people you know me," said Jesus. "Then I'll tell God's angels I know you. Are you afraid to tell people you know me? Then I'll tell God's angels I don't know you.

"People might bring you into the towns' worship houses," said Jesus. "They might take you to the leaders. But don't worry about what you'll say. The Holy Spirit will tell you what to say."

The Rich Man's Barns
LUKE 12:13-21

Somebody in the crowd said, "Teacher! Tell my brother to share with me."

"Who made me your judge?" asked Jesus.

Then he said to the people, "Be careful. Guard yourself against wanting more and more things. Life is not made of how many things you have."

Then Jesus told this story. "A rich man grew lots of crops on his farm. 'What should I do?' said the rich man. 'I don't have a place to keep all my crops.'

"Then the rich man said, 'I know! I'll take down my old barns. I will build bigger barns. Then I can store all my crops. I'll have plenty of good things stored away. They'll last for many years to come. I can take life easy. I can eat. I can drink. I can be happy.'

"But God said, 'You are foolish. You will die tonight. Then who will get the things you kept for yourself?'

"This is the way it is for some people," said Jesus. "They are people who aren't rich in giving to God. They store up things for themselves instead."

The Wise Servant
LUKE 12:35-48

"Be ready to help and serve," said Jesus. "Being ready is like keeping your lamp turned on.

"Be like servants waiting for their master," said Jesus. "The master comes back from a wedding party. He taps on the door. His servants open it right away. Their master sees the servants waiting for him. That makes the servants look good.

"Then the master will serve and help them," said Jesus. "He will tell them to sit at the table. He will wait on them. It's good if the servants are ready for him. They should be ready even if he comes at midnight.

"A robber comes when no one is watching," said Jesus. "You need to be ready. I'll come when you're not thinking about it."

Peter said, "Lord, is this story just for us? Or is it for everybody?"

"It's for people who do what they say they will do," said Jesus. "That's what a wise servant does. His master puts him in charge of all the servants. He even gives them their food. A good servant does what his master tells him. He will be following orders when his master comes back. His master will put him in charge of everything.

"Think about it," said Jesus. "What if he says, 'My master is taking too long'? Then he begins to eat and drink. He gets drunk. He even beats the other servants. Then the master comes back. The servant wasn't thinking about him. The master will throw him out. He will be sent away forever. He will go to the place where people don't believe in God.

"The servant knows what his master wants," said Jesus. "If he doesn't do it, he will get in trouble. What if the servant doesn't know what his master wants? He will still get in trouble, but not as badly.

"The master may give his servant a lot," said Jesus. "Then he will want his servant to give a lot too."

Clouds from the West

LUKE 12:51-56; 13:6-9

"Do you think I came to bring peace?" asked Jesus. "No. I came to shake things up. From now on, families will fight each other. Three will be against two. Two will be against three.

"Fathers will turn against sons," said Jesus. "Sons will turn against fathers. Mothers will turn against daughters. Daughters will turn against mothers. Mothers-in-law will be against daughters-in-law. Daughters-in-law will be against mothers-in-law.

"You watch clouds coming up from the west," said Jesus. "Then you say it's going to rain, and it does. A south wind blows. Then you say it will be hot, and it is. You can tell what's happening with the earth and sky. Why can't you tell what's happening now?"

Then Jesus told a story. "A man planted a fig tree in his garden. Sometimes he'd go back to look at it. He was watching for fruit to grow on it. But there was no fruit.

"At last the man talked to his gardener about it. He said, 'I've been coming here for three years. I've been looking for fruit on this fig tree. But I haven't found any. So cut it down. It's just using up the soil.'

"But the gardener spoke up. 'Sir, leave the fig tree alone one more year. I'll see what I can do. I'll dig around it. I'll make the soil richer. Maybe it will give you fruit next year. If it doesn't, you can cut it down.'"

The Woman Who Couldn't Stand Up Tall

LUKE 13:10-17

One worship day, Jesus was teaching in a town's worship house. A woman there was all bent over. She couldn't stand up tall. A bad spirit had kept her bent for 18 years.

Jesus saw her. He called her to come over to him. He said, "You're now set free from your sickness." Then he put his hands on her. Right away, she stood up tall. She praised God.

The man in charge was mad. He was mad because Jesus made this woman well on the worship day. So the man in charge talked to the people. "There are six days for

work," he said. "You can come and be made well any other day. But don't come to be made well on the worship day."

Then Jesus said, "All of you work on the worship day! Don't you take your ox or donkey outside on the worship day? Don't you lead it to water so it can drink? Satan kept this woman bent over for 18 years. Shouldn't she be set free on this worship day?"

Jesus' enemies felt put down when they heard this. But the other people were glad. They loved the wonderful things Jesus did.

Seeds and Dirt

MATTHEW 13:1-23; MARK 4:1-20; LUKE 8:4-15

Jesus went out to sit by the lake. Many people came to listen to him. So he got into a boat. The people stood on the shore. Then Jesus told them many stories.

"Once there was a farmer," said Jesus. "He went out to plant his seeds. He threw them here and there. Some of the seeds fell on a path. Birds came and ate them up.

"Some of the seeds fell on rocky dirt. These seeds grew up fast. But there wasn't much dirt. Then the sun came out. It was hot on the little plants. They dried up. They didn't have good roots.

"Some seeds fell around weeds. Those seeds grew up. But the weeds grew up too. The weeds grew over the new plants. The new plants couldn't grow.

"Some seeds fell on good, rich dirt. A crop of good plants came up. The farmer got much more than he planted. Listen, if you have ears."

Jesus' friends came to him. "Why do you tell people stories?" they asked.

Jesus said, "You can understand the secrets of God's kingdom. Other people can't. Some people want to know and understand. They'll be able to understand even more. Some people don't want to know or understand. They'll understand less and less.

"That's why I tell stories," said Jesus. "The people seem to see. But they're not really looking. They seem to hear. But they're not really listening. They don't understand.

"What the prophet Isaiah said has come true:

"You will hear but never
    understand.
You will see, but you won't know
    what it means.
These people's hearts are hard.
    They can't hear very well with
        their ears.
    Their eyes are closed.
If their ears and eyes were open,
    they might see.

They might hear.
Their hearts might understand.
Then they would turn, and I would
    make them well."

Jesus said, "Good things have come to your eyes. Your eyes see. Good things have come to your ears. They hear. There were many prophets long ago. There were many others who did right. They all wanted to see what you see. But they didn't get to see it. They all wanted to hear what you hear. But they didn't get to hear it.

"So listen to what the story of the farmer means. Some people hear the message about God's kingdom. But they don't understand it," said Jesus. "Then Satan comes. He takes away what was planted in that person's heart. This is the seed that fell on the path.

"Then there was the seed that fell on rocky dirt. It's like the person who hears. He is glad to take God's word into his heart. But he doesn't grow. He has no roots. So this person lasts just a short time. He is quick to leave God when trouble comes.

"Then there was the seed that fell around weeds. It's like the person who hears God's words. But he has lots of things to worry about. His riches make him worry too. That pushes God's words away.

"But some seed fell on good dirt. It's like the person who hears God's words. He understands. He is like a plant that comes up. A great crop grows. It may be 30, 60, or even 100 times bigger than what was planted."

Weeds

Matthew 13:24-30, 36-43; Mark 4:26-29

Jesus told his friends another story. "God's kingdom is like this," he said. "A farmer planted wheat seeds in his field. One night while he was sleeping, his enemy came. His enemy planted weeds in the field. Then he crept away.

"Now the wheat began to come up. It got tall. But the weeds came up too.

"The farmer's servants came to him. 'Sir, didn't you plant good wheat seeds?' they asked. 'Where did all these weeds come from?'

"The farmer said, 'The enemy did that.'

"The servants asked, 'Do you want us to pull the weeds?'

"The farmer said no. He said, 'You might pull up some wheat, too. Let the wheat and the weeds grow together. Soon it will be time to bring in the crops. You can bring

in the weeds first. You can pile them up and tie them together. Then you can burn the weeds. After that, you can bring in the wheat. You can put it in the barn.'"

Now Jesus left the group of people. He went into a house. His friends went with him. They asked, "Remember the story of the weeds and wheat? What does it mean?"

Jesus said, "I'm the one who planted good seed. The field is the world. The good seeds are the people in God's kingdom. The weeds are the people who follow Satan. Satan is the enemy who plants those weeds.

"Bringing in the crop happens at the end of time. The angels are the ones who bring in the crops. The weeds are pulled up," said Jesus. "They're burned in the fire. That's how it will be at the end of time.

"I'll send out my angels," said Jesus. "They'll take sinful people out of God's kingdom. The sinful people will be thrown into the fire. They will cry about it.

"But think of the people who do what's right," said Jesus. "They will shine like the sun in God's kingdom. Hear this if you have ears.

"Here's what God's kingdom is like," said Jesus. "A farmer plants seeds. Night and day the seeds are growing. They grow while the farmer sleeps. They grow when he is awake. They grow even if he doesn't understand how. All by itself, the ground grows wheat.

"First the stem comes up," said Jesus. "Then it makes a head. The farmer cuts it when it's ripe. That's the time to bring in the crops."

Seeds, Yeast, Pearls, and Nets

MATTHEW 13:31-35, 44-52; MARK 4:30-34; LUKE 13:18-21

"God's kingdom is like a mustard seed," said Jesus. "A man took the seed and planted it. Now the mustard seed is the smallest seed of all. But it grows into the biggest plant in the garden. It becomes a tree. The birds fly to it. They sit in its branches.

"God's kingdom is like yeast," said Jesus. "A woman mixed the yeast with a lot of flour. She mixed it all through the batter.

"God's kingdom is like riches in a field," said Jesus. "The riches were hidden under the ground. A man who was digging found them. He covered them up again. He was very glad to find the riches. So he sold everything he owned to buy that field.

"God's kingdom is like a man shopping for fine pearls. One day, he found a very special pearl. There was no other pearl like it in the world. It was the best. It cost a lot of money. So the man sold everything he owned. He bought the pearl.

"God's kingdom is like a net in the lake," said Jesus. "Many different kinds of fish swam into it. They filled the net. So the men who were fishing pulled the net up to the shore. Then they took the fish out of the net. They put the good fish in baskets. They threw the bad fish away.

"That's how it will be when time ends," said Jesus. "Angels will come. They'll keep people who did what's right. They'll throw out sinful people. Then the sinful people will cry.

"Do you understand what I'm saying?" Jesus asked.

"Yes," they said.

"Some teachers know about God's kingdom," said Jesus. "They're like people who own houses. They have rooms where they store things. Sometimes they bring new things out of their rooms. Sometimes they bring old things out of their rooms."

Jesus told many other stories. He said hardly anything to the people without a story. But he told his friends what the stories meant. So the psalm came true. "I'll talk in stories. I'll tell secrets hidden since the world was made."

Foxes Have Dens

MATTHEW 8:19-22; LUKE 9:57-62

A teacher came up to Jesus. This teacher knew God's law. He said, "I will follow you anywhere you go."

"Foxes sleep in dens," said Jesus. "Birds sleep in nests. But I don't have a place to sleep."

Jesus told another man, "Follow me."

But the man said, "Lord, let me wait. I can't come until my father grows old and dies."

Jesus said, "Let people whose love for me is dead wait for that. You need to follow me. Tell other people about God's kingdom."

Another man said, "I'll follow you, Lord. But first I want to have some time with my family."

Jesus said, "You're like a farmer. He was getting his field ready for planting. He looked back and wished he had stayed home. Anyone who thinks that way isn't ready to serve in God's kingdom."

The Storm

MATTHEW 8:23-27; MARK 4:35-41; LUKE 8:22-25

The sun began to go down. "Let's go across the lake," Jesus told his friends.

So they got into a boat. They left the crowd of people. Some other boats went with them.

But a roaring storm blew in. Waves crashed over the boat. Water almost filled it. All this time, Jesus was in the back of the boat. He was sleeping on a pillow.

Jesus' special friends woke him up. "We're about to die in this water! Don't you even care?" they asked.

Jesus got up. He spoke firmly to the wind. He spoke firmly to the waves. He said, "Be quiet. Be still."

Then the wind died down. Everything became still.

Jesus looked at his friends. "Why are you so scared?" he asked. "Could it be that your faith is still very small?"

Jesus' friends were afraid. They said to each other, "Who is this Jesus? The wind obeys him! The water obeys him!"

The Man Who Lived by Graves

MATTHEW 8:28-34; MARK 5:1-20; LUKE 8:26-39

Jesus and his friends landed their boat. Jesus got out. A man came up to meet him.

This man was controlled by a bad spirit. He lived by the graves, where dead bodies were placed. No one could control him. Many times people put chains on his hands and feet. But he just tore the chains off. No one was strong enough to hold him down.

This man would shout loudly around the graves and hills. Every day and every night, he would call out. He would use stones to cut himself.

But this man saw Jesus a little way off. He ran to Jesus.

Jesus said, "You bad spirit, come out of this man!"

The man fell down in front of Jesus. He shouted as loudly as he could. "Jesus, Son of God Most High! What do you want with me? Please promise you won't hurt me!"

Then Jesus asked the spirit, "What's your name?"

"Many," answered the spirit. "There are many of us." The spirits begged Jesus not to send them out of that land.

Pigs were eating on a hill nearby. "Let us go into the pigs," said the bad spirits.

So Jesus let them go into the pigs.

There were about 2,000 pigs. The spirits went into them. Then all the pigs ran down the hill. They jumped into the lake and drowned.

The people who had been taking care of the pigs saw this. They ran to town right away. They told everyone in town what had happened.

The people went out to see it for themselves. It wasn't long before they reached Jesus. There was the man, sitting with Jesus. He had been controlled by bad spirits. But now he was dressed. His mind seemed to be working just fine.

The people were scared. They begged Jesus to leave their land.

So Jesus got back into the boat.

The man asked if he could go with Jesus.

"Go home to your family," said Jesus. "Tell your family what God did for you. Tell them about God's kindness."

So the man went home. He told people what Jesus had done for him. People were very surprised.

The Sick Little Girl

MATTHEW 9:1, 18-26; MARK 5:21-43; LUKE 8:40-56

Jesus took the boat to the other side of the lake. A big crowd of people came to see him.

A leader from the town's worship house was in the crowd. His name was Jairus. He bowed down in front of Jesus. "My little girl is sick," he said. "She is going to die. Please come with me. Touch my little girl so she will live."

So Jesus went with Jairus. Many people followed them. The people pushed in around Jesus.

A woman was in the crowd. She had been sick for 12 years. Many doctors had tried to make her well. In fact, she had given all her money to doctors. But instead of getting better, she got sicker.

This woman had heard about Jesus. So she pushed her way through the crowd. She crept up right behind Jesus. Then she reached out. "I just need to touch his clothes!" she thought. "Then I'll be well." So she touched Jesus' coat.

Right away she was well. She could feel it.

Jesus could tell that power had gone out of him. So he looked around. He asked, "Who touched me?"

"Many people are pushing against you," said his friends. "Why are you asking who touched you?"

Jesus kept looking around. Then the woman came up to Jesus. She bowed down at his feet. She was so scared, she was shaking. But she told Jesus everything.

"You are well because you believe," said Jesus. "Go home now. You will have peace."

Jesus was still talking to the woman when some men came to Jairus. "Your little girl has died," they said. "Don't bother Jesus anymore."

Jesus didn't listen to them. He told Jairus, "Don't be afraid. Just believe."

People were crying loudly at Jairus's house.

Jesus went in. He let only Peter, James, and John go with him.

"Why is everyone crying?" asked Jesus. "Why are you making so much noise? This little girl isn't dead. She is just sleeping."

The people laughed at him.

So Jesus sent them all out. He took Peter, James, and John with him. He took the little girl's mother and father, too. Then he went into the little girl's room.

Jesus held the girl's hand. He said, "Little girl, get up."

Right away, the girl got up and walked! She was about 12 years old.

The people were very surprised. Jesus told them to bring her something to eat. He said, "Don't tell anyone else about this."

Two Men Who Could Not See

MATTHEW 9:27-33

Two men who could not see began to follow Jesus. They called out, "Jesus, be kind to us! Make us well!"

Jesus kept walking. He went inside a house. But the men followed him.

"Do you believe I can do this?" Jesus asked.

"Yes, Lord," they said.

Then Jesus touched their eyes. He said, "You believe. So you will see."

And they could see again.

"Don't let anybody know about this," Jesus said.

But they left and told everybody about it.

Then another man came in. He was controlled by a bad spirit. He couldn't talk. A friend brought him to Jesus.

So Jesus sent the bad spirit out of the man. Then the man could talk.

People were surprised. "We've never seen anything like this," they said.

Sheep with No Shepherd

MATTHEW 9:35-38; 13:53-58;
MARK 6:1-6

Jesus went back to the town where he grew up. He took his friends with him. The worship day came. So he taught in the town's worship house. Many people heard him there. They were surprised.

"How can he say all these things?" they asked. "How can he be so wise? He even does wonders. Didn't he work in the wood shop when he was growing up? Isn't he Mary's son? He is the brother of James, Joseph, Judas, and Simon. All his sisters live here!" Thinking about Jesus bothered them.

"Nobody says good things about a prophet in his own town," said Jesus.

Jesus made a few sick people well there. But that's all he could do. He couldn't do any other wonders. He could hardly believe that their faith was so small.

Jesus traveled through many towns. He taught in the towns' worship houses. He told about the Good News of God's kingdom. He made people well.

Jesus looked out at the crowds of people. He was sad for them. It seemed like they had no one to help them. They were like sheep with no shepherd.

"These people are like crops in the farmer's field. It's time to bring in the crops," Jesus said to his friends. "But there aren't very many workers. Ask God to send workers into the field. The workers can bring in the people."

Like Sheep Going Where Wolves Are

MATTHEW 10:1-16, 40-42; MARK 6:7-11; LUKE 9:1-5

Jesus called his 12 special friends. He told them to go out two by two. He gave them power that was stronger than bad spirits. They could send bad spirits away. They could make people well.

"Go to the Jews," said Jesus. "Teach God's message. Tell people that the kingdom of heaven is near.

"Heal people who are sick," said Jesus. "Make people alive again after they have died. Send bad spirits away from people.

"You were given what you have, for free," said Jesus. "Now give it away for free. Don't take gold or silver. Don't take a bag for your trip. Don't take more than one shirt. Don't take more than one pair of shoes. Don't take a walking stick. You are a worker. People should help you out.

"Go into the towns," said Jesus. "Look for people who will help you. Stay with them until you leave that town. Go into their homes. Be friendly and pray for peace to come to them. If they welcome you, keep praying for peace. If they don't welcome you, don't pray for peace for them.

"What if people won't listen to you?" said Jesus. "Then shake the dust off your feet when you leave that town. The truth is, someday God will judge the world. Then the bad city of Sodom will be better off than that town.

"You're like sheep going where the wolves are," said Jesus. "So be as smart as snakes. But be as peaceful as doves.

"People who are friendly to you are being friendly to me. People who welcome me are welcoming God," said Jesus.

"Welcome a prophet just because he is a prophet. Then God will give you the same good things he gives the prophets," said Jesus. "Welcome people who do what's right because of the right things they do. Then God will give you the same good things he gives them.

"You follow me. So you might give just a cup of cold water to someone. But you'll still get good things from God."

John in Trouble

MATTHEW 14:1-12; MARK 6:14-29; LUKE 9:7-9

John, who baptized people, was still around. He had talked to many people about God's way. He had even talked to King Herod.

King Herod had married his own brother's wife. Her name was Herodias. John had told Herod, "It's not right to marry your brother's wife." So King Herod had put John into jail. Herodias was angry at John too. In fact, she wanted to have him killed, but she couldn't. That's because Herod was afraid of John. And he was afraid that people would be upset. So he kept John safe.

King Herod knew that John was a good man. He knew that John did what was right. Herod liked to listen to John. The things John said were like a mystery to him.

One day King Herod had a party. It was his birthday. All the leaders of the land came. Herodias had a daughter who came too. She danced for the people. They all liked the way she danced.

So Herod promised to give her anything she wanted. "Just ask me," he said. "I'll give you whatever you want. You can even have half of my kingdom."

The girl went out and told her mother. "What should I ask for?" she said.

"Ask Herod to kill John," said Herodias. "Tell him you want John's head!"

So the girl went back to King Herod. "I want John's head on a plate! Right now!" she said.

This made Herod very upset. But he had promised. He didn't want to say no in front of everyone. So he sent a man to the jail. He gave the man orders to kill John. So he did.

Then the man put John's head on a plate. He brought it to King Herod. The king gave it to the girl. She gave it to her mother.

John's friends came and got his body. They put it in a grave.

Jesus and his friends were traveling from town to town. They told people the Good News about Jesus. They made many people well, too. People talked about Jesus everywhere. Even King Herod heard about Jesus.

Some people kept saying, "Jesus is really John. He came back to life! That's why great powers work in him."

Other people said, "Jesus is really Elijah!"

Other people said, "Jesus is a prophet. He is like one of the prophets from long ago."

When Herod heard about Jesus, he said, "It's John! I cut his head off, but he is alive again!" Herod tried to see Jesus for himself.

Bread for Everyone

MATTHEW 14:13-21; MARK 6:30-44; LUKE 9:10-17; JOHN 6:1-14

Now Jesus' 12 special friends had been going from town to town. After some time, they came back. They told Jesus what they had done. But many other people were around them. They didn't even have time to eat.

"Come to a quiet place with me," said Jesus. "Let's get some rest."

They got into a boat. They sailed across Lake Galilee. They headed to a place away from the crowds.

People saw them leave. They knew it was Jesus and his friends. So they came from all the towns. They ran to the place where Jesus would be landing. They got there before Jesus did.

When Jesus and his friends landed, there were the people. They stood in a big crowd. Jesus felt sorry for them. They looked like sheep who had no shepherd. So he started teaching them. He told them about God's kingdom. He made the sick people well.

It got later and later. Jesus' friends came to him. "It's getting late," they said. "We're not in town. We need to send the people back to town. Then they can buy their supper."

Jesus looked at the crowd of people. Then he looked at Philip. "Where can we get bread for these people?" he asked. He asked just to see what Philip would say. Jesus already knew what he was going to do.

"We would need lots of food," said Philip. "We could work for eight months. We still wouldn't have the money to buy enough food. We wouldn't have enough for each person to have one bite!"

"Look at this little boy," said Andrew. "He brought his own supper. He has five rolls and two small fish. But that won't feed many people."

Then Jesus told his friends to put the people into groups. Some people got in groups of 100. Some got in groups of 50. They sat down on the grass.

Jesus took the five rolls and the two fish. He looked up to heaven. He thanked God. Then he began to hand out the rolls. He gave them to his helpers. There were a lot more than just five rolls!

Jesus' friends began to give the rolls to the people. Then Jesus handed the fish to his friends. They gave fish to the people too. There was more than enough! All of the people got to eat as much as they wanted.

After supper, Jesus' friends cleaned up the leftovers. They filled up 12 baskets. About 5,000 men had eaten there. Women and children had eaten there too. They said, "This is the prophet we've been looking for!"

On Top of the Water

MATTHEW 14:22-36; MARK 6:45-56; JOHN 6:15-21

Jesus sent his special friends out in the boat. Then he sent the crowd of people home. He knew they wanted to make him their king.

He went up on a hill to be alone and pray.

It was already dark. Out on the lake, a strong wind was blowing. The water was getting wavy.

From the hill, Jesus saw his friends in their boat. They were rowing hard. They were trying to go one way. But the wind was blowing them the other way.

About three o'clock in the morning, Jesus went out to them. He walked right on top of the water.

Jesus' friends had rowed about three and a half miles. Now they looked up and saw Jesus coming. In fact, he was just about to pass them! They got scared when they saw him. They yelled! They thought he was a ghost.

"It's just me," said Jesus. "Don't be afraid."

"If it's really you, tell me to come to you," said Peter. "Let me walk on the water too."

"Come on," said Jesus.

So Peter got out of the boat. He stepped onto the water. He began to walk to Jesus. Then he saw the waves. He got scared, and he started going down into the water.

"Lord! Save me!" Peter cried.

Right away, Jesus reached out to Peter. He lifted Peter up. "Your faith is so small!" said Jesus. "Why didn't you believe?"

They both climbed into the boat. Then the wind stopped blowing so hard.

Jesus' friends were surprised. They hadn't really understood the wonder Jesus did with the rolls and the fish. Their hearts were still a little hard. But now they worshiped Jesus. They said, "You really are God's Son!"

At last they reached the other side of the lake. When they left their boat, people saw Jesus. They knew who he was. So they ran through the land telling everyone.

Everybody brought their sick friends to Jesus. When he was in the country, they brought sick friends. When he was in town, they brought sick friends. They wanted just to touch the edge of his coat. Everyone who touched him got well.

Bread from Heaven

JOHN 6:22-71

Some people had stayed on the other side of the lake. The next day, they wondered where Jesus was. They knew only one boat had left. They knew Jesus wasn't in it. So they began to look for him.

At last they got into some boats. They went to the other side of the lake. There was Jesus. "When did you get here?" they asked.

"You're looking for me because I gave you food," said Jesus. "Don't work for food that will rot. Work to get life that lasts forever. It's like food that lasts. I can give it to you because God is pleased with me."

"What does God want us to do?" they asked.

"Here's God's work for you," said Jesus. "Believe in me, because God sent me."

"Show us a wonder," they said.

"Then we can believe in you. Long ago, God's people got food in the desert. It was bread that came down from heaven."

"You know, it wasn't Moses who gave them bread from heaven," said Jesus. "It was God, my Father. Now he gives you true bread from heaven. I'm like bread from heaven. I give life to the world."

"We'd like to have this bread," they said. "We'd like to have it from now on."

"I am the Bread of Life," said Jesus. "Come to me. Then your heart will never be hungry. Believe in me. Then your spirit will never be thirsty. But you saw what I did, and you still don't believe.

"I'll never send away people who come to me," said Jesus. "I didn't come from heaven to do what I want. I came to do what God wants. He wants me to care for people who trust me. He wants me to give them life that lasts forever."

Now God's people began to give Jesus a hard time. It's because he said he was the Bread of Life from heaven. They said, "This is Jesus. He is Joseph's son. We know his father and mother. So how can he say that he came from heaven?"

"Stop making a fuss," said Jesus. "People can't come to me unless my Father brings them. I will give them life that lasts forever.

"Isaiah the prophet wrote that God will teach everyone. So people come to me when they hear from God. They come to me when they learn from my Father.

"I'm the only one who is from God," said Jesus. "I'm the only one who has seen the Father. The truth is, the person who believes has life forever.

"I am the Bread of Life," said Jesus. "Long ago, God's people ate manna in the desert. But they still died. I came from heaven too, like the manna. But you'll never die if you eat this kind of bread. This kind of 'bread' is my body. I'll give up my body so the world can live."

Then the Jews fussed among themselves. "How can he give us his body to eat?" they asked.

Jesus said, "I'll give my blood for you too. My body and my blood give life. You must let this gift fill you like food. If you don't, you won't live very long. This gift can feed your spirit like food feeds your body. So let your spirit feed on my gift. Then you'll have life forever. Your last day on earth will come. Then I'll make you live again."

Jesus talked about this at the town's worship house that was in Capernaum. Many of Jesus' followers said, "This is too hard to understand. Who can go along with this?"

Jesus knew they were talking about what he said. "Does this upset you?" he asked. "What if you see me go where I was before? You see, it's the Spirit who gives life. The body doesn't count for anything. The words I speak are spirit. They are life. But some of you don't believe."

Many people turned away after he said this. They didn't follow him anymore. Jesus already knew which followers wouldn't believe. He'd known from the first who would become his enemy.

Jesus talked to his 12 close friends. "Do you want to leave too?" he asked.

"Lord, where would we go?" asked Peter. "You teach us about life that lasts forever. We believe you. We know that you are God's Son."

"I chose 12 of you," said Jesus. "But one of you is a devil." He was talking about Judas. Jesus had chosen him as one of his 12 special friends. But later, he would turn against Jesus. He would become an enemy.

The Leaders' Rules
MATTHEW 15:1-20; MARK 7:1-23; JOHN 7:1

There was a special way that Jewish leaders washed their hands. They wouldn't eat until they had washed in this way. They even made a washing rule. Everyone had to wash that same way.

The leaders had many other rules like this. They had a rule for washing cups, jugs, and pots. The rule told the special way to wash these things.

Now some of the leaders had seen Jesus' friends eating. Jesus' friends hadn't washed their hands that special way. So the leaders went to Jesus. They asked, "Why don't your friends follow the leaders' rules? They don't wash their hands like we do."

"Isaiah talked about you," said Jesus. "He was right. He gave this message from God: 'These people say good things about me. But their hearts are far away from me. They worship me for nothing. Their teachings are just rules made by people.'

"You're not obeying God's rules," said Jesus. "Instead, you're following your own rules. Moses said, 'Treat your mother and father like important people.' But you say you don't have to help your mother and father. You tell them you'll give your help to God instead. So you make God's rules seem like nothing. It's all because of the rules your people made up."

Later, Jesus' followers came to him. "The leaders were angry when you said that!" they said.

"Plants that God didn't plant will be pulled up by the roots. Just leave them alone," said Jesus. "They are leaders. But they can't see. What happens when someone who can't see leads someone else who can't see? They both fall down."

Jesus went on. "Nothing a person eats can make him dirty from sin. That's because it's not going into his heart. It's going into his stomach. Then it goes out of his body."

"What do you mean?" asked Peter.

"Don't you understand yet?" Jesus asked. "It's the words that come out of a person that make him dirty. Bad thoughts come from inside him, from his heart.

"Sinning with sex, stealing, and killing come from the heart. Being greedy, hating, and lying come from the heart. Wanting what someone else has comes from the heart. Bragging and foolish thinking come from the heart. All of these come from inside a person. That's what makes a person dirty," said Jesus.

Then Jesus went to Galilee. He stayed away from Judea. Some of the leaders of God's people there were waiting to kill him.

More Wonders and Stories from Jesus

Making People Well

MATTHEW 15:21-31; MARK 7:24-37

Jesus went to a town called Tyre. He went to a house there. He didn't want anyone to know he was there. But he couldn't keep it a secret.

A woman who was not Jewish lived near there. She came to Jesus. She cried, "Lord, be kind to me! Bad spirits control my daughter!"

But Jesus didn't answer her. So Jesus' friends said, "This lady keeps crying to us. Tell her to go away!"

Jesus looked at the lady. "I was sent only to God's people," he said.

The woman bowed down to Jesus. "Lord, help me," she said.

"I shouldn't take what belongs to God's people," said Jesus. "I shouldn't toss it to the dogs. It wouldn't be right."

"Yes, Lord," she said. "But even dogs get tiny bits of food. They eat what falls off their master's table."

Then Jesus said, "You have a lot of faith. I'll give you what you asked for."

At that very moment, her daughter got well.

Then Jesus traveled to the Ten Cities.

Some people led a man to Jesus. This man couldn't hear. He could hardly talk. The people asked Jesus to put his hand on this man.

So Jesus took the man away from the people. He put his fingers into the man's ears. Then Jesus spit. He touched the man's tongue. Jesus looked to heaven. He took a deep breath. "Open up," he said.

Right away, the man's ears opened. His tongue was set free. He started talking clearly.

Jesus told the crowd not to tell anybody. But the more Jesus said, "Don't tell," the more they told.

People were very surprised. "Jesus does everything just right," they said. "He can even make people hear. He can make people talk."

561

Big crowds of people came to Jesus. They brought people who couldn't walk or see. They brought people who couldn't hear or talk. Jesus made them well. People who couldn't walk before ended up walking. People who couldn't see ended up seeing. People who couldn't hear or speak were listening and talking. Everyone was very surprised. The people cheered for God.

Seven Rolls

MATTHEW 15:32–16:4; MARK 8:1-12

The crowd around Jesus hadn't had anything to eat. So Jesus called his friends to him.

"I feel sorry for these people," said Jesus. "They've been with me for three days. They don't have anything left to eat. Many of them came a long way to get here. They'll get hungry if I send them home. They might be too weak to get home."

"We're not close to any town," said his friends. "Where can we get enough bread to feed all these people?"

"How much bread do you have?" Jesus asked.

"We have seven rolls," they said.

Jesus told the people to sit on the ground. He took the seven rolls. He thanked God. Then he pulled the rolls apart. He gave them to his friends. His friends gave them to the people.

Someone had a few small fish there. Jesus gave thanks for them, too. Then he told his friends to pass the fish to everyone. All the people got plenty of food. There were about 4,000 men. There were many women and children, too.

After they were finished, Jesus' friends picked up the leftovers. All in all, they got seven baskets full of leftovers.

Then Jesus sent the people away. He got into a boat with his friends. They sailed across the lake.

Now the leaders wanted to test Jesus. They wanted him to show them a wonder.

Jesus said, "You say, 'The evening sky is red. So we'll have good weather tomorrow.' You say, 'The morning sky is red. There are clouds. So we will have a storm today.'

"You know what will happen by looking at the sky. But you're not looking around you," said Jesus. "What's happening right now? Sinful people look for wonders. But you'll get just one sign. It will be Jonah's sign."

Yeast

MATTHEW 16:5-12; MARK 8:13-21

Jesus got into the boat. He sailed back to the other side of the lake.

Jesus' friends had only one loaf of bread. They had it in the boat.

"Be careful about the leaders' yeast," said Jesus.

His friends looked at each other. "Is it because we're running out of bread?" they whispered.

Jesus knew what they were saying. "Why are you talking about not having any bread? Don't you understand?" he said. "Are your hearts hard? Don't your eyes see? Don't your ears hear? Don't you remember?

"I gave five rolls to 5,000 people. How many baskets of leftovers did we have?" he asked.

"Twelve," they said.

"I gave seven rolls to 4,000 people," said Jesus. "How many baskets of leftovers did we have?"

"Seven," they said.

"Don't you understand?" asked Jesus. "I wasn't talking to you about bread. Be careful about the leaders' yeast."

Then they understood. They saw that he wasn't talking about the bread's yeast. He meant, "Be careful about what the leaders teach."

Keys

MATTHEW 16:13-20; MARK 8:22-30; LUKE 9:18-21

Some people led a man to Jesus. The man couldn't see. The people asked Jesus to touch the man and help him see.

So Jesus took the man's hand. He led the man to a place outside the town.

Then Jesus spit on the man's eyes. He put his hands on the man. "Can you see anything?" asked Jesus.

The man looked. "I see people," he said. "They look like walking trees."

Jesus put his hands on the man's eyes again. Then the man could see clearly.

Jesus sent the man home. He said, "Don't go into town."

Jesus traveled on with his friends. "Who do people say I am?" he asked.

"Some people say you're the John who baptized," they said. "Other people say you're Elijah. Other people say you're Jeremiah. Some say you're one of the other prophets."

"Who do you think I am?" asked Jesus.

"You're the one God promised to send," said Peter. "You're the Christ. You're the Son of the Living God."

Jesus said, "God will be good to you, Peter. My Father in heaven showed you who I am. You're Peter. You are like a rock. I'll build my church on this rock. The power of hell will never get rid of it.

"I'll give you the keys to God's kingdom," said Jesus. "Lock up anything on earth. It will be locked up in heaven, too. Open up anything on earth. It will be open in heaven, too."

"Don't tell anyone I'm the one God promised to send," said Jesus.

What's Coming

MATTHEW 16:21-28; MARK 8:31–9:1; LUKE 9:22-27

Jesus now began to get his friends ready. He let them know what was going to happen. He told them he had to go to Jerusalem. He said the leaders and teachers of God's laws would treat him badly. He said he would be killed. But he'd come alive again on the third day.

Peter pulled Jesus to one side. "Never, Lord," he said. "This will never happen to you."

"Get out of my way, Satan!" said Jesus. "This does not help me. You're not thinking of what God wants. You're thinking of what you want."

Then Jesus called to everyone around him. "Do you want to be with me? Then you'll have to give up what you want. You'll have to do what God chose you to do.

"Do you just want to save your own life? Then you'll end up losing it," said Jesus. "Give up your life for me. Give up your life for God's kingdom. That's the way to save your life.

"What if you got all the riches in the world? What if you then lost your soul?" said Jesus. "What good would your riches be? What could you give to buy your soul back?

"Some people don't feel good about me," said Jesus. "They don't feel good about my words. So I won't feel good about them when I come again. That's when I'll come with angels and with my Father's power.

"Some people here will see God's kingdom," said Jesus. "They'll see it before they die."

SEPTEMBER 8

As White As Light

MATTHEW 17:1-13; MARK 9:2-13; LUKE 9:28-36

Six days later, Jesus took Peter, James, and John. They went up on a high mountain.

All of a sudden, Jesus changed. It happened right in front of Peter and James and John. Jesus' face started shining. It was as bright as the sun. His clothes turned as white as light.

Then Moses and Elijah showed up. They talked with Jesus.

"Lord!" said Peter. "It's wonderful to be here. If you want, I can make three tents here. I'll make one for you. I'll make one for Moses. I'll make one for Elijah!"

Then a bright cloud came down around them. A voice came from the cloud. It said, "This is my Son. He is the Son I love. I'm happy with him. Listen to him."

Peter, James, and John fell to the ground. They didn't look up. They were afraid.

But Jesus came over. He touched them. He said, "You can get up. Don't be afraid."

They looked up, and they saw no one but Jesus.

Then they all came down the mountain. Jesus said, "Don't tell anybody what you just saw. I will die. But I'll come back to life. Then you can tell about it."

"The Jewish leaders say Elijah has to come first," they said. "Why?"

"Elijah already came," said Jesus. "They didn't know him. They treated him any way they wanted to. They'll treat me badly too."

Then Jesus' friends understood what he was saying. He was talking about John, who baptized people. Jesus was calling him Elijah.

Peter, James, and John did what Jesus asked. They didn't tell anybody what they saw on the mountain.

Everything Is Possible
MATTHEW 17:14-21; MARK 9:14-29; LUKE 9:37-43

Jesus walked back with Peter, James, and John. They looked for their other friends. They found them with a big crowd around them. Some teachers of God's law were there too. The teachers were fussing at Jesus' friends.

When the people saw Jesus, they ran to meet him.

"What are you fussing about?" asked Jesus.

One man said, "I brought my son here to see you. A bad spirit controls him. It won't let him talk. It throws him to the ground. His teeth rub together. His arms and legs get tight. I asked your friends to send the spirit away. But they couldn't."

"You people don't believe in me," said Jesus. "How long will I have to put up with you? Bring me the boy." So they brought the boy to him.

When the spirit saw Jesus, it threw the boy down. He fell on the ground and rolled around.

"How long has he been like this?" asked Jesus.

"This started when he was very little," said his father. "Sometimes the bad spirit throws him into the fire. Sometimes it throws him into the water. It tries to kill him. Please be kind to us. Help us if you can."

"If I can?" said Jesus. "Everything is possible for the person who believes."

"I do believe!" said the father. "Help me get past the part of me that doesn't believe."

Now Jesus saw that a crowd was gathering. So he talked to the bad spirit. He said, "You spirit, come out of that boy. Never go into him again!"

The spirit yelled. It shook the boy. Then it came out.

The boy looked like he was dead. That's what many people thought. They said, "He is dead."

But Jesus took the boy's hand. Then the boy stood up.

Jesus went into a house. His friends asked, "Why couldn't we send the spirit away?"

"It's because your faith is very small," said Jesus. "Even faith the size of a small mustard seed is strong. With it, you can move a mountain. You can say, 'Move from here to there!' It will move. Nothing will be impossible for you. But this kind of spirit comes out only by prayer."

Fishing for Money

MATTHEW 17:22-27; MARK 9:30-32; LUKE 9:44-45

Jesus and his friends traveled through Galilee. Jesus was teaching these friends. He didn't want anybody to know where they were.

"One of my 12 special friends will turn against me," said Jesus. "He will take money from some of the leaders. Then he will show them where I am. They will kill me. But on the third day, I'll come back to life."

Jesus' friends didn't understand what he was talking about. They were afraid to ask Jesus about it.

They came to the town of Capernaum. Some tax men saw them and came up to Peter. They said, "Doesn't Jesus pay the worship-house tax?"

"Yes, he does," said Peter. Then Peter went to Jesus.

But Jesus talked first. "What do you think, Peter?" he said. "Who do kings get taxes from? Do they get taxes from their own family? Or do they get taxes from other people?"

"From other people," said Peter.

"Then their own family doesn't pay taxes," Jesus said. "But we don't want to make these men mad. So go fishing. Throw your line out into the lake. Take the first fish you catch. Open its mouth and look inside. You'll find money in there. Then you can pay our taxes."

Who Is the Greatest?

MATTHEW 18:1; MARK 9:33-35; LUKE 9:46; 17:7-10

Jesus and his friends were walking down the road. His friends began fussing with each other. So Jesus asked them, "What are you fussing about?"

Jesus' friends didn't answer. They had been fussing over who was the greatest.

Jesus sat down. "Do you want to be first?" he asked. "Then make yourself last. Serve others.

"Suppose you had a servant," said Jesus. "Let's say this servant was taking care of your garden. Or he was watching your sheep in the field. At the end of the day, he comes in. Would you say, 'Come in. Sit down. Have something to eat'?

"He is your servant," said Jesus. "So you would say, 'Make my supper first. Serve me while I eat and drink. Then you may have your supper.'

"Let's say your servant does what you tell him to do. Is that anything special? I don't think so," said Jesus.

"It's that way with you, too," said Jesus. "You say you only did what you were told to do. To be a great servant, you must do more than you were told."

A Little Child and a Little Sheep

MATTHEW 18:2-20; MARK 9:36-41; LUKE 9:47-50; 17:1-2

Jesus called a child to come to him. Jesus' 12 special friends were there too. He asked the child to stand with them. Then Jesus said, "You must change from what you're like now to go into God's kingdom. You must become like little children.

"A little child knows there are others who are greater. So treat others like they're greater than you are," said Jesus. "Then you'll be the greatest in God's kingdom.

"If you welcome a little child, you are welcoming me," said Jesus. "If you welcome me, you are welcoming God.

"If you make a child sin, you're in trouble. It would be better to drown in the deepest sea. Don't treat these little ones as if they aren't important. Their angels are always with their heavenly Father. They always see his face," said Jesus.

"Suppose you had 100 sheep. One walked off and got lost. Wouldn't you leave 99 sheep on the hill?

Wouldn't you look for your lost sheep?

"What would you do if you found that sheep?" said Jesus. "You'd be happy about that one sheep. You'd be happier for it than for 99 that didn't walk off. That's the way your Father in heaven is. He doesn't want any little ones to be lost.

"How sad it is for the world that there are things that make people sin. These things will always be around," said Jesus. "But how sad it is for the people who make others sin. They should know they'll get in trouble with God."

John said, "We saw a man sending bad spirits away. He was doing it by saying your name. We told him to stop, because he is not one of us."

"Don't stop him," Jesus said. "He does wonders in my name. That means he won't be saying bad things about me. Anyone who isn't against us is for us.

"Someone may give you water in my name. They may do it because you're my friend," said Jesus. "If they do, God will do good things for them.

"Someone may do something wrong to you," said Jesus. "Then you should go to see him. Show him what he did wrong. Keep it just between the two of you. If he listens, then you have won a friend.

"If he won't listen, go back later," said Jesus. "Take one or two people with you. Maybe he will listen to them. If he doesn't listen to them, tell my followers. If he doesn't listen to my followers, stop trying. He is like a tax man. He is like someone who doesn't believe in God.

"Two of you might agree when you pray. Agree about anything you ask for. Then my Father in heaven will do it for you," said Jesus. "Two or three people might come together in my name. Then I'm right there with them."

The Servant Who Would Not Forgive

MATTHEW 18:21-35; LUKE 17:3-4

Peter came to Jesus. "How many times should I forgive somebody for doing wrong? Seven times?" asked Peter.

"Not just seven times," said Jesus. "Seventy-seven times. Someone may do something wrong to you. Then tell him what he did. If he is sorry, forgive him. He may sin against you seven times in one day. He may come back seven times saying, 'I'm sorry.' So forgive him.

"God's kingdom is like a king," said Jesus. "This king wanted his servants to pay what they owed him. One man owed him millions.

But he couldn't pay the money back.

"The king said he would sell that man. He would sell the man's whole family. He would sell everything the man owned. Then the king would have the money the man owed him.

"But the servant bowed down in front of the king. He begged, 'Please wait a little while longer! I'll pay all the money back!'

"The king felt sorry for the man. So he told the man not to worry about what he owed. The king wouldn't make him pay it back. He let the man go.

"So the servant left. He didn't owe all that money anymore! But the servant met a man who owed him just a little money. He caught this man and started choking him. 'Pay me what you owe me!' he said.

"The man got down and begged. 'Please wait a little while longer,' he said. 'I'll pay you back!'

"But the servant wouldn't listen to him. Instead, he had the man put in jail.

"Other servants saw what happened. They were very angry. They went and told the king about it.

"The king called the servant. 'You are a sinful servant!' he said. 'I did not make you pay what you owed me. That's because you begged me not to. I was kind to you. So

shouldn't you have been kind to this other man?'

"The king was angry. He sent his servant to jail. He wouldn't let him out until he paid everything back."

"Forgive other people from your heart," said Jesus. "If you don't, my Father in heaven will treat you this same way."

SEPTEMBER 10

Whispering about Jesus
JOHN 7:2-31

The Holiday of Tents was coming up soon. Jesus' brothers told him, "You should go to Judea for the holiday. Then your followers can see your wonders. You want people to know who you are, don't you? Don't keep these things a secret.

"You can do all these wonderful things," they said. "So why don't you show yourself to all the world?" Jesus' brothers said this, but they didn't really believe in him.

"The right time hasn't come yet," said Jesus. "Any time is all right for you. The world can't hate you. But the world hates me. It's because I tell them that they sin. You go on to Judea. I'm not going yet."

So Jesus stayed in Galilee. His brothers went to Judea. Later, Jesus went too. But he didn't let anybody know he was going. He went in secret.

569

Now the leaders of God's people watched for Jesus at this holiday. "Where is that man?" they asked.

There was a lot of whispering about Jesus. "He is a good man," said some people. "He is just fooling everybody," said others. But nobody would say anything out loud about him. They were afraid of the leaders.

Jesus stayed out of sight until halfway through the holiday. Then he went to the worship house. He began to teach.

The people at the worship house were surprised. They said, "How did this man learn so much? He didn't learn these things in school."

"This isn't my teaching," said Jesus. "It comes from God. God sent me. Choose to do what God wants. Then you'll find out if my teaching is from God.

"If I speak just for me, then I make myself important. But if I make God important, what I say is true. Moses gave you God's laws," said Jesus. "But you don't obey them. Why are you trying to kill me?"

"Who is trying to kill you?" the crowd asked. "We think a bad spirit must be in control of you!"

"I did a wonder on the worship day," said Jesus. "I made a man well. Everybody was surprised. But you also work on the worship day. You do it to keep some of God's rules. So don't judge things just by the way they look."

Then some of the people began to talk about Jesus. "Aren't our leaders trying to kill him?" they asked. "Here he is! He is speaking out loud in the crowds. The leaders aren't stopping him. Do they think he really is the one God promised to send?

"We know where this man is from," they said. "When the Promised One comes, nobody will know where he is from."

"Yes, you know me," said Jesus. "You also know where I'm from. But it wasn't my idea to come here. God sent me. He is true. You don't know him, but I know him. I came from him."

Then the leaders of God's people tried to find a way to catch Jesus.

But nobody could, because it wasn't time yet.

Lots of people believed in Jesus. "He must be the one God promised to send," they said. "Look at all the wonders he has done."

Streams of Living Water
JOHN 7:32–8:1

The Jewish leaders heard people whisper about Jesus. So they sent the worship-house guards to catch him.

"I'm here for just a little while," said Jesus. "Then I'll go back to the one who sent me. You'll look for me. But you won't find me. You can't come where I'm going."

"Where does he think he can go? Where could we not find him?" asked the leaders. "Will he go to another land to teach? What does he mean?"

The last day of the holiday was the most important. Jesus stood up in front of the people that day. He talked loudly.

"If you're thirsty, come to me," said Jesus. "Believe in me. Then streams of living water will flow out of you."

Jesus was talking about God's Spirit. God was going to give his Spirit. God would send him to people who believed in Jesus. But God hadn't given them the Spirit

yet. That's because Jesus wasn't finished with his work yet.

"We're sure Jesus is the Prophet," said some people. Others said, "He is the one God promised to send!"

Others said, "How could the Promised One come from Galilee? The Promised One is supposed to come from King David's family. They come from Bethlehem. That's the town where David lived."

The people didn't agree about Jesus. Some wanted to catch him, but nobody even touched him.

At last, the worship-house guards went back to the leaders.

"Why didn't you bring Jesus with you?" asked the leaders.

"Because nobody ever talked the way he talks," they said.

"Did he fool you, too?" the leaders asked. "Have any leaders believed in him? No! It's this foolish crowd! They don't know anything about the Law! Bad things will happen to them."

Nicodemus was one of the leaders. He had gone to visit Jesus one time. He asked, "What does our Law say? Can people be blamed before we even hear them? First we should find out what he is saying and doing."

"Are you from Galilee too?" asked the other leaders. "Look it up!

You'll find out that a prophet doesn't come from Galilee."

Then the leaders went home. Jesus went to Olive Mountain.

Writing on the Ground

JOHN 8:2-11

Jesus was at the worship house by sunrise the next day. Lots of people gathered around him. So he sat down and started teaching them.

But the worship-house leaders pushed a woman in front of him. They had found her sleeping with a man the way a wife would. This man wasn't her husband. Now here she was, in front of everyone.

"We found this woman sleeping with a man the way a wife would. He isn't her husband," they told Jesus. "The Law says we're to throw rocks to make her die for that. What do you say about it?"

The leaders were trying to trap Jesus with their question. They wanted to have a reason to blame him for what he said.

Jesus bent down. He started writing in the dirt with his finger.

But they kept on asking him about it. So Jesus stood up tall. "Is there anyone here who has never sinned?" he asked. "If you've never

sinned, you can go first. You can be first to throw a rock at her."

Then Jesus bent down again. He wrote in the dirt some more.

People started leaving, one at a time. The older people left first.

Soon only Jesus was left. The woman was still standing there.

"Where did everyone go?" asked Jesus. "Is there anyone left to blame you for what you've done?"

"No one, sir," she said.

"Then I won't blame you," said Jesus. "Go on home. But don't sin anymore."

The World's Light

JOHN 8:12-59

Jesus talked to the people at the worship house again. "I'm the World's Light," he said. "Follow me. Then you won't live in the dark. You'll have the light of life."

"You're telling about yourself," said the leaders. "So what you say can't be true."

"I may be telling about myself," Jesus said. "Still, what I say is true. The Law says to have two people tell about something. Then you know it's true. So I tell you about myself. My Father tells you about me also. That makes two."

"Where is your father?" they asked.

"You don't know me," said Jesus. "You don't know my Father. If you

572

knew me, you'd know my Father, too."

"Who are you?" they asked.

"I'm just who I said I am," Jesus told them. "You'll lift me up. Then you'll know I'm who I said I was."

Many people believed in Jesus. "Keep believing what I'm teaching," Jesus told them. "Keep obeying me. Then you'll really be my followers. You'll know the truth. The truth will set you free."

"We've never been anybody's slaves," they said. "So how could we be set free?"

"Anybody who sins is a slave to sin," said Jesus. "A slave is not one of the family. Only a son belongs to the family forever. If the Son sets you free, you really are free.

"I know you're ready to kill me," said Jesus. "You don't have any room in your hearts for my word. I do what I've heard from my Father. You do what you've heard from your father."

"Our father from long ago was Abraham," they said.

"Then you should do what Abraham would have done," said Jesus. "You want to kill me. Abraham didn't do things like that."

"At least we have a father," they said. "Our only true father is God."

"Then you should love me," said Jesus. "I came from God. But you belong to your father, the devil. You do what he says. He was a killer from the very beginning. He never had a bit of truth in him. Lies are the language he speaks. He is a liar, and he is the father of lies.

"I tell the truth," said Jesus. "But you don't believe me. If you belong to God, then hear what God says. You don't hear because you don't belong to God."

"We are right," said the leaders. "A bad spirit controls you."

"No," said Jesus. "I'm following my Father and making him the important one. Now he wants to make me the important one. He is the judge. If you obey my word, you'll never die."

"Now we know a bad spirit controls you," they said. "Abraham died. All the prophets died. But you say that whoever obeys your word will never die. Are you greater than Abraham? He died. So did the prophets. Who do you think you are?"

"My Father is the one you call your God," said Jesus. "He makes me the important one. Your father Abraham was happy to think about seeing me here. He did see this, and he was glad."

"You're not even 50 years old," the leaders said. "When did you see Abraham?"

"The truth is," said Jesus, "I lived before Abraham was born."

When Jesus said that, they picked up rocks to throw at him. But Jesus hid. Then he quietly left the worship house.

Seeing for the First Time
JOHN 9:1-7

As Jesus walked along, he came to a man who couldn't see. He'd been that way since he was born.

Jesus' followers asked, "Why can't he see? Did he sin? Did his mother and father sin?"

"It's not because of anyone's sin," said Jesus. "It happened so God can show his power. I have to do God's work while it's day. Night will be coming. Then nobody can work. While I'm here, I'm the Light of the World."

Then Jesus spit on the dirt and made some mud. He put it on the man's eyes.

"Go," said Jesus. "Wash the mud off in the pool."

The man went to the pool. He washed the mud off. When he came back, he could see!

How Could This Happen?
JOHN 9:8-17

People were used to looking at this man who couldn't see. They used to watch him beg. But he could see now. The people said to each other, "Isn't this the same man? He couldn't see before. He used to sit and beg."

Some said he was the same man. Other people said, "No, he just looks like that man."

But he said, "I am that man."

"How can you see now?" they asked.

"The man named Jesus made some mud," he said. "Jesus put the mud on my eyes. Then he told me to go to the pool and wash. So I did. Then I could see!"

"Where is Jesus?" they asked.

"I don't know," said the man.

Then the people took the man to the leaders at the worship house. That's because this was a worship day.

The leaders asked the man how he could see.

"A man put mud on my eyes," he said. "I washed it off. Now I can see!"

Some of the leaders were angry. "The man who did this can't be from God. He is not obeying the law of the worship day."

Other leaders said, "He is not from God? Then how could he do such a wonder?"

The leaders didn't agree.

At last they turned to the man who couldn't see before. "What do you have to say about this man?"

they asked. "It was your eyes that he made well."

"I think he is a prophet," said the man.

The Men Who Could Not Believe

JOHN 9:18-38

The leaders still couldn't believe it. A man couldn't see before. Now he could see. The leaders called for the man's mother and father.

"Is this your son?" they asked. "Could he see when he was born? How can he see now?"

The man's mother and father were afraid of the leaders. That's because the leaders had a rule. People couldn't call Jesus the Promised One. If they did, they'd be kicked out of their town's worship house.

His mother and father said, "We know he is our son. We know he couldn't see when he was born. We don't know why he can see now. We don't know who made him well. You'll have to ask him. He is old enough. He can speak for himself."

So the leaders called again for the man who had been made well. They said, "Tell us the truth. We know the man who made you well is a sinner."

"I don't know if he is a sinner or not. I do know one thing. I couldn't see before," said the man. "But now I can see."

"What did he do to you?" they asked. "How did he make you see?"

"I told you already," said the man. "You didn't listen. Do you want to hear it again? Do you want to follow him too?"

Then the leaders made fun of the man. "You follow the man who made you well," they said. "We follow Moses. We know God spoke to Moses. But we don't even know where this man comes from."

"That's funny," said the man. "You don't know where this man comes from. But he made me well. We know God doesn't listen to sinners. God listens to people who do what he says. Who ever heard of someone making a person see? This man had to come from God. If he didn't, he couldn't have made my eyes well."

"You were a sinner when you were born," they said. "How dare you tell us what's wrong and what's right!" Then they kicked him out.

Jesus heard what happened. So he looked for the man and found him. "Do you believe in God's Son?" asked Jesus.

"Who is he?" the man asked. "Tell me so I can believe in him."

"You've already seen him," said Jesus. "He is the one talking to you right now."

"Lord!" said the man. "I do believe!" Then he worshiped Jesus.

The Shepherd's Voice

JOHN 10:1-21

"One man goes into the sheep pen. He goes in by the gate," said Jesus. "He is the shepherd. The guard will open the gate for the shepherd. Another man climbs in another way. He is a robber.

"The sheep listen for the shepherd's voice," said Jesus. "He calls his sheep by their names. He leads them out. All of them come out. Then he walks on in front of them.

"The sheep follow the shepherd," said Jesus. "They know his voice. They'll never follow a stranger. In fact, they run from strangers. They don't know the stranger's voice."

Jesus told this story. But people didn't understand what he was talking about.

So Jesus said, "I am like a gate for the sheep. People are like the sheep. Anyone who goes in through me will be saved. He can come in and go out. He will find green fields.

"The robber comes only to steal," said Jesus. "He comes to kill. He comes to tear things apart. I came so my sheep can have a full life.

"I am the Good Shepherd," said Jesus. "The Good Shepherd will die to save his sheep.

"Some people are paid to watch sheep," said Jesus. "They're not like the shepherd who owns the sheep.

"What if the paid person sees a wolf? Then he runs away," said Jesus. "He leaves the sheep with the wolf. The wolf jumps at the sheep. The sheep run this way and that. The man runs too. He is only being paid to watch sheep. He doesn't really care about them.

"But I am the Good Shepherd," said Jesus. "I know my people. They are my sheep. My sheep know me, just like the Father knows me. I know the Father. I will even die to save my sheep.

"I have other sheep," said Jesus. "They're not in this sheep pen. I'll bring them, too. They'll listen to my voice. Then there will be one group of sheep. There will be one shepherd.

"My Father loves me, because I give up my life. Nobody is going to take my life away from me. I choose to give it up," said Jesus.

The leaders who heard Jesus

couldn't agree. Some said, "A bad spirit controls him. He is mad. Why do we listen to him?"

Others said, "Listen. He wouldn't talk this way if a bad spirit controlled him. A man couldn't see before. But now he can see. Can a bad spirit make a man see?"

Ten Men and One Thank-You
LUKE 17:11-19

Jesus headed toward Jerusalem. As he came near a town, he saw 10 men.

These men had a very bad skin sickness. So they stood a little way off. They called out loudly, "Jesus! Master! Feel sorry for us!"

"Go to the priests," Jesus called. "Let them look at your skin."

So the men started out to see the priests. While they were walking, they looked at their skin. Their skin was well!

One of the men ran back to Jesus. He cheered loudly for God. He bowed down at Jesus' feet. He thanked Jesus. He wasn't even Jewish. He was from Samaria.

"Weren't there 10 men who got well?" asked Jesus. "Where are the nine other men? Are you the only one who came back to praise God?"

Then Jesus said, "You can get up and go. You're well because you believed in me."

Seventy-Two Men
MATTHEW 11:25-30; LUKE 10:1-11, 16-21

Jesus chose 72 helpers. He put them in pairs. He sent them ahead of him two by two. They went to every town where Jesus was going.

Before they went, Jesus spoke to them. "People are ready to come into God's kingdom," he said. "It's like the time when farmers bring crops in. But there aren't many workers. Ask God to send workers into the fields.

"You are like lambs going into a world of wolves. Don't take a bag or shoes," said Jesus. "Don't stop to talk with people on the road.

"Don't move from house to house," said Jesus. "Stay in one house. Eat whatever the people feed you. Drink whatever they give you. They should give you food for the work you do. Your work is to make sick people well. Tell people that God's kingdom is near.

"You might go into a town where you're not welcome. Then stand in the street. Say, 'We wipe the dust of this town off our feet! But you can be sure that God's kingdom is near.'

"Anyone who listens to you is

listening to me," said Jesus. "Anyone who won't listen to you is not listening to me. He is not listening to God, who sent me."

Sometime later, the 72 helpers came back to Jesus. They were full of joy. They said, "Lord! Even the bad spirits left in your name."

"I saw Satan fall from heaven like a flash of lightning," said Jesus. "I've given you power to walk over snakes and spiders that can kill you. I've given you power greater than the power of Satan, the enemy. Nothing will hurt you.

"But don't be glad just because the spirits follow your orders. Be glad because your names are written in heaven," said Jesus.

Then Jesus was full of joy. He said, "I praise you, Father. You're the Lord of heaven and earth. You hid your truth from people who thought they were wise. You showed this to people who look foolish to the world. Yes, Father, this is what you enjoy."

Then Jesus said, "Come to me if you're tired. Come to me when you have too much to do. I'll give you rest. Learn by watching and listening to me. I'm thoughtful and kind. My heart is not proud. You'll find your soul can rest with me. I'll be easy on you."

The Neighbor

LUKE 10:25-37

One day, a man who knew the Law stood up. He tried to test Jesus. "What do I have to do to live forever?"

"What does the Law say?" Jesus asked.

"Love the Lord your God with all your heart. Love him with all your soul," said the man. "Love him with all your strength. Love him with all your mind. Love your neighbor as much as you love yourself."

"You're right," Jesus said. "You'll live if you do that."

But the man wanted to show that what he did was right. So he asked, "Who is my neighbor?"

Then Jesus told him a story. "There once was a man who was on a trip. He was going from Jerusalem to Jericho. But robbers jumped out at him. They took his clothes. They beat him. Then they left. There the man was, lying by the road. He was half dead.

"Soon a priest came down the road. He saw the hurt man. But he moved to the other side of the road. He just passed by.

"A man who knew the Law came down the road. He saw the hurt man too. But he moved to the other side of the road. He passed by.

"Then a man from another land came down the road. He was a Samaritan. He saw the hurt man too. He felt sorry for the hurt man. The Samaritan went over to him and took care of his hurts. Then he put the hurt man on his own donkey. He took the man to an inn. This was a place with rooms where people could stay. The man could rest there until his hurt places were well.

"The next day, the Samaritan took out his money. He gave some to the person in charge of the inn. 'Take care of this man,' he said. 'I'll come back. I'll pay back what it costs to take care of him.'

"Which man was a neighbor?" asked Jesus.

The man who knew the Law said, "The man who was kind."

"Right," said Jesus. "Now you go and do the same thing."

All This Work
LUKE 10:38-42

Jesus and his followers came to a town called Bethany. A woman named Martha lived there. She said Jesus was welcome to stay at her house. So Jesus did.

Martha had a sister named Mary. She sat down at Jesus' feet. She listened to what he said.

But Martha was thinking. She thought about all the things she had to do. She wanted things to be just right for Jesus' visit.

At last, Martha came to Jesus. "Lord," she said. "My sister left me to do all the work by myself. Don't you care? Tell Mary to help me."

"Martha, Martha," said Jesus. "You're upset. You're worried about so many things. There is only one thing that's important right now. That's what Mary chose to do. She is taking time to be with me. I won't take that away from her."

Throwing Rocks
JOHN 10:22-33, 39-42

It was winter. There was a special holiday time in Jerusalem. So Jesus went. A covered porch called Solomon's Walk was at the worship house. Jesus began walking there.

The leaders of God's people came up to Jesus. "How long will you make us guess?" they asked. "If you're the Promised One, then just say so."

"I told you," said Jesus. "You didn't believe me. I do wonders in my Father's name. Those wonders tell you who I am. But you don't believe me. That's because you're not my sheep.

"My sheep listen to me," said Jesus. "I know them. They follow me. I give them life that lasts forever. They will never die.

Nobody can take them out of my hand. That's because my Father gave them to me. He is greater than anyone or anything. My Father and I are one and the same."

The leaders at God's house began to pick up rocks. They were going to throw them at Jesus. "I've done great wonders," said Jesus. "I've done them with my Father's power. Which wonder makes you want to throw rocks at me?"

"We're not throwing rocks at you for doing wonders. We're throwing rocks at you because you're just a man. But you're calling yourself God," they said.

The leaders tried to catch Jesus again. But he got away. He went back across the Jordan River. That's where John had baptized people. That's where Jesus stayed now. Many people came to see him there.

People said, "John never did a wonder. But everything he said about Jesus is true." Many people believed in Jesus.

Like a Hen Gathering Chicks

LUKE 13:22-35

Jesus went through many towns. He was teaching people on his way to Jerusalem.

Someone came to Jesus with a question. "Will only a few people be saved?"

"Try to go in at the narrow door," said Jesus. "Lots of people will try to go in. But they'll find out they can't.

"It's like a man who owns a house," said Jesus. "He closes the door. People may stand outside and tap on the door. They may call, 'Open the door for us.'

"But the owner will say, 'I don't know you. I don't know where you came from.'

"They'll answer, 'We ate where you were eating. We drank where you were drinking. We heard you teach.'

"The owner will say, 'Maybe you ate where I ate. Maybe you heard me teach. But you didn't get to know me. You still sin. You do what's wrong.'

"People will come from the east," said Jesus. "People will come from the west. They'll come from the north and south. There will be places for them in God's kingdom. They will come and sit at the dinner party. The ones who are last now will be first then. The ones who are first now will be last then."

"You'd better leave town," said some Jewish leaders. "King Herod wants to kill you."

"Tell that fox I'm going to send bad spirits away," said Jesus. "I'm going to make people well today and tomorrow. On the third day, I'll finish my plan.

"Whatever happens, I have to keep going," said Jesus. "It's not right for a prophet to die outside Jerusalem!

"Jerusalem, Jerusalem!" said Jesus. "You killed the prophets. You hurt the people God sent to you.

A hen gathers chicks under her wings. I've often wanted to get your children together like that. But you wouldn't come.

"Look!" said Jesus. "You have nothing left. You won't see me again until you call to me. You'll say, 'Let God bring good to you. You come in the Lord's name!'"

A Dinner Party in Heaven

LUKE 14:1, 7-24

On a worship day, Jesus went to a dinner party. It was at a Jewish leader's house.

Jesus was sitting at the table. He watched some of the people there. They took the best places at the table.

Then Jesus spoke to the people.

"What if somebody asks you to come to a wedding party? Then don't take the best seat at the table. Somebody more important than you might come in. The person in charge will come to you. He will say, 'Give this person your seat, please.' Then you'll feel put down. You'll have to move to a different seat.

"Instead, take a place that's not important," said Jesus. "The person in charge will come to you. He will say, 'Hello, friend. Move to one of these better seats.' Then you'll feel important in front of everyone.

"You see, some people try to make themselves important. But they will end up feeling like nothing," said Jesus. "Some people make others more important than themselves. They will end up feeling great."

Then Jesus talked to the man in charge of the dinner. "Let's say you want to ask people to come to lunch. Or you want people to come for dinner," said Jesus. "Don't ask friends or family or rich neighbors. Later, they'll ask you to come to lunch with them, too. They'll pay you back.

"Instead, ask poor people to come to your party," said Jesus. "Ask people who can't walk or see. Then God will bring good to you. Those people can't pay you back, but God can."

A man at the table heard what Jesus said. The man said, "I know what will make people happy. They'll be happy if they eat at the party in God's kingdom!"

"Once a man planned a party," said Jesus. "He asked lots of people to come. But no one showed up when it was time.

"So the man sent his servant to say, 'Come on. The party's ready.' But people gave different reasons for why they couldn't come.

"The first man said, 'I just bought a field. I need to go and see about it.'

"Another person said, 'I just bought 10 oxen. I'm on my way to try them out.'

"Another person said, 'I just got married. So I can't come.'

"The servant came back. He told his master what the people said.

"The master got angry. 'Quick!' he said. 'Go out to the streets all over town. Get poor people. Get people who can't walk or see. Bring them to my party.'

"The servant went to the streets. He asked people to come to the party. Then the servant came back. 'I did what you told me,' he said. 'But there is still room.'

"The master said, 'Then go out to the roads. Go into the country.

Bring people in. Let's fill my house! None of the people I asked first can come. They won't even get to taste my food!'"

Building and Going to War
LUKE 14:25-33

Big crowds of people traveled with Jesus. He turned to them. "There's only one way you can follow me," said Jesus. "I have to be the most important person in your life. I have to be more important than your family. I have to be more important than your own life. You must choose what is most important to you.

"What if you wanted to build a tall building?" said Jesus. "First you'd find out how much it would cost. Then you'd know if you had enough money to finish.

"What if you started the building and couldn't finish it? Everybody would make fun of you. People would say, 'He couldn't finish what he started!'

"What if a king was planning to fight another king? First he'd see if he had enough men to win. If he didn't, he'd call some of his men. He'd send them to the other king to make peace.

"So you must give up everything for me," said Jesus. "If you don't, you can't follow me."

Lost and Found

LUKE 15:1-10

Tax men and sinners came to hear Jesus. So the Jewish leaders and teachers said, "This man welcomes sinners. He even eats with them."

Then Jesus told some stories.

"Suppose you're a shepherd. You have 100 sheep. But one of them gets lost. Wouldn't you leave the other 99 sheep out in the open? Wouldn't you look for the lost sheep until you found it?

"Then you'd be so happy. You'd carry the sheep home on your shoulders. You'd call all your friends and neighbors. You'd say, 'Be glad with me! I found my lost sheep!'

"It's the same way in heaven," said Jesus. "The angels are very happy about one sinner who is sorry. They're happy when one sinner turns to God. It's better than knowing 99 people who do what's right. Those people don't even need to say they're sorry.

"Suppose a woman has 10 silver pieces of money. But she loses one," said Jesus. "Won't she light a lamp? She will clean house. She will look carefully until she finds her money. When she finds it, she will call her friends. She will call her neighbors. She will say, 'Be glad with me! I found the money I lost!'

"It's the same way in heaven," said Jesus. "The angels are very glad when one sinner is sorry. They're glad when one sinner turns to God."

Pig Food

LUKE 15:11-32

"A man had two sons," said Jesus. "Someday, the father's money would belong to his sons. But his younger son came to him one day. 'Father, give me my share of the money now,' he said.

"So the man gave the younger son his part of the money. He gave his older son the other part.

"Soon after that, the younger son left home. He took his part of the money. He moved to a land far away.

"He lived a wild life there. He used up all his money. He had another problem too. There wasn't enough food in that land. So he couldn't get enough to eat. He was hungry. He needed clothes. He needed a place to stay.

"So the young man looked for a job. The only job he could get was feeding pigs. By that time, he was very hungry. He even wanted to eat the pigs' food. But no one would let him.

"At last he started getting smart. He said, 'People who work for my father have plenty to eat. Here I sit, dying of hunger! I'm going home. I'll tell my father that I've sinned against heaven and against him. I'll say that I'm not good enough to be called his son.'

"So the young man got up. He went back home. He wasn't even close to his house yet. But his father saw him coming. His father was full of love for his son. He ran to his son. He hugged and kissed him.

"The son said, 'Father, I've sinned against heaven. I've sinned against you. I'm not good enough to be called your son.'

"But the father called his servants. 'Hurry!' he said. 'Bring me the best robe we have! Let's put it on my son! Put a ring on his finger! Put shoes on his feet!'

"The father went on. 'Remember the meat we were saving for a special time? Cook it!' he said. 'Let's have a party! I thought I would never see my son again! It's like he was lost. But now he is found!'

"So they had a big party. All this time, the older son was out in the field. He heard music and dancing coming from the house. He called one of the servants. 'What's happening?' he asked.

"The servant said, 'Your brother came home. Your father is having a welcome-home party for him.'

"Then the older brother got angry. He wouldn't go to the party.

"So his father went out. He begged his older son to come in. 'Look,' said the older son. 'I worked for you all these years. I always did what you told me to do. But you never gave me a party. Now my brother comes home. He used up all the money you gave him. But you have a party for him!'

"The father said, 'You don't understand, Son. You're always with me. Everything I have is yours. But I thought I'd never see your brother again. So we need to have a party! We need to show our joy. He was lost, but now he is found!' "

SEPTEMBER 17

A Little and a Lot
LUKE 16:1-12

"There once was a rich man," said Jesus. "He heard something about the man in charge of his business. He heard that this man was using up his money. So the rich man called his worker. 'What's this I hear about you?' he asked. 'Tell me what you're doing with my money. If you're using it up, you can't be in charge.'

"The worker was worried. He thought, 'What will I do now? My boss will take my job away. I'm not strong enough to dig. I'd feel bad about having to beg for food. I know what I'll do. I'll make friends with people who owe my boss money. I'll lose my job. But these people will let me come to their houses.'

"So the worker called one man. 'How much do you owe my boss?' he asked.

"The man said, 'I owe him 800 jugs of olive oil.'

"The worker told him, 'Take your bill and change it. Make it just 400 jugs.'

"The worker asked another man, 'How much do you owe?'

"The man said, 'I owe 1,000 baskets of wheat.'

"The worker told him, 'Take your bill and change it. Make it just 800.'

"The boss saw what his worker had done. He said it was a witty idea. He said the worker had been wise. Worldly people are wise when they deal with worldly people. They're wiser than God's people in dealing with the world.

"Use worldly money to get friends," said Jesus. "Someday, the money will be gone. But you will have friends.

"What happens when you can be trusted with a little? Then you can be trusted with a lot," said Jesus. "What happens when you can't be trusted with a little? Then you can't be trusted with a lot.

"What if people can't trust you with worldly riches? Do you think you'll be trusted with heaven's riches? What if people can't trust you with things that belong to them? Do you think you'll get things of your own?"

Lazarus and the Rich Man
LUKE 16:14-15, 19-31

Jesus talked to the leaders of God's people. "You try to make people think you're always right. But God knows what's in your hearts," said Jesus. "People may think you're special. But what's special to people is nothing to God.

"Once there was a rich man," said Jesus. "He wore fine purple clothes. He had everything he wanted.

"A beggar man named Lazarus sat at his gate. Lazarus had hurt places all over his body. Dogs would come and lick his hurt places.

"Lazarus was hungry, too. Little bits of food fell off the rich man's table. Lazarus would have loved to eat those bits.

"One day, Lazarus died. Angels came and got him. They took Lazarus to sit by Abraham.

"Sometime later, the rich man also died. But he went to hell. He felt terrible there. He hurt all over.

"The rich man looked up. He saw Abraham far away. Lazarus was sitting beside him. So the rich man called to Abraham. 'Father Abraham!' he cried. 'Be kind to me. Tell Lazarus to dip the tip of his finger in water. Then send him here to cool my mouth with the water. All this fire is too much for me!'

"But Abraham said, 'Remember the way you lived? You got your good things on earth. Lazarus got bad things. But now he is feeling good and you're not.'

"Abraham went on. 'Even if Lazarus wanted to come, he couldn't. There is a big space between us and you. Nobody can cross from us to you. And nobody can cross from you to us.'

"The rich man begged. 'Then please send Lazarus to my brothers,' he said. 'There are five of them. Ask Lazarus to tell them what happened to me. Maybe then they won't have to come to this fearful place!'

"Abraham answered, 'They know the Law. They know what the prophets said. So they should know how to live already.'

"The rich man said, 'They don't listen to the Law. But they know Lazarus is dead. If he went to see them, they'd change.'

"Abraham told the rich man, 'Your brothers don't listen to the Law. They don't listen to the prophets. So they won't believe anybody, even if someone comes alive again.'"

Like Lightning

LUKE 17:20-37

One time, some Jewish leaders came to Jesus. They asked when the kingdom of God would come.

"Watching for God's kingdom won't make it come," said Jesus. "People won't say, 'Here it is!' They won't say, 'There it is!' That's because God's kingdom is inside people."

Then Jesus talked to his followers. "One of these days, you'll wish I were with you. But you won't see me," he said. "People may say, 'There he is!' They may say, 'Here he is!' But don't follow them.

"I'll come back like a flash of lightning. I'll light up the whole sky. Before that, I'll go through a lot of pain. People won't believe me," said Jesus. "It will be like the time when Noah lived. People ate and drank while Noah went into the ark. They thought it was a day like any other day. Then the flood came. It got rid of all of them.

"The same thing happened when Lot lived," said Jesus. "People ate and drank. They bought things. They sold things. They planted fields. They built buildings. But when Lot left the city of Sodom, fire came down from heaven. It got rid of all of them.

"People will be living like this when I come back. What if a man is up on his roof when I come? All his things are inside his house. He shouldn't try to run inside to get his things.

"People may be at work in their fields," said Jesus. "They shouldn't try to go home to get things. Remember Lot's wife? People trying to hold on to life will give up real life. People who give up life for me will have real life.

"When I come, two people may be in one bed. One will go with me," said Jesus. "The other will be left behind. Two women may be making grain into flour. One will go with me. The other will be left behind."

"Where will this happen?" asked Jesus' friends.

"Think about it," said Jesus. "The wild birds come wherever there is something dead."

The Judge
LUKE 18:1-8

Jesus told his followers another story. He wanted them to see that they should always pray. He wanted them to know that they should never give up.

"Once there was a judge," said Jesus. "He didn't worship God. He didn't care about people.

"There was a lady who lived in his town. Her husband had died. The lady kept coming to see the judge. 'My enemies aren't treating me right,' she would say. 'Help me, please.'

"Time after time she came. But the judge wouldn't listen to her.

"At last the judge thought, 'I don't worship God. I don't care about people. But this lady keeps bothering me. So I'll make sure she is treated fairly. Then she won't wear me out by coming so much.'

"Listen," said Jesus. "Won't God help his people? They call him night and day. Will he send them away? No. He will make sure they are treated right. He will be fast about it. But I wonder. Will I find people who believe in me when I come back?"

The Proud Prayer
LUKE 18:9-14

Some people were sure they did what was right. They were proud of doing right. They thought they were more important than anyone else. So Jesus told them a story.

"Once there were two men," said Jesus. "They went to the worship house to pray. One man was a leader of God's people. The other man was a tax man.

"The leader stood up tall. He prayed about himself. 'God, thank you that I'm not like other men. I'm not a robber. I don't sin. I'm not like this tax man. I go without food to worship God two times a week. I give God one out of every 10 pieces of money I earn.'

"The tax man stood a little way off. He wouldn't even look up. He pounded his chest. 'God, be kind to me,' he said. 'I'm a sinful person.'

"God forgave the tax man," said Jesus. "It was just as if he'd never sinned. But God didn't forgive the leader.

"Some people think they're great. God will make those people feel like they're not important. Some people don't act like they're important. God will make those people feel great."

Workers Who Fussed

MATTHEW 20:1-16

"Here's what the kingdom of heaven is like," said Jesus. "It's like a farmer who had a grape field. He went to town early in the morning. He got men to come and work in his field. He told them what he'd pay them for the day. Then he sent them out to work in his field.

"At nine o'clock that morning, the farmer went back to town. He saw more people standing there. They were in the market place, but they weren't doing anything.

"So the farmer took them with him. 'You can work in my field too,' he said. 'I'll pay you whatever is right.' So they went to work.

"The farmer got more workers at noon. He got more workers at three o'clock in the afternoon. At five o'clock, the farmer still found people standing around. He asked them, 'Why did you stand around all day doing nothing?'

"They said, 'Nobody asked us to work.'

"The farmer said, 'You can work in my field.' So they did.

"It wasn't long until evening came. 'Call the workers,' said the farmer to the head servant. 'Pay them. Start with the last men who came to work. Then go on to the first men.'

"The workers who went to work at five o'clock came. Each one got paid for a whole day's work.

"Then the early morning workers

came. They thought they would get more money. But the farmer paid each worker for one day's work.

"The workers who had worked all day started fussing. 'You gave the same pay to those workers,' they said. 'They worked only one hour. You treated them just like us. We worked all day long in the hot sun.'

"The farmer said, 'I'm being fair to you. I asked you to work for me. I told you what I would pay you. You said you would work for that much.'

"The farmer went on. 'Take your money and go,' he said. 'I want to give the others what I gave you. It's my money. Can't I do what I want with it? Or are you mad because I'm being kind to them?'

"The last will be first," said Jesus. "The first will be last."

A Trip to Bethany

JOHN 11:1-17

Mary and Martha were from a town named Bethany. They had a brother named Lazarus. One day, Lazarus got sick. Mary and Martha sent a message to Jesus. "Lord, Lazarus is sick."

Jesus got the message. "This sickness won't end in death. It's to show God's great power," he said.

Jesus loved Mary and Martha and Lazarus. But he didn't go see them right away. He stayed where he was

for two more days. Then he said to his friends, "Let's go to Judea."

"But the Jewish leaders tried to throw rocks at you there. Are you going back?" his friends asked.

"The light shines for 12 hours each day. Right?" said Jesus. "People won't fall down if they walk in the daytime. They see the world's light. They fall when they walk at night. They have no light then.

"Our friend Lazarus is sleeping," said Jesus. "I'm going to wake him up."

"If he is sleeping, he will get better," said Jesus' friends.

Jesus meant that Lazarus had died. But Jesus' friends thought he meant that Lazarus really was just sleeping. So then Jesus made it clear. "Lazarus is dead," he said. "When I think of you, I'm glad I wasn't there. Now you'll believe in me. But we need to go to Bethany."

Sometime later, Jesus got to Bethany. Lazarus was dead. His body had been in the grave for four days.

SEPTEMBER 19

Out of the Grave

JOHN 11:18-54

The town of Bethany was only about two miles from Jerusalem. So lots of people went to see Mary and

Martha. The people hoped they could make the two sisters feel better.

Someone said that Jesus was coming. Martha went to meet him, but Mary stayed home.

"Lord!" Martha said. "If you'd been here, Lazarus wouldn't have died. But I know God gives you whatever you ask for. He will give it even now."

"Your brother will come to life again," said Jesus.

"I know," said Martha. "He will come back to life at the end of time."

"I hold the power of coming alive again," said Jesus. "I am new life. People who believe in me will live even after they die. People who live and believe in me will never really die. Do you believe what I'm saying?"

"Yes, Lord," said Martha. "I believe that you are the one God promised to send. You are God's Son."

Then Martha went back to her house. She told Mary, "Jesus is here. He wants to see you."

Mary got up quickly. She went to see Jesus. He hadn't come into town yet. He was still at the place where Martha had seen him.

People at Mary's house were trying to cheer her up. But they saw how fast she got up. They thought she was going to Lazarus's grave to cry. So they followed her.

Mary went to the place where Jesus was. She bowed down at Jesus' feet. "Lord," she said. "If you'd been here, Lazarus wouldn't have died."

Mary began to cry. The people who had followed Mary began to cry too.

Jesus felt their deep sadness. "Where is the grave?" he asked.

"We'll show you," they said.

Then Jesus cried too.

"Look at how much Jesus loved Lazarus," said the people.

But some of them said, "He has made people's eyes well. Couldn't he have kept Lazarus from dying?"

Soon Jesus came to the grave. He felt the deep sadness again.

The grave was a cave. A big stone blocked the opening. "Take the stone away," Jesus said.

"But, Lord!" said Martha. "He has been in there four days! By this time it will smell bad in there."

"Remember what I told you," said Jesus. "If you believe in me, you'll see God's power."

So they took the stone away.

Then Jesus looked up. "Father," he said, "thank you for hearing me. I know you always hear me. But saying this will help people believe you sent me."

Jesus called loudly, "Lazarus, come out!"

Then Lazarus came out! Cloth covered his hands and feet. There was a cloth around his face.

"Help him out of his grave clothes," said Jesus.

Many people who saw this chose to believe in Jesus.

But some of them went to the Jewish leaders. They told the leaders what Jesus had done.

These leaders of God's people called a meeting. "What good are we doing?" they asked. "Here is this man doing lots of wonders. What if everybody starts believing in him? Then the Romans will come. They'll take away our nation! They'll take over our worship house!"

One of the leaders was the high priest that year. He said, "You don't know anything. It's good for one man to die for the people. It's better than the whole nation dying."

Now he didn't think about saying this himself. His words were a message from God. Jesus would die for the whole nation. He would die for all people. That way, they could be God's children.

From then on, the leaders made plans to kill Jesus. So Jesus didn't go where he could be seen in public anymore.

A Camel and a Needle

MATTHEW 19:13-26; MARK 10:13-27; LUKE 18:15-27

People started bringing little children to Jesus. They wanted Jesus to touch them and pray for them. But Jesus' friends got mad at the people.

Jesus saw this, and he was upset. He said, "Let the little children come to me. Don't stop them. God's kingdom belongs to those who are like these children.

"People must welcome God's kingdom like a child does," said Jesus. "If they don't, they won't get to go into it."

Then Jesus picked up the children. He held them in his arms. He touched them. He prayed that God would bring good things to them.

As Jesus left, a man ran up to him. The man bowed down in front of Jesus. "Good Teacher," said the man. "What do I need to do to live forever?"

"Why are you calling me good?" Jesus asked. "God is the only one who is good. Are you calling me God?

"But to answer your question, you know the laws," said Jesus. "Don't kill. Stay with the one you marry. Don't take things that belong to someone else. Don't lie. Be kind to your father and mother."

"I've done these things," said the man. "I've done them since I was a boy."

Jesus took a good look at the man. Jesus loved him. "There is one more thing for you to do," said Jesus. "Go and sell everything you have. Take the money you get and give it to the poor. Your riches will be in heaven. You can come and follow me."

When Jesus said this, the man got sad. That's because he was very rich.

Jesus turned to his followers. "It's hard for rich people to come into God's kingdom. It's harder than a camel going through the hole in a needle."

Jesus' followers were surprised. "Who can be saved?" they asked.

"It's impossible for people to do it," said Jesus. "But anything is possible with God."

To Sit at Your Right Hand

MATTHEW 20:17-28; MARK 10:32-45; LUKE 18:31-34

Jesus headed for Jerusalem. His 12 special friends and other followers went with him. Jesus' special friends were surprised to see him going to Jerusalem. His other followers were afraid.

Jesus called his 12 friends to him. He told them what was about to happen. "We're on our way to Jerusalem," he said. "One of my friends will turn against me. He will tell the leaders at the worship house where I am. They will take me. They will blame me. They will say I should die.

"These leaders will send me to the Romans," said Jesus. "The Romans will make fun of me. They will beat me. They will kill me. But on the third day, I will come back to life."

Jesus' friends didn't understand any of this. They didn't know what Jesus was talking about.

Then James and John's mother brought them to Jesus. She bowed down. She asked Jesus to do something special for her.

"What do you want?" Jesus asked.

"Someday you'll be the king," she said. "Let one of my sons sit at your right side. Let my other son sit at your left side."

"You really don't know what

you're asking," said Jesus. "Can you do what I'm about to do?"

"We can," said James and John.

"And you will," said Jesus. "But I'm not the one to say who will sit at my right or left."

Jesus' other friends heard what James and John wanted. They got angry at James and John.

So Jesus called them all together. He said, "You know, the world's rulers boss everyone around. They tell everyone what to do. But you're not supposed to act like that.

"Instead, if you want to be great, you'll serve people," said Jesus. "Anybody wanting to be first has to be a servant. Even I didn't come to earth to be served. I came to serve. I came to give up my life. Then I can set people free from sin."

Up in a Tree

LUKE 19:1-10

Jesus came to the town of Jericho. A man named Zacchaeus lived there. He was a tax man. He was very rich.

Zacchaeus heard that Jesus was coming. He wanted to see who Jesus was. But Zacchaeus was a short man. So he couldn't see around the crowd.

Zacchaeus knew which way Jesus was going. So he ran ahead of the crowd. He climbed up into a tree.

He wanted to make sure he could see Jesus.

Jesus did come that way. When he got to the tree, he stopped. He looked up. "Zacchaeus!" he called. "Come down right away. I need to stay at your house today."

So Zacchaeus came down. He was glad to welcome Jesus into his house.

The other people began to fuss. "Jesus has gone to stay with a sinner!" they said.

But Zacchaeus was making things right. "Look, Lord," he said to Jesus. "I'll give half of everything I own to poor people. Did I trick people into giving me too much? Then I'll pay them back. I'll pay four times what I took!"

"Someone has been saved today at this house!" said Jesus. "This is why I came. I came to look for people who lost their way. I came to save them!"

By the Side of the Road

MATTHEW 20:29-34; MARK 10:46-52; LUKE 18:35-43

Jesus and his friends were leaving Jericho. A big crowd of people followed them.

A man was sitting by the side of the road. He could not see. His name was Bartimaeus. He was begging for money.

Bartimaeus heard people say that Jesus was coming. So he started shouting, "Jesus! Be kind to me!"

Lots of people got mad at him. They told him to be quiet.

Bartimaeus just shouted louder. "Jesus!" he called. "Be kind to me!"

Jesus stopped walking. He said, "Tell that man to come here."

The people called to Bartimaeus. "Stand up!" they said. "You can cheer up now! Jesus is calling you!"

Bartimaeus threw his coat off. He jumped up and went over to Jesus.

"What do you want me to do?" Jesus asked.

"I want to see!" said Bartimaeus.

"All right," said Jesus. "You are well because you believe in me!"

Right away, Bartimaeus could see. He followed Jesus, cheering for God.

All the people saw it. They cheered for God too.

SEPTEMBER 21

The Servants and the Money

LUKE 19:11-27

Jesus and his followers were getting close to Jerusalem. His followers thought about God's kingdom coming. They thought it would show up right away. So Jesus told them a story.

"Once there was an important man. He had to go to a land far away. He was going to have the people there make him their king. Then he would come back home. He'd be the king.

"So the man called 10 servants. He gave each of them some money. 'Use this money to get more money,' he said. 'See how well you can use it until I come back.'

"Now some of the people hated this man. Some of them followed him to the land far away. They said, 'We don't want this man to be king.'

"But the man was made king anyway. Then he came home.

"He sent for the servants who had the money he'd given them. He wanted to find out what they'd done with it.

"The first servant came to him. He said, 'Sir, I made more money for you. You gave me one piece of money, and I got 10 more.'

"'Well done!' said the king. 'You are a good servant! I see I could trust you with a little bit. Now you may be in charge of 10 cities.'

"The second servant came to the king. He said, 'Sir, I made more money for you. You gave me one piece of money, and I got five more.'

"'Well done!' said the king. 'You may be in charge of five cities!'

"Then another servant came to the king. He said, 'Sir, here's the money you gave me. I hid it in a piece of cloth. I was afraid, because you are a hard man to work for. You take what doesn't belong to you. You bring in crops you didn't plant.'

"The king said, 'I see! So you know I'm a hard man to work for. Then why didn't you put my money in the bank? I could have made more money in the bank.'

"Other people were standing nearby. The king said, 'Take the money away from this man. Give it to the servant who has 10 pieces of money.'

"The people said, 'But he already has 10.'

"The king answered, 'Everybody who has something from me will get more. But what if it means nothing to him? Then he won't be allowed to have more. Even what I gave him will be taken away.'

"Then the king looked for his enemies. They were the ones who didn't want him to be king. He told his men to bring the enemies to him and kill them.'"

A Jar of Perfume

MATTHEW 26:6-13; MARK 14:1-11; LUKE 19:28; JOHN 11:55–12:11

Jesus kept traveling toward Jerusalem. It was almost time for the Pass Over holiday. So lots of people were coming to Jerusalem. They were getting ready for the holiday. They were looking for Jesus, too.

People were standing around the worship house. They were asking each other, "What do you think? Do you think he will come for the holiday?"

But the leaders at the worship house sent word to the people. Anybody who knew where Jesus was had to tell these leaders. They were looking for a way to catch Jesus.

It was six days before the Pass Over holiday. Jesus came to Bethany. That was the town where Mary, Martha, and Lazarus lived. Lazarus was the man who had been brought back to life by Jesus.

A man named Simon also lived in Bethany. He had a dinner party for Jesus. Martha served the food. Lazarus ate at the table with Jesus.

But Mary took out a jar of nard. It was perfume that cost a lot of money. She tipped the jar over. She let perfume flow out onto Jesus' feet. Then she wiped his feet with her hair. The air was filled with the sweet perfume smell.

Judas, one of Jesus' 12 helpers, said, "Why didn't Mary sell this perfume? Think of the money she could have made! It would have been enough to pay a working person for a year. She could have given the money to poor people!"

Now Judas didn't really care about poor people. He was a robber. He kept the money bag for Jesus and his friends. He would take out whatever he wanted for himself. Judas was the one who would turn against Jesus.

"Leave Mary alone," said Jesus. "It was right for Mary to save this perfume. She got my body ready for the grave. Poor people will always be around you. But I won't always be here. I'm going to die.

"The news about me will be shared all over the world. Then people will hear what Mary did tonight," said Jesus.

Many people found out that Jesus was in Bethany. So they went to Bethany. They didn't go just to see Jesus. They went to see Lazarus, too. It was because Jesus had brought him back to life.

The leaders at the worship house made plans to kill Jesus and Lazarus. They were angry about Lazarus. Many people had seen that Lazarus was alive again. They believed in Jesus because of Lazarus.

SEPTEMBER 22

A Colt

MATTHEW 21:1-9; MARK 11:1-10; LUKE 19:29-40; JOHN 12:12-16

Now Jesus came to Olive Mountain. Jesus asked two of his 12 special friends to do something. He asked them to go into the next town. "You'll see a donkey with her colt

just as you go into town. Nobody has ever ridden the colt before," said Jesus. "It will be tied up there. Untie it, and bring it to me. Someone might ask you what you're doing. Just tell them the Lord needs it."

Jesus' two friends went to town. They found the colt. It was in the street, tied by a door. They untied it.

Some people were standing there, watching. They said, "What are you doing? Why are you untying that colt?"

Jesus' friends told them just what Jesus had said. Then the people let them take the colt.

Jesus' friends took the colt to Jesus. They put their coats on the little donkey's back. Then Jesus got on it. Off they went, down the road.

That made the words of the prophet Zechariah come true. He wrote to Jerusalem, "See? Your king is coming to you. He is kind and good. He rides on a donkey. It's a colt, a donkey's baby."

Jesus' friends didn't understand why he wanted a colt. They understood later, after Jesus died and came to life again. Then they knew that the prophet had written about him. They saw that they had helped these words come true.

Lots of people were in Jerusalem for the Pass Over holiday. They heard that Jesus was on his way to Jerusalem. So they got big branches from palm trees. Then they went to meet Jesus.

"God save us!" the people shouted. "May good things come to the King of God's people! May good things come! He is coming in the Lord's name!" They began to follow him.

Some leaders of God's people were in the crowd. They said to Jesus, "Tell your followers to be quiet!"

"If they're quiet, the stones will shout!" said Jesus.

A Fig Tree and a Hiding Place for Robbers

MATTHEW 21:10-16; MARK 11:11-18; LUKE 19:45-48; JOHN 12:17-19

Jesus went into Jerusalem. Everybody in the city was talking about him. "Who is this?" they asked.

"This is Jesus," said the people who had followed him. "He is the prophet from Nazareth."

People told how Lazarus had come back to life. Lots of people who heard about it went to see Jesus.

"Look how everybody in the world is following him. This isn't getting us anywhere," said the Jewish leaders.

Jesus went to the worship house. He looked around. But it was late. So Jesus and his 12 good friends went back to Bethany. They spent the night there.

The next day, they headed for Jerusalem again. Jesus was hungry. He saw a fig tree ahead. It had leaves on it. So Jesus went to see if it had any fruit. But when he got there, he found only leaves. It wasn't the season for figs to grow yet.

Jesus spoke to the tree. "No one will ever get fruit from you again." Jesus' good friends heard him say this.

When he got to Jerusalem, Jesus went to the worship house. People were buying and selling animals there. Others were trading money that people brought from different places. They traded it for money that people could use to buy things.

Jesus started chasing those people out. He turned over tables. That's where men traded money from other places for money that people could use. Jesus turned over the seats of the people selling doves. He wouldn't even let people carry things across the yards at the worship house.

"My house is supposed to be a

house of prayer. It's a house of prayer for all people," said Jesus. "But you turned it into a hiding place for robbers!"

The leaders at the worship house heard this. They wanted to kill Jesus. They were afraid of him.

But there were crowds of people around Jesus. People were listening to what he said. People who couldn't see came to Jesus at the worship house. People who couldn't walk came. Jesus made them well. So it was hard for the leaders to catch Jesus.

The leaders saw the wonderful things Jesus was doing. They saw children shouting. "Cheer for the King!" called the children.

The worship-house leaders were upset. They talked to Jesus about it. "Do you hear what these children are saying?" they asked.

"Yes," said Jesus. "Haven't you read from the psalm? It says that God planned for children and babies to praise him."

A Seed

JOHN 12:20-36

Some people from the land of Greece came to Jerusalem. They were going to worship. They found Philip and said, "Sir, we want to see Jesus."

So Philip went to tell Andrew. Then Andrew and Philip went to tell Jesus.

Jesus talked to Andrew and Philip. "It's time for God to show his greatness in me. It's time for the whole world to see who I am.

"A wheat seed falls to the ground," said Jesus. "It dies. It's just a little seed. But it will make many other seeds. It will send out roots and grow. It will live again.

"Some people want to serve me," said Jesus. "Anyone who wants to do that will have to follow me. Then that person will be where I am. If someone serves me, my Father will make that person feel special.

"Right now I feel troubled," said Jesus. "What can I say? 'Father, save me from what's going to happen'? No. I came into the world because of what's going to happen. So I say, 'Father, show how great you are in me. Let the world see you.'"

Just then a voice came from heaven. "I have shown how great I am. And I will show how great I am again."

People who were standing there heard the voice. Some of them said it was just thunder. Other people said it was an angel talking.

"This voice was for you, not for me," said Jesus. "It's time for the world to be judged now. It's time to chase away Satan, the world's sinful prince. I'll be lifted up from the earth. Then I'll draw all people to me." Jesus was talking about how he would die.

"The Promised One will stay with us forever," people said. "How can you talk about being lifted up?"

"You have the light just a little while longer," said Jesus. "Walk while you have the light. The dark is going to come. People in the dark don't know where they're going. Trust in the light while it's here. Then you can be children of light."

Then Jesus left Jerusalem. The people didn't know where he went.

Two Sons and a Grape Garden

MATTHEW 21:20-32; MARK 11:20-33; LUKE 20:1-8

Morning came. Jesus and his friends headed back to Jerusalem. They passed the fig tree Jesus had talked to. It had dried up.

Peter remembered what Jesus had said to the fig tree. "Look!" said Peter. "You talked to the fig tree. You said no one would get fruit from it. It dried up!"

Jesus' friends were surprised to see it. "How did it dry up so fast?" they asked.

"You can do the same thing if you have faith. You can tell a mountain to jump into the sea. It will," said Jesus.

"Believe in God," said Jesus. "Then you'll get whatever you ask for when you pray. But when you pray, ask yourself if you are angry at someone. Forgive that person. Then your Father in heaven will forgive you."

They came to Jerusalem. Jesus went to the worship house again.

The leaders there came to Jesus. "Who gave you the right to do the things you do?"

"Let me ask you a question," said Jesus. "If you answer me, then I'll answer you. Tell me. John baptized people. Was that his idea? Or did God tell him to do that?"

The worship-house leaders talked to each other. "What if we say it was God's idea? Then he will say, 'Why didn't you believe John?' What if we say it was John's idea? Then we're in trouble." They were afraid of all the people who were around. The people had been saying that John really was a prophet.

At last the leaders answered, "We don't know."

"Then I won't answer your question," Jesus said.

Jesus went on. "Think about this. There once was a man who had two sons. The man talked to his first son. 'Go work in the grape garden today,' he said.

"His first son said no. Later, he changed his mind. He did go.

"The man talked to his other son. 'Go work in the grape garden today,' he said.

"His other son said, 'Yes, sir. I will.' But he didn't go.

"Which son did what his father wanted?" asked Jesus.

"The first one did," they said.

"John came to show you the right way to live," said Jesus. "Tax men and sinners believed John. They will get into God's kingdom. But you wouldn't believe John and be sorry for the wrong things you did. So tax men and sinners will get into God's kingdom before you will."

SEPTEMBER 24

The Farmers and the Grape Garden

MATTHEW 21:33-46; MARK 12:1-12; LUKE 20:9-19

"Once a man planted a garden of grape bushes," said Jesus. "He built a wall around his field. He built a tall tower for watching over the field. Then he let some farmers rent the field. He went away on a long trip.

"In time, the grapes were ready to be picked. So the man sent a servant to get some. But the farmers caught the servant. They beat him up. They sent him away without any fruit.

"The man sent another servant to the farmers. But the farmers hit him on the head. They were very mean to him.

"The man sent another servant. But the farmers killed him.

"The man sent lots of other servants. The farmers beat some of them up. They killed others.

"At last, there was only one person left to send. It was the man's son. He loved his son very much. 'They will listen to my son,' he said. So he sent his son to them.

"But the farmers said, 'Aha! This is his son! Come on! Let's kill him! Then the field will be ours!' So they killed the son. They threw him out of the field.

"What will the owner of the field do?" asked Jesus. "He will come and kill those farmers. He will give his field to somebody else."

"We hope this never happens," said the people.

Jesus said, "Have you read this psalm?

"There was a stone that the builders
     didn't want.
Now that stone holds up the whole
     building.
God made this happen.
We think it's wonderful!

"God is going to take his kingdom away from you. He will

give it to people who will follow him. They'll obey him."

The leaders at the worship house heard this story. They knew Jesus was talking about them. So they looked for a way to catch him. But they couldn't, because the people said Jesus was a prophet. The leaders were afraid of the crowd.

Tricks

MATTHEW 22:15-22; MARK 12:13-17; LUKE 20:20-26

Some Jewish leaders tried to think of ways to trick Jesus. They wanted to make him say the wrong thing. Then they could blame him. They could have the Roman leaders take him to jail.

So the Jewish leaders sent some people to trick Jesus. They said, "We know you tell the truth. You teach about God. You don't follow people's ideas. So tell us something. Should we pay taxes to the king?"

Jesus knew what they were trying to do. He said, "Why are you trying to trick me? Show me the money you pay your taxes with."

They showed him the money.

"Whose picture is on it?" asked Jesus. "Whose name is on it?"

"The king's," they said.

"Then give the king what belongs to him," said Jesus. "And give God what belongs to God."

The people couldn't trick Jesus. In fact, they were surprised by what Jesus said. They couldn't think of anything else to say.

More Tricks

MATTHEW 22:23-46; MARK 12:18-25, 28-37; LUKE 20:27-44

The same day, some other leaders of God's people came to see Jesus. These leaders didn't believe that people go to heaven after they die. So they tried to trick Jesus too.

They said, "Here's a problem. Moses told what should happen if a man dies. The man's brother has to marry the wife of the man who died. His brother has to have children for him.

"Now there were seven brothers. The first brother got married and then died. But he didn't have any children. So the second brother married the wife of the man who died.

"But the second brother died. He didn't have any children. So the third brother married the woman.

"Then this brother died. He didn't have any children. So the fourth brother married the woman.

"Then he died. And the fifth brother married the woman. But the same thing kept happening.

"All seven brothers married the woman. All died. There were no children. At last, the woman died.

"Now, what if people live again?" said the leaders. "What if they go to heaven? Whose wife will the woman be? She married all seven brothers."

"You're thinking the wrong way," said Jesus. "You don't understand what God says. You don't know God's power. People will come back to life. Then they won't marry. And they won't die. They'll be like the angels in heaven."

One teacher of God's laws saw that Jesus had given a good answer. So he said, "There are many rules. Which one is the most important?"

"The most important rule is this one," said Jesus. "The Lord is the only God. Love the Lord with all your heart. Love him with all your soul. Love him with all your mind. Love him with all your strength. The next important rule is to love your neighbor like you love yourself. No other rule is greater than these."

"You answered that very well," said the teacher. "You're right to say that there is only one God. It's important to love him with all our heart. We must love him with all our soul, mind, and strength. It's important to love our neighbor, too. All of this is more important than any gift we could give God."

Jesus could tell that this man was wise. "You're not very far from God's kingdom," said Jesus.

The Jewish leaders were standing there together. So Jesus asked, "What do you think about the Promised One? Whose son is he?"

"He is King David's son," they said.

"Then how could David call him his Lord?" asked Jesus. "Remember what David wrote in the psalm? David called the Promised One 'Lord.' So how could he be David's son?"

Nobody could answer Jesus. After that, nobody dared to ask any more questions.

SEPTEMBER 25

The Most Money

MARK 12:41-44; LUKE 21:1-4

Jesus sat down at the worship house. He was across from the place where people gave money. He was watching people put money into the offering box.

Lots of rich people came by. They threw in lots of money. Then a poor woman walked up. Her husband had died. She dropped in two small pennies.

"Look!" said Jesus to his friends. "This woman put the most money into the offering box. It's more than what the rich people put in! The other people gave only part of their riches. This poor woman gave all the money she had.

Days to Come
MATTHEW 24:1-36; MARK 13; LUKE 21:5-36

Jesus and his helpers left the worship house.

"Look!" said one of his friends. "Look how big the stones in the worship house are! What wonderful buildings!"

"Yes, look at all these big buildings," said Jesus. "Someday they will be torn down. Not one stone will be left on top of another."

Jesus walked up Olive Mountain. He sat down. From there, he could see the city across the valley. He could see the worship house.

Peter, James, John, and Andrew came up to Jesus. They said, "When will that happen? And what will happen to let us know you're coming again? How will we know when the end of time is coming?"

"Be careful," said Jesus. "Don't let anyone trick you. You'll hear people say, 'I am the one God promised to send.' They'll fool lots of people. You'll also hear about wars. Don't be scared. This has to happen. That doesn't mean the end of time has come yet.

"Nations will fight each other," said Jesus. "Kingdoms will fight each other. Sometimes there won't be enough food. The ground will shake in different places. This is just the beginning.

"You'll have to be careful," said Jesus. "People will send you to judges. They'll beat you. It's because of me. Then you'll tell rulers and kings about me. I'll help you know what to say.

"There will be more and more sin," said Jesus. "Most people's love will grow cold. People will hate you because you belong to me. But keep loving me, and you will be saved.

"The Good News of the kingdom will be told. It will be told all over the world," said Jesus. "All nations will hear it. Then the end will come.

"One day, you will see armies all around Jerusalem. Then you'll know bad times are coming for Jerusalem. People living nearby will need to run to the mountains. People in the city should get out. People in the country shouldn't go back to the city. This will pay God's people back for their sins.

"Pray that you won't have to leave in winter. Pray that you won't have to leave on a worship day. There will be lots of trouble," said Jesus. "Things will be worse than they have been since time began. Things will never be that bad again.

"Some people will be killed," said

Jesus. "Others will be taken to live in other lands. People who aren't Jewish will control Jerusalem for a while. This won't last long. If it did, no one would live through it. The time will be short because of God's people.

"Someone might say, 'Look! Here's Jesus!' They might say, 'There he is!' Don't believe them. Fake promised ones and fake prophets will come. They'll even do great wonders. They'll try to fool God's people if they can.

"See?" said Jesus. "I've told you all this before it happens. Someone might say, 'There is Jesus. He is out in the desert!' Don't go there. They might say, 'Here he is. He is in one of the rooms in this building!' Don't believe it.

"When I come, it will be like lightning," said Jesus. "You can see it when you're in the east. You can see it when you're in the west.

"Right after the hard times, the sun will turn dark. The moon will not shine its light. Stars will fall from the sky. Then my sign will show up in the sky.

"Nations will cry," said Jesus. "They'll see me coming through the sky on clouds. I'll come with power. I'll send my angels out with a loud call from a horn.

"The angels will bring my people together," said Jesus. "They'll come from one end of the sky to the other. There will be signs in the sun. There will be signs in the moon. There will be signs in the stars.

"The sea will roar and toss. People will wonder about it. People will be afraid of what's coming.

"Look up when this starts happening. Watch!" said Jesus. "That means it's time for you to be saved. Learn a lesson from the fig tree. You see its leaves coming out. So you know summer will soon be here. You may see these things I've talked about. Then you'll know the time is coming soon.

"One day there will be an end to the sky," said Jesus. "There will be an end to the earth. But there will never be an end to my words.

"Nobody knows when this will happen," said Jesus. "Even the angels in heaven don't know. Even I, the Son, don't know. Only the Father knows. I'm telling everyone the same thing. Watch!"

SEPTEMBER 26

Ten Lamps

MATTHEW 25:1-13

Jesus told a story. It was about the time when he would come back. "The kingdom of heaven will be like 10 young people," he said. "They weren't married. But they were going to a wedding party. They were going to be with the groom.

"All the young people brought their lamps with them. Five of these young people were foolish. They didn't bring any oil to keep their lamps lit up. Five of them were wise. They brought oil in jars.

"It took a long time for the groom to come. All the young people got sleepy. In fact, they went to sleep.

"In the middle of the night, a voice called out. 'Here comes the groom! Come and meet him!'

"All the young people woke up. They lit their lamps. But the foolish ones had run out of oil. They said, 'Our lamps! They're going out! Give us some of your oil!'

"The wise ones said, 'No. We don't have enough for us and for you, too! You'll have to go to the store. Buy your own oil.'

"So the foolish people went to the store. While they were gone, the groom came. The young people who were there went with him. They went to the wedding party. The door closed behind them.

"Sometime later, the other young people came back. They called, 'Open the door. Let us in.'

"But the groom said, 'I don't know you.'

"So watch. You don't know when I'll come," said Jesus.

Sheep and Goats

MATTHEW 25:31-45

"I'll come back," said Jesus. "All the angels will come with me. All the nations will come together in front of me. They'll see me as the king of my kingdom. Then I'll put the people into different groups.

"A shepherd puts his sheep into one group," said Jesus. "He puts the goats into another group. I'll put people who are my sheep into one group. They'll be on my right. I'll put people who are like goats on my left.

"Then I'll talk to the people on my right. I'll say, 'Come! My Father has good things for you. So come and get what he is giving you. It's his kingdom. It's been ready for you since the world was made.'

"I'll say, 'I was hungry, and you gave me food. I was thirsty, and you gave me a drink. I needed a place to stay, and you asked me to come in. I needed clothes, and you gave me clothes. I was sick, and you took care of me. I was in jail, and you came to see me.'

"The people who did what's right will wonder. They'll say, 'Lord, when did we see you hungry? When did we give you food? When did we give you a drink? When did you need a place to stay? When did we ask you to come in? When did we give clothes to you? When were you sick? When were you in jail? When did we come to see you?'

"Then I'll say, 'You did these things for other people. You did these things for people who don't seem important at all. That's when you did them for me.'

"Then I'll talk to the people on my left. 'Go away from me,' I'll say. 'Go into the fire that burns forever. It's been made ready for the devil and his helpers.'

"I'll say, 'I was hungry. But you didn't give me any food. I was thirsty. But you didn't give me anything to drink. I needed a place to stay. But you left me outside. I needed clothes. But you didn't give me any. I was sick. I was in jail. But you didn't take care of me.'

"The people who didn't do what's right will wonder too. 'Lord, when did we see you hungry or thirsty? When did you need clothes, or a place to stay? When were you sick or in jail?'

"Then I'll say, 'You never did these things for others. You never did these things for people who don't seem important. So you left me out too.' "

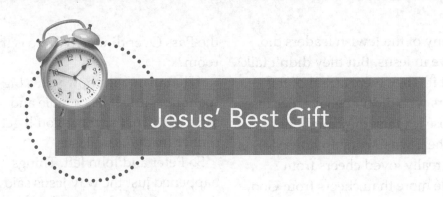

Jesus' Best Gift

Thirty Silver Coins

MATTHEW 26:3-5, 14-16; MARK 14:1-2, 10-11; LUKE 21:37–22:6; JOHN 12:37-47

The leaders of God's people got together at the high priest's palace. They made plans to catch Jesus by some trick. Then they would kill him. They planned carefully. "We won't do it while the Pass Over holiday is going on. If we do, the people might start fights against us," they said.

Judas was one of Jesus' 12 special friends. But Satan took control of Judas now. So Judas went to the

leaders at the worship house. He told them he could show them where Jesus was. "What will you give me if I do?" he asked.

The leaders counted out 30 silver coins for Judas. Judas took the money. Then he waited and watched. He looked for a time when no crowds were around.

Every day, Jesus went to the worship house to teach. People came out early in the morning to hear him. At the end of every day, he left the city. He spent the night on Olive Mountain.

People had seen Jesus do many wonders. But many people still would not believe in him. So Isaiah's words came true. Isaiah said, "Who believed our news? Who did God show himself to?"

Isaiah said something else. "Their eyes can't see. Their hearts are dead. They don't see or understand. If they did, I would make them well." When Isaiah said this, he was talking about Jesus.

Many of the Jewish leaders did believe in Jesus. But they didn't talk about it. They were afraid of the leaders who didn't believe. Because of those leaders, they might not get into the towns' worship houses. They really loved cheers from people more than cheers from God.

"People who believe in me also believe in my Father. When you look at me, you see God," said Jesus. "I came to the world to be a light. People who believe in me don't stay in darkness.

"Some people hear what I say," said Jesus. "But they don't do what I say. I'm not here to blame them. I came to save them."

The Room Upstairs

MATTHEW 26:17-20, 26-29;
MARK 14:12-17, 22-25; LUKE 22:7-20;
JOHN 13:1

At last, the Pass Over day came. Jesus sent Peter and John into the city. "Go find a place to eat the Pass Over dinner," he said. "Get everything ready for the dinner."

"Where?" they asked.

"Go into the city," said Jesus. "You'll see a man carrying a jar of water. Follow him. He will go into a house. Find the owner of the house. Tell him, 'Jesus wants to know something. Where can he eat the Pass Over dinner? Where is the room?'

"That man will show you a big room upstairs. It has a table and seats in it. That's where you'll get dinner ready," said Jesus.

So Peter and John left. Things happened just the way Jesus said they would. So they got the Pass Over dinner ready.

Dinner time came. Jesus and his 12 special friends gathered around the table. "I wanted to eat Pass Over dinner with you," said Jesus. "A time of pain is coming for me. I won't eat this Pass Over dinner again. Not until it has a new meaning in the kingdom of God."

Jesus held up a cup of wine. He thanked God. "Take this," he said to his friends. "Share it with each other. I won't drink wine again until God's kingdom comes."

Then Jesus picked up the flat bread. He thanked God. He broke some off to give to his friends. "This will help you remember my body," he said. "I'm giving my body for you. Eat this to remember me."

They finished dinner. Then Jesus picked up the cup of wine. "This shows God's new special promise," he said. "It's a promise made with my blood. I will give my blood for you."

Jesus knew it was time to leave the world. It was time for him to go to his Father. He loved his friends very much. They were his own people here in the world. He was about to show how much he loved them.

Clean Feet

MATTHEW 26:21-25; MARK 14:18-21; LUKE 22:21-23; JOHN 13:3-30

Jesus knew God had given him power over all things. He knew he had come from God. He knew he was going back to God.

Jesus got up from the table. He took a long cloth. He tied it around himself like a belt. Then he got a big bowl of water. He started washing his friends' feet. He dried their feet with the long cloth.

Soon it was Peter's turn. But Peter said, "Lord, are you going to wash my feet?"

"I know you don't understand now," said Jesus. "But someday you'll understand."

"No," said Peter. "I can never let you wash my feet."

"That means you won't belong to me," said Jesus. "You won't be part of what I'm doing."

"Then don't just wash my feet, Lord," said Peter. "Wash my hands and my head, too!"

Jesus said, "People who had a bath only need to wash their feet. The rest of their body is already clean. So you're clean now. But not all of you are clean." Jesus knew which friend had turned against him. He was talking about this person's heart.

Jesus finished washing his friends' feet. Then he went back to his place. "Do you understand what I just did?" he asked. "You call me Teacher. You call me Lord. That's right. That's what I am. Your Lord and Teacher just washed your feet. So you need to wash each other's feet too.

"I'm showing you the way to treat others," said Jesus. "The master is always greater than the servant. The person who sends a message is important. He is greater than the one who takes the message.

"Look at what you know now," said Jesus. "God will bring good to you if you do what you know."

Then Jesus became sad. "One of you has turned against me," he said. "This will make David's psalm come true. 'The person who shares my bread has turned against me.' I'm telling you about this before it happens. Then when it happens, you'll believe that I'm God's Son."

Jesus' friends were sad. One after another they said, "I'm sure it's not me."

"It's the one who ate from the bowl with me. He is the one who has turned against me," said Jesus.

"How sad it is for him. It would be better if he'd never been born."

Jesus' friends looked at each other. They didn't know what he was talking about. Peter whispered to John, "Ask Jesus who he is talking about."

John moved close to Jesus. "Lord, who is it?" he asked.

"I'll dip my bread in the dish," said Jesus. "Then I'll give it to someone. He is the one I'm talking about."

Jesus dipped his bread in the dish. He gave it to Judas. Judas took the bread. Right away, Satan took control of him. Judas said, "I'm sure I'm not the one."

"Yes, you are," said Jesus. "Do what you planned. Do it now."

Nobody understood why Jesus said that to Judas. But Judas was in charge of the money. So some of them thought Jesus sent Judas out to buy something. Some thought Jesus sent him to give money to poor people.

Right after Judas took the bread, he left. It was night.

Where Are You Going?

MATTHEW 26:34-35; MARK 14:29-31; LUKE 22:31-38; JOHN 13:31–14:21, 26-31

Judas was gone. Jesus said, "Now God is going to show his greatness in me. I'll be here just a little longer. You'll look for me. But you can't come to the place where I'm going.

"Here's a new rule for you. Love each other," said Jesus. "Love each other like I love you. Everyone will know you're my friends if you love each other."

"Lord, where are you going?" asked Peter.

"You can't follow me," said Jesus. "You'll come later."

"Why can't I follow you?" asked Peter. "I'll even die for you."

"Peter, Peter!" said Jesus. "Satan wants to toss you around like bits of wheat. But I prayed for you, Peter. I prayed that you'll keep believing in me. Then you can help others to be strong."

"Lord, I would go to jail for you," said Peter. "I would even die for you!"

But Jesus said, "Peter, something will happen before the rooster crows today. You'll say you don't know me. You'll say it three times.

"Don't worry," said Jesus to his friends. "Trust me. Trust God. There are many rooms in my Father's house. I wouldn't say that unless it was true. I'm going there to get a place ready for you. So you can be sure I'll come back for you. I'll take you with me. You know the way to the place where I'm going."

"We don't even know where

you're going," said Thomas. "How can we know the way?"

"I'm the way," said Jesus. "I'm the truth. I'm the life. I'm the only way to get to the Father. You know me. So you know the Father. You've seen him."

"Show us the Father," said Philip. "That will be enough for us."

"Don't you know me yet, Philip?" asked Jesus. "I've been with you such a long time. Anybody who has seen me has seen the Father. How can you say, 'Show us the Father'? Don't you believe that I'm in the Father? Don't you believe that the Father is in me?

"This isn't just my idea," said Jesus. "The Father lives in me. So he gives me his ideas and words.

"You can believe me because of what I say. Or you can believe because of the wonders I do," said Jesus. "But all people who believe in me will do what I've been doing. In fact, they'll do even greater things. That's because I'm going to the Father. I'll do whatever you ask in my name. That way, I can show how great God is.

"You'll obey me if you love me," said Jesus. "I'm going to ask the Father to give you another Helper. He will be with you forever. He is God's Spirit of truth.

"The world can't believe that this Spirit is real," said Jesus. "They don't see the Spirit. They don't know the Spirit. But you know the Spirit. He lives with you, and he will be in you."

Then Jesus said, "I won't leave you by yourselves. I'll come to you. In a little while, the world won't see me. But you'll see me. Because I'm alive, you'll be alive too. That's when you'll know that I'm in the Father. You're in me, and I'm in you.

"Know my rules. Obey me," said Jesus. "Then I'll know you love me. The Father will love whoever loves me. I'll love them too. I'll show myself to them.

"My Father will send the Holy Spirit in my name. He will help you," said Jesus. "He will teach you everything. He will help you remember everything I've told you.

"I'm giving you my peace," said Jesus. "Don't worry. Don't be afraid.

"I've told you what's going to happen before it happens. So you can believe when it really does happen. I won't talk to you much longer," said Jesus. "Satan, the world's sinful prince, is coming. He can't hold on to me. The world has to learn that I love the Father. They have to know I'll do whatever he tells me."

Then Jesus said, "Remember when I sent you out two by two? Remember when I sent you to teach? I told you not to take a bag or shoes. Did you need anything?"

"No," they said.

"Now take a bag with you," said Jesus. "You'd better get a sword, too. Isaiah said, 'They treated him like a sinner.' This is coming true about me."

"We have two swords here," said Jesus' friends.

"That will be enough," said Jesus. "Let's leave now."

The Vine

MATTHEW 26:30; MARK 14:26; LUKE 22:39; JOHN 15:1-16; 16:7-8, 20-33

Jesus and his friends sang a song. Then they headed for Olive Mountain.

"I'm like a vine," said Jesus. "You are like the branches. My Father is the one who takes care of the garden. He cuts off the branches that don't grow fruit. He trims the branches that do grow fruit. That way they will grow even more fruit.

"So stay in me," said Jesus. "Then I will stay in you. Branches can't grow fruit by themselves. They have to stay on the vine. You'll grow a lot of fruit if you stay in me.

"You can't do anything without me," said Jesus. "So what happens if you don't stay in me? You're like a broken branch. It dries up and gets thrown away. Then it gets burned up in the fire.

"Stay in me, and let my words stay in you. If you do that, you can ask for anything you want. And it will be given to you.

"Be like a branch that grows a lot of fruit. Show everyone that you are my followers. Then people will see what my Father is like. They will see how great my Father is.

"I love you the way my Father loves me," said Jesus. "Stay in my love. You do this by obeying me. That's how it is with my Father and me. I obey my Father's rules. I stay in his love.

"I've told you this so you can have joy. The joy that I have will be in you, too.

"This is my rule. Love each other like I love you. There is one thing that shows the greatest love. It's giving up your life for your friends. You're my friends if you do what I say.

"I'm not calling you servants anymore," said Jesus. "I'm calling you friends. I've told you everything I learned from my Father. I chose you. You didn't choose me. I chose you to go out and be like a tree that grows fruit. Grow fruit for God by doing things for him that will last.

"I'm going away," said Jesus. "That's really the best thing for you. Then I can send the Helper to you. He will show the people of the world that they've sinned. He will show what it's like to be right with God.

"You'll cry while the world is happy," said Jesus. "You'll cry, but your crying will turn into joy. It's like a woman who's going to have a baby. It hurts when it's time for the baby to be born. But then the baby comes. She forgets the hurting. She is so happy that the baby is born.

"So now is your time to cry. But I will see you again. Then you'll be happy. No one will be able to take your joy away.

"I've been talking in stories," said Jesus. "But someday I'll tell you clearly about my Father. I came from him. Now I'm going back to him."

"You are talking clearly," said Jesus' friends. "We believe that you come from God."

"At last you believe!" said Jesus. "Soon each of you will go back home. You'll leave me all alone. But I won't really be alone. My Father is with me.

"You'll have trouble in this world," said Jesus. "But be happy! The world has lost. I have won."

Out of the World
JOHN 17

Then Jesus looked up toward heaven. He prayed. "Father, it's time now. Show your greatness in me. Show who I am so I can show who you are.

"You put me in charge of all people. You did it so I could give life that lasts forever. I can give it to everyone you gave me. This life comes from knowing you and me. You are the only real God. And I'm the one you sent," said Jesus.

"I've shown your greatness. I've done the work you sent me to do. So now, Father, show who I am. Give me the place I had with you before the world started.

"I've shown you to the people you gave me," said Jesus. "They were yours. You gave them to me. They obey your word. I told them the words you told me. They believed that you sent me. I'm praying for them.

"They're still in the world," said Jesus. "But I'm coming to you. Father, keep them safe. Keep them safe by the power of your name. I kept them safe. Only one of them turned away. I'm not asking you to take them out of the world. I'm asking you to keep them safe from Satan.

"My prayer isn't just for them," said Jesus. "I'm praying for all people who will believe in me. I pray that they will all work together. I pray they'll work together like you and me, Father. You're in me, and I'm in you. So let them be in us. That way, the world can believe that you sent me.

"Father, I want my friends to be with me. I want them to see my greatness. It's the greatness you gave me because you loved me. You loved me before the world was made.

"The world doesn't know you," said Jesus. "But I know you. I've told them about you. I'll keep showing you to them. That way your love for me can be in them. Then I can be in them too."

OCTOBER 1

Praying in the Garden
MATTHEW 26:36-46; MARK 14:32-42; LUKE 22:39-46; JOHN 18:1

Jesus and his friends crossed the valley. There was an olive garden on the other side. That's where they went. The garden was called Gethsemane.

"Sit here," said Jesus. "I'm going to go pray."

Jesus took Peter, James, and John with him. "Stay here and watch," he told them.

Jesus was beginning to feel very sad. He walked just a little way from Peter, James, and John. It was close enough to throw a stone.

Jesus got down on his knees. He started praying. "Father, if you will, don't let this happen," he said. "But do whatever you think is best. I want to do what you want."

Then an angel came from heaven. He helped Jesus to be strong.

Jesus was so sad. He prayed even harder. His sweat fell on the ground in big drops.

Jesus got up. He went back to his friends. They were sleeping. They were tired because they were so sad.

"Couldn't you men watch for just one hour?" Jesus asked Peter. "Watch! Pray, so you won't think about doing wrong."

Jesus went to pray again. "Father," he said. "Do whatever you think is best. I want to do what you want."

Jesus walked back to Peter, James, and John. They were sleeping again. So he walked back to pray a third time. He told God the same thing he said before.

Then he came back to his friends. "Are you still sleeping?" he asked. "It's almost time. I'm about to be given to sinful people. Get up! Let's go! Here comes the one who is showing them where I am."

Judas and the Guards

MATTHEW 26:47-56; MARK 14:43-52; LUKE 22:47-53; JOHN 18:2-11

Judas knew where Jesus was. Jesus and his friends often went to the olive garden. So Judas led guards and officers from the worship house to the garden. It was dark. They held lamps and sticks with fire on the end.

Judas had made a plan with the worship-house leaders. He would show them which man was Jesus. He had told them, "The man I kiss will be Jesus. Have the guards take him away."

So now Judas walked up to Jesus to kiss him.

Jesus said, "Judas! Are you going to turn against me by kissing me?"

Judas said, "Teacher!" Then he kissed Jesus.

Jesus knew what was going to happen to him. So he asked, "Who are you looking for?"

"We're looking for Jesus," they said.

"I'm Jesus," he said.

Everyone stepped back. Some even fell to the ground.

"Who are you looking for?" Jesus asked again.

"We're looking for Jesus," they said.

"I told you," said Jesus. "I'm Jesus. I'm the one you're looking for. Let these other men go."

Then the guards took hold of Jesus.

Jesus' friends saw what was happening. "Lord, should we fight with our swords?" they asked.

Peter had a sword. He pulled it out. He swung it at Malchus, the high priest's servant. Peter cut off the servant's right ear.

"Put your sword back," said Jesus. "People who fight with swords die by swords. Don't you know? I could call out to my Father. Then thousands of angels would come. They would do anything I asked. But this is what is supposed to happen. So no more fighting."

Then Jesus touched Malchus's ear. Malchus was well again.

Jesus talked to the officers and guards. "Am I leading people against you? You've come after me with swords and clubs. I was at the worship house every day. You didn't even touch me. Of course, you do your work after dark."

Then the guards and officers took Jesus. They also held on to a young man. He'd been with Jesus.

The young man was wearing just a cloth around him. But he ran away. He left his cloth behind. So he ran away with no clothes on. All of Jesus' other friends ran away too.

The Rooster Crows

MATTHEW 26:57-75; MARK 14:53-72;
LUKE 22:54-65; JOHN 18:12-27

The guards tied Jesus up. They took him to the high priest's house.

Peter and John followed. John knew the high priest. So he went into a closed-in yard with Jesus. Peter had to wait outside by the gate.

Later, John came back. He talked to the girl who was in charge. She let him bring Peter inside the yard.

The high priest was asking Jesus questions about his followers. He asked about what Jesus taught.

"All my teaching has been done where anyone could hear," said Jesus. "I've told it to the whole world. I taught at worship places. That's where God's people gather. I didn't teach anything in secret. So why are you asking these questions? Ask the people who heard me. They know what I said."

One of the Jewish officers was standing close to Jesus. He hit Jesus' face. "Is that how to answer the high priest?" he asked.

"Did I say something wrong?" asked Jesus. "Tell me what it was. Why did you hit me if I'm telling the truth?"

There was a fire in the middle of the big closed-in yard. Peter sat down there.

A servant girl saw Peter sitting in the fire light. She looked at him very closely. She said, "This man was with Jesus."

"I don't even know him," said Peter. He got up and went out to the gate.

The Jewish leaders were looking for something wrong that Jesus had done. They wanted a reason to kill him. But they couldn't find anything wrong. Lots of people said he had done wrong, but they were lying. They didn't agree with each other.

Then somebody stood up to talk. "Jesus said he would tear down this worship house that man has made. He said he'd build another one in three days. He said it wouldn't be made by man."

Even then the people couldn't agree.

Then the high priest turned to Jesus. "Aren't you going to answer?" he asked. "What are these people saying about you?"

Jesus was quiet. He didn't say a word.

"Are you the one God promised to send?" asked the high priest.

"I am," said Jesus. "Someday you'll see. I'll be sitting at God's right hand. You'll see me coming on the clouds of heaven."

"Do we need to hear any more?"

asked the high priest. "You heard him. What do you think?"

Everybody said Jesus should die.

The guards around Jesus began to make fun of him. They covered his eyes. They began to beat him. Then they said, "Tell us who is hitting you." They laughed at him.

An hour passed. People were standing around Peter. They looked at him. "We're sure you're one of Jesus' followers!" they said. "The way you talk tells us that you are!"

"I don't know the man," said Peter.

Now, one of the high priest's servants was from Malchus's family. Malchus was the man whose ear Peter had cut off. This servant looked at Peter. "Didn't I see you with Jesus in the olive garden?"

"Man, I don't know what you're talking about," said Peter.

Right then, while Peter was talking, the rooster crowed. Jesus turned and looked at Peter. Then Peter remembered what Jesus had told him. Jesus had said, "Something will happen before the rooster crows today. You'll say you don't know me. You'll say it three times."

Then Peter went outside and cried hard.

The Son of God

MATTHEW 27:1, 3-10; MARK 15:1; LUKE 22:66-71

The sun began to come up. The leaders at the worship house had a meeting. They brought Jesus in. They said, "If you are the Promised One, then tell us."

"I could tell you," said Jesus. "But you won't believe me. From now on I'll be sitting by God's right hand."

"Then are you God's Son?" they asked.

"You're right," said Jesus.

"We don't need to have others tell about him," they said. "We've heard it now from his own mouth." Then they planned for sure to have Jesus killed.

Judas saw that they really were going to kill Jesus. He understood what was happening, and he was sorry. He took the 30 silver coins back to the leaders at the worship house. "What I did was wrong," he said. "I turned against a man who didn't do anything wrong."

"So what?" the Jewish leaders said. "That's your problem."

Judas threw the money into the

worship house. He left. Then he went and killed himself. He hung himself on a tree.

The leaders picked up the money Judas had thrown down. "We can't put this back into the money box. It's money paid to kill a man," they said. So they used the money to buy the potter's field.

The potter's field became a grave yard. Graves were made there for people from other lands. Then the field was called "Blood Field."

That made Jeremiah's words come true. He had said, "They took the 30 silver coins. It was the price God's people sold him for. They used the coins to buy the potter's field."

Pilate

MATTHEW 27:2, 11-14; MARK 15:1-5; LUKE 23:1-7; JOHN 18:28-38

The Jewish leaders took Jesus to Pilate. He was the Roman leader in charge of the people in Jerusalem.

It was early in the morning now. Pilate was not Jewish. So the Jewish leaders wouldn't go into Pilate's palace. If they went in, they couldn't eat the Pass Over dinner.

So Pilate came out to them. "What did this man do wrong?" he asked.

"This man has turned against our whole nation," they said. "He tells us we shouldn't pay taxes. He says he is the one God promised to send. He says he is a king."

"Take him yourselves," said Pilate. "You can judge him by your own law."

"We aren't allowed to kill anybody," the Jewish leaders said.

Pilate went back into his palace. He called Jesus to him. "Are you really the King of the Jews?" he asked.

"Do you want to know for yourself?" asked Jesus. "Or are you asking because somebody else wanted you to?"

"Am I Jewish?" Pilate asked. "Your people and leaders brought you here. I'm telling you what they told me. What have you done?"

"I have a kingdom," said Jesus. "But it's not from this world. What would happen if my kingdom were from this world? My servants would be fighting right now. I wouldn't have been caught by the Jewish leaders. But my kingdom is from a different place."

"Then you are a king?" asked Pilate.

"Yes," said Jesus. "That's why I was born. That's why I came to the world. I came to show the truth. Anybody who wants truth will listen to me."

"What is truth?" Pilate asked. Then he went back out to the Jews.

"I see no reason to blame this man for anything," he said.

But the Jewish leaders from the worship house kept blaming Jesus. Jesus wouldn't say anything to answer them.

"Don't you hear what they're saying about you?" asked Pilate.

Jesus still didn't say anything. Pilate was surprised.

The leaders kept saying, "This man is fooling the people. He gets them to follow him. He started in Galilee. Now he has come all the way down here."

King Herod was the Roman leader in charge in Galilee. So Pilate thought maybe Herod should question Jesus. Herod happened to be in Jerusalem at that time.

A Dream
MATTHEW 27:15-23; MARK 15:6-14; LUKE 23:8-23; JOHN 18:39-40

Herod was happy to see Jesus. He had wanted to see Jesus for a long time. He had heard about Jesus. He hoped he could see Jesus do a wonder. So he asked Jesus lots of questions. But Jesus wouldn't answer him.

The Jewish leaders were standing there. They were telling Herod that Jesus had done wrong things. So Herod's guards made fun of Jesus. They put a king's robe on him. Then they sent Jesus back to Pilate. Herod and Pilate had been enemies. But that day, they became friends.

Now Pilate's wife sent him a message. It said, "Don't have anything to do with Jesus. He hasn't done anything wrong. I had a dream about him, and it made me feel terrible."

So Pilate called the Jewish leaders together. He said, "You brought this man to me. He may have upset the people. He may have gotten people to follow him. But I talked with him. I can't find that he has done anything wrong.

"Herod didn't find that he'd done anything wrong," said Pilate. "Herod sent him back to us. Jesus hasn't done anything he should be killed for. So I'll have some men beat him. Then I'll let him go."

Every year, Pilate set someone free. He let one person out of jail. This person was always someone the people asked for.

"How about the King of the Jews?" asked Pilate. "Shall I let him go free?" He was talking about Jesus. He knew why the worship-house leaders had brought Jesus to him. They wished people would follow them instead of Jesus.

These leaders got the crowd upset. The leaders told the people to ask for Barabbas instead. So the crowd shouted, "No! Not Jesus! We want Barabbas!" They cried out, "Take Jesus away! Set Barabbas free! Give Barabbas to us!"

Now Barabbas had made lots of people turn against the king. His followers had even killed people in their fights. That's why Barabbas was in jail.

"Then what should I do with Jesus?" asked Pilate.

"Kill him!" they cried.

"Why?" asked Pilate. "What has he done that's so bad?" Pilate wanted to let Jesus go.

The crowd just shouted, "Kill him! Kill him!"

OCTOBER 4

The King of the Jews
MATTHEW 27:24-30; MARK 15:15-19; LUKE 23:24-25; JOHN 19:1-16

The people's yelling won. Pilate had some men beat Jesus. Then lots of Roman guards got together. They took Jesus' clothes off. They put a purple robe on him. Then they made a crown out of sharp thorns. They put it on Jesus' head.

The guards put a walking stick in Jesus' right hand. They bowed in front of him. "Here's the King of the Jews!" they called. They spit on him. They took the stick he held. They hit him on the head with it. They hit him again and again.

Then Pilate went back out to talk to the Jewish leaders. "Look," said Pilate. "I'm bringing this man out to you. I don't see any reason to kill him."

Pilate brought Jesus out. He was wearing the crown of sharp thorns and the purple robe. Pilate said, "Here's your man."

As soon as the leaders saw Jesus, they shouted, "Kill him! Kill him!"

"You kill him yourselves," said Pilate. "I can't find a reason to kill him."

The Jews would not change their minds. "We have rules," they said. "Our rules say he has to die. It's because he said he was God's Son."

Pilate really got scared now. He went back into his palace. "Where are you from?" he asked Jesus.

Jesus didn't answer.

"You won't talk to me?" asked Pilate. "Don't you know I have power? I can set you free or kill you."

Jesus looked at Pilate. "You have power only because God gave it to you."

From then on, Pilate tried to set Jesus free. But the people kept shouting at him. "You're not the king's friend if you let Jesus go! Jesus says he is a king. So he is against our king!"

It was about six o'clock in the morning. It was the day for getting ready for Pass Over week. Pilate brought Jesus out. Then Pilate sat on the judge's seat. It was at a place called the Stone Pavement.

"Here's your king," said Pilate.

"Take him away!" the people called. "Take him away and kill him!"

"You want me to kill your king?" Pilate asked.

"We have just one king. That's Caesar," they said.

Pilate could see he wasn't getting anywhere with the people. Instead, the people were getting louder and louder.

So Pilate got some water. He washed his hands in front of the people. "Nobody can blame me for killing him," said Pilate. "I'll have nothing to do with it. You are the ones choosing this."

"That's fine," said all the people. "We'll take the blame."

So Pilate gave them what they wanted. He let Barabbas go free, and he gave Jesus to them so they could have him killed.

Skull Hill

MATTHEW 27:31-38; MARK 15:20-27; LUKE 23:26-34; JOHN 19:17-24

The guards made fun of Jesus. Then they took the purple robe from him. They put his own clothes back on him. Then they took him out to kill him on a cross. But they made him carry his own cross.

A man named Simon was walking along the road. He was on his way to Jerusalem from the country.

The guards stopped Simon. They made him carry the cross for Jesus.

They took Jesus to a hill. It was called Skull Hill. Lots of people followed Jesus there. Some women were there, crying for him.

Jesus turned to them. "Don't cry for me," he said. "Cry for yourselves and your children. Someday you'll tell the mountains, 'Fall on us!' You'll tell the hills, 'Cover us!' People do bad things when times are good! So what will happen when times are bad?"

Two other men were going to be killed that day. They had done many wrong things. The guards took them to be killed with Jesus.

They all came to Skull Hill. There they nailed Jesus and the two other men to crosses. One man was on Jesus' right side. The other man was on his left side. It was nine o'clock in the morning.

"Father, forgive the people who are doing this," said Jesus. "They don't know what they're doing."

People tried to give Jesus wine with something bitter in it. But he wouldn't drink it.

Pilate told someone to make a

sign. He said to put it on Jesus' cross. The sign said, "Jesus of Nazareth. The King of the Jews."

The sign was written in three languages. It was written in the Jews' language. It was also written in Latin and Greek. Many people read the sign. That's because Jesus was killed close to the city.

The Jewish leaders said, "Don't write 'The King of the Jews.' Write that he said he was King of the Jews."

"The sign is already written," said Pilate. "That's the way it will stay."

The four guards who killed Jesus took his clothes. Each guard got one thing. But his long shirt was left. It was all one piece of cloth, top to bottom. There was no line on the cloth because nothing had been sewn together.

So the guards said, "Don't tear the shirt. Let's roll dice for it. Let's see who wins the shirt."

This made one of the psalms come true. "Each one took part of my clothes. They rolled dice for them." That's just what the guards did.

OCTOBER 5

Close to the Cross

MATTHEW 27:39-44; MARK 15:29-32; LUKE 23:35-37, 39-43; JOHN 19:25-27

People passed by the crosses. They yelled bad words at Jesus. Some of them shook their heads.

"You were going to tear down the worship house," they yelled. "You said you'd build it again in three days! So why don't you save yourself! Come down from the cross if you're God's Son!"

The leaders of God's people made fun of Jesus too. "He saved other people," they said. "Why can't he save himself? Is he the King of God's people? Then let him come down from the cross. We'll believe in him if he does. He trusts in God. Let God save him now. After all, Jesus said he is God's Son."

The guards made fun of Jesus too. They asked him if he wanted some sour wine. They said, "If you're the Jews' king, save yourself."

One of the men being killed made fun of Jesus. "Aren't you the

Promised One?" he asked. "Then save yourself. Save us, too!"

The other man being killed got mad at the first man. "Aren't you afraid of God?" he asked. "You are going to die too!"

The man went on. "This is happening to us because we've done wrong. We're getting what was coming to us. But Jesus didn't do anything wrong," he said. "He shouldn't be killed." Then the man said, "Jesus! Remember me when you get to your kingdom."

"You'll get to be with me in heaven today," said Jesus.

Jesus' mother stood close to the cross. His aunt was there too. Another Mary and Mary Magdalene were also there. Jesus looked out. He saw his mother. He saw his friend John there too.

"Dear woman!" Jesus said to his mother. "John will be like your son now."

"Take care of her," he told John. "Care for her like you'd care for your own mother."

After that, John let Jesus' mother stay at his house. He took care of her.

Open Graves
MATTHEW 27:45-54; MARK 15:33-39; LUKE 23:44-48; JOHN 19:28-30

Now the sky got dark around noon. Darkness covered the land until about three o'clock in the afternoon. At that time, Jesus gave a loud cry. He cried, "My God, my God, why did you leave me?"

"He is calling for Elijah!" said some of the people.

Jesus knew his time on earth was finished. "I'm thirsty," he said.

Right away, somebody ran to get a cloth. He got it wet with sour wine. Then he put it on a stick. He held it up to Jesus so he could drink it.

"Leave him alone," said the other people. "Let's see if Elijah will come and save him."

Jesus drank some of the sour wine. Then he said, "It's finished!" He cried out in a loud voice. He said, "Father, I give my spirit to you." Then he bowed his head. And he died.

Inside the worship house there hung a big, long cloth. It hung in front of the Most Holy Place. It kept people out of that room. But at the moment Jesus died, it tore in half. The tear started at the top. It ripped all the way down to the bottom.

The earth shook. Rocks broke. Graves came open. Dead people came back to life! These were people who had done right while they lived. Their bodies came out of the graves. They went into the city of Jerusalem. Lots of people saw them.

The guards at Skull Hill saw the earth shake. They were very scared.

"He really was God's Son!" they said.

The other people who had been watching felt very sad. They pounded their chests and walked away.

The Grave
MATTHEW 27:57-61; MARK 15:42-47; LUKE 23:50-56; JOHN 19:31-42

The next day was a special worship day. The Jews didn't want bodies left on crosses that day. So they asked Pilate if they could break the men's legs. Then they could take them off the crosses sooner.

The guards came and broke the first man's legs. Next they broke the legs of the other man with Jesus. Then they came to Jesus. But he was already dead. So they didn't break his legs. Instead, one guard put a spear into Jesus' side. Blood and water flowed out.

This happened so the words of the psalm would come true. "None of his bones will be broken." It was like Zechariah said. "They will look at the one they hurt with a spear."

A man who saw this happen told about it. He knew he told the truth. He told it so you can believe.

Evening came. A man named Joseph went to see Pilate. Joseph was a Jewish leader. But he was watching for God's kingdom to come. He was very brave. He asked Pilate if he could have Jesus' body.

Pilate was surprised to hear that Jesus was already dead. He called for the man in charge of the guards. He asked if it was true. Was Jesus already dead?

The man in charge said Jesus really was dead. So Pilate said Joseph could take Jesus' body.

Nicodemus went with Joseph. Nicodemus was the man who once came to see Jesus at night. He and Joseph took 75 pounds of spices with them.

They took Jesus' body. They covered the body with spices. Then they put clean cloth all around the body. This was the Jewish way to get a body ready. Then they put it in a grave.

Joseph put Jesus' body in his own new grave. He had cut it out of rock in a garden.

The worship day was the next day. The grave was close by. So that's where they put Jesus' body. They rolled a big stone in front of the opening. Then they left.

The women who had come with Jesus from Galilee followed Joseph. They saw the grave. They saw how Jesus' body was put inside.

Then the women went home. They got some spices ready for Jesus' body too. But then they had to rest. It was the worship day. The Law said they had to rest on the worship day.

Angels

Matthew 27:62–28:8; Mark 16:1-8; Luke 24:1-3; John 20:1

Some of the Jewish leaders went to talk to Pilate. "We remembered something," they said. "Before Jesus died, he said he'd come back to life after three days.

"Jesus was lying," they said. "But send some guards over to his grave. Tell them to make sure the grave stays closed. We don't want Jesus' friends to take his body. Then they'd tell everyone that he came back to life again. That would be a bigger problem for us than we had before."

"All right," said Pilate. "Take some guards. Make sure no one takes the body."

Guards went to the grave. They made sure the stone was in place. It was in front of the opening into the grave. Then they sealed the stone so people would see that the grave had stayed closed. Then the guards stood by the grave.

The next day was the first day of the week. The sun was just coming up. Suddenly, the earth began to shake. An angel came down from heaven.

The angel went to the grave. He rolled away the stone at the opening. Then he sat on it. The angel looked like lightning. His clothes were as white as snow.

The guards saw the angel. They were so afraid that they shook. Then they fell down. They looked like they were dead.

Mary Magdalene, another Mary, and Salome left for the grave. They started on their way right after the sun came up. They were taking spices to the grave. They were going to put them on Jesus' body. But they wondered, "Who will roll the stone away? Who will roll it from the opening of the grave?"

They came to the grave. They saw the big stone. It had already been rolled away! So they went inside the grave.

The women saw a young man sitting there. He was wearing a white robe. They were surprised and scared.

"Don't be afraid!" he said. "You're looking for Jesus, who was killed. But he is not here! He is alive again! You can see the place where he was.

"But don't stay here," said the young man. "Go tell Peter and Jesus' other friends what happened. Tell them that Jesus is going to Galilee. They can see him there. Say that it's just the way Jesus told them it would be."

The women were shaking. They didn't know what to think. They left there in a hurry. At first, they didn't tell anybody what had happened. They were too scared.

Running to the Grave

JOHN 20:2-18

Mary Magdalene went running to Peter and John. "Someone took Jesus' body out of the grave!" she said. "We don't know where he took it!"

Peter and John ran to the grave. John ran faster than Peter. So he got there first. But he didn't go in. He just bent over and looked inside. He saw the cloth that had been around Jesus' body.

Then Peter got there. He went right in. He saw the cloth lying there too. He saw the cloth that had been around Jesus' head. It was folded up and was lying by itself.

At last, John went inside. He saw the grave, and he believed.

Peter and John still didn't understand. They hadn't known Jesus would come back to life.

Peter and John went home. But Mary Magdalene stayed there. She stood outside the grave. She cried.

Then she bent over and looked inside the grave. There she saw two angels. They wore white clothes. They sat where the body of Jesus had been. One angel sat where his head had been. The other angel sat where his feet had been.

"Why are you crying?" asked the angels.

"Somebody took Jesus' body away," said Mary. "I don't know where they took it."

Mary turned around. She saw a man. It was Jesus standing there. But Mary didn't know it was Jesus.

"Why are you crying?" asked Jesus. "Who are you looking for?"

Mary thought he was the gardener. She asked, "Did you take Jesus' body away? If you did, please tell me where you put it. I'll come and get it."

"Mary," said Jesus.

Mary looked at Jesus. "Teacher!" she cried.

"Don't try to hold on to me," said Jesus. "I haven't gone back to my Father yet. Go find my friends. Tell them I'm going to my Father and your Father. I'm going to my God and your God."

So Mary hurried to find Jesus' friends. "I've seen Jesus!" she said. And she told them what Jesus had said to her.

The Guards' Story

MATTHEW 28:11-15

Some of the guards went back into the city. They told some leaders at the worship house what happened.

The leaders made a plan. They paid the guards lots of money to tell a lie.

The leaders made up a story for the guards to tell. "Say that Jesus' friends came while it was night and you were sleeping. Say that Jesus' friends took his body away.

"Pilate might hear what happened," said the Jewish leaders. "But we'll take care of Pilate. We'll make sure you stay out of trouble."

So the guards took the money. They said just what the leaders told them to say. They told their story to many of the Jewish people. And these people still tell that story, even today.

OCTOBER 8

Two Friends on the Road

MARK 16:12-13; LUKE 24:13-33

Now there was a little town called Emmaus. It was about seven miles away from Jerusalem. Two of Jesus' friends were walking to Emmaus. They were talking about the bad things that had happened to Jesus.

While they were talking, Jesus came up to them. He began to talk with them. But they were kept from knowing who he was.

"What are you talking about?" asked Jesus.

The two friends stopped walking.

They stood still. Their faces were very sad.

One was Cleopas. "Are you the only person in Jerusalem who hasn't heard?" he asked. "Don't you know what's been happening there?"

"What?" asked Jesus.

"It's about Jesus," they said. "He was a prophet. What he said was powerful. What he did was powerful. But our leaders at the worship house had him killed. We hoped he would save our nation.

"Now two days have passed," they said. "It's the third day since this happened. Women from our group told us something surprising. Early this morning they went to the grave. But Jesus' body wasn't there. The women said they saw angels. These angels told them Jesus is alive!

"Then some men from our group went to the grave," they said. "It was just like the women said. They didn't see Jesus!"

"You have a lot to learn!" said Jesus. "It takes you a while to believe what the prophets said! Didn't the Promised One have to go through these things?"

Then Jesus began telling them about Moses and the prophets. He made it all very clear. He told them what God's Word said about himself.

They came to the town where

they were going. Jesus acted like he would go on from there.

"Stay with us," said the two followers. "The day is almost over."

So Jesus went to stay with them.

When they sat down to eat, Jesus picked up the bread. He thanked God for it. Then he started giving it to his friends. That's when they were able to see it was Jesus! Suddenly, he was gone!

The two followers looked at each other. "Wasn't it wonderful when he talked on the road?" they said. "It was wonderful when he told us what God's Word meant."

They got up and hurried back to Jerusalem.

In a Locked Room
MARK 16:14; LUKE 24:33-44; JOHN 20:19-29

Cleopas and the other follower from Emmaus found Jesus' followers. Jesus' special friends were there too. They were together in a locked room. They kept the doors locked. They were afraid of their own Jewish leaders.

"It's true," Jesus' friends said. "Jesus has come back to life. Peter saw him."

The two from Emmaus told what happened to them. They told how Jesus shared the bread. They told how they knew then that he was Jesus!

They kept talking about this. All of a sudden, there was Jesus! He was standing right there with them.

"Be at peace!" Jesus said.

They were scared. They thought they were seeing a ghost.

"Why are you scared?" asked Jesus. "Why do you wonder if I'm real? Look at my hands. Look at my feet. It's me! Touch me. See? A ghost doesn't have skin and bones like I have."

Then Jesus showed them his hands. He showed them his feet. They were surprised. They were full of joy. But they could hardly believe their eyes.

"Do you have anything to eat here?" Jesus asked.

They brought him some cooked fish. He ate it.

"Remember when I was still with you?" said Jesus.

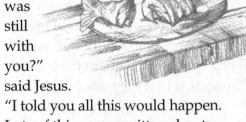

"I told you all this would happen. Lots of things are written about me in God's Word. Moses wrote about me. The prophets wrote about me. The psalms are about me. Everything written about me has to come true."

Then Jesus said, "God the Father

sent me. Now I'm sending you."
Jesus breathed on them. "I'm giving
the Holy Spirit to you," he said.

Thomas wasn't there that night.
Jesus' other friends told him, "We
saw the Lord!"

Thomas said, "I don't believe it. I'm
not going to believe. First I'd have to
see the nail marks in his hands. I'd
have to touch the places where the
nails were. I'd have to put my hand
on his side where the spear went in."

A week later, Jesus' friends were in
the same house. Thomas was there
too. They still kept the doors locked.

Jesus came again. He stood with
his friends. "Be at peace!" he said.

Then he turned to Thomas.
"Thomas, put your finger here," he
said. "Touch my side. Look at my
hands. Stop thinking that this is just
a story. Believe!"

"My Lord and my God!" said
Thomas.

"You believe because you see
me," said Jesus. "Some people don't
see me. They believe anyway. God
will send good things to them."

OCTOBER 9

Going Fishing

JOHN 21:1-12

Peter, Thomas, Nathanael, James,
John, and two other friends were
together.

"I think I'll go fishing," said Peter.
"We'll go with you," said the
others.

So off they went. They got into
their boat and went fishing. But that
night they didn't catch anything.

At last the sun began to come up.
There was Jesus, standing on the
shore. But his friends couldn't tell it
was Jesus.

"Don't you have any fish, my
friends?" Jesus called to them.

"No," they called back.

"Throw your net into the water
on the right side of your boat. You'll
find some fish there," said Jesus.

So they threw their net over on
the boat's right side. Lots of fish got
caught in the net. The net got very
heavy. Jesus' friends couldn't even
pull it in.

"It's the Lord!" said John.

Peter heard John. Right away, he
pulled his clothes around him. He
had taken most of them off. Then
he jumped into the water.

The other friends followed in
the boat. They were only about 100
yards from the shore. They had the
net full of fish with them.

A camp fire was going when
they got near the shore. Fish were
cooking on it. There was bread, too.

"Bring some of the fish you
caught," said Jesus.

Peter climbed back into the boat.
He pulled the net to the shore. The

net was full. There were 153 big fish! But the net didn't break.

"Come have some breakfast," said Jesus.

Jesus' friends didn't dare ask him, "Who are you?" They knew he was Jesus.

Do You Love Me?

JOHN 21:13-24

Jesus gave his friends bread and fish for breakfast. They ate it.

Then Jesus turned to Peter. "Peter, do you love me more than anyone else?" he asked.

"Yes," said Peter. "You know I love you."

"Then feed my lambs," said Jesus.

"Peter, do you really love me?" asked Jesus.

"Yes," said Peter. "You know I love you."

"Then take care of my sheep," said Jesus.

Jesus asked again, "Peter, do you love me?"

Now Peter was upset. Jesus had asked three times, "Do you love me?"

"You know everything, Lord," said Peter. "You know I love you."

"Then feed my sheep," said Jesus. "You were younger once. You dressed yourself. You chose where to go, and you went. But someday you'll be old. Then you'll reach out

your hands. Somebody else will dress you. They'll take you where you don't want to go." Jesus was talking about the way Peter would die.

Then Jesus said to Peter, "Follow me."

Peter looked around. He saw John following them. "What about John?" Peter asked.

"What if I want him to stay alive? What if he lives until I come back?" said Jesus. "What does that have to do with you? You just follow me."

Now some of Jesus' followers began saying John wouldn't die. But Jesus didn't say John wouldn't die. He only said, "What if I want him to stay alive?"

John is the one who wrote this. He saw and heard these things. So we know that what he wrote is true.

Going into the Clouds

MATTHEW 28:18-20; MARK 16:15, 19; LUKE 24:45-53; Acts 1:6-11

"I've been given the right to be in charge. I'm in charge of heaven and earth," Jesus told his 11 special friends. "So I'm telling you to go. Make followers for me in all nations. Baptize them in the Father's name, the Son's name, and the Holy Spirit's name. Teach people to obey everything I've told you.

"I'll always be with you," said

Jesus. "Even to the very end of time."

Jesus helped his friends understand what God's Word meant. "It was all written down," said Jesus. "God's Word says that the Promised One would die. It says he would come back to life.

"God's Word says people will teach about him in all nations. Then people will be sorry about their sins. They'll change their ways," said Jesus. "They'll be forgiven. All this will start in Jerusalem. You've seen it all. You can tell about it.

"I'll send you the gift my Father has promised," said Jesus. "But stay in Jerusalem for a while. Stay there until the Father gives you power."

Jesus led his special friends to a place close to Bethany. Then he lifted his hands up. He prayed for God to bring good to them.

"Is it time now?" asked Jesus' friends. "Will God's people be a kingdom again?"

"You can't know the times," said Jesus. "You can't know when things are going to happen. The Father has planned them. He is in charge. But you'll get power when the Holy Spirit comes to you. You'll tell people about me.

"You'll teach about me in Jerusalem," said Jesus. "You'll teach about me in Judea. You'll teach about me in Samaria. In fact, you'll teach about me all over the world."

Then Jesus went up off the ground. His friends watched until a cloud hid him. They peered up into the sky.

Suddenly, they saw two men standing by them. The men were dressed all in white.

"Men from Galilee!" said the two men. "Why are you just standing here? Why are you peering into the sky? Jesus has gone up into heaven. He will come back the same way you saw him go."

Jesus' special friends worshiped him. Then they went back to Jerusalem. Their hearts were full of joy. They stayed at the worship house. They cheered for God there.

God's Kingdom Grows

Another Leader

ACTS 1:1-5, 12-26

To the one who loves God,

Once before, I wrote a book about Jesus. It told about what Jesus said and did until he went to heaven. Before he left, Jesus told his best friends what to do.

Jesus had gone through a lot of pain. He had died. Then he showed up alive. His followers saw him many times for 40 days. He told them about God's kingdom.

Once Jesus said to his friends, "Don't leave Jerusalem. Wait for the gift my Father promised to give you. You heard me talk about it. John baptized people with water. But soon you'll be baptized with the Holy Spirit."

Now Jesus had gone back to heaven. After he left, his best friends went back to Jerusalem. It wasn't even a mile away from the place where Jesus left them.

Jesus' friends went to the house where they were staying. They went upstairs to their room.

Peter was there. John, James, and Andrew were there. Philip was there with Thomas, Nathanael, and Matthew. The other James was there too. Simon and the other Judas were there. They kept praying together. Jesus' brothers and his mother, Mary, met with them. And some other women were there.

About 120 other people were there too. They were all people who believed in Jesus.

Peter stood up in the group. He said, "God's Word about Judas had to come true. Judas was one of us. He helped with the work we did. But our leaders paid Judas money. So he showed them where Jesus was.

"The Holy Spirit helped David write about Judas long ago," said Peter. "David wrote, 'Let another person be a leader in his place.' So we have to choose someone to take the place of Judas.

"Who has been with us from the start?" asked Peter. "Who has been with us since John started baptizing people in water? Who was with us when Jesus went back to heaven? It must be someone who can tell what he has seen. He must tell how Jesus came back to life."

Now Justus had been with them from the start. Matthias had too. So they prayed. "God, you know what's in people's hearts. Show us the man you choose. He will take the place of Judas."

Then they rolled dice. Matthias won. So he became one of the 12. These 12 helpers were now called apostles. That's because they were being sent to tell everyone about Jesus.

Wind, Fire, and Different Languages

ACTS 2:1-24, 31-33, 36-47

It was time for the Holiday of Weeks. Jesus' friends got together at someone's house.

All of a sudden, they heard a sound. It sounded like a strong wind blowing. The sound came from heaven. It filled the whole house.

Then they saw something that looked like fire. The fire broke into

different parts. It came to sit on each of them.

Then God's Holy Spirit filled them. They started talking in different languages. God's Spirit made them able to do this.

Jews from every country were in Jerusalem. They had come for the holiday. They were people who worshiped God. They heard the sound too. They wondered about it.

Soon a crowd of people gathered around Jesus' friends. They heard Jesus' friends talking in languages they could understand.

The people were very surprised. "Aren't these men from around here?" they asked. "Why do we hear them talking in our own language? People from all nations hear them talking about God's wonders. We can understand them!"

The people didn't know what to think. "What do you think it means?" they asked each other.

Some people laughed at Jesus' friends. "They've just had too much wine to drink," they said.

Peter stood up with the other 11 apostles. He talked loudly to the big crowd. "Let me tell you about this," he said. "Listen very carefully. These men are not drunk like you think they are. After all, it's only nine o'clock in the morning!

"Long ago, Joel told about God's

plans," said Peter. "You are seeing what the prophet Joel wrote about. He wrote what God said:

"My Spirit will flow out on all
      people.
   Your children will tell my plans.
Your old men will dream dreams.
   Your young men will have
      dreams even when they are
      awake.
My Spirit will flow out on all my
      servants.
   Men and women will tell my
      plans.
I'll show you wonders in the sky.
   I'll show you signs on the earth.
The sun will get dark.
   The moon will look like blood.
That will happen before the Lord's
      great day comes.
   Everyone who calls on the Lord's
      name will be saved.

"So listen, you people of God," said Peter. "God showed you how special Jesus is by the wonders he did. God did these through Jesus.

"God had a plan," said Peter. "Because of God's plan, Jesus was given to you. Sinful men helped you kill him on the cross. But God brought him back to life again. He set Jesus free from death. There was no way death could keep him down.

"Jesus was not left in the grave," said Peter. "His body did not waste away. God brought him back to life again. All of us can tell you we saw him.

"Jesus is beside God now," said Peter. "His Father gave him the Holy Spirit as he promised. And Jesus has now given us that Spirit. That's what you are seeing and hearing now.

"You killed Jesus," said Peter. "But God has made him the Lord."

People were very sad when they heard this. "What will we do?" they asked Jesus' friends.

"Be sorry," said Peter. "Change your ways. Be baptized in Jesus' name. All of you. Then he will forgive your sins. Then you'll get the gift of God's Holy Spirit. That's a promise. This gift is for you and your children. It's for people near and far. It's for anybody God calls into his kingdom."

Peter talked to the people about lots of things. "Save yourselves from this sinful world," he begged.

People who believed were baptized. About 3,000 people came into God's kingdom that day. Those people listened to Jesus' helpers teach. They got together to talk and eat and pray. Everybody had a feeling of wonder.

Jesus' 12 helpers did lots of wonders. People who believed shared what they had. They even sold what they had. Then they gave to people who needed help.

They kept meeting every day at the worship house. They ate together in their homes. They were happy, and their love for Jesus was real. They praised God.

All people said good things about Jesus' followers. Every day, more people were saved. God added them to his kingdom.

The Man at Beautiful Gate

ACTS 3

Peter and John went to the worship house one afternoon. It was about three o'clock. It was time for people to come and pray.

Some people came in carrying a man. They were taking him to the gate called Beautiful Gate. It led to the worship house.

This man couldn't walk. So he sat at the gate every day. People going in the gate could see him. He'd beg for money there.

The man saw Peter and John. They were about to go in the gate. So he asked them for money.

Peter and John looked right at the man. "Look at us!" said Peter.

The man looked at them. He thought they were going to give him some money.

"I don't have any silver or gold," said Peter. "But I do have something else. That's what I'll give you. In Jesus' name, get up and walk."

Then Peter reached out and took the man's right hand. Peter helped the man get up.

Right away, the man's feet got strong. He jumped up and started walking.

The man went with Peter and John. They all went into a closed-in yard outside the worship house.

Now the man was not only walking. He was jumping, too! And he was praising God.

All the people saw him. They saw who he was. He was the man who used to beg at the gate. People were very surprised. They wondered how he could walk.

The man held on to Peter and John. People came running up to them.

Peter said, "Why are you surprised? You're looking at us as if our power made him well. But God did this. He showed the power and greatness of Jesus.

"You let Jesus be killed," said Peter. "Pilate wanted to let him go. But you wouldn't stand up for Jesus. Instead, you asked Pilate to let a killer go free. You killed the one who gave you life. But God made Jesus alive again. We saw it happen.

"Now you see a man you know," said Peter. "He is well because we believe in Jesus. Jesus' name and this man's faith made him well. You can see for yourselves.

"You didn't know what you were doing when you killed Jesus. Your leaders didn't know what they were doing," said Peter. "So be sorry. Come back to God. Then your sins can be cleaned out of your hearts. God can make you feel like new.

"Jesus has to stay in heaven until the right time," said Peter. "When it's time, God will make everything new again. He promised it long ago. Moses said, 'God will send someone who tells his plans. He will be someone from your own people. Listen to everything he says. If you don't, you'll be left out of God's kingdom.'

"All God's prophets told about what was coming," said Peter. "Now you have it! You have what God promised long ago to Abraham. God promised that he would bring good to everyone. He said he'd do it through Abraham's family.

"Now God has brought good to you. He has sent Jesus to help you turn away from sin."

Plain Men and Proud Leaders

ACTS 4:1-24, 29-37

The priests and other leaders at the worship house walked up. The captain of the guards was with them. They heard Peter and John. They were very upset. That's because Peter and John were saying Jesus was alive again. So the leaders put Peter and John in jail.

But lots of people had heard Peter and John. So lots of people believed in Jesus. There were now more than 5,000 people who believed.

The next day, the leaders met together. They brought Peter and John in. They began to ask them questions. "What power did you call on? Whose name did you use to make the man well?"

Peter was full of the Holy Spirit. He said, "We did something kind for a man who couldn't walk. Now we are here, being asked questions. So I'll tell you the answer. The man was made well by the name of Jesus.

"You killed Jesus," said Peter. "But God brought him back to life again! He is like 'a stone the builders didn't want. Now that stone holds up the whole building.' Nobody else can save you. There is no other name under heaven that can save."

The worship-house leaders could tell several things about Peter and John. They could tell that these men hadn't gone to school very much. They were plain men. But they were being very brave. The leaders were surprised about that. They could tell that Peter and John had been with Jesus.

The leaders could clearly see the man who had been made well. He was standing there with Peter and John. So there wasn't anything they could say.

The leaders told Peter and John to leave for a few minutes. Then they had a talk. "What should we do about these men?" they asked. "Everyone in the city knows about this wonder. We can't say it didn't happen. But we must stop these men from saying Jesus is alive."

So they told Peter and John to come back in. Then they told them not to teach about Jesus.

But Peter and John had an answer for the leaders. "What do you think God would say? Is it right to obey you or God?" they asked. "We can't stop talking about what we saw and heard."

The leaders tried to scare Peter and John. "You'll be sorry if you keep this up," they said.

Then they let Peter and John go. They couldn't think of what to do. All the people were praising God for what he had done. The man who was made well was not young. He was more than 40 years old.

Peter and John went back to their friends. They told them what the leaders at the worship house had said. Then everyone prayed. "Great God, you made heaven, earth, and sea. You made everything in them.

"Now look at what our leaders are saying," they prayed. "Make us brave. Then we can say what you want us to say. Reach out to make people well. Do your wonders by the power of Jesus' name."

When they finished praying, the room shook. God's Holy Spirit filled all of them. So they became brave and talked about God.

Everyone who believed in Jesus felt the same. Nobody said that what he owned was just his. Instead, Jesus' followers shared what they had.

The 12 apostles kept telling people that Jesus was alive. They spoke with great power. God's kind love was with them.

No believer was so poor that he didn't have the things he needed. That's because some people sold their land or buildings. Then they gathered the money they made. They gave it to the men who had been with Jesus, his apostles. The apostles gave it to people who needed it.

OCTOBER 13

A Locked Jail

ACTS 5:1–6:1

Ananias and his wife, Sapphira, sold some of their land. They kept part of the money for themselves. But they didn't tell anyone else that they kept some of it. They gave the rest of the money to the apostles.

"Ananias," said Peter. "How did your heart get so full of Satan? You lied to the Holy Spirit. You kept some of the money for yourself.

"Didn't the land belong to you?" said Peter. "Then you sold it. You could have done whatever you wanted with the money. Why did you need to lie? You haven't lied to people. You have lied to God."

Then Ananias fell down and died. Everybody who heard about it was afraid. Some young men came and covered his body. They took it out and put it in a grave.

Three hours passed. Then Sapphira came in. She didn't know what had happened to her husband, Ananias.

"Tell me something," said Peter. "Is this how much money you got for your land?"

"Yes," said Sapphira. "That's how much we got."

"How could you and your husband plan this lie together? How could you test God's Holy Spirit?" asked Peter. "Some men are at the door. They just put your husband's body in a grave. They'll carry your body out too."

Then Sapphira fell down at Peter's feet. She died. The young men came in. They put Sapphira's body in a grave too.

All of Jesus' followers were afraid. So was anyone else who heard about what happened.

The 12 apostles did lots of wonders. All of Jesus' followers met together at the worship house. They met at a place called Solomon's Walk. Nobody dared to meet with them. But people said good things about them.

More and more people believed in Jesus. So people began to bring sick people out to the streets. They would lay them on mats. They would watch for Peter to walk down the street. They hoped Peter's shadow would pass over some of the sick people.

Crowds of people came from nearby towns. They brought sick people with them. They brought people who were bothered by bad spirits. All of the people got well.

The high priest and his friends were mad. They wanted people to forget about Jesus and his friends. So they put the apostles in jail.

That night, an angel opened the jail doors. He brought the men out of jail. He said, "Go on. Stand in the yards of the worship house. Tell the people all about the new life they can have."

So when morning came, the apostles went to the worship house. They started teaching people again.

The high priest and his friends got together. The other Jewish leaders were there too. They sent some men to the jail to get the apostles.

But the men couldn't find the apostles in jail. The men went back to the high priest. "The jail was locked tight," they said. "Guards were standing at the doors. So we opened the doors, but nobody was in there."

The leaders couldn't figure it out. They wondered what would happen next.

Then somebody came in. "Look at this!" he said. "The people you put in jail are at the worship house. They're teaching the people again."

Then the captain of the worship-house guards took some guards with him. They brought the apostles back. They treated them nicely. They didn't want to be too hard on them. They were afraid of what the people might do.

They took the apostles to the high priest. "We told you not to teach about Jesus," he said. "But you are filling this city with your teaching. You are blaming us for killing Jesus."

"We have to obey God, not men,"
said Peter and the others. "God made Jesus come back to life. You had him killed on a cross. But God lifted him up to sit at his right side.

"Jesus is the Prince," said Peter. "He saves us. He forgives our sins. We've seen these things happen. The Holy Spirit shows us that these things are true. God gives the Holy Spirit to people who obey him."

The leaders were very angry to hear this. They wanted to kill the apostles.

But there was one leader named Gamaliel. He was a teacher. Everyone looked up to him. He stood up. He asked the apostles to step outside for a minute.

Then Gamaliel talked to the other leaders. "Think carefully about what you plan to do," he said. "Remember Theudas? He said he was somebody important. About 400 people followed him. But Theudas was killed. And his followers stopped making trouble for us.

"Then there was Judas from Galilee," said Gamaliel. "Judas led a group of people against us. He was killed too. And his followers stopped making trouble for us.

"So I say we should leave these men alone," said Gamaliel. "What if this teaching is just their idea? Then they won't keep it up for long. But what if it's God's idea? Then you won't be able to stop them no matter what you do. You'll be fighting God."

What Gamaliel said made sense to the leaders. So they brought the apostles back in. They had some men beat them. The leaders told them not to talk about Jesus anymore. Then they let the men go.

The apostles were glad when they left. They were glad to be good enough to go through all of this. They were glad to do it for Jesus. Every day, they went to the worship house. They went to people's houses, too. They kept teaching the Good News about Jesus. The number of followers kept growing and growing.

OCTOBER 14

Stephen Sees Jesus

ACTS 6:1–8:2

Now there were some women whose husbands had died. Every day, the apostles would bring these women some food. But some of the women began to fuss. They said they weren't getting any of the food.

So Jesus' 12 apostles got together with the other followers to talk about it. "Our job is to teach God's Word," they said. "Instead, we take time to put food on people's tables. Let's choose seven men to do that job.

They should be men full of God's Spirit. They should be wise. They can take care of the food. Then we can use our time to pray and teach."

That sounded good to everyone. So the people chose Stephen. He was full of faith and the Holy Spirit. Then they chose Philip and five other men. The apostles put their hands on these men and prayed for them.

Then God's Word was shared in more places. More people believed. Many priests became followers of Jesus too.

Now Stephen was full of God's kind love and power. He did great wonders.

Leaders of some of the Jews got mad at Stephen. They questioned him.

But Stephen was very wise. He talked with the Spirit's help. The leaders could not win against him by talking.

So the leaders got together in secret. They told some men to say that Stephen was against God. They told them to say that he was against Moses. So that's what these men said.

People got angry when they heard this. So they took Stephen to the Jewish leaders. They brought in the men who lied.

The men said, "Stephen never stops talking against God's law. He says bad things about the worship house. He says Jesus will tear this place down. He says Jesus will change the way we live."

The leaders looked firmly at Stephen. "Is this true?" they asked.

Stephen said, "Listen! God went to Abraham long ago. He said, 'Leave your country. Leave your people. Go to the land I show you.'

"So Abraham left his land," said Stephen. "God sent him to the land where we are now. Remember what Abraham did. Remember Isaac, Jacob, and Joseph. Remember Moses and Joshua, David and Solomon. It was Solomon who built the worship house.

"But God doesn't live in houses that men make," said Stephen. "Isaiah wrote what God said:

"Heaven is where I rule.
Earth is where I rest my feet.
What kind of house will you build
        for me?
Where will I rest?
My hand made all these things.

"You people are set in your ways!" said Stephen. "You have hearts and ears like people who don't believe in God. You're just like your families from long ago. You always go against the Holy Spirit!

"Long ago, people from your families hurt God's prophets," said Stephen. "They killed people who said Jesus would come. And now

you have killed Jesus. You have the Law that angels put in place. But you have not obeyed it."

The leaders were so angry they couldn't stand it. But Stephen was full of the Holy Spirit. He looked up to heaven. There he saw God's shining greatness.

"Look!" said Stephen. "I see heaven! It's open. Jesus is standing at God's right side!"

The leaders covered their ears. They began yelling as loudly as they could. They ran toward Stephen. They pulled him out of the city. They started throwing rocks at him.

The rocks were hitting Stephen. But he prayed, "Lord Jesus, take my spirit." He bowed down. He called, "Lord, don't blame them for this sin." After he said that, he died.

There was a young man watching all this. His name was Saul. He said that killing Stephen was the right thing to do.

Some of Jesus' followers put Stephen's body in a grave. They were very sad about what had happened.

OCTOBER 15

Simon, the Magic Man
ACTS 8:1, 3-25

This was the beginning of hard times for Jesus' followers. People turned against them and hurt them in many ways. That's why many of Jesus' followers left the city. They went here and there to live. Only the apostles stayed.

Saul tried to get rid of Jesus' followers. He went from one house to another. He pulled men and women out of their houses. He put them in jail.

But Jesus' followers who left the city taught about Jesus.

Philip went to a city in Samaria. He told the people there about Jesus. He did wonders. Big crowds of people listened carefully to him. Bad spirits would yell and come out of people. People who could not move or walk were made well. The people were very glad.

Now a man named Simon lived there. Simon had done magic for a long time. The people watched him with wonder. Simon bragged that he was somebody great. Everybody listened to him.

People said, "Simon has the power of the gods. He is called the Great Power." They followed him because they liked to watch his magic.

But now people believed the Good News that Philip told them. They believed in God's kingdom, and they believed in Jesus. They were baptized.

Even Simon believed. He was baptized, too. He followed Philip wherever he went. Simon was very surprised by the wonders he saw.

The apostles in Jerusalem heard what was happening. So they sent Peter and John to Samaria.

When Peter and John got there, they prayed for the people. They prayed for the people to get the Holy Spirit. That's because the Holy Spirit had not come on them yet. They had only been baptized in Jesus' name.

So Peter and John put their hands on people. Then the Holy Spirit came to the people.

Simon watched. He talked to Peter and John about it. He wanted to pay them so he could do what they did. "Give me this power," he said. "I want to put my hands on people. Then I want them to get the Holy Spirit."

"You should die and take your money with you," said Peter. "You think you can buy God's gift with money! You're not part of what we do. The way God sees it, your heart doesn't want to do what's right.

"Be sorry for your sins," said Peter. "Change. Pray to God. Maybe he will forgive you for even thinking you could buy this gift. I can tell your heart is full of anger. Sin has control of you."

"Pray to God for me," said Simon.

"Then nothing you talked about will happen to me."

Peter and John taught about God's Word. Then they went back to Jerusalem. They stopped in many towns in Samaria on the way. They taught the Good News to many people.

A Chariot Ride

ACTS 8:26-40

One of God's angels came to Philip. "Go to the road south of here," he said. "It's the desert road."

Philip found the road. He started traveling down it. On his way, he met a man from Ethiopia. This man was an important leader. He was in charge of Queen Candace's riches. He had been to Jerusalem to worship. Now he was on his way home in his chariot. As he rode, he read the book Isaiah wrote.

The Spirit said to Philip, "Go up to that chariot. Stay close to it."

So Philip ran up to the chariot. He heard the man reading the book Isaiah wrote. "Do you understand what you're reading?" Philip asked.

"How can I understand?" asked the man. "I don't have anyone to tell me what it means." Then he asked Philip to sit with him in the chariot.

The man was reading this part of Isaiah:

He was taken like a sheep to be killed.
A sheep is quiet
    while the farmer cuts off its wool.
    He was quiet too.
They treated him like nothing.
    What they did to him was not fair.

"Tell me something," said the man from Ethiopia. "Who is Isaiah talking about? Is he talking about himself? Or is he talking about somebody else?"

Then Philip answered him.

He began by talking about the book that Isaiah wrote. Philip told about the part that the man was reading. He told the man about Jesus' Good News.

As they traveled, they came to some water. "Look," said the man. "Here's some water. I see no reason why I can't be baptized." He told the driver to stop the chariot.

Philip and the man went down into the water. Philip dipped him in the water.

They came up out of the water. Then God's Spirit took Philip away. The man didn't see Philip again. But the man was happy. He went on his way.

Philip showed up in the city of Azotus. He began to travel through many towns. In every town, he told people about Jesus.

A Bright Light and a Voice

ACTS 9:1-31

All this time, Saul was planning ways to hurt Jesus' followers. He went to the high priest in Jerusalem. He asked him to write some letters. The letters would go to the worship houses in Damascus. The letters would give Saul the right to take Jesus' followers to jail.

Saul headed for Damascus. All of a sudden, a bright light came from heaven. It shone down on Saul.

Saul fell down. He heard a voice. "Saul, Saul, why are you hurting me?"

"Who are you?" asked Saul.

"I'm Jesus," said the voice. "I'm the one you're hurting. Get up. Go into the city of Damascus. Someone there will tell you what to do."

The men who were with Saul just stood there. They didn't know what to say. They heard the sound of the voice. But they couldn't see anybody.

Saul got up and opened his eyes. But he couldn't see anything. So his friends took his hand. They led him into the city.

Saul couldn't see for three days. All that time, he didn't eat or drink anything.

Now there was a man named Ananias in Damascus. He was a follower of Jesus. Jesus called to him, "Ananias!"

"Here I am, Jesus," said Ananias.

"Go to Straight Street," said Jesus. "Go to the house of a man named Judas. Ask for a man named Saul. He is praying there. He saw a man with your name in a dream. In his dream, you put your hands on him. Then he could see again."

"I've heard about Saul," said Ananias. "Lord, he has hurt your people in Jerusalem. He is here to put your people in jail."

"Go!" said Jesus. "I chose this man to serve me. He will tell people who aren't Jews about me. He will tell their kings. He will tell Jews, too. I'll show him how much he will have to face for following me."

Ananias found the house. He went in and put his hands on Saul. "Saul," he said. "The Lord Jesus came to you on the road. He sent me here so you can see again. He sent me so you can be filled with God's Holy Spirit."

Right away, a small, thin cover fell off Saul's eyes. Now he could see again. He got up, and he was baptized. Then he ate and felt stronger.

Saul stayed in Damascus for a few days. Right away, he started teaching in the town's worship houses. He told everyone that Jesus is God's Son.

People were surprised. "Isn't he the man who made trouble in Jerusalem?" they asked. "He made trouble for Jesus' followers there. And he came here to put Jesus' followers in jail."

Saul got better and better at teaching about Jesus. The Jews in Damascus couldn't understand it. Saul was showing people that God sent Jesus to save them.

Many days passed. The Jews made plans to kill Saul. Every day and night, they watched the city gates. The gates were in the wall around the city. The Jews were going to kill Saul when he left.

Saul found out about their plan. So one night, Saul's friends took him to the city wall. Saul got into a big basket. His friends put the basket through an open place in the wall. Then they let it down to the ground.

Saul went back to Jerusalem. There he tried to meet with Jesus'

followers. But they were afraid of him. They didn't believe he had really become a follower of Jesus.

But Barnabas took Saul to the apostles. Barnabas told them about Saul's trip to Damascus. He told them how Jesus talked to Saul. He told them how Saul taught people about Jesus. So they let Saul stay with them.

Saul went wherever he wanted to go in Jerusalem. He was brave. He taught in Jesus' name. He talked to Jews from Greece about Jesus. But they tried to kill him. So some of Jesus' followers sent Saul to Tarsus. That was his home town.

Then things were peaceful for Jesus' followers. They grew stronger. The Holy Spirit made them brave. Many people became Jesus' followers. They worshiped the Lord.

Peter Travels

ACTS 9:32-43

Peter traveled from place to place. He went to see God's people in Lydda. A man who could not move lived there. He'd had to stay in bed for eight years. Peter went to see him.

"Jesus makes you well," said Peter. "Get up, and make up your bed."

Right away, the man got up. The people who lived there saw him walking. They started believing in Jesus.

A woman named Dorcas lived in Joppa. She did good things. She helped poor people. But she got sick and died. Her body was put in an upstairs room.

Jesus' followers in Joppa heard that Peter was in Lydda. The towns were close together. So the followers sent two men to see Peter. "Please come right away!" they said.

So Peter went with them to the place where Dorcas was. They took him upstairs. Women were standing around. They showed Peter the clothes Dorcas had made.

Peter told them to leave the room. Then he got down and prayed. He looked at the woman. "Dorcas, get up," he said.

Dorcas opened her eyes. When she saw Peter, she sat up.

Peter held her hand and helped her stand up. Then he called her friends in. He gave Dorcas back to them. She was alive again!

Everybody in town found out what had happened. So lots of people believed in Jesus.

Peter stayed there for a while with a man named Simon.

OCTOBER 17

Animals in a Big Sheet

ACTS 10

There was a Roman army captain named Cornelius. He lived in the city of Caesarea. He and his family were good people who believed in God. He prayed to God often. And he gave a lot of his money to poor people.

One afternoon around three o'clock, Cornelius saw one of God's angels. He saw it very clearly.

The angel came to him and said, "Cornelius!"

Cornelius was afraid. "What, Lord?" he said.

"Your prayers have been a gift to God," said the angel. "Your gifts to poor people have been gifts to God. Now send some men to Joppa. Ask them to bring Peter back. He is staying with Simon in a house by the sea."

The angel left. Cornelius called in two servants and one army man. He told them what had happened. Then he sent them to find Peter in Joppa.

The next day Peter was praying. He was up on the flat roof of Simon's house. It was about noon. The men Cornelius sent were coming into the city.

As Peter was praying, he got hungry. So someone in the house started making lunch for him. While Peter waited, he saw a picture in his mind. It was a picture God was showing him.

Peter saw heaven open up. Something that looked like a big sheet came down. It was held up by its corners. Different kinds of animals were in the sheet. There were animals with four feet. There were animals like snakes and turtles. And there were birds.

A voice said, "Get up, Peter. Choose one of these to eat."

"I can't, Lord!" said Peter. "These are not the animals you allow us to eat."

Then the voice talked again. "God says it's all right. So don't say you can't."

The same thing happened three times. Then the sheet was pulled back up into heaven. Peter wondered what this meant.

Now the men sent by Cornelius found where Simon's house was. They stopped by the gate. They called, "Is Peter staying here?"

At the same time, the Holy Spirit told Peter, "Get up. Go downstairs. Three men are here. They are looking for you. I sent them here, so go with them."

Peter went down to see the men. He said, "I'm Peter. Why are you here?"

"Cornelius sent us," they answered. "He is a captain in the Roman army. He is a good man. He believes in God. All the Jews say good things about him. An angel told Cornelius to bring you to his house. Then he can hear what you have to tell him."

Peter asked the men to come into Simon's house. They stayed there that night.

The next day, Peter went with them. Some of Jesus' other followers went too. The day after that, they came to the town where Cornelius lived.

Peter went to see Cornelius at his house. Cornelius was waiting for him and bowed down at Peter's feet.

"Stand up," said Peter. "I'm just a man like you are!"

Peter and Cornelius talked. Then they went inside. Peter saw many people there. Cornelius had asked his family and some good friends to come over.

Peter began to talk to them. "You know the law of Jewish people. We're not supposed to visit someone who is not Jewish. But God showed me that it's all right with him. So I would not say I couldn't come. Now I'm here. Why did you ask me to come?"

Cornelius told Peter about the angel he saw. "I sent for you right away," said Cornelius. "It's good that you came. We are all here. We want to listen to whatever God wants you to say."

So Peter talked to them. "I see now that it's true," he said. "God doesn't love one person more than another. He loves people from every nation. He welcomes everyone who looks up to him and does what is right.

"God sent the Good News to his people. It's Good News about the peace Jesus brings," said Peter. "Jesus is the Lord of everything. You know how God gave Jesus his Holy Spirit. God gave him power. You know the good things Jesus did. You know how he made people well. That's because God was with him.

"We saw what Jesus did," said Peter. "He was killed on a cross. But God made him alive again. Some of us saw him. We even ate and drank with him.

"Jesus told us to teach people," said Peter. "He told us to say he is the one God chose. God chose Jesus to judge people. All the prophets tell about him. They say he forgives the sins of everyone who believes in him."

Suddenly, the Holy Spirit came on Cornelius and the others. They talked in other languages. They praised God.

The Jews with Peter were surprised. That's because Cornelius and his friends were not Jewish.

"Can we stop them from being baptized?" asked Peter. "They got the Holy Spirit just like we did."

So they were dipped in water in Jesus' name. Then they asked Peter to stay with them for a while.

OCTOBER 18

The Same Gift

ACTS 11

It wasn't long before the other apostles and followers heard about Cornelius. They heard that people who weren't Jews believed in Jesus.

The Jewish followers fussed at Peter when he came to Jerusalem. "Cornelius and his family aren't Jews," they said. "But you went into their house."

Then Peter told them everything. He told them about his prayer. He told them about the picture in his mind. It was the picture of a sheet with animals. It came down from heaven. He told about the men that Cornelius sent. He told them about his visit with Cornelius and his family. He told how the Holy Spirit had come to them.

"God gave them the same gift he gave us," said Peter. "So how could I stand in God's way?"

Then the Jews who believed in Jesus cheered for God. "God is even saving people who aren't Jews!" they said.

Now Jesus' followers had moved to cities here and there. They had moved after Stephen was killed. They told the Good News about Jesus in many places. But they told it only to Jews.

Then some of Jesus' followers went to Antioch. They started telling the Good News to Greek people. Many of the Greek people believed in Jesus.

Jesus' followers in Jerusalem heard about this. So the church there sent Barnabas to Antioch.

Barnabas saw that it was true. God's kind love was going to the Greeks. Barnabas was glad. He told them to keep believing with their whole hearts.

Barnabas was a good man. He was full of God's Holy Spirit. He was full of faith. Barnabas went to look for Saul in Tarsus. Barnabas found Saul and brought him to Antioch.

Barnabas and Saul stayed in Antioch for a year. They taught lots of people about Jesus. People in Antioch started calling Jesus' followers Christians.

Some prophets came to Antioch from Jerusalem. One of them was named Agabus. He stood up. The Holy Spirit was working in him. He told what was going to happen. He said that bad times were coming. No food would grow.

This came true when Claudius was ruling over the Roman kings. So Jesus' followers thought they'd help God's people in Judea. They got a gift together. They sent the gift to Judea with Barnabas and Saul.

The Angel in the Jail
ACTS 12

King Herod put some of Jesus' followers in jail. He planned to give Jesus' followers lots of trouble. He had James killed with a sword. James was John's brother. He was one of Jesus' 12 apostles.

The Jewish people were glad that James was killed. So Herod took Peter, too. He put Peter in jail.

It was time for one of the Jewish holidays. Herod sent four groups of guards to watch Peter. Each group had four men in it.

Herod's plan was to judge Peter after the holiday. So he kept Peter in jail. But Jesus' followers were praying hard for Peter.

One night, Peter was sleeping in jail. The next day Herod was going to judge him. One guard was sleeping beside Peter on his right. Another guard was sleeping beside Peter on his left. Peter was chained between them. There were also guards at the door.

All of a sudden, an angel was there. A light shone into the jail room. The angel tapped Peter's side and woke him up.

"Hurry!" said the angel. "Get up!" Peter's chains fell off.

"Put your clothes on," said the angel. "Put your shoes on."

So Peter did.

"Put your coat around you. Then follow me," said the angel.

Peter followed the angel out of the jail. But Peter thought he was dreaming. He didn't know it was really happening.

They walked past the first guard. They passed the next guard. They came to an iron gate that led to the city. It opened by itself. They walked right through. They walked down one street. Then the angel left.

Now Peter saw that he wasn't dreaming. "The Lord sent his angel!" said Peter. "He saved me from Herod. He saved me from everything the Jewish people were planning!"

Peter went to the house where John Mark's mother lived. That's where lots of people were praying that night. Peter tapped on the door.

A servant girl came to the door. Her name was Rhoda. She heard Peter's voice and knew it was him. She was so happy, she forgot to open the door.

Rhoda ran back to the others. "Peter is at the door!" she said.

"You're crazy," they said.

But Rhoda promised it was Peter. "Maybe it's his angel," they said.

Peter kept tapping at the door.

At last they opened the door. They saw that it really was Peter. They were very surprised.

Peter held his hand up to show they should be quiet. He told them how God had saved him. "Tell

Jesus' brother James about this," he said. "Tell the others, too." Then he left the house. He stayed somewhere else that night.

The next morning there was trouble at the jail. No one knew what had happened to Peter. Herod made everybody look carefully for him. But no one found him. So Herod asked the guards what had happened. Then he gave orders for the guards to be killed.

Now Herod went to Caesarea. He stayed there for a while. He had been fussing with people from Tyre and Sidon. So people from these cities got together. They went to see Herod. They were going to ask Herod for peace. They needed food from Herod's country.

The day of the meeting came. Herod put on his kingly clothes. He sat on his throne. Then he talked to all the people who came.

They shouted, "His voice is the voice of a god!"

Herod let them praise him. He didn't give the praise to God. So at once, an angel from God made him sick. Then worms began to eat him up, and he died.

God's Word was being told everywhere.

Barnabas and Saul finished their job in Jerusalem. Then they went back to Antioch. They took John Mark with them.

Being Bold

ACTS 13:1-16, 23, 27-33, 38-52

There were many prophets and teachers among Jesus' followers in Antioch. Barnabas, Saul, and several others lived there. One of the men had grown up with King Herod.

One day these men were worshiping the Lord. They went without food that day. The Holy Spirit said, "Pick Barnabas and Saul. Send them to do the work I chose them to do."

The men prayed. They put their hands on Barnabas and Saul. Then they sent them on their way.

Barnabas and Saul took John Mark with them. He was their helper.

First they sailed to Cyprus. There they taught God's Word in the towns' worship houses. They went all over the island.

At last they came to the city of Paphos. A Jewish man who did magic lived there. The governor lived there too. He was the leader of the island.

The governor was a smart man. He sent for Barnabas and Saul. He wanted to hear God's Word.

But the man who did magic worked against them. He tried to keep the governor from believing them.

Saul was full of God's Holy Spirit.

He looked right at the man who did magic. "You are Satan's child," he said. "You're an enemy of what's right! You're full of lies and tricks. Won't you ever stop trying to change the right ways of God? Now God is against you. You will lose your sight. You won't be able to see the sunlight."

All of a sudden, the man could not see. He felt for things around him. He tried to find somebody to take his hand. He needed someone to lead him.

When the governor saw that, he believed the teaching about Jesus.

Now Saul was starting to be known as Paul. He and his friends sailed to another city. Then John Mark went back to Jerusalem.

Barnabas and Paul went on to the next town. There they went into the town's worship house. It was the worship day. So they sat down.

The worship leaders read from the Law. They read from the prophets' books. Then they talked to Barnabas and Paul. They said, "You may talk, if you have a message for us."

Paul stood up. He talked to people who were Jewish. And he talked to people who weren't Jewish. "Listen!" he said. "God sent someone to save his people. That's just what he promised to do. But people didn't think God sent Jesus. They blamed Jesus. They didn't have any reason to kill him. But they killed him on a cross. Then they put his body in a grave.

"But God made Jesus come alive again," said Paul. "Many people saw him after that. We are telling you Good News. God made a promise. He kept his promise by making Jesus alive again.

"Jesus can forgive your sins," said Paul. "It can be just as if you'd never sinned. The Law can't do that for you. But be careful that what the prophets said doesn't happen to you."

Then Paul told the people these words. The words were from God to the prophet Habakkuk.

"Look, you people who doubt and laugh.
Watch and be surprised.
I'm going to do something in your days.
You won't believe what I'm going to do.
You wouldn't believe even if somebody told you it would happen."

After the worship time, people asked Paul and Barnabas to talk to them again. Then Paul and Barnabas left, and many of the people went with them. So Paul and Barnabas talked with them. They told them to keep on following God.

The next worship day came. Almost everybody in the town came to the town's worship house. They came to hear about Jesus.

Now the Jewish leaders saw how many people were there. That made them angry. They wished all those people had come to follow them. So they said horrible things about what Paul was saying.

Paul and Barnabas were bold. They said, "We had to tell this message to Jews first. But you are turning against it. You don't think you're good enough to live forever. So we'll tell this message to people who aren't Jewish.

"God told us to do this," said Paul. "Isaiah said God's words this way:

"I made you a light for people who
    aren't Jews.
Show people all over the earth how
    to be saved."

People who were not Jewish heard what Paul said. They were glad. They thought God's Word was important. Many of them believed. So God's Word went through the whole land.

But the Jewish leaders got some important women upset about it. They got the leaders of the city upset. They had some people do mean things to Paul and Barnabas. They sent the two men out of the city.

Paul and Barnabas went to the city of Iconium. Jesus' followers were filled with joy and the Holy Spirit.

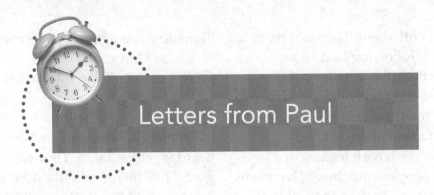

Letters from Paul

OCTOBER 20

People Who Wanted to Worship Paul

ACTS 14

In Iconium, Paul and Barnabas went to the town's worship house. They did a good job of speaking. Many Jews and many people who weren't Jews believed in Jesus.

But some Jewish people would not believe. They upset some of the people who weren't Jews. The Jewish people put bad ideas in the minds of the other people. The bad ideas were against Jesus' followers.

Paul and Barnabas stayed in the town for a while. They talked boldly for God. God showed that their message was true. He let them do wonders.

The people could not agree with each other. Some believed the Jews. Some believed Paul and Barnabas.

Now the leaders and some others made a plan. They planned to throw big stones at Paul and Barnabas. They planned to kill them this way.

Paul and Barnabas found out about the plan. So they ran away to the city of Lystra. They told God's Good News there.

A man in Lystra could not walk. He had been that way since he was born. Paul talked, and this man listened.

Then Paul looked right at the man. Paul knew that the man believed he could get well. So Paul said, "Stand up on your feet!"

The man jumped up. He started walking!

The crowd saw this. They shouted, "The gods are here! They are in human bodies!" They called Barnabas "Zeus." They called Paul "Hermes." That's because Paul did most of the talking.

There was a worship house for the fake god Zeus outside the city. The priest of Zeus brought bulls to the city gates. He brought circles of green leaves. The people wanted to offer worship gifts to Paul and Barnabas.

Paul and Barnabas heard about this. They ran out to the crowd. "What are you doing?" they asked. "We are just people like you. We're telling you good news. Don't worship things that aren't good for anything. Worship the living God."

"God made the sky, the earth, and the sea," said Paul. "He made everything in them. He used to let nations do whatever they wanted. But God has shown who he is. He is kind to you. He gives you rain and crops that grow. He gives you plenty of food. He gives you joy in your hearts."

Paul tried to stop the crowd. But he had a hard time. People still wanted to offer worship gifts to him and Barnabas.

Then some Jews came to town from Antioch and Iconium. They began talking to the crowd. The crowd soon believed those people and began to throw stones at Paul. They pulled him outside the city. They thought he was dead.

Jesus' followers came and stood around Paul. Then he got up. He went back into the city.

The next day, Paul and Barnabas left. They went to Derbe. There they told the Good News about Jesus. Lots of people believed.

Then Paul and Barnabas went back to Lystra, Iconium, and Antioch. They helped Jesus' followers to be strong and to keep believing. "People will give us a hard time," Paul said. "That's because we follow Jesus."

Paul and Barnabas chose leaders in each church. They went without food for a while to worship God. They prayed for the new leaders. They trusted God to lead these men.

At last, Paul and Barnabas sailed back to Antioch. That's where they had started their trip to many different places. Their trip was over now. So the church people in Antioch got together. Paul and Barnabas told these followers of Jesus what God had done. They told how God had helped them teach people to believe in Jesus. They said they had taught people who weren't Jews.

Paul and Barnabas stayed in Antioch with Jesus' followers for a long time.

OCTOBER 21

Looking and Acting like Jews

ACTS 15:1-35

Now some men came to Antioch from Judea. They said people had to become like Jews. If they didn't, they couldn't be saved from their sins. Paul and Barnabas did not agree. They said so.

So Jesus' followers in Antioch sent Paul and Barnabas to Jerusalem in Judea. Some other followers went with them. They went to see what the apostles and other leaders thought.

Jesus' followers in Jerusalem welcomed the followers from Antioch. Paul and Barnabas told about everything God had done. They said that many people who weren't Jews believed in Jesus.

Some of Jesus' followers in Jerusalem stood up. They said, "People who are not Jewish  still must obey. They must obey the laws God gave to Moses. They must look and act like Jews."

So the apostles and other leaders got together. They talked about it.

At last, Peter talked to the group. "God wants people who aren't Jewish to hear his Good News about Jesus. I taught some of them. They believed.

"God knows what's in each person's heart," said Peter. "He showed us he welcomes people who aren't Jewish. He gave the Holy Spirit to them like he did to us. He didn't treat them a different way. He made their hearts sinless by their faith.

"We Jews can't follow the Law," said Peter. "Jews who lived before us couldn't follow the Law. But you're trying to make these people follow the Law! The Law can't save us. We believe that Jesus' kind love saves Jews from their sins. That's the way people who aren't Jewish are saved too."

Everybody got quiet to listen to Paul and Barnabas. The two men told about wonders God had done. They said he had done wonders for people who weren't Jewish.

Then James spoke. "Listen," he said. "Peter just showed us how God welcomes people who aren't Jewish. The prophets' words agree with this."

James told about God's message to the prophet Amos. "God said that he would come back. Then God said that people who aren't Jewish can look for him.

"So here's what I think," said James. "We shouldn't make it hard for people who aren't Jewish. They're coming to God. So we should just tell them a few things.

"They should not eat food given to idols," said James. "They shouldn't sin with sex. They shouldn't eat meat from animals that were choked to death. They shouldn't eat blood. God's laws have been taught for a long time everywhere. People read his laws in the towns' worship houses every worship day."

So the group in Jerusalem chose two men to go to Antioch. Their names were Judas and Silas. They went back with Paul and Barnabas. They took this letter with them.

To the believers who are not Jewish,

Hello!

We heard that people came from Judea and upset you. So now we send Judas and Silas with Barnabas and Paul. We only ask you to do a few things. Don't eat food given to idols. Don't eat blood. Don't eat meat from animals that were choked to death. Don't sin with sex. It's good for you to stay away from these things.

Good-bye.

From the apostles and other leaders, part of God's family.

Judas and Silas went with Barnabas and Paul to Antioch. They called Jesus' followers together and gave them the letter. The people read it. It made them feel better.

Judas and Silas stayed there for a while. Then they went back to Jerusalem.

But Paul and Barnabas stayed in Antioch. They taught God's Word. Many others did too.

A Different Good News

GALATIANS 1

While he was in Antioch, Paul wrote a letter. It was to some of Jesus' followers in Lystra, Derbe, and Iconium. These cities were in a land called Galatia. So his letter was to the Galatians. And that's what his letter is called.

To Jesus' followers in Galatia,

I pray for God's kind love and peace to be with you. Jesus died for our sins. He did it because our Father in heaven wanted to save us. He wanted to save us from all that's bad.

I'm surprised at you. You're leaving the one who chose you. You're turning to a different kind of good news. It's not really good news at all.

Some people are saying things that mix you up. Don't let anybody change the Good News about Jesus. Not us. Not an angel. Not anybody. People who try to change it will be in trouble with God. They'll be in trouble now and always.

The Good News I taught isn't something people made up.

Nobody taught it to me. Instead, Jesus showed it to me.

You heard about how I used to live. As a Jew, I believed the way Jews did. I tried to get rid of people who followed Jesus. I worked hard teaching about Jewish beliefs.

But God chose me from the day I was born. He was kind and loving to me. He showed me his Son, Jesus. That was so I could teach people about Jesus. I could teach people who were not Jewish.

Three years went by. I wanted to get to know Peter. So I went to Jerusalem. I stayed with Peter for 15 days.

Then I traveled. I met many of Jesus' followers.

People said, "That's the man who hurt us. He is teaching about Jesus now." They thanked God because of me.

OCTOBER 22

The Law and the Good News

GALATIANS 2

After 14 years, God told me to go to Jerusalem again. This time I went with Barnabas and Titus. I went because God told me to.

I quietly talked to Jesus' close friends. I told them what I was teaching people who aren't Jewish.

I told only the leaders of Jesus' followers. I was afraid people might get upset.

Titus was with me. He was not Jewish. That was a problem to some people. They came into our group to spy on us. They wanted us to be like Jews.

Peter was sent to teach Jews about Jesus. I was sent to teach people who aren't Jewish. God was with Peter's work, and God was with my work.

People said James, Peter, and John were strong men of God. These men saw that God's kind love was with me, too. So they welcomed Barnabas and me.

They told us to keep teaching people who aren't Jewish. They would keep teaching the Jews. They only asked us to do one thing. They asked us to keep helping poor people. That's just what I wanted to do.

Then Peter came to Antioch. I had come back here too.

Peter sometimes ate with people who were not Jewish. Then some Jews came to see Peter. Peter was afraid of what they would think. So he stopped eating with people who were not Jewish.

That's not what the Good News is all about. So I talked to Peter in front of everyone. "You are Jewish," I said. "But you don't do everything that Jews once did. So why do you expect people who aren't Jewish to do that?

"We were born Jews. We followed God's law. We know that following the Law doesn't take away sins. Sins are taken away by believing in Jesus. Now it's just as if we'd never sinned. It's not because we keep laws. It's because we believe in Jesus.

"What if we still sin? Does that mean Jesus makes us sin? Not at all!

"I let my sins die with Jesus. So it's not me living by myself anymore. Instead, Jesus lives in me. I live by believing in God's Son. He loved me, and he died for me.

"What if I could be made right with God by following the Law? Then Jesus died for nothing! I don't treat God's kind love as nothing."

Believing What You Heard

GALATIANS 3:1-14, 19, 24-28

I want to know one thing from you people in Galatia. Did you get God's Spirit by following the Law? No. It was by believing what you heard about Jesus.

You began with the Spirit's help. Now are you trying to live for God by yourself? Why does God give you his Spirit? Why does he work wonders? Is it because you keep the Law? No. It's because you believe what you heard.

Think about Abraham. He believed God. That made him right as God sees it. Try to understand this. People who believe in God belong to Abraham's family.

God's Word said God would save people who aren't Jewish. He saves them because they believe in him. That's good news.

It's clear. Nobody is made right with God by the Law. The prophet Habakkuk wrote, "People who are right with God live by believing in him." The Law has nothing to do with believing.

What if you choose to live by the Law? Then you have to keep it up. If you don't, you've sinned. Then you get in trouble.

But Jesus kept us from getting in trouble. He got in trouble for us when he died on a cross. He saved us. Now everyone can believe in Jesus. We can trust in God and get the Spirit he promised.

So what good was the Law? God made the Law because people sinned. But then Jesus came.

The Law was in charge of us at one time. It led us to Jesus. Now the Law is not in charge anymore. Jesus is.

You are all God's children. That's because you believe in Jesus. You were baptized into Jesus, soaked in him, covered with him.

Being Jewish or not Jewish

doesn't matter. Being a slave or being free doesn't matter. Being a man or a woman doesn't matter. Everyone is together in Jesus.

Promised Children

GALATIANS 4:1-9, 13-25, 28

Think about what I'm saying. What happens when a son is a little boy? He might own the whole house. But he is no different than a servant. He still has to obey the people in charge. He obeys until his father says he can have the house.

We were like servants. We followed the world's way. But at the right time, God sent his Son. He came to save God's people. Now it's like we're children. We can get everything a son should get. So God sent his Son's Spirit into your hearts. His Son's Spirit calls, "Daddy! Father!"

When you didn't know God, you were servants. But now you know God. Better than that, God knows you.

So why are you going back to the Law? It's not strong. It can't make you happy. Do you want to follow it again?

I was with you the first time because I was sick. That's when I told you the Good News. My sickness was hard on you. But you didn't treat me badly. You didn't

laugh at me. Instead, you welcomed me. You treated me as if I were God's angel. You treated me as if I were Jesus.

What happened to your joy? You would have given me your own eyes if you could have. Am I your enemy now for telling the truth?

Those who want to change the Good News are trying hard to win you. They want you on their side. But it's no good. They want to make us enemies. They want you to work hard for them. It's fine to work hard. But it should be for a good reason.

I wish I could be with you now. I wish I didn't have to say these things. I don't know what to do with you!

Some of you still want to follow the Law. Don't you know what the Law tells you? It says in God's Word that Abraham had two sons. One was the son of Sarah's servant. He was born like all other children.

The other son was Sarah's boy. Sarah was not a servant. She was free. God promised that she'd have a son. So he was born because of God's promise.

It's like that with God and his people. The servant mother is like the Law. People who follow the Law all their lives are its servants.

But you are like Sarah's son. You

are God's children because of God's promise.

A Good Tree Growing Good Fruit

GALATIANS 5

Jesus set us free. So don't carry the heavy load of serving the Law.

Listen carefully! Just looking Jewish won't do you any good. Let's say you try to be like a Jew. Then you have to obey every bit of the Law. You try to get your heart clean from sin by obeying laws. But that takes you away from Jesus. It takes you away from God's kind love.

With Jesus it doesn't matter if you're a Jew. What matters is loving others to show you believe in him.

It's as if you were running a race. You were doing a good job. Who got in your way? Who moved you away from following the truth? It wasn't God.

"A little yeast mixes into all the batter." I'm sure you'll agree with me. Whoever is mixing up your thinking will pay for it.

What if I were still teaching people to be Jews? Then the Jews wouldn't be mad at me. They wouldn't be upset when I talk about the Cross.

God planned for you to be free. But don't sin just because you're free. Instead, love and help each other. The whole Law can be said in one rule. "Love your neighbor the same way you love yourself."

What if you keep fussing at each other? It's like you're biting each other. Be careful or you'll get rid of each other.

So here's what I say. Live by what God's Spirit shows you. Then you won't try to sin. The sinful part of us wants something different than what God's Spirit wants. The sinful part of us and God's Spirit fight each other inside us. Let God's Spirit lead you. Then the Law won't be in charge of you.

It's easy to see what sin is: Using sex in the wrong way. Worshiping idols. Following witches. Hating. Fussing and fighting. Wanting what other people have. Showing great anger. Being selfish. Talking against each other. Getting drunk. Having wild parties. Things like that. So be careful. People who do these things won't be in God's kingdom.

God's Spirit helps you act a different way. You can be like a good tree growing good fruit. Loving. Showing joy. Having peace. Waiting quietly. Being kind. Being good. Keeping promises. Treating people with care. Having control of yourself. There is no law against these things.

People who belong to Jesus have put their sinful self to death. And wanting to sin has been put to death. It's all been put on Jesus' cross.

We live by God's Spirit. So let's follow the Spirit. Let's not think we're the best. Let's not make each other mad. Let's not want what other people have.

Big Letters

GALATIANS 6; 1:1-2

What if somebody sins? You can show him the right way to act. Be kind about it. But watch out! You might want to sin too.

Help each other with your problems. That way you'll do what Jesus wants.

What if you think you're important when you're not? Then you lie to yourself. Be careful how you act.

Don't worry about doing what other people do. Each person should take care of his own work.

Let's say you learn God's Word from a teacher. Then share good things with your teacher.

Don't believe a lie. You can't make fun of God. A farmer will get the kind of plant he planted. It's the same with you. The person who sins will get trouble. But let's say the person lives to please God's Spirit. Then he will get life from the Spirit. It will be life that lasts forever.

Don't get tired of doing good things. Someday we'll get paid back for doing good. But we must not give up. Let's do good whenever we can. Most of all, let's do good to God's people.

See the big letters I'm making as I write to you? I'm writing with my own hand!

Some people want to look good to everyone. They try to do it by saying you have to be like Jews. They have a reason for saying this. They're afraid they will be hurt by Jewish people. They might be hurt for believing Jesus died on the cross to save people.

It's funny. Even people who are like Jews don't obey the Law. But they want you to become like Jews! That's so they can brag about you.

There is only one thing I want to brag about. It's how Jesus died on the cross for me.

It doesn't matter if you are like a Jew or not. What matters is Jesus making you new. God, give your peace and kind love to people who think this way. Give these things even to God's own Jewish people!

I pray that Jesus' kind love will be in your spirit. Yes! Amen!

From Paul and all God's people who are with me.

The Earth Shakes

ACTS 15:36–16:40

Some time passed. One day Paul said to Barnabas, "Let's go back. Let's go to the towns where we taught God's Word. Let's visit our friends there. Let's see how they're doing."

Barnabas wanted to take John Mark, too. Paul didn't think that was wise. John Mark had left them once before. He hadn't kept working with them.

Paul and Barnabas began to fuss with each other about it. They couldn't agree. So they chose not to go with each other.

Barnabas took John Mark with him. They went to Cyprus. Paul chose to take Silas with him. They began to travel together.

Paul and Silas went many places. They helped Jesus' followers to believe more strongly.

On one trip, Paul and Silas went back to Lystra. There was a follower of Jesus there named Timothy. His mother was Jewish, and she believed in Jesus. His father was Greek.

Everyone said good things about Timothy. So Paul wanted to take him on the trip too.

They traveled from town to town. They told people what the leaders in Jerusalem had said. So the people's faith grew stronger. Many more people believed in Jesus.

Paul and his friends traveled through Galatia. The Holy Spirit wouldn't let them teach in Asia. They ended up in a town called Troas.

That night, Paul had a dream. He saw a man from Macedonia in his dream. The man said, "Come to Macedonia. Come and help us."

Right away, Paul and his friends got ready to go. They knew God wanted them to teach in Macedonia. So they sailed across the sea. They traveled to Philippi.

Philippi was a place where some Roman people had come to live. It was the main city in Macedonia. Paul and his friends stayed there for a while.

The worship day came. Paul and his friends went out of the city. They went to the river. They thought they'd find a place of prayer there.

Some women were by the river. So Paul and his friends sat down. They started talking to the women.

One woman was named Lydia. She sold purple cloth. She was a worshiper of God.

God worked in Lydia's heart. She

was ready to hear about Jesus. She believed what Paul said. Lydia and her family were baptized. Lydia asked Paul and his friends to stay at her house. So they did.

One day, Paul and his friends went to the prayer place. On their way, a slave girl met them. A bad spirit lived in her. It made her able to say what was going to happen. She was a fortune teller.

This girl belonged to her masters. She made lots of money for them. People paid to find out what would happen to them.

The slave girl followed Paul and his friends. She shouted to others, "These men serve the Most High God. They can tell you how to be saved." She did this day after day.

At last, Paul had enough. He turned around to her. He talked to the bad spirit. "Come out of this girl. I tell you to do this in Jesus' name!" he said. Right away, the spirit left her.

The girl's owners didn't like this. Now they couldn't make money from her fortune telling. They took Paul and Silas to the city leaders. The owners said, "These men are Jewish. They are saying things that upset the people in our city. They tell us to do things that Romans shouldn't do. It's against our law."

There was a crowd of people.

They turned against Paul and Silas too.

The Roman leaders had Paul and Silas beaten. They were beaten very badly. Then the leaders had them put in jail. The jailer was told to guard the two men very carefully.

So the jailer put Paul and Silas in the inside jail room. He chained their feet in holes on a wooden board.

At midnight, Paul and Silas were praying. They were singing songs to God. The other people who had been put in jail were listening.

All of a sudden, the earth began to shake hard. The floors of the jail shook. Everybody's chains fell off.

The jailer woke up. He saw that the jail doors were open. He thought the people in jail had gotten out. He pulled out his sword. He was getting ready to kill himself.

But Paul called, "Don't hurt yourself! We're all here!"

The jailer called for someone to bring lights in. Then he ran into the jail room where Paul was. He fell down in front of Paul and Silas. He was shaking.

The jailer took Paul and Silas out of jail. "How can I be saved?" he asked.

"Believe in Jesus," they said. "Then you'll be saved. Your family can be saved too." Paul and Silas told him the Good News about Jesus. Everyone in his house listened.

The jailer washed the two men's hurt places. Then right away, he and his family were baptized.

The jailer took Paul and Silas into his house. He brought food for them to eat. He was full of joy. He and his whole family now believed in God.

Day came. The leaders sent officers to the jailer. They ordered, "Let those men go."

The jailer went to Paul. "The leaders say you and Silas can go," he said. "So leave now, and go in peace."

But Paul told the officers, "The leaders beat us. Everyone saw it. They put us in jail. But we are Romans. That's no way to treat Romans. Do they think we'll leave quietly? No! They'll have to come and take us out."

The officers went back. They told the leaders what Paul said.

The leaders were shocked. They didn't know Paul and Silas were Romans! The leaders came right away to try to make peace. They

helped the two men out of jail. Then the leaders asked the men to leave their city.

Paul and Silas went back to Lydia's house. They met with Jesus' followers there. They cheered them up. Then they left the city.

OCTOBER 25

Paul Visits Many Towns
ACTS 17:1–18:4

Paul and his friends went through other towns. Then they came to Thessalonica. This town had a worship house for Jews. So Paul went in.

On three worship days, Paul told the people about God's Word. He told them that Jesus had come to save them. He said Jesus had died for them. He told how Jesus came back to life again.

Some Jews believed. They went with Paul and Silas. A lot of Greeks believed. Many important women believed too.

Some Jewish people were angry. They didn't want anyone to believe Paul and Silas. These Jewish people went to the market place. They got some bad men to help them. Together, they upset a crowd of people.

All the people ran to the house of a man named Jason. They were looking for Paul and Silas. They planned to pull them out into the crowd. But they didn't find Paul and Silas. So they pulled Jason and some others out. They took them to the city leaders.

They shouted, "Paul and Silas made trouble all over the world. Now they've come to our city. Jason let them stay at his house. They are breaking the law. They say there is another king. They call him Jesus."

The crowd yelled when they heard this. They made Jason and the others pay to be set free. Then they let them go.

When it got dark, Paul and Silas left. They went to the town of Berea.

People in Berea were nicer. They welcomed Paul and Silas and their message. They read God's Word every day. They wanted to find out if what Paul said was true. Lots of Jews believed there. Many Greeks believed too.

But the Jews in Thessalonica heard where Paul was. They heard he was teaching about Jesus. So they went to Berea. They began to upset the crowds there.

Right away, Jesus' followers sent Paul to the sea side. But Silas and Timothy stayed in Berea.

The men with Paul took him to Athens. Paul sent them back with a message for Silas and Timothy. It said to come to Paul as soon as they could.

Paul waited for Silas and Timothy in Athens. He was upset to see so many idols in that city. So he went to the city's worship house. He talked to the Jews about it. He talked to Greeks who believed in God. He went to the market place every day. He talked with whoever was there.

There were some wise thinkers in Athens. They began to talk with Paul. Some said, "He doesn't make sense. What's he trying to say?"

Other people said, "He seems to be talking about gods of other nations." The reason they said that was because Paul was talking about Jesus. He was telling how Jesus came back to life.

Then they took Paul to a special meeting. They said, "Tell us what this new teaching is. These are strange ideas. We want to know what it all means." The people of Athens talked about new ideas all the time.

So Paul stood up. He said, "I see that you think about the spirit world. I walked around your city. I looked carefully at what you worship. I even found an altar with a different sign. It says, 'To a God We Don't Know.' I'll tell you about this God you don't know.

"God made the world and everything in it," said Paul. "He is the Lord of heaven and earth. He doesn't live in houses built by people. People don't bring him things he needs. Instead, he gives people what they need. He gives life and breath and everything.

"God made all nations from one man," said Paul. "He planned for people to live all over the world. He planned when and where they would live. God did it so people would look for him. He wanted people to reach out to him. He knew they'd find him."

Paul said, "God is not far from any of us. 'That's because we live in him. We move in him. We're alive because of him.' Some of your writers said it this way. 'We are his children.'

"We are God's children," said Paul. "So we shouldn't think God is made of gold. He is not made of silver or stone. He is not a figure that people made.

"God used to let people get away with this foolish thinking," said Paul. "But now he tells everyone everywhere to change. He tells them to be sorry for doing wrong. He has planned for a day when he will judge the world. He has chosen the one who will do the judging. He has shown who this is by bringing him back to life."

Some people laughed when they heard about coming back to life. But some said, "We want to hear more."

A few people believed Paul.

Then Paul left Athens and went to Corinth. He met a Jew there whose name was Aquila. This man had lived in Rome with his wife, Priscilla. But they had to move to Corinth. The ruler of Rome had told the Jewish people to leave his city.

Paul went to visit Aquila and Priscilla. They made tents. Paul did too. So Paul stayed and worked with them. He went to the city's worship house every worship day. He tried to get Jews and Greeks to believe in Jesus.

OCTOBER 26

Paul's Dream

ACTS 18:5-11

At last, Silas and Timothy came. Paul worked hard at teaching. He kept trying to tell Jewish people about Jesus. He told them God sent Jesus to save them. But the Jewish people wouldn't believe. They started being mean to him.

Paul said, "You are to blame. I've

done what I could. From now on, I'll teach people who aren't Jewish."

Paul left the city's worship house. He went next door. Justus lived there. He believed in God, but he wasn't Jewish.

Crispus was the leader at that city's worship house. He and his family believed in Jesus. Many others believed too. They were baptized.

One night, God talked to Paul in a dream. "Don't be afraid," he said. "Talk to these people. Don't be quiet. I'm with you. Nobody will hurt you. I have lots of people here in this city."

So Paul stayed in Corinth for one year and six months. He taught the people God's Word.

We Remember

1 THESSALONIANS 1

From Corinth, Paul wrote some letters to Jesus' followers.

To the followers of Jesus in Thessalonica,

We pray for God's kind love and peace to be with you.

We always thank God for you. We remember the work you've done for him. You were able to work because you believe in God. You wanted to work because you love God. And you kept working because you hope in Jesus.

God loves you, and he chose you. We know this because of how our Good News came to you. It didn't just come with words. It came with power. It came with the Holy Spirit.

We lived near you so we could teach you. You learned to live like Jesus. You had hard times. But you were glad to welcome the message. The Holy Spirit helped you to be glad. You showed others what following Jesus is like.

People everywhere hear about your faith in God. We don't need to tell them about it. They tell us!

People tell how good you were to us. They tell how you left idols. They tell how you began worshiping the true God. They say you're waiting for Jesus to come back.

Like a Mother

1 THESSALONIANS 2:2-4, 7-8, 13-14

We were brave when we told you the Good News. Many people tried to stop us. But we weren't trying to trick you. We weren't after more and more things for ourselves. It's not people that we're trying to make happy. We're trying to make God happy. He sees what's in our hearts.

We could have made things hard

on you. But we were kind. We were like a mother taking care of little children. We loved you very much. So we were happy to share God's Good News with you.

We always thank God because you believed. You began to live like God's people.

Hard Times

1 THESSALONIANS 3

We've wanted to see you for a long time. At last we couldn't take it anymore. So we sent Timothy. He worked to help you have a strong faith. In these hard times, he helped you keep believing.

You knew hard times were coming. We told you it would happen. And it did. So I sent Timothy. He came to see how your faith was holding up.

Now Timothy just came back. He tells us good news about your faith. He tells us about your love. He says you're happy when you think of us. He says you want to see us, just as we want to see you.

We are having hard times too. So what Timothy told us helped us feel better about you. You are strong in Jesus. How can we give enough thanks to God for that?

We pray night and day that we can visit you. We want to see you

again. We want to help build your faith up.

We hope God shows us how to visit you. We hope Jesus will make your love grow. Love each other like we love you.

We hope God will make your hearts strong. Then no one can say bad things about you. You'll have no sin when Jesus comes back.

A Quiet Life

1 THESSALONIANS 4:1-8, 11-18

We told you how to live to make God happy. That's just the way you're living.

God wants your hearts to be clean from sin. Stay away from using sex in a wrong way. God wants you to control your own bodies. He wants people to be able to look up to you.

Don't be like people who don't know God. Don't treat people the wrong way. God will bring trouble to you if you sin like this. God didn't plan for us to have dirty minds. He plans for us to live sinless, good lives.

What if you don't live good lives? Then you're turning away from God. It's God who gives you his Holy Spirit.

Try to live a quiet life. Mind your own business. Work with your hands. That way, people who don't know God will look up to you. Then you won't need other people's help.

Now we want you to know about dying. What if someone dies? Then don't be sad like people who don't have any hope. Here's what we believe. Jesus died and came back to life again. So God will bring people back to life again too. They'll get to be with Jesus.

What if we're still alive when Jesus comes back? We'll go with him. But we won't go ahead of the people who died before us. Jesus himself told us this.

Jesus will come down from heaven. The angel in charge will shout with a loud voice. He will tell us what to do. God's horn will call us. Jesus' followers who died will go up first. Then people who are alive will go up with them. We'll go up in the clouds. We'll meet Jesus in the air. Then we'll live with Jesus forever.

Help each other remember this. It will cheer you up.

People Will Be Surprised

1 THESSALONIANS 5; 1:1

When will Jesus come back? We don't need to write about that. You know that people will be surprised when Jesus comes. People are surprised when a robber comes

during the night, too. People don't look for a robber. And they won't be looking for Jesus.

It's like a woman who is going to have a baby. She doesn't know when. But all of a sudden, it's time. It's time for the baby to come. No one can stop it.

But you don't live in the darkness. So you shouldn't be surprised when Jesus comes again. You are children of the light. You are children of the day. So let's be watching. Let's control ourselves.

Let's have faith and love. They are like a hard, metal vest that keeps us safe. Let's put our hope in being saved. That's like a hard helmet on our head.

God didn't choose us so he could be angry at us. He chose us to be saved by Jesus. Jesus died for us. That way, if we die, we live with him. And if we live, we live with him.

So help each other. Cheer each other up just like you're doing.

Show the leaders of your group that you think they're important. They work hard. They are in charge of you. They show you how to live. Make them feel important. Love them for their work.

Live with each other in peace. Tell people who are lazy that they should work. Help shy people to be bold. Help people who are weak. Wait quietly for people.

What if people do wrong to you? Don't pay them back by doing wrong to them. Instead, try to be kind to everybody.

Always show your joy. Always pray. Always thank God. This is what God wants you to do.

Let God's Holy Spirit work in you. Don't turn away from him.

Other people may tell you what God's plans are. Follow God's plans, but test things. Find out what's good, and hold on to it. Stay away from any kind of sin.

God is the God of peace. I hope he will make your whole heart clean from sin. Then nobody will speak badly about you when Jesus comes.

Pray for us. Tell God's people hello by giving them a godly kiss. Read this letter to them.

From Paul, Silas, and Timothy.

Bright Fire and Strong Angels

2 THESSALONIANS 1

To Jesus' followers in Thessalonica,

We pray that God's kind love and peace will fill you.

We should always thank God for you. That's because your faith is growing more and more. Your love is growing too. So we talk about you to Jesus' followers. We talk about how you keep going in hard times. We talk about how you keep believing.

It just shows that what God does is right. He will keep you in his kingdom. People give you a hard time for believing in God. But God is fair. He will give trouble to people who give you trouble. And he will take our troubles away. That will happen when Jesus comes back.

Jesus will appear. He will come from heaven. Bright fire will be around him. His strong angels will be with him.

Some people never knew Jesus. Some people never obeyed him. They won't get to be with him. They won't get to see the greatness of the King's power. They will be shut out on the day Jesus comes back.

When Jesus comes, his power will shine in his people. Everybody who believed will look at him with wonder. You will too, because you believed what we told you.

We always pray for you. We want God to count you as part of his people. He can help with your good plans. We pray that people will be able to see Jesus' greatness in you.

A Time of Trouble

2 THESSALONIANS 2:1-10, 13

Now let's talk about Jesus coming again. Don't get upset or mixed up.

Some people told you that we said Jesus already came back. Don't believe that lie. He won't come back yet.

Before Jesus comes back, there will be a time of trouble. Many people will turn against Jesus. Then the man of sin will come. He will come to fight against God. And he will even say he is greater than God. He will go into God's worship house. But he will be thrown out.

Remember? I've told you this before. You know what keeps him from coming. He will show up when it's time. Sin's secret power is working already. But someone is keeping it back. He will keep it back and then be moved out of the way. Then the sinful man will show up. But Jesus will get rid of him with his breath and his greatness.

This sinful man will come to do Satan's work. He will show wonders that are not from God. He will do sinful things that trick people who aren't following God. They will die because they said no to God. They enjoyed being sinful. They would not love truth. So they couldn't be saved.

We should thank God for you. God chose you from the very first. He chose you to be saved. He chose you to be cleaned from sin by his Spirit. You were saved by believing the truth.

Lazy Busybodies

2 THESSALONIANS 3:1-13, 16-17; 1:1

Pray for us. Pray that God's message will go out fast. Pray that others will think it's important, like you did. Pray that God will save us from sinful, mean people.

Not everybody believes. But God keeps his promises. He will make your faith stronger. He will keep you safe from Satan. We're sure that you'll keep doing what God wants. We're sure that he will lead you into his love. And you'll stay with him in hard times.

Stay away from God's people who are lazy. We weren't lazy when we were with you. We paid for the food we ate. We worked hard day and night. We didn't want to be any trouble to you.

It would have been all right for you to help us. But we wanted to show you how to live. We told you this rule. "If a person won't work, then he shouldn't eat."

We've heard that some of you are being lazy. You're not busy. Instead, you're busybodies. You just think about what other people should be doing. Stop this. Work for what you eat.

Some of you are good followers of Jesus. Don't get tired of doing what's right.

God is the God of peace. I pray that he will always give you peace.

I, Paul, am writing this part with my own hand. This is the way I write. So you can always tell when you're getting a letter from me.

From Paul, Silas, and Timothy.

A Judge and a New Jewish Teacher

ACTS 18:12-28

Now the Jews came against Paul. They brought him to Gallio. Gallio was the ruler in Corinth.

The Jewish people spoke against Paul. "This man teaches people to worship God in wrong ways."

Paul was just about to talk. But Gallio spoke instead. "I'd listen to you Jewish people if this were about some crime. But it's just about your words, names, and laws. So take care of it yourselves. I won't judge things like this."

Gallio threw them all out of the building.

Then the Jewish people beat the ruler of the town's worship house. They beat him right in front of the judge's building. But Gallio didn't seem to care at all.

Paul stayed for a long time in Corinth. Then he and Aquila and Priscilla sailed to Ephesus.

Paul went into the town's worship house at Ephesus. He talked to the Jews. They asked him to stay and talk some more. But he wouldn't. "I'll come back if God wants me to," said Paul.

Paul left Aquila and Priscilla in Ephesus. He sailed on. He ended his trip back in Antioch.

Some time later, Paul traveled again. He went from town to town. He cheered up Jesus' followers wherever he went.

While Paul was traveling, a man named Apollos went to Ephesus. He was Jewish. He was very smart. He knew God's Word well. Apollos told people about Jesus. But he only knew about baptizing like John did.

Apollos talked in the town's worship house. Aquila and Priscilla heard him. They asked him to come home with them. They taught him more about Jesus.

Apollos wanted to go to Corinth. Jesus' followers said that was a good idea. They even wrote letters to Jesus' followers in Corinth. The letters said people should welcome Apollos.

When Apollos got to Corinth, he helped Jesus' followers a lot. He was very good at talking with people. He used God's Word. He showed that Jesus could save people.

Seven Sons and Lots of Magic Books

ACTS 19:1-22

While Apollos was in Corinth, Paul went to Ephesus. He met 12 men there. They were learning about Jesus.

Paul asked, "Did you get the Holy Spirit when you believed?"

"No," they said. "We didn't even know there was a Holy Spirit."

"Why were you dipped in water?" asked Paul.

"We were baptized because of what John said," they answered.

"John's baptizing was for saying you're sorry," said Paul. "But then John told people to believe in Jesus."

So the men were baptized in Jesus' name. Then Paul put his hands on them. They began to talk in different languages. They told about God's plans.

Paul went to the town's worship house. He taught there for three months. He told people about God's kingdom. Some people would not believe. They said bad things about Jesus' followers. So Paul left the town's worship house.

Paul and Jesus' followers talked every day. They met in a large hall. It was a special place for speaking. They met there for two years. All the Jews and Greeks around there heard God's Word.

God did surprising wonders through Paul. People would get cloths that Paul had touched. They'd take them to sick people. The sick people would get well. Bad spirits would leave people.

Now some Jewish people also tried to get bad spirits out of people. They used Jesus' name to do it. They'd say, "In Jesus' name, the one Paul teaches about, come out."

One of the Jewish leaders had seven sons. All of them tried to get bad spirits out of people. But one day a bad spirit talked back to them.

"I know Jesus," said the spirit. "I know about Paul. But who are you?"

Then the man with the bad spirit jumped on them. He was stronger than all of them. He pulled their clothes off. He beat them up.

The seven sons ran out of the

house. They had no clothes. They were bleeding.

People in Ephesus heard about this. It made them very scared. They wondered about Jesus' name.

Lots of believers came and told what they'd done wrong. Many of them had done magic by the power of bad spirits. So they brought their magic books and burned them. They added up how much the books had cost. It was about 50,000 (fifty thousand) silver pieces of money.

God's Word went out all over the place. Its power grew.

Then Paul made plans to go to Jerusalem. "After that, I need to go to Rome," he said.

Paul had two helpers named Timothy and Erastus. He sent them to Macedonia. Paul stayed in Asia a little longer.

OCTOBER 29

Where Is the Thinker?

1 CORINTHIANS 1:2, 5-7, 10-28

From Asia, Paul wrote this letter.

To Jesus' followers in Corinth,

Any way you look at it, God has made you rich. You're rich in everything you say. You're rich in everything you know. You have every gift God wanted to give you.

Here's what I beg you to do in Jesus' name. Try to get along with each other. Then you're not working against each other. You can agree together.

Somebody from Chloe's family told me what you're doing. You're fussing with each other. One of you says, "I follow Paul." Another person says, "I follow Apollos." Someone else says, "I follow Peter." Somebody else says, "I follow Jesus."

Is Jesus broken into different parts? Was Paul killed on a cross for you? Were you dipped into water in Paul's name? I'm glad I baptized only two of you. That way, people can't say they were baptized in my name. Oh, yes. I also baptized the family of Stephanas. I don't remember if I baptized anybody else.

Jesus didn't send me to dip you into water. He sent me to teach his Good News.

Some people don't follow God. What do they think? They think the news about the Cross is foolish. But we are being saved. So to us the Cross is power. Isaiah said it like this. "Wise people won't think they're so wise anymore. Smart people won't think they're so smart anymore."

Where is the wise person? Where is the thinker? God made the world's wise thinking look foolish. All of people's wise thinking did not show them God.

God saved people who believed what they were taught about him. The things they were taught seemed foolish. But that's the way God wanted to do it.

The Jews want wonders. The Greeks want wise thinking. But we teach about how Jesus died. It doesn't make sense to Jewish people. It seems foolish to other people. But some Jews and some Greeks believe in Jesus. So to them, Jesus is the power of God. He is God's wise thinking.

What if God could be foolish? He'd still be wiser than wise people. What if God were not strong? He'd still be stronger than strong people.

Think about what you were like when God chose you. Not many of you were wise. Not many of you were strong. Not many of you were from rich, important families.

God chose things that look foolish to the world. That way, wise people don't seem so important. God chose things that look weak to the world. He chose things the world doesn't like. That way, what the world thinks is important looks like nothing.

No Eye Has Seen It
1 CORINTHIANS 2:1-2, 4-5, 7, 9-16

I came to see you before. I told you about God. But I didn't come with great, wise thinking. I chose to talk about one thing. I chose to talk about Jesus. I chose to talk about how he died for us.

My message showed the Spirit's power, not my wise thinking. You believed because of God's power. God planned to show his power in us before time began.

Isaiah said it this way. "No eye has seen what God has planned. No ear has heard what God has planned. No mind has thought of God's plans. His plans are for people who love him."

God showed us his plans by his Spirit. Only a person's spirit knows that person's thoughts. It's the same with God. No one knows what God is thinking. Only God's Spirit knows his thoughts.

We didn't get the spirit of the world. We got God's Spirit. Now we can understand what God freely gave us.

We don't use words that wise thinking taught us. We use words the Spirit taught us. We talk about truth with the Spirit's words.

Some people don't have God's Spirit. They don't believe what comes from God's Spirit. It seems foolish to them. They can't understand it. You have to understand it with your spirit.

Isaiah said it this way. "Who knows what's in God's mind? Who ever told him what he should do?"

But we have the same mind that Jesus has.

Like Seeds in a Field

1 CORINTHIANS 3:1-7, 16-20

You have not been able to understand things about the spirit. That's because you think like people of the world. You're just babies in God's family. So the words I've said have been like milk for a baby. You have not been ready for more.

You still act and think like the world. You try to be like other people. You fuss with each other. One of you says, "I follow Paul." The other says, "I follow Apollos." Aren't you acting like people of the world?

After all, who is Apollos? Who is Paul? We are just servants. We work for God.

The Good News about Jesus is like a seed. I planted the seed. Apollos watered it. But God made it grow. The person who plants isn't important. The person who waters isn't important. God is important. He makes things grow.

Did you know that all of you are God's worship house? Did you know God's Spirit lives in you? What if someone tears down God's worship house? Then God will tear that person down. That's because

God's worship house is special. That's you.

Don't fool yourself. You may think you are wise. But to God, the world's wise thinking is foolish. The psalm says it this way. "Wise people's thoughts aren't good for anything."

At the End of the Parade

1 CORINTHIANS 4:6-14, 16-20

I told you about Apollos and me for your good. You can learn from us. You can learn what this means. "Do only what God says to do in his Word." Then you won't brag about one person being greater than another.

Who makes you different from other people? God does. What do you have that you didn't get from him? Nothing. If God gave it to you, why brag about it?

You have everything you want already. You're already rich. You live like kings without us! I wish you really were kings. Then we could be kings with you!

But the other apostles and I seem to be at the end of the parade. God shows us to everyone. We're something for everyone in the world to look at. We're here even for the angels to look at.

We are fools for Jesus. But you think you're so wise in Jesus! We're not strong. But you think you are! People think you're important. But they don't think we're important!

Even now, we go hungry. We get thirsty. We dress in rags. People are mean to us. We have no homes. We work hard.

But we pray for people who speak badly of us. Some people are mean to us. We take it. We answer kindly when people say bad things about us. We are like the dirt of the earth. We're like the trash of the world.

I'm not writing this to make you feel bad. I'm just telling you where the danger is. I feel like you're my dear children.

So I beg you. Do what I do. This is why I'm sending Timothy to you. I love him like a son. He keeps his promises to God. He will help you remember my way of living in Jesus. I do what I say.

Some of you brag. It's as if I weren't going to come see you. But I will come see you. I'll come very soon, if God lets me. Then I'll find out what these proud braggers are saying. I'll see how strong they are. God's kingdom isn't talk. It's power.

Don't Eat with People like That
1 CORINTHIANS 5:1-3, 9-13

I hear that some people in your group sin with sex. A man is sleeping with his father's wife the way only a husband should. People who don't believe in God don't even do that! And you are proud of yourselves! Shouldn't you be sad instead? Shouldn't you send this man away from your group?

I may not be with you. But I've already judged the man who did this. It's just as if I were there with you.

I wrote a letter to you. It said not to be with people who sin with sex. I didn't mean people of this world. They sin with sex. They want more and more things. They lie to get money. They worship things, not God. If you weren't around them, you'd have to leave this world.

Now someone might say he follows Jesus. But he sins with sex. He wants more and more things. He worships things, not God. He says bad things about other people. He gets drunk. He lies to get money. Don't be friends with him. Don't even eat with him.

It's not my job to judge people who don't follow Jesus. God will judge people who don't follow him. But you're supposed to judge people who do follow Jesus. God's Word says, "Send the sinful person away from you."

Who Gets into God's Kingdom?

1 CORINTHIANS 6:1-7, 9-13, 15, 18-20

Let's say some of you fuss with each other. Do you dare talk about it with someone who doesn't follow Jesus? Do you dare to have that person say who is right? You should ask Jesus' followers to help.

Jesus' followers will judge the world. So can't you judge smaller things? Don't you know we'll judge angels? Then I'm sure we can judge things of this life!

Take your problems to God's people. Let them say who is right and who is wrong. You can even take problems to people who don't seem important.

Can it be that nobody is wise enough? Can no one say what's right and what's wrong? Instead, one of Jesus' followers gets mad at another one. Then they go to a judge who doesn't follow Jesus!

When Jesus' followers take each other to a judge, nobody wins. Why not let the other person do wrong to you? Why not let him lie to you?

Sinful people won't get into God's kingdom. Don't be fooled. People who sin with sex won't get into God's kingdom. People who worship idols won't get in. People who rob others won't get in. People who want more and more things won't get in. Drunks won't get in. People who say bad things about others won't get in. People who lie to get money won't get in.

Some of you used to do those things. But your hearts were washed. Your hearts were made clean from sin. It was just as if you'd never sinned. It happened in Jesus' name. It came by God's Spirit.

I might say, "I'm allowed to do everything." But not everything is good for me. And I will not let anything control me.

Our bodies weren't made for using sex the wrong way. Our bodies were made for the Lord. The Lord cares about our bodies. They belong to Jesus. So should we use our bodies to sin with sex? Never!

Run away from sinning with sex. Other kinds of sins happen outside your body. But sinning with sex is sinning against your own body.

Your body is the Holy Spirit's worship house. The Holy Spirit is in you. God gave him to you. You don't belong just to yourself. God bought you. He paid for you by giving his Son, Jesus. That was a big price to pay. So let God know how great you think he is. Show it by the way you act with your body.

To Marry or Not to Marry

1 CORINTHIANS 7:1-3, 6-16, 23-35, 39-40

Here are some answers to questions you asked when you wrote me.

It's good for people not to marry. But many people think about using sex the wrong way. So each man should have his own wife. Each woman should have her own husband. The husband should have sex with his wife. The wife should have sex with her husband.

Here's a good idea, but it isn't a rule. I wish everyone could be happy not to be married, like me. But each person is different. All of us are the way God made us.

You may not be married. Maybe your wife or husband died. Then I say it's good to stay unmarried. But some people can't control themselves. So they should marry. It's better to marry than to wish for sex all the time.

Here's the rule for married people. This is God's rule, not mine. A husband is not to leave his wife. A wife is not to leave her husband. If she does, she should stay unmarried. Or she should go back to her husband.

Here's what I have to say. It's my idea, not God's. Let's say a man who believes in Jesus has a wife. But she doesn't believe in Jesus. What if she wants to stay with him? Then he shouldn't leave her. God helps the wife who doesn't believe. God helps her because of her husband.

Let's say a woman who believes in Jesus has a husband. But he doesn't believe in Jesus. What if he wants to stay with her? She shouldn't leave him. God helps the husband who doesn't believe. God helps him because of his wife.

But let's say the wife or husband leaves. The one who leaves doesn't believe in Jesus. Then let that person leave. The one who believes in Jesus isn't tied to the one who left.

God wants us to live in peace. If you're the wife, you never know. You might save your husband. If you're the husband, you never know. You might save your wife.

Jesus paid a big price for you. So don't follow people. Each person should stay where God puts him.

Now I'll tell you about people who have never married. This isn't God's rule. But I tell it the way I see it. Because of Jesus, you can trust me. Times are hard today. There are many problems. So it's good for you to stay like you are.

Are you married? Don't leave your wife or husband. Are you not married? Don't look for a wife or husband. If you do marry, that's not a sin. But when you marry, you face many troubles in this life. I'd like to save you from that.

Here's what I mean. Time is short. Don't live just to make your wife or husband happy. Don't buy things just to have things. Don't use your time thinking about things of the world. The world is not going to last forever.

I'd like you to be free from worry. A man who is not married thinks about what God wants. He thinks about how he can make God happy. But a married man thinks about things of the world. He thinks about how he can make his wife happy. So his thoughts go two ways.

A woman who isn't married thinks about what God wants. She tries to belong to God in body and spirit. But a married woman thinks about things of the world. She thinks about how she can make her husband happy.

I say this for your own good. I'm not trying to tie you down. I want you to live the right way. Give your whole heart to God.

A wife should stay with her husband as long as he lives. What if he dies? Then she is free to marry anyone she wants. But her new husband must follow Jesus. Here's how I see it. She'd be happier if she doesn't marry again. I think I have these words from God's Spirit.

Food for Idols

1 CORINTHIANS 8

We all know things. But knowing things only puffs us up and makes us feel important. Some people think they know a lot. They don't know all they should know. It is love that builds us up. People who love God grow close to him. God knows them well.

So what about eating food that was given to idols? We know an idol is nothing. There is only one God. People may worship things and call them gods or lords. But for us, there is only one God. He is the Father. All things came from him. We live for him. There is only one Lord. That's Jesus. All things came from him. We live because of him.

But not everyone knows that. Some people are still used to idols. They think food given to idols is bad for you. But food doesn't make us closer to God. It's not bad if we don't eat this food. It's not better if we do eat it.

Be careful. We might think we are free to do something. But we don't want others to do something they think is wrong.

What if someone's faith is not strong? He sees you eating food that was given to an idol. You know it's all right. But you don't want to tear down his faith. Jesus died for him. What if you hurt his faith when it's weak? Then you're sinning against Jesus.

What if the food I eat makes someone sin? Then I'll never eat that food again. That way, I won't make anyone lose his faith.

Let the Ox Eat

1 CORINTHIANS 9:1, 3-11, 13-27

Am I free? Yes. Am I an apostle? Yes. Have I seen Jesus our Lord? Yes.

Some people try to judge me. But here's what I tell them. Isn't it all right for us to eat and drink? Wouldn't it be all right for a wife to come with us? Wives follow Jesus too. The other apostles take their wives. Jesus' brothers do. Peter does.

Are Barnabas and I the only ones who work for a living? If you plant grapes, you get to eat them. If you keep goats, you get to drink goat milk. The Law that God gave Moses says it this way. "Let the ox eat the wheat it's working on."

God wasn't just thinking about oxen. He was thinking about the farmer who works in the field. The farmer should get to have part of what he grows. God was thinking about us, too. We are planting God's seed. It's seed for the spirit. So shouldn't we get something for it?

The priests who serve at the altar get a share of what's given. It should be the same way for us. We teach God's Good News. God says that everyone who does that should get paid for it.

But I haven't taken any pay. And I'm not writing this so you'll pay me.

I teach the Good News because I have to teach. How sad it would be for me if I didn't do it. What if I teach because that's what I want to do? Then God has a gift for me. What if I teach because I have to do it? Then I'm only doing what I know I should.

So what is the gift I get? Only this. I can teach the Good News for free. No one has to pay me for doing it.

I'm free. I don't belong to any person. But I serve everyone. I want to help lots of people believe in Jesus.

I became like a Jew to help Jews believe in Jesus. I became like a person who follows the Law. I did it to help Law followers believe in Jesus. I became like a person who doesn't follow the Law. That way, I could help people who don't follow the Law. I could help them believe in Jesus. I became weak. I did it to help weak people believe in Jesus.

I have become all things to all people. That way, I have the best chance to save some people. I do it all for the Good News about Jesus. I want to share the good things that it brings.

All the runners in a race run. But only one of them will win. Run well so you will win.

All people who race have to practice hard before they run. They do it to win something that won't last. But we're like runners for God's kingdom. We run to get something that will last forever.

I don't run like a man running for no reason. I taught other people how to live. So I don't want to lose the race myself!

A Way to Say No

1 CORINTHIANS 10:1, 5-15, 23-28, 31-33

I want you to know something. God's people who lived in Moses' time followed God's cloud. But God wasn't happy with most of them. Most of them died in the desert.

This happened to teach us that we shouldn't want to sin. That's what they did. Don't worship idols. Some of them did. God's Word tells about it. "The people ate and drank. Then they had a wild party."

We shouldn't use sex in a wrong way. Some of them did. What happened to them? Twenty-three thousand (23,000) of them died in one day.

We shouldn't test God to see how much we can get away with. Some of them did. What happened to them? Snakes killed them.

Don't make a fuss about things. Some of them did. What happened to them? God sent an angel to get rid of them.

These things happened to teach us. God had someone write about these things to tell us of danger. Time is moving on. God's promises are coming true. So if you think you are doing well, be careful. You might sin in these ways too!

The only sins that come to your mind are sins everyone has problems with. God won't let a sin come to your mind unless he knows you can say no to it. Let's say a sin comes to your mind. Then God gives you a way to say no. That way, you can win over sin.

Run away from the worship of idols. You have a good mind. Think about it and choose what's right.

I might say, "Everything is all right." But not everything is good for me. I might say, "Everything is all right." But not everything makes me a better person. Nobody should look for what's good just for himself. Look for what's good for other people.

Eat anything the meat market sells. Don't ask questions about it being right or wrong. David said it this way in a psalm. "The earth and everything in it belong to God."

Let's say you know someone who doesn't follow Jesus. He asks you to eat with him. So you do. Eat whatever he puts on your plate. Don't ask if it's right or wrong.

But let's say he tells you about it. He says, "This food was a gift to an idol." Then don't eat it.

You may eat. You may drink. But whatever you do, do it to show how great God is.

Don't make other people do anything they think they shouldn't do. I try to make everyone happy. I'm not looking for what's good for me. I'm looking for what's good for many people. That way, they can be saved from their sins.

Remembering

1 CORINTHIANS 11:3, 5, 7, 9-12, 14-15, 17-34

I want you to know something. Jesus is the leader of every man. Man is the leader of woman. God is the leader of his Son, Jesus.

A woman should cover her head when she prays. She should cover her head when she tells what God wants people to know.

But a man should not cover his head. He shows what God is like. He shows how great God is. But the woman shows how great the man is. Man wasn't made for woman. Woman was made for man. Covering her head shows that she has a leader.

Here's how it is in God's kingdom. A woman doesn't live on her own apart from man. Man doesn't live on his own apart from woman. Woman came from man. But man is born from woman. Everything comes from God.

It's bad for a man to have long hair. But it's good for a woman to have long hair. Long hair is for covering her.

There are some things you do that aren't good. You meet because you are followers of Jesus. But your meetings hurt more than they help. First of all, I hear that you don't get along with each other. Of course, not everyone agrees. That shows that some of you are doing what God wants. Some aren't.

You eat together. But it's not the Lord's Supper. Some of you start eating before the others. You don't wait for each other. So one person stays hungry. Another person gets drunk. Don't you have homes where you can eat and drink?

Jesus ate bread with his friends one night. That same night Judas told the Jewish leaders where Jesus was. But Jesus gave thanks. Then he pulled the bread apart. He said, "When you eat this bread, remember my body. I will give up my body for you."

After supper, Jesus held a cup of wine. He said, "This shows God's new special promise. It's a promise made with my blood. When you drink this wine, remember my blood. I will give up my blood for you."

Now you eat the bread, and you drink the wine. That's one way you tell about why Jesus died. You do it until he comes back.

Let's say someone eats the bread. But he doesn't remember Jesus. Let's say he drinks the wine. But he doesn't remember Jesus. Then he is sinning. People should think about what's in their hearts. They should think about it before they eat the bread. They should think about it before they drink the wine.

What if people don't think about Jesus? Then they show how wrong they are. That's why lots of you are weak. That's why lots of you are sick. Some of you have even died.

What if we think about our hearts? Then no one else will judge us. When Jesus judges us, he shows us how to live. Then we won't get in trouble like the other people in the world.

Wait for each other when you get together to eat the Lord's Supper. Hungry people should eat at home. Then you won't be in trouble when you get together.

What If Your Whole Body Were an Eye?

1 CORINTHIANS 12

I want you to know about God's gifts. There was a time when you believed in idols. But when God's Spirit is in control, people worship Jesus. They don't say bad things about Jesus. Only people who have God's Spirit say "Jesus is Lord."

There are different kinds of gifts. But they all come from the same

Spirit. There are different ways to help. But it's all for the same Lord. There are different kinds of work. But the same God does the work through everyone.

A gift from God's Spirit can be seen in each person. It's for everybody's good. God gives some people wise messages through his Spirit. He makes other people know many things. By the same Spirit, God gives other people faith.

God gives some people the gift of making people well. It comes from the same Spirit. He gives other people the power to do wonders. He lets other people tell what he has to say. He lets others know whether a spirit is good or bad. God lets some people talk in different languages. He lets others tell what those languages mean.

It's all the Spirit's work. God's Spirit gives these gifts. He chooses which gift to give each person.

Your body is all one body. But it's made of many different parts. All the parts together make one body.

It's like that with Jesus. God's Spirit puts us all into one group, one body. We may be Jewish or not Jewish. We may be slaves or free people. God gave all of us his one Spirit. It's as if we all drink from the same river.

Your body isn't just one part. It's many parts. Let's say your foot says,

"I'm not a hand. So I don't belong to this body." That wouldn't stop it from being part of your body.

Let's say your ear says, "I'm not an eye. So I don't belong to this body." That wouldn't stop it from being part of your body.

What if your whole body were an eye? How would you hear? What if your whole body were an ear? How would you smell anything?

God put all the parts of your body together. He did it just like he wanted. What if they were all one part? Then where would your body be? So there are many parts. But there is only one body.

The eye can't tell the hand, "I don't need you!" The head can't tell the feet, "I don't need you!" Some parts seem like they are weak. But you can't do without them.

We may think some parts aren't as special as others. But we take special care of parts we can't show. Then we have parts we can show. They don't need to be treated in a special way.

God put your body together. There are parts that don't seem so special. But God makes them important.

So the parts of the body should work together. If one part hurts, all the parts hurt. If one part is cared for, all the parts show their joy.

Now, Jesus' followers are like the

body of Jesus. Each person is a part of this body. God gives the parts of this body different work.

God planned for some people to be apostles. Some are prophets. Some are teachers. Some do wonders. Some can make others well. Some can help others. Some can be in charge of the work. Some talk in different languages.

Not everyone is an apostle. Not everybody is a prophet. Not everyone is a teacher. Not everyone does wonders. Not everyone can make people well. Not everyone speaks in other languages. Not everyone tells what the languages mean.

But I hope you want the greatest gifts. So I will show you the best way.

NOVEMBER 3

Love

1 CORINTHIANS 13

Let's say I talk in different languages. It could be languages of people or angels. But what if I don't love people? Then I'm only like a bell with a loud ring. It rings for no reason.

Let's say I can tell you what God wants people to know. Or I can understand all kinds of mysteries. Let's say I know everything. Let's say I have faith big enough to move mountains. But I don't love people. Then I'm nothing.

What if I give everything I have to poor people? What if I give up my whole life for Jesus? But I don't love people. Then it doesn't do me any good.

Love waits quietly. Love is kind. It doesn't want what others have. It doesn't brag. It isn't proud. It has good manners. It doesn't think of itself ahead of others. It doesn't get angry very fast. It doesn't try to remember who was wrong.

Love isn't happy with sin. Instead, it's happy to know the truth.

Love always takes care of people. It always trusts. It always hopes. It always keeps going. Love never fails.

Telling what God has to say will stop someday. Talking in different languages will stop. Knowing things will stop. Right now we only know part of what there is to know. We can only tell part of what God has to say.

Someday we'll know all about God. What's good and clean and right will come. Then what's not good or clean or right will fade away.

Once I was a little child. I talked like a child. I thought like a child. Then I grew up. So I wasn't like a child anymore.

What I see now seems dim and fuzzy. I only know a part. It's like being a child. But someday I'll see

687

God face to face. That's like growing up. Then I'll know all about God just like God knows all about me.

Three things will always be with us. They are faith and hope and love. But love is the best.

Words That People Understand

1 CORINTHIANS 14

Follow love's way. I hope you want gifts for your spirit. But I hope you want one thing more than anything. That's to have the gift of telling what God has to say.

People who pray in different languages talk to God. But they don't talk to other people. Nobody understands them. They talk with their spirits. It's all a mystery.

People who tell what God has to say do talk to other people. God's words help other people to be strong and brave. His words help others feel better. The person who prays in a different language helps himself. But the person who tells what God has to say helps Jesus' followers.

I wish everybody could pray in different languages. But more than that, I wish everyone could tell what God has to say. People who can do that are greater.

Let's say I come to you. I pray in another language. What good will that do unless I teach you something?

Think about things that make music. There are pipes like flutes. There are harps with many strings. They aren't alive, but they make sounds. What if the different notes are not played clearly? How will people know what the song is?

It's the same way with you. What if we can't understand your language? How will we know what you're saying? You'll just be talking to the air.

There are all kinds of languages in the world. The words all have meaning. But maybe I don't understand what somebody is saying. Then I might as well be from another land.

It's the same way with you. You want gifts for your spirits. So try to get gifts that help God's people.

People who talk in different languages need to pray. They should pray that they can tell what they're saying. If I pray in a different language, my spirit prays. But my mind doesn't understand.

So what can I do? I'll pray with my spirit. But I'll pray with my mind, too. I'll sing with my spirit. But I'll sing with my mind, too.

What if you praise God only with your spirit? Others hear you, but they don't understand you. So how can they say "Yes"? They don't know what you're saying. You may be doing a good job of giving thanks to God. But that doesn't help the other people.

I thank God that I can talk in different languages. But sometimes I meet with Jesus' followers. Then I'm glad to say five words that people understand. That way, I can teach them. That's better than 10,000 (ten thousand) words people don't understand.

So what can we say? You get together, and everybody has something to share. Someone sings a song. Someone has something to teach. Someone has something to say that God showed him. Someone talks in a different language. Someone tells the meaning of the language. It should all be done to help God's people.

What if people talk in different languages? Two or three people should talk. They should take turns, and somebody should tell what they mean.

What if there isn't anybody to tell what they mean? Then the person with the different language should be quiet. He should just talk to himself and to God.

What if there are people who tell what God has to say? Then two or three should talk. The others should think carefully about what they said.

What if God shows something to somebody who is sitting down?

Then the first person should stop talking. You can all take turns. That way, everyone can learn things and be cheered up.

God doesn't make things go out of order. He makes things happen in peace.

Don't tell people they can't talk in different languages. Just do everything the right way. Take turns and do it in order.

Coming Back to Life

1 CORINTHIANS 15:1, 3-10, 12, 14-17, 19-20, 23-26, 28, 32-44, 50-58

I want to help you remember the Good News about Jesus. I told you about it. You believed it.

I taught you the most important thing I ever learned. Jesus died for our sins. It happened just like God's Word said it would. He was put in a grave. He came back to life on the third day.

Jesus let Peter see him. Then the rest of Jesus' special friends saw him. After that, Jesus came to more than 500 friends at the same time. Most of them are still alive. But some of them have died.

Jesus let James see him. Then all the apostles saw him. Last of all, he let me see him too. I was like a person who was born later.

I'm not an important apostle. I really shouldn't even be called an apostle. That's because I used to hurt Jesus' followers. But I am what I am because of God's kind love.

God's kind love changed me. I worked hard. But it wasn't me. It was God's kind love that was with me.

We told you Jesus came back to life again.

What if Jesus didn't come back to life? Then our teaching is good for nothing. Your faith is good for nothing. What's more, we are lying about God.

What if dead people don't live again? Then God didn't make Jesus live again. What if Jesus isn't alive? Then you're still lost in your sins. What if we have hope just in this life? Then people should feel more sorry for us than for anybody.

But Jesus really has come back to life. He was the first to die and come back to life forever.

Jesus lives. So he will come back again. His followers will come back to life too. Then the end will come. Jesus will get rid of every other power. He will be in charge until he controls all his enemies. The last enemy he will get rid of is death. Then Jesus will give the kingdom to God the Father. God will be in charge of everything.

What if dead people don't come back to life? Then some people say, "Let's eat and drink as much as we want. Tomorrow we'll just die." Don't believe a lie like that. "Bad friends mess up the good in you." Wake up and think! Stop sinning. Some people don't even know who God is.

Someone may ask, "How do dead people come back to life? What kind of body will they have?" That's silly! A seed you plant has to die first. Then it comes to life. God gives it the plant body he planned for it. He gives each kind of seed its own plant body.

All bodies aren't the same. People have one kind of body. Animals have another kind of body. Birds have another kind. Fish have another kind.

There are heavenly bodies. There are earthly bodies. Heavenly bodies have one kind of beauty. Earthly bodies have another kind.

The sun has one kind of beauty. The moon has another kind. The stars have another. Even stars are different from each other in how they shine.

Coming back to life will be the same way. The body will die one day. But it will come alive again. After that, it will never die.

Before it dies, the body grows like a plant. It's not very important. After it dies, it comes back to life showing God's power. Before it dies, it is weak. When it comes back to life, it is strong. Before it dies, it is a human body. When it comes back to life, it is a spirit body.

Human bodies can't get into God's kingdom. Things that die don't fit where things never die.

Listen! I'm telling you a mystery. We won't all die. But we will all be changed. We'll be changed in a flash, as quick as a wink. It will happen when the last horn sounds.

The horn will play. Then dead people will come back to life. They'll never die again. People who are alive will be changed. Things that die must become things that never die.

When that happens, Isaiah's words will come true. "We have won over death!" Hosea said it this way. "Death, what did you win? Now where is your power to hurt?"

Death hurts because of sin. Sin has power. That's because the Law says we're in trouble if we sin. But thank God! Jesus took our place when he died for us. So we don't have to get in trouble! Jesus helps us win over sin!

Stay with Jesus. Don't let anything move you away. Always do your best work for the Lord. You know that none of the work you do for him is for nothing.

Choosing How Much to Give

1 Corinthians 16:1-6, 8-21, 24; 1:1

Now let's talk about giving money for God's people. Each person should give some of his money. Do it on the first day of each week. People can choose how much to give. They can choose by looking at how much money they make.

Save some money. Then you'll have it ready when I come. I'll write letters to God's people in Jerusalem. Choose some men to take the letters and the money. They can take it to Jerusalem as a gift. I might go too, if it seems like I should. Then I'll come back to see you. I might even stay all winter. That way, you can help me get ready for my next trip.

I'll stay here in Ephesus until the Holiday of Weeks. It's possible for me to do some good work here. It's like a door that's open for me. But many people are against me.

Timothy may come to see you.

691

Make sure he doesn't worry about anything. He is doing God's work just like I am. Everybody should welcome him. Then send him on his way. He can come back to me.

Let me tell you about Apollos. I tried to get him to go and see you. But he didn't want to go right now. He will go some other time when he can.

Be careful. Keep a strong faith. Be brave. Be strong. Do everything with love.

The family of Stephanas was the first to follow Jesus in Greece. They help God's people. I hope you will let them lead you. Follow everyone who is hard at work for God.

I was glad when Stephanas came with two other men. They gave me what you couldn't give me. They made my spirit feel new again. We should listen to men like them.

Jesus' followers in Asia say hello. Aquila and Priscilla send a warm hello in the Lord. So do all of God's people who meet at their house.

God's people here say hello. Tell each other hello with a godly kiss.

I, Paul, am writing this hello with my own hand. I send my love to all of you in Jesus. Yes! Amen!

From Paul and Sosthenes, followers of Jesus.

The Silver Worker

ACTS 19:23–20:1

Now some problems came up in Ephesus. There was a man who worked with silver. His name was Demetrius. He made silver worship figures for a fake god. It was a woman goddess. She was called Artemis. Other silver workers helped make the figures. They got lots of money for doing it.

Demetrius got the other workers together one day. "We get lots of money in our business," he said. "But Paul tells people not to believe in Artemis. He says the gods we make are not real. People won't think our business is important anymore. People won't even think our great goddess Artemis is important."

The silver workers were very angry. They began to shout, "Artemis is great! She is the goddess of Ephesus!" Soon the whole city went along with them.

Two men had been traveling with Paul. The people pulled them into the crowd. The crowd took them to the meeting place.

Paul wanted to go to the crowd. He wanted to talk to them. But Jesus' followers wouldn't let him.

Some of the leaders of the land were Paul's friends. They sent him a message. They begged Paul not to go into the meeting place.

Most people didn't really know what was going on. Some were shouting this. Some were shouting that. Most of them didn't even know why they had come.

The Jews made a man named Alexander go up front. Some of them shouted at him, telling him what to do.

Alexander waved his hand. He wanted everyone to be quiet so he could talk.

But the people found out Alexander was Jewish. So they all began shouting together, "Artemis is great!" For about two hours they shouted, "Artemis is great!"

At last, a city leader got them quiet. He said, "Everybody knows our city guards the worship house of Artemis. So be quiet. Don't do anything you'll be sorry for later.

"You brought these men here," he said to the people of Ephesus. "They didn't rob the worship house. They didn't say anything bad about our goddess. Do Demetrius and the other silver workers have a problem with somebody? They can tell the judge.

"We are in danger here," said the city leader. "We might all be blamed for starting a panic. We wouldn't be able to tell why. There is no good reason for it." Then he told everybody to go home.

After all this, Paul called the believers together. He cheered them up. Then he said good-bye. He left for Macedonia. From there, he wrote another letter to Jesus' followers in Corinth.

Cheer Up
2 CORINTHIANS 1:1, 3-11, 15-24

To Jesus' followers in Corinth,

Cheer for God! He makes us feel better about our troubles. Now we can help other people feel better about their troubles. We give them the same love we got from God.

We share the hard times Jesus had. But we share his love and kindness, too. His love and kindness make us feel better.

If we have hard times, it's so you'll feel better. It's so you'll be saved from sin. If we cheer up, it's so you'll cheer up too. That helps you wait when times get hard.

We know you share our hard times. So we know you share our good times too.

We want you to know about our troubles in Asia. It was very hard. It was more than we could take. We really thought we would die. But this happened so we wouldn't lean on ourselves. We had to lean on God.

God is so great, he makes people come back to life. He is the one who

693

saved us from danger. He will keep saving us too. We put our hope in him. You help us by praying for us.

Two times I made plans to visit you. I wanted to help you. Did I plan this without thinking? Do I plan like people of the world do? Do I say yes and no at the same time? God always keeps his promises. That's for sure. And we don't say yes and no at the same time. That's just as sure.

Jesus never says yes and no at the same time. It has always been "Yes" with Jesus. God has made many promises. They are all answered with a "Yes" because of Jesus. Through Jesus, we say yes too. That shows how great God is.

God chose us. He showed that we belong to him. He put his Spirit in our hearts. That's something he gives us to show what's coming. It's a sign of his promise.

God knows that I didn't want you to worry. So I didn't come back to Corinth. I'm not your boss. Instead, I work with you. That way, you can have joy. Your faith will keep you strong. It will keep you following God.

Like Winners in a Parade
2 CORINTHIANS 2:1-2, 4-8, 10-11, 14-17

I chose not to visit you. It would only hurt. I might cry for you.

I was upset when I wrote to you. My heart was very sad. I had cried many tears. But I didn't write to make you sad. I wrote so you'd know how much I love you.

Someone there with you made me sad. In a way, he has made everybody sad. See the way everyone has acted toward him? That has paid him back for what he has done. That's enough.

Now you need to forgive him. Try to cheer him up. That way, sadness will not be too much for him. So let him know you love him.

If you forgive, then I forgive too. I forgive because of Jesus and because of you. That way, Satan won't be too smart for us. We know that he tries to plan bad things.

Thank God. He always leads us like winners in a parade with Jesus. He uses us to show everyone how sweet it is to know Jesus. It's like we offer a sweet smell that goes all through the air to God.

To people who don't believe, we're like a deadly smell. But to people who believe, we're the sweet smell of life.

We're not like a lot of people. We don't try to sell God's Word to make money. Instead, Jesus helps us say what is true. God sent us. He knows that.

A Letter from Jesus

2 CORINTHIANS 3:2-13, 18

You are like a letter that tells how we've helped you. Everybody knows you. Seeing you is like reading a letter from Jesus. This letter wasn't written with ink. It was written with God's living Spirit. God doesn't write on stone. He writes on human hearts.

We can't brag, because we're not able to do anything by ourselves. Being able to do something comes from God. He made us able to tell about his new special promise. It didn't come written down. It came from the Spirit.

The Law was the old way to tell about God. It was written on stone. But it didn't bring life.

The Law came with God's greatness. Moses' face was bright from seeing God. It was so bright that God's people couldn't keep looking at Moses. Even then, the brightness was fading.

Won't the Spirit's way to tell about God be greater? Won't it show more of God's shining greatness? That's the way of the Spirit. He brings life that's right with God.

God shows up so brightly now! His power from long ago doesn't seem bright at all anymore. The Law was fading away. But still it came with God's shining greatness. God's Spirit will never fade away. He will shine even brighter.

This is what we hope for. We are very brave. We aren't like Moses. His face was shining. He covered it until the brightness wore off. But our faces are not covered. So we share the Lord's shining greatness. We are being changed. We are becoming like him. He shines brighter and brighter in us every day. This is a gift from the Lord. He is the Spirit.

Clay Jars Full of Riches

2 CORINTHIANS 4:1-10, 13-14, 16-18

We work for God because of his kind love. We don't give up. Instead, we stop our secret, bad ways. We don't lie. We don't change God's Word. We tell the truth.

Our Good News about Jesus may be hidden. But it's hidden only to people who don't love God. Satan, the fake god of this world, closes their minds. So they can't see the Good News. They can't see the shining greatness of Jesus, who is just like God.

We don't teach about us. We teach about Jesus. He is Lord. He is the reason we serve and help you. When time began, God said, "Let light shine from the dark." Now God has made his light shine in our hearts. So we know Jesus shines with God's greatness.

This makes us rich! We are like clay jars full of riches from God. It's clear that this great power inside us comes from God, not from us.

We get pushed hard on every side. But we don't break. We wonder about things. But we don't give up. We get hurt. But God doesn't leave us. We get pushed down. But we're not killed. We are alive. But we always face death for Jesus. That way, people see Jesus living in us.

The psalm says, "I believed. So I speak." We believe with that same kind of faith. So we speak too. We know that God brought Jesus back to life. We know that he will bring us back to life too. Then we will be with you when we see God.

So we don't give up. Our bodies may be getting older. But inside, we are being made new every day.

Our troubles are not too bad. They only last a little while. These troubles will bring us greatness. It's a greatness that shines brighter than troubles.

This greatness will last forever. So we don't look at things we can see.

We look at what we can't see. Things we can see last only a short time. Things we can't see last forever.

Our Tent

2 CORINTHIANS 5:1-2, 4-12, 16-21

Our bodies are like tents we live in on earth. What if a body dies? Then we have a house in heaven. It's built by God, not by people. Until we get it, we think about it. We want very much to have our heavenly tent.

It's not that we want to get rid of this body. But we do want our heavenly body. We'll trade our dying bodies for bodies that live forever. This is the reason God made us. He gave us his Spirit as a promise. The Spirit is a promise of what's coming.

When we're in this body, we're away from Jesus. That means we live by believing, not by seeing. We'd like it better the other way. We'd like being away from this body and home with Jesus.

We may be in this body. We may be away from it. Both ways, we try to please Jesus. That's because one day, we'll be in front of him. He will judge us. Then each person will get what's coming to him. He will be paid back for what he did in this body. He may have done good things. Or he may have done bad things.

God sees clearly what we're like. Some people are proud of things that can be seen. But they're not proud of what's in their hearts. We want you to be proud of us. Then you can let those people know what we're really like.

We don't look at people the way the world does. If anyone follows Jesus, he has been made new. The old is gone. The new is here!

God brought us to himself through Jesus. Our job is to bring people to God. God does not count people's sins against them. He gave us that message. So we tell it to people. It's like God is calling other people through us.

So we beg you for Jesus. Come back to God. Jesus had no sin. He took our sin for us. Now we can be right with God.

NOVEMBER 7

A Fair Trade

2 CORINTHIANS 6:4-18

We want to show that we're God's followers. We keep on following him. We follow God in troubles. We follow him in hard times. We follow him in worries.

We follow God when people beat us. We follow him when they put us in jail. We follow him when they get together and shout at us. We follow him when we work hard. We follow him when we don't get to sleep at night. We follow him when we're hungry. We follow him when we do what's right. We follow him when we understand. We follow him when we wait quietly. We follow him when we're kind.

We follow God's Holy Spirit. We follow God with true love. We follow him by telling the truth. We follow him in his power.

We are true. But people think we lie. People know us. But they treat us as if they didn't know us. We are left for dead. But we keep living. People beat us. But we're not killed. We are sad. But we always show our joy. We are poor. But we make many people rich. We have nothing. But we have everything.

We are not keeping our love from you. But you're keeping your love from us. So let's make a fair trade. I'm talking to you as if you were my children. Open your hearts wide too.

Don't get tied down with people who don't believe in God. Can right and wrong fit together? Can light and darkness be together? Do Jesus and Satan agree? Does a believer agree with someone who doesn't believe? Is God's worship house the same as idols' worship houses?

We are God's living worship

house. God said long ago, "I will live with them. I will walk among them. I will be their God. They will be my people.

"Come away from other people. Be different," says God. "Don't get near anything bad. Then I will welcome you. I will be your Father. You will be my sons and daughters."

Make Room in Your Heart

2 CORINTHIANS 7:1-9, 11

We should think about God's promises, dear friends. Then we'll want to make our hearts clean. Let's get rid of everything sinful that makes our spirits dirty. Let's become right and good, because we look up to God.

You know that we haven't hurt anyone. So make room for us in your hearts. I'm not saying this to blame you. I said before that you have a big place in our hearts. We would live with you or die with you. I'm very proud of you. No matter what troubles we have, my joy is great.

Here's what happened when we got to Macedonia. We had no rest. Instead, we were bothered everywhere we turned. We had problems on the outside. We had fear on the inside.

But God helps people when they're down. He helped us feel better by sending our friend Titus. Titus told us

that you wanted to see me. He told me how sad you were. He told me how worried you were about me. That made me happier than ever.

I may have made you sad by my letter. I'm not happy because you were sad. But I'm happy that your sadness led you to change and do right.

See what being sorry in a godly way has done for you? You want very much to be clean and good. You are upset by sin. It scares you. You want very much to do what's right.

The First to Give

2 CORINTHIANS 8:1-11, 13-14

God's people in Macedonia had very hard times. They were very poor. But they ended up giving a lot. They gave as much as they could. They even gave more than they could. They begged us to let them share. First they gave themselves to God. Then they gave to us. That's just what God wanted.

So we asked Titus to help you also with your giving. You do a great job in everything. You're good at believing. You're good at talking. You're good at knowing things. You're good at wanting to do right.

You're good at loving us. So do a great job in your giving, too.

I'm not ordering you to do this. But I want to see how much you truly love. You know about Jesus' kind love. He was rich, but he became poor to help you. Because he did this, you can have his riches.

Last year you were the first to give. You wanted to give. So finish what you started. Look at what you have. Then give whatever you can.

We don't want others to be rich while you're poor. We want everyone to have enough. Right now, your riches can give poor people what they need. Someday, their riches can give you what you need.

The Big Gift

2 CORINTHIANS 9:2-7, 11, 15

You're ready to help. I've been bragging about it to the people in Macedonia. I told them you've been ready to give for a year. They know you want to give, so most of them are giving too.

I said you'd be ready to give. But I'm sending some men so you really will be ready. Some people from Macedonia might come with me. What if you weren't ready? Then we would feel bad. You'd feel bad too.

So I think it's good to send these men.

Remember this. If you plant a little, you will grow a little. If you plant a lot, you will grow a lot. People should give because they want to, not because they have to. God loves people who are happy to give.

God will make you rich in every way. Then you can give a lot any time. Your big giving will bring thanks to God.

And we thank God for his Son. He is the best gift!

Face to Face

2 CORINTHIANS 10:1-5, 8-13, 17-18

You say I'm shy when I'm face to face with you. You say I'm bold when I'm away! I have to be bold with some people. They're people who think we live the world's way.

We may live in the world. But we don't fight the way the world does. What we fight with has power from God. It tears down the enemy's strong places.

We fight anything that comes against knowing God. We catch every thought. We make those thoughts obey Jesus.

Sometimes I tell about how God put us in charge. That's to build you up, not to pull you down. I won't feel bad about that.

I don't want to scare you with my letters. Some people say, "He writes powerful letters. But when you see him, he is nothing." That's not true. When we come, we'll do what we've said in our letters.

We don't dare act like some people. They say how good they are. But they measure themselves by themselves. That's not wise.

We won't brag more than we should. We will brag only about what God has given us. Jeremiah said it this way. "If you brag, brag about God."

We can say that we're good. But that doesn't make us right with God. God will say who is good. That's the person who is right with him.

In Danger

2 CORINTHIANS 11:2-5, 13-15, 21-33

I want to give you to Jesus. I want you to be clean from sin for him. But I'm afraid. Maybe you believed a lie like Eve believed the snake's words. Maybe you went away from the true, clean love you had for Jesus.

What if somebody teaches you about a different Jesus? What if you follow a different spirit? What if you look for a different kind of Good News?

Some people think they are greater than apostles. They must be "super apostles." I don't think I'm less important than they are. These people aren't true apostles. They lie. They pretend they are apostles of Jesus. It's no wonder. Even Satan pretends he is an angel of light. So I'm not surprised when his servants pretend they're servants of what's right. They'll end up getting what's coming to them.

Think about what others brag about. I will also dare to brag. Are they Jewish? So am I. Are they God's people? So am I. Are they from Abraham's family? So am I. Do they serve Jesus? I serve Jesus even more.

I'm silly to talk this way. But I worked harder. I've been in jail more often. I've been beaten harder. I've been left for dead again and again.

Five times, Jewish people beat me. Each time, they hit me 39 times. Three times they beat me with rods. They threw rocks at me once. Three times I was in a ship that crashed. For a night and day, I was in the sea. I have moved around all the time.

I've been in danger from rivers. I've been in danger from robbers. I've been in danger from my own people and from people who aren't Jewish. I've been in danger in the city and in the country. I've been in danger at sea. And I've been in danger from people who were not true believers.

I've worked hard. Lots of times I've gone without sleep. I've been hungry and thirsty. I've often had no food. I've been cold. There were times when I didn't have enough clothes.

Every day I worry about Jesus' followers. When others aren't strong, I don't feel strong. When others sin, I get upset.

In Damascus, the man in charge wanted to catch me. So he set guards up all around the city. But my friends put me in a basket. Then they let the basket down out of a window in the wall. So I got away.

I may brag. But I'll brag about things that show I'm weak. God knows this is not a lie.

NOVEMBER 9

Bragging

2 CORINTHIANS 12:1-12, 14, 20-21

I have to brag some more. It won't do much good. But I'm going to tell about things God showed me.

I know a follower of Jesus. He went up to a part of heaven 14 years ago. Maybe just his spirit went. I don't know. Only God knows. But I know that this man went there. He heard things he can't even tell. They are things that God won't let people talk about.

I'll brag about a man like that. But I won't brag about myself. I'll just talk about how I'm not strong.

What if I did brag? I wouldn't be a fool. I'd just be telling the truth. But I won't brag about myself. Then no one will think I'm better than I am.

God gave me something to keep me from being proud. It's a place that hurts in my body. It comes from Satan. It's here to bother me. Three times I asked Jesus to take it away. But Jesus said, "My kind love is enough for you. My power shows up best when you're weak."

So I'm glad to brag that I'm weak. Then Jesus' power can stay with me. That's why I'm glad to be weak. I'm glad when people say bad things about me. I'm glad to have hard times. I'm glad that people want to hurt me. I'm glad to have trouble. I may not be strong by myself. But I'm very strong in Jesus.

I'm sounding like a fool. But you made me do it. You should have told about the good I've done. I'm not less important than the "super apostles," even though I'm nothing.

There is a way to tell that someone is an apostle. You can tell by signs and wonders. When we were with you, we did these.

Now I'm ready to visit you again. This will make three times. I won't be any trouble to you. I don't want your things. I want you.

I'm afraid you may be fussing. You may be wanting things that others have. You may be acting in anger. You may be in groups, against each other. You may be saying bad things about each other. You may be proud.

Then I'll be sad about people who sinned and haven't changed. They haven't chosen to do right. They use sex in a wrong way. Their hearts aren't clean and good.

Live in Peace

2 CORINTHIANS 13:1-5, 7-13; 1:1

This will make three times I've come to see you. I told you what would happen the last time I was with you. I'll tell you again. I won't be easy on the people who sinned before.

Jesus is strong enough to deal with you. He may not have seemed strong when he died on the cross. But he is alive now because of God's power.

We may not seem very strong. But by God's power, we'll live with him and serve you.

Look at yourselves. See if you are believers. Test yourselves. Don't you know that Jesus is in you? He is in you unless you don't believe.

We pray that you won't do anything wrong. We want you to do what's right. It's not that we worry

about looking like we failed. But we can't do anything against the truth. We can work only for the truth.

We're glad if we're weak and you're strong. We pray that you will do what's right. That's why I'm writing to you. I don't want to be hard on you. God put me in charge. But I should build you up, not tear you down.

At last, I want to say good-bye. Try to be clean from sin and to be good. Listen to what I say. Agree together. Live in peace. Then the God of love and peace will be with you.

When you tell each other hello, give a kiss that's godly. All God's people say hello.

From Paul and Timothy.

A Letter from Greece

ACTS 20:1-3; ROMANS 1:7, 10, 13, 15-32

Paul traveled through Macedonia. He cheered up Jesus' followers there. At last he came to Greece. He stayed there for three months.

While Paul was in Greece, he 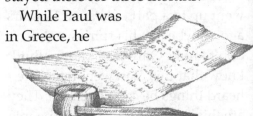 wrote a letter. He sent it to his friends in Rome.

To my friends in Rome,

I'm praying that God will let me come see you. Lots of times I made plans to come see you. But I haven't been able to come.

I want to teach you the Good News about Jesus.

I'm not shy about the Good News. It's God's power. It saves everybody who believes. First, it saves the Jewish people. Then it saves people who aren't Jewish. God shows how we can be right with him. We can be right by believing.

God is showing his anger. He is against anything that leaves him out. He is against sinful people who hide the truth by their sins.

These people know about God. God clearly showed who he is. He showed his greatness. People can see his greatness by looking at what he made. So there is no reason for people not to believe.

These sinful people knew God. But they didn't show how great he was. And they didn't thank him. Their thoughts were no good. Their hearts were foolish and dark. They said they were wise. But they were really fools. They made figures of people and animals. They said these idols were God. They didn't worship and serve their Maker. Instead, they worshiped and served what they made.

So God let them go. He let them have the sin their hearts wanted. They didn't even care about their own bodies. Instead, they sinned with sex. They threw away the truth of God. They held on to a lie.

God let them do what they wanted so badly to do. He let them do things that made them feel like nothing. Men wanted sex with men. Women wanted sex with women. This is not the way God made it to be. In their bodies, they were paid back for their sin.

They didn't think it was important to know God. So he let them have minds full of nothing important. He let them do what they shouldn't do.

Sinful people are now full of all kinds of sin. They want what others have. They kill. They fuss and fight. They lie. They hate people. They say bad things about others. They hate God. They are rude. They are proud. They brag. They make up new ways to sin. They don't obey their parents. They don't think. They don't believe. They seem to have no feelings. They aren't kind.

They know what's right. They know what God says. They know they should die for what they've done. But still they do those things. They think it's all right when other people do those things too.

Rules That Are in the Heart

ROMANS 2:1-11, 25-29

You have no reason to blame others for what they do. When you blame others, you blame yourself. You do the same kinds of things they do.

When God blames people for doing wrong, he is right. You are only a person. So when you blame others, watch out. You do the same things.

God will judge what's right and what's wrong. Then do you think you'll get away with what you've done? Do you treat God's wonderful kind love like it's nothing?

God waits for you. Do you think that's nothing? God waits so you will follow him and stop doing wrong.

What if you say, "I won't follow. I won't change." Then you're just asking God to be angry at you. Someday, God will say who has done right or wrong. God "will give each person what he should get."

What if we keep doing good? What if we show how great God is? Then he will give us life that lasts forever. But what if we think only about what we want? What if we follow sin? Then God will be angry.

There are problems for people who sin. But greatness and peace come to people who do good. This is for Jewish people and for people who aren't Jewish. God does not have favorites.

Being Jewish is great. But that's true only if you obey God's laws. If you don't, you might as well not be Jewish. Let's say people obey God's laws. But they aren't Jewish. Then to God, they are his people. They make you look bad. You are Jewish. You know God's laws. But you don't obey them.

People aren't Jewish just because they look Jewish. A real Jew has the heart of a Jew. He loves God in his heart. This comes from God's Spirit. It doesn't come from words written down in laws. This person wants God to cheer for him. He doesn't look for praise from people.

Even If Every Person Lies

ROMANS 3:1-2, 9-18, 21-31

What makes it special to be Jewish? Many things do! But the most important thing is that God gave Jews his words.

What should we say? Are we Jews better than other people? No. Jewish people sin, and people who aren't Jewish sin. The psalms and Isaiah put it this way.

"Nobody does what is right.
  Nobody.
Nobody understands.

Nobody looks for God.
Nobody does good things. Nobody.
They open their mouths to lie.
    Their lips are like snake bites.
They say bad words. They are angry.
    They hurt others.
They leave sadness wherever they
    go.
    They don't know how to have
    peace.
They don't think God is important
    at all."

But now God is showing us how to be right with him. It has nothing to do with the Law. It's being right with God by believing in Jesus.

Everyone sins. No one is good enough for God's greatness. But everyone is made clean from sin by God's kind love. This is free. It's just as if we had never sinned. It's all because God gave Jesus as a gift. Jesus paid for our sins by dying for us.

God showed how fair he is. Somebody has to get in trouble for what people have done wrong. So God sent Jesus to die on the cross for our sin. That pays for our sin. It also makes us clean from sin. If we believe in Jesus, it's just as if we'd never sinned.

So how can we brag? We can't. Did we obey all the rules? No. We believed. People are cleaned from sin by believing in Jesus. It has nothing to do with obeying God's laws.

Is God only the God of Jews? Isn't he also the God of people who aren't Jewish? Yes. There is only one God. He makes all people right with him when they trust him. Does that mean that God's laws aren't important? No. We obey his laws!

Believing the Promise
ROMANS 4:1-8, 13, 17, 19-25

So then what about Abraham? Was he made right with God by the good work he did? If he was, he would have had something to brag about. That's because when you work, you get paid. Your pay is not a gift. You're supposed to get paid.

But it is written that "Abraham believed God. That's what made everything right between Abraham and God." So trust God. Then you'll be right with him, because you believe.

This is what David said.

"People are happy when their sins
    are forgiven.
    Their sins are erased.
People are happy when God throws
    away the list of their sins.
    God doesn't hold their sins
    against them."

God gave Abraham a promise. God promised that his family would become a big nation. Then good things would come to the world. This promise didn't come by God's rules. It came because Abraham believed God.

Abraham knew he was too old to have children. In fact, he was almost 100 years old. He knew his wife, Sarah, was old too. But he believed God's promise anyway.

Abraham's faith was strong. He believed God had the power to do what he promised. That's why God said Abraham was right with him.

All of this happened not just for Abraham. It happened for us, too. We can learn from Abraham. We can believe in God also. When we do, God says we are right with him.

God gave the promise to Abraham. "I made you a father of many nations," said God. To God, Abraham is the father of all of us.

Jesus died for our sins. God made him alive again. So now we can live just as if we'd never sinned.

At the Right Time
ROMANS 5:1-4, 6-11

We believe. So it's just as if we'd never sinned. Now we have peace with God. This peace comes to us through Jesus, who brought us to God. Now we live in God's kind love by believing in Jesus.

We show our joy, because we hope in God's power. We're happy even when we have hard times. That's because we know hard times teach us how to keep going. When we keep going, we grow to be good people. When we are good people, we have hope. We hope for life that lasts forever.

You see, we could not save ourselves. We had no power. But at the right time, Jesus came. He died for people who sin. Sometimes a person will die for someone who does what's right. Sometimes a person will die for another good person. But we were sinners. Jesus died for us anyway. That shows just how much God loves us.

Now it's just as if we'd never sinned. It's all because of Jesus' blood. What's more, we'll be saved from God's anger! We were God's enemies. But now he lets us be his children, because Jesus died. His life saves us. That's why we show our joy. We can have life forever. It's all because of Jesus our Lord.

Into the Water
ROMANS 6:1-6, 9-13, 15-18, 21-23

Should we sin so God can be kinder to us? No! We died to sin. We can't live in sin anymore.

Being baptized is like going into the grave with Jesus. We go into the water. Then we come out again. We can live a new life. It's just like Jesus did when he came back to life again.

We were dipped in water. So we shared Jesus' "grave." Our old self died with him. Now sin is gone from us.

Sin doesn't control Jesus. When he died, the power of sin died. He is alive now, living for God. You're like that too. You're dead to the power of sin. Now you live for God.

So don't let sin control you. Don't obey it. Don't give your body to sin. Don't be a tool for what's bad. Give yourself to God. He has brought you from death to life.

Should we sin because God is so kind? No! Don't you know? You are the servant of the one you obey. When you served sin, what good did it do? Sin just ends in death!

But thanks to God, you have obeyed his teaching. Now you are free from sin. So you serve God. What good does that do? A lot of good! You become special and good. Serving God leads to life that lasts forever.

The pay for sin is death. But God gives us a gift. It's life that lasts forever. It comes to us because of Jesus.

Doing What I Don't Want to Do

ROMANS 7:5-7, 10, 15, 17, 21-25

Sin used to control us. We wanted to do what was wrong. The Law let us know it was wrong. Sin just ended in death.

But now we don't have the Law telling us what to do. Now God's Spirit tells us what's right. We serve God now because the Spirit tells us to. We don't do it because a law says to.

So does that mean the Law is bad? No! The Law is right and good. It showed me what sin was. It showed me that sin is terrible, because it brings death.

I want to do good, but I can't. Instead, I do things I don't want to do. Sin must be living in me. It's right beside me. But inside me, I love God's law. But another law works in me. It fights me. I feel like I'm in sin's jail. This is terrible! Who will save me? Thank God through Jesus! He will save me.

More than Winners

ROMANS 8:1-9, 11-15, 21, 23, 26-29, 31-35, 37-39

People who follow Jesus don't get blamed for their sins. That's because the law of God's Spirit makes us free from sin's law. It makes us free from death.

The old Law didn't have that power. It wasn't strong enough to get rid of sin in us.

But God was strong enough to set us free from death. God sent his own Son, Jesus. Jesus lived in a body like a man. He was a special gift God gave to pay the price of sin. The Law says if you sin, you die. We sinned, so we should die. But Jesus died instead. He did it for us. Now we don't live by sin. We live by the Spirit.

Some people live by sin. They just think about what they want. When sin controls a mind, there is death.

But some people live by the Spirit. They think about what the Spirit wants. When the Spirit controls a mind, there is life and peace.

A sinful mind doesn't like God. It doesn't follow God's law. It can't. When sin controls people, they can't please God.

But sin does not control you.

God's Spirit controls you, if his Spirit lives in you.

God made Jesus come back to life. Let's say his Spirit lives in you. Then he will give life to your body too!

So we have a job to do. It's not our job to sin. That brings death. Our job is to live by the Spirit. People who follow God's Spirit are God's children. So we can call to him, "Daddy! Father!"

Someday, everything God made will be free. Things he made won't grow old or break down. They won't die or rust or rot.

Our hard times are nothing when we think about what's coming. We wait to have our bodies made new. That's what we hope for.

God's Spirit helps us. We don't know what we should pray for. But the Spirit does. So he prays for us. He tells God things we don't know how to say. God looks into our hearts. He knows what the Spirit has in mind. The Spirit prays for what God wants for us.

We know God makes everything turn out for our good. He does this for people who love and follow him. God knew us before we were born. He planned for us to grow to be like Jesus. That way, Jesus will be his first Son. But we can be God's children too. We can be Jesus' brothers and sisters.

If God is for us, who can be against us? He didn't keep back his own Son. He gave up Jesus for all of us. So don't you think he will give us everything we need?

Who will blame us for anything? God chose us. He makes us good and right with him. So who can say we do what's wrong?

Jesus died. What's more, he came back to life. Now he is at God's right side. Jesus prays for us too.

So who can take us away from Jesus' love? Can trouble take us away? Can hard times? What if people treat us badly for doing good? Can that take us away from Jesus' love? Can needing food take us away from Jesus' love? What if we need clothes? Can that take us away from his love? Can danger take us away? No. These things will never take us away from Jesus' love. We are more than winners because he loved us.

I am sure of this. Death can't keep us from God's love. Life can't. Angels can't. Bad spirits can't. Nothing with us right now can keep God's love away. Nothing that can happen will keep God's love away. No power can keep God's love away, nothing high or low. Nothing in the world can keep God's love from us. We'll always have this love from Jesus.

A Sad Heart

ROMANS 9:2-5, 24-25, 30-32

My heart is very sad. It's because of my people, the Jews. I could let myself be taken away from Jesus. I'd do it if it would bring the Jewish people to him. He chose them to be his children. God's promises belong to them. He gave them the Law and worship. Their family from long ago were God's people. Jesus even comes from their family line.

But God didn't just choose Jewish people. He also chose people who are not Jewish.

God gave this message to Hosea the prophet.

"There are some who are not my
    people.
But I will call them my people.
There are some who are not my
    loved ones.
But I will call them my loved
    ones."

So what can we say? The Jewish people tried to be right by keeping the rules. But that didn't make them right with God. That's because they didn't believe. People who aren't Jewish didn't even try to be right with God. But God made them right with him anyway. That's because they believed God.

Beautiful Feet

ROMANS 10:1-4, 8-10, 12-15, 18-21

Here's what my heart wants. Here's what I ask God to do for the Jews. I pray that they will be saved.

I can tell you about the Jewish people. They work hard for God. But they don't really know what they're doing. They tried to be right on their own. But being right is a gift from God. The Jewish people wouldn't let God give it to them.

The Law was given to the Jews. It was given so they'd come to Jesus. Then they could be right with God like everyone who believes.

God's Word is near you. It's in your mouth. It's in your heart. That's the faith we're talking about.

So say it with your mouth. "Jesus is Lord." Believe that God made him come back to life again. Then you will be saved. When you believe with your heart, it's just as if you'd never sinned. When you say with your mouth that you believe, you are saved.

Jewish people are no different than people who aren't Jewish. God is the Lord of both. He gives good things to everyone who calls on him. Joel said it this way. "Everyone who calls on the name of the Lord will be saved."

But they can't talk to Jesus if they don't believe in him.

They can't believe in Jesus if they never heard of him.

They can't hear about Jesus if nobody tells them.

Nobody can tell them unless someone sends people to tell them.

Isaiah wrote this. "People's feet are beautiful when they bring Good News!"

Did the Jewish people hear? Yes. The psalm says it this way. "It was as if everything God made could talk. The words went around the world."

Next question. Didn't the Jewish people understand? Moses wrote these words from God. "I'll use people who are not Jewish. They'll make Jewish people want what they have."

Isaiah wrote these words from God. The words are about people who aren't Jewish. "People who didn't look for me found me. I showed who I am to people who didn't ask for me."

Here's what God said about the Jewish people. "I have held out my hands to these people all day long. But they won't come to me."

NOVEMBER 13

A Wild Olive Branch

ROMANS 11:1-5, 7-8, 11-12, 17-26, 28-29, 33-34, 36

Next question. Did God turn his people away? No! I'm Jewish

myself. I came from the family line of Abraham. I'm from the family group of Benjamin. God didn't turn his people away. He knew them long ago.

God's Word tells us about Elijah. He cried to God about the Jewish people. "Lord, they killed your prophets! They tore your altars down. I'm the only prophet left. They're trying to kill me, too!"

What did God tell Elijah? "I still have 7,000 Jewish people who belong to me. They don't worship idols."

It's the same way now. There are a few people God chose. He chose them by his kind love.

The Jews tried so hard. They tried to see how to be right with God. But they missed it. Some of them didn't care about God anymore. Isaiah said, "God gave them foggy minds. He gave them eyes that couldn't see. He gave them ears that couldn't hear. They're like that even now."

Next question. Did Jewish people fall too far away from God? Did they fall so far that they can't get back to him? No! They sinned. Then God planned that other people would be saved. These are people who aren't Jewish. God planned that this would make his people want what the others have.

The Jews sinned. That means other people can get God's great riches. So what will it mean when the Jews turn to God? The riches will be even greater!

The Jews are like branches on God's tree. They were broken off of the tree. You are like a wild olive branch. You were put onto the plant where the old branch was. Now you get to have sap from the olive root.

But don't brag about being better than the first branches. Think about this. You don't hold up the root. The root holds you up.

You'll say, "Branches were broken off so I could be put on." That's true. But they were broken off because they didn't believe. You were put on because you do believe.

So don't brag. Be careful. God broke off the first branches. So he can break you off too, if you turn away from him.

Let's say the Jews believe and turn to God again. Then God will put them back on his tree. God can do it. You were a wild olive branch. God put you on the tree. So it's easy for him to put them back. It's their own tree!

I want you to know about this mystery. Then you won't think you're better than the Jews. Here's part of the reason why the Jews turned away from God. It's so other people could come into God's kingdom. Then the Jews will be saved. God loves the Jews. He doesn't change his mind about who he chooses.

How great God's riches are!
How wise he is!
How much he knows!
We don't know how he chooses.
We can't tell which way he will go!

Isaiah said, "Who knows what's in God's mind?
Who ever told him what he should do?"

Everything comes from God.
Everything lives through him.
Everything belongs to him.

God will be the greatest forever. Yes! Amen!

Stick with Each Other
ROMANS 12:1-2, 4-21
So think about God's kind love. Then give yourself to him. Be a living gift. Be special and clean. Make God happy. This is the way your spirit worships him.

Don't be like people of the world. Be changed by letting God make your mind new again. Then you'll know what God wants. You'll know what's good. You'll know what makes God happy. You'll know what's right.

Every person has one body. Each body has many parts. All of the parts do different things.

It's like this with Jesus. There are many of us who follow Jesus. Together we are like a body. We belong together. But each of us is made to be different.

God made some people good at telling his words to others. So they should tell God's words. They should do it by using the faith God gives them.

God made some people good at helping. So they should help.

God made some people good at teaching. So they should teach.

God made some people good at making others feel better. So that's what they should do.

God made some people good at giving to others. So they should give a lot.

God made some people good leaders. So they should lead people as well as they can.

God made some people to be kind

and loving. So they should gladly be kind and loving.

Your love should be real. Hate sinful things. Hang on to good things. Stick with each other. Love each other like brothers and sisters. Treat other people as if they're better than you.

Always be in a hurry to do what's right. See that your spirit keeps wanting to serve the Lord.

Be happy because of the hope you have. Wait in peace when you have troubles. Keep praying. Share with God's people who need things. Welcome people into your house.

Pray for good things to happen to people. Pray for people even if they treat you badly.

Be happy with people who are happy. Be sad with people who are sad. Live at peace with each other.

Don't be proud. Be happy to be with people who don't seem important. Don't think you're the best.

Make sure you do what's right. Live at peace with everybody if you can.

Don't try to get back at people. Let God do it. In God's Word the Lord says, "It's my job to pay people back. I'll take care of it."

God's Word also has this wise saying.

"What if your enemy is hungry?
Feed him.

What if he is thirsty?
Give him a drink.
Do good to your enemy.
It's like putting fire on his head."

Don't let sin get control of you. Win over sin by doing good.

Wake Up!
ROMANS 13:1, 3-14

People should obey the leaders of their country. Leaders were put in charge by God. Leaders make sure people follow the rules. People who obey don't have to be afraid. But people who do wrong should be afraid.

You don't want to be afraid of people in charge. So do what's right. Then they'll tell you that you've done a good job. They're God's servants. They're supposed to do good for you.

So obey the people in charge. Do it not just because you'll get in trouble if you don't. Do it because it's what God wants. You'll feel better when you do what's right.

That's why you pay taxes. It's because the people in charge are God's servants. They make sure everyone obeys the rules.

Give people what you're supposed to give them. Are you supposed to pay them your taxes? Then pay them. Are you supposed to treat them as important people? Then treat them as important people.

Pay back anything you owe to someone. But you'll always owe people your love. If you love people, you've done what God wants.

Remember God's rules? "Have sex only with your wife or husband." "Don't kill." "Don't steal." There are other rules too. But one rule takes care of all the others. That rule says, "Love your neighbor the same way you love yourself." Love doesn't hurt people. Love helps you obey God's laws.

You need to understand what's happening now. It's time to wake up! It's time to watch. The time when we'll be saved is near. It's closer than it was when we first believed. It's as if the night is almost over. The day when we'll be saved is almost here.

So let's stop doing things that are bad. Bad people try to hide what's bad. Let's do what's right. We don't mind people seeing what's right.

Let's not have wild parties. Let's not get drunk. Let's not have sex with anyone but the person we marry. Let's not work to get things that belong to others.

Let's get close to Jesus. Let's not think about things that might make us sin.

Your Friend's Faith

ROMANS 14:1-14, 17-19, 22-23

Some people don't have much faith. But don't judge them. Some people believe they can eat everything. Other people eat only vegetables. The person who eats everything shouldn't think people who don't are silly. The person who doesn't eat everything shouldn't blame people who do. They belong to God too.

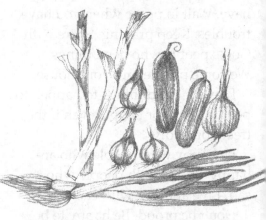

How can you judge a follower of God? God will say if his follower is standing close to him. God will say if the person has fallen away from him. But we know that the person will stand close. God can help him do it.

Some people think one day is more important than another. Other people think every day is alike. Both ways are fine. Each person needs to choose what he thinks is right.

Somebody thinks one day is more special. So he thanks God for it. Somebody eats meat. He thanks

God for it. Somebody doesn't eat meat. He thanks God too.

Nobody lives by himself. Nobody dies by himself. If we live, we live for God. If we die, we die for God. Both ways, we belong to God.

That's why Jesus died. That's why he came back to life again. He did it so he could be the Lord. He is Lord of people who die and people who live.

So why do you judge others? Why do you treat them like they're not important? All of us will stand in front of God someday. He will judge us all.

Isaiah wrote down these words from God.

"You can be sure that everyone will
    bow down in front of me.
Every mouth will tell that I am God."

Then each person will have to tell God what he did. He will have to tell why he did it.

Let's stop blaming each other. Don't make people do things they think are wrong. I'm sure it's all right to eat any kind of food. But some people think it's a sin to eat some foods. So for them, those aren't good foods to eat.

God's kingdom isn't made of eating and drinking. It's made of what's right. It's made of peace. It's made of joy in God's Holy Spirit.

God is happy with people who serve Jesus this way. Other people are happy with them too.

So let's try to do things that bring peace. Let's do things that are good for everybody.

Be careful of the things you say yes to. Make sure they're not things you can be blamed for.

Good things will come if you do what's right. But if you think something is wrong, don't do it.

NOVEMBER 15

One Heart

ROMANS 15:1-7, 13-15, 23, 25-26, 28, 30-33

Some people have a lot of faith. They should be kind to people who don't have so much faith.

We shouldn't try to make just ourselves happy. We should try to make others happy. We should try to do good for them and help them. Even Jesus didn't try to make himself happy.

God's Word from long ago is there to teach us. It helps us keep living the right way. It makes us brave. That gives us hope.

I pray that God will help you work together to follow Jesus. That way, it will seem like you have one heart. Together you can show God's greatness.

Jesus made you his friend. So be friends with each other.

God is the God of hope. Trust in him. Then he can fill you with joy and peace. Hope can flow in and out of you by the power of God's Spirit.

I'm sure you are full of what's good. You know all you need to know. You can teach each other. I've been brave to write about some of these things. I'm helping you remember them again.

I've wanted to come see you for a long time. But right now I'm on my way to Jerusalem. I'll help God's people there. I'm taking money that others sent to help the poor people. I'll make sure God's people get it. Then I'll go on to Spain. I'll visit you on the way.

Please help me by praying for me. Ask God to save me from people who don't believe. Ask God to make my work helpful.

Then, if God wants, I can come see you. I'll be full of joy. Being with you will make me feel like new! I pray that the God of peace will be with you all. Yes! Amen!

A Godly Kiss

ROMANS 16:1-24, 27; 1:1

I want you to know that Phoebe is a good person. She helps Jesus' followers. So welcome her the way God's people should be welcomed. Give her any help she needs. She has helped many people. I'm one of them.

Say hello to Priscilla and Aquila. They worked with me for Jesus. They put their lives in danger for me. I'm thankful for that. Say hello to the church that meets at their house.

Say hello to Epenetus. He is my dear friend. He was the first person in Asia to believe in Jesus.

Say hello to Mary. She worked very hard for you.

Say hello to the two people who are part of my family. They have been in jail with me. They are great people in the group of Jesus' friends. They believed in Jesus before I did.

Say hello to Ampliatus. I love him in the Lord.

Say hello to the people who work with us in Jesus.

Say hello to Apelles. He has had his faith tested. But he still believes and belongs to Jesus.

Say hello to the families that believe in Jesus.

Say hello to the women who work hard for Jesus.

Say hello to my dear friend Persis. She is another woman who works very hard for Jesus.

Tell Rufus hello. Jesus chose him and his mother. She has been like a mother to me, too.

Say hi to all the brothers and sisters.

Say hello to all of God's people. When you say hello, give everyone a godly kiss.

All of Jesus' churches say hello.

Please watch out for people who start fights. They'll try to keep you from doing what you should. Stay away from them. People like that are not serving Jesus. They serve themselves. They say nice things. They tell you how they like you. But they lie. People who don't see through their lies believe them.

Everybody has heard how you obey. I'm happy about that. But I want you to be wise about what's good. Don't have anything to do with what's sinful.

Soon God will pound Satan down under your feet.

I pray that Jesus' kind love will be with you.

Timothy works with me. He says hello. So do the three men here who are in my family.

My name is Tertius. Paul is telling me what to write down. I say hello to you in the Lord.

Gaius is making me feel welcome at his house. The whole church here feels welcome at his house! Gaius says hi!

Erastus is in charge of some of the work in the city. He and Quartus say hi!

Our only wise God is great forever through Jesus! Yes! Amen!

From Paul, Jesus' servant.

NOVEMBER 16

Falling Out the Window

Acts 20:6-12, 16-25, 27-38

Paul and his friends traveled to the city of Troas. They stayed there for seven days.

On Sunday, they met together for the Lord's Supper. Paul taught the people there. He planned to leave town the next day. So he kept talking until after midnight.

They were in a room upstairs on the third floor. Lots of lamps were in the room. One young man sat in a window. His name was Eutychus.

Now Paul talked and talked and talked. Eutychus went to sleep. Soon he was very sound asleep. All of a sudden, he fell out the window. He fell to the ground.

When the people picked Eutychus up, he was dead.

Paul went downstairs too. He hugged the young man. "Don't worry," Paul said. "He is alive!"

Then Paul went back upstairs. He ate and started teaching again. He talked until after the sun came up. Then he left.

The people went home. So did the young man. He was alive. All the people were very glad.

Paul and his friends sailed to a place near Ephesus. Paul was in a hurry to get to Jerusalem. So he didn't go into Ephesus. He just sent for the church leaders there.

The church leaders came out of the city to see Paul.

Paul said, "You know how I lived with you. I served the Lord. I wasn't proud. The Jewish people made plans against me. But I kept teaching.

"I went from house to house," said Paul. "I taught you things that would help you. I told Jews and Greeks to turn to God. I told them to be sorry for the wrong they'd done. I told them to believe in Jesus.

"Now God's Spirit wants me to go to Jerusalem," said Paul. "I don't know what will happen there. But I do know this. Wherever I go, God's Holy Spirit tells me to watch out. Hard times are coming, even time in jail.

"But my life doesn't mean anything to me," said Paul. "I only want to finish the job Jesus gave me to do. That's the job of telling the Good News about God's kind love.

"I know you won't see me again," said Paul. "So I wanted to tell you this. I have told you all that God wants. Take care of yourselves, and take care of God's people. Be shepherds of God's church. He bought the church with his own blood.

"After I leave, other teachers will come," said Paul. "But they'll be like wolves in a group of sheep. Even men who meet with you now will bend the truth. They will try to get people to follow them. So be careful!

"Now I give you to God and his kind love. God's words can build you up," said Paul. "I haven't wanted anybody's silver or gold. I haven't wanted anybody's clothes. I worked to get everything my friends and I needed. I showed you how to work hard to help people who aren't strong. Remember Jesus' words. 'It is better to give than to get,' he said."

Then Paul and the church leaders all bowed and prayed. The people cried and hugged Paul. They were sad because he said they'd never see him again. Then they went with Paul to his ship.

Crowds and Shouts

ACTS 21:1-24, 26-40

Paul and his friends sailed to a place where they found another ship. That ship was sailing to a city near Jerusalem. So they sailed on that ship.

The ship stopped for a few days at Tyre. They met some of Jesus' followers in that city. They stayed with them for a week.

These people asked Paul not to go to Jerusalem. But Paul went anyway. All the people walked out of the city with Paul. Even the children went. They all prayed on the beach. Then they said good-bye to each other. Paul and his friends got on their ship. They sailed on.

They landed at Caesarea. There they stayed with a man named Philip. He was a man who taught the Good News. He had four daughters who were not married yet. They could tell people God's words.

One day, another prophet who could tell God's words came to town. This was a man named Agabus. He took Paul's belt. Agabus tied up his own hands and feet with it. He said, "The Holy Spirit says that Paul will be tied up like this. Jewish leaders in Jerusalem will send Paul to people who aren't Jewish."

Then everyone there begged Paul not to go to Jerusalem.

"Why cry?" asked Paul. "Why break my heart? I'm ready to be in chains for Jesus. I'm even ready to die for Jesus." Paul would not change his mind.

So his friends gave up. "We pray that what God wants will be done," they said.

Some of Jesus' followers from Caesarea went with Paul to Jerusalem. They took him to a house where he and his friends could stay. The man who lived there was from Cyprus. He was one of the first people from Cyprus to follow Jesus.

Jesus' followers in Jerusalem were glad to see Paul.

The next day, Paul and his friends went to see James. All the leaders of Jesus' followers were there. Paul told them about his trip. He told them what God had done for people who weren't Jewish. He told all about the work God had helped him do.

The leaders praised God. Then they told Paul something. "Thousands of Jews have believed in Jesus," they said. "But they still follow the Law. They heard that you teach Jews to stop following the Law. The Jews who follow the Law will hear that you're in town.

"So we have an idea," said the leaders. "Four men here have made a special promise to God. It's a vow. They must do some special things at the worship house. So go with them. Pay for what they need. Then people will see that you obey the Law too. They'll know that what they heard about you isn't true."

So Paul went to the worship house.

But some Jews from Asia saw him there. They got the whole crowd upset. They pulled Paul into the group. They shouted, "Help us! This man teaches everybody to go against the Law. He even brought people who aren't Jewish into this worship house!"

They had seen Paul before with a man from Ephesus. They thought

Paul had brought him into the worship house. But he hadn't.

The whole city was upset now. People came running from everywhere. They pulled Paul out of the worship house. They closed the gates. They began beating Paul. They were trying to kill him.

The captain of the Roman army heard about it. He heard that the whole city was in a panic. So he took guards with him. He ran to the crowd.

The crowd saw the captain and his guards. So they stopped beating Paul.

The captain walked up and took Paul. He told the guards to put chains on him. Then he asked who Paul was. He asked what Paul had done.

Some people shouted this. Some shouted that. The captain couldn't find out the truth. There was too much noise. So he told the guards to take Paul away. The guards came to take him into one of the army buildings.

They got Paul to the steps of the building. But the crowd was being mean. So the guards had to carry him. The crowd kept shouting, "Get rid of him!"

The guards were just about to take Paul into the building. Paul spoke to the captain. "May I tell you something?" he asked.

"Do you speak Greek?" asked the captain. "Aren't you the man from Egypt? Didn't you start a panic? Didn't you lead a lot of men out into the desert?"

"No," said Paul. "I'm Jewish. Please let me talk to the people."

The captain said Paul could speak. So Paul stood on the steps. He held his hand up. The people got quiet. Then Paul talked to them in their own language.

Tossing Dust into the Air
ACTS 22

"Listen to me," said Paul.

The crowd heard their own language. So they got very quiet.

"I'm a Jew," said Paul. "I grew up in this city. I went to school here. Gamaliel was my teacher. He taught me the Law.

"I worked hard for God and his Law," said Paul. "I worked hard just like you do. I was hard on the followers of Jesus. I had many of them killed. I took men and women to jail. I even went to Damascus to catch more of them.

"I was on my way to Damascus," said Paul. "About noon, a bright light shone down on me from heaven. I fell down, and I heard a voice. 'Saul! Saul! Why are you hurting me?' said the voice."

Paul told the crowd his story. He told them how Jesus had talked to him. He told about how he couldn't see. He told them that he went to Damascus. He told them about Ananias coming to see him. He told them how he got his sight back. He told them that he was baptized. He told how he had gone back to Jerusalem.

"I was praying at the worship house," said Paul. "I was awake, but it was as if I was dreaming. I saw the Lord. He was talking to me. He said, 'Quick! Leave Jerusalem right away. They won't believe what you say about me.'

"I said, 'Lord, they know I hurt your followers. When they killed Stephen, I was glad. I guarded their coats for them while they did it.'

"The Lord talked to me again. 'Go. I'm sending you far away to people who aren't Jewish,' he said."

The crowd listened to Paul until he said that. Then they yelled, "Get rid of him! He is not good enough to live!" They threw their coats off. They tossed dust into the air.

The captain told the guards to take Paul into the army building. The captain said to beat Paul. Then he said to ask Paul why people were shouting. So the guards got ready to beat him.

But Paul said, "Isn't it against the law to beat a Roman? No one showed you that I did anything wrong."

The guard went to the captain. "This man is a Roman," he said. "Now what are you going to do?"

The captain went to Paul. "Are you really a Roman?" he asked.

"Yes," said Paul. "I am."

"I paid lots of money to become a Roman," said the captain.

"I was born a Roman," said Paul.

The guards had planned to ask Paul questions. But now they left right away. Even the captain was worried. He had put a Roman in chains.

The captain wanted to know what the Jews were blaming Paul for doing. He asked the Jewish leaders to get together. Then he brought Paul to them.

The Secret Plan

ACTS 23

Paul looked right at the leaders. He said, "I know I have done what God wants me to do. I've even done what he wants today."

The high priest told the people near Paul to hit him. He told them to hit Paul on the mouth.

"You fake!" said Paul. "You're the one who will get hit, and God will do it. You sit there to judge me by the Law. But you break the Law by telling them to hit me!"

The people near Paul said, "How dare you talk that way! That's the high priest you're talking to!"

"I didn't know he was the high priest," said Paul. "The Law says not to say bad things about the ruler of God's people."

Paul knew that these leaders often fussed with each other. They fussed about what they believed. So Paul said, "I'm here because of what I believe. I believe that the dead will come back to life again."

Then the leaders began to fuss with each other. Some of them believed the dead don't come back to life. Others believed they do. Some didn't believe in angels or spirits. Others did. So there was lots of noise.

Some of the leaders believed like Paul did. They stood up. "Nothing is wrong with this man," they said. "What if a spirit talked to him? What if he heard from an angel?"

The fussing was getting out of control. The captain was afraid that Paul would be torn to pieces. So he told the guards to take Paul back to the army building.

The next night, Jesus came to Paul. He said, "Be brave, Paul! You have told people in Jerusalem about me. Now you must tell people in Rome, too."

The next day, the Jews got together. There were more than 40 of them. They made a promise to each other. They wouldn't eat or drink anything until they killed Paul.

They told their Jewish leaders about their promise. "Ask the captain to bring Paul to you," they said to the leaders. "Say you want to know more about him. We'll kill him before he gets here."

Now, Paul had a sister, and she had a son. Her son heard about the Jews' plan. He told Paul about it.

Paul called one of the guards. He said, "This young man has something to tell the captain."

The guard took the young man to the captain. The captain took his hand. They stepped away from the others. "What do you want to tell me?" the captain asked.

"The Jews will ask you to bring Paul to their leaders tomorrow. But don't do it," he said. "More than 40 men will be waiting to kill Paul."

"Don't let anybody know you told me this," said the captain.

The captain called two guards. "Get 200 soldiers ready," he said. "Also get 70 soldiers who ride horses. And get 200 soldiers with spears. Send them to Caesarea at nine o'clock tonight. Give Paul a horse. Take him safely to Governor Felix."

Then the captain wrote a letter.

To the Best Governor, Felix,

Hello.

The Jews were going to kill this man. But I saved him with my guards. I knew he was a Roman. I wanted to find out what the Jews' problem was. So I took this man to the Jewish leaders. They blame him for doing things against their Law. But he did nothing he should die for. He didn't even do anything to be put in jail for. I found out that the Jews planned to kill him. So I sent him to you right away. I told the Jews to come see you about it.

From Claudius Lysias.

The guards followed the captain's orders. That night, they took Paul part of the way. The next day, soldiers on horses took him to Caesarea. They gave the letter to the governor. They gave Paul to him too.

The governor read the letter. He said, "I'll find out more about this. But wait until the people who blame you get here."

Then the governor sent Paul to Herod's palace. He ordered guards to watch him there.

Felix and His Wife

ACTS 24

Five days passed. Then the Jewish leaders from Jerusalem came to Caesarea. They brought a lawyer with them. They went to Governor Felix. He called for Paul.

The lawyer told Felix what they blamed Paul for doing. "We've had peace for a long time," he said. "You have ruled us well. You have brought good things to this nation. We are very thankful to you. Now we don't want to bother you. So we'll make this quick.

"This man makes trouble," said the lawyer. "He gets crowds of Jewish people into a panic. He does this all over the world. He is a leader of a group that makes trouble. He even treats the worship house as if it were nothing. So we have tried to stop him. Ask him about it yourself. You'll find out that we're telling the truth."

The Jewish people agreed with the lawyer. They said it was true.

Felix held his hand out toward Paul. That showed it was Paul's turn.

Paul said, "You've judged this nation for many years. So I'm glad to speak to you. It was just 12 days ago that I went to Jerusalem to worship. You can ask around. You'll find that this is true.

"I didn't make a fuss at the worship house," said Paul. "I didn't gather a crowd anywhere in the city. These men can't show you that anything they say is true.

"Here's what is true," said Paul. "I worship God. I'm a follower of Jesus. I believe the Law and the prophets. I hope in God just like these men do. I believe the dead will come back to life again. Both good people and bad people will come back to life. So I try to make sure I'm always doing what's right.

"I was away from Jerusalem for many years," said Paul. "I came back to bring gifts for poor people. I came to give my offerings. I was doing all this in the right way. There wasn't a crowd with me. I didn't start a panic.

"Instead, some Jews came from Asia to start trouble," said Paul. "They're the ones who should be here today. They should say why they blame me. If they don't, the people here should tell what they found out.

"There was one thing that did upset them," said Paul. "I told them why I was there. It's because I believe the dead will live again someday."

Felix knew a lot about Jesus and his followers. So he sent everyone away. He said, "The captain who wrote to me will come. Then I'll choose what to do with you."

Felix ordered the guard to watch Paul. But Felix said to let Paul have some freedom. Felix said Paul's friends could bring him whatever he needed.

A few days passed. Then Felix asked Paul to come see him again. Felix's wife, Drusilla, was with him. She was Jewish. She and Felix listened to Paul.

Paul talked to them about believing in Jesus. Paul talked about how to be right with God. He talked about self-control. He talked about how God would judge people someday.

Felix felt afraid. "That's enough!" he said. "Leave for now. I'll ask you to come again another time."

Felix hoped Paul would pay him money to be set free. So he often called Paul to come talk with him.

Two years went by. A new governor came. He took the place of Felix. His name was Festus.

Felix wanted to do the Jews a favor. So he left Paul in jail.

Judges and Rulers
ACTS 25:1-26

Festus was in town for three days. Then he went to Jerusalem. The Jewish leaders there told him about the things they blamed Paul for.

They asked Festus to send Paul back to Jerusalem. They really wanted to kill Paul on the way.

Festus said, "Paul is in jail in Caesarea. I'm going there soon. Some of your leaders should come with me. They can blame Paul there, if he has done wrong."

Eight or ten days later, Festus went back to Caesarea. The next day, he called for Paul.

The Jews from Jerusalem had also come. They stood around Paul. They blamed him for many wrong things. But they couldn't show that anything they said was true.

"I haven't done anything wrong," said Paul. "I've done nothing against the Jewish Law. I've done nothing against the worship house. I've done nothing against Rome's great ruler, Caesar."

But Festus wanted to do the Jewish people a favor. So he said, "Will you go to Jerusalem? Will you let them judge you there?"

Paul said, "You are a Roman judge. So here's where I should be judged. I haven't done anything wrong to the Jews. You know that. Did I do something I should die for? Then I won't stop you from killing me.

"But what if these Jewish people are lying?" said Paul. "Then you shouldn't give me to them. The great ruler in Rome should be the judge! I ask for Caesar!"

Festus talked with his helpers about this. Then he said, "You asked for Caesar, so you'll go to Caesar!"

A few days passed. King Agrippa and his wife, Bernice, came to Caesarea. They came to see Festus. They were there for many days. Festus talked to the king about Paul.

"Felix left a man in jail here," said Festus. "I went to Jerusalem. The Jewish leaders there blamed him for many things. They asked me to blame him too. They want to kill him.

"But that's not the way it's done in Rome," said Festus. "I told them that. We let people in jail answer for themselves. So the Jewish leaders came here. The man was brought in. Then the Jews blamed him for many things.

"They didn't talk about crimes he'd done," said Festus. "That's what I thought they'd do. Instead, they fussed about what they believe. They talked about a dead man named Jesus. Paul kept saying Jesus is alive.

"I didn't know what to do about this," said Festus. "So I asked Paul to go to Jerusalem to be judged. But he asked to be judged by the ruler of all the Romans. So I'm keeping him in jail. He will be there until I can send him to our ruler, Caesar."

"I'd like to hear this man talk," said King Agrippa.

"You can hear him tomorrow," said Festus.

The next day, King Agrippa and Bernice met with Festus. They made a big show coming into the room. The city leaders were with them.

Then Festus called for Paul. Paul was brought in.

"See this man?" said Festus. "The Jewish people say he should die. I don't think he has done anything he should die for. He asked for Caesar to be his judge. So I'm going to send him to Rome.

"I think I should tell Caesar why I'm sending him. But I'm not sure what I can say," said Festus. "So you listen to him, King Agrippa. Maybe you can tell me what I should write."

NOVEMBER 20

You're out of Your Mind!

ACTS 26

Then King Agrippa turned to Paul. "You may speak for yourself," he said.

Paul began his story. "King Agrippa, I'm happy to talk to you today. I know you understand the Jews' laws and their problems. So please listen carefully.

"The Jews know about my life," said Paul. "They can tell you that I lived as a Jew. I went by the laws. I

hope in what God promised our people. That's why I'm being judged today.

"The 12 family groups of Jews are waiting for God's promise," said Paul. "That's why they worship God night and day. That's why they are blaming me. But is it surprising that God makes the dead alive again?

"At one time, I thought I should be against Jesus. I put his followers in jail," said Paul. "I spoke against them. I had them killed. I tried to make them say bad things about God. I even went to cities in other countries to catch them.

"I was on one of these trips, going to Damascus," said Paul. "About noon, a light shone on me. It was brighter than the sun. I fell down, and I heard a voice in my language. It said, 'Saul, Saul, why are you hurting me? It's hard on you when you go the wrong way.'

"I asked, 'Who are you?'

"He said, 'I'm Jesus, the one you're hurting. Now stand up. You are going to serve me. You'll tell what you've seen. I'll save you from your own Jewish people. I'll save you from people who aren't Jewish. I'm sending you to show them how to leave sin. Show them how to turn away from Satan. Show them how to come to me. Then their sins can be forgiven. They can be with others who believe.'

"I obeyed," said Paul. "I taught people everywhere to turn to God. I told them to show they had changed by acting like it. That's why some Jewish people pulled me out of the worship house. That's why they tried to kill me. But God is helping me, even today.

"Moses said this would happen," said Paul. "The prophets said this would happen. They said Jesus would die. They said he would come back to life again. They said he'd be like a light to show God's kingdom. He'd show it to his own Jewish people and to people who aren't Jewish."

Then Festus shouted, "You're out of your mind, Paul! You've learned so much, your mind is gone!"

"I'm not out of my mind," said Paul. "I'm telling the truth. It makes sense. King Agrippa knows about these things. I can talk to him. I'm sure he knows about what

happened. These things were not hidden from people. Do you believe the prophets, King Agrippa? I know you believe."

"You've talked for just a little while," said King Agrippa. "Do you think I'll become a Christian in that short time?"

"It may be short," said Paul. "It may be long. But I pray to God. I pray that you and everyone listening will become Christians like me. But I hope you don't go to jail like me."

The king and Bernice got up and left the room. Festus and the other people left too. They began talking with each other. "This man isn't doing anything he should be killed for. He isn't doing anything he should be in jail for."

"I could have set him free," said King Agrippa. "But he has asked for Caesar to judge him."

NOVEMBER 21

Stormy Seas!

ACTS 27

The time came to sail to Rome to see Caesar. Paul and some others were taken out of jail. They were given to an army captain named Julius.

Some of Paul's friends went with him. They got on a ship and sailed out to sea. The next day, they landed at Sidon.

Julius was kind. He let Paul go to see his friends in Sidon.

Soon it was time to sail again. They sailed across the open sea and landed at Myra.

Julius found another ship there. It was headed for Rome. So he took Paul and his friends on that ship.

The sailing went very slowly for many days. The wind wouldn't push them the way they wanted to go. So they sailed along the shore of Crete Island. It was still hard for them to sail that way. So they landed at Fair Havens.

They had lost a lot of time, and now winter was coming. It would not be safe to be on the sea in winter.

Paul said, "Our trip will be full of danger. The ship will break down. The load we carry will be torn up. Our lives will even be in danger."

But Julius didn't listen to Paul. He listened to the ship's captain. He listened to the owner of the ship too. Fair Havens was a bad place to keep ships in winter. So they chose to sail on as soon as they could.

The ship's captain hoped to get to Phoenix. That town faced the southwest and the northwest. They could stay there for the winter.

A soft wind began to blow from the south. This was just what the captain wanted. So they set sail. They sailed along the shore of Crete. It wasn't long before a strong wind began to blow. It was called a "northeast wind." It blew like a hurricane from the island.

The storm pushed the ship along. The ship couldn't head into the wind. So they let the ship go wherever the storm drove it.

They tried to tie their life boat to the ship. But they couldn't get it tight. So they pulled it inside.

They tied ropes around the ship. That might keep it from falling apart. Then they let the anchor down. That's because they were afraid they'd hit sand bars in the water.

The storm tore into the ship. So the next day, they made the ship lighter. They threw the load they were carrying into the sea. The day after that, they threw out ropes. They threw out other things that belonged to the ship.

But the storm kept blowing. For days, they couldn't see the sun or the stars. At last, they gave up. They all thought they'd die.

The men had not eaten for a long time. Finally Paul stood up. "You should have listened to me," he said. "You would have saved yourself from all this trouble. But be brave. The ship won't make it, but the people will.

"Last night, an angel came to me," said Paul. "He was from God. I belong to God. I serve God. God's angel stood by me. He said, 'Don't be afraid. You have to let Caesar judge you. God is kind. He will let the people who sail with you live.'

"So be brave," said Paul. "I believe in God. It will happen just the way he said. But we'll have to crash on an island somewhere."

After 14 days, the storm was still driving them along. About midnight, the sailors thought they might be near land. So they checked. They found out the water was 120 feet deep. They checked again a little later. It was 90 feet deep.

They were afraid the ship would crash on rocks. So they let four anchors down into the water. Then they prayed for day to come.

Now the sailors tried secretly to get off the ship. They said they were going to let anchors down. Instead, they put the life boat into the water.

Paul talked to Julius and the soldiers. "You can't be saved unless the sailors stay with the ship."

So the soldiers cut the ropes to the life boat. It fell into the sea without anyone in it.

It was almost morning. Paul tried to talk everyone into eating. "You haven't eaten in 14 days," he said. "You've been so worried. Please eat something. You'll need food to stay alive. No one will lose even one hair from his head."

Then Paul picked up some bread. He thanked God in front of everybody. He started eating. The men felt better when they saw Paul eat. They ate some food too.

There were 276 people on the ship. After they had finished eating, they made the ship lighter. They threw the wheat into the sea.

Morning came. They couldn't tell what land they were near. They saw a bay with a sandy beach.

They wanted to let the ship wash up on the beach. So they cut the anchors loose. They left the anchors in the sea. Then they put the sail up in the front of the ship. They headed for the beach.

But the ship hit a sand bar in the water. It got stuck there. The pounding waves began to break the ship apart.

The soldiers planned to kill the men they were guarding. They didn't want them to get away. But Julius wanted to save Paul's life. So he wouldn't let the soldiers kill anyone.

Julius asked who could swim. He told those people to jump into the sea first. He told them to swim to land. He told everyone else to hold on to boards from the ship. Then they could get to land. So everybody got to the beach safely.

A Snake in the Fire

ACTS 28:1-11, 14-31

They were on an island called Malta. It was raining, and it was cold. But the people on the island were very kind. They welcomed the men from the ship.

The island people built a fire for them. Paul helped by carrying some sticks. He put the sticks on the fire.

The fire was hot. The heat made a snake crawl out of the sticks. The snake bit Paul's hand and held on. The island people saw this. "That man must be a killer," they said. "He got away from the sea. Now he is paying for his crime. He won't live."

But Paul shook the snake off. It fell into the fire. Paul was fine.

The people thought Paul would get sick. They thought he might fall down dead all of a sudden. They watched him for a long time. But nothing bad happened.

So the people changed their minds. They said Paul was a god.

Now there was a big house nearby. It belonged to the leader of the island. He welcomed Paul and his friends to his house. He treated them very well. They were there for three days.

The leader's father was sick. He was in bed and felt very hot. Paul went to see him.

Paul prayed. Then he put his hands on the man. And the man got well.

After this, the other sick people came to see Paul. They got well too. So everyone looked up to Paul and his friends.

Three months went by. It was time to sail again.

A ship had stayed in the island all winter. The ship had the figures of twin gods on the front. Julius, Paul, and his friends got on that ship. The island people gave them what they needed for the trip. Then they sailed off to Italy, where Rome was.

In a few days, they came to a town in Italy. Some of Jesus' followers there asked them to stay a week. So they did. But at last they got to Rome.

Jesus' followers in Rome had heard that Paul was coming. They traveled out of the city to meet Paul. Just seeing them cheered Paul up. He thanked God.

Paul got to live in a house in

Rome. But a guard had to be with him.

Three days passed. Then Paul asked the Jewish leaders to come together.

Paul told them, "I've done nothing wrong against our Jewish people. I've done nothing wrong against our way of life. But the Jews in Jerusalem took me to the Romans.

"The Romans asked me questions," said Paul. "They wanted to let me go. That's because I didn't do anything I should be killed for. But the Jewish people wouldn't let them set me free. So I had to ask for Caesar to judge me.

"I don't have anything against my own people, the Jews. But I'm chained up because I believe in Jesus," said Paul. "That's why I wanted to talk to you."

"We didn't get any letters about you," said the Jewish leaders. "Nobody said anything bad about you. But we do want to hear what you have to say. Lots of people say things against Jesus' followers." They made plans to meet Paul another day.

When that day came, even more Jews came to Paul's house. Paul talked about God's kingdom from morning until night. He showed how the Law and prophets told about Jesus.

Some people believed Paul.

Others wouldn't believe. They could not agree.

At last, Paul said that the Holy Spirit spoke through Isaiah. He told the truth. Isaiah said to tell God's people these words.

You'll hear,
    but you won't understand.
You'll see,
    but you won't know what it
        means.
That's because the hearts of my
        people are hard.
    They don't care about me.
Their ears can hardly hear.
    Their eyes are closed.
If their eyes were open,
    they would see.
If their ears were open,
    they would hear.
Their hearts would understand.
    They would turn back to me.
    Then I would make them well.

"I want you to know something," said Paul. "God will let people who aren't Jewish know about Jesus. They will listen and be saved!"

After Paul said this, the Jews began to leave.

Paul rented his own house in Rome. He stayed there for two years. He welcomed anyone who came to visit him. He was brave. He taught about God's kingdom. He taught about Jesus. Nobody stopped him.

Paul Writes Again

Kingdom of Light

COLOSSIANS 1:2-4, 9-10, 12-19, 21-27

From Rome, Paul wrote a letter to Jesus' followers in Colosse.

To God's special people in Colosse, who keep following Jesus,

We pray that God will give you his kind love and peace. We thank God the Father that you believe in his Son, Jesus. We thank God that you love all of Jesus' followers.

We've prayed for you ever since we heard about you. We ask God to help you know what he wants. We ask him to make your spirits wise.

Then you can live a life God would be proud of. You can make God happy in everything you do.

You can be glad to thank God the Father. He made you good enough to get all that he will give his followers.

God saved us from the kingdom of darkness. He brought us into the kingdom of light. It's his Son's kingdom.

God loves his Son, Jesus. Because of Jesus, God forgives our sins.

We can't see God. Jesus shows what God is like. Jesus is in charge of everything. He made everything in heaven and on earth. He made things we can see and things we can't see. He made kings, powers, rulers, and anyone in charge. Everything was made by him and for him.

Jesus was around before anything else. Everything holds together because of him. He is like the head of a body. The body is the church, his followers.

Jesus is the beginning. He was the first to die and come back to life that lasts forever. That makes him greater than all others. God was happy to give everything he had to Jesus. All of God was in Jesus.

You were away from God in the past. It was because of the sinful way you acted. But now God has

733

made peace between you and him. He made peace by Jesus' death.

Now, as God sees it, you are clean and sinless. There is nothing wrong between you and God. You are spotless. You won't be blamed for bad things you've done if you keep believing.

Stay firm and sure. Keep the hope that the Good News gives you. This Good News has been told to everyone. And I, Paul, have been serving God by telling people the Good News.

Jesus was hurt for you. I'm glad for you. I sometimes get hurt for Jesus, too. I also get hurt for his people. They are his church, which is called his body.

I serve Jesus' followers. I serve the church. That's what God told me to do. He wants me to tell you everything about his Word.

God wants me to tell about a mystery. It's been hidden for a long time. But now God's people see what the mystery is. God even shows it to people who aren't Jewish. The mystery is that Jesus lives in you. This is your hope of being part of his greatness.

Like a Tower

COLOSSIANS 2:1-7, 9-15, 18, 20-23

I want you to know something. I work very hard for you. I work hard for people who haven't even met me yet. I work so they'll feel better in their hearts. I work so they'll get together and love each other. I work so they can understand all God wants them to know.

Riches are hiding in Jesus. His riches are wise thinking and knowing what's true.

I'm telling you this so you won't believe lies. Don't believe them, no matter how great they sound.

My body may not be with you, but my spirit is. I'm very glad to see that you follow God's plan. I'm glad that your faith in Jesus is strong.

You believed in Jesus. So keep living in him. Be like a plant. Let your roots go deep into Jesus. Be like a tower. Be built up in Jesus. Be strong in your faith. That's what you were taught. Let thanks to God flow out of you.

All of God lives in Jesus' body. And you have all of Jesus. He is in charge of every power and ruler.

You left sin behind. You were baptized, dipped in water. It was like being put in the grave with Jesus. After that, you were new and clean. It was like being brought back to life again. It happened because you believed in God's power. He is the one who brought Jesus back to life.

Sin made you as good as dead.

Then God made you alive with Jesus.

God forgave all our sins. The Law was against us. It blamed us for our sins. But Jesus took away the blame. It was like nailing the Law to the cross. Jesus took away the strength of any evil ruler that would blame you. He made evil power look bad. He won with the Cross.

Some people pretend they're not proud. But they really are proud. Some people worship angels instead of God. Don't let them lead you away from Jesus. These people talk a lot about what they see. They are puffed up with ideas that don't get them anywhere.

It's as if you died with Jesus. You died to the world. So why go by its rules? It says, "Don't touch this! Don't taste that! Don't hold on to this!" These are human rules. They won't last forever. They look like wise rules. They tell when and where to worship. They tell people how to work hard with their bodies. But they aren't any good at keeping people from sinning.

NOVEMBER 24

A New Self

COLOSSIANS 3

You have been made alive with Jesus. So think about things that are from Jesus. He is above, sitting at God's right side. Think about things that are above. Don't think about things of the earth. You died to the world. Now your life is with Jesus in God.

Jesus is your whole life. Someday, Jesus will appear in all his greatness. You'll be there too.

Some things show that the world is still in you. Let those things die. Those are things like using sex in a wrong way. Having a heart that's not clean from sin. Wanting to do wrong. Wanting more and more things, which is just like worshiping idols. God will get angry because of these things.

You used to live that way. But now you need to get rid of that way of life. Get rid of strong anger. Get rid of hate. Get rid of saying bad things about others. Get rid of dirty talk. Don't lie to each other. Your old self is gone.

You have a new self now. You are being made like new so you'll be like Jesus. It doesn't matter if you're Jewish or not. It doesn't matter if you're a slave or a free person. Jesus is the important one.

God chose you to be his people. You are special to him. He loves you dearly. So be kind. Don't be proud. Treat other people with care. Be glad to wait.

Work with each other. Forgive each other. Forgive like Jesus forgave you. And more than all this, love each other. Love will help us do all these good things together.

All of you are like parts of one body. God wants you to live together in peace. So let Jesus' peace control your hearts. Be thankful, too.

Let Jesus' words live in you like riches. Teach each other with wise thinking. Sing psalms and songs from your spirit. Be thankful to God in your hearts. Do everything in Jesus' name. It may be what you say. It may be what you do. But do it in Jesus' name, giving thanks to God.

If you're a wife, let your husband lead. It's the right thing to do in Jesus' kingdom. If you're a husband, love your wife. Don't be hard on her.

Children, always obey your mother and father. That will make Jesus happy.

Fathers, don't upset your children so much that they give up.

Servants, obey your human masters. Do whatever they say. Don't obey just when they're looking. Don't obey just to make them treat you nicely. Obey with a good, true heart. Obey, showing that you look up to Jesus.

Whatever you do, do it with your whole heart. Do it as if you were working for Jesus. He has good things planned for you. It's really Jesus you're serving.

People who do wrong will get what's coming to them. Jesus doesn't have favorites.

True Friends

COLOSSIANS 4; 1:1

If you're a master, give your servants what is right. Give them what's fair. Remember that you have a Master in heaven.

Work at praying. Watch. Be thankful. Pray for us, too. Ask God to give us times when we can tell our message. Then we can talk about the mystery of Jesus. It's because of this mystery that I'm in jail. Pray that I can tell about it clearly. That's how I need to tell it.

Be wise about how you act toward people who don't believe in Jesus. Use every minute to show that Jesus lives in you. Talk kindly. Be wise. Then you'll know how to answer people.

Tychicus will tell you all about me. He is a true friend. He helps me serve Jesus. I'm sending him to you. Then you'll know what's happening with us. He will help you feel better about us. Onesimus will be with him. He is also a true friend. These two men will tell you what's happening here.

The one who is in jail with me says to tell you hi. So does Mark, the cousin of Barnabas. Make him feel welcome if he comes. Justus says hello. These are the only Jewish men who are working with me. They help to make me feel better.

Epaphras serves Jesus with us. He says hello too. He prays hard for you. He prays that you will keep following what God wants. He prays that you will be grown up and wise. He prays that you will be sure of your faith. I can tell you that he works hard for you. He works hard for others, too.

Luke, the doctor, is a special friend of ours. He and Demas say hello.

Say hi to God's people in the town next to you. Tell Nympha hello. Say hi to God's people who meet at her house.

After you read this letter, send it to the next town. Then you can read the letter I sent them.

Give this message to Archippus. "Make sure you finish what Jesus wants you to do."

I, Paul, am writing this part with my own hand. Remember me in jail. I hope God's kind love will be with you.

From Paul and Timothy.

Like a Son

PHILEMON 1:1, 4-25

Paul also wrote a letter from Rome to a man named Philemon. Philemon's servant, Onesimus, had run away. Paul met Onesimus in Rome.

To Philemon,

I remember you when I pray. I thank God for you. I heard about how you believe in Jesus. I heard about how you love God's people. I'm praying that you'll tell a lot of other people what you believe.

I feel much better because of your love. You have made God's people feel like new. That makes me happy.

I want to ask you something out of love. I could be bold. I could order you to do what you should do. But I, Paul, am just asking you as an old man. I'm now in jail for Jesus.

I'm asking you for Onesimus. He is like a son to me. I grew to love him here in jail. Once he was no good to you. But he is doing lots of good for me now. He can do lots of good for you, too.

I'm sending him back to you. But he is like my own heart. I wish I could keep him with me. Then he could help me here in jail.

But I won't do that. I couldn't,

unless you said it was all right. That way it would be what you wanted. It wouldn't be something I made you do.

Maybe there is a reason he was away from you for a while. Maybe it was so you could have him back for good. Now he won't be a servant. He will be better than a servant. He will be like a brother.

Onesimus is very special to me. He will be even more special to you. Now he is like your brother in God's family.

Do you think of me as a worker with you? Then welcome Onesimus like you would welcome me.

Did he do anything wrong to you? Does he owe you anything? Then let me pay it back. I, Paul, write this myself. I will pay you back. But then, you do owe me your whole self. So I want to get something good from you.

Make my heart feel new. I'm sure you'll obey. That's why I'm writing to you. I know you'll do more than I'm asking.

I want to ask one more thing. Get a room ready for me. I hope I can come back to you. I know that will be an answer to your prayers.

Epaphras is in jail with me. He says to tell you hi. Mark, Luke, and the others who work here with me say hello too.

I pray that Jesus' kind love will be with you.

From Paul.
And from Timothy.

Super Great Power
EPHESIANS 1:1, 4-23

From Rome, Paul also wrote a letter to Jesus' followers in Ephesus.

To God's people in Ephesus,

God loved us. That's why he chose us. He planned to make us his children through Jesus. He wants to. He is happy to. So we praise him for his powerful, kind love.

God's kind love for us is free because of Jesus. Jesus forgives us for the bad things we do. God's love flows over us. His love brings us all his wise thinking and understanding.

God even lets us know the mystery of his plan. God will make it all happen at the end of time. Here is God's mystery. Everything in heaven and earth will come together. Jesus will be in charge.

God works everything out by this plan. He chose us so we could praise him. He chose us so we could show how great he is.

You heard the truth. It's the Good News of how to be saved. You believed in Jesus. Then God put his mark on you. His mark is his Holy Spirit, who is the one he promised to you.

God gives you his Holy Spirit. The Holy Spirit is a promise inside you. The Holy Spirit lets you know that God will save his people. He shows how great God is.

I heard that you believe in Jesus. I heard about how you love God's people. So I keep thanking God for you.

I remember you when I pray. I ask God to give you his wise Spirit. I ask him to show you his plans. Then you can know God better.

I'm also praying that God will open your heart. Then you'll know the riches he will give his people someday. You'll know his super great power. His power is for people who believe. It's the power he used to bring Jesus back to life.

God lets Jesus sit beside him in heaven. Jesus is more important than all rulers or kings. He is more important than any other power. He is more important than any other leader now or ever. God put him in charge of everything.

Jesus is in charge of his followers. They are called "the church." Jesus is like the head. His followers are like his body.

Born to Do Good Things

EPHESIANS 2

What about you? You were sinning. It's like you were dead. That's because you used to follow the world's ways. You followed Satan, who rules the kingdom of the air. He is the spirit who is working in people who don't obey God.

We were all like that once. We sinned the way we wanted to. So God was angry at us.

But God loves us very much. He is full of kind love. It's like we were dead because of our sin. But we've been saved by God's kind love.

God brought us back to life again with Jesus. God lets us sit with Jesus in heaven. That's so he can show how great his kindness is. It's all because of Jesus.

God's kind love saves you when you believe. This isn't something you do. It's a gift from God. You can't work to get it. So you can't brag about having it.

You were made by God. He made you to do good things. God planned this before you were born.

You people who aren't Jews should remember something. Remember that in the past you were not with Jesus. You were not God's people. You didn't know God's promise. You didn't have hope. You didn't have God. You were far away from him then. But now Jesus has brought you close to God.

Jesus brings peace. He brings together Jews and people who aren't Jews. There is nothing to keep them apart now. There's no reason for them not to get together.

Jesus brought people together when he died. That got rid of the Law. Now people can make peace with each other.

Jesus made a way for everyone to come to God. Jesus taught peace to all of you. We can all come to his Father by his Spirit.

Now you're not strangers anymore. You're part of God's people. You're in God's family.

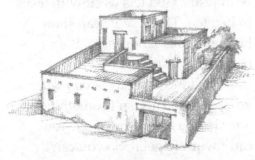

God's family is like a building. The apostles and prophets are like the base of the building. Jesus is the most important part. The whole building fits together in him. The building grows tall. It turns into a special worship house for God.

You're like a house. You're a house that God's Spirit lives in.

Wide, Long, High, and Deep

EPHESIANS 3:1-3, 6, 8-12, 14-21

I'm in jail for Jesus. It's because I helped you people who aren't Jewish. I'm sure you heard how God gave me his kind love. He showed me a mystery.

And here's the mystery. People who aren't Jewish get to be in God's kingdom. They can be in God's kingdom just like Jews can. They all share God's kingdom together because of Jesus.

I'm not as important as the rest of God's people. God gave me his kind love anyway. His kind love lets me teach people who aren't Jewish. I teach them about the riches they can have from Jesus.

God's kind love makes his mystery clear. God hid the mystery for a long time. His plan was to show how wise he is. That can be seen by looking at his people. God's plan was for rulers in heaven to see his wise thinking. His plan did not fail. It worked because of Jesus.

We believe in Jesus. So we can come to God freely and bravely.

I bow down to God the Father. His family in heaven is named for him. His family on earth is named for him. He has great, powerful riches.

I'm praying that God will make you strong with his power. He will do this by his Spirit inside you. That way Jesus can live in your hearts. He lives in your hearts because you believe in him.

I'm also praying that you'll know Jesus' love. I want you to know how wide his love is. I want you to know how long it is. I want you to know how high and how deep it is. God's love is greater than you can know. Still, I want you to know as much of it as you can. I want you to be filled to the top with God.

God can do much more than anything we ask or think. It's all because his power works in us.

Let God's greatness shine in his people. Let it shine in Jesus forever and ever! Yes! Amen!

We Won't Be Babies

EPHESIANS 4:1-8, 11-24, 26-32

Live the way God wants you to live. Live like others are better than you. Wait quietly when you need to. Put up with each other and love each other. Try to work together in God's Spirit. Be at peace with each other.

There is one Spirit. There is one group of God's people, one "body." God promised one hope to all of his people. There is one Lord. There is one faith. There is one baptism. There is one God. He is our Father. He is in charge of everything.

God is kind to all of us. The psalm says, "He gave gifts to people." He made some people to be apostles. He made some to be prophets. He made some to lead others into his kingdom. He made some to take care of others. He made some to teach.

God gave these gifts to make his people ready to serve. These gifts build up Jesus' followers, his "body." God gave gifts to help us all agree about what we believe. The gifts help us really know Jesus. They help us grow up in how we think and act. Now we can grow until we are filled to the top with Jesus.

Then we won't be babies. We won't toss back and forth like we were riding on a wave. We'll know what to do. We won't blow here and there like wind. We won't keep changing our minds. We won't believe everything we hear or read or see.

Some people fool others with their lies. But we will talk lovingly about the truth. We'll grow up to be like Jesus.

Jesus is like the head. We are like the body. Each part of the body helps the whole body. When each part does its work, the body grows. Its love gets stronger.

So here's what I say. Stop living

like people who don't follow God. Their thinking isn't good for anything. They don't understand. They live apart from God because they don't know him. They don't know him because they don't care about him. Their hearts are hard.

They can't tell right from wrong anymore. They do whatever feels good at the moment. So they do sinful things that make their hearts dirty. They sin, and they want more sin.

You didn't get to know Jesus by acting that way. I'm sure you heard about Jesus. Someone told you the truth that's in him.

Someone told you to stop your old way of life. That's because your life was being torn up by sin. You were told to think a new way. You were told to put on a new self. You were made to be like God. You were made to be truly right and good.

The psalm says, "Don't sin when you're angry." Get rid of your anger before the sun sets. Then Satan won't have a place to work in your heart.

If you steal, stop stealing. Work. Do something useful with your hands. Then you'll have something to share with people who need help.

Don't say things that hurt people. Instead, say things that will cheer them up. Say things they need to hear. That will help them.

Don't make God's Holy Spirit sad. God gave you his Spirit as a promise that you belong to him.

Get rid of anger. Maybe you've had anger deep inside for a long time. It may be anger that comes out loudly. It may be a dangerous anger. But get rid of it.

Get rid of fighting and saying bad things about others. Get rid of hate. Be kind to each other. Forgive each other like God forgave you by sending Jesus.

Children of the Light
EPHESIANS 5:1-23, 25-33

Be like God. After all, you are his children. He loves you very much. So live a life full of love like Jesus did. Jesus loved us. He gave his life for us. It was his gift to God.

Don't even think about using sex in a wrong way. Don't think dirty thoughts. Don't look at things that make you think about sin. Don't let yourself want more and more things. These things are not right for God's special people.

Don't tell dirty jokes. They don't fit you. Instead, talk about what you're thankful for.

You can be sure of one thing. People who sin with sex won't be in God's kingdom. People who keep wanting more and more things won't be there. They worship things as if they were idols. Don't let anybody lie to you. People who live this way are not obeying God. God is angry with them. So don't go along with them. That would be like living in the dark.

In the past, you lived in the dark. But now you live in God's light. So live like children of the light. Light brings things that are good, right, and true.

Find out what makes God happy. Don't have anything to do with the dark, bad life. It doesn't do anyone any good. Instead, show these things for what they are. People do these things in secret. It's not even good to talk about what they do.

But these things will show up in God's light. That's why it has been said, "Wake up, sleepy head. Come back to life again. Then Jesus will shine on you."

So be very careful about how you live. Live like a wise person, not like a fool. Do as much as you can that's good. We live in sinful times. So understand what it is that God wants.

Don't get drunk. Drunks often just do what feels good at the moment. Instead, let God's Spirit fill you. Talk to each other by saying psalms. Sing about God to each other. Fill your heart with songs and music to the Lord.

Always thank God the Father for everything. Give thanks in Jesus' name.

Let each other be leaders. And follow each other because Jesus is important to you.

If you are a wife, let your husband lead you. Let him lead you the same way you let Jesus lead you. That's because the husband is the leader of his wife. The husband leads his wife like Jesus leads his followers.

If you are a husband, love your wife. Love her like Jesus loves his followers, who are called "the church." Jesus gave his life up for his followers. That's so he could make them special, right, and good. Now his followers can shine clean, spotless, and without blame.

Husbands should love their wives this same way. They should love their wives like they love themselves. People never hate themselves. They feed themselves and take care of themselves. Jesus takes care of his followers. That's because we are like Jesus' body.

God's Word says, "This is why a man leaves his mother and father. He lives with his wife. The two of them become like one person." This is a big mystery. But it's like Jesus and his followers. Anyway, each husband should love his wife like he loves himself. Each wife should look up to her husband.

Putting on God's Armor

EPHESIANS 6; 1:1

Children, obey your mother and father. This is what's right in God's kingdom. God's rules say, "Treat your father and mother like they are important." This is the first command that comes with a promise. It says, "Things will go well for you. You'll enjoy a long life here on earth."

Fathers, don't make your children angry. As they grow, teach them how to live as God's people.

If you're a servant, obey your master. Care about him. Follow him with a true heart like you would obey Jesus. Don't obey your master only when he is looking. Don't obey him just so he will like you. Obey him the way you obey Jesus. Serve with all your heart.

If you're a master, treat your servant kindly. Don't say you'll treat him badly if he doesn't obey. You know that God is your Master. He is your servant's Master too. God doesn't love one person any better than another.

Be strong in God. Be strong in his great power. It's like putting on God's heavy, metal armor. Then you can stand up against Satan's plans.

We don't fight people. We fight rulers, kings, and powers of this dark world. We fight bad, sinful spirits in places around the heavens.

So put on God's whole armor. Days filled with sin may come. But you'll be able to keep your place in God's kingdom. After you do everything you can, you'll still be standing. So stand firm.

Make truth like a belt around you. Being right with God will cover your chest to keep it safe. The Good News of peace makes your feet ready. Hold faith like a shield in front of you. Your faith will put out arrows of fire that the enemy shoots.

Jesus saved you. That's like a helmet for your head. Your sword will be the Spirit's sword, God's Word.

Pray with the Spirit's help anytime. Pray all kinds of prayers. Ask for all kinds of things. Remember this, and watch. Always keep praying for all God's people.

Pray for me, too. Pray that when I talk, God will tell me what to say. That way, I'll talk without being afraid. Then I'll tell about the mystery of God's Good News. It's because of this news that I'm in jail right now.

Tychicus is a servant in God's

kingdom. He keeps his promises. He will tell you everything that's happening here. Then you'll know what I'm doing. You'll know how I am, and you'll feel better. That's why I'm sending him to visit you.

Tell everyone that I pray they're living in peace. I pray that their love will never die.

From Paul.

In Chains for Jesus

PHILIPPIANS 1:1-18

From Rome, Paul also wrote to Jesus' followers in Philippi.

To God's people at Philippi,

I pray for God's kind love and peace to be with you.

I thank God whenever I remember you. I always pray with joy when I pray for you. That's because you're my friends. You welcomed the Good News the first day I met you. You still believe it and help me tell others about it.

God began doing good work in you. I know he will finish what he started. He will work in you until the day Jesus comes again.

It's right for me to feel this way about you. You're in my heart. I may be in jail. I may be standing up for the Good News. I may be speaking

God's Word. Whatever I'm doing, you're enjoying God's kind love along with me. God knows just how much I want to be with you. I love you with Jesus' love.

Here's what I pray. I pray that your love will grow. I pray that you'll know and understand more and more. Then you'll be able to choose what's best. Your hearts will be clean from sin. You'll be without sin until Jesus comes again. You'll be full of good things.

Good things come from being right with God. Being right with him comes through Jesus. It brings praise to God and shows God's greatness.

Now I want you to know something. I'm in jail. But this helps people hear the Good News. All the guards know I'm in jail for Jesus. Everyone else knows that too.

Most of God's people are brave now, because I'm in jail. They're not afraid to speak God's Word.

But there are some people who want to be important. So they teach about Jesus just to be important. Other people teach because of their good hearts. They speak in love. They know why I'm here in jail.

People who want to be important teach just to get what they want. They think they can make trouble for me. It doesn't matter. The important thing is that they teach about Jesus. They may have good reasons. They may have bad reasons. But at least they speak about Jesus. I'm glad about that.

What Should I Choose?

PHILIPPIANS 1:18-24, 27-28

Yes, I'll keep on showing my joy. I know you're praying for me. Jesus' Spirit helps me. So what has happened to me will turn out good. I'll be saved.

I hope I'll be brave enough to make Jesus look great. I hope I can show his greatness now and always. I hope I can show it if I live or if I die.

I may go on living. That means good things will come from my work. Should I choose to live or die? I don't know! I want both. I want to leave and be with Jesus. That's the best for me. But it's better for you if I live.

Whatever happens, live the way you should. Then I'll know that you're going to keep telling others the Good News.

You'll work together as if you were one person. You won't be afraid of anyone who works against you. This will show them that they won't be saved, but you will be.

NOVEMBER 29

Shining like Stars

PHILIPPIANS 2:3-18

Don't do anything just to get something you want. Don't do anything because you feel you're better than others. Instead, look at other people as being better than you.

You shouldn't think only about what matters to you. You should also think about what matters to others.

You should look at things the same way that Jesus does.

He was God.
But he didn't hold on to being God.
He made himself into nothing.
He became a servant.
He became a human.
He looked like a man.
He put himself in a low place.
He obeyed, and he died on a cross.
So God made him great.
God gave him the highest place.
God gave him a name better than all other names.
All people will bow down when they hear Jesus' name.
Everyone in heaven will bow.
Everyone on earth and under the earth will bow.
Every voice will say that Jesus Christ is Lord.
This will show that God the Father is great.

My dear friends, you have always obeyed. You obeyed while I was with you. Now that I'm gone, you still obey. So keep working out your lives. Keep looking up to God, because he is saving you.

God is working in you to help you think and act right. He is helping you fit into his good plans.

Do everything without fussing and fighting. Then you can be sinless and clean. You'll be without sin in a bent and needy world.

You'll shine like stars in the sky. You'll shine because you show God's Word and talk about it. God's Word brings life.

Jesus will come back. Then I can say that I did my work well. I won't need to say it was for no reason.

You're giving and serving because of your faith. And I may need to give up my life. It will be like pouring a drink for God.

I'm happy along with all of you. You should be happy along with me.

Brothers and Workers

PHILIPPIANS 2:19-30

I want to hear news about you. That will cheer me up. So I hope I can send Timothy to you soon. I don't have anyone else like Timothy. He really cares about you.

It seems like people look only for what they want. They don't care about what Jesus wants.

But Timothy shows that he is a good man. He worked with me to tell the Good News. He worked like a son would work with his father.

First I'll see what's going to happen to me here. I'm sure I can come and see you soon.

I think I should send Epaphroditus back to you. He is like a brother to me. He is a worker and a fighter with me. He is also the one you sent with your message. You sent him to take care of whatever I needed.

But he wants to go back to be with you. He is upset because you heard he was sick. He really was sick. He almost died, but God was kind to him. That was a good thing for me. God saved me from being sad.

So I do want to send him to you. When you see him again, you'll be glad. Then I won't be so worried.

Be glad to welcome him. Look up to people like him. He nearly died for Jesus' work. He  was giving me the help you couldn't give. That's when he almost gave his life.

The End of the Race

PHILIPPIANS 3:1-14, 18-21

Show how happy God makes you! It's no trouble for me to write the same things to you over and over. The words I write help guard you and keep you safe.

Watch out for people who do sinful things. They're like dogs. They say we must be like Jews to be God's children. But we are God's children. His Spirit helps us worship him. It's Jesus who makes us great and strong.

We don't brag about being like Jews. I could brag if I wanted to. I am a Jew. I'm from Benjamin's family group. I know the Law. I was a leader of the Jews. I wanted to do the right thing. So I hunted people who believed in Jesus. I put them in jail. I made sure I kept every bit of the Law.

But if good came from that, it's good for nothing. I don't mind losing all of that for Jesus. Nothing is more important than knowing Jesus. Everything else is trash. I want Jesus.

I'm not made right with God by keeping laws. I'm right with God because I believe in Jesus. Being made right comes from God. It comes by faith.

I want to know Jesus. I want to know his power. It's the same power that brought Jesus back to life again. I want to be his friend and share his troubles. I'll even face death like he did. I want, somehow, to come back to life again someday.

There is a reason Jesus took hold of me. I'm going for it. I want what Jesus planned for me. I don't think I have it yet.

But there is one thing I do. I forget what happened in the past. I push toward what's coming. I push on to get to the end of the race. God called me toward heaven. I want to win the gift he has for me.

I've told you this before. I'm sad to have to say it again. Many people live like enemies of Jesus' cross. They are headed toward death. Their belly is their god. They try to be great by doing dirty, sinful things. Their minds are on things of the earth.

But we belong to heaven. We can hardly wait for the one from heaven. He will save us. He is Jesus the Lord. He has the power to control all things. By his power, he will change the bodies we have now. We'll have bodies like his body, shining with greatness.

NOVEMBER 30

Show Your Joy!

PHILIPPIANS 4:4-8, 10-19, 21-23; 1:1

Always show how happy God makes you! I'll say it again. Show your joy! Let everybody see clearly how kind you are.

God is near. So don't worry about anything. Instead, pray and ask God for everything. Thank him when you tell him what you need. Then God's peace will guard your hearts and minds. God's peace is greater than anyone can understand.

Think about things that are true and good. Think about things that are right and clean. Think about beautiful things. Think about things you can look up to. If anything is the best, think about it. If it's something to cheer for, think about it.

I'm glad you're thinking about me. You wanted the best for me. You just didn't have any way to show it.

I don't really need anything. I've learned how to be happy no matter what. I know what it's like to need things. I know what it's like to have more than enough.

I've learned the secret of being happy all the time. I can be happy if I'm well fed. I can be happy if I'm hungry. I can be happy if I have all I need. I can be happy if I need things. The secret is this. I can do everything with Jesus' help. He makes me strong.

You were kind to help me in my troubles. Remember when you first heard the Good News? You were the only church that shared with me. You gave to me again and again when I needed it.

I'm not looking for a gift. I'm looking for the good that you do. I want God to bring good to you for any good you do.

I've been paid enough. You sent Epaphroditus with your gifts. God is happy with these gifts. God will give you all you need. He gives out of his great riches. Jesus brings these riches.

Tell all God's people hello. All God's people here say hi. Most of all, the ones in Caesar's house say hello.

I pray that Jesus' kind love will be with you. Yes! Amen!

From Paul and Timothy.

The Biggest Sinner
1 TIMOTHY 1:2-4, 6-9, 12, 15-19

Sometime later, Paul wrote to his friend Timothy.

Dear Timothy,

I've told you this before. Stay in Ephesus. Then you can tell people there not to teach lies. It just brings fussing and fighting. It doesn't do God's work any good.

Some people talk about things that aren't important. They want to teach God's Law. But they don't know what they're saying.

We know the Law is good. It's

good if you use it the right way. The Law wasn't made for people who do right. It was made for people who do wrong.

Jesus makes me strong. I thank him for that. He thought I could follow him no matter what. So he chose me to serve him.

Here's a saying you can believe. Jesus came to the world to save sinners. I'm the biggest sinner of all. But that's why Jesus was kind to me. It shows how he waits for people. He waits for them to come to him.

God is the King who will live forever. He will never die. Let the King be great forever. He can't be seen by human eyes. He is the only God. Yes! Amen!

Timothy, you are like a son to me. Follow what I teach. Then life will be like fighting a good fight. You will keep believing no matter what. You'll know you are doing right.

Some people have turned away from what I teach. Their faith is like a ship that has crashed.

Listen and Learn

1 TIMOTHY 2:1-6, 8-15

Pray for everybody. Ask God to give people what they need. Thank God for them. Pray for kings. Pray for anybody who is in charge. Pray that we can be godly and clean in our hearts. Pray so our lives can be full of peace and quiet.

When we pray for these things, God is happy. He wants everybody to be saved. He wants everybody to know the truth. There is one God. There is one person who talks to God for people. That's Jesus. He gave his life to buy us back from sin.

I want all people to lift up their hands to pray. They should do it without being angry. They shouldn't fuss with each other.

Women should wear clothes that cover enough of their bodies. Women shouldn't be known just for the way they wear their hair. They shouldn't be known for their gold or pearls. They shouldn't be known for clothes that cost a lot of money. Women should be known for the good things they do. They should act like people who worship God.

A woman should listen and learn. She should obey her leaders. I don't let a woman teach or lead a man. She should be quiet. That's because God made Adam first. Then he made Eve. Adam didn't believe Satan's lie. Eve did. She sinned.

Women will have children and will be saved. They are to keep believing and loving. They are to have hearts that are clean from sin.

The Leaders of Jesus' Followers

1 TIMOTHY 3:1-12, 14-16

Here's a saying you can believe. It's good when people want to be leaders in God's church. The leader needs to live the right way. Then no one can blame him for anything. He should have only one wife. He shouldn't overdo anything. Instead, he should control himself. He should be the kind of man people can look up to.

A leader should welcome people into his house. He should be a good teacher. He shouldn't get drunk. He shouldn't hurt people or things. He shouldn't fuss and fight. He shouldn't love money.

A leader should lead his own family well. His children should obey him and look up to him. It would be bad if he couldn't control his own family. Then how could he take care of God's church?

A leader in God's church should not be a new believer. If he is, he might get proud. Then he'd get judged like Satan did. Even people who don't believe should speak well of a church leader.

Choose men to help the leaders. They should be men that people look up to. They should say and do what's true. They shouldn't drink too much wine. They shouldn't try to get rich by doing wrong. They should keep believing. They should know they are doing right. Try them out first. If they are good men, they can be helpers.

Their wives should be women that people look up to. They shouldn't say bad things about other people. They shouldn't overdo things. They should be women you can trust.

A man who helps leaders should have only one wife. He should be a good leader for his family.

I hope I can come see you soon. But I might not be able to. That's why I'm writing these things to you. Now you'll know how people should act in God's family. His family is the church.

There is no question about it. Being like God is a big mystery.

God appeared in a human body.
His Spirit showed that he was right. Angels saw him.
The nations heard about him. People in the world believed in him.
He went up to heaven, shining with greatness.

Train Yourself

1 TIMOTHY 4:1-4, 6-16

What the Spirit says is clear. Some people will turn away from God. They'll follow spirits that lie.

People who lie don't know right from wrong anymore. They tell people they can't get married. They tell them they can't eat this or that. But God made food for us. We should eat and be thankful for it. Everything God made is good.

Show God's people these things. Then you'll be doing a good job of serving Jesus.

You grew up knowing the truth. You follow good teaching. Don't listen to made-up stories that lead away from God. Instead, teach yourself to be who God wants you to be.

You can train your body. That does a little good. But also train yourself to live like God wants. That does lots of good. It's good for your life now and forever.

Here's a saying you can believe. We hope in the living God. He wants to save everyone. Most of all, he saves people who believe.

Teach people these things. Tell people these are rules to live by. And don't let anybody put you down for being young. Instead, show God's people how to talk. Show them how to live. Show them how to love. Show them how to believe. Show them how to have hearts that are clean from sin.

Work at getting people together. Read God's Word to them. Work at teaching.

Remember when the church leaders put their hands on you? They told God's message for you. Use the gift you got then.

Stay busy doing these things for God. Do them with all your heart. Then everybody can see how you're growing.

Watch your life carefully. Watch what you teach. Keep following Jesus even when times are hard. Then you'll save yourself. You'll save the people who hear you too.

Older Women and Younger Women

1 TIMOTHY 5:1-5, 8-11, 13-15, 17-23

You can tell an older man what's wrong. But don't be hard on him when you do. Teach him as if he were your father. Treat younger men like brothers. Treat older women like your mother. Treat younger women like sisters. Be good and right in the way you treat them.

Sometimes a woman's husband dies. Find out if a woman like this really needs help. Let's say she has children or grandchildren. She has done a lot for them. Now it's their turn to help her. This makes God happy.

Sometimes a woman has no family to help her. Then she hopes in God. She prays. She asks God to help her.

Keep a list of women whose husbands have died. These women should be more than 60 years old. They are women who stayed with their husbands as long as they lived. People know them for the good things they have done. They took good care of their children. Or they welcomed people into their houses. Or they did good things for God's people. Or they helped people in trouble.

Don't put younger women on this list. They often want to get married again. They get lazy. They talk about other people. They don't mind their own business. They say things they shouldn't say.

So I tell younger women to get married. They should have children. They should take care of their homes. Then Satan won't have a chance to send lies around.

What if people don't work for what their families need? What if they don't work for what their children need? That shows that they don't really believe in Jesus. Even people who don't believe are better off than they are.

Some people have already turned away from God. They're following Satan.

Some leaders take care of the business of the church. They should be treated as very important people. Most of all, treat leaders who teach as important people. God's Word says it this way. "Let the working ox eat some of the grain." It also says, "Pay a worker for his work."

Don't listen when someone says something bad about a leader. Listen if two or three people say it's true. Let's say a leader sins. Then the people should get together and tell him. That way, other people can learn from it.

Do what I tell you. Don't treat some people better than others.

Don't be too fast to put your hands on people to pray. Don't be a part of other people's sins. Keep your heart clean.

Don't just drink water. Drink a little bit of wine. That will help your stomach. It will help the sickness you have so often.

DECEMBER 2

Loving Money

1 TIMOTHY 6:1-12, 15-21

Are you a servant? Then care about your master with all your heart.

That way, people will say good things about God.

Let's say your master believes in Jesus. That doesn't mean you act like he is less important. Instead, you serve him better. That's because the person you serve is special to you. Teach the people these things.

What if people teach lies? What if they don't believe the teaching about Jesus? Then they are proud. They don't understand anything. They want to fuss and fight about words.

All of this brings angry talking. These people want what others have. They think being good is a way to get rich.

Here's what is best. It's being good and being happy with what you have. We didn't bring anything into the world with us. We can't take anything out of the world with us. We should be happy to have food and clothes.

People who want to get rich have problems. It's like getting into a trap. They get pulled into doing wrong things. They begin wanting foolish things. They want things that end up hurting them.

Loving money brings all kinds of trouble. Some people wanted money so badly, they stopped believing Jesus. Then they had lots of problems that made them sad.

You are a man of God. Run away from all these sinful things. Go for what's right. Go for what's godly. Go for believing. Go for love. Try to keep your faith even in hard times. Try to be kind.

Sometimes it's hard to keep believing. Try hard to believe. Fight for it. Fight a good fight. Hold on to life that lasts forever. This is what God chose for you.

God is the only Ruler. He is the King of kings. He is the Lord of lords. Only God never dies. He lives in light that we can't even get near. Nobody has seen him, and nobody can see him. He will be called great forever. He will have power forever. Yes! Amen!

Tell rich people not to be proud. Tell them not to hope in their riches. Riches can be here today and gone tomorrow. So tell them to hope in God. He is rich. He gives us everything to enjoy.

Tell rich people to do good things. Tell them to give a lot. Tell them to be happy to share. That way, they'll really be making riches for themselves. These riches bring life that truly is life.

Timothy, take care of what God gave you. Stay away from talk that is not godly. Stay away from ideas that are against God. People say these ideas are the right things to know. Some people believed these ideas. Then they stopped believing in God.

I pray that God's kind love will be with you.

From Paul.

Leaders in Every Town
TITUS 1:4-16

Paul also wrote a letter to Titus, who was in Crete.

Dear Titus,

I left you in Crete. I wanted you to take care of God's work that wasn't finished there. I wanted you to choose leaders for the church in every town.

A church leader must not do anything to be blamed for. He must have only one wife. His children should believe. They shouldn't be wild. They should obey him.

God trusts leaders to do his work. Those who are leaders over others can't be bossy. They shouldn't get angry too fast. And they shouldn't get drunk. They shouldn't be mean. And they shouldn't try to get money by tricking others.

Instead, they should welcome people into their houses. They should love what's good and control themselves. They should be good and right. Their hearts should

be sinless. They should keep their lives in order.

Leaders should keep believing God's message the way they learned it. Then they can help others grow stronger by teaching God's way. They can tell people what's wrong with turning against God.

Lots of people turn against God. They talk a lot. They lie. They tear apart whole families by teaching wrong things. They do it to get rich.

One of their own prophets said it this way. "People from Crete always lie. They are sinful and mean. They are lazy. They eat too much." It's true.

Tell them they're wrong. Tell them firmly. Then they can believe what's right. Don't listen to the stories Jewish people make up. Don't listen to the laws of people who go against truth.

When your heart is clean from sin, everything is clean. But some people's minds are dirty from sin. They say they know God. But the way they act shows they don't know him. They are not good to be around. They don't obey. They can't do anything good.

Teaching Us to Say No
TITUS 2:1-14

You should teach what's right. Teach older men not to overdo things. They should act right so people can speak well of them. They should control themselves. They should have a strong faith and love others. They should keep believing even in hard times.

Teach older women to show that they look up to God. They shouldn't say bad things about others. They shouldn't drink too much wine. They should teach good things.

Older women can teach younger women how to love their husbands. They can teach them how to love their children. They can teach self-control. They can teach how to have a heart that's clean from sin. They can teach how to work at home. They can teach how to be kind. They can teach how to let husbands lead. That way, nobody will say bad things about God's Word.

Help young men grow stronger in self-control. Show them how. Do good things. Teach truth. Mean what you say, and say what you mean. Then nobody can blame you for what you say.

Teach servants that they should always obey their masters. They should try to make their masters happy. Teach them not to talk back to their masters. They shouldn't steal from their masters. Their masters should be able to trust them. That way, the teaching about God will look good.

God's kind love saves people. It's for everyone. His kind love teaches us to say no to bad things. It teaches us to say no to things the world loves. It teaches us to have self-control. God's kind love teaches us to do what's right. It teaches us how to be good.

We wait and hope for Jesus to come again. He died to save us from sin. He died to make his people clean and spotless. He wants his people to belong just to him. He wants them to be ready to do good things.

DECEMBER 3

Making Us New

TITUS 3:1-5, 7-15

Help people remember to obey the rulers in charge. People need to be ready to do good. They shouldn't say bad things about others. They should make peace. They should be thoughtful. They should treat other people as the important ones.

We were foolish once. We didn't obey. We lied. We did only what felt good at the moment. We wanted bad things to happen to other people. We wanted what others had. We hated them, and they hated us.

But God was kind and loving to us. He saved us. He didn't save us because we did the right things. He saved us just because of his kind love.

God saved us by making us new. It's like being born again. He made us new with his Holy Spirit.

We have a hope. We can live forever! I want you to make sure people know this. That way, people who trust God can work at doing good.

Stay away from fussing and fighting over God's laws. That does no good.

What if somebody wants to turn people against each other? Tell him once to stop. Then tell him again. Then stay away from him. You can be sure of one thing. That kind of person's thinking is sinful.

I'll send two of my friends to see you. Then try your best to come see me in Greece. I'm going to stay there for the winter.

Do all you can to help Zenas. He is the lawyer. Help Apollos, too. These men are traveling. Make sure they have whatever they need.

God's people have to learn to work hard doing good. That way, they'll get lots of things done. And they can have what they need each day.

Everybody here says to tell you hi. Say hello to God's people who love us.

I pray that God's kind love will be with you all.

From Paul.

A Powerful Spirit

2 TIMOTHY 1:2-12, 15-17

Paul was put in jail again in Rome. He wrote another letter to Timothy from jail.

Dear Timothy,

You are like a son to me. I pray that God's kind love and peace will fill you.

I always remember you when I pray, night and day. I remember how you cried. I want very much to see you. Then I'll be happy.

I remember your true faith. Your grandmother, Lois, believed. Your mother, Eunice, believed. You believe too. That's why I want God's gift to grow stronger in you. You got this gift when I put my hands on you.

God didn't give us a shy spirit. He gave us a powerful spirit. He gave us a spirit of love. He gave us a spirit of self-control.

Don't be afraid to tell about Jesus. Don't feel bad because I'm in jail for Jesus. Instead, work with me in these hard times.

God gave his kind love to us before time began. Now we see this kind love because Jesus came. Jesus got rid of death. He brought us life that lasts forever.

God chose me to tell this message. He chose me to be an apostle and a teacher. That's why I'm having hard times. But I don't feel bad about it. I know who I believe in. I've given my life to him. I know he can take care of me.

Everybody in Asia left me. You know that.

I pray that God will be kind to Onesiphorus and his family. He helped me. He didn't forget about me because I was in jail. Instead he looked hard for me in Rome. And he found me.

A Good Soldier
2 TIMOTHY 2:1, 3-4, 8-17, 21-24

So be strong in Jesus' kind love. Keep on believing even when times get hard. You'll be like a good soldier for Jesus. A soldier wants to make his captain happy.

Remember Jesus. He came back to life again. This is the Good News I bring. It's the reason I'm having hard times. It's why I'm tied up like someone who has done wrong.

But God's Word is not tied up. So I'll keep on believing when times are hard. I'll do it for God's people. Then they can be saved by Jesus too. They can have his great power. It lasts forever.

Here's a saying you can trust.

If our old selves died with Jesus,
    we will live with Jesus.
If we keep on believing when we
        have hard times,
    we'll rule with him.
If we turn away from him,
    he will turn away from us.
If we don't keep our promises,
    he will still keep his.
    That's because he is who he is.
    He will always be true to himself.

Keep helping people remember these things. Tell them not to fuss about words. It doesn't do any good. It just hurts people who listen to them.

Try your best to live a good life. Be a worker who doesn't feel bad about his work. Be a person who teaches what's right about God's Word. Stay away from busy talk that isn't about God.

Some people do lots of busy

talking. They just become less and less like God. What they teach will sink into other people like sickness.

We can clean ourselves up. We can stop doing sinful things that make our hearts dirty. Then our Master can use us. We'll be ready to do good works. That's what he planned for us.

Run away from the sins that young people want to do. Go for what's right. Go for faith and love and peace. Be with others who follow God with hearts that are clean from sin.

Stay away from silly fussing and fighting. That happens when people try to show that other people are wrong. God's servants are not supposed to fuss and fight.

Instead, God's servants should be kind to everybody. They should be able to teach. They should not stay angry at anyone.

DECEMBER 4

Earth's Last Days

2 TIMOTHY 3

Listen! Think about this. Earth's last days will be full of trouble. People will love themselves. They will love money. They will brag. They will be proud.

They will hurt others. They won't obey their parents. They won't be thankful. Their hearts will be full of sin. They won't love others. They won't forgive each other. They will say bad things about other people.

They won't control themselves. They'll be mean. They won't love what's good. They'll trick people. They'll do things without thinking. They'll think they're the best.

They'll do what feels good at the moment. They won't love God. They'll do things to look like they're godly. But they won't believe in God's power. Stay away from them.

These people trick their way into homes. They get control of people who can't say no. Those people are full of sin. They follow whatever bad things they want to do.

People who are full of sin are always learning. But they can never say what the truth really is. They fight against the truth. They have dirty minds. People who have faith want nothing to do with them. Those sinful people won't get very far. Others will clearly see how foolish they are.

You know about my teaching. You know how I live. You know what I live for. You know how I wait quietly. You know my faith and love. You know how I keep believing even in hard times. You know how I've been hurt.

You know my troubles. You know what happened to me in cities

I visited. I was hurt, but I kept going. Jesus saved me from all the danger.

The fact is that everyone who wants to be godly will get hurt. Sinful people will get more and more sinful. They will lie, and they will be lied to.

But you need to keep following what you have learned. Keep doing the things you know you should.

You've known God's Word since you were a baby. God's Word will make you wise. Then you'll be saved because you believe in Jesus.

All of God's Word is given to us by God. We can use it to teach. We can use it to show people what's right and wrong. We can use it to train people how to live. Then God's people can be ready to do good.

Like a Race

2 TIMOTHY 4:2-22; 1:1

Teach people carefully. One of these days they won't listen to good teaching. They'll do what they want. They'll get their own teachers. These teachers will say what the people want to hear. The people won't listen to truth. Instead, they'll listen to made-up stories.

But you should use your head. Think, no matter what happens. Keep going even when it's hard.

Teach the Good News. Follow God's plans for your life.

I'm like a drink that's being given as a gift to God. I'm flowing out, and it's time for me to leave. My life has been like a fight. I fought well. It's been like a race. I finished the race. I kept believing all the way.

Now God has a crown for me. It's a crown that shows I'm right with him. Jesus, the judge who does right, will give it to me. I'm not the only one to have a crown. There is one for everybody who wants Jesus to come back.

Come to see me as soon as you can. Demas loved this world. He left me. He went to Thessalonica. Crescens went to Galatia. Titus went to Dalmatia. Luke is the only one with me.

Bring Mark with you. He can help with the work God wants me to do. I sent Tychicus to Ephesus. I left my coat at Troas. Bring it with you when you come. Bring my writings, too.

Alexander the metal worker made lots of trouble for me. God will pay him back for what he did. You should watch out for him too. He was very much against our message.

I tried to show I was right. At first nobody helped me. Everybody left me. I hope God doesn't hold it against them. But Jesus stood beside me. He made me strong so I could tell the whole message. That way, all the people who aren't Jewish could hear it.

God saved me from the lions. He will save me from everything bad that comes against me. He will bring me safe to heaven, to his kingdom. Let God's greatness shine for ever and ever. Yes! Amen!

Say hello to Priscilla and Aquila and to Onesiphorus and his family. Erastus is staying in Corinth. I left Trophimus in Miletus. He was sick.

Try to come before winter.

Linus, Claudia, and all God's people here say hello.

I pray that Jesus will be with your spirit. I pray that his kind love will be with you.

From Paul.

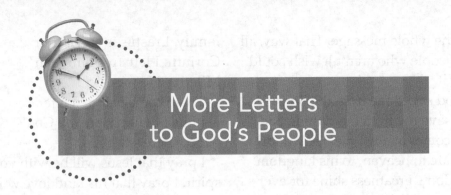

More Letters to God's People

Like a Sea Wave

JAMES 1:1-15, 17, 19-27

James was one of Jesus' brothers. He was a leader of Jesus' followers. He wrote this letter to them.

To God's people here and there in all the nations,

Hello!

Think of hard times as happy times. Your faith is being tested. That helps you learn to keep on believing, no matter what happens. When you believe no matter what, you're grown up. Your faith fills you. There is nothing more you need.

Do you need to be wise? Ask God. He gives plenty of wisdom to everyone. He doesn't blame you for asking. God will make you wise.

But you should believe when you ask God. Don't think he can't do it. If that's what you think, you're like a sea wave. The wind blows waves here and there. If you're like that, don't think God will give you anything. Your mind would be going different ways at one time. Your faith in Jesus wouldn't be strong.

If someone is poor, he should be glad. That's a high place in God's kingdom. If someone is rich, he should be glad too. But that's a low place in God's kingdom.

The rich person is like a wild flower. He will soon fade away. The sun comes up, burning hot. The plant bends over. Its flower falls off. It's not as beautiful anymore. Rich people are the same way. They'll seem to fade away, even while they're busy.

God brings good things to people who keep believing no matter what. Someday their troubles will be over. Then God will let them live forever. This life that lasts forever will be like a crown from God. God promises this crown of life for everybody who loves him.

What if a sin comes to your mind?

Then we shouldn't say, "God is trying to make me sin." Nothing sinful can make God want to sin. And he doesn't try to make anyone else want to sin.

People sin when sin looks good to them. Sin leads them on. First they think about it. Then they sin. Sin grows. It ends up in death.

God sends every good gift. He sends every gift that is clean and sinless. God is the Father of heaven's lights. He doesn't change like shadows that move around.

Remember this. People should be in a hurry to listen. They shouldn't be in such a hurry to talk. They shouldn't get angry very fast. Being angry doesn't help us live the way God wants.

God wants us to live a life that's right. So stop being around things that make you think dirty thoughts. Sin is everywhere. Stay away from it. Welcome God's Word. You know it as if it had been planted in you. It can save you.

Don't just listen to God's Word. Instead, do what God's Word says. Let's say you listen to God's Word. But you don't do what it tells you. Then you are like a person looking into a mirror. You see yourself. Then you leave and forget what you look like.

But let's say you look carefully at God's way. You keep looking. You don't forget what you heard. You do it. Then whatever you do, God will bring good things to you.

Let's say you think you're following God. But you don't control what you say. Then you're lying to yourself. You're not following God.

What does God want us to do? Take care of children who have no mother and father. Take care of women whose husbands have died. Keep our hearts from getting dirty in the world's sin.

Rich Man, Poor Man
JAMES 2:1-5, 8-9, 14-26

You believe in Jesus. So don't treat some people better than others.

Let's say someone comes to your meeting place. This person wears a gold ring and has very nice clothes. Then someone who is poor comes in. This person wears worn-out clothes. Let's say you're very nice to the rich person. You say, "Here's a good place for you to sit." But you tell the poor person to stand. Or you let that person sit on the floor next to your feet. Haven't you treated one better than the other? That's a sinful way to treat people.

Listen. God planned for poor people to be rich in faith. He chose them. He will give them the riches of his kingdom. This is what he promised to people who love him.

God's Word says, "Love your neighbor like you love yourself." That's the law of our King. If you do this, you're doing the right thing.

But what if you treat some people better than others? Then you are sinning. You're breaking the law.

What if a person says he believes? But he doesn't obey. Then what good does it do for him to believe? Can that kind of believing save him?

Let's say one of God's people has no clothes. Or the person has no food. You say, "Go on your way. I hope the best will come to you. Stay warm! Get plenty to eat!" But you don't do anything to help the person stay warm. You don't share any of your food. What good is your faith?

If all you do is believe, it won't do any good. You also have to do what God wants. Faith by itself is nothing. It's dead.

Somebody might say, "You have faith. But I do what God wants."

Try to show me that you have faith but do nothing for God. And I'll show you my faith by doing what God wants. You say you believe there is one God. That's good! But even bad spirits believe that. They shake to think about it.

Faith by itself does no good. You have to do what God wants. Think about Abraham. He was right with

God, and he showed it. He gave his son Isaac to God.

See? Abraham believed God, so he did something. Faith was just part of it. Obeying was the other part. So God's Word came true. "Abraham believed God. That made everything right between Abraham and God." God said Abraham was his friend.

See? It's just as if you had never sinned. That's because you do what God wants. It's not just because you believe.

It was the same way with Rahab. She let two of God's people stay at her house. She sent the soldiers one way. She sent God's people another way.

A body is dead without its spirit. Faith is dead without doing what God wants.

A Small Fire in a Big Forest

JAMES 3:3-18

We can put bits into horses' mouths. That's the way we make them obey us. We turn the whole horse around by using the bit.

Think about ships. They are so big! Strong winds blow them across

764

the water. But there is a small rudder on each ship. It makes the ship go wherever the captain wants.

It's the same way with your mouth. Your mouth is a small part of your body. But it talks big! A small fire can burn down a whole forest. Your mouth is like a fire.

Think of all the parts of your body. Your mouth can bring the most pain. It can make you sin. The bad things you say come from hell. It's as if hell sets your mouth on fire.

People can train all kinds of animals. They can train sea animals, birds, and animals that crawl. But nobody can train a mouth. It doesn't rest. It can be full of hurtful things to say.

We praise God with our mouths. Then we turn around and say bad things about people. They are people God made to be like him.

Good words and bad words come from the same mouth. It shouldn't be this way. Can fresh water and salt water flow down the same river? No! Can you get olives from a fig tree? No! Can you get figs from a grape vine? No!

Are you wise? Do you understand? Then show it by living God's way. Do things that are wise.

What if anger lives deep in your heart? What if it's there because you want to be like other people? What if you just think about yourself?

What if you want to make yourself great? Then don't say it's not so. And don't brag about it. That wouldn't be wise. That's what worldly people do.

Satan starts things like that. When you want to be like others, you're asking for trouble. When you just think about yourself, you're asking for trouble. When you want to be great, you're asking for trouble. Things will get out of order. It brings all kinds of sin.

Here's what comes with heaven's wise thinking. First, you're spotless and clean, without sin. Then you love peace. You put others first. You let your leaders lead you. You are full of kindness. Good things happen when you're around. You are fair. You say what's true.

People who make peace are like farmers. They plant peace. Then they pick a crop of doing what's right.

Like a Fog
JAMES 4:1-10, 13-17

What makes you fuss and fight? Fussing and fighting come from wanting things. You want something, but you don't get it. You don't have it, because you don't ask God for it. When you ask God, you don't get it. That's because you ask for the wrong reasons. You want it just to make yourself feel good.

You are turning away from God. Don't you know? If you are the world's friend, you hate God. People who are the world's friends are God's enemies.

People have a problem of wanting to be like others. But God is kind to us. The wise saying from God's Word puts it this way.

"God is against people who think
     they're the greatest.
God is kind to people who know
     they're not great."

Let God lead you. Turn away from Satan. Then he will run away from you. Come close to God. Then he will come close to you.

You people who sin, clean up your hearts. Be sorry. Cry. Stop laughing about it. Stop being glad for what you've done. Let God know he is the most important to you. Then he will make you important to him.

You say, "Today we'll go here. Tomorrow we'll go there. We'll have a business. We'll make money." But you don't really know what's going to happen tomorrow.

Your life is like a fog. It comes for a little while. Then it fades away. So you should say, "If God wants, we'll do this. If God wants, we'll do that." But you brag. That's wrong.

Sometimes we know we're supposed to do good. But we don't do it. We are sinning.

Rotten Riches

JAMES 5:1-9, 13-18; 1:1

Now you rich people, listen. You can cry because of what's coming to you. You'll see that your riches are rotten. Moths ate up your clothes. Your gold and silver rusted away. It all shows that you held on to your riches.

Look! You didn't pay the people who worked for you. That says bad things about you. The workers cried about it, and God heard them.

You lived with riches all around you. You bought whatever you wanted. You made yourselves fat. Now it's time to pay for it.

You blamed people who did nothing wrong. You killed people who were not even against you.

But everyone who follows Jesus should wait quietly. Wait until the Lord comes. Look at the farmer. He waits for a good crop to grow. He waits for rain in the spring and the fall. So you can wait too. Hold on. The Lord is coming soon.

Don't fuss at each other. If you do, God will judge you for it. He is right at the door.

Are you in trouble? Pray. Are you happy? Sing praise songs. Are you sick? Ask the leaders of the church to pray for you. Ask them to put oil on you in Jesus' name.

Believe and pray, and sick people will get well. God will make them well. If they've sinned, God will forgive them.

If you've sinned, say so. Pray for each other. Then God will make you well. A person who is right with God can pray a powerful prayer. It does a lot of good.

Elijah was a person just like us. He prayed with all his heart that it wouldn't rain. And it didn't. It didn't rain for three and a half years! Then he prayed again, and rain came. Crops grew again.

From James.

DECEMBER 7

Like Wild Waves in the Sea
JUDE

Jude was another brother of Jesus. He wrote to Jesus' followers too.

To the people God chose,

You are dear friends to me. Please fight for your faith. Jesus trusted his people to keep believing.

Some people have quietly come into your group. They don't obey God. They say, "God is kind, so we can sin all we want." They don't believe in Jesus. But he is our only Lord and King.

Remember. God saved his people from Egypt. Later, some of those same people didn't believe in him. So he got rid of them.

Some of the angels didn't obey. They didn't stay where God put them in charge. They left their own home. So God sent them into the darkness. They are in chains there. They'll be there until the day God judges.

The people in the town of Sodom sinned with sex. We can look at what happened in Sodom. We can see what happens when people get in trouble with God. God pays them back with fire.

The people who have come into your group have big dreams. But they make their own bodies dirty from sin. They turn away from anyone who is in charge. They say bad things about heaven's beings.

Michael is the head angel. He fussed with Satan about Moses' body. But even Michael didn't dare say bad things about Satan. Instead, he said, "The Lord will put you down!"

But these people say bad things against anything they don't understand. Trouble will come to these people. They are like dirt spots that show up when you meet together. They have no problem eating with you. But they're like shepherds who feed only themselves.

They are like clouds that the wind blows in. But they don't bring any rain.

They are like trees in the fall. But they didn't grow the fruit they were supposed to have. And they've been pulled up by the roots.

They're like wild waves that toss high in the sea. Everybody sees the waves. And everybody sees the sin these people should feel bad about.

They are like stars that fly here and there. They're heading for the deepest, blackest darkness. It's been saved for them. It will last forever.

Long ago, Enoch talked about these men. He said, "See? The Lord is coming. Thousands and thousands of his sinless people are with him. He will judge everybody. He will blame sinful people for the wrong they've done. He will blame them for saying bad, angry things about him."

These people fuss and fight. They do whatever sinful things they want to. They brag about themselves. They trick other people into liking them. That way, they can use those people for their own good.

Remember what Jesus' apostles said before. "When the last days come, people will make fun of others. They will do only the sinful things they want to do."

These are the people who make you turn against each other. They don't have the Spirit. So they just do what they feel like doing.

Be kind to people who don't believe. Lead people away from wrong. Be kind to others, but be afraid of sin. Hate even the clothes people wear when they sin.

God can keep you in his kingdom. He can let you see his greatness. You'll come to him with a heart he has made clean and sinless. You'll come with great joy. God saves us. He is our only God.

God will shine with greatness forever. He rules as the King. He is strong. He is in charge. He comes to us through Jesus our Lord. He lived before all time. He lives now, and he will live forever! Yes! Amen!

From Jude.

Richer than Gold

1 PETER 1:1-9, 13-23, 25

Peter also wrote letters. He wrote this one to Jesus' followers in many different lands.

To the people God chose,

Cheer for God! He has been very kind to us. He gave us a new hope. It's all because Jesus came back to life. For us, it's like being born all over again.

Now we get what God planned to give his children. It will never fade away. It will never rot. It will never die. God keeps it in heaven for you.

You believe. So God's power is like a shield for you. Everyone will see that he saves you in the end.

You show your great joy about this, even though you're having hard times. These hard times will last for just a while.

Your faith is richer than gold. Gold won't last. But your faith will last even through hard times. That will show how important Jesus is to you. His greatness will shine. He will come back again. Then people will see him for who he is.

You haven't seen Jesus, but you love him anyway. You believe in him. You are full of joy. It's better than words can tell. It shines in you. That's because your souls are being saved. You are getting what you wanted from your faith.

So get your minds ready. Control yourselves. Put all your hope in Jesus' kind love. He will be kind to you when he comes.

Be children of God who obey. Don't keep doing the sinful things you wanted to do. You wanted to do these things when you didn't understand. But God is clean from sin. So you be clean from sin too. Don't sin in anything you do. God says in his Word, "Be sinless and holy, because I'm sinless and holy."

God is a Father who judges each person. He is fair. He doesn't treat any person better than another. So live like you belong to heaven, not to earth. Treat God like the important Father he is.

The way your fathers lived did no good. But you were saved from that way of life. You weren't saved because someone paid with silver or gold. You were saved because Jesus paid with his blood. Jesus was clean, sinless, and holy.

God chose Jesus before he made the world. Years later, God sent him to earth. God sent him for you.

You believe in God because of Jesus. God made Jesus come back to life and showed how great Jesus is. So you believe and hope in God.

Now you're clean from sin. You've obeyed the truth. So you

truly love God's people. Have a deep love for each other. Love with your whole heart.

It's like you've been born again. You haven't been born again into a family that dies. You've been born again into a family that never dies. God's Word lives and lasts forever. Isaiah said it this way. "God's Word stays fresh forever."

Living Stones

1 PETER 2:1-7, 9-14, 16-25

So get rid of hate. Get rid of lies. Stop saying one thing and doing something different. Stop wanting to be like other people. Stop saying bad things about people. You have seen how good God is. So be like a baby that's just been born. Then you can grow up in God's kingdom.

Come to Jesus. People didn't want him, but God chose him. Jesus is important to God.

Isaiah says it this way.

"See? I am putting a stone down in
    my land.
It's a stone I chose.
It's an important stone.

It holds the walls together at the
    corner.
Whoever trusts in him will never
    have to feel bad."

You believe in Jesus. He is important to you. But what about people who don't believe? The psalm puts it like this.

"The builders didn't want the stone. But this stone is now the most
    important stone."

That's Jesus.

You are like stones that are alive too. God is building you into a house. It's a spirit house. God wants you to serve him like priests. You can give gifts to God.

God chose you. You are like the king's priests. You are a nation of people with no sins. You belong to God. So you can praise him. He brought you out of the dark. He led you into his wonderful light.

In the past, you were not God's people. But now you are. In the past, you didn't have his kind love. But now you do.

You are my dear friends. You don't belong to the world. So I beg you to stay away from sinful things. They fight against your soul. Live good lives. Then people who don't believe will see the good you do.

Let every leader you have lead you. There is a reason they are leaders. It's so they can get rid of sinful people. They can speak up for good people.

Live like a servant of God. Show people that they're important. Love God's people. Treat God as the most important one. Say good things about the king.

If you're a servant, obey your master. Don't just obey masters who are good and kind. Obey masters who are hard on you too.

Let's say you haven't done anything wrong. It's still good to deal with the pain of hard times. Hard times are good if you're thinking about what God wants.

Let's say your master beats you for doing something wrong. That makes you look like a bad person. Even if you deal with it all right, you look bad.

But let's say you do good. What if your master is still mean to you? Then deal with it. Keep on going. That makes you look good.

Jesus was hurt when he died for you. He showed you how to deal with hard times. So you should do like he did.

Isaiah said this about Jesus.

"He didn't sin.
He didn't lie."

People said terrible things about Jesus, but he didn't talk back. They hurt him, but he didn't say he'd hurt them back. Instead, he trusted God, because God is a fair judge.

Jesus took our sins as if they were his sins. He died on the cross. He died to get rid of our sins. He died so we could live for what's right.

You have been made well because Jesus was hurt. You were like sheep. You were going here and there, away from your Shepherd. Now you have come back to the Shepherd. He is Jesus. He is the one who takes care of your soul.

What Makes You Beautiful
1 PETER 3

If you're a wife, let your husband lead you. Then if he doesn't believe God's Word, he will see how you act. He will see how sinless your life is. He will see how much you look up to God. Then you won't even have to say anything. He will learn to believe in Jesus.

The way you look shouldn't be what makes you seem beautiful. It shouldn't matter if you wear your hair in a braid. It shouldn't matter if you wear gold or not. It shouldn't matter if you have the best clothes. What should matter is the real you that's inside your body.

Your beauty should come from your kind, quiet spirit. That kind of beauty doesn't fade away. That kind of beauty is what's important to God.

That's the way women from long ago were beautiful. They hoped in God. They let their husbands lead them. Think of Sarah. She did what Abraham said. She even called him her master. So be like Sarah. Do what's right, and don't be afraid.

If you're a husband, be kind to your wife. Show that she is important to you by how you act. You work together as a team. You have the strong place on the team.

God is kind. He lets both of you live as his children. So act like it. Then nothing will get in the way when you pray.

All of you, live peacefully with each other. Try to understand each other's feelings. Love each other as if you were family. Be kind.

Don't act like you're the greatest. Don't do wrong to others because they did wrong to you. Instead, do good things for others. That's what God chose you to do. That way, God can bring good to you.

The psalm says it this way.

"If you want to love life,
    don't say bad things.
If you want to have good days,
    don't lie.
Turn away from what's wrong.
    Do good.

Look for the way of peace,
    and follow it.
God watches people who do what's
    right.
He listens when they pray.
But God turns his face away from
    people who sin."

Who will hurt you if you want to do good? Let's say someone does hurt you for doing good. God will still bring good to you. Isaiah put it this way. "Don't be afraid of the things sinful people are afraid of. Don't be scared."

In your heart, make Jesus your Lord. Always be ready to tell people why you hope in him. But tell them kindly. Make them feel important.

Be sure you are doing what's right. People might say bad things about how you act. But they will feel bad for saying these things.

It's not good when you're hurt for doing wrong. It's better when you're hurt for doing good. That might be what God wants.

Jesus died for our sins. He died one time. He died for everyone. He died once and for all. Jesus has always done what's right. He died for people who do what's wrong. He did it to bring you to God.

In Noah's time, only eight people were saved in the ark. They went through all that water, and they were saved. The water you're dipped into when you're baptized is like that water.

Being baptized is not for washing dirt off your body. It's for washing sin from your heart. Then you know things are right between you and God. You are saved because Jesus came back to life. He went into heaven. He is at God's right side. He is in charge of all the angels and other powers.

In Trouble for Following Jesus

1 PETER 4:1-5, 7-19

People hurt Jesus because he obeyed God. You should look at your troubles the same way. What if people hurt you for obeying God? Then it shows that you got rid of sin. Now you don't live to get what you want. You live to do what God wants.

You used to live like people who don't believe in God. You did anything that felt good at the moment. You tried to get whatever you wanted. You got drunk. You had wild parties. You worshiped idols.

People who don't believe in God think you're strange now. You don't do those things anymore. So they make fun of you. They'll have to answer to God. He is ready to judge people, alive or dead.

Time is coming to an end. So have a clear mind and control yourself. Then you can pray. Most of all, have a deep love for each other. Love can make up for lots of sins.

Welcome each other into your homes. Don't fuss about it. God has given each of you a gift in your spirit. Use your gift to help people. Show God's kindness in different ways.

Some people teach about God. They should teach as if they're saying God's own words.

People who serve should let God make them strong. That way, God will get the praise. God will have power forever. We will see his shining greatness forever. Yes! Amen!

Don't be surprised that you're having hard times. This brings lots of pain to you. But don't think it's strange. Instead, be glad that you share Jesus' pain. Then you'll be even more glad to see his greatness.

What if people make fun of you because of Jesus? Then God will bring good to you. God's Spirit is with you.

If you're in trouble, it shouldn't be because you stole something. It shouldn't be because you killed someone. It shouldn't be because you got into someone else's business. It shouldn't be for anything wrong.

If you're in trouble for following

Jesus, you shouldn't feel bad about it. Instead, praise God that you belong to Jesus.

It's time for God to judge his people. If it begins with us, where will it end? What will happen to people who don't believe God's Good News? The wise saying from God's Word puts it this way.

"It's hard for people who do right to be saved.
So what will happen to people who sin?"

People who get hurt for obeying God should trust him. God keeps his promises. These people should keep doing good.

The Chief Shepherd
1 PETER 5; 1:1

I want to tell you leaders something. I'm a leader in the church too. I also saw Jesus being hurt. So we will share the great power that he will show us.

Be like shepherds to God's people. They are like your sheep. You take care of them. Help them and watch over them. Don't do it because you have to. Do it because you want to.

God wants you to be happy to lead. Don't do it because you want money. Do it because you want to

help. Don't be bossy. Live a good life that people can see. That way, they'll live the way you do.

Jesus, the Chief Shepherd, will come someday. Then he will help you shine like he does. It will be like getting a shining crown from him. The crown will never fade.

If you're a young man, let the older men lead. Don't act like you're the best. Treat other people as if they are the important ones.

A wise saying from God's Word puts it this way.

"God is against proud people.
But his kind love comes to people who make others feel important."

So treat others as the important ones. Then God will let you have an important place someday.

Tell God about all your worries. Then trust him to take care of those worries. God cares about you.

Control yourself. And watch out. Satan is your enemy. He is like a roaring lion. He creeps around and looks for somebody to get his teeth into. So push him away. Keep believing in Jesus.

God is the God of kind love. He called you to live in his greatness forever. You may have trouble for a while. But he will make up for it. He will make you strong. He will keep you on track. All power will belong to him forever. Yes! Amen!

I wrote this letter to you with the help of Silas. He believes in God and keeps following him.

This is just a short letter. It's to help you feel better. It's to tell you that God's kind love is with you. So keep living in God's kind love.

Mark says hi. Tell each other hello with a kind kiss.

I pray that God will send you his peace.

From Peter.

DECEMBER 10

The Morning Star in Your Hearts

2 PETER 1:1, 3-21

Some time later, Peter wrote another letter to Jesus' followers.

To people who know how special faith is,

Jesus' godly power gave us all we need to live. It gave us all we need to grow to be like God. We know God. He showed us how great and good he is. He called us to come to him.

God gave us great promises. They're very special. So you can live as a child of God. You can get away from the rotting world. The world is

rotting away because people want what's wrong.

So try your best to add goodness to your faith. Then add knowing God's ways. Then add self-control. Then add obeying God no matter what. Then add growing to be like God. Then add being kind to God's people. Then add love.

Live like this, and what you do will be important. You'll do lots of good. That's because you'll know Jesus.

If these things aren't in your life, you can't see. You only see things right in front of you. You don't see things that are far behind or far ahead. You forget that Jesus cleaned sin out of your heart.

Keep doing what God wants you to do. Then you won't ever be away from God. He will give you a warm welcome into Jesus' kingdom, which lasts forever.

I'll help you remember all of this, even if you already know it. You are following the truth. But it's all right for me to remind you.

I know I'll die soon. Jesus clearly told me that. So I'll try my best to remind you of things. Then after I'm gone, you'll remember.

We didn't make up the stories about how Jesus came. We didn't make up the stories about his power. We really saw his kingly greatness.

God made Jesus important. God

showed how great Jesus is. A voice came from the Great King. He said, "This is my Son. I love him. I'm happy with him." We were up on the mountain with Jesus. We heard God's voice. It came from heaven.

We also know what the prophets wrote long ago. You should think about their words. They're like light shining in a dark place. They will shine until day comes. They will shine until Jesus, the morning star, comes back. Then his light will shine in your hearts.

Most of all, understand this. None of God's Word is a story made up by prophets. They said what God told them to say. The Holy Spirit was leading them.

Like Mean Animals
2 PETER 2:1-7, 9-22

Some prophets were fake prophets. They lied. There will be teachers who lie too. They will teach in secret. They will teach things that tear down your faith. They will even say Jesus is not the Lord. They will say that, even though he died for them. They will end up tearing themselves down.

Lots of people will follow these lies. People will make God's truth sound bad. They will want more and more things. They will trick you with stories they invent. But they will be blamed for their wrong. Their sin will catch up with them.

Some of the angels sinned. God didn't save them. He sent them to hell. He put them into dark pits. They will have to stay there until God judges them.

Long ago in Noah's time, people turned away from God. God didn't save the world then. But he did save Noah and his family. That's because Noah did what was right.

God burned the city of Sodom because of its sin. He showed what happens to people who turn away from him. But he saved Lot. Lot was a man who did what was right. He was upset by the sins in Sodom.

So God knows how to save godly people from trouble. But he remembers sinful people. He will judge them someday. Even now, they're paying for their sins.

This happens most often to people who do only what they want. They won't follow their leaders. They hate for anyone to tell them what to do. They are bold. They are proud braggers. They're not even afraid to say bad things about heavenly beings.

Angels are stronger. They have more power. But even angels don't say such things around God.

The teachers who lie don't understand what they're talking about. They're like mean animals.

They just do what they feel like doing. They'll get paid back for the bad things they do.

Their idea of fun is acting wild with people watching. They eat with you, but they are like dirty spots. They enjoy whatever feels good to them at the moment. Their eyes see the wrong they can do. They never stop sinning.

These teachers lead others into their sin. They lead those who aren't strong in their faith. They are good at wanting more and more things. They are a group going down hill. They're off the path. They go here and there looking for wrong to do.

They are like Balaam. He loved sin. But a donkey talked to him with a man's voice. The donkey kept him from doing wrong.

Teachers who lie are no better than rivers that have dried up. They are like fog that a storm blows around. The darkest dark is saved for them.

They brag. They say things that have no meaning. They try to get you to do what they want. They try to get someone who has stopped sinning to start again. They say this will make the person free.

But they're not free themselves. They serve sin. A person serves whatever is his master.

Let's say that people come out of the world's sin. They get to know Jesus. But they get mixed up in sin again. Then they end up in a darker spot. It's darker than where they were at first. It would be better if they'd never known what's right.

But they knew what was right. They still turned away from God. There are some sayings about these people.

"The dog goes
    back to where it threw up."
"The pig was washed clean.
    But she went back to roll in the
    mud."

DECEMBER 11

Coming like a Robber
2 PETER 3

You are my dear friends. This is the second letter I'm writing to you. Both my letters are to help you remember. They should help you think about good things.

Remember what God's prophets said long ago. Remember what your apostles have taught you about Jesus.

First, understand this. In the last days, people will make fun of others. They will sin any way they want. They'll say, "If Jesus promised to come, where is he? Every day goes by just the same. He hasn't come back yet."

But they forgot something. Long ago God made the sky with his words. He made the earth out of water. He also got rid of the world with water in Noah's time.

The earth and sky will hear God's words again. This time his words will bring fire. The fire will come when God judges the world. He will get rid of people who don't follow him.

Don't forget one thing. To God, a day is like a thousand years. A thousand years are like a day. God is not slow about keeping his promise. He is not slow the way people think of being slow. He is waiting for you. He doesn't want anybody to die and never live again. He wants everybody to be sorry and turn away from their sins. He wants everybody to come into his kingdom.

The day that Jesus comes back will come like a robber comes. A robber surprises you.

Someday there will be a roar. The sky will suddenly be gone. Everything in it will burn up. The earth and everything in it will be uncovered.

Everything is going to be torn down. So what kind of people should you be? You should be good and clean and sinless.

You should look for that day of God. Help it come soon. The sky will burn up with fire that's very hot. Everything will melt.

But God keeps his promise. So we look for a new sky and space. We look for a new earth. It will be the home of people who are right with God.

You are watching for this. So try to have clean, spotless hearts. Try to be at peace with God. Remember that God is waiting so people will be saved.

Paul wrote you about this. God made him wise to know these things. He writes all his letters the same way. He talks about this.

Sometimes Paul's letters are hard to understand. Some people change the meaning of his letters. They change the meaning of other things God said too. In the end, they get hurt for doing it.

Watch out. Make sure you don't get pulled into sin. Be sure you're in God's kingdom. Grow in Jesus' kind love. Grow to know Jesus better. Let him be seen for who he is. He is great now and forever! Yes! Amen!

From Peter.

Angels
HEBREWS 1

(No one knows for sure who wrote this letter. Maybe Paul did. Or Luke. Or

Barnabas. Or Apollos. It was written in Italy. It was sent to Jesus' Jewish followers.)

A long time ago, God talked to our people through prophets. He talked in different ways.

Now God has talked to us through Jesus. God chose Jesus. God promised that everything would belong to Jesus. In fact, God made everything with Jesus.

God's Son, Jesus, shines brightly with God's greatness. Jesus shows just what God is like. And Jesus keeps everything going with his powerful Word.

Jesus made a way for hearts to be clean from sin. Then he sat down beside the King of heaven. So he is greater than angels. Even his name is greater than theirs.

Did God ever say this to an angel?

"You are my Son.
Today I became your Father."

God brought his Son into the world. He said,

"All you angels, worship him."

Here's what God says about angels.

"He makes his angels to be like wind.
   He makes his servants to be like
      fire."

But here's what God says about his Son.

"You will be King forever and ever.
   You will do what's right when
      you rule your kingdom.
You love what's right.
   You hate what's wrong.
So your God gave you a place
      greater than others.
   He let joy flow over you."

God says this to his Son.

"Lord, in the beginning you made
      the earth.
   Your hands made the sky and all
      of space.
They won't last forever.
   But you will.
They will wear out like clothes.
   You'll roll them up as if they were
      a robe.
   They will be changed like you
      change clothes.
But you stay the same.
   Your life never ends."

Did God ever say this to an angel?

"Sit at my right side.
I'll make your enemies like a stool.
   You can rest your feet on them."

The angels are spirits that God sends. He sends them to serve his people.

Jesus' Brothers and Sisters

HEBREWS 2

We should be careful. We should think about what we heard. That way we won't turn away from God.

Everyone had to obey the message that angels brought from God. Those who did not obey got what was coming to them.

Now we have heard how to be saved. We can't get away with pretending we never heard it. Jesus was the first to say we could be saved. Then people who heard him said it was true. And God showed it was true. He did wonders. He gave the Spirit's gifts to people the way he wanted.

Someday, someone will be in charge of the world. But it won't be angels. The psalm says it this way.

"I wonder why you even think
    about people.
I wonder why you care about
    your Son,
who became a man.
You made him a little lower than
    angels.
You showed your greatness in
    him.
You made him important.
You put him in charge of
    everything."

So God put Jesus in charge of everything. He didn't leave out anything.

Right now, we don't see Jesus being in charge of everything. But we do see him. He was made to be a little lower than angels for a while. But now he shines with greatness. Jesus gets to be called great. That's because he died to show God's kind love. He felt death for everybody. It was right for God to make his Son, Jesus, perfect. God did this as Jesus followed God's whole plan. Jesus was hurt because of what we did wrong. He died to save us from sin.

Jesus makes people's hearts clean and spotless. Jesus' heart is clean and spotless too. We are in the same family. So Jesus doesn't feel bad about calling us his brothers and sisters.

Jesus says it this way in the psalm.

"I'll tell God's name to my brothers
    and sisters.
I'll sing praises to God when the
    people get together."

Now people have human bodies. So Jesus became human too. That way, when he died, he could get rid of Satan.

Satan holds death's power. People were afraid of death. But Jesus died to set people free from being afraid. He wasn't helping angels when he died. He was helping people. So he had to be human.

Jesus had to become human like us. That's so he could understand us. Now he can tell God what it's like to be human.

It hurt Jesus to have sins come to his mind. He had to say no to sin. Sins come to our minds too. But Jesus knows what that's like, so he can help us.

Hard Hearts

HEBREWS 3:1-2, 6, 12-18

God has a heavenly plan for your life. So keep thinking about Jesus. He brought the Good News. He is the one who shows us the way to God. We tell about him. He always followed God.

We are in God's family, if we keep following God. We must stay brave. We must keep our hope.

Make sure you don't have a sinful heart. Make sure you believe. Don't turn away from the living God. Instead, help each other want to do what's right every day. Don't let sin's lies make your hearts hard so you don't care about God.

We share a place with Jesus. We must keep following him to the end. We must keep knowing for sure we're right. It's like the psalm says.

"Do you hear God's voice today? Then don't let your hearts get hard."

The people Moses led out of Egypt let their hearts get hard. God was angry at them for 40 years. So they had to live in the desert all of their lives. God said they would never have peace.

Rest

HEBREWS 4:1-4, 9-16

God plans for us to have his peace. Let's be careful so we can have this peace. God's people in the desert didn't believe God. But we believe. So we have that peace from God.

God said,

"I was angry.
I promised that they would never
    have my peace."

But God made the world. Then he rested on the seventh day.

There is a special rest for God's people. They can rest from their work. They can rest like God rested from his work. So let's try to get that special rest. Don't turn away from God by not obeying him.

God's Word is alive. It's doing its work. It is sharper than a sword with two edges. It can go right into a person. It can go right through a person's soul and spirit. It can cut to the bone. It can show if a person's thoughts are right or wrong.

Nothing in all the world can hide from God's eyes. He sees everything. We'll have to answer for everything we do and say.

Jesus is like the high priest for us. He is the person who takes us right to God. He is God's Son. So let's keep believing no matter what.

Jesus understands us. He faced every sin that looks good to us. But he said no every time. He did not sin.

So let's go to the kind, loving King in heaven. We can be sure he will understand. He will be kind and loving to us. He will help us when we need him.

DECEMBER 13

Our Priest

HEBREWS 5:1-6, 8-12, 14

God chose human priests to serve him. They talk to God for the people. They give gifts to God so he will forgive people. They are kind to people who go away from God. The people go away because they don't know any better. These priests can do these things because they're human themselves. They know what it's like to sin. They even have to bring gifts to God for their own sins.

No one chooses himself to be a priest. God chooses. He chooses like he chose Aaron. It was the same with Jesus. He didn't choose himself. A psalm tells us what God said to Jesus.

"You're my Son.
I've become your Father today."

Another psalm says it this way.

"You are a priest forever."

Jesus learned to obey by the hard times he had. He didn't sin. That way, he could save everyone who obeys him. God chose him to be our priest.

It's hard to tell you about this. You should be teachers yourselves by now. But you still need somebody to teach you. You still need to learn the simple parts of God's Word. Grown-up teaching is for people who live what they're taught. They train themselves to tell right from wrong.

Like a Ship's Anchor

HEBREWS 6:4-6, 9-15, 17-20

What if some people have seen how good God's Word is? What if they already know the power that's coming? But what if they turn away from God? Then nobody can bring them back.

Nobody can change that kind of people. It's like they have killed Jesus all over again. They're making Jesus look like nothing.

We're sure you're doing better than this. You're doing things that fit people who are saved by God. God is fair. He won't forget your work. He won't forget your love.

Keep on working hard to the very end. We don't want you to start being lazy. We want you to be like other people who believe. We want you to wait for what God promised.

God made a promise to Abraham. He said, "You can be sure I will bring good things to you. I will give you a big family." Abraham waited, and he got what God promised.

God doesn't change. He doesn't lie. So we hope in him. We feel better, because God keeps his promise. This is our hope.

Hope is like a ship's anchor. An anchor keeps the ship where it's supposed to be. Our hope keeps us where we're supposed to be. Our hope is with Jesus. He has gone to see God, our King. Jesus is our priest forever.

Jesus Is Better

HEBREWS 7:1-3, 11, 18-19, 21-27

Long ago, Melchizedek was the king of Salem. He was also God's priest. His name means "king of what's right." It also means "king of peace." Nobody knew when he was born or when he died. It was like he was a priest for all time.

God gave his Law to Moses later. The Law said to have men be priests. But priests could not make people's hearts clean and sinless.

So the Law was put to one side. It couldn't clean sin out of people's hearts. Jesus is better. He helps us come close to God. God told Jesus, "You're a priest forever, just like Melchizedek."

Priests of long ago got old and died. New priests had to come. So there were lots of them. But Jesus lives forever. So he can be our priest forever. He can save us in every way. That's because he will always be alive. He talks to God about what's happening with us.

This kind of high priest is just what we need. He has no sin. No one can blame him for anything wrong. His heart is clean through and through. He is not like the other priests.

Other high priests have to pay for their own sins. So they bring gifts to God. Then they bring gifts to pay for other people's sins. They sin again and again. So they have to bring gifts again and again. But Jesus never sinned. So he gave a gift one time. It paid for everybody's sins. Jesus gave himself. He died for us.

Like a Shadow

HEBREWS 8:1-6, 10, 12

Here's the point. We have a high priest. It's Jesus. He sat down beside the King in heaven. He serves in the true house of God. It's a house that is set up by God, not by people.

All high priests were chosen to bring gifts. So Jesus had to give a gift too. What if Jesus lived on earth now? Then he wouldn't be a priest. There are already priests to give gifts like the Law said.

These priests served at God's house on earth. It was the worship tent. But the worship tent is like a shadow. It shows what's in heaven. That's why God told Moses to build it just right. "Make everything the way I showed you," said God.

But Jesus' job is greater than the priests' job. God has made a new special promise. Jesus makes this promise come true between God and us. The new promise is better than the old one.

God said,

"I'll put my laws in people's minds.
    I'll write my rules in their hearts.
I'll be their God.
    They'll be my people.
I will forgive their sins.
    I won't remember their sins anymore."

DECEMBER 14

Better Gifts

HEBREWS 9:1-20, 22-26, 28

The first promise between God and people had rules for worship. There was a worship house here on earth. A worship tent was put up. A lamp stand and table were in the first room. This room was the Holy Place. A long cloth hung between this room and the next room.

The next room was the Most Holy Place. A gold altar was in there. God's gold ark box was there too. Figures with wings were over the ark box.

Everything was put in its right place. Then the priests did their work in the Holy Place.

Only the high priest went into the Most Holy Place. And he went in only one time a year. He always took a gift with him. It was animal blood. He gave this gift to pay for his sins. The gift also paid for the sins of other people.

People couldn't get into the Most Holy Place. No one but the high priest could go in. As long as the worship tent was around, this was true. But the high priest's gift couldn't take sins away for long.

Then Jesus came. He became our high priest. He went into a different worship tent. It wasn't made by people. He didn't go in with animal blood. Jesus went into the real Most Holy Place in heaven just one time. He went for all people. He went with his own blood. He got people's sins taken away forever.

Animal blood made people sinless for a while. But then Jesus died for us. Jesus never sinned. So his blood makes us sinless forever. Now we can be servants of the living God!

That's why Jesus is between us and God. He makes the new special promise come true. Now we are part of God's family forever! Jesus died to pay for sin. So God's people are free from sins they did before.

Think about a will. That's a paper that someone leaves behind when he dies. A will tells what he leaves for other people. But you have to show that the person really died. A will is good only if the person died. It's never used when the person is still alive.

That's why blood was given when the first promise was made. That promise was the Law. Moses told the Law to everybody. Then he tossed animal blood over the written words. Then he tossed it out to the people. He said, "This blood shows we're making a promise. God has told you to keep his Law. So keep this promise."

The Law said things had to be made clean by a gift of blood. Nobody was forgiven without blood.

These things from earth are like things in heaven. But the things in heaven are better. So there had to be better gifts. Jesus didn't go into a worship tent made by people. Jesus went right into heaven. He went face to face with God for us.

Priests on earth had to give gifts over and over again. But Jesus didn't have to give himself over and over again. That would have meant that Jesus had to die again and again. But Jesus came one time. He came for everybody. He got rid of sin once and for all. He did it by giving himself.

Jesus will come back again. This time it won't be to take people's sins. He will come to save the people who wait for him.

Keep Following

HEBREWS 10:19-39

Now we can go into the Most Holy Place where God is. It's all because of Jesus' blood. He opened a new way. He did it by giving his body. Now he is a great priest for all God's people.

So let's come close to God. Let's be sure of what we believe. Let's have hearts that are clear of doing wrong. Let's have clean bodies. Let's hang on to the hope we have. God promised, and he keeps his promises.

Let's think about how to help each other love. Let's think about how to help each other do good. Let's not stop meeting together. Let's see how we can help each other want to do what's right.

We know the truth. But what if we keep sinning because we want to? Then no gift can make us clean. We can only look forward to being judged. We can only look forward to burning fire. That's what happens to God's enemies.

People who turned away from Moses' Law died. So think how bad it is to turn away from Jesus. He is God's Son. People who turn away from him show what they think. They think Jesus' blood is not important. They say bad things about God's kind Spirit.

God says, "It's my job to pay people back for their sins." It's terrible to be an enemy of the living God.

Remember the first days after you believed? You kept following God even in the hard times. People said bad things about you in front of others. They hurt you.

Sometimes you stood beside other people who were being hurt. You were sad with people who were in jail for Jesus. People took things away from you. But you still showed your joy. You knew God had better things ready for you.

So keep trusting in God. Be sure of what you believe. Don't toss that away. God has wonderful things ready for you. Keep following him no matter what. Do what God wants. Then you'll get what he promised.

It won't be long. Habakkuk says it this way.

"He is coming.
　He won't stay away.
My people who do what's right
　will live by what they believe.
If they turn away, I won't be happy
　with them."

We're not people who turn away. We believe, and we're saved.

Faith
HEBREWS 11:1, 3-14, 16-40

Now faith is being sure of what you hope for. It's being sure of things you don't see.

We have faith. So we understand that God made the world and all of space. He told it to happen, and it happened. He made things we see out of things we don't see.

Abel had faith. So he gave God a better gift than Cain did. God said this made Abel right with him. Abel's faith still teaches us today, even though Abel is dead.

Enoch had faith. God took him from the earth. Enoch didn't have to die. That's because God was so happy with the way he lived. No one can make God happy without having faith.

People who come to God have to believe two things. First, they must believe that God really lives. Then they must believe that God brings good to people who look for him.

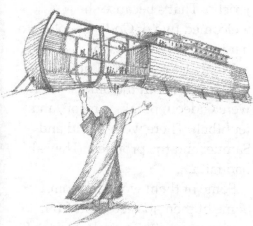

Noah had faith. God told him what was coming. So Noah built an ark to save his family.

Abraham had faith. God chose a place for him to live and told him to move there. Abraham obeyed God. He didn't know where God was leading him. But he went to the Promised Land. He lived in a tent there.

Isaac and Jacob lived in tents too. They got the same promise Abraham got. Abraham was looking ahead. His spirit saw a city built by God. Abraham knew he would live in it someday.

Abraham had faith. He was too old to have children. Sarah was too old too. But God gave them a child. So Abraham became a father. It was all because he believed God's promise.

Then a whole nation was started. Abraham's son had sons. So his family grew to have as many people as the stars in the sky. There were as many people as the sand on the beach.

These people believed God all their lives. They were still believers when they died. They didn't get all God promised. They just knew it was coming.

They said they were strangers here on earth. People who say that mean they're looking for a different land. They're looking for a better land. It's a heavenly land. God is glad that they call him their God. He has made a city ready for them.

God tested Abraham's faith. God

asked him to give Isaac as a gift on the altar. Abraham had gotten Isaac by God's promise. But he was going to give him back to God. Isaac was his only son.

God had said, "Your family will come from Isaac." Then God asked for Isaac as a gift. Abraham believed that God could bring Isaac back to life. In a way, God did.

Isaac had faith. When he was old, he prayed a special prayer for his sons, Jacob and Esau. He prayed for good things for them.

Jacob had faith. When he was old, he prayed a special prayer for his grandsons. They were Joseph's sons. He prayed for good things for them. He worshiped God before he died.

Joseph had faith. So before he died, he told God's people about leaving Egypt. He said, "Take my bones with you when you go."

Moses' mother and father had faith. After Moses was born, they hid him for three months. They could see he was special. They weren't afraid of the mean king's law.

Moses had faith. He grew up in the palace. But he wouldn't let himself be in the king's family. He chose to be one of God's people. That got him into trouble.

Moses could have enjoyed sin for a little while. But he knew it was better to be treated badly for God. It was better than all the riches of Egypt. Moses was looking for good things from God.

Moses had faith. So he left Egypt. He wasn't afraid of the angry king. He kept on believing no matter what. In his heart, he saw God.

Moses had faith. So he obeyed God by having blood put around the doors. That way, the first sons of each Jewish family would live.

God's people had faith. So they walked across dry ground at the Red Sea. The army of Egypt tried to go across too. But the sea water flowed back. The people from Egypt died.

God's people had faith. So the walls around the city of Jericho fell down. The people had marched around the walls for seven days.

Rahab had faith. So she wasn't killed with the other people of Jericho. That's because she welcomed two of God's people into her house. She hid them.

What else can I say? I don't have time to tell about the others. There were Gideon, Barak, Samson, and Jephthah. There were David and Samuel and the prophets. They all had faith.

Some of them won kingdoms. Some of them judged right from wrong among the people. Some of them went and got what God promised them. Some of them closed lions' mouths.

Some put out roaring fires. Some

got away from people who were killing others. Some were powerful fighters. Some chased away armies from other lands. Some women saw their families brought back to life again.

Some were hurt very badly. They stayed in jail. They wanted a life that lasts forever. They wanted this more than they wanted to be free. Some were laughed at. Some were beaten. Some were tied up in jail. Some were hit with stones until they died. Some were sawed in half. Some were killed with swords.

Some were very poor. They wore only the skin of sheep or goats. They were treated very badly. This world was not good enough for them. They went here and there in deserts and mountains. They went to caves. They went to holes in the ground.

They all had great faith. But none of them got what had been promised. God had something better. He planned to give it to us and to them. That would finish God's plan.

DECEMBER 16

Keep On Running

HEBREWS 12:1-5, 7-12, 14-16, 18-19, 21-28

These people are all around us. They're like a big cloud of people. They've seen it all. So let's toss away things that keep us from moving on. Let's get rid of sin. It's so easy to get mixed up in sin.

Life is like a race. So let's run the race that God has made for us. Let's keep on running no matter what.

Let's keep looking at Jesus. Our faith started with him. He will help us keep our faith all the way.

Jesus saw the joy that was waiting for him. So he kept on going, even to the cross. He didn't care that it made him look bad. When it was over, he sat down beside God. He is sitting at the King's right side.

Think about Jesus. Many sinful people were against him. Think about him so you won't get tired. Think about him so you won't give up.

You have been fighting against sin. But you haven't lost any blood over it yet. Don't forget Solomon's wise saying that will help you feel better. It calls you children.

"My children, know that it's important when God trains you.
Don't give up when he points out something you did wrong."

Fathers train their children. Everybody is trained in some way. So if you're not trained, then you're not really God's children.

We've all had human fathers. We

looked up to them when they trained us. God is the Father of our spirits. So it's even more important to let him train us.

Our fathers trained us for a while. They did it in the way they thought was good. But God trains us so we can be sinless like he is.

When you're being trained, it may not seem fun. It might be hard. Later, we see the good it does. People who have been trained know and do what's right. They have peace.

So make your arms strong. Make your knees strong. Try your best to live at peace with everyone. Try not to sin. People who live in sin won't see God.

Make sure nobody misses God's kind love. Don't let anger grow and get you in trouble. It can hurt many people.

Make sure nobody sins with sex. Make sure no one turns away from God.

You haven't come to a mountain you can touch. You haven't come to a mountain burning with fire. You haven't come to the dark or to fog. You haven't come to the storm. You haven't come to the call of a horn. That happened when Moses went up the mountain. Moses said, "I'm shaking with fear."

But you have come to God's land. It's the Jerusalem of heaven. It's the city of the living God.

You have come to thousands and thousands of angels. They're meeting together, and they're full of joy.

You have come to Jesus' church. The names are written in heaven.

You have come to God. He will judge all people.

You have come to the spirits of people. These are people who are right with God. He has made their hearts clean and spotless.

You have come to Jesus. He is in the middle between us and God, making the new promise work.

Don't turn away from the one who is talking to you. On earth, God told people what was coming. They didn't listen, so they got in trouble. Now God is telling us from heaven what's coming. What if we don't listen? We'll get in trouble too.

Long ago, God's voice made the earth shake. Now he makes us another promise. "I will shake the earth one more time. But I won't just shake the earth. I'll shake all of space, too."

God says, "One more time." That means he will get rid of whatever shakes. If something can shake, it's not firm. Things that don't shake can stay.

We have a kingdom that will not shake. So we should thank God. We should worship him and tell how great he is. We should wonder at his greatness. God is like a burning fire.

Yesterday, Today, and Tomorrow

HEBREWS 13:1-9, 12-20, 23-24

Keep loving each other. Love like a family. Don't forget to welcome people you don't know. Some people welcomed strangers. They didn't know they were really welcoming angels.

Remember people who are in jail. Feel bad for them as if you were in jail too. Remember people who are hurting. Feel bad for them as if you were hurting too.

People should show how special it is to be married. They should have sex only with the one they marry. God will judge people who sin with sex.

Don't love money. Be happy with what you have. God has given us a promise. "I'll never leave you." So we say what the psalm says.

"God helps me.
  I won't be afraid.
What can people do to me?"

Remember your leaders. They told you God's Word. Think about how their lives will turn out. Try to have a faith like theirs.

Jesus is the same today as he was yesterday. He will always be the same.

Don't follow strange teachings. Special foods can't make our faith strong. Our faith gets strong from God's kind love.

Jesus died outside the city. That's how the leaders showed he wasn't important to them. But let's follow Jesus anyway. It's all right for people to think we're not important.

Cities here on earth don't last. But Jesus' heavenly city does last. That's where we're headed.

Let's keep giving God a gift of praise. Let's tell who he is. Don't forget to do good things. Share with other people. God likes those kinds of gifts.

Obey your leaders. Let them lead you. They watch over you. They have to answer for what happens to you. Obey them. That way they'll be happy with their work. Their work won't be too hard for them. If their work's too hard, that's not good for you.

Pray for us. We're sure we are living the right way. We want people to be able to look up to us. Pray that I can come back to you soon.

God is a God of peace. He made Jesus come back to life again. Jesus is like the main Shepherd. We are his sheep.

Timothy is out of jail now. He may come to see me soon. Then we'll both come to see you.

Tell all your leaders hello. Say hi to all God's people there. God's people here in Italy say to tell you hello.

Nothing Dark

1 JOHN 1:1-2, 5-9

(John was old when he wrote this letter to Jesus' followers.)

We're telling you what's been around from the start. We're telling you what we heard and saw. We're telling you what we touched with our hands.

We're telling you about the Word of life. We saw it. It's life that lasts forever. The Father had this life with him. He showed it to us.

Here's the message he told us. God is light. There is nothing dark in him. If we keep sinning, we are living in darkness. We might say we are God's friend. But that would be a lie.

If we follow God in his light, we are friends with each other. Jesus' blood cleans the sin from our hearts.

If we say we don't sin, we are lying. But what if we say we sin, and we're sorry? Then God keeps his promise. He forgives us. He cleans our hearts from the wrong we've done.

Living in the Light

1 JOHN 2:1-6, 9-17, 27, 29

You are like dear children to me. I'm writing to you so you won't sin. But what if you do sin? Then Jesus talks to God the Father for you. Jesus is the One Who Does What's Right. He makes us right with God. We're right with God because Jesus died for our sins.

How do we know that we really know him? We obey what he tells us. What if somebody says, "I know him"? But this person doesn't do what God says. Then that person is lying. What if a person obeys God? Then God's love fills him.

Here's how we know we are in Jesus' kingdom. We act like Jesus acted.

Someone might say, "I'm living in God's light." But if he hates somebody else, he is still in the dark.

If you love, it's like living in God's light. Nothing makes you sin against God. But if you hate, it's like living in the dark. You don't know where you're going. You can't see.

I'm writing to you, children,
because Jesus forgave your sins.
You believe in Jesus' name.
I'm writing to you, fathers,
because you know Jesus.
He has been around from the start.
I'm writing to you, young men,
because you're strong.
God's Word lives in you.
You have won over Satan.

Don't love the world. Don't love anything in the world. What if someone loves the world? Then the Father's love isn't in him.

In the world, there are sinful things people want. They brag about what they did and what they're doing. These things don't come from the Father. They come from the world.

The world and what it wants will fade away. The person who does what God wants will live forever.

God chose you. He cleaned sin out of you. That tells you everything. He truly chose you. It's not a lie. He has told you that you're his. So stay with him.

God is sinless. He does what's right. So everybody who does what's right belongs to him. They're his children.

God's Children
1 JOHN 3:1-2, 4-11, 13-24

The Father's love is so great! He calls us his children! We really are his children! Why doesn't the world know us? It's because the world didn't know him.

We know that Jesus will come back again. When he does, we'll be like him. That's because we'll see him like he really is.

Everybody who sins is breaking the Law. That's what sin is. But Jesus came to take our sins away. There is no sin in Jesus. People who belong to him will stop sinning. People who keep sinning have not seen Jesus. They don't know Jesus.

Don't believe lies. When people do right, things are right between them and God. People who sin belong to Satan. That's because Satan sinned from the start. The reason Jesus came was to get rid of Satan's work.

People who belong to God won't keep sinning. That's because God is in them. They can't keep sinning. They've been born into God's family.

Here's how we know who Satan's children are. People who don't do right aren't God's children. People who don't love God's people aren't God's children.

Here's the message. You heard it from the start. Love each other.

Don't be surprised if the world hates you. We know we've left the kingdom of death behind. We live in the kingdom of life. We know this is true because we love God's people.

People who don't love stay in the kingdom of death. People who hate are killers. You know that no killer lives forever with Jesus.

Here's how we know what love is. Jesus gave up his life for us. We should give up our lives for God's people too.

Let's say someone owns lots of things. He sees one of God's people who needs something. But he doesn't feel sorry for that person. How can we say God's love is in him?

Let's show love not just by what we say. Let's show love by what we do. That's how we know we belong to God. What if our hearts start blaming us? We can feel peace, because we've shown love. We can feel peace, because God is greater than our hearts. He knows everything we say and do.

If our hearts don't blame us, we feel sure about talking to God. He gives us what we ask for. That's because we are obeying him. We are doing what makes him happy.

Here's what God wants. He wants us to believe in Jesus, his Son. Then he wants us to love each other.

People who obey God live in his kingdom. And God lives inside them. How do we know he lives inside us? He gave us his Spirit.

Spirits

1 JOHN 4:1-14, 16, 18-21

Don't believe every spirit. Test spirits. See if God sent them. Many fake prophets in the world have lied. Here's how you can tell if it's God's Spirit. God's Spirit says Jesus came into the world as a man. Other spirits don't say that. So they aren't from God.

You are from God. So you have won over bad spirits in the world. Jesus is in you, and he is great. He is greater than Satan, the sinful one in the world.

Bad spirits that lie are from the world. So they say things the way the world sees it. The world listens to what they say. But we're from God. People who know God listen to us. People who aren't from God don't listen to us.

Let's love each other. Love comes from God. People who love have been born into God's family. They know God. People who don't love don't know God. That's because God is love.

Here's how God showed us his love. He sent his only Son to the world. He did it so we could live. That's love. It's not that we loved God. It's that he loved us. So he sent his Son as a gift. He sent Jesus to die for our sins. God loved us that much! So we should love each other.

Nobody has seen God. But he lives in us if we love each other. That's how God can show his full love in us. We know we belong to God, and he lives in us. We know it, because God gave us his Spirit.

We saw how God sent Jesus to save the world. We tell about it. We know how much God loves us. We count on his love.

If you love, you don't have to be afraid. Love pushes fear away. Fear comes from thinking God will make us get in trouble for sin. So the person who is afraid isn't full of love yet.

God loved us first. So we love others. People might say that they love God. But what if they hate somebody? Then they're lying. They don't love someone they can see. So how can they love God when they can't see him? We have this rule from God: If we love him, we have to love his people, too.

Who Wins?

1 JOHN 5:1-5, 11-15, 18-21

People who love the Father love his child, too. That's how we know we love God's children. We love God. We do what he says.

Here's how we love God. We obey him. What he tells us to do isn't too hard for us. That's because people born into his family are strong. They're so strong they win over the world.

Faith makes us win over the world. Who wins over the world? It's the people who believe that Jesus is God's Son.

God gives us life forever. This life comes from his Son. If you have Jesus, you have life. If you don't have Jesus, you don't have life.

I'm writing so people who believe

in Jesus will know they have life forever.

If we ask for what God wants for us, he hears us. So we know he gives us what we asked for.

We know that people born into God's family don't keep sinning. Jesus keeps them safe. Satan can't hurt them, even though Satan controls the whole world.

We know that we're God's children.

We know that God's Son, Jesus, has come. We belong to him. Jesus is the way to the true God. He is the way to live forever.

You're like dear children to me. So stay away from idols.

DECEMBER 19

Be Careful

2 JOHN 1:1-2, 4-13

(John wrote two more short letters. One was to a lady. The other was to his friend Gaius.)

To the lady who was chosen, and to her children,

I love you all because of the truth. Everyone who knows the truth loves you. That's because the truth lives in us. It will always be with us.

I'm very glad that some of your children follow God's truth. They're doing just what the Father told us to do.

You are a dear lady. I'm not writing anything new to you. I'm writing something we've known from the start. We should love each other.

Here's what love is. It's obeying what God tells us. You heard it from the beginning. His rule is that we love.

Many people who lie are in the world. They say Jesus hasn't come as a man. Any person like this is against Jesus.

Watch out! Don't lose what you worked for. Be careful to get the good things God planned for you.

Some people don't wait for God. They don't keep following Jesus' teaching. So they don't have God with them. But what about people who keep following Jesus? God the Father and Jesus, his Son, are with them.

Let's say somebody comes to you and doesn't teach this. Then don't let that person stay at your house. Don't welcome that kind of person. If you do, you are helping with that person's sinful work.

I have a lot to say to you. But I don't want to write it. I want to come see you. I want to talk with you in person. Then both of us can be full of joy.

Your sister's children say to tell you hello.

From the leader.

Saying Bad Things and Good Things

3 JOHN

To Gaius, my dear friend,

I truly love you. I'm praying that you'll enjoy good health. Then your body will do well just like your soul is doing well.

Some of God's people came and told me about you. They said you keep following God's truth. What makes me happier than anything? It's hearing that people I taught keep obeying God.

You keep helping God's people from other places. You do it even though you don't know them. They have told us how you showed your love.

Keep treating God's people like God wants you to. Help people who are traveling so they can keep going. They began this trip because they believe in Jesus. People who don't believe in God have not helped them. So we need to welcome them. That way, we can work together for the truth.

I wrote to Jesus' followers. But Diotrephes loves to be first. He won't listen to us. So I might come.

Then I'll point out what he is doing. He is telling other people bad things about us.

That's not all he is doing. He won't welcome God's people from other places. He won't let anyone else welcome them. Some people want to welcome them. If they do, he won't let them be in the church.

Don't do the sinful things that others do. Instead, do what's good. People who do what's good are from God. People who sin haven't seen God.

Now Demetrius is another follower of Jesus. Everybody says good things about him. He follows the truth. That makes him look good. We say good things about him too. You know that what we say is true.

I have a lot to say to you. But I don't want to write it. I hope I can come see you soon. Then we'll see each other face to face. We'll talk then.

I pray that God will give you his peace. Your friends here say to tell you hello. Tell each of our friends there hello too.

From the leader.

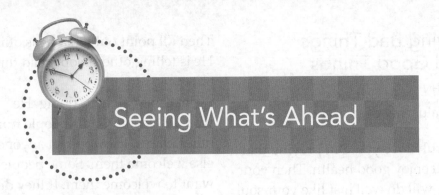

Seeing What's Ahead

A Voice like a Waterfall, a Face like the Sun

REVELATION 1

(John wrote one more letter to Jesus' followers.)

To the seven churches in Asia.

God gave this message to Jesus so he would show it to us. It shows what has to happen soon. God showed it by sending his angel to John. And John told about everything he saw.

God will bring good things to people who read God's plan. He will bring good things to people who hear and believe it. The time for these things to happen will be soon.

God is God now. He always was God. He always will be God. Seven spirits come near to God. Jesus sees it all. He tells the truth about what he sees. Jesus died, but he came back to life again. So he is like the first one born to live forever. He rules as king over all other kings.

Jesus loves us. He died for us. So we are free from sin's power. He made us into a kingdom for God. We serve God, his Father. Let Jesus' greatness and power shine forever! Yes! Amen!

Look! He is coming in the clouds.
Everyone will see him.
Even the people who killed him will see him. Yes! Amen!

"I'm the first and the last," says God. "I'm the one who lives now. I have always lived. I always will live. I am the one with all power."

Now I, John, am speaking. I'm in God's family like you are. I have trouble because I follow Jesus, just like you. I'm in God's kingdom because of Jesus, just like you. I quietly wait and believe no matter what happens, just like you.

I was on the island called Patmos. I was sent away there so I couldn't tell about Jesus. It was the Lord's Day. My spirit was meeting with God's Spirit. I heard a loud voice behind me. It sounded like a horn. It said, "Write about the things you see. Then send it to the seven churches."

I turned around so I could see who was talking. I saw seven lamps on gold stands. Someone was standing among the lamps. He looked like a man. He wore a robe. It went all the way down to his feet. A wide gold cloth went around his chest.

His hair was like wool. It was as white as snow. His eyes shone like fire. His feet were like brown metal. They glowed like metal does in a hot fire. His voice sounded like a waterfall.

He was holding seven stars in his right hand. A sharp sword with two edges came from his mouth. His face was like the sun shining its brightest.

When I saw him, I fell down like a dead man. I was down at his feet. But he touched me with his right hand. He said, "Don't be afraid. I'm the First and the Last. I'm the One Who Is Alive. I was dead. But see? I'm alive now. I'll live forever and ever. I keep the keys to death and the place of death.

"So write about what you saw. Write what's happening now. Write what will happen later.

"Here's the mystery of the seven stars I hold. Here's the mystery of the seven gold lamps. The seven stars stand for the angels of seven churches. The seven lamps stand for the seven churches."

DECEMBER 21

To the Angels of the Churches

REVELATION 2

Then the one who looked like a man said this. "Write this to the angel of the church in Ephesus.

"This is from the one who holds seven stars. He walks among the seven gold lamps. Here's what he says. I know what you do. I know how hard you work. I know how you keep going no matter what.

"I know you can't stand sinful people. I know you checked out people who said they were apostles. They were not who they said they were. You found that out.

"You have kept believing. You've gone through lots of hard times for me. You haven't gotten tired.

"But there is something wrong. You forgot the love you had at first. Remember how far you've fallen away from that love! Be sorry. Change. Do what you used to do. What if you don't change? Then I'll come and take your lamp away.

"But here's something good about you. You hate the sinful things that some people do. These people are part of the church. I hate what they do too.

"Do you have ears? Then listen to what the Spirit tells the churches. Keep following me, no matter what. Then I'll let you eat fruit from the tree of life. It's in God's heavenly land.

"Write this to the angel of the church in Smyrna.

"This is from the one who is First and Last. He died and came back to life. He says this. I know your troubles. I know how poor you are. But you're really rich.

"I know there are people who say they are Jews. But they aren't. They are from Satan's worship place. They say bad things about you.

"Don't be afraid of hard times that will come. Satan will send some of you to jail. That will test you. People will hurt you for 10 days.

Keep believing in me, even if it looks like you'll die. I'll give you life forever.

"Do you have ears? Then listen to what the Spirit tells the churches. Keep following me, no matter what. Then you won't be hurt one bit by what happens after death.

"Write this to the angel of the church in Pergamum.

"This is from the one who has the sharp sword. This sword has two edges. He says this. I know where you live. You live where Satan rules. But you keep following me. You didn't stop believing, even when one of my followers was killed in your city. He kept telling the truth about my kingdom.

"But there are a few things that are wrong. Some of your people act like Balaam. He led people into sin. He got them to sin with sex. He got them to eat food given to idols.

"Some of your people believe the teachers who do what's wrong. These teachers are part of the church. So change! Be sorry, and start doing right. If you don't, I'll come soon. I'll fight against these people with my mouth, which is like a sword.

"Do you have ears? Then listen to what the Spirit tells the churches. Keep following me, no matter what. Then I'll give each person heavenly food. I'll also give each person a white stone. It will have a new name on it. Only the one who gets the stone will know the name.

"Write this to the angel of the church in Thyatira.

"This is from the Son of God. His eyes shine like fire. His feet are like brown, shining metal. Here's what he says. I know what you do. I know how you love. I know how you believe and serve. I know you keep following God's way, no matter what. You do more now than you first did.

"But there is something wrong. You let the woman named Jezebel be in your group. She says she tells what God has to say. But she leads my people to do what's wrong. She is getting my people to sin with sex. She is getting them to eat food given to idols.

"I gave her time to change. But she doesn't want to change. So I'll send trouble to her. People who follow her will be in trouble too. They'll be in trouble unless they're sorry and stop doing wrong.

"Jezebel's children will die. Then the churches will know who I am. I'm the one who looks into people's hearts and minds. I'll pay you back for what you've done. Now some of you don't follow her. So hold on to what you believe until I come.

"Keep believing. Keep obeying me, no matter what. Keep on until the very end. Then I'll let you rule the nations. I'll let you rule like my Father lets me rule. I'll give you the morning star, too. Do you have ears? Then listen to what the Spirit tells the churches."

DECEMBER 22

From the One Who Holds Seven Stars

REVELATION 3

"Write this to the angel of the church in Sardis.

"This is from the one holding God's seven spirits. He holds the seven stars. He says this. I know what you do. People say you are alive. But you are dead in your spirit.

"Wake up your spirit! There is part of you that still has some life. But it's about to die. Make it stronger. To God, what you do isn't all good.

"So remember the teaching you heard. Obey it. Change. Stop doing wrong. Start doing right. What if you don't wake up? Then I'll come to you the way a robber does. You won't know when it will be.

"But a few people there have clean hearts. They'll walk with me. They'll be dressed in white. They have done what's right. So they can be with me.

"Keep following me, no matter what. Then you'll be like them. You'll dress in white. I'll never take your name out of the Book of Life. I'll tell my Father and his angels about you. Do you have ears? Then listen to what the Spirit tells the churches.

"Write this to the angel of the church in Philadelphia.

"This is from the one who is sinless and true. He holds King David's key. When he opens something, nobody can close it. When he closes something, nobody can open it.

"Here's what he says. I know what you do. See? I put an open door in front of you. Nobody can close it. I know you're not very strong. But you keep following me. You keep believing.

"There are some people who say they're Jews. But they lie. They're from Satan's worship place. I'll make them bow down at your feet. I'll make them agree that I loved you.

"You obeyed me. You waited quietly and kept believing in me. So I'll save you from the trouble that's coming. Everyone on earth at that time will have hard times that test them.

"I'm coming soon. Hold on to what you believe. Then nobody will take away your crown. Keep following me, no matter what. Then you'll be like strong posts in God's worship place. You can live there forever.

"I'll write God's name on you. I'll write the name of God's city. It's the new Jerusalem. It will come down from God in heaven. Do you have ears? Then listen to what the Spirit tells the churches.

"Write this to the angel of the church in Laodicea.

"This is from the one who says yes by keeping his promises. He says yes by telling the truth about what he has seen. He rules over all God made.

"Here's what he says. I know what you do. You're not cold. You're not hot. I wish you were hot or cold. But you are in between, not hot and not cold. So I'm going to spit you out of my mouth.

"You say, 'I'm rich. I worked to get lots of riches. I don't need anything.' You don't know that you're broken down. People should feel sorry for you. You're poor. You can't see. You have no clothes.

"Here's what I tell you. I have real gold for you. Come to me and you can be rich. I have white clothes you can wear. I can make your eyes see.

"I point out what's wrong for people I love. I train them in the way that's right. So change. Feel it strongly in your heart. Start doing right.

"I'm here! It's like I'm standing at your door and tapping on it. I'm calling for you. Hear my voice. Open the door of your heart. I'll come in. I'll be with you, and you can be with me.

"Keep on following me, no matter what. Then you can sit with me where I rule as King. Follow me like I kept following my Father. I sat down with my Father. I sat where he rules as King. Do you have ears? Then listen to what the Spirit tells the churches."

An Open Door

REVELATION 4

Then I, John, looked up. There was a door in front of me. It was in heaven. It was standing open.

The same loud voice talked to me again. "Come up here," it said. "I'll show you what has to happen after this."

Suddenly, my spirit was meeting with God's Spirit. I saw somebody sitting on the King's throne in heaven. He looked like beautiful, shiny green and red stones. A rainbow fanned out over where he

sat. It glowed like a shiny green stone.

Twenty-four other king's chairs were around where he sat. One leader sat on each of these thrones. The leaders wore white clothes. They had gold crowns on their heads.

Flashes of lightning came from where the King sat. Thunder rolled and boomed. Seven lamps blazed in front of the King. They were God's seven spirits. There was a shiny sea in front of the King too. It was clear. It looked like glass.

Four living beings were in the middle, around the King. They had eyes all over them. They had eyes in front and eyes in back. One living being was like a lion. The next was like an ox. The next one had a man's face. The last one was like a flying eagle. The living beings each had six wings. They even had eyes under their wings.

These living beings always call, "Holy, holy, holy. God is clean, sinless, and holy. He has all power. He is holy. He lived before. He lives now. He will always live." The living beings tell how important the King is. They show his greatness. They thank him.

Then the 24 leaders bow down in front of the King. They worship the one who lives forever and ever. They put their crowns down in front of him.

The leaders say,

"You're our Lord and our God.
Nothing is better than you.
Your greatness shines.
We show how important you are.
You have power.
You made everything.
You wanted to.

So all things were made.
They are what they are because
of you."

DECEMBER 23

Who Can Open the Roll of Paper?

REVELATION 5

Then I saw something in the King's right hand. It was a rolled-up paper. Both sides of the paper had writing on them. Seven pieces of wax kept the paper rolled up and closed.

Then I saw a strong angel. He called out loudly, "Who is good enough to break the wax seals? Who is good enough to open the paper roll?" But nobody was good enough. Nobody in heaven or on earth was good enough. They weren't even good enough to look inside. So I cried and cried.

Then one of the leaders said, "Don't cry! See? Jesus is good enough. He is called the Lion of Judah. He is called the Root of King David. He has won over sin. He can open the wax seals and the paper roll."

Then I saw a Lamb. He looked like he had been killed. He was standing in the middle by the King's throne. The four living beings and the leaders were around him. He had seven horns. He had seven eyes. They were God's seven spirits. The seven spirits go through the whole earth.

The Lamb came and took the paper roll from the King. Then the four living beings and the 24 leaders bowed down. They bowed in front of Jesus, the Lamb. Each one of them had a harp. Each one held a golden bowl. A sweet smell came from each bowl. It was the prayers of God's people.

The leaders sang a new song.

"You are good enough to open the
     wax seals on the paper.
It's because you were killed.
You bought people for God.
   You bought them from every
        nation and every language.
   You bought them from every
        group.
You made them into a kingdom.
   You made them God's servants.
   They will rule on the earth."

Then I looked around. I heard many angels' voices. There must have been thousands and thousands. Ten thousand times ten thousand. They went around the King and the beings and the leaders.

The angels sang loudly,

"Jesus is good enough.
   He was killed.
So now he has power.

He has riches.
He is wise.
He is strong.
We worship him.
   His greatness shines.
   We praise him!"

Then I heard all the living beings in heaven and earth. I heard all the living beings under the earth. I heard all the living beings in the sea. They were singing.

"We worship the King and Jesus,
     the Lamb.
   We praise them.
   Their greatness shines.
   They have power forever and ever!"

The four beings said, "Yes! Amen!" The leaders bowed down. They worshiped the King and the Lamb.

The First Six Wax Seals
REVELATION 6:1-5, 7-17

I watched. Jesus opened the first wax seal. Then one of the four living beings said, "Come!" His voice sounded like thunder. So I looked.

There in front of me was a white horse! The rider of the horse was holding a bow and arrow. A crown was given to him. He rode out. He went like a strong fighter, planning to win.

Jesus opened the second seal. The

second living being said, "Come!" Another horse came out. He was red, like fire. The rider of this horse had power. He could take earth's peace away. He had power to make people kill each other. A big sword was given to him.

Jesus opened the third seal. The third living being said, "Come!" A black horse passed in front of me! The rider of this horse had scales to weigh things on.

Jesus opened the fourth seal. The fourth living being said, "Come!" A light colored horse stood in front of me. The rider of this horse was named Death. He had power to kill. He could do it in one out of every four parts of the earth. He could kill some with a sword and some by hunger. He could kill some by sickness and some by wild animals.

Then Jesus opened the fifth seal. I saw the souls of people who had been killed. They were killed because they believed in God. They had kept telling about God until the very end.

The souls were under the altar. They called loudly, "How long will it be, Lord? How long until you judge people on earth? How long before you pay them back for killing us?" Then they were given white clothes. They were told to wait awhile.

Jesus opened the sixth seal. The earth shook. The sun turned black.

The moon turned red as blood. The stars fell from the sky to the earth. They fell like figs blown off a tree by the wind. The sky rolled up like a roll of paper. Mountains and islands were pushed out of place.

Then kings and princes hid in caves. Rich and powerful people hid. Servants and free people hid in rocky mountains. They even cried out to the mountains. "Fall on top of us," they cried. "Hide us from the King's face! Hide us from Jesus' anger! It's the great day of their anger! No one can stand up against them!"

Four Angels and Four Winds

REVELATION 7:1-4, 9-17

Then I saw four angels. They stood at the north and the south of the earth. They stood at the east and the west. They held back the earth's winds from all four directions. They kept wind from blowing on the trees. They kept wind from blowing on land or sea. They had power to hurt the land and sea.

Another angel came from the east. He had God's seal. He called loudly to the four angels. "Don't hurt land or sea or trees yet," he called. "Wait! We must put a seal on the head of each of God's servants."

Then I heard how many servants would get seals. There were 144,000 (one hundred forty-four thousand) from all the family groups of Israel.

I saw a great crowd of people. No one could count them. They were from all nations and groups. They spoke all languages. They stood in front of the King and Jesus, the Lamb. They wore white clothes. They held palm branches. They called loudly,

"God rules as King!
God and his Son, the Lamb, are the
    only ones who can save."

All the angels stood around the King. They stood around the leaders and the four beings. They bowed their faces to the ground. They worshiped God. They said,

"Yes! Amen!
Praise God and show his greatness.
He is wise.
Thank him.
Show how important he is.
Show his greatness forever and ever.
Yes! Amen!"

Then one of the leaders came to me. "Who are the ones in white clothes?" he asked. "Where did they come from?"

"You know the answer to that," I said.

So he told me. "They have come from the time of great trouble on earth. The blood of the Lamb has made them clean from sin.

"Now they stay in front of the King.
    They serve him in his worship
        house day and night.
The King puts his tent over them.
They won't get hungry anymore.
    They won't be thirsty anymore.
The sun won't shine too hot on them.
Jesus will be their Shepherd.
    He will take them to rivers of
        living water.
    God will wipe off all their tears."

The Last Seal

REVELATION 8

Jesus opened the last seal. After that, heaven was quiet for half an hour. Then I saw the seven angels who stand in front of God. They were given seven horns to blow.

Another angel came. He had a gold bowl. He came over to the altar and stood there. He was given sweet-smelling prayers from God's people. He put them on the altar. Sweet-smelling smoke came up in front of God.

The angel filled the bowl with fire from the altar. He threw it down to the earth. Then thunder boomed. Lightning flashed. The earth shook.

The seven angels got ready to blow their horns.

The first angel blew his horn. Hail came. Fire mixed with blood was thrown onto the earth. Part of the earth burned. Part of the trees burned. All the green grass burned.

Then the second angel blew his horn. A blazing mountain was thrown into the sea. Some of the sea became blood. Some of the animals in the sea died. Some of the ships were torn apart.

Then the third angel blew his horn. A great blazing star fell out of the sky. Its name was Wormwood. It fell on rivers and springs of water. Some of the water got a sour taste. Lots of people died from drinking the sour water.

The fourth angel blew his horn. Then part of the sun, moon, and stars turned dark. Part of the day didn't have any light. Part of the night didn't have any light.

Then I heard an eagle flying in the air. It called loudly, "How terrible! How terrible for you people on earth! The next three angels are going to blow their horns!"

DECEMBER 25

Smoke and Horses

REVELATION 9

The fifth angel blew his horn. Then I saw a star. It had fallen out of the sky. It was on the earth. The star had a key. The key was for the tunnel into the bottomless pit.

The star opened the bottomless pit. Smoke came up out of it. It was like smoke from a huge fireplace. The smoke made the sun and sky dark.

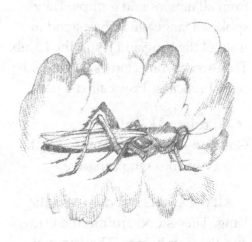

Big grasshoppers called locusts came out of the smoke. They came down onto the earth. They had power like earth's big spiders called scorpions. They were not allowed to hurt grass, plants, or trees. But they could hurt people who didn't have God's seal. They couldn't kill them. But they could make them hurt for five months. The pain was like a scorpion's sting. When all of this happens, people will want to die, but they won't be able to.

The locusts looked like horses ready to fight. They wore something on their heads. It looked like gold crowns. Their faces looked like people. Their hair looked like women's hair. They had lions' teeth. They had vests over their chests. These looked like iron.

The locusts flew. Their wings sounded like horses and chariots. They sounded like thundering horses running out to fight. They had tails like scorpions. They had stings like scorpions. Their king was the angel of the bottomless pit.

That's the first terrible thing. The other two are still going to come.

The sixth angel blew his horn. Then a voice spoke. It came from between the corners of the gold altar. "Four angels are tied up at the Euphrates River. Let them go," said the voice.

So it happened. The four angels had been waiting for this time. They went out. They killed some of the people on earth.

I saw horses and their riders. I heard there were 200,000,000 (two hundred million) of them. It was like a dream, but I was awake. The vests the riders wore were red, dark blue, and yellow. The horses' heads looked like lions' heads. Fire, smoke, and yellow acid came out of their mouths.

Some people were killed by the fire, smoke, and yellow acid. The horses' power was in their mouths and tails. Their tails were like snakes. Their tails had heads. So they could hurt people.

The rest of the people weren't killed by these. They still were not sorry for their sins. They didn't stop worshiping bad spirits. They worshiped gold, silver, metal, stone, and wood idols. These idols can't see or hear or walk.

The people didn't stop killing. They didn't turn away from sinful magic. They didn't stop using sex in a wrong way. They didn't stop stealing.

Eating a Roll of Paper
REVELATION 10

Then another strong angel came down from heaven. He was wearing a cloud. A rainbow was above his head. His face looked like the sun. His legs looked like posts of fire. He held a small roll of paper. The paper was open in his hand.

The angel put his right foot on the sea. He put his left foot on the land. He shouted so loud, he sounded like a roaring lion.

Then seven thunders talked. When they talked, I was going to write. But a voice from heaven said, "Don't write it down. Close and lock what the seven thunders said."

Then there was the angel with his feet on land and sea. He held up his right hand. He made a promise in God's name.

Now God lives forever and ever.

He made the sky and all of space and everything in it. He made the earth and everything in it. He made the sea and everything in it. So the angel promised in God's name.

"There will be no more waiting!" he said. "The last angel will blow his horn. Then God's mystery will be done. It will be just like he told his prophets."

Then the voice from heaven said to me, "Go! Take the roll of paper from the angel."

So I went to the angel. I asked him to give me the roll of paper. He said, "Take it. Eat it. It will make your stomach feel sour. But it will taste as sweet as honey in your mouth."

I took the small roll of paper. I ate it. It did taste as sweet as honey in my mouth. But after I ate it, my stomach felt sour.

Then a voice said, "You must tell God's plans again. Tell God's plans for people, nations, languages, and kings."

The Animal from the Bottomless Pit

REVELATION 11

Then someone gave me a stick to measure with. I was told, "Go. Measure God's worship house.

Measure the altar. Count how many people worship there. But don't measure the outside yard that has walls around it. It belongs to people who aren't Jewish. They'll march over the holy city for 42 months.

"I'll give power to two people who see and tell the truth. They will tell my plans for 1,260 days." There are two olive trees in front of the Lord. They stand for these two people. There are two lamps in front of the Lord. They stand for these people too.

What if somebody tries to hurt them? Then fire comes out of their mouths. It burns up their enemies. People who want to hurt them will die this way.

These two men have power to close the sky. It won't rain while they tell God's plans. They have power to turn water into blood. They have power to send sickness to the earth. They can do it as much as they want.

They will finish telling about God. Then the animal from the bottomless pit will come up. It will jump on them and kill them. Their bodies will stay in the city street. It's the city where Jesus was killed.

People from everywhere will look at their bodies. Nobody will put their bodies in a grave. The people will be glad they're gone. They'll send gifts to each other because of it. That's because these men had upset them.

I saw that three and a half days passed. Then God's breath of life came into them. They stood up. People who saw them were very scared.

Then they heard a loud voice out of heaven. It said, "Come here." These two men went to heaven in a cloud. Their enemies watched it.

Right then, the earth shook wildly. Part of the city fell down. Seven thousand people were killed. The other people were as scared as they could be. They said God in heaven was the great one.

The second terrible thing has passed now. The third one will come soon.

The last angel blew his horn. Loud voices in heaven called out:

"The world's kingdom is now the
    Lord's kingdom.
He will rule as King forever and
    ever."

The 24 leaders sat on their thrones in front of God. They bowed their faces to the ground. They worshiped God. They said,

"We thank you, Lord God of all
    power.
You are the One who lives now.
    You lived before.

We thank you.
You are starting to rule with your
    great power.
It's time to judge people.
Bring good to all your people, small
    and great.
But get rid of people who destroy
    the earth."

Then God's heavenly worship house opened. Inside was the ark, the box of his promises. Lightning flashed. Thunder rolled and crashed. The earth shook. Hail fell from the sky.

The Dragon

REVELATION 12

Then I saw a great sign come into the sky. It was a wonderful sign. It was a woman. She wore the sun. The moon was under her feet. She had a crown of 12 stars on her head. She was going to have a baby.

Then another sign came into the sky. It was a huge red dragon. It had seven heads. It had 10 horns. It had seven crowns on its heads.

The dragon's tail pushed stars from the sky. It tossed them onto the earth.

The dragon stood in front of the woman. She was going to have her baby soon. But he was going to swallow her baby.

The woman had a baby boy. He

will be King of all the nations. He will rule firmly and strongly. This baby was quickly taken up to God. He was taken to where God rules as King.

The woman ran away into the desert. God had made a place ready for her. That's where she went. There, she could be taken care of for 1,260 days.

Then there was a war in heaven. Michael and his angels fought the dragon. The dragon and his angels fought back. But the dragon wasn't strong enough. He and his angels lost their place in heaven. The great dragon was thrown down. He is that old snake called the devil or Satan. He leads the whole world to do wrong. He and his angels were thrown to the earth.

Then a voice from heaven called loudly.

"Now it's time for God to save.
    It's time for his power and his
        kingdom to come.
    It's time for Jesus to be in charge.
The one who blames God's people
        is thrown down.
    He blames them day and night.
But God's people won over him
        because of Jesus' blood.
    They won by telling the truth
        about God.

"God's people didn't love their lives
        too much.
    They didn't turn away from God.
They followed God even when they
        knew they could be killed for it.

"So, heavens, you can show your
        joy.
But earth and sea, you can be sad.
    That's because Satan is down
        with you.
He is very angry.
    He knows he only has a little
        time."

The dragon saw he'd been tossed down onto the earth. So he chased the woman who had the baby.

But the woman was given two great eagle wings. That way, she could fly to the desert. A place was ready for her there. She'd be taken care of for a while. The dragon could not get her there.

Then the dragon sent out a river of water. The river flowed out of his mouth. He tried to catch the woman in the wild water.

But the earth helped the woman. The earth opened up. It drank the dragon's river.

That made the dragon roar with anger. He left to fight the rest of the woman's children. They are the ones who follow God's way. They believe in Jesus.

At the Edge of the Sea

REVELATION 13

Then the dragon stood at the edge of the sea. An animal came up out of the sea. It had seven heads. It had 10 horns. Ten crowns were on its horns. Each horn had a bad name against God on it. The animal looked like a leopard. But it had a bear's feet. It had a lion's mouth.

The dragon gave its own power to the animal. He let the animal rule.

It looked like one of the animal's heads was hurt. It looked like it was hurt badly enough to die. But the hurt place had gotten well.

All the world was surprised. They followed this animal. People worshiped the dragon. That's because he let the animal rule. They worshiped the animal, too. They said, "No one is greater than the animal. No one can fight him and win."

The animal was able to rule for 42 months. He said bad things about God. He said bad things about where God lives. He said bad things about all who live in heaven.

The animal had power to fight against God's people. He had power to win over God's people. He could rule over all people and groups. He could rule over all languages and nations.

People whose names are in God's Book of Life won't worship the animal. But all other people on earth will worship it.

Do you have ears? Then listen. God's people must quietly wait. This means they must keep following God, no matter what.

Then another animal came out of the earth. He had two horns like a lamb. But he talked like a dragon. He ruled for the first animal. He made people worship the first animal. He even did great wonders. He made fire come from heaven to earth. Everybody could see it. So he fooled people.

He said people had to build an idol. It had to be an idol of the first animal. It was to show that the first animal was great. The second animal made the idol talk. If anybody wouldn't worship it, they would be killed.

He made all people get a mark on their right hand or forehead. People might be small or great. They might be rich or poor. They might be free people or slaves. But they all had to get the mark.

Nobody could buy anything without the mark. They couldn't sell anything without the mark. The mark is the animal's name. Or it's the number of his name.

Think wisely. If anybody understands, he can figure out the

animal's number. It's man's number. His number is 666.

A Man on a Cloud

REVELATION 14

Then I looked up. Jesus, the Lamb, was standing on Zion Mountain. He was right in front of me. The 144,000 (one hundred forty-four thousand) people stood with him. Jesus' name and God the Father's name were written on their heads.

Then the sound of roaring water came from heaven. I heard the sound of loud thunder. I heard the sound of people playing harps. They stood in front of the King. They stood in front of the four living beings and the leaders. They were singing a new song.

Only the 144,000 (one hundred forty-four thousand) people could learn the song. They had been saved from the earth. They had kept their hearts clean and sinless. They follow the Lamb, no matter where he goes. He bought them. They're the first ones given to God and his Son, the Lamb. They didn't lie. They haven't done anything wrong that anyone can blame them for.

Then another angel came flying in the air. He had the Good News that never ends. He was going to tell it to everybody on earth. He would tell it to all nations and groups. He would tell it to all languages and people.

The angel called out loudly, "Look up to God. Let his greatness shine. It's time for him to judge. Worship him. He made the sky and all of space, earth, seas, and rivers."

A second angel called out, "Fallen! Great Babylon has fallen! This city turned away from God. All the nations have been hurt by Babylon's sin."

A third angel called loudly, "What happens if someone worships the animal? What if someone worships his idol? What if someone gets his mark on the hand or forehead?

"Then that person will feel God's anger. That person will have times of trouble and hurting forever. People who worship the animal will never get to rest. People who get his mark won't get to rest."

This means people who obey God will have to wait quietly. They'll have to keep following Jesus, no matter what.

Then a voice from heaven called,

"Write this. God will bring good things to his people who die from now on."

"Yes," said the Spirit. "They will rest from their work. The good things they do go with them."

A white cloud came in front of me. Someone who looked like a man was sitting on it. He wore a gold crown on his head. He held a sharp blade in his hand.

Then another angel came out of God's worship house. He called loudly, "Take your blade. The crop has grown. It's ready now. It's time to cut it and gather it in."

The man swung his blade over the earth. The crop was gathered in.

An angel came out of God's worship house. He had a sharp blade, too. Then another angel came from the altar. He called loudly to the one with the sharp blade. "Take your sharp blade," he said. "Gather up the grapes from the earth's vine. Its grapes are ready."

So the angel swung his blade over the earth. He gathered the grapes. He threw them into a big tub. It was a tub that showed God's anger. That's where the grapes would be pressed to make wine. They were pressed down in the big tub. Blood flowed out of the press tub. It got as high as the mouths of the horses.

A Sea of Glass

REVELATION 15

I saw another great, wonderful sign in heaven. Seven angels were there with the seven last troubles. These were last because after this, God stops being angry.

There was a sea of glass mixed with fire. People who won over the animal stood by the sea. They had harps that God gave them.

These people sang Moses' song and Jesus' song.

"The things you do are great and
 wonderful.
 You have all the power.
You are fair and true.
 You are the King of all time.
Everyone will look up to you, Lord.
 All people will show how great
 you are.
You're the only one who is sinless
 and clean.
All nations will worship you.
 They saw the things you did that
 were right."

Then heaven's worship house opened. Seven angels with the seven troubles came out. They wore clean, shining clothes. A wide, gold cloth lay across each one's chest.

One of the four living beings gave

them seven gold bowls. The bowls were full of God's anger.

Then the worship house filled with smoke from God's greatness. It was smoke from his power. Nobody could go inside until the seven troubles were over.

Tipping the Bowls Over
REVELATION 16

A loud voice came from the worship house. It spoke to the seven angels. "Go," it said. "Tip God's bowls of anger over. Let what's inside flow out onto the earth."

So the first angel tipped his bowl over. It flowed out onto the land. Ugly hurt places showed up on people who worshiped the animal.

The second angel tipped his bowl over. It flowed out onto the sea. The sea turned into blood. All things that lived in the sea died.

The third angel tipped his bowl over. It flowed out on the rivers. The rivers turned into blood, too.

Then the angel in charge of the water spoke.

"You live now.
   You lived before.
You are the Holy One.
   The way you judge is fair and right.
They killed your people.
   So you gave them blood to drink.
That's what was coming to them."

The altar answered,

"Yes, Lord of all power.
When you judge, it is true and fair."

The fourth angel tipped his bowl over. It flowed out on the sun. Then the sun had power to burn people with fire. It was so hot, they were burned. So they said bad things about God. That's because these troubles were under his power. But people would not say they were sorry. They would not change. They would not agree that God is the greatest.

The fifth angel tipped his bowl over. It flowed over the place where the animal ruled as king. His whole kingdom turned dark.

People chewed their own tongues. That's because they were hurting so badly. They said bad things about God because of their pain. But they would not say they were sorry. They would not change.

The sixth angel tipped his bowl over. It flowed out on the Euphrates River. The water dried up. That made a place for kings from the east. They could come across there.

Then one bad spirit came out of the dragon's mouth. One came out of the animal's mouth. One came out of the lying prophet's mouth. The spirits looked like frogs.

These bad spirits do wonders. They go to the world's kings. They get them to come together to fight. But God has all power. The fight will happen on his great day.

"Look! I'll surprise you like a robber does! But good things will come to people who stay awake. Good things will come to people who are ready."

Then bad spirits brought the kings to a place called Armageddon.

The last angel tipped his bowl over. It flowed out into the air. A voice from the worship house called loudly, "It's finished!"

Then lightning flashed. Thunder roared. The earth shook hard.

The earth never shook that hard before. It was so hard, the great city broke. It broke into three parts. Cities from all nations fell down. God judged the city of Babylon. He gave the city all his anger.

Then all the islands ran away. There were no more mountains. Huge hail fell from the sky. Each hail stone was about 100 pounds. The hail stones fell on people. People said bad things about God, because it was so terrible.

The Woman Sitting on a Red Animal

REVELATION 17

One of the seven angels came up to me. He said, "Come on. I'll show you the great one who left God. I'll show you how she gets in trouble. She sits on lakes and rivers and seas. Earth's kings followed her instead of God. People were full of the bad things she did."

Then the angel took me away in the Spirit. He took me to a desert. There I saw a woman sitting on a red animal.

Bad names against God covered the animal. He had seven heads. He had 10 horns.

The woman wore purple and red clothes. She shone with gold and beautiful stones. She held a gold cup. But it was full of ugly things. It was dirty with the bad things she had done.

Here's what was written on the woman's forehead. "Mystery. Babylon the Great. The Mother of People Who Leave God. The Mother of the Ugly Things of the Earth." The woman was drunk with the blood of God's people.

I was surprised when I saw the woman. The angel said, "Why are you surprised? I'll tell you the mystery of the woman. I'll tell you about the animal she is riding.

"Once the animal was alive," said the angel. "He doesn't live now. But he will come up out of the bottomless pit. He will go to be torn up.

"Some people's names are not in

God's Book of Life. They will be surprised when they see the animal.

"It takes a wise mind to understand this. The seven heads stand for seven hills. The woman sits on these hills. The heads also stand for seven kings.

"Then there is the animal who lived once. He doesn't live now. But he is king number eight. He is with the other seven. He will be torn up.

"The 10 horns stand for 10 kings. They don't have kingdoms yet. But they'll be kings with the animal for one hour. There is one reason for them. They will give their power to the animal. He will be in charge.

"They will come against Jesus in a war. But Jesus, the Lamb, will win over them. That's because he is the Lord of lords. He is the King of kings. The people he chose will be with him. They are the ones who keep following him.

"The lakes, rivers, and seas stand for people, nations, and languages.

"The animal and the 10 horns will hate the woman. They'll leave her with no clothes on. They'll eat her and burn her with fire. God said they could rule if they would get rid of her. But they can rule only until God's words come true. The woman is the great city that rules the kings of earth."

Babylon the Great

REVELATION 18:1-18, 21

Then another angel came down from heaven. His brightness lit up the earth. He shouted with a strong voice. He cried,

"Fallen! Great Babylon has fallen!
    Now bad spirits live there.
She turned nations away from God.
    Earth's kings followed her.
    Buyers and sellers got rich off of her.
She had things she didn't even need."

Another voice came from heaven.

"Come away from her, my people.
    Then you won't sin with her.
    You won't have the troubles she
        will have.
Her sins are piled as high as the sky.
    God remembers the wrong things
        she has done.

"Do to her what she did to others.
    Pay her back two times as much.
    It's all because of what she did.
She made herself great.
    She took much more than she
        needed.
So give her that much pain and
    sadness.

"She brags to herself.
She says, 'I'm the queen. I rule. I'll
    never cry.'

So trouble will come over her all in one day.
There will be death.
There will be crying.
There will not be enough food.
She will be burned up in fire.
That's because the Lord God judges.
He has all power.

"Earth's kings who followed her will see the smoke. It comes from Babylon burning. The kings will cry about it. They will be afraid, too. They'll stand back and cry,

"'How terrible for Babylon, the strong city.
Your end came in one hour!'

"Buyers and sellers will cry about it. That's because nobody buys what they sell anymore. No one buys their gold and silver and beautiful, shiny stones. No one buys their purple and red cloth. No one buys their wood, ivory, metal, and marble.
"No one buys their cinnamon and spice. No one buys their wine, oil, flour, and wheat. No one buys their cows, sheep, horses, and carts. No one buys the people they sell as slaves.
"They'll say, 'Your riches and beauty have left you. You can't get them back.'
"Buyers and sellers will cry out,

'All these riches were torn down in one hour!'
"All the sea captains will stand back. Sailors and sea travelers will stand back too. They will see the smoke. They'll say, 'There was never a city as great as this.'"
Then a strong angel picked up a huge stone. It was like a big stone that mashes wheat at the mill. The angel threw the stone into the sea. He said, "This is how hard Babylon will be thrown down."

The White Horse and Its Rider

REVELATION 19:1, 4-16, 19-21

Then I heard a roaring sound. It was like a great crowd of people in heaven. They shouted,

"Praise the Lord!
Show God's greatness!
He is strong. He saves."

The 24 leaders and the four living beings bowed down. They worshiped God, the King. They cried, "Yes! Amen! Praise the Lord!"

Then a voice came from where the King sat.

"All his servants, cheer for our God!
People who worship him, cheer for
    him!
Small and great, cheer for him!"

Then I heard a big crowd again. They sounded like a roaring waterfall. They sounded like loud, rolling thunder.

They shouted,

"Praise the Lord!
Let's be glad!
It's time for the Lamb's wedding.
    His bride is ready.
She is wearing clean, bright clothes."

The clothes stand for the right
    things God's people do.

Then the angel told me, "Write this. Some people will be asked to come to Jesus' wedding supper. God will bring good things to them."

Then I bowed down at the angel's feet. I was going to worship him. But he said, "Don't! I'm a servant like you and all who follow Jesus. Worship God! Jesus is the reason for telling God's plans."

I saw heaven. It was open. There was a white horse in front of me. The horse's rider is called the True One. He is called the One Who Keeps Promises. He judges fairly. He goes to war.

His eyes are like burning fire. Many crowns are on his head. There is a name written on him. But only he knows what it is. He wears clothes that were dipped in blood. His name is the Word of God.

Heaven's armies follow him. They ride on white horses. Their clothes are white and clean.

A sharp sword comes out of his mouth. He can cut the nations down with it. "He will rule them with power."

A name is on Jesus' clothes and on his leg. It is "King of kings and Lord of lords."

Then I saw that the animal, earth's kings, and their armies got together. They went to fight against the horse rider and his army.

But the horse rider and his army

caught the animal. They caught the lying prophet. He had tricked people who had gotten the animal's mark. So the animal was thrown into the lake of fire. That's where the lying prophet was thrown too.

All the others were killed by the sword. It came from the mouth of the horse rider. Then the birds swallowed them.

DECEMBER 30

Into the Bottomless Pit

REVELATION 20:1-14

An angel came down from heaven. He held the key to the bottomless pit. He also held a big chain. He caught the dragon. That dragon is the old snake, the devil, or Satan. The angel put the chain on him. It had to stay on him for 1,000 (one thousand) years.

Then the angel threw him into the bottomless pit. The angel locked the pit and covered it. That would keep Satan from lying to the nations anymore. He was there until the thousand years were over. Then he'd have to be set free for a little while.

I saw kings' thrones. People who were judges sat there. Then I saw souls. They had been killed because they talked about Jesus. They hadn't worshiped the animal or his idol. They hadn't gotten his mark on their heads or hands. So they came back to life again. They ruled with Jesus for 1,000 (one thousand) years.

After that, the rest of the dead people came to life again. This is when people came back to life for the first time. God brings good things to these people. They are clean and sinless. The second death won't happen to them. Instead, they will serve God and Jesus. They will rule with him for 1,000 (one thousand) years.

After the thousand years, Satan will be let out of the pit. He will go around the earth. He will lie to the nations. He will get them together to fight a war.

There were many people in this war. There were as many as the sand on the beach. They marched all over the earth. They stood in a circle around God's people's camp. That's the city that God loves.

But fire came out of heaven. It burned them up. Then Satan was thrown into the burning lake of yellow acid. That's where the animal and lying prophet were thrown before. They'll always be in pain, forever and ever.

Then I saw the King. He was sitting on his great white throne. The earth ran away from him. The sky ran away from him. Everyone who had died stood in front of the King.

God's Book of Life was opened. Other books were opened too. The people were judged for what they had done. It was written in the books. Then death was thrown into the burning lake of fire.

A New Heaven and a New Earth

REVELATION 21

Then I saw a new heaven. I saw a new earth. The first heaven and earth were gone. There wasn't a sea anymore.

I also saw the Holy City. It was a new Jerusalem. It was coming down from heaven. It was like a bride with beautiful clothes on.

A loud voice came from where the King was. "Now God will live with people. That's where his house will be. They will be his people. He will be their God.

"God will wipe all their tears away. They won't die anymore. They won't cry anymore. They won't hurt anymore. The old way of doing things is gone."

The King said, "I'm making everything new!" Then he said, "Write this down. You can trust what I say. It's true.

"It's finished," he said. "I'm the First and the Last. I'm the Beginning and the End. Thirsty people can drink from the river of living water. I'll give it to them free. People who keep following Jesus get all this. I'll be their God. They'll be my children.

"But people who aren't brave enough to follow me go to a different place. So do people who don't believe and people who kill. So do people who use sex in a wrong way. So do people who do magic in a sinful way. So do people who worship idols, and people who lie. Their place will be in the burning acid lake. That's the second death."

Then one of the seven angels talked to me. He is the one who had one of the bowls of trouble. He said, "Come on! I'll show you the bride. She belongs to Jesus."

Then he took me away in the Spirit. We went to a big, high mountain. There he showed me the Holy City. It was Jerusalem. It was coming down from heaven. It was shining with God's power. It was bright. It was like beautiful, shiny stones. It was like a clear green stone.

There was a big, high wall around the city. Twelve gates were in the wall. Twelve angels were by the gates. On the gates were names of the 12 family groups of Israel. Three gates were in the east wall. Three gates were in the north wall. Three were in the south wall. Three were in the west wall.

The city was built on 12 flat floors or bases. The names of the Lamb's 12 apostles were on the bases.

The angel had a gold stick to measure with. The city was square. It was as long as it was wide. The angel measured it. It was 1,400 miles long. It was 1,400 miles wide. It was 1,400 miles high. Its walls were 200 feet thick. The wall was made out of clear green stone. The city was made of gold, as spotless as glass.

The bottom parts of the city walls had beautiful stones on them. The first part had clear green stone. The second had blue stone. The next had shiny green stone. Then came dark green stone, then orange red, then red, then yellow. Next came sea blue stone. Then came a clear gold stone. Then there was apple green and blue purple. The last floor was purple.

The city gates were pearls. Each of the gates was one big pearl. The main street was made all of gold. It was as clear as glass.

I didn't see a worship house in the city. That's because God and his Son, the Lamb, are the worship place. The city doesn't need the sun or moon. God's greatness shines so bright, it lights up the city. Jesus is the city's lamp. The nations will be in its light.

Earth's kings will bring their beautiful things to the city. Its gates will never be closed. That's because it will never be night there.

Nothing dirty or sinful will ever get into the city. People who do wrong or lie won't get in. Only people whose names are in Jesus' Book of Life can come in.

DECEMBER 31

No More Night

REVELATION 22

Then the angel showed me the river of living water. It was as clear as it could be. It was flowing from where the King and the Lamb sat. It went down the middle of the main city street.

The tree of life grew on each side of the river. Every month it made fruit, ready to pick. The tree's leaves will make people well. Nothing bad will happen again.

The King and Jesus will live in the city. The King's servants will serve him there. They'll see his face. His name will be on their foreheads.

There won't be any more night. The people won't need lamp light or sun light. That's because God will give them the light they need. They will rule forever and ever.

Then the angel said, "You can trust these words. They're true. The Lord sent me to show what will happen soon."

Jesus said, "Look and listen! I'm coming soon! God will bring good things to people who remember this book."

I'm John. I'm the one who heard and saw all of this. After I heard it and saw it, I bowed down. I started to worship at the angel's feet.

But the angel said, "Don't! I'm God's servant too. Worship God!

"Don't close and lock these words about God's plans," he said. "It's almost time for it to happen. People who do what's wrong can keep doing wrong. People who are mean can keep being mean. People who do what's right should keep doing right. People who are sinless should keep being sinless."

"Look and listen!" said Jesus. "I'm coming soon! I have my gifts with me. I'll see what everybody has done. Then I'll give them the good things they are to have. I'm the First and the Last. I'm the Beginning and the End.

"God will bring good things to people who keep themselves clean from sin. They can go to the tree of life. They can go into the city.

"But people who do sinful magic must stay outside the city. People who sin with sex must stay out. People who kill must stay out. People who worship idols must stay out. Anybody who lies must stay out.

"I'm Jesus. I've sent my angel to tell you these things. Now you can tell it to my followers. I'm called King David's Child. I'm called the bright Morning Star."

The Spirit says, "Come on!" The bride says, "Come on!" Whoever hears it should say, "Come on!" If you're thirsty, come. If you want to, you can have living water. It's free.

Be careful if you hear God's plans from this book. If you add to them, God will add troubles to you. What if you take away from them? God will take away your part of the tree of life. He will take away your part of the Holy City.

Jesus says these things are true. He says, "Yes. I'm coming soon."

Yes! Amen! Come, Lord Jesus.

Jesus will be kind and loving to all his people. Yes! Amen!

New Testament

Old Testament

100 MAIN EVENTS, PASSAGES AND TEACHINGS

100 FAVORITE BEDTIME STORIES

Karyn Henley is an award-winning author and children's communicator. She is best known as the author of the original *The Beginner's Bible*, which has sold more than four million copies, and *God's Story*, a chronological Bible for young readers ages seven and up. Her PLAYSONGS® video series for ages two to five is an increasingly popular resource for use in home and child-care settings. Karen's most recent releases include *My Thank-You Bible* and *Rag Baby*, a picture book for young children.

In 2001 *Children's Ministry* magazine named Karyn Henley a Pioneer of the Decade, in response to a readers' poll that identified Karyn as one of the top ten people who have most changed the face of children's ministry. In 1997 the International Network of Children's Ministry honored Karyn with their Excellence in Children's Ministry Award, recognizing her long-term commitment to children's ministry.

An accomplished songwriter, Karyn coauthored *My First Hymnal*, an illustrated easy reader that introduces young children to classic hymns and worship choruses. The companion audio recording was nominated for a Dove Award in 1995, the same year that a video version was released. In 1990 Karyn received an Emmy Award as music composer for a children's television special.

Karyn has created numerous resources for parents and teachers, including *100 Ways to Teach Your Child About God* and *Sword*

Fighting, a Scripture-memory devotional book. Her Bible-class curriculum includes PLAYSONGS® Bible Time for preschoolers, and Foundations for first through fifth grade.

Karyn's career as a teacher and author began at the age of fourteen when her mother asked her to teach a class for eighteen-month-old children. Now, more than thirty years later, her Child Talk™ Seminars and PLAYSONGS® concerts take her all over the U.S.

A graduate of Abilene Christian University, Karyn lives in Nashville, Tennessee, with her husband, Ralph, where they raised their two grown sons. Karyn is currently working on her Master of Fine Arts in Writing for Children at Vermont College.

For more information about Karyn's insightful seminars, go to www.karynhenley.com, or call 1-888-573-3953.